W9-AOW-299

SIXTH EDITION

Exceptional Children

▲ ▲ ▲

Introduction to Special Education

DANIEL P. HALLAHAN
JAMES M. KAUFFMAN

University of Virginia

ALLYN AND BACON
Boston ▲ London ▲ Toronto ▲ Sydney ▲ Tokyo ▲ Singapore

EDITOR-IN-CHIEF, EDUCATION: Nancy Forsyth
SENIOR EDITOR: Ray Short
DEVELOPMENTAL EDITOR: Alicia Reilly
EDITORIAL ASSISTANT: Christine Shaw
COVER ADMINISTRATOR: Linda Dickinson
EMM SUPERVISOR: Andrew Walker
PAGE LAYOUT ARTIST: Timothy Ries
COMPOSITION BUYER: Linda Cox
MANUFACTURING BUYER: Louise Richardson
PRODUCTION COORDINATOR: Deborah Brown
TEXT DESIGNER: Karen Mason
PHOTO RESEARCHER: Susan Duane
COVER DESIGNER: Studio Nine

CHAPTER OPENING QUOTES: (1) and (4) Richard H. Hungerford, "On Locusts," *American Journal of Mental Deficiency,* 1950, *54.* 415–418. (2) Bob Dylan, "The Times They Are A-Changin,'" 1963 Warner Bros. Inc. (Renewed). All rights reserved. Used by permission. International copyright secured. (3) Marian Wright Edelman, *The Measure of Our Success: A Letter to My Children and Yours.* Copyright © 1992 by Marian Wright Edelman. Reprinted with permission of Beacon Press. (5) Neil Diamond, "Brooklyn Roads." Copyright © 1968 Stonebridge Music. All rights reserved Used by permission. International copyright secured. (6) Neil Diamond, "Shilo." Copyright © 1967 Tallyrand Music, Inc. All rights reserved. Used by permission. International copyright secured. (7) D. Shields, *Dead Languages.* New York: Alfred A. Knopf, Inc. (8) Helen Keller, *The Story of My Life.* New York: Doubleday, 1954. (9) Leonard Gershe, "Butterflies Are Free." Copyright by Leonard Gershe. (10) Words by Chuck Mangione. Copyright © Gates Music, Inc. All rights reserved. (11) Excerpt from *The Autobiography of Mark Twain,* edited by Charles Neider. Copyright 1927, 1940, 1958, 1959 by the Mark Twain Company, copyright 1924, 1955, 1952 by Clara Clemens Somossoud, copyright 1959 by Charles Neider. Reprinted by permission of HarperCollins Publishers Inc. (12) Christopher Nolan (1987). *Under the Eye of the Clock: The Life Story of Christopher Nolan.* London: Weidenfeld & Nicholson Limited. pp. 37–38. Reprinted with permission.

PHOTOGRAPH AND ART CREDITS: see page 536.

Library of Congress Cataloging-in-Publication Data

Hallahan, Daniel P., 1944–
   Exceptional Children: introduction to special education/Daniel
P. Hallahan, James M. Kauffman.—6th ed.
     p.   cm.
   Includes bibliographical references and indexes.
   ISBN 0–205–14917–0
   1. Special Education—United States.   I. Kauffman, James M.
II. Title.
LC3981.H34 1994
371.9'073—dc20   93–27213
                                      CIP

Printed in the United States of America
10 9 8 7 6 5 4 3 2 1   98 97 96 95 94 93

CONTENTS

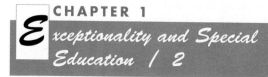

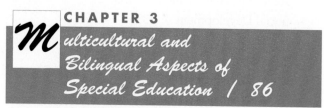

CHAPTER 4

Mental Retardation / 114

CHAPTER 5

Learning Disabilities / 158

CHAPTER 9

Visual Impairment / 340

CHAPTER 10

Physical Disabilities / 384

CHAPTER 11
G̶iftedness / 444

CHAPTER 12
Parents and Families / 490

Contents

PREFACE
▲ ▲ ▲

This book is a general introduction to the characteristics of exceptional persons and their education. (*Exceptional* is the term that has traditionally been used to refer to persons with disabilities as well those who are gifted.) Although students preparing to be special educators will undoubtedly find this text useful, we have written it with those preparing to be general educators in mind. We place major emphasis on classroom practices, as well as cover the psychological, sociological, and medical aspects of disabilities and giftedness.

We begin with an introductory chapter in which we present an overview of exceptionality and special education, including definitions, basic legal requirements, and the history and development of the field. In Chapter 2, we discuss major current issues and trends, including inclusion, transition to adulthood programming, and early childhood programming. In Chapter 3, we present issues pertaining to multicultural and bilingual aspects of special education. Following that are eight chapters covering the major categories of special education—mental retardation, learning disabilities, emotional or behavioral disorders, communication disorders, hearing impairment, visual impairment, physical disabilities, and giftedness. The last chapter pertains to parents and families of persons with disabilities.

MAJOR CHANGES FOR THIS EDITION

More Emphasis on Integration

Although previous editions have contained much material on integration of students with disabilities into general education, we have added even more information on this important topic. Students preparing to be special or general educators should find this coverage useful. We have added material pertinent to integration in each of the chapters as well as presented an extended section on integration, including full inclusion, in Chapter 2, Current Trends and Issues.

New Chapter on Multicultural and Bilingual Aspects of Special Education

In the previous edition, we covered the topic of multicultural special education in the chapter on trends and issues. In this edition, we have emphasized this topic by devoting an entire chapter (Chapter 3, Multicultural and Bilingual Aspects of Special Education) to it. We discuss multicultural issues relative to assessment, instruction, and socialization.

Expanded Coverage of Transition to Adulthood and Early Childhood

Researchers and practitioners in the field of special education continue to expand their concerns at both ends of the age spectrum. In order to reflect this activity, we have increased our attention to issues related to transition to adulthood as well as early childhood. Two of the major sections in Chapter 2, Current Trends and Issues, concern transition to adulthood and early childhood, respectively. In addition, we have added new information pertaining to these two topics in each of the categorical chapters as well as Chapter 12, Parents and Families.

Glossary in the Margins

In this edition, in addition to the Glossary in the back of the text, we have included glossary definitions in the margins. We believe readers will find this useful as a pedagogical aid.

Issues In Special Education Boxes

Also new to this edition, this boxed feature occurs in every chapter, highlighting contemporary issues that confront individuals as they become more and more integrated into the larger society. Complementary CNN news clips for each box are available on videotape.

In Their Own Words Boxes

New to this edition, this boxed feature appears in each of the categorical chapters, featuring an individual who has lived with the disability discussed in the chapter. Included is a brief biographical sketch of the person profiled, and an excerpt from his or her published autobiography.

MAJOR FEATURES RETAINED FOR THIS EDITION

Based on responses from students and instructors, we have preserved some of the popular features from previous editions:

Suggestions for Teaching Students in General Education Classrooms

For the fifth edition, we asked Dr. E. Jane Nowacek, an experienced resource teacher and currently a teacher educator at Appalachian State University, to write a section at the end of each categorical chapter. Written specifically for the general education teacher and updated thoroughly for the sixth edition, Dr. Nowacek's contributions provide a variety of teaching ideas and strategies. In addition to many practical, how-to-do-it suggestions, she provides lists of additional resources, books, and software. While not everything a teacher needs to teach students with disabilities is included, we do think, however, that these sections serve as an excellent starting place for general education teachers faced with their first mainstreamed students.

Collaboration: A Key to Success

Also introduced in our last edition, for each categorical chapter we asked two expert teachers, one from general education and one from special education, to write about how they collaborate to provide effective integration of exceptional students into the mainstream. (For Chapter 12, Parents and Families, we asked a parent and a family educator.) We believe these sections serve as models of best practices for integration. For this edition, we have substituted new teachers for two of the boxes.

Boxed Material on Misconceptions

We start each chapter with a box of myths and facts. These serve as excellent advance organizers for material covered in the chapter. Although some of the myths and facts have changed over the years, this is a feature that we have used since our first edition in 1978.

Chapter Opening Quotes

In our first edition we introduced excerpts from literature and songs (some of which we have replaced over the years) at the beginning of each chapter. We draw upon these quotes in the opening paragraphs to begin our discussion of some of the topics covered in the chapter. Students have continued to tell us that they find this an effective way of grabbing their attention and leading them into some of the issues contained in the chapter.

Boxed Material on Special Topics

Sprinkled throughout the text are boxes of three types: some highlight research findings and their applicability to educational practice; some discuss issues facing educators in the field; and some present the human side of having a disability.

SUPPLEMENTS

Study Guide

Written by Arthur and Sandra Rathgeber of Nipissing University, the study guide includes key points, learning objectives, exercises, practice tests, and enrichment activities to reinforce text concepts.

ACKNOWLEDGMENTS

We are thankful to the reviewers of the sixth and fifth editions and readers of drafts of our revised chapters:

Sixth Edition:

Robert Rueda
University of Southern California

Michael S. Rosenberg
Johns Hopkins University

John Lagone
The University of Georgia

William N. Bender
The University of Georgia

Steven F. Warren
George Peabody College for Teachers, Vanderbilt University

Gayle L. Nash
Eastern Michigan University

Hilda R. Caton
University of Louisville

Ann L. Lee
Bloomsburg University

Gary A. Davis
University of Wisconsin-Madison

Timothy E. Heron
The Ohio State University

Jean Kueker
Northwestern State University

Fifth Edition:

Rebecca Dailey Kneedler
University of Virginia

Ann Turnbull
University of Kansas

June H. Elliot
Lyndon State College

Carol Jo Yanek
Howard Community College

Charlene Lingo
Pittsburgh State University

Linda C. Knicker
College of DuPage

Louise Pitt
Florida Southern College

Jerome J. Schultz
Lesley College

Antoinette Heppler
Nova University

B. C. Moore
Arizona State University

Linda Reese
Northeastern State University

Deborah Gartland
Towson State University

Ann C. Candler
Texas Tech University

T. Hisama
Southern Illinois University

Rhoda Cummings
University of Nevada

Kay Butler
Syracuse University

Mara Sapon-Sevin
University of North Dakota

Jeanne E. Legan
Joliet Junior College

Joseph S. Renzulli
University of Connecticut

Agnes Rainwater
Eastern Michigan University

Patricia Mulhearn Blasco
University of North Carolina

Donald F. Moores
Gallaudet University—Research Institute

Carolyn Callahan
University of Virginia

Rebecca R. Fewell
Tulane University

Ruth Buehler
Millersville University

Bruce L. Mallory
University of New Hampshire

Richard M. Gargiulo
University of Alabama at Birmingham

Steward Ehly
University of Iowa

We thank Kerri Frymier for her assistance on various phases of the project. At Allyn & Bacon, we are grateful to Ray Short, Deborah Brown, and Christine Shaw for their help during the project. Also at Allyn & Bacon, we are appreciative of Alicia Reilly's and Christine Shaw's contributions to the Issues in Special Education and In Their Own Words boxes.

Finally, we thank those instructors and students who have given us feedback on our previous editions. Your comments are always welcome.

Daniel P. Hallahan

James M. Kauffman

ALLYN AND BACON is once again privileged to include original artworks from Very Special Arts for the sixth edition of *Exceptional Children*. These works, which include painting and sculpture, appear in the chapter openers. A brief biography of each artist appears below the art. The artists chosen for this edition have shown their work around the country and abroad.

Very Special Arts provides opportunities in drama, dance, literature, and the visual arts for people with mental and physical disabilities. An international organization that extends to 55 countries, Very Special Arts was founded in 1974 as an educational affiliate of The John F. Kennedy Center for the Performing Arts in Washington, D.C. Since 1991, Allyn and Bacon has featured original artworks from artists with disabilities on its covers and as part of interior illustration.

Exceptional Children

CHAPTER ONE

MARY THORNLEY

Mary Thornley is a nationally recognized visual artist. She describes her work as "art about life, about being a deaf person, about being different." Her work often incorporates themes and images related to hearing impairment.

*O*nly the brave dare look upon the gray—
upon the things which cannot be explained easily,
upon the things which often engender mistakes,
upon the things whose cause cannot be understood,
upon the things we must accept and live with.
And therefore only the brave dare look upon difference
without flinching.

➤ Richard H. Hungerford
"On Locusts"

Exceptionality and
Special Education

▲ ▲ ▲

*T*he study of exceptional children is the study of *differences*. The exceptional child is different in some way from the "average" child. In very simple terms, such a child may have problems or special talents in thinking, seeing, hearing, speaking, socializing, or moving. More often than not, such a child has a combination of special abilities or disabilities. Today over 4 million such "different" children have been identified in public schools throughout the United States. About one out of every ten children in U.S. schools is considered exceptional. The fact that even many so-called normal children also have school-related problems makes the study of exceptionality very demanding.

The study of exceptional children is also the study of *similarities*. Exceptional children are not different from the "average" in every way. In fact, most exceptional children are average in more ways than they are not. Until recently, professionals, and laypeople as well, tended to focus on the differences between exceptional and nonexceptional children, almost to the exclusion of the ways in which all children are alike. Today we give more attention to what exceptional and nonexceptional children have in common—to similarities in their characteristics, needs, and ways of learning. As a result, the study of exceptional children has become more complex, and many so-called facts about children with disabilities and those who have special gifts or talents have been challenged.

Students of one of the hard sciences may boast of the difficulty of the subject matter because of the many facts they must remember and piece together. The plight of students of special education is quite different. To be sure, they study facts, but the facts are relatively few compared to the unanswered questions. Any study of human beings must take into account inherent ambiguities, inconsistencies, and unknowns. In the case of the child who deviates from the norm, we must multiply all the mysteries of normal human behavior and development by those pertaining to the child's exceptionalities. Because there is no single accepted theory of normal child development, it is not at all surprising that relatively few definite statements can be made about exceptional children.

There are, however, patches of sunshine in the bleak gray painted by Hungerford (see page 3). It is true that in the vast majority of cases we are unable to identify the exact reason why a child is exceptional, but progress is being made in determining the causes of some disabilities. In a later chapter, for example, we discuss the detection of causal factors in Down syndrome—a condition resulting in the largest number of children classified as having moderate mental retardation. Likewise, **retinopathy of prematurity (ROP)**—at one time a leading cause of blindness—has been greatly reduced since the discovery of its cause. The cause of mental retardation associated with a metabolic disorder— **phenylketonuria (PKU)**—has been discovered. Soon after birth, infants are now routinely tested for PKU so that mental retardation can be prevented if they should have the disorder. More recently, the gene responsible for cystic fibrosis, an inherited disease characterized by chronic respiratory and digestive problems, has been identified. The specific genes governing many other diseases and disorders will also likely be located. The location of such genes raises the possibility of gene therapy to prevent or correct many disabling conditions. Besides these and other medical breakthroughs, research is bringing us a more complete understanding of the ways in which the child's psychological, social, and educational environments are related to learning. For example, special educators,

The goals of special education have become more ambitious, seeking to enable individuals with disabilities to succeed in mainstream society.

➤ **retinopathy of prematurity (ROP).** Formerly referred to as retrolental fibroplasia, a condition resulting from administration of an excessive concentration of oxygen at birth; causes scar tissue to form behind the lens of the eye.

➤ **phenylketonuria (PKU).** A metabolic genetic disorder caused by the inability of the body to convert phenylalanine to tyrosine; an accumulation of phenylalanine results in abnormal brain development.

EXCEPTIONAL CHILDREN

MYTH ➤ Public schools may choose not to provide education for some students.

FACT ➤ Federal legislation specifies that to receive federal funds, every school system must provide a free, appropriate education for every student regardless of any disabling condition.

MYTH ➤ By law, the student with a disability must be placed in the least restrictive environment (LRE). The LRE is always the regular classroom.

FACT ➤ The law does require the student with a disability to be placed in the LRE. However, the LRE is *not* always the regular classroom. What the LRE does mean is that the student shall be segregated as little as possible from home, family, community, and the regular class setting while appropriate education is provided. In many, but not all, instances this will mean placement in the regular classroom.

MYTH ➤ The causes of most disabilities are known, but little is known about how to help individuals overcome or compensate for their disabilities.

FACT ➤ In most cases, the causes of disabilities are not known, although progress is being made in pinpointing why many disabilities occur. More is known about the treatment of most disabilities than about their causes.

MYTH ➤ People with disabilities are just like everyone else.

FACT ➤ First, no two people are exactly alike. People with disabilities, just like everyone else, are unique individuals. Most of their abilities are much like those of the "average" person who is not considered to have a disability. Nevertheless, a disability is a characteristic not shared by most people. It is important that disabilities be recognized for what they are, but individuals with disabilities must be seen as having many abilities—other characteristics that they share with the majority of people.

MYTH ➤ A disability is a handicap.

FACT ➤ A disability is an inability to do something, the lack of a specific capacity. A handicap, on the other hand, is a disadvantage that is imposed on an individual. A disability may or may not be a handicap, depending on the circumstances. For example, inability to walk is not a handicap in learning to read, but it can be a handicap in getting into the stands at a ball game. Sometimes handicaps are needlessly imposed on people with disabilities. For example, a student who cannot write with a pen but can use a typewriter or word processor would be needlessly handicapped without such equipment.

psychologists, and pediatricians are increasingly able to identify environmental conditions that increase the likelihood that a child will have learning or behavior problems (Patterson, Reid, & Dishion, 1992; Werner, 1986).

Educational methodology has also made strides. In fact, compared to what is known about causes, we know a lot about how exceptional children can be taught and managed effectively in the classroom. Although special educators constantly lament that all the questions are not answered, we do know considerably more today about how to educate exceptional children than we did ten or fifteen years ago.

Before moving to the specific subject of exceptional children, we must point out that we vehemently disagree with Hungerford on an important point: We must certainly learn to "live with" disabling exceptionalities, but we must never "accept" them. We prefer to think there is hope for the eventual eradication of many of the disabling forms of exceptionality. In addition, we believe it is of paramount importance to realize that even children whose exceptionalities are extreme can be helped to lead a fuller life than they would without appropriate education.

We must not let people's disabilities keep us from recognizing their abilities. Many children and youths with disabilities have abilities that go unrecognized because their disabilities become the focus of our concern and we do not give enough attention to what they *can* do. We must study the disabilities of exceptional children and youths if we are to learn how to help them make maximum use of their abilities. Some students with disabilities that are not obvious to the casual observer need special programs of education and related services to help them live full, happy, productive lives. However, we must not lose sight of the fact that *the most important characteristics of exceptional children are their abilities.*

Most exceptional individuals have a disability, and they have often been referred to as "handicapped" in laws, regulations, and everyday conversations. We make an important distinction between disability and handicap. A disability is an inability to do something, a diminished capacity to perform in a specific way. A handicap, on the other hand, is a disadvantage imposed on an individual. A disability may or may not be a handicap, depending on the circumstances.

One of the challenges to special educators is that individuals with disabilities are otherwise as diverse a group as any other.

Likewise, a handicap may or may not be caused by a disability. For example, blindness is a disability that can be anything but a handicap in the dark. In fact, in the dark the person who has sight is the one who is handicapped. Needing to use a wheelchair may be a handicap in certain circumstances, but the disadvantage may be a result of architectural barriers or other people's reactions, not the inability to walk. Others can handicap people who are different from them (in color, size, appearance, language, and so on) by stereotyping them or not giving them an opportunity to do the things they are able to do. When working and living with exceptional individuals who have disabilities, we must constantly strive to separate the disability from the handicap. That is, our goal should be to confine their handicap to those characteristics and circumstances that cannot be changed and to make sure that we impose no further handicap by our attitudes or our unwillingness to accommodate their disability.

EDUCATIONAL DEFINITION OF EXCEPTIONAL CHILDREN AND YOUTHS

For purposes of their education, *exceptional children and youths are those who require special education and related services if they are to realize their full human potential.* They require special education because they are markedly different from most children in one or more of the following ways: They may have mental retardation, learning disabilities, emotional or behavioral disorders, physical disabilities, disorders of communication, autism, traumatic brain injury, impaired hearing, impaired sight, or special gifts or talents. In the chapters that follow, we define as exactly as possible what it means to have an exceptionality.

Two concepts important to our educational definition of exceptional children and youths are (1) diversity of characteristics and (2) need for special education. The concept of diversity is inherent in the definition of exceptionality; need for special education is inherent in an educational definition.

Children and youths with exceptionalities are an extraordinarily diverse group compared to the general population, and relatively few generalizations apply to all exceptional individuals. Their exceptionalities may involve sensory, physical, cognitive, emotional, or communication abilities or any combination of these. Furthermore, exceptionalities may vary greatly in cause, degree, and effect on educational progress, and the effects may vary greatly depending on the individual's age, sex, and life circumstances. Any individual we might present as an example of our definition is likely to be representative of exceptional children and youths in some respects but unrepresentative in others. Consider the two students, Tony Hensley and Matt Radcliffe, who are described in the box on pages 8 and 9. How are these students typical and how are they atypical of the general population? How are they typical and atypical of students with disabilities? In what ways do they fit our educational definition of exceptionality? We do not provide answers to these questions here; they are intended as food for thought, and we hope you will reflect on them as you continue reading and studying.

The *typical* student who receives special education has no immediately obvious disability. He (more than half of the students served by special education are males) is in elementary or middle school and has persistent problems in learning and behaving appropriately in school. His problems are primarily academic and social or behavioral. These difficulties are not apparent to many teachers until

*C*OUNTY GRADUATES DEFY ODDS TO REALIZE GOALS ➤ by Tammy Poole

PROGRESS PHOTO BY MATT GENTRY

Tony Hensley says he'd like to study business administration in college.

With a 3.8 grade-point average, Hensley is in the top 10 percent of his class.

Young photographer focuses on attending a more accessible UVa

The University of Virginia should be more accessible to Tony Hensley in a couple of years.

The problem is not academic. Right now, parts of UVa's campus are not physically accessible for the Western Albemarle High School senior.

Hensley was born with a muscular condition that left him weak, and he started using a wheelchair after he was injured in an automobile wreck.

"I plan to attend Peidmont Virginia Community College for two years and transfer to UVa," he said. "With the Americans with Disabilities Act, it should be more accessible in a couple of years."

In 1986, nine months after having two metal rods placed in his back to help correct curvature of the spine, Hensley was injured in a car accident.

He was trapped in the vehicle for 45 minutes, and his leg was broken in three places.

Being the only senior at WAHS in a wheelchair has not hindered his progress in any way, Hensley said.

The school is accessible for people with disabilities, he said. And his disability is no big deal to his classmates. He said he gets treated the same as everyone else.

He and his 215 classmates graduate tonight at 8 p.m. in Warrior Stadium at the High School.

With a 3.8 grade-point average, Hensley is in the top 10 percent of his class. He is a member of the National Honor Society and the French Honor Society and has won various academic awards. Hensley loves photography and stays busy photographing weddings and other events. He also was hired to photograph several senior portraits this year.

He became interested in photography while on the yearbook staff at Heritage Christian School.

Hensley drives a van and often goes on the Blue Ridge Parkway to take photographs that he mats and sells.

He is not sure whether photography would be profitable enough to make a living. "I'm interested in business administration," he said. "Eventually I'd like to be a business owner of some sort."

Hensley lives in North Garden with his parents, John M. and Betty Jo Hensley.

For cancer survivor at AHS, college hurdle remains a challenge

Matthew Radcliffe is a fighter.

In 1985, doctors discovered a malignant tumor at the stem of his brain. At the tender age of 10, he was given a 40 to 60 percent chance of surviving.

"Before that, I was a perfect kid who had everything," he said. "I could run really well and I played soccer."

The operation was successful, but Matthew had to wear an eye patch and suffered from double vision. He temporarily lost the use of some of his motor skills. His head was shaved, and he had a huge scar from the surgery.

He went back to school almost immediately.

Some of his classmates were afraid of him. They thought he was going to die.

"For some reason, I never thought I would die," he said. "I had a lot to live for—my family and my future. I wanted to graduate from school, go to college, and have a family some day."

Tonight, Matthew accomplishes one of those goals as he graduates form Albemarle High School.

But the fight isn't over.

With a 3.89 grade-point average, Matthew is in the top 10 percent of his 362-member class. He is a member of the National Honor Society, is in the Beta Club, and was named to Who's Who Among American High School Students for two years.

But he said his low SAT scores kept him from getting into the colleges he wanted to attend.

"I applied to James Madison University, the University of Virginia and William and Mary, but I wasn't accepted," he said.

His dream was to go to JMU in Harrisonburg.

"This is my greatest disappointment," he said. "I don't think SAT scores show my ability to succeed in college."

He said he can't help but feel bitter about the rejection, but he will not give up.

He plans to live at home with his parents, Jan and Mike Radcliffe, and attend Peidmont Virginia Community College. He hopes to transfer to a larger college.

He received the George and Ruth Huff Scholarship for $1,000 last week. He does not know what kind of a career

PROGRESS PHOTO BY MATT GENTRY

Matthew Radcliffe will graduate from AHS with a 3.89 grade-point average.

he wants but said he would probably end up working with children.

"I feel like I missed my childhood," he said. "While the other kids were playing, I was fighting for my life."

In middle school, some kids teased him because of his scar and called him nicknames like "hammerhead."

The scar has faded but the teasing he suffered still bothers him.

"Anybody can get cancer—kids or adults," he said. "You can't catch it. People who have cancer are just like everybody else."

SOURCE: The Daily Progress, June 12, 1992, pp. C1, C2. Copyright © 1992. Reprinted with permission.

they have worked with him for a period of weeks or months. His problems persist despite teachers' efforts to meet his needs in the regular school program in which most students succeed. He is most likely to be described as having a learning disability or to be designated by an even broader label indicating that his academic and social progress in school are unsatisfactory due to a disability.

By federal law, an exceptional student is not to be identified as eligible for special education until careful assessment indicates that he or she is unable to make satisfactory progress in the regular school program without special services designed to meet his or her extraordinary needs. Federal special education laws and regulations include definitions of several conditions (categories such as learning disability, mental retardation, hearing impairment, and so on) that *might* create a need for special education. These laws and regulations require that special services be provided to meet whatever special needs are created by a disabling condition and cannot be met in the regular educational program. They do *not* require that special education be provided simply because a student has a disability.

When you read the article about Tony Hensley and Matt Radcliffe, you may have wondered whether these young men, both of whom obviously acquired disabilities at some point in their school careers, received special education. Remember that having a disability does not necessarily mean special education is required. Tony did not receive special education; his regular classroom teachers made minor adjustments to meet his needs related to his physical condition. His progress in elementary and high school was not affected by his physical problems. He decided to attend a community college for two reasons: (1) it was readily accessible and (2) he wanted to explore various academic and career options before entering the University of Virginia or another four-year college or university. If and when he enters the University of Virginia, it will be more readily accessible to someone in a wheelchair than it was in 1992. Its increased accessibility will be due in part to the Americans with Disabilities Act, a federal law we will discuss later. Matt did not receive special education. His regular classroom teachers helped him keep up with his work during his illness. Obviously, he had the cognitive capacity and emotional strength to deal successfully with the disabilities caused by his illness and attain an outstanding academic record without special education services. The primary school-related problems he experienced were the fear and insensitivity of some of his classmates (see his essay in Chapter 10, page 430). When he graduated from high school, his educational goals were thwarted—only temporarily, we hope—by college and university admissions officers' emphasis on SAT scores rather than his academic record.

Tony and Matt illustrate the fact that special education may not be necessary just because a student has a disability. They also illustrate another point we made earlier: Educators must focus on exceptional students' abilities, not just accommodate their disabilities. Students with disabilities typically have ordinary or extraordinary abilities as well. We discriminate against students with disabilities when we do not foster the full development of their abilities.

Now consider another exceptional student, one with a severe disability who, nevertheless, achieved a high level of academic and athletic success. Aaron Farley (see box on page 11) needed and received special education because of the extraordinary difficulty a student's profound deafness imposes on teaching and learning in a classroom in which all the other students can hear. The extraordinary difficulty we refer to is the difficulty in communication. Individuals with severely impaired hearing often need to learn to communicate in the language of

U P TO THE CHALLENGE ➤

by Steve Lewis

Deaf pitcher doesn't let disability stand in way of success

Hitters and pitchers look for them. Catchers and coaches give them. Everyone tries to steal them. Signs are as much a part of the game of baseball as the bat and ball.

And in a society that does not always accommodate the hearing impaired, baseball—with its endless parade of signs and gestures—is an oasis where the hearing and deaf alike attend on equal footing.

Aaron Farley is deaf. He also happens to have been raised on baseball. The name given at birth—Aaron (as in Hank) Matthew (as in Eddie, only without the 's') Farley (as in Aaron's father Bob, big Braves' fan)—left little doubt that baseball would constitute a huge part of his life.

Make no mistake about it, when Farley takes the mound in this weekend's 17-18 year old Babe Ruth state tournament in Purcellville, the 18-year-old C.B. Baker all-star will be just another baseball player.

"Baseball is one of those beautiful sports that rely so much on symbols," said Bob Farley, who also serves as all-star coach. "When the game starts we all speak a different language, anyway."

If baseball is unique in that sense, then it owes a good deal to deaf individuals such as William Hoy. An act so central to the national pastime—the umpire's animated strike call—was prompted by Hoy, a turn-of-the-century National League outfielder, who required hand signals to know if the pitch was a ball or a strike.

The symbolic code that has developed in the years since is a language Farley probably understands better than most.

Born profoundly deaf—the most severe degree of hearing impairment—Farley is capable of hearing high-decibel sounds like thunder, but little else. So he compensates with eyes. Farley confidently states that no one on the playing field sees as much as he does. His father doesn't remember him ever missing a sign.

His own safety, in fact, requires that Farley rigidly adhere to the proverbial command—keep your eye on the ball.

"He has to focus and concentrate on the entire game," said the elder Farley. "I don't know if it makes him better, but it sure makes him tired."

Moreover, it makes him intensely competitive. As one not distracted on the field, he expects nothing less from his teammates. "I don't want to make a mistake, I don't want my teammates to make a mistake," Aaron said. "I want to win."

Win he has. During the C.B. Baker regular season, Farley posted a perfect 4-0 record for champion Ruritan, the best mark in the league. He was equally successful at the plate with a .360 batting average.

Progress photo by Matt Gentry

Aaron Farley of the C. B. Baker League All-Star team has not let deafness keep him from enjoying success as a pitcher. The 18-year-old is 6–0 this summer (1992) in regular season and tournament play.

In last weekend's District 5 tournament, Farley added two more wins—including Sunday's 12-6 championship victory—to help put the Charlottesville squad in today's first-round game against the District 7 champions.

On the subject of stats, try this one: 3.60. Not ERA, but GPA. In June, Farley graduated with honors from Charlottesville High School and will attend Rochester (N.Y.) Institute of Technology this fall with plans to major in computer science and math.

A message blackboard in Farley's bedroom frequently carries this admonition from his father: "Most limitations are self-imposed." The son has taken the saying to heart. Consequently, Aaron Farley has not allowed his disability to get in the way of on- or off-field achievement.

He rejects the notion, however, that he is any sort of role model, but the message is clear: Being deaf is no excuse not to participate, or succeed.

SOURCE: The Daily Progress, July, 17, 1992, pp. C1, C3. Copyright © 1992. Reprinted with permission.

signs—a manual language with its own grammar. Others use a combination of speech and cues called *cued speech*. Few hearing people are fluent in sign language or cued speech; in fact, most know virtually no signs or cues. Teachers without extensive training are not able to help most students with severely impaired hearing become fluent in any language. Thus it is imperative that students with severe hearing impairments receive specialized instruction so they can learn to communicate fluently, typically through a combination of signing, speech, and speech reading or cued speech (see Chapter 8 for further discussion).

Aaron Farley's hearing impairment was diagnosed when he was two years old. He attended a special preschool program at the University of Virginia from ages three to five years old. There, he began learning cued speech, which combines manual cues with speech (see Chapter 8). From kindergarten through elementary school, Aaron attended a special class for children with impaired hearing and also received special instruction from a speech-language therapist. The speech-language therapist helped Aaron with speech reading, articulation, and vocabulary. Beginning in middle school, he attended a special class for several hours each day and received speech-language therapy. Both these services continued through grade 12. In high school, he attended the special class for two hours per day and spent a half hour each day with a speech-language therapist. The rest of the day he attended regular classes with a cued speech transliterator—a person with special training in translating spoken English into the combination of speech and cues known as cued speech. The transliterator made sure that Aaron could understand the speech of others, interpreted nonspeech sounds for Aaron, and expressed Aaron's ideas to others.

Aaron and his father list the following aids as especially helpful aspects of his education: his cued speech transliterator; note takers (hearing classmates who took notes for him in regular classes); his speech-language therapy; and having, in grades 10, 11, and 12, a high school special education teacher who is deaf. This teacher became Aaron's confidant and provided a good role model for him.

Without the special education he received, Aaron likely would not have learned the academic and social skills necessary to graduate with honors and continue his academic career at the Rochester Institute of Technology. His high intelligence and athletic skills may have gone undeveloped, and a handicap would have been imposed on him by not providing the means to nurture his potential.

PREVALENCE OF EXCEPTIONAL CHILDREN AND YOUTHS

Prevalence refers to the percentage of a population or number of individuals having a particular exceptionality. The prevalence of mental retardation, for example, might be estimated at 2.3 percent, which means that 2.3 percent of the population, or twenty-three people in every thousand, are assumed to have mental retardation. If the prevalence of giftedness is assumed to be between 3 percent and 5 percent, we would expect somewhere between thirty and fifty people in a sample of a thousand to have special gifts of some kind. Obviously, accurate estimates of prevalence depend on our ability to count the number of people in a given population who have a certain exceptionality.

At first thought, the task of determining the number of children and youths who have exceptionalities seems simple enough, yet the prevalence of most exceptionalities is uncertain and a matter of considerable controversy. Factors

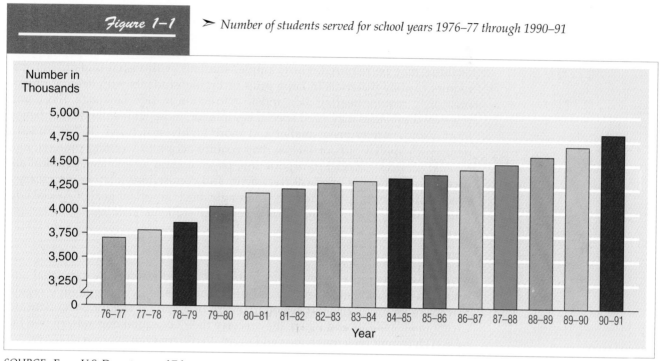

Figure 1-1 ➤ *Number of students served for school years 1976–77 through 1990–91*

SOURCE: From U.S. Department of Education, 1992, p. 4.

making it hard to say with great accuracy and confidence just how many exceptional individuals there are include vagueness in definitions, frequent changes in definitions, and the role of schools in determining exceptionality—matters we discuss in later chapters.

Government figures show that about 10 students out of every 100 are receiving special education (U.S. Department of Education, 1992). The total number of students served by special education is nearly 5 million. Increases from 1976 to 1991 in the number of students served by special education are shown in Figure 1–1. Most of these children and youths are between the ages of six and seventeen. Although preschoolers and youths eighteen to twenty-one are being identified with increasing frequency as having disabilities, school-age children and youths in their early teens make up the bulk of the identified population. The distribution of certain disabilities has changed considerably in the past two decades. As shown in Figure 1–2, the percentage of students with disabilities in the specific learning disabilities category has doubled since the mid 1970s. There has been a slight increase in the percentage categorized as having serious emotional disturbance. In contrast, the percentage of students whose primary disability is speech or language impairments has declined substantially, and the percentage identified as having mental retardation is now about half of what it was in 1976. No one has an entirely satisfactory explanation of these changes. However, they may reflect, in part, alterations in definitions and diagnostic criteria for certain disabilities and the growing social acceptability of the learning disabilities label. In subsequent chapters, we discuss the prevalence of specific categories of exceptionality.

1/4 in self contained class rooms

2/3 in "regual class"

7% day schools & residential prog.

DEFINITION OF SPECIAL EDUCATION

Special education means specially designed instruction that meets the unusual needs of an exceptional student. Special materials, teaching techniques, or equipment and/or facilities may be required. For example, students with visual impairment may require reading materials in large print or Braille; students with hearing impairment may require hearing aids and/or instruction in sign language; those with physical disabilities may need special equipment; those with emotional or behavioral disorders may need smaller and more highly structured classes; and students with special gifts or talents may require access to working professionals. Related services—special transportation, psychological assessment, physical and occupational therapy, medical treatment, and counseling—may be necessary if special education is to be effective. The single most important goal of special education is finding and capitalizing on exceptional students' *abilities.*

Where and by Whom Special Education Is Provided

Several administrative plans are available for the education of exceptional children and youths, from a few special provisions made by the student's regular teacher to twenty-four-hour residential care in a special facility. Who educates exceptional students and where they receive their education depends on two factors: (1) how and how much the child or youth differs from average students; and (2) the resources of the school and community. We describe various administrative plans for education according to the degree of physical integration—the extent to which exceptional and nonexceptional students are taught in the same place by the same teachers.

Beginning with the most integrated intervention, the *regular classroom teacher* who is aware of the individual needs of students and skilled at meeting them may be able to acquire materials, equipment, and/or instructional methods that

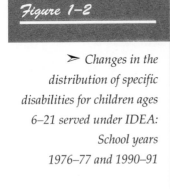

➤ *Changes in the distribution of specific disabilities for children ages 6–21 served under IDEA: School years 1976–77 and 1990–91*

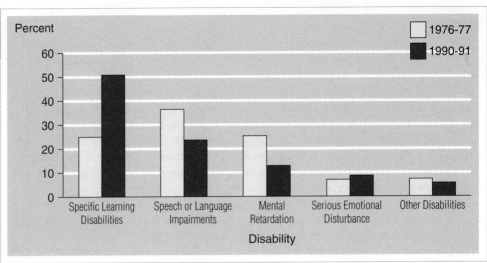

SOURCE: From U.S. Department of Education, 1992, p. 9.

The emphasis today in special education is to provide services tailored to individual needs.

are appropriate. At this level, the direct services of specialists may not be required—the expertise of the regular teacher may meet the student's needs.

At the next level, the regular classroom teacher may need consultation with a *special educator* or other professional (e.g., school psychologist) in addition to the special materials, equipment, or methods. The special educator may instruct the regular teacher, refer the teacher to other resources, or demonstrate the use of materials, equipment, or methods.

Going a step further, a special educator may provide *itinerant services* to the exceptional student and/or the regular classroom teacher. The itinerant teacher establishes a consistent schedule, moving from school to school and visiting the classroom to instruct students individually or in small groups. This teacher provides materials and teaching suggestions for the regular teacher to carry out, and consults with the regular teacher about special problems.

At the next level, a *resource teacher* provides services for the students and teachers in only one school. The students being served are enrolled in the regular classroom and are seen by the specially trained teacher for a length of time and at a frequency determined by the nature and severity of their particular problems. The resource teacher continually assesses the needs of the students and their teachers and usually teaches students individually or in small groups in a special classroom, where special materials and equipment are available. Typically, the resource teacher serves as a consultant to the regular classroom teacher, advising on the instruction and management of the child or youth in the classroom and perhaps demonstrating instructional techniques. The flexibility of the plan and the fact that the student remains with nondisabled peers most of the time make this a particularly attractive and popular alternative.

Diagnostic-prescriptive centers go beyond the level of intervention represented by resource rooms. In this plan, students are placed for a short time in a special class in a school or other facility so their needs can be assessed and a plan of

*T*able 1–1 ➤ **Examples of Service Alternatives for Special Education**

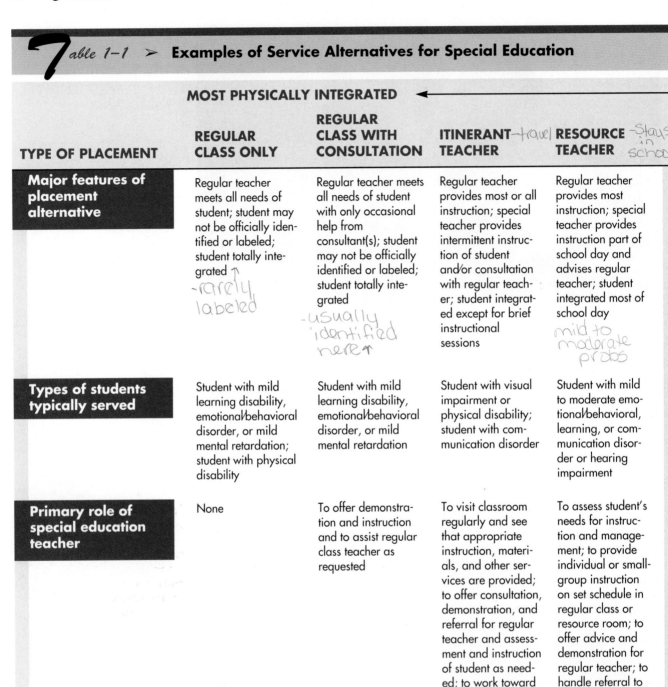

MOST PHYSICALLY INTEGRATED ◄────────────

TYPE OF PLACEMENT	REGULAR CLASS ONLY	REGULAR CLASS WITH CONSULTATION	ITINERANT TEACHER —travel	RESOURCE TEACHER —stays in school
Major features of placement alternative	Regular teacher meets all needs of student; student may not be officially identified or labeled; student totally integrated ↑ *-rarely labeled*	Regular teacher meets all needs of student with only occasional help from consultant(s); student may not be officially identified or labeled; student totally integrated *-usually identified here ↑*	Regular teacher provides most or all instruction; special teacher provides intermittent instruction of student and/or consultation with regular teacher; student integrated except for brief instructional sessions	Regular teacher provides most instruction; special teacher provides instruction part of school day and advises regular teacher; student integrated most of school day *mild to moderate probs*
Types of students typically served	Student with mild learning disability, emotional/behavioral disorder, or mild mental retardation; student with physical disability	Student with mild learning disability, emotional/behavioral disorder, or mild mental retardation	Student with visual impairment or physical disability; student with communication disorder	Student with mild to moderate emotional/behavioral, learning, or communication disorder or hearing impairment
Primary role of special education teacher	None	To offer demonstration and instruction and to assist regular class teacher as requested	To visit classroom regularly and see that appropriate instruction, materials, and other services are provided; to offer consultation, demonstration, and referral for regular teacher and assessment and instruction of student as needed; to work toward total integration of student	To assess student's needs for instruction and management; to provide individual or small-group instruction on set schedule in regular class or resource room; to offer advice and demonstration for regular teacher; to handle referral to other agencies for additional services; to work toward total integration of student

LEAST PHYSICALLY INTEGRATED

DIAGNOSTIC PRESCRIPTIVE CENTER	HOSPITAL OR HOMEBOUND INSTRUCTION	SELF-CONTAINED CLASS	SPECIAL DAY SCHOOL	RESIDENTIAL SCHOOL
Special teacher provides most or all instruction for several days or weeks and develops plan or prescription for receiving teacher; student totally segregated while in center but may be partially or totally integrated following diagnosis and prescription *rarely used*	Special teacher provides all instruction in hospital or home until student is able to return to usual school classes (regular or special) from which he or she has been temporarily withdrawn; student totally segregated for short period *reg or spec Ed teacher*	Special teacher provides most or all instruction in special class of students; regular teacher may provide instruction in regular class for part of school day; student mostly or totally segregated *in reg ed school*	Special teacher provides instruction in separate school; also may work with teachers in regular or special classes of regular school; student totally or mostly segregated *restricted school*	Same as special day school; special teacher also works with other staff to provide a total therapeutic environment or milieu; student totally or mostly segregated *- lives their 24 hrs a day -restricted*
Student with mild disability who has been receiving no services or inadequate services *-offers advice to teachers -sent to work out of school shortly*	Student with physical disability; student undergoing treatment or medical tests	Student with moderate to severe mental retardation or emotional/behavioral disorder	Student with severe or profound physical or mental disability	Student with severe or profound mental retardation or emotional/behavioral disorder
To make comprehensive assessment of student's educational strengths and weaknesses; to develop written prescription for instruction and behavior management for receiving teacher; to interpret prescription for receiving teacher and assess and revise prescription as needed	To obtain records from student's school of attendance; to maintain contact with teachers (regular or special) and offer instruction consistent with student's school program; to prepare student for return to school (special or regular)	To manage and teach special class; to offer instruction in most areas of curriculum; to work toward integration of students in regular classes	To manage and teach individuals and/or small groups of students with disabilities; to work toward integration of students in regular school	Same as special day school; also to work with residential staff to make certain school program is integrated appropriately with non-school activities

action can be determined on the basis of diagnostic findings. After an educational prescription is written for the pupil, the recommendations for placement may include anything from institutional care to placement in a regular classroom with a particularly competent teacher who can carry out the plan.

Hospital and homebound instruction is most often required by students who have physical disabilities, although it is sometimes employed for those with emotional or behavioral disorders or other disabilities when no alternative is readily available. Typically, the youngster is confined to the hospital or the home for a relatively short time, and the hospital or homebound teacher maintains contact with the regular teacher.

One of the most visible—and in recent years, controversial—service alternatives is the *special self-contained class.* Such a class typically enrolls fifteen or fewer exceptional children or youths with particular characteristics or needs. The teacher ordinarily has been trained as a special educator and provides all or most of the instruction. Those assigned to such classes usually spend the whole school day segregated from their nondisabled peers, although sometimes they are integrated with nondisabled students during part of the day (perhaps for physical education, music, or some other activity in which they can participate well).

Special day schools provide an all-day, segregated experience for exceptional children and youths. The day school is usually organized for a specific category of exceptional students and may contain special equipment necessary for their care and education. These students return to their homes during nonschool hours.

The final level of intervention is the *residential school.* Here exceptional students receive twenty-four-hour care away from home, often at a distance from their communities. These children and youths may make periodic visits home or return each weekend, but during the week they are residents of the institution, where they receive academic instruction in addition to management of their daily living environment.

The major features of each type of placement or service alternative, examples of the types of students most likely to be served in each, and the primary roles of the special educators who work there are shown in Table 1–1. Note that although these are the major administrative plans for delivery of special education, variations are possible. Many school systems, in the process of trying to find more effective and economical ways of serving exceptional students, combine or alter these alternatives and the roles special educators and other professionals play in service delivery. Furthermore, the types of students listed under each service alternative are *examples only*; there are wide variations among school systems in the kinds of placements made for particular kinds of students. Note also that what any special education teacher may be expected to do includes a variety of items not specified in Table 1–1. We discuss these expectations for teachers in the following section.

Special education law requires placement of the student in the **least restrictive environment (LRE).** What is usually meant is that the student should be segregated from nondisabled classmates and separated from home, family, and community as little as possible. That is, his or her life should be as "normal" as possible, and the intervention should be consistent with individual needs and not interfere with individual freedom any more than is absolutely necessary. For example, students should not be placed in a special class if they can be served

➤ **least restrictive environment (LRE).** A legal term referring to the fact that exceptional children must be educated in as "normal" an environment as possible.

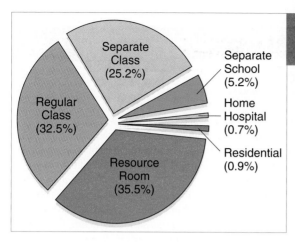

Figure 1–3

➤ *Percentage of all students with disabilities ages 3–21 served in six educational placements: School year 1989–90*

SOURCE: From U.S. Department of Education, 1992, p. 23.

adequately by a resource teacher, and they should not be placed in an institution if a special class will serve their needs just as well. Although this movement toward placement of exceptional students in the least restrictive environment is laudable, the definition of *least restrictive* is not as simple as it seems. Cruickshank (1977) has pointed out that greater restriction of the physical environment does not necessarily mean greater restriction of psychological freedom or human potential. In fact, it is conceivable that some students could be more restricted in the long run in a regular class where they are rejected by others and fail to learn necessary skills than in a special class or day school where they learn happily and well. It is important to keep the ultimate goals for the pupil in mind and to avoid letting "least restrictive" become a hollow slogan that results in shortchanging them in their education. As Morse has noted, "The goal should be to find the most productive setting to provide the maximum assistance for the child" (1984, p. 120).

Although considerable variation in the placement of students with disabilities is found from state to state and among school systems within a given state, most exceptional students are educated in regular classes. Nationwide, over two-thirds of exceptional children and youths are served primarily in regular classes. Most of these students receive special instruction for part of the school day from special education resource teachers. In the United States, about one-fourth of all children and youths with disabilities are placed in separate special classes, and only about 7 percent are segregated in separate schools or other environments (e.g., institutions, hospital schools, and homebound instruction; see Figure 1–3).

Children under the age of six less often receive education in regular classes and more often attend separate schools than do children who have reached the usual school age. Special classes, separate schools, and other environments such as homebound instruction are used more often for older teenagers and young adults than for students of elementary and high school age. We can explain these differences by two facts. First, preschoolers and young adults who are identified for special education tend to have more severe disabilities than students in kindergarten through grade 12. Second, some school systems do not have regular classes for preschoolers and young adults, and thus placements in other than regular classes are typically more available and more appropriate.

*W*HAT SHOULD I DO BEFORE I MAKE A REFERRAL? ➢

Probably the most important thing you should do is to contact the student's parents if you are thinking about referring him or her. If you cannot reach them by phone, try a home visit or ask the visiting teacher (or school social worker, psychologist, or other support personnel) to help you set up a conference. It is very important that you discuss the student's problems with the parents *before* you refer. Parents should never be surprised to find that their child has been referred; they should know well in advance that their child's teachers have noticed problems. One of the most important things you can do to prevent conflict with parents is to establish and maintain communication with them regarding their child's progress.

Before making a referral, check *all* the student's school records. Look for information that could help you understand the student's behavioral or academic problems.

Has the student ever:
- had a psychological evaluation?
- qualified for special services?
- been included in other special programs (e.g., programs for disadvantaged children or speech or language therapy)?
- scored far below average on standardized tests?
- been retained?

Do the records indicate:
- good progress in some areas, poor progress in others?
- any physical or medical problem?
- that the student is taking medication?

Talk to the student's other teachers and professional support personnel about your concern for the student.

Have other teachers:
- also had difficulty with the student?
- found ways of dealing successfully with the student?

The analysis of information obtained in these ways may help you teach and manage the student successfully, or help you justify to the parents why you believe their child may need special education.

Before making a referral, you will be expected to document the strategies that you have used in your class to meet the student's educational needs. Regardless of whether the student is later found to have a disabling condition, your documentation will be useful in the following ways: (1) you will have

evidence that will be helpful to or required by the committee of professionals who will evaluate the student; (2) you will be better able to help the student's parents understand that methods used for other students in the class are not adequate for their child; and (3) you will have records of successful and/or unsuccessful methods of working with the student that will be useful to you and any other teacher who works with the student in the future.

Your documentation of what you have done may appear to require a lot of paper work, but careful record keeping will pay off. If the student is causing you serious concern, then you will be wise to demonstrate your concern by keeping written records. Your notes should include items such as the following:

- exactly what you are concerned about
- why you are concerned about it
- dates, places, and times you have observed the problem
- precisely what you have done to try to resolve the problem
- who, if anyone, helped you devise the plans or strategies you have used
- evidence that the strategies have been successful or unsuccessful.

In summary, make certain that you have accomplished the following before you make a referral:

1. Held at least one conference to discuss your concerns with the parents (or made extensive and documented efforts to communicate with the parents).
2. Checked all available school records and interviewed other professionals involved with the child.
3. Documented the academic and behavioral management strategies that you have tried.

Remember that you should refer a student only if you can make a convincing case that the student may have a disability and probably cannot be served appropriately without special education. Referral for special education begins a time-consuming, costly, and stressful process that is potentially damaging to the student and has many legal ramifications.

SOURCE: From Patricia L. Pullen and James M. Kauffman, *What should I know about special education? Answers for classroom teachers* (Austin, TX: Pro-Ed, 1987). © 1987 by P. L. Pullen and J. M. Kauffman. Reprinted with permission.

The environment that is least restrictive depends in part on the individual's exceptionality. There is almost never a need to segregate in a separate class or separate school a student whose primary disability is a speech impairment. Most students with learning disabilities can be appropriately educated primarily in regular classes. On the other hand, the resources needed to teach students with severe impairments of hearing and vision may require that they attend separate schools or classes for at least part of their school careers.

WHAT TEACHERS ARE EXPECTED TO DO

We have noted that most students in public schools who have been identified as exceptional are placed in regular classrooms for at least part of the school day. Furthermore, there is good reason to believe that a large number of public school students not identified as disabled or gifted share many of the characteristics of those who are exceptional. Thus all teachers must obviously be prepared to deal with exceptional students.

The roles of general and special education teachers are not always clear in a given case. Sometimes uncertainty about the division of responsibility can be extremely stressful; for example, teachers may feel uneasy because it is not clear whose job it is to make special adaptations for a pupil or just what they are expected to do in cooperating with other teachers.

Relationship Between General and Special Education

During the 1980s, the relationship between general and special education became a matter of great concern to policymakers, researchers, and advocates for exceptional children. Proposals for changing the relationship between general and special education, including radical calls to restructure or merge the two, came to be known as the **regular education initiative (REI)**. Moderate proponents of the REI suggested that general educators take more responsibility for many students with mild or moderate disabilities, with special educators serving more as consultants or resources to regular classroom teachers and less as special teachers. More radical proponents of the REI recommended that special education be eliminated as a separate, identifiable part of education. They called for a single, unified educational system in which all students are viewed as unique, special, and entitled to the same quality of education. Although many of the suggested reforms have great appeal and some could produce benefits for exceptional students, the basis for the integration of special and general education and the ultimate consequences have been questioned (Goodlad & Lovitt, 1993; Lloyd, Singh, & Repp, 1991).

One reason behind the proposals known as the REI is concern for pupils who are considered at risk. "At risk" is often not clearly defined, but it generally refers to students who perform or behave poorly in school and appear likely to fail or fall far short of their potential. Some advocates of reform suggest that at-risk students can not be or should not be distinguished from those with mild disabilities. Some argue that the problems of at-risk students tend to be ignored because special education siphons resources from general education. Should special education and general education merge for the purpose of making general education better able to respond to at-risk students? Or should special education maintain its separate identity and be expanded to include at-risk students? Should general

> **regular education initiative (REI).** A philosophy that maintains that general education, rather than special education, should be primarily responsible for the education of students with disabilities.

*E*ducators in regular
classrooms must
be tuned into their
students as individuals, since
special education referrals
often begin with their
recommendations.

education be expected to develop new programs for at-risk students without merging with special education? There are no ready answers to these and other questions about the education of students at risk.

We discuss the REI, inclusion, and their implications further in Chapter 2. Regardless of one's views, the controversy about the relationship between special and general education has made teachers more aware of the problems of deciding just which students should be taught specific curricula, which students should receive special attention or services, and where and by whom these should be provided (Ysseldyke, Algozzine, & Thurlow, 1992). There are no pat answers to the questions about how special and general education should work together to see that every student receives an appropriate education. Yet it is clear that the relationship between them must be one of cooperation and collaboration. They must not become independent or mutually exclusive educational tracks. Neither can we deny that general and special educators have somewhat different roles to play. With this in mind, we summarize some of the major expectations for all teachers, as well as for special education teachers in particular.

Expectations for All Educators

Whether specifically trained in special education or not, a teacher may be expected to participate in educating exceptional students in any one of the following ways:

1. *Make maximum effort to accommodate individual students' needs.* Teaching in public schools requires dealing with diverse students in every class. All teachers must make an effort to meet the needs of individuals who may differ in some way from the average or typical student in their classroom. Flexibility, adaptation, accommodation, and special attention are to be

expected of every teacher. Special education should be considered necessary only when a teacher's best efforts to meet a student's individual needs are not successful.

2. *Evaluate academic abilities and disabilities.* Although psychologists or other special school personnel may give a student formal standardized tests in academic areas, adequate evaluation requires the teacher's assessment of the student's performance in the classroom. Teachers must be able to report specifically and precisely how the student can and cannot perform in all academic areas for which they are responsible.

3. *Refer for evaluation.* By law, all public school systems must make extensive efforts to screen and identify all children and youths of school age who have disabilities. Teachers must observe students' behavior and refer those they suspect of having disabilities for evaluation by a multidisciplinary team. *We stress here that a student should not be referred for special education unless extensive and unsuccessful efforts have been made to accommodate his or her needs in regular classes. Before referral, school personnel must document the strategies that have been used to teach and manage the student in general education. Only if these strategies have failed is referral justified* (see the box on p. 20).

4. *Participate in eligibility conferences.* Before students are provided special education, their eligibility must be determined by an interdisciplinary team. Therefore, teachers must be ready to work with other teachers and with professionals from other disciplines (psychology, medicine, or social work, for example) in determining a student's eligibility for special education.

5. *Participate in writing individualized education programs.* A written individualized program for his or her education must be on file in the records of every student with a disability. Teachers must be ready to participate in a conference (possibly including the student and/or parents, as well as other professionals) in which the program is formulated.

6. *Communicate with parents or guardians.* Parents (sometimes surrogate parents) or guardians must be consulted during the evaluation of their child's eligibility for special education, formulation of the individualized education program, and reassessment of any special program that may be designed for their child. Teachers must contribute to the school's communication with parents about their child's problems, placement, and progress.

7. *Participate in due process hearings and negotiations.* When parents, guardians, or students with disabilities themselves are dissatisfied with the school's response to educational needs, they may request a "due process" hearing or negotiations regarding appropriate services. Teachers may be called on to offer observations, opinions, or suggestions in such hearings or negotiations.

8. *Collaborate with other professionals in identifying and making maximum use of exceptional students' abilities.* Finding and implementing solutions to the challenges of educating exceptional students are not the exclusive responsibility of any one professional group. General and special education teachers are expected to share responsibility for educating students with special needs. In addition, teachers may need to collaborate with other professionals, depending on the student's exceptionality. Psychologists,

In addition to regular teaching skills, special educators must possess highly specialized skills.

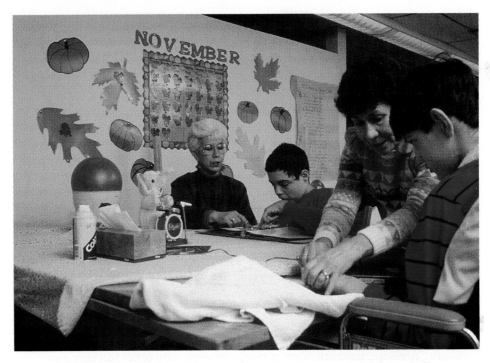

counselors, physicians, physical therapists, and a variety of other specialists may need the teacher's perspective on the student's abilities and disabilities, and they may rely on the teacher to implement critical aspects of evaluation or treatment.

A high level of professional competence and ethical judgment is required to conform to these expectations. Teaching demands a thorough knowledge of child development and expertise in instruction. Furthermore, teachers are sometimes faced with serious professional and ethical dilemmas in trying to serve the needs of students and their parents, on the one hand, and in attempting to conform to legal or administrative pressures, on the other (Howe & Miramontes, 1992). For example, when there are indications that the child may have a disability, should a teacher refer that child for evaluation and possible placement in special education, knowing that only inadequate or inappropriate services will be provided? Should a teacher who believes strongly that teenage students with mild retardation need sex education refrain from giving students any information because sex education is not part of the prescribed curriculum and is frowned on by the school board?

Expectations for Special Educators

In addition to being competent enough to meet the preceding expectations, special education teachers must attain special expertise in the following areas:

1. *Academic instruction of students with learning problems.* The majority of students with disabilities have more difficulty learning academic skills than do those without disabilities. This is true for all categories of disabling conditions because sensory impairments, physical disabilities, and mental

or emotional disabilities all tend to make academic learning more difficult. Often the difficulty is slight; sometimes it is extreme. Special education teachers must have more than patience and hope, though they do need these qualities; they must have the technical skill to present academic tasks so that students with disabilities will understand and respond appropriately.

2. *Management of serious behavior problems.* Many students with disabilities have behavior problems in addition to their other exceptionalities. Some, in fact, require special education primarily because of their inappropriate or disruptive behavior. Special education teachers must have the ability to deal effectively with more than the usual troublesome behavior of students. Besides understanding and empathy, they must possess the mastery of techniques that will allow them to draw out particularly withdrawn students, control those who are hyperaggressive and persistently disruptive, and teach critical social skills.

3. *Use of technological advances.* Technology is increasingly being applied to the problems of teaching exceptional students and improving their daily lives. New devices and methods are rapidly being developed, particularly for students with sensory and physical disabilities. Special education teachers need more than mere awareness of the technology available; they must also be able to evaluate its advantages and disadvantages for teaching the exceptional children and youths with whom they work.

4. *Knowledge of special education law.* For good or ill, special education today involves many details of law. The rights of students with disabilities are spelled out in considerable detail in federal and state legislation. The laws, and the rules and regulations that accompany them, are constantly being interpreted by new court decisions, some of which have widespread implications for the practice of special education. Special education teachers do not need to be lawyers, but they do need to be aware of the law's requirements and prohibitions if they are to be adequate advocates for students with disabilities.

We caution here that the specific day-to-day expectations for special education teachers vary from school system to school system and from state to state. What are listed here are the general expectations and areas of competence with which every special educator will necessarily be concerned.

HOW AND WHERE SPECIAL EDUCATION BEGAN

There have always been exceptional children, but there have not always been special educational services to address their needs. During the closing years of the eighteenth century, following the American and French revolutions, effective procedures were devised for teaching children with sensory impairments—those who were blind or deaf (Winzer, 1986). Early in the nineteenth century, the first systematic attempts were made to educate "idiotic" and "insane" children—those who today are said to have mental retardation and emotional or behavioral disorders. In the prerevolutionary era, the most society had offered children with disabilities was protection—asylum from a cruel world into which they did not fit and in which they could not survive with dignity, if they could survive at all. But as the ideas of democracy, individual freedom, and egalitarianism swept

America and France, there was a change in attitude. Political reformers and leaders in medicine and education began to champion the cause of children and adults with disabilities, urging that these "imperfect" or "incomplete" individuals be taught skills that would allow them to become independent, productive citizens. These humanitarian sentiments went beyond a desire to protect and defend people with disabilities. The early leaders sought to "normalize" exceptional children to the greatest extent possible and "confer on them" the human dignity they presumably lacked.

The historical roots of special education are found primarily in the early 1800s. Contemporary educational methods for exceptional children can be traced directly to techniques pioneered during that era. And many (perhaps most) of today's vital, controversial issues have been issues ever since the dawn of special education. In our discussion of some of the major historical events and trends since 1800, we comment briefly on the history of people and ideas, professional and parent organizations, and legislation.

People and Ideas

Most of the originators of special education were European physicians. They were primarily young, ambitious people who challenged the wisdom of the established authorities, including their own friends and mentors (Kanner, 1964). Jean Marc Gaspard Itard (1775–1838), a French physician who was an authority on diseases of the ear and on the education of students who were deaf, is the person to whom most historians trace the beginning of special education as we know it today. In the early years of the nineteenth century, this young doctor began to educate a boy of about twelve who had been found roaming naked and wild in the forests of France. Itard's mentor, Philippe Pinel (1745–1826), a prominent French physician who was an early advocate of humane treatment of "insane" persons, advised him that his efforts would be unsuccessful because the boy, Victor, was a "hopeless idiot." But Itard persevered. He did not make Victor nondisabled, but he did dramatically improve the wild child's behavior through patient, systematic educative procedures (Itard, 1962).

Itard's student, Edouard Seguin (1812–1880), emigrated to the United States in 1848. Before that, Seguin had become famous as an educator of "idiotic" children, even though most thinkers of the day were convinced that such children could not be taught anything of significance.

The ideas of the first special educators were truly revolutionary for their times. These are a few of the revolutionary ideas of Itard, Seguin, and their successors that form the foundation for present-day special education:

- *Individualized instruction,* in which the child's characteristics rather than prescribed academic content provide the basis for teaching techniques.
- *A carefully sequenced series of educational tasks,* beginning with tasks the child can perform and gradually leading to more complex learning.
- *Emphasis on stimulation* and awakening of the child's senses, the aim being to make the child more aware of and responsive to educational stimuli.
- *Meticulous arrangement of the child's environment,* so that the structure of the environment and the child's experience of it lead naturally to learning.
- *Immediate reward for correct performance,* providing reinforcement for desirable behavior.

*Jean Marc Gaspard Itard—*Victor

- *Tutoring in functional skills*, the desire being to make the child as self-sufficient and productive as possible in everyday life.
- *Belief that every child should be educated to the greatest extent possible*, the assumption being that every child can improve to some degree.

↓ Montessori - one of the early founders - beliefs carried over to now.

So far we have mentioned only European physicians who figured prominently in the rise of special education. Although it is true that much of the initial work took place in Europe, many U.S. researchers contributed greatly during those early years. They stayed informed of European developments as best they could, some of them traveling to Europe for the specific purpose of obtaining first-hand information about the education of children with disabilities.

Among the young U.S. thinkers concerned with the education of students with disabilities was Samuel Gridley Howe (1801–1876), an 1824 graduate of Harvard Medical School. Besides being a physician and an educator, Howe was a political and social reformer, a champion of humanitarian causes and emancipation. He was instrumental in founding the Perkins School for the Blind in Watertown, Massachusetts, and was also a teacher of students who were deaf and blind. His success in teaching Laura Bridgman, who was deaf and blind, greatly influenced the education of Helen Keller. Howe was also a force behind the organization of an experimental school for children with mental retardation in Massachusetts in the 1840s and was personally acquainted with Seguin.

When Thomas Hopkins Gallaudet (1787–1851), a minister, was a student at Andover Theological Seminary, he tried to teach a girl who was deaf. He visited Europe to learn about educating the deaf, and in 1817 established the first American residential school, in Hartford, Connecticut, for students who were deaf (now known as the American School of the Deaf). Gallaudet University in Washington, D.C., the only liberal arts college for students who are deaf, was named in his honor.

The early years of special education were vibrant with the pulse of new ideas. It is not possible to read the words of Itard, Seguin, Howe, and their contemporaries without being captivated by the romance, idealism, and excitement of their exploits. The results they achieved were truly remarkable for their era. Today, special education remains a vibrant field in which innovations, excitement, idealism, and controversies are the norm. Teachers of exceptional children—and that includes, as discussed earlier, all teachers—must understand how and why special education emerged as a discipline.

Thomas Hopkins Gallaudet

Growth of the Discipline

Special education did not suddenly spring up as a new discipline, nor did it develop in isolation from other disciplines. The emergence of psychology and sociology, and especially the beginning of the widespread use of mental tests in the early years of the twentieth century, had enormous implications for the growth of special education. Psychologists' study of learning and their prediction of school failure or success by means of tests helped focus attention on children with special needs. Sociologists, social workers, and anthropologists drew attention to the ways in which exceptional children's families and communities responded to them and affected their learning and adjustment.

As the education profession itself matured and as compulsory school attendance laws became a reality, there was a growing realization among teachers and school administrators that a large number of students must be given something beyond the ordinary classroom experience. Elizabeth Farrell, a teacher in New York City in the early part of the century, was highly instrumental in the development of special education as a profession. She and the New York City superintendent of schools attempted to use information about child development, social work, mental testing, and instruction to address the needs of children and youths who were being ill-served in or excluded from regular classes and schools. Farrell was a great advocate for services for students with special needs. Her motives and those of the teachers and administrators who worked with her were to see that every student—including every exceptional child or youth—had an appropriate education and received the related health and social services necessary for optimum learning in school (Hendrick & MacMillan, 1989; MacMillan & Hendrick, 1993). In 1922, Farrell and a group of other special educators from across the United States and Canada founded the Council for Exceptional Children, today still the primary professional organization of special educators.

Contemporary special education is a professional field with roots in several academic disciplines—especially medicine, psychology, sociology, and social work—in addition to professional education. It is a discipline sufficiently different from the mainstream of professional education to require special training programs but sufficiently like the mainstream to maintain a primary concern for schools and teaching.

Professional and Parents' Organizations

Individuals and ideas have played crucial roles in the history of special education, but it is accurate to say that much of the progress made over the years has been achieved primarily by the collective efforts of professionals and parents. Professional groups were organized first, beginning in the nineteenth century. Effective national parents' organizations have existed in the United States only since 1950.

The earliest professional organizations having some bearing on the education of children with disabilities were medical associations founded in the 1800s. With the organization of the Council for Exceptional Children (CEC) and its many divisions, educators have a professional association devoted to special education. Today CEC has a national membership of over 50,000, including about 10,000 students. There are state CEC organizations and hundreds of local chapters. Divisions of CEC have been organized to meet the interests and needs of members who specialize in a particular area.

Although the parents' organizations offer membership to individuals who do not have exceptional children of their own, they are made up primarily of parents who do have such children and concentrate on issues of special concern to them. Parents' organizations have typically served three essential functions: (1) providing an informal group for parents who understand one another's problems and needs and help one another deal with anxieties and frustrations; (2) providing information regarding services and potential resources; and (3) providing the structure for obtaining needed services for their children. Some of the organizations that came about primarily as the result of parents' efforts include the ARC (formerly the Association for Retarded Citizens), the National Association for Gifted Children, the Learning Disabilities Association, the

Autism Society of America, and the Federation of Families for Children's Mental Health.

Legislation

Laws have played a major role in the history of special education. In fact, much of the progress in meeting the educational needs of children and youths with disabilities is attributable to laws requiring states and localities to include students with special needs in the public education system. We focus here on recent legislation that represents a culmination of decades of legislative history.

Two landmark federal laws were passed in 1990: the **Individuals with Disabilities Education Act (IDEA)** and the **Americans with Disabilities Act (ADA)**. IDEA amended a federal law passed in 1975, the Education for All Handicapped Children Act, also commonly known as **PL 94–142**.* IDEA ensures that all children and youths with disabilities have the right to a free, appropriate public education. ADA ensures the right of individuals with disabilities to nondiscriminatory treatment in other aspects of their lives; it provides protections of civil rights in the specific areas of employment, transportation, public accommodations, state and local government, and telecommunications.

IDEA (sometimes cited as PL 101–476) and another federal law focusing on intervention in early childhood (PL 99–457) now mandate a free, appropriate public education for every child or youth between the ages of three and twenty-one regardless of the nature or severity of the disability he or she may have. PL 99–457 also provides incentives for states to develop early intervention programs for infants with known disabilities and those considered at risk. Together, these laws require public school systems to identify all children and youths with disabilities and to provide the special education and related services they may need.

As mentioned earlier, IDEA amended an earlier law, commonly known as PL 94–142 (the Education for All Handicapped Children Act). PL 94–142 was revolutionary. It was the first federal law mandating free, appropriate public education for all children with disabilities. Its basic provisions, which are now incorporated in IDEA, are described in the box on page 32. IDEA altered PL 94–142 in several significant ways, three of which are particularly important for our discussion here. First, the language of the law was altered. "Children" became "individuals," reflecting the fact that some of the students involved are young adults, not children. The terminology "handicapped" was changed to "with disabilities," acknowledging the difference between limitations imposed by society (handicaps) and inability to do certain things (disabilities; recall our earlier discussion, p. 6–7). Use of the phrase "with disabilities" also signifies that we think of the person first; the disabling condition is only one characteristic of an individual, who has many other characteristics as well. Second, special emphasis was placed on transition. PL 94–142 required an individualized education program for every child with a disability; IDEA requires that every older student with a disability (usually beginning at age 14 or 16) have an individualized plan for making the transition to work or further education following high school. Third, two additional categories of disability were recognized as distinct

> ➤ **Individuals with Disabilities Education Act (IDEA).** The Individuals with Disabilities Education Act of 1990; replaced PL 94–142.

> ➤ **Americans with Disabilities Act (ADA).** Civil rights legislation for persons with disabilities ensuring nondiscrimination in a broad range of activities.

> ➤ **PL 94–142.** The Education for All Handicapped Children Act, which contains a mandatory provision stating that to receive funds under the act, every school system in the nation must make provision for a free, appropriate public education for every child between the ages of three and eighteen (now extended to ages three to twenty-one) regardless of how, or how seriously, he or she may be disabled.

*Legislation is often designated PL (for public law), followed by a hyphenated numeral, the first set of digits representing the number of the Congress that passed the bill and the second set representing the number of that bill. Thus PL 94–142 is the 142nd public law passed by the 94th Congress.

*I*ndividuals with disabilities
have been empowered by
recent legislation to use
legal channels to ensure their rights
to equal opportunities.

➢ **autism.** A disorder
characterized by extreme
withdrawal, self-stimulation,
cognitive deficits, language
disorders, and onset before
the age of thirty months.

➢ **traumatic brain injury.**
Injury to the brain, not
including conditions present
at birth, birth trauma, or
degenerative diseases or
conditions, resulting in total
or partial disability or
psychosocial maladjustment
that affects educational
performance; may affect
cognition, language, memory,
attention, reasoning, abstract
thinking, judgment, problem
solving, sensory or perceptual
and motor disabilities,
psychosocial behavior,
physical functions,
information processing, or
speech.

entities—**autism** and **traumatic brain injury**. These categories had previously
been subsumed under other categories.

In special education, as in other areas of professional practice, laws and law
suits are numerous and technical. We do not try to lead you through the thicket
of legislation and litigation. Our purpose is to describe general trends and leave
you with a sense of the direction legislation and litigation have taken.

TRENDS IN LEGISLATION AND LITIGATION

Trends in Legislation

Legislation has historically been increasingly specific and mandatory. In the
1980s, however, the renewed emphasis on states' rights and local autonomy, plus
a political strategy of federal deregulation, led to attempts to repeal some of the
provisions of IDEA (then still known as PL 94–142) and loosen federal rules and
regulations. Federal disinvestment in education and deregulation of education
programs were hallmarks of the Reagan administration (Clark & Astuto, 1988;
Verstegen & Clark, 1988), so it is not surprising that federal mandates for special
education came under fire. Dissatisfaction with federal mandates is due in part to
the fact that the federal government contributes relatively little to the funding of
special education. Although the demands of IDEA are detailed, state and local
governments must pay most of the cost of special education programs.

Issues in Special Education

An Act of Transformation: Law for Disabled to Change Workplace

CNN

The most far-reaching civil rights law since the 1960s takes effect Sunday, promising to force the kind of wholesale changes that would make the American workplace far more hospitable to workers with physical and mental disabilities.

The new law, the second phase of the Americans With Disabilities Act, outlines changes that companies must make to nearly every facet of employment, from job applications and interviews, to health insurance plans, compensation and work schedules—all designed to extend to the disabled the same rights that women and minorities won nearly three decades ago.

At many companies in the Washington area and across the country, managers already are bending and flexing to meet the needs of disabled workers.

Marriott Corp. uses interpreters to help a hearing-impaired employee at its Bethesda headquarters understand what is being said at staff meetings. A blind manager at Nordstrom's Pentagon City store has a scanner attached to his computer that reproduces ordinary documents in Braille.

In Atlantic City, owners of the Trump Castle casino altered a blackjack table to help a dealer who uses a wheelchair. And Continental Insurance, a New York-based property and casualty company, has an enlarging device attached to a computer so that a clerical worker with poor vision can see her keyboard more clearly.

Since it affects all industries, and ultimately touches millions of businesses, the act has a scope matched by few other laws. Generally, it is being praised by businesses as an effort to reach out to a disenfranchised segment of society. But it also has drawn criticism from industry groups that fear it could open the floodgates to litigation and subject businesses to large financial judgments by juries . . . .

The law does not state precisely what a company must do or spend to ensure that it does not discriminate, since what is appropriate for a commercial giant like IBM might not be for a small retailer. What the law does require is that employers make "reasonable accommodations" to assure that qualified applicants with physical or mental disabilities are not discriminated against, unless the employer can show that the accommodation would put an "undue hardship" on its operations.

For a large law firm, that could mean providing a reader for a lawyer who is blind; for a computer company, it could mean widening doorways or adjusting a desk's height to accommodate a systems analyst in a wheelchair.

The law goes well beyond traditional notions of disability by including any person with an impairment that substantially limits a major life activity. It protects people with AIDS, with cosmetic disfigurements, with dyslexia, even those who suffer from stress or depression if their condition is so severe as to be considered disabling by a psychiatrist . . . . To prepare themselves for the July 26 deadline, companies in recent weeks have been doing everything from scrutinizing the wording of job applications to reviewing hiring and promotion practices to ensure nothing they do could be considered discriminatory.

Under the new law, for example, applicants cannot be asked whether they have a disability, only whether they are able to perform specific functions that are considered essential to a job. For employers, that often means determining just exactly what are the essential functions of each job.

"Is it essential for a painter in a wheelchair to be able to reach the ceiling? Probably not, if we have a crew of 30 other painters who can do it," said Roger Wagner, president of Trump Castle, which is reviewing some 600 distinct jobs to determine their essential functions . . . .

Even with the force of the act on their side, many advocates for the disabled say it will be some time before the fortunes of that community improve significantly. The unemployment rate among those with disabilities is estimated to run as high as 60 percent and, as a result, many lack the skills necessary to compete for jobs.

"It is a Catch-22," said Peter Blanck, a University of Iowa law professor who is involved in a study of persons with disabilities. "If you haven't been in the work force, you won't have the skills needed for a lot of jobs."

The act does not mandate job quotas; it only requires that employers hire and promote qualified candidates, whether they have a disability or not.

To Mary Beth Chambers, a deaf employee who works the cosmetics counter at Nordstrom's Pentagon City store, the struggle for equality in the work place is well worth it.

"It's not people's fault that they're hearing-impaired," said Chambers, who reads customers' lips.

"Companies don't know what they're missing," she said. "These people are capable of doing anything, and if they keep trying, their dreams will come true."

SOURCE: Liz Spayd, *The Washington Post,* Sunday, July 26, 1992, pp. C1, C9. © 1992, The Washington Post. Reprinted with permission.

AJOR PROVISIONS OF IDEA (PL 94–142) ➢

Each state and locality must have a plan to ensure

Identification	Extensive efforts must be made to screen and identify all children and youths with disabilities.
Full service, at no cost	Every student with a disability must be assured an appropriate public education at no cost to the parents or guardians.
Due process	The student's and parents' rights to information and informed consent must be assured before the student is evaluated, labeled, or placed, and they have a right to an impartial due process hearing if they disagree with the school's decisions.
Parent/guardian surrogate consultation	The student's parents or guardian must be consulted about the student's evaluation and placement and the educational plan; if the parents or guardian are unknown or unavailable, a surrogate parent to act for the student must be found.
LRE	The student must be educated in the least restrictive environment that is consistent with his or her educational needs and, insofar as possible, with students without disabilities.
IEP	A written individualized education program must be prepared for each student with a disability. The program must state present levels of functioning, long- and short-term goals, services to be provided, plans for initiating and evaluating the services, and needed transition services (from school to work or continued education) for students at an appropriate age (usually by age 14 or 16).
Nondiscriminatory evaluation	The student must be evaluated in all areas of suspected disability and in a way that is not biased by the student's language or cultural characteristics or disabilities. Evaluation must be by a multidisciplinary team, and no single evaluation procedure may be used as the sole criterion for placement or planning.
Confidentiality	The results of evaluation and placement must be kept confidential, though the student's parents or guardian may have access to the records.
Personnel development, in-service	Training must be provided for teachers and other professional personnel, including in-service training for regular teachers, in meeting the needs of students with disabilities.

Detailed federal rules and regulations govern the implementation of each of these major provisions. The definitions of some of these provisions—LRE and nondiscriminatory evaluation, for example—are still being clarified by federal officials and court decisions.

Special education laws survived the deregulation of the 1980s, and the trend in legislation has been increasingly to extend civil rights to citizens with disabilities. The enactment of IDEA (the Individuals with Disabilities Education Act) and ADA (the Americans with Disabilities Act) in 1990 represents a continuing commitment to require schools, employers, and government agencies to recognize the abilities of people with disabilities. These laws require reasonable accommodations that allow those who have disabilities to participate to the fullest extent possible in all the activities of daily living that individuals without disabilities take for granted. The requirements of ADA are intended to grant equal opportunity to people with disabilities in employment, transportation, public accommodations, state and local government, and telecommunications. ADA is as revolutionary for business in the 1990s as PL 94–142 was for education when it was enacted in the 1970s (see box page 31, "An Act of Transformation"). You may recall that in the article about his plans for higher education, Tony

Hensley mentioned how ADA will make a difference for him (see box page 8). Clearly, ADA has great implications for many young adults with disabilities as they leave high school for work or higher education, and for the everyday lives of all individuals with disabilities who live in our communities.

Relationship of Litigation to Legislation

Legislation requires or gives permission to provide special education, but it does not necessarily result in what legislators intended. Whether the laws are administered properly is a legal question for the courts. That is, laws may have little or no effect on the lives of individuals with disabilities until courts interpret the meaning of those laws—exactly what the laws require in practice. Exceptional children, primarily through the action of parents' and professional organizations, have been getting their day in court more frequently since IDEA and related federal and state laws were passed. Thus we must examine trends in litigation to complete the picture of how our legal system may safeguard or undermine appropriate education for exceptional children.

Trends in Litigation

Zelder (1953) noted that in the early days of public education, school attendance was seen as a *privilege* that could be awarded or withheld from an individual child at the discretion of local school officials. The courts typically found, during

*H*opes are that recent legislation will go far to make full participation in the education system a realistic goal for students with disabilities.

the late nineteenth and early twentieth centuries, that disruptive children or those with mental retardation could be excluded from school for the sake of preserving order, protecting the teacher's time from excessive demands, and sparing children the "pain" of seeing others who are disabled. In the first half of the twentieth century, the courts tended to defend the majority of school children from a disabled minority. But now the old excuses for excluding students with disabilities from school are no longer thought to be valid. Today, the courts must interpret laws that define school attendance as the *right* of every child, regardless of his or her disability. Litigation is now focused on ensuring that every child receives an education *appropriate for his or her individual needs.*

Litigation may involve legal suits filed for either of two reasons: because special education services are not being provided for students whose parents want them, or because students are being assigned to special education when their parents believe they should not be. Suits filed *for special education* have been brought primarily by parents whose children are unquestionably disabled and are being denied any education at all or being given very meager special services. The parents who file these suits believe that the advantages of their child's identification for special education services clearly outweigh the disadvantages. Suits *against special education* have been brought primarily by parents of students who have mild or questionable disabilities and who are already attending school. These parents believe that their children are being stigmatized and discriminated against rather than helped by special education. Thus the courts today are asked to make decisions in which the individual student's characteristics are weighed against a specific educational program.

Parents want their children with disabilities to have a free public education that meets their needs but does not stigmatize them unnecessarily and that permits them to be taught in the regular school and classroom as much as possible. The laws governing education recognize parents' and student's rights to such an education. In the courts today, the burden of proof is ultimately on local and state education specialists, who must show in every instance that the student's abilities and disabilities have been completely and accurately assessed and that appropriate educational procedures are being employed.

One court case of the 1980s deserves particular consideration. In 1982 the U.S. Supreme Court made its first interpretation of PL 94–142 in *Hudson v. Rowley*, a case involving a child who was deaf, Amy Rowley. The Court's decision was that "appropriate" education for a child with a disability does not necessarily mean education that will produce the maximum possible achievement. Amy's parents had contended that she might be able to learn more in school if she were provided with a sign language interpreter. But the Court decided that because the school had designed an individualized program of special services for Amy and she was achieving at or above the level of her nondisabled classmates, the school system had met its obligation under the law to provide an "appropriate" education. Court cases in the 1990s will undoubtedly help to clarify what the law means by "appropriate" education and "least restrictive" environment (Yanok, 1986).

The Intent of Legislation: An Individualized Education Program

The primary intent of the special education laws passed during the past two decades has been to require educators to focus on the needs of individual stu-

NDIVIDUALIZED EDUCATION PROGRAM (IEP) ➤

WHAT IS AN IEP?

An IEP is a written agreement between the parents and the school about what the child needs and what will be done to address those needs. It is, in effect, a contract about services to be provided for the student. By law an IEP must include the following: (1) the student's present levels of academic performance; (2) annual goals for the student; (3) short-term instructional objectives related to the annual goals; (4) the special education and related services that will be provided and the [*—trans- portation*] extent to which the child will participate in regular education programs; (5) plans for starting the services and the anticipated duration of the services; and (6) appropriate plans for evaluating, at least annually, whether the goals and objectives are being achieved.*

*Note: IDEA added transition planning as a requirement for older students.

ARE TEACHERS LEGALLY LIABLE FOR REACHING IEP GOALS?

No. Federal law does not require that the stated goals be met. However, teachers and other school personnel are responsible for seeing that the IEP is written to include the six components listed above, that the parents have an opportunity to review and participate in developing the IEP, that the IEP is approved by the parents before placement, and that the services called for in the IEP are actually provided. Teachers and other school personnel are responsible for making a good-faith effort to achieve the goals and objectives of the IEP.

SOURCE: From Patricia L. Pullen and James M. Kauffman, *What should I know about special education? Answers for classroom teachers* (Austin, TX: Pro-Ed, 1987). © 1987 by P. L. Pullen and J. M. Kauffman. Reprinted with permission.

dents with disabilities. The **Individualized Education Program (IEP)** is the most important aspect of this focus; it spells out just what teachers plan to do to meet an exceptional student's needs, and the plan must be approved by the student's parents or guardian. IEPs vary greatly in format and detail and from one school district to another. Some school districts use computerized IEP systems to help teachers determine goals and instructional objectives and to save time and effort in writing the documents. Many school systems, however, still rely on the teachers' knowledge of students and curriculum to complete handwritten IEPs on the district's forms. Federal and state regulations do not specify exactly how much detail must be included in an IEP, only that it must be a *written* statement developed in a meeting of a representative of the local school district, the teacher, the parents or guardian, and, whenever appropriate, the child, and that it must include certain elements (see the box above).

Figure 1–4 shows excerpts from an IEP written by teachers in a school district that does not use computer-generated goals or objectives. We estimate that the IEP that follows is about average in specificity. It is not perfect, and we caution that IEPs sometimes omit important information, are poorly written, or do not represent what the student actually receives. The information in this excerpt is taken verbatim from the IEP, except that all the personally identifying information has been changed. We have excerpted five pages (from a total of 18) to illustrate how an IEP might be organized and the various components that must be included. The first four pages are followed by goals and objectives in each area of the curriculum. Figure 1–4 includes only goals and objectives for reading and math. Note the additional areas of Ann's educational program in special and general education that are listed on page 3 of her IEP. Ann's actual IEP included

➤ **Individualized Education Program (IEP).** PL 94–142 requires an IEP to be drawn up by the educational team for each exceptional child; the IEP must include a statement of present educational performance, instructional goals, educational services to be provided, and criteria and procedures for determining that the instructional objectives are being met.

written agreement

Figure 1-4

➤ *Individualized Education Program*

CURRY PUBLIC SCHOOLS
Department of Pupil Personnel Services
1417 Broadway, Curry, Virginia 23234
(804) 666-9876

INDIVIDUALIZED EDUCATION PROGRAM

Name Amy North   DOB 7-7-83   Grade 2
Parent/Guardian John/Sandra North   School Eugene Field
Address 1400 Perth Road 23456   Phone: HOME 945-4546   WORK 886-1234
Handicapping Condition(s) mild mental retardation   Most Recent Eligibility Date 1-24-91
IEP Purpose: _____ Initial Placement ✓ Continued Placement _____ Dismissal from _____

PRESENT LEVEL OF EDUCATIONAL PERFORMANCE:

Amy reads stories of approximately 100 words on first grade level using phonics skills to decode unfamiliar words. She answers factual comprehension questions. She does not copy from the board but completes reading seatwork legibly. She spells C-V-C words from dictation but does not write stories using inventive spelling. In math she solves horizontal & vertical addition & subtraction problems and knows no. facts plus-1, plus-0, plussing numbers to 10 (10 + 4 = ☐). Her math seat work is more accurate when she remembers no. facts than when she uses manipulatives. She has some difficulty with some self-help skills: buttons & zippers. She eats her lunch independently opening her juice & applesauce. She independently negotiates her school environment and participates in regular P.E. w/adaptations as needed. Amy tends to be telegraphic in responses & spontaneous responses are often inappropriate. It is very difficult to evaluate her language abilities. She indicates a higher level of expressive language during creative play. She is non-compliant frequently. Amy is mildly delayed in manipulative skills & mild-to-moderately delayed locomotor and balance skills. Successfully participates in regular P.E.

Communication Severity Rating Scale: N/A 1 2 3 4 5 ⑥

White Copy: Dept. of Spec. Ed/Student Services   Yellow Copy: School   Pink Copy: Parent

---

Name Amy North   School Eugene Field   Page 2

ASSURANCE OF LEAST RESTRICTIVE ENVIRONMENT

The IEP Committee has discussed the following issues in determining an appropriate placement:

✓ Placement in the same school the student would attend if not disabled
✓ Placement in a mainstream class with the use of supplementary aids/services
✓ Placement in a special education class located in a building serving general education students (as opposed to a building serving disabled students exclusively)
✓ Quality and extent of services to meet the IEP goals
✓ Appropriateness of the placement to meet IEP goals, taking into account the potential negative effects of the placement
✓ School and class placement with chronologically age appropriate peers
✓ Physical education with non-handicapped, chronologically age appropriate peers
✓ Travel time and distance to school.
✓ Educational integration with non-handicapped, chronologically age appropriate peers
✓ Placement essentially outside the mainstream based on the individual needs of the student

Having considered the issues relating to least restrictive environment, the IEP Committee has selected the following option on the continuum below as the most appropriate placement:

_____ General education placement with monitoring/consultation
_____ Direct instruction within general education
✓ General education placement with service in a special education setting for less than 50% of the day
✓ Special education placement for more than 50% of the day
_____ Separate day school serving both handicapped and non-handicapped students
_____ Separate day school for the handicapped
_____ Public and/or private residential facility
_____ Homebound instruction
_____ Hospital

This placement is deemed most appropriate due to
Amy's general cognitive delays
Amy's general social skills

PARTICIPATION IN TESTING PROGRAMS:

Literacy Passport   Yes   No (N/A)
Virginia State Assessment Program   Yes   No (N/A)
Charlottesville Assessment Program   Yes   No (N/A)

ACCOMMODATIONS / RATIONALE FOR EXCLUSION:

_____
_____
_____

White Copy: Dept. of Spec. Ed/Student Services   Yellow Copy: School   Pink Copy: Parent

Name _Amy North_   School _Eugene Field_   Page 3

EDUCATIONAL PROGRAM / SPECIAL EDUCATION AND RELATED SERVICES:

Insruction/Service	Amount of Time in Instructional Week	Percent of Instructional Week	Projected Date for Initiation of Service	Anticipated Completion Date
Speech/Language ✗	4 ✗ x 30 min.	5% – 6%	9-8-92	6-16-93
self-contained MiMR	27 hours	71%	9-8-92	6-16-93
physical therapy	consult as needed		9-8-92	6-16-93
occupational therapy	1 x 25 min.	2%	9-8-92	6-16-93
adaptive phys. ed.	1 x 30 min.	2%	9-8-92	6-16-93

Unless otherwise noted, the services listed above will be provided within the Charlottesville Public Schools by school personnel or qualified personnel contracted by the school division

Transportation: ✓ Regular _____ Special: _Services available in the school_

EDUCATIONAL PROGRAM / GENERAL EDUCATION:

_____ All educational options, except those listed above, provided with non-handicapped students

Academic/Non Academic/ Extracurricular Activities	Amount of Time in Instructional Week	Percent of Instructional Week
art	1 x 45 min.	3%
physical education	2 x 30 min.	3%
music	2 x 30 min.	3%
library	1 x 45 min.	3%
soc. st./science/health	3 x 45 min.	8%
lunch, recess,	5 x 60 min.	
~~assemblies~~		

FAMILY LIFE EDUCATION:

✓ Provided in general education setting ~~with the following adaptations/exclusions~~:

_____

_____ Provided in special education setting with the following adaptations/exclusions:

_____

_____ No Participation

White Copy: Dept. of Spec. Ed/Student Services   Yellow Copy: School   Pink Copy: Parent

---

Name _Amy North_   School _Eugene Field_   Page 4

MEETING PARTICIPANTS:

	Signature	Relationship to Student	Date
Sandra North	_Sandra North_ Thomas	Parent	5-26-92
John J. North	_John J. North_	Parent	5-26-92
Judy C. Franks	_Judy C. Franks_	Speech/Language Pathologist	5-26-92
Anne Hanks	_Anne Hanks_	Adapted P.E. teacher	5-26-92
Elaine Sails	_Elaine Sails_	Physical Therapist	5-26-92
Patty Kauffman	_Patty Kauffman_	Primary MiMH teacher ✗	5-26-92
Valerie C. Padgett	_Valerie C. Padgett_	Principal ✗	5-26-92

*has to be their - by law - input must be there if body is not (therapist etc.)

┌─────────────────────────────────────┐
I GIVE PERMISSION for my child,
  Amy North
_____
to be enrolled in the special education program described in this Individualized Education Program. I understand the contents of this document and I have been informed of my due process rights. I understand that I have the right to rewiew my child's records and to request a change in the IEP at any time. I also understand that I have the right to refuse this placement and have my child continue in his/her present placement pending further action.

 5 / 26 / 92   John J. North _John J. North_
Month Day Year   Signature of Parent(s)/Guardian(s) or Surrogate
└─────────────────────────────────────┘

┌─────────────────────────────────────┐
I DO NOT GIVE PERMISSION for my child,
_____
to be enrolled in the special education program described in this Individualized Education Program. I understand that I have the right to review his/her records and to request another placement. I understand that the action described above will not take place without my permission or until due process procedures have been exhausted. I understand that if my decision is appealed, I will be notified of my due process rights in this procedure.

 __ / __ / __   _____
Month Day Year   Signature of Parent(s)/Guardian(s) or Surrogate
└─────────────────────────────────────┘

SUMMARY OF COMMUNICATION(S) TO ESTABLISH IEP MEETING

Dates(s)/Method(s)/Results(s): _____

L - Letter   T - Telephone with confirmation letter   P - Personal contact with confirmation letter

White Copy: Dept. of Spec. Ed/Student Services   Yellow Copy: School   Pink Copy: Parent

(continued to next page)

Name ___Amy North___   School ___Eugene Field___   Page 5

Annual Goal ___Reading – To demonstrate growth in reading as measured by informal reading inventories___

Short Term Objectives	Evaluation Procedure and Criteria	Review Schedule	Completion Date
① will read following sounds in isolation & in words on her reading level: ă, ā, b, c, ĕ, ē, f, g, h, ĭ, ī, k, l, m, n, ŏ, ō, p, r, s, t, u, v, w, sh, th, ch	teacher observation of oral reading – 100%	daily	
② will read following sounds in isolation & in words: ing, er, ar, al, ou, y, oo, j, ū	teacher observation of oral & written responses – 90%	daily after presentation	
③ will answer oral & written comprehension questions seeking concrete information about stories on her level (Who is in the story? What happens? When? Why?)	tchr. observation of oral & written responses – 90%	daily	
④ will predict outcomes suggested in reading stories	teacher observation of oral responses	daily	
⑤ will sight-read stories on her level at 60 words/minute	teacher observation of oral responses – no more than 2 errors per reading	weekly after 1/93	

Annual Goal ___Math – to demonstrate growth in math skills as measured by teacher-made tests___

Short Term Objectives	Evaluation Procedure and Criteria	Review Schedule	Completion Date
① will solve simple horizontal & vertical addition & subtraction & missing addend problems	teacher observation of written responses – 90%	daily	
② will solve 2-digit addition without regrouping	tchr. observ. of written responses – 90%	daily after present'n 10/92	
③ will add a column of 3 numerals	tchr. observ. of written responses – 90%	daily – 12/92	
④ will state & write addition facts: plus-1, plus-2, plus-3, plus-4, plus-5 to numerals 1-9	teacher observation of written & oral responses – 90%	daily	
⑤ will translate a simple fraction into an oral statement, represent/write a fraction that describes a picture	teacher observation of oral & written responses – 90%	weekly after presentation	
⑥ will solve word problems written on her level	tchr. ob. of oral & written resp. – 90%	daily	
⑦ will tell time on the hour & half hour	tchr. observ. of oral responses – 90%	daily	

White Copy: Dept. of Spec. Ed/Student Services   Yellow Copy: School   Pink Copy: Parent

12 additional pages of goals and objectives for spelling, health, science, social studies, language arts and computer instruction, speech and language therapy, and motor skills related to physical and occupational therapy. Ann's teacher and all others who signed the IEP (see Figure 1–4, p. 37) reviewed the IEP with Ann's parents before Mr. and Mrs. North were asked to sign it.

The process of writing an IEP and the document itself are perhaps the most important features of compliance with the spirit and letter of IDEA. When the IEP is prepared as intended by the law, it means that

- the student's needs have been carefully assessed;
- a team of professionals and the parents have worked together to design a program of education to best meet the student's needs; and
- goals and objectives are clearly stated so that progress in reaching them can be evaluated.

Government regulation of the IEP process has always been controversial. Some of the people who were influential in formulating the basic law (IDEA) have expressed great disappointment in the results of requiring IEPs (Goodman & Bond, 1993, p. 413). Others question whether the requirement of long-term and short-term objectives is appropriate.

The IEP assumes that instructors know in advance what a child should and can learn, and the speed at which he or she will learn . . . This is a difficult projection to make with nondisabled children of school age—for preschool children with cognitive, emotional, and social disabilities, it is near impossible. (Goodman & Bond, 1993, p. 415)

A major problem is that the IEP—the educational *program*—is too often written at the wrong time and for the wrong reason (Bateman, 1992). As illustrated in Figure 1–5, the legal IEP is written following evaluation and identification of the student's disabilities and *before* a placement decision is made; what the student needs is determined first, then a decision is made about placement in the least restrictive environment in which the needed services can be provided. Too often, we see the educationally wrong (and illegal) practice of basing the IEP on an available placement; the student's IEP is written *after* available placements and services are considered.

Writing IEPs that meet all the requirements of the law and are also educationally useful is no small task. Computerized IEPs and those based on standardized testing or developmental inventories are extremely likely to violate the requirements of the law or be of little educational value or both (Bateman, 1992; Goodman & Bond, 1993). However, much of the controversy about IEPs and the disappointment in them appear to result from misunderstanding of the law or lack of instructional expertise or both. Within the framework of IDEA and other regulations, it is possible to write IEPs that are both legally correct and educationally useful (Bateman, 1992).

Legislation and litigation were initially used in the 1960s and 1970s to include exceptional children in public education with relatively little regard for quality. In the 1980s and 1990s they have been used to try to ensure individualized education, cooperation and collaboration among professionals, parental participation, and accountability of educators for providing high-quality, effective programs. *ON TEST*

PL 99–457 and IDEA, for example, are noteworthy for their expansion of the idea of individualized planning and collaboration among disciplines. PL 99–457 mandated an **Individualized Family Service Plan** (IFSP) for infants and toddlers with disabilities. An IFSP is similar to an IEP for older children in that it requires assessment and statements of goals, needed services, plans for implementation. As we discuss in Chapter 2, it also requires more involvement of the family, coordination of services, and plans for making the transition into preschool. IDEA mandated the inclusion of plans for transition from school to work for older stu-

> ➤ **Individualized Family Service Plan (IFSP).** A plan for services for young children with disabilities (under 3 years of age) and their families drawn up by professionals and parents; similar to an IEP for older children, mandated by PL 99-457. *Birth- 3yrs.*

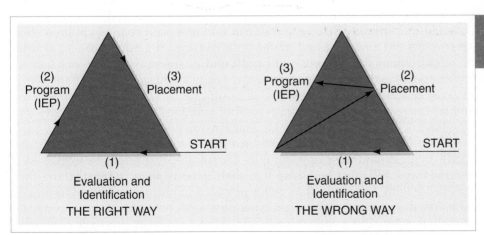

Figure 1–5

> ➤ *The right way and the wrong way to determine placement*

SOURCE: From B. D. Bateman, (1992). Better IEPs, Copyright © 1992 by Otter Ink, Creswell, OR. Reprinted with permission. p. 19.

dents as part of their IEPs. Other provisions of IDEA are intended to improve the quality of services received by children and youths with disabilities.

A PERSPECTIVE ON SPECIAL EDUCATION'S PROGRESS

Special education has come a long way since it was introduced into American public education over a century ago. It has become an expected part of our public education system, a given rather than an exception or an experiment. Much progress has been made since PL 94–142 (now IDEA) was enacted about two decades ago. Now parents and their children have legal rights to free, appropriate education; they are not powerless in the face of school administrators who do not want to provide appropriate education and related services. The enactment of PL 94–142 (IDEA) was one of very few events in the twentieth century that altered the power relationship between schools and parents (Sarason, 1990).

We can best illustrate some of the progress special education has made by returning to an example we used in discussing the educational definition of exceptional children and youths. Recall our earlier discussion of the accomplishments of Aaron Farley and the special education he received (see pp. 10–12). Aaron's special education was important in helping him achieve what he has. Nevertheless, his education was not all that it might have been. Had Aaron been born a decade later, his education might have allowed him to achieve even more. Aaron's father, a special education teacher of students with emotional and behavioral disorders, notes the positive changes that have occurred since Aaron was an infant. Aaron's brother John, who is 11 years younger than Aaron and also deaf, is receiving better educational services. His hearing impairment was diagnosed at the age of two weeks (recall that Aaron's was not diagnosed until he was two years old). John's special training, therefore, began much earlier than Aaron's. John was fitted with an auditory trainer (a type of hearing aid; see Chapter 8) at a very early age, and he uses this device constantly in school, an advantage Aaron did not have. He goes to a resource room for an hour each day and receives speech-language therapy in addition; the rest of the time he is in regular classes and uses his auditory trainer. John is also accompanied by a cued speech transliterator, who allows him to have equal access to all speech communication and environmental sounds at all times. Compared to Aaron, he is included much more of the school day in activities with hearing children. Now seven years old and in second grade, he is reading on grade level—an unusual accomplishment for students with profound deafness who have not had the advantages of early diagnosis and intensive early language training. Aaron never attained grade-level reading skills, although he clearly has high intellectual ability; his reading level is more typical of students who are profoundly deaf who have not had early, intensive language instruction.

The differences between Aaron's and John's education, their academic and social progress, and their opportunities for socialization might be explained in several ways. We must be aware that their parents were "educated" by their experience with Aaron and thus better prepared to nurture and be advocates for John. Yet their parents' greater preparedness for John's education does not tell the whole story. The public schools, too, were "educated" by their experience with Aaron and other students with disabilities and were encouraged by legislation and parent advocacy to provide better programs. Aaron was born before PL

94–142 (IDEA) was enacted. The law went into effect in 1978, four years after Aaron's birth. By the time John was born in 1981, schools had already been implementing the law for several years. By then, school administrators and teachers knew more about accommodating students with disabilities and working with parents to provide the services that these students' parents agree are appropriate. Whereas Aaron was provided a full-time cued speech transliterator only after his parents secured a court order through a law suit, John has been provided this service without court action.

In spite of the fact that IDEA and related laws and court cases have not resulted in flawless programs for exceptional children, they have done much to move American public schools toward providing better educational opportunities for those with disabilities. Laws like PL 99–457 (see p. 29) help to ensure that, like John Farley, all infants and toddlers with disabilities will receive early intervention. Laws like ADA (see p. 29) help to ensure that young adults like Aaron Farley will not be discriminated against in our society. Laws and court cases cannot eliminate all problems in our society, but they can certainly be of enormous help in our efforts to equalize opportunities and minimize handicaps for people with disabilities.

We have made much progress in special education, but making it all that we hope for is—and always will be—a continuing struggle. In Chapter 2, we discuss current trends and issues that highlight dissatisfaction with the way things are and represent hope for what special education and related services might become.

Summary

The study of exceptional children is the study of similarities and differences among individuals. Exceptional children differ from most other children in a specific way, but they are also similar to most others in most respects. Children's exceptionalities—their differences—must not be allowed to obscure us to the ways in which they are like other children. We distinguish between an exceptionality that is a disability and one that is a handicap. A disability is an inability to do something. A handicap is a disadvantage that may be imposed on an individual. A disability may or may not be a handicap.

For purposes of education, *exceptional children and youths* are defined as those who require special education and related services if they are to realize their full human potential. Special education strives to make certain that students' handicaps are confined to those characteristics that cannot be changed.

Current government figures show that approximately one student in ten is identified as exceptional and receiving special education services. Most children and youths identified as exceptional are between the ages of six and seventeen, although identification of infants and young adults with disabilities is increasing.

Special education refers to specially designed instruction that meets the unusual needs of exceptional children and youths. The single most important goal of special education is finding and capitalizing on exceptional students' abilities. Special education may be provided under a variety of administrative plans. Some exceptional students are served in regular classrooms by their regular classroom teacher, in some cases, in consultation with other professionals, such as psychologists or teachers with more experience or training. Some are served by an itinerant teacher who moves from school to school or by a resource teacher. Itinerant and resource teachers may teach students individually or in small groups for certain periods of the school day and provide assistance to regular classroom teachers. Sometimes children are placed in a diagnostic-prescriptive center so their special needs can be determined. The special self-contained class is used for a small group of students, who are usually taught in the special class all or most of the day. Special day schools are sometimes provided for students whose disabilities necessitate special equipment and methods for care and education. Hospital and homebound instruction are provided when the student is unable to go to regular classes. Finally, the residential school provides educational services and management of the daily living environment for students with disabilities who must receive full-time care.

Present law requires that every exceptional child and youth be placed in the least restrictive environment so that educational intervention will be consistent with individual needs and not interfere with individual freedom and the development of potential. Today, therefore, most students with exceptionalities are educated primarily in regular classes.

All teachers need to be prepared to some extent to deal with exceptional students because many of these students are placed for part of the day in regular classrooms. Furthermore, many students not identified as exceptional share some of the characteristics of disability or giftedness. Although the relationship between general and special education must be one of collaboration and shared responsibility for exceptional students, the roles of special and general educators are not always clear. Both may be involved in educating exceptional students by making maximum efforts to accommodate individual students' needs, evaluating academic abilities and disabilities, referring students for further evaluation, participating in eligibility conferences, writing individualized education programs, communicating with parents, participating in due process hearings, and collaborating with other professionals. In addition, special educators must have particular expertise in instructing students with learning problems, managing serious behavioral problems, using technological aids, and interpreting special education law.

Systematic attempts to educate children with disabilities, especially those with mental retardation and emotional and behavioral disorders, began in the early 1800s. European physicians like Itard, Pinel, and Seguin pioneered in these educational efforts. Their revolutionary ideas included individualized instruction, carefully sequenced series of educational tasks, emphasis on stimulation and the awakening of the child's senses, meticulous arrangement of the child's environment, immediate reward for correct perfor-

mance, tutoring in functional skills, and the belief that every child should be educated to the greatest extent possible. Howe and Gallaudet brought special education techniques and ideas to the United States.

Many other disciplines, especially psychology and sociology, were involved in the emergence of special education as a profession. Much of the progress in special education has resulted from the efforts of professional and parents' organizations. The Council for Exceptional Children (CEC) is an influential group with many divisions devoted to such things as the study of specific exceptionalities; the administration, supervision, and implementation of special programs; teacher training and placement; and research. Organizations such as the ARC provide parents, schools, and the public with information about exceptionalities and the structure for obtaining needed services.

The legal basis of special education has evolved over the years from permissive legislation, allowing public funding of special programs for exceptional children, to mandatory legislation, requiring such expenditures. The contemporary commitment to the principle that every individual has the right to as normal a life and education as possible has prompted much legislation and litigation in the 1970s and 1980s. Special education legislation has historically been increasingly specific and mandatory. The Individuals with Disabilities Education Act (IDEA) mandates that in order to receive funds under the act, *every school system in the country must make provision for a free, appropriate education for every child with a disability.*

Laws and regulations may have little effect until their meanings are interpreted by the courts through litigation. Litigation today focuses on ensuring that every exceptional child and youth receives an education that is appropriate for his or her individual needs. Suits filed *for* special education have tended to be filed on behalf of students who are unquestionably disabled but are receiving no education at all or only meager services. Suits filed *against* special education have tended to be filed on behalf of students whose disability is mild or questionable and for whom special education is thought to be more stigmatizing and discriminatory than helpful. Future court cases will undoubtedly result in clarification of the term *appropriate* with reference to education for exceptional students.

The primary intent of special education legislation has been to require educators to focus on the needs of individual students. Thus, a central feature of IDEA is the requirement that every student receiving special education under the law must have an individualized education program (IEP). An IEP is a written plan, which must be approved by the child's parents or guardian, that specifies the following: (1) the student's current level of performance; (2) annual goals; (3) instructional objectives; (4) special services to be provided and the extent to which the student will participate in regular education; (5) plans for starting services and their expected duration; (6) plans for evaluation; and (7) for older students, the services needed to ensure a successful transition from school to work or higher education.

Special education has made much progress during the past century. It is now an expected part of American public education, not an exception or experiment. Parents of students with disabilities now have more involvement in their children's education. In part, this progress has occurred because of laws requiring appropriate education and other services for individuals with disabilities.

ALEX WILHITE

Alex Wilhite is a visual artist living and working in New York City, whose paintings have received national attention. Born and educated in Alabama, he considers among his greatest accomplishments "to be seen as an artist, especially a deaf artist, and to be able to survive in New York is something to be proud of."

*C*ome writers and critics
Who prophesy with your pen
And keep your eyes wide,
The chance won't come again.
And don't speak too soon
For the wheel's still in spin
And there's no tellin' who
That it's namin'
For the loser now
Will be later to win
For the times they are a-changin'.

➤   Bob Dylan
"The Times They Are A-Changin'"

Current Trends and Issues

▲   ▲   ▲

Bob Dylan could have written his song, "The Times They Are A-Changin'" (see excerpt on previous page) for the field of special education. Special education has a rich history of controversy and change. In fact, controversy and change are what make the teaching and study of people with disabilities so challenging and exciting. The 1980s and 1990s have seen especially dramatic changes in the education of people with disabilities, and current thinking indicates that the field is poised for still more changes.

In this chapter, we explore three major trends in the field and issues related to them. The first trend is for people with disabilities to be more integrated with the larger, nondisabled society. The second is for there to be a greater emphasis on early intervention. And the third is for there to be a greater emphasis on programming for transition from secondary school to adulthood.

INTEGRATION

Integration, sometimes referred to as mainstreaming, involves the movement of people with disabilities from institutions to community living, from special schools to regular public schools, from special classes to regular classes. As a broadly supported social issue, integration began in the 1960s and is going stronger than ever today. In the 1960s and 1970s, champions of integration were proud of the fact that they were able to reduce the number of people with disabilities residing in institutions and the number of special education students attending special schools and special self-contained classes. Some of today's more radical proponents of integration, however, will not be satisfied until virtually all institutions, special schools, and special classes are eliminated. They propose that all students with disabilities be educated in regular classes. And even today's more conservative advocates of integration are recommending a much greater degree of interaction between students with and without disabilities than was ever dreamed of by most special educators in the 1960s and 1970s.

This movement toward more integration has led to some of the bloodiest professional battles ever waged in the field of special education. The disputes between radical integrationists and those of a more conservative persuasion have threatened to rip apart the field of special education. No matter whose point of view ultimately prevails, it is fair to say that there will be dramatic changes over the next few years in how, and especially where, we educate students with disabilities.

Philosophical Roots: The Principle of Normalization

➤ **normalization.** A philosophical belief in special education that every individual, even the most disabled, should have an educational and living environment as close to normal as possible.

A key principle behind the trend toward more integration of people with disabilities into society is normalization. First espoused in Scandinavia (Bank-Mikkelsen, 1969) before being popularized in the United States, **normalization** is the philosophical belief that we should use "means which are as culturally normative as possible, in order to establish and/or maintain personal behaviors and characteristics which are as culturally normative as possible" (Wolfensberger, 1972, p. 28). In other words, under the principle of normalization, both the means and the ends of education for students with disabilities should be as much like those for nondisabled students as possible. Regarding the means, for example,

PERSONS WITH DISABILITIES

MYTH ➤ Normalization, the philosophical principle that dictates that the means and ends of education for students with disabilities should be as culturally normative as possible, is a straightforward concept with little room for interpretation.

FACT ➤ There are many disagreements pertaining to the interpretation of the normalization principle. As just one example, some have interpreted it to mean that all people with disabilities must be educated in regular classes, whereas others maintain that a continuum of services (residential schools, special schools, special classes, resource rooms, regular classes) should remain as options.

MYTH ➤ All professionals agree that technology should be used to its fullest to aid people with disabilities.

FACT ➤ There are some who believe that technology should be used cautiously because it can lead people with disabilities to become too dependent on it. Some believe that people with disabilities can be tempted to rely on technology rather than develop their own abilities.

MYTH ➤ Research has established beyond a doubt that special classes are ineffective and that mainstreaming is effective.

FACT ➤ Research comparing special versus mainstream placement has been inconclusive because most of these studies have been methodologically flawed. Researchers are now focusing on finding ways of making mainstreaming work more effectively.

MYTH ➤ Professionals agree that labeling people with disabilities (e.g., retarded, blind, behavior disordered) is more harmful than helpful.

FACT ➤ Some professionals maintain that labels help professionals communicate, explain the atypical behavior of some people with disabilities to the public, and spotlight the special needs of people with disabilities for the general public.

MYTH ➤ People with disabilities are pleased with the way the media portrays people with disabilities, especially when they depict extraordinary achievements of such persons.

FACT ➤ Some disability rights advocates are disturbed with what they believe are too frequent overly negative *and* overly positive portrayals in the media.

MYTH ➤ Everyone agrees that teachers in early intervention programs need to assess parents as well as their children.

FACT ➤ Some authorities are now of the opinion that, although families are an important part of intervention programming and should be involved in some way, special educators should center their assessment efforts primarily on the child and not the parents.

MYTH ➤ Everyone agrees that good early childhood programming for students with disabilities should follow the same guidelines as that for nondisabled preschoolers.

FACT ➤ There is considerable disagreement about whether early intervention programming for children with disabilities should be child-directed, as is typical of regular preschool programs, or should be more teacher-directed.

MYTH ➤ Professionals agree that all students with disabilities in secondary school should be given a curriculum focused on vocational preparation.

FACT ➤ Professionals are in conflict over how much vocational versus academic instruction students with mild disabilities should receive.

we should place students with disabilities in educational settings as similar to those of nondisabled students as possible. And we should use treatment approaches that are as close as possible to the ones we use with the rest of the student population. Regarding the ends, we should strive to help students with disabilities weave into the larger fabric of society.

Although on the face of it, the principle of normalization seems simple enough, numerous controversies have swirled around the implementation of this important concept. We shall mention three of the more hotly contested issues. First, the phrase "as culturally normative as possible" is open to interpretation. Even though the originators of the normalization principle saw the need for a variety of service delivery options, including residential institutions, special schools, and special classes, more recently some have interpreted normalization to mean the abolishment of such segregated settings.

Second, there are some groups of people with disabilities who are leery about being too closely integrated with nondisabled society. For example, some people who are deaf, because of their difficulty in communicating with the hearing world, prefer associating with other people who are deaf. For them, normalization does not translate into integration with the larger society (Lord, 1991; Padden & Humphries, 1988).

Third, some have questioned whether the rapidly expanding use of technology to assist people with disabilities is actually working against the goal of normalization. Technology is, undoubtedly, changing the way professionals work with exceptional persons. In addition, it is changing how people with disabilities themselves participate in society, from leisure to job activities. Throughout this book, we provide numerous examples of how technology has bettered the lives of people with disabilities. In particular, some technologies have helped people with disabilities lead more independent lives. By allowing for greater independence, technology is making it possible for more and more people with disabili-

Protest activities among disability rights groups share similar goals and a similar flavor to the civil rights protests of earlier times.

ties to take part in activities that previously were inaccessible to them. Thus, technology serves in many instances as a means for achieving normalization.

Yet, some people with disabilities have expressed concerns about the misuse of technology. First, they point to the danger that some people with disabilities might be too quick to rely on technology for assistance instead of working to improve their own abilities. Reliance on artificial means of interacting with the environment when more natural means are possible could jeopardize a person's quest for normalization. Just how sensitive some people with disabilities are to the issue of technology and independence is captured in the following incident. The National Federation of the Blind of New Mexico was upset about an electronic guidance system being used at the University of New Mexico. In this system wires under the floor transmit a signal to an electronic cane. The cane acts as a receiver, beeping whenever it is near a wire. Fred Schroeder, president of the federation, wrote a letter to the developer of the electronic system in which he listed his complaints:

> The guidance system which you have installed . . . poses a limitation to independent travel rather than an opening of new freedom of movement for the blind.
>
> The fundamental problem with an electronic guidance system is the philosophical premise upon which it is based. The underlying attitude behind its creation stems from an image of the hopeless, helpless blind groping their way timidly through the world fraught with danger and uncertainty.
>
> By installing an electronic guidance system the public is reinforced in its belief that the blind are unable to travel without elaborate accommodation. . . . Our success in improving social and economic conditions for the blind has come from our ability to adapt ourselves to the world rather than relying on the benevolence of the world to adapt to us.

Second, some professionals fear that an emphasis on technology may be dehumanizing (McMurray, 1986). They argue there is a danger that a heavy stress on technology leads to viewing people with disabilities as "broken persons," like broken machines whose parts need fixing (Cavalier & Mineo, 1986). An indication of this dehumanization, they claim, is the tendency for technologists to concentrate on trying to fit people with disabilities into existing technology rather than developing technology to fit the needs of individuals.

Although most technology does not usurp the independence of exceptional individuals and technology need not lead to dehumanization, a couple of points are worth keeping in mind. First, those who develop technology for people with disabilities need to consult with them at every stage of research and development. The consumer needs to be considered.

As technology becomes ever more sophisticated, the issue of independence will become ever more important. One general guideline might be that if the technology allows people with disabilities to do something they could not do without it, then the technology is in their best interest. If, however, it allows them to do something new or better but at the same time imposes new limitations, then one might need to rethink the technology's benefits.

Historical Roots: Deinstitutionalization and the Regular Education Initiative

The idea of integrating people with disabilities into society is hardly new. Professionals have been advocating for and implementing programs of integra-

*C*UTTING THROUGH PREJUDICIAL BARRIERS WITH HUMOR ➤

Most special education professionals and people with disabilities would agree that there are many ways to break down attitudinal barriers toward those who have disabilities. Humor may be one of the most effective weapons against such prejudices, especially if humor and disability are merely coinciden-

Others make frontal attacks on attitudinal barriers through humor in which disability is central, not incidental. One of the best known cartoonists taking this approach is John Callahan, who is quadriplegic (as a result of an auto accident) and a recovering alcoholic. His cartoons, which often feature black

For Better or For Worse® by Lynn Johnston

SOURCE: FOR BETTER OR FOR WORSE copyright 1992 Lynn Johnston Prod., Inc. Reprinted with permission of UNIVERSAL PRESS SYNDICATE. All rights reserved.

tal. In her syndicated cartoon feature "For Better Or For Worse," Lynn Johnston occasionally includes a teacher who uses a wheelchair. This teacher experiences the frustrations and successes of any other in managing and teaching students, and her use of a wheelchair is typical of humor in this vein.

humor about disability, have appeared in *The New Yorker, Penthouse, National Lampoon, American Health,* and a variety of other magazines, newspapers, and books. Callahan's autobiography, *Don't Worry, He Won't Get Far on Foot,* is a book that some may find offensive but others find liberating in its irreverence and ability to make people laugh at disability.

➤ **deinstitutionalization.** A social movement of the 1960s and 1970s whereby large numbers of persons with mental retardation and/or mental illness were moved from large mental institutions into smaller community homes or into the homes of their families; recognized as a major catalyst for integrating persons with disabilities into society.

tion for 30 or 40 years. Although the amount of interaction between people with and without disabilities has increased relatively steadily over this time, there are two "movements" that have helped speed up integration: deinstitutionalization and the regular education initiative.

Deinstitutionalization

At one time it was common to place children and adults with retardation and/or mental illness in residential institutions, especially if they had relatively severe problems. The 1960s and 1970s, however, witnessed a systematic drive to move people out of institutions and back into closer contact with the community. Referred to as **deinstitutionalization**, this movement caused more and more children with disabilities to be raised by their families. Smaller facilities, located within local neighborhoods, are now common. Halfway houses exist as a placement for individuals with emotional disturbance who no longer need the more isolated environment of a large institution. For people with mental retardation, group homes house small numbers of individuals whose retardation may range from mild to severe. More and more people with disabilities are now working, with assistance from "job coaches," in competitive employment situations.

A major impetus for deinstitutionalization was the recognition by both the general public and the special education profession that many large institutions of the 1960s were offering grossly inadequate care. The publication of the classic, *Christmas in Purgatory* (Blatt & Kaplan, 1966), a pictorial essay on the squalid conditions of institutional life, did much to raise the sentiment against institutions. This book and others like it have shown how bad residential living *can be* for persons with disabilities.

We emphasize *can be* because there are some professionals who maintain that residential institutions, even large ones, need not be sordid (Crissey & Rosen, 1986; Landesman & Butterfield, 1987; Zigler, Hadapp, & Edison, 1990). They point out that not all institutions are alike. Smallness and proximity to the community does not guarantee high quality. Some very small homes, located in community settings, they maintain, can be every bit as dehumanizing as large institutions. And some large institutions can provide very humane treatment for their residents.

Some professionals have asserted that deinstitutionalization has been implemented, in some cases, without much forethought. They maintain that, although deinstitutionalization has the potential to improve the quality of life for most people who, in previous generations, would have been lifelong residents of institutions, it has failed some people because of poor planning. Turning people with disabilities out of institutions onto the streets places them in even greater jeopardy.

Is research on deinstitutionalization needed? Among special educators, there tend to be two camps on the issue of whether we need research on deinstitutionalization. Some believe, for example, that "the issue of whether institutionalization, even under the best conditions, is inherently damaging to the mentally retarded child . . . remains very much alive" (Bybee, Ennis, & Zigler, 1990, p. 216). Others, however, see no need for research. For them, deinstitutionalization is morally and ethically the right thing to do: "Deinstitutionalization is a highly desirable policy whose time has come. Researchers should focus on how to implement it most successfully instead of trying to demonstrate that it may not work" (Greenspan & Cerreto, 1989, p. 448).

There appears to be an impasse between those who see the need for more research on this matter and those who do not. Perhaps we can best summarize the controversy in the following way:

> What is at issue is whether any institution can provide a humane, habilitating environment that allows maximum personal freedom and self-actualization for any individual. One perspective on this issue is that institutions are inherently incompatible with achieving these goals for anyone; another is that an institution can be the most effective structure for achieving these ends for some individuals. What has been empirically documented in many sources is that (a) over the past quarter century the number of residents of institutions has been dramatically reduced; (b) the vast majority of residents remaining in institutions have severe or profound disabilities; and (c) movement of persons with mental disabilities from institutions to community settings has not always been accompanied by the development of effective human services, meaning that much still needs to be accomplished to improve the quality of life for these individuals even though they have been released from institutional care. (Kauffman & Hallahan, 1992, p. 300)

The Regular Education Initiative

The **regular education initiative (REI),** was first formally introduced by former Assistant Secretary of Education, Madeleine C. Will. Through speeches and articles, Will (1986) called for general educators to become more responsible for the education of students who have special needs in school, including those who are economically disadvantaged and those who are bilingual, as well as those with disabilities. Although for several years numerous professionals had been advocating *mainstreaming,* the practice of placing students with disabilities into regular education classes, Will was going a step further. She was questioning the legitimacy of special education as a system of education distinct from general education.

As a high-ranking government official, Will lent official sanction to the notion that regular education should take over many of the functions traditionally thought the province of special education. During Will's tenure as assistant secretary of education, the funding priorities of the federal government shifted dramatically to include many more projects focusing on mainstreaming.

The REI, as articulated by Will, was vague with regard to how much regular education should assume responsibility for the education of students with disabilities. And this vagueness has contributed to the current raging debate about the roles of special versus regular education in educational programming for students with disabilities. Today, views on integration of students with disabilities range from **full inclusion**—the belief that *all* students with disabilities should be educated solely in the regular classroom—to the belief in the maintenance of a full range of service delivery options—residential institutions, special schools, special classes, resource rooms, regular classes.

Full Inclusion Versus a Continuum of Services

Educational programming for students with disabilities has traditionally been built upon the assumption that a variety of service delivery options need to be

➤ **regular education initiative (REI).** A philosophy that maintains that general education, rather than special education, should be primarily responsible for the education of students with disabilities.

➤ **full inclusion.** The belief that all students with disabilities should be educated in regular classrooms in their neighborhood schools.

Advocates of the regular education initiative favor full integration of children with disabilities into the regular education system.

available. Special education law, for example, stipulates that schools place students with disabilities in the least restrictive environment (LRE). The notion of LRE assumes that there are alternatives along a continuum of restrictiveness, with residential institutions on one end of the continuum and regular classes on the other. For the most part, special educators have been proud of this continuum of services. They have viewed the LRE concept as the lifeblood of special education. LRE was something they fought hard to get enacted into law. Before LRE was enacted into law, school personnel were free to claim that they did not have services for children with disabilities and to deny these children access to regular classes.

In recent years, however, some special educators have begun to argue vehemently against the notion of the LRE. Although still a minority, this group is growing ever stronger and more vociferous in their attack on the LRE. These professionals believe in what they refer to as full inclusion (Laski, 1991; Sailor, 1991; Stainback & Stainback, 1992). The basic components of most full inclusion models are:

1. All students attend the school to which they would go if they had no disability.
2. A natural proportion (i.e., representative of the school district at large) of students with disabilities occurs at any school site.
3. A zero-rejection philosophy exists so that typically no student would be excluded on the basis of type or extent of disability.
4. School and general education placements are age- and grade-appropriate, with no self-contained special education classes operative at the school site.
5. Cooperative learning and peer instructional methods receive significant use in general instructional practice at the school site.
6. Special education supports are provided within the context of the general education class and in other integrated environments. (Sailor, 1991, p. 10)

Key to the full inclusion philosophy, then, is the notion that students with disabilities should be educated in their home school and in regular classes. Some professionals are in favor of the total elimination of special education. Others hold that special educators, speech therapists, physical therapists, and so forth are still needed, but their main duties should be carried out in regular classes along with general education teachers. Thus, advocates of full inclusion favor the elimination of a continuum of services.

> Three generations of children subject to LRE are enough. Just as some institution managers and their organizations—both overt and covert—seek refuge in the continuum and LRE, regional, intermediate unit, and special school administrators and their organizations will continue to defend the traditional and professionally pliable notion of LRE. The continuum is real and represents the status quo. However, the morass created by it can be avoided in the design and implementation of reformed systems by focusing all placement questions on the local school and routinely insisting on the home school as an absolute and universal requirement. In terms of placement, the home-school focus renders LRE irrelevant and the continuum moot. (Laski, 1991, p. 413)

Premises of Full Inclusion

Those who advocate full inclusion base their position on at least the following four premises: (1) labeling of people is harmful; (2) special education pull-out programs have been ineffective; (3) people with disabilities should be viewed as a minority group; and (4) ethics should take precedence over empiricism.

*F*ulfilling the special needs
of individuals shouldn't
saddle them with labels
that separate them from other
educational opportunities.

Labeling is harmful. Some people fear that a "special education" label can cause a child to feel unworthy or to be viewed by the rest of society as a deviant, and hence grow to feel unworthy. This fear is not entirely unfounded. Most of the labels used to designate students for special education carry negative connotations. *Retarded, disturbed,* and other labels that designate disabilities associated with special education are not kind words. Being so described may lower a person's self-esteem or cause others to behave differently toward the labeled person. Consequently, advocates for people with disabilities have suggested using different labels or, to the extent possible, avoiding the use of labels altogether.

Antilabeling sentiment is based in part on the theory that disabilities are a matter of social perceptions and values, not inherent characteristics. Bogdan (1986) suggests that disability is a socially created construct. Its existence depends on social interaction. Only in a very narrow sense, according to Bogdan, does a person *have* a disability. For example, the fact that a person cannot see only sets the stage for his or her being labeled blind.

Once we call a person blind, there are a variety of undesirable consequences. Our interactions are different because of the label. That is, we view the person primarily in terms of the blindness. We tend to interpret everything the blind person can or cannot do in terms of the blindness, and the label takes precedence over other things we may know about the individual. This labeling opens the door for viewing the person in a stereotypical and prejudicial manner because, once labeled, we tend to think of all people with blindness as being similar to one another but different from the rest of society.

Research on the effects of labeling has been inconclusive (Brantlinger & Guskin, 1987). On the one hand, studies indicate that people tend to view a labeled person differently from a nonlabeled one. People are more likely both to expect deviant behavior from labeled individuals and to see abnormality in nondisabled individuals if told (incorrectly) that the nondisabled persons are deviant. On the other hand, labels may also make nondisabled people more tolerant of those with disabilities. That is, labels may provide explanations or justifications for differences in appearance or behavior for which the person with a disability otherwise might be blamed or stigmatized even more (Fiedler & Simpson, 1987). For example, it is probably fairly common for the nondisabled adult to tolerate a certain degree of socially immature behavior in a child with mental retardation while finding the same behavior unacceptable in a nondisabled child.

In addition to serving as an explanation for unusual behavior, some special educators have defended the use of labels on other grounds. First, they have argued that the elimination of one set of labels would be replaced by another set. In other words, they believe that individuals with special problems will always be perceived as different. Second, they have contended that labels help professionals communicate with one another. In talking about a research study, for example, it helps to know with what type of population the study was conducted. Third, they assert that labels help spotlight the special needs of people with disabilities for the general public: "Like it or not, it is a fine mixture of compassion, guilt, and social consequence that has been established over these many years as a conditioned response to the label 'mental retardation' that brings forth . . . resources [monies for specialized services]" (Gallagher, 1972, p. 531). The taxpayer is more likely to react sympathetically to something that can be labeled.

Special education pull-out programs have been ineffective. Some special educators have asserted that research shows **pull-out programs** to be ineffective. They maintain that students with disabilities have better, or at least no worse, scores on cognitive and social measures if they stay in regular classes than if they are pulled out for all (self-contained classes) or part (resource rooms) of the school day.

Many research studies have compared students with disabilities in more and less segregated settings; over the past 30 years, there have been more than 50 such studies. Results, when taken at face value, have not been very supportive of pull-out programs. Critics of this research, however, have argued that taking these investigations at face value is highly questionable (Kauffman & Hallahan, 1992). The biggest problem with this line of research is that most of the studies are methodologically flawed. For example, in only two studies did the researchers randomly assign students to the different treatment groups. For ethical reasons, school personnel are hesitant to leave placement decisions to chance. It is difficult, however, to compare students who have been assigned to a self-contained class to those left in a regular class because the former, if appropriately placed, are probably more severely disabled and have a poorer prognosis for improvement. Critics maintain that, unless students are randomly assigned, students from the less restrictive setting will invariably have an advantage over students from more restrictive settings.

> ➤ **pull-out programs.** Special education programs in which students with disabilities leave the regular classroom for part or all of the school day, e. g., to go to special classes or resource rooms.

Children with disabilities should not be restricted from exploration of their environment and participation in activities.

People with disabilities as a minority. Advocates of full inclusion tend to see people with disabilities as members of a minority group rather than as individuals who have difficulties as an inherent result of their disability. In other words, they see the problems that people with disabilities face to be the result of society's discrimination and prejudice. The Stainbacks typify this point of view:

> In the past, educators have assumed a "functional limitations" approach to services. This paradigm locates the difficulty within students with disabilities when they experience problems in learning or adapting in general education classrooms. From this perspective, the primary task of educators is to remediate these students' functional deficits to the maximum extent possible. That is, educators attempt to fix, improve, or make ready the students who are being unsuccessful by providing them with the skills to be able to succeed in a mainstreamed educational environment that is *not* adapted to meet their particular needs, interests, or capabilities. And if this is not possible, they must be relegated to special, separate learning settings. In the "functional limitations" paradigm the student is expected to fit into the existing or educational environment.
>
> This paradigm is gradually being replaced by a minority group paradigm. The minority group paradigm of school operation locates the principle [sic] difficulties of students with disabilities as not residing in the student, but rather in the organization of the general education environment. That is, school failure is the result of such things as educational programs, settings, and criteria for performance that do not meet the diverse needs of students. From this perspective, the problem is with the educational organization or environment that needs to be fixed, improved, or made ready to address the diverse needs of all students. (Stainback & Stainback, 1992, p. 32)

The notion of people with disabilities as a minority is consistent with the views of disability rights activists. Disability rights activists are a part of the **disability rights movement**, which is patterned after the civil rights movement of the 1960s. Disability activists claim that they, like African Americans and other ethnic minority groups, are an oppressed minority. They have coined the term *handicapism*, a parallel of *racism*. **Handicapism** is a "set of assumptions and practices that promotes the differential and unequal treatment of people because of apparent or assumed physical, mental, or behavioral differences" (Bogdan & Biklen, 1977, p. 14).

Although more and more people with disabilities—and nondisabled professionals too—are supporting the disability rights movement, there are several impediments to its achieving the same degree of impact as the civil rights movement. Some believe that the political climate in the United States has not been conducive to fostering yet another rights movement. Whereas the civil rights movement of the 1960s was spawned in an era of liberal ideology, the disability rights movement has coincided with a more conservative climate (Gartner & Joe, 1986). Activists themselves have been unable to agree on the best ways to meet the movement's general goals. For example, some believe that individuals with disabilities should receive special treatment in such things as tax exemptions or reduced public transportation fares. Others maintain that such preferential treatment fosters the image that people with disabilities are dependent on the nondisabled for charity (Gartner & Joe, 1986).

People with disabilities are an incredibly heterogeneous population. Although general goals can be the same for all people with disabilities, specific needs vary greatly, depending to a large extent on the particular type and severity of disability the person has. The *particular* problems an adolescent with severe retardation and blindness faces are considerably different from those of a Vietnam veteran who has lost the use of his or her legs. Although activists admit

➤ **disability rights movement.** Patterned after the civil rights movement of the 1960s, this is a loosely organized effort to advocate for the rights of people with disabilities through lobbying legislators and other activities. Members view people with disabilities as an oppressed minority.

➤ **handicapism.** A term used by activists who fault the unequal treatment of individuals with disabilities. This term is parallel to the term racism, coined by those who fault unequal treatment based on race.

it would not be good for the public to believe that all people with disabilities are alike any more than they already do (Gartner & Joe, 1986), the heterogeneity does make it more difficult for people with disabilities to join forces on specific issues.

But perhaps what has been missing most and what is hardest to achieve is a sense of pride. The civil rights movement for African Americans and the women's movement fostered a sense of pride. For example, there has been no equivalent of the "Black is beautiful" slogan within the disability rights movement, although the movement is attempting to develop a sense of identity and community. One of the vehicles for accomplishing this is a publication, *The Disability Rag*, which highlights disability as a civil rights issue (see the box on pp. 58–59).

In fact, the following article from *The Disability Rag* targets pride as a major problem for people with disabilities:

Ten women sat around a conference table on a Saturday afternoon, engrossed in the faces and voices on the videotape. They watched and listened as, one after another, women on the screen talked about their lives, their loves, their work and themselves. In the meeting room, the expressions on the faces of those watching showed recognition and relief, as the women saw and heard their own lives mirrored and validated.

The women on the video, like the women at the conference table, had a variety of disabilities. The video, produced by Access Oregon, Portland's independent living center, was called "Don't Go To Your Room, and Other Affirmations for Disabled Women." I had been asked to co-present a session on feminism and disability issues for a group of women being trained as peer counselors at the Center for People with Disabilities in Boulder, Colo. We used the video as part of our presentation, and once again saw how powerful it could be in opening women to the truth and strength of their own lives.

When it finished, silence filled the room for a few minutes.

Then a middle-aged woman with multiple sclerosis, who had been disabled for several years, said, "This is the first time I have felt proud since I became disabled."

Her comment struck me deeply at the time, and has stayed with me ever since. At first I was tempted to read it as typical of a "new crip," someone who hadn't yet turned to disability cool, or come to terms with her own life as a woman with a disability. But I soon acknowledged her words as an expression of a sentiment that is pretty common among my friends and colleagues who have disabilities, and that I saw even in myself.

More and more I have realized how familiar it is within the disability community, that feeling of no pride. Those of us in the movement don't talk about it much—either to each other, for fear of being politically incorrect, perhaps compromising our leadership status; or to others, for what we say might somehow be used against us, to confirm the assumptions of the nondisabled that our shame is an inevitable, and therefore permanent, outgrowth of our disabilities.

But don't we all, like the woman in the training, struggle for a sense of pride? How many of us truly live in that place, where everyone has the right to live: a place of power, effectiveness, validation, connection, beauty—in other words, in pride?

It's a feeling that is not easy to come by in this segregated, inaccessible, often discriminatory world. Even the coolest of us do our share of internalizing the oppression all around us. A week or so after that presentation in Boulder, I caught myself doing it.

I was interested in a writing workshop being offered by a local "free university," so I telephoned to find out if it was accessible. It wasn't, so I asked whether that workshop could be switched to another one on the same day, in order to hold it in one of the organization's many other locations.

That was impossible, I was told. I argued for awhile with the program director, and then I hung up. I then called the workshop instructor, a well-known local

▶ ▶ ▶ FROM RAGS TO RAGES ➤   by David McGinty

A David among magazines raises a mighty voice for people with disabilities

A Hollywood writer scripting a movie that will star William Hurt needs some quick, authoritative insight into the world of the disabled. She calls The Disability Rag.

The Easter Seal Society of Canada wants to know which terms disabled people find acceptable and objectionable. They query The Disability Rag.

The British Broadcasting Corp. is gathering material for a documentary on a movement in Berkeley, Calif., in the 1970s and 80s to make independent living possible for the disabled. The phone rings at The Disability Rag.

"It's really funny when these people contact us," says managing editor Sharon Kutz-Mellem. "They think we're this whole big staff."

By which she means that it is not really funny at all. Ironic, maybe.

Begun in Louisville on an impulse 12 years ago, the Rag has come to the attention of a selective but international audience for its coverage of disability issues. Universities—Harvard, Yale and Vienna among them—subscribe to it. So do social workers in Greece and Sweden. Requests for information have come from China and India.

And yet, as its reputation grows, one thing about the Rag stays the same.

It struggles to survive.

Although its readership has been estimated at 28,000, its paid following hovers at a very modest—if devoted—4,000 to 5,000 subscribers. Its present staff is at an all-time high of two full-timers and two part-timers, which seems hardly enough. Its financial condition cycles with almost annual regularity between leanness and desperation.

"It ekes by," says Cass Irvin, one of the magazine's founders. "One of my biggest regrets is that the community has not supported it the way I'd like to see." The Rag is, she sighs, "Louisville's best-kept secret."

If you sought out the Rag on a local newsstand—and you could look far before locating it—you would find it at first blush unprepossessing.

It's bimonthly and these days runs to 30- or 40-odd pages. It has clean but unremarkable layout, no color, few pictures and virtually no ads. It is printed on inexpensive newsprint. It looks like nothing so much as one of those cheeky counterculture publications common in the 1960s and early '70s.

The resemblance is not coincidence. To read the Rag is to take a bracing plunge into '60s-style advocacy.

The magazine has a clear, unwavering premise: The disabled are America's last, great, unacknowledged, oppressed minority, and it's time they banded together and asserted themselves.

In pushing this message, the Rag has been vigorous, iconoclastic and unabashed. A few years ago exercise guru Richard Simmons, in a moment of raised consciousness, wrote a book on exercise programs for the disabled and promoted it on national television. He said proceeds from the book would go to build special fitness centers for the disabled.

A wonderful idea? Not to the Rag, which believes the disabled should be able to go to the same fitness centers as everybody else. "Simmons doesn't understand what it is he's promoting," wrote Rag staffer Lauri Klobas. "He's allowing the non-disabled public to avoid making way for their friends, neighbors and relatives who have disabilities. Even worse . . . he's becoming a spokesman on this special form of 'apartheid.'"

There was more. Simmons had, in his enlightenment, begun picking up phrases like "physically challenged" and "handi-capable." Writer Mary Jane Owen found these terms "particularly odious" for their glossing over of the real problems faced by disabled people and concluded, with table-pounding fervor, "Move over, Richard! You're irrelevant—and you're in our way!"

All of which was, for the Rag, mere batting practice. "We've gone after some pretty big boys," notes Kutz-Mellem.

The Rag has taken on telethons that raise money for people with disabilities, in particular the Jerry Lewis Labor Day Telethon, for presenting the disabled in what it considers a pitiable, demeaning fashion. It reports tenaciously, and with discernible relish, on protests against Lewis and the Muscular Dystrophy Association, and on the association's "whining" and "crybaby" responses.

It has also curled a lip at Mother Teresa's Missionaries of Charity order, because the order's New York shelter was not accessible to the disabled; at the National Organization on Disability, which has taken, in the Rag's opinion, a Milquetoast approach to disability issues; and at the mass media for various sins, including portrayals of the disabled as brave conquerors of adversity—the "supercrip" syndrome . . .

Julie Shaw Cole, a contributing editor and longtime Rag supporter, says a key function is to provide a forum in which the disabled can speak their minds. "The Rag gives them that opportunity."

And they seize it. Debate buzzes through the Rag's letters pages. Readers write in to approve, suggest, cheer, dispute.

"By golly, the March/April Rag has a right-on article," writes Kandy Penner of Gainesville, Fla.

But Geeta Dardick of North San Juan, Calif., thinks the Rag may be getting too soft on questions of terminology: "Get the point, Rag, Give us a break! Keep supporting all of the language rules the leaders of the disability movement have agreed upon."

But Damian Anthony Rheaume, of Greendale, Wis., has had enough. "I received a renewal form for your magazine. Renew? Are you Kidding? . . . Good luck. May your lives be as bitter as your outlook on life."

Then there is another letter, a short one posted on a wall in the Rag's offices. The writing is an uneven scrawl that struggles across the page, but the message is clear and strong: "Please continue to fight oppression and tyranny towards the disabled. It's stuff like that that feeds your sanity. . . . I need a lot of fuel to fight this uphill battle."

It is signed, "Monica."

Throughout its existence the Rag has heard quietly and often from the Monicas of the world, says Mary Johnson. "We get almost a standard letter all the time from people saying, 'We've been so isolated, I never knew other people felt this way.'"

Those letters, for Johnson, validate what she has done. She is the mother of the Rag, and to this day she sounds slightly bemused by how she came to do it.

Johnson is not disabled. But a number of years ago she became involved in disability issues through an activist friend who was disabled, and she came to see how hard it was to organize the disabled and get them to envision their problems as a civil-rights issue.

And then one day in 1980, Johnson says, "I was just sitting in my house, and I thought, 'Well, I'm going to put this thing out.' There was no planning. It was totally spur of the moment."

"This thing" was a four-page newsletter called The Disability Rag—the name, like the idea, just came to her, Johnson says. The first issue, she recalls, printed a long article that had been circulating among disability activists.

"It was sort of like a call to arms," Johnson remembers, "It was a florid piece of writing."

She sent the newsletter out to perhaps 30 or 40 people she knew in the local disabled community. Anonymously. "I was very keen on being anonymous at the time," she says. Why? "Paranoia, I guess."

She was not sure how some of the radical notions in the newsletter would be received. The Rag was, in a sense, a way of finding out. She kept putting it out, and things happened. She attached her name to it. She joined forces with Irvin, a quadriplegic and disability activist.

The Rag grew, Johnson credits Irvin with putting it on a business-like footing. They incorporated, began to sell subscriptions nationwide and discovered an audience for what they were saying.

Under the auspices of its publisher, The Advocado Press, the Rag now prints a variety of disability-related educational materials, including a newsletter explaining the Americans with Disabilities Act and cards that can be slapped on the windshields of cars improperly parked in handicapped-only parking spaces. The cards are a popular item.

But the magazine's finances remain hitched to a yo-yo. Until recently the Rag did not take advertising. Because many disabled people live on meager incomes, its subscription rates have always been low. One year costs $12—unless you take the $16 "generous-person rate" or the $8 "tight-budget rate."

The Rag tries to cajole much of the money it needs to survive from foundations. In the last 1 $1/2$ years, Cole says, it has written to hundreds of potential donors, but "there is not a lot of non-profit money going anywhere right now."

And, she adds, "funders do not fund controversy."

Last year, the magazine was starting to lose money and Johnson was convinced it was going to fold. The Rag put out an appeal to its readers. More than $30,000 came in and the Rag survived.

"I guess that made all of us say, 'We're here for some reason,' Johnson says.

For the moment, the Rag is between crises. It has a $139,000 budget and no worries about making it through the fiscal year, which ends in December. It is perking along with customary feistiness. Articles in the May/June issue take a few more cuts at the Jerry Lewis telethon . . .

Around the country, "there were pools of this kind of thinking," Irvin says. "There were people saying, 'Yeah, this is right.'"

In 1984, in an act of faith, Johnson quit other work to devote full time to the Rag. She and Irvin published it out of their homes, surviving on bare-bones budgets. In the mid-'80s it had a subscription list of about 2,000 and a growing national reputation.

It was quoted in The Atlantic magazine and The Village Voice. The Ladies Home Journal cited Irvin as one of 50 "American Heroines." Major newspapers like The Washington Post and The Wall Street Journal wrote stories about the Rag.

The press helped. So did a grant, which enabled the Rag to mount a genuine marketing campaign for subscriptions. The magazine's circulation increased to its present level. Its scope broadened.

columnist, to see if she could be persuaded to support my cause by pressuring the school to change the location. Instead, she offered to meet with me privately, for the same price as the workshop. She said she wanted to avoid a "political brouhaha." I said I would think about it.

I called the school back to try once again reasoning with the director. She still refused to budge. She told me I was looking at the situation "very simplistically." I angrily replied that the issue here was not only logistics, but rights—my rights. She couldn't understand why I insisted on integration and equality—perhaps she's never known their opposites. "I don't see why you don't just accept the offer of a private session," she said.

Her words and her tone carried an obvious message: She saw me as a spoiled child, mad because I didn't get my own way, even when something else was offered to placate me. I began to feel that way myself, losing some of my angry energy to creeping embarrassment and contrition.

In the end I went with the private session, ostensibly for the pragmatic reason that the personal contact might help me break into the local writing market. Partly, my decision may have been due to a failure of pride. I think, though, and I hope, that I recovered enough of my original anger to know I was making a compromise, and that I didn't have to. I delivered a long lecture to the program's director, full of righteous indignation and unsolicited advice, about the rights of people with disabilities.

I felt okay about it afterwards. But the experience remained with me as a lesson in how easily my personal sense of dignity could be messed with by some stranger.

The thing about pride is that you can work like crazy to find it, but when you finally do, that doesn't mean you have it forever. It can slip away from you unless you guard it. We may be at different levels in integrating our disabilities into our lives; some of us, lucky enough to have supports, or skills, or knowledge, or whatever it takes, might have a little better handle on our roles and our self-image than some others. But we all, in one way or another, sometimes struggle with a personal shortage of pride.

Don't we? Let's talk about it for once. This is an important issue both personally, for every one of us, and politically: Without pride our movement can never develop. What do other people think and feel about pride?

Here's how I've started to resolve the issue for myself: Maybe it is important to differentiate between a feeling of pride, or no pride, and the deeper reality of existential pride. I might go through periods of self-doubt, but on a deeper level I know I'm worthy and powerful. The emotional experience of shame is strong, difficult to endure, and quite real, but it doesn't define my whole life. There's a more lasting knowledge available to me that transcends those painful moments. (Hershey, 1991, pp. 1, 4–5)

People in the disability rights movement have been active on a variety of fronts, ranging from lobbying legislators and employers to criticizing the media for being guilty of representing people with disabilities in stereotypical and inaccurate ways. Disability activists have been particularly critical of television and movies (Klobas, 1985; Longmore, 1985). They argue that the depictions are typically overly negative or overly positive. On the negative side, electronic media often treat people with disabilities as criminals, monsters, potential suicides, maladjusted people, or sexual deviants. These portrayals offer the viewer absolution for any difficulties faced by persons with disabilities and allow the nondisabled to "blame the victims" for their own problems. Rarely do movie themes acknowledge society's role in creating attitudinal barriers for people with disabilities. When television attempts to portray people with disabilities in a positive light, it often ends up highlighting phenomenal accomplishments—a one-legged skier, a wheelchair marathoner, and so forth. The superhero image, according to some disability activists, is a mixed blessing. It does promote the notion that being disabled does not automatically limit achievement. Such human interest stories, however, may make other more "ordinary" people with disabilities somehow feel inferior because they have not achieved such superhuman goals. These stories also imply that people with disabilities can prove their worth only by achieving superhuman goals and reinforce "the view that disability is a problem of individual emotional coping and physical overcoming, rather than an issue of social discrimination against a stigmatized minority" (Longmore, 1985, p. 35).

Although disability activists, for the most part, have been extremely displeased with television's handling of disabilities, they have been more complimentary of TV advertising that uses characters with disabilities. Beginning in the mid-1980s, advertisers began to experiment with the use of persons with disabilities in some of their ads. The last few years have seen a dramatic increase in actors with disabilities in TV advertising, whether out of corporate America's desire to be more socially responsive or their recognition of the large market of buyers with disabilities. (See box on p. 62.)

Ethics over empiricism. Full inclusion proponents emphasize people with disabilities as a minority group who have undergone discrimination. The proponents tend to approach issues of integration from an ethical rather than an empirical perspective. Many proponents of full inclusion are not interested in pursuing the question of whether full inclusion is effective. For them, empirical data on the comparative effectiveness of full inclusion versus pull-out programs is irrelevant. Apparently, even if one were to find, through well-controlled research, that pull-out programs lead to better academic and social outcomes than do full inclusion programs, these advocates would still favor full inclusion on ethical grounds. For them,

> by far the most important reason for including all students into the mainstream is that it is the fair, ethical, and equitable thing to do. It deals with the value of EQUALITY. As was decided in the *Brown versus Board of Education* decision, SEPARATE IS NOT EQUAL. All children should be part of the educational and community mainstream.
>
> It is discriminatory that some students, such as those labeled disabled, must earn the right or be prepared to be in the general education mainstream or wait for

While positive media portrayals are inspiring to all, they can create unrealistic expectations for "regular" people with disabilities.

▶ 7 HIS AD'S FOR YOU ➤   by Elizabeth Roberts and Annetta Miller

Madison Ave. discovers disabled consumers

Meet Jack, a dedicated athlete sweating through a strenuous workout with his comely girlfriend providing inspiration. "One more," she urges, spotting him on the free weights. Sex, physical prowess, beer—nothing new in this Budweiser commercial—until the camera pulls back and shows Jack leaving the gym in a wheelchair. Cut to a local bar. Jack and his lady are celebrating his completion of the wheelchair marathon over a beer with friends, when she turns to him and asks. "What's next?" "Tomorrow," Jack says, "we're sleeping in."

Sleeping in? A guy in a wheelchair with a beautiful girl? Most of the time, television commercials barely acknowledge the existence of disabled people, let alone depict them as sexually desirable. But new legislation and a largely untapped market of disabled Americans has advertisers taking a fresh look at a group that lives, loves and shops like everyone else. The Eddie Bauer catalog of outdoor wear includes a skier with an artificial leg. Citibank advertisements show a deaf woman getting her lost Visa card replaced by signing on a telecommunications device for the deaf. Disney depicts a disabled man picking up his college diploma, who, when asked what he's going to do next, says exuberantly, "Go to Disney World."

What's spurring marketers to open their eyes to the disabled? "This is a way that a company or product can demonstrate some humanity," says Howard Liszt, president of Campbell-Mithun-Esty Advertising in Minneapolis. But the motives go far beyond altruism. An estimated 43 million disabled people now live in the United States. The recently implemented Americans with Disabilities Act—which broadens disabled people's access to everything from buses to the top shelves at grocery stores—is expected to provide them entree to places and products never before accessible. Says Sandra Gordon, a spokeswoman for the National Easter Seal Society, "Companies have started seeing that there are disabled people out there who are working and have money . . . and squeeze the Charmin [like everyone else]."

Companies have traditionally shied away from the practice of featuring disabled people in their advertising for fear it might alienate consumers. "We were concerned that we might be viewed as exploiting children with disabilities," says George Hite, spokesman for the Target clothing store chain, a pioneer in using children with disabilities in its ads. In fact, that concern has proved to be unwarranted. Target has received hundreds of letters, many from the parents of disabled children, complimenting the company on its vision. Sales have reflected the public's approval. "Merchandise that these young models are wearing has sold extremely well," says Hite, "certainly as well as, and, in some cases, better than, other advertised merchandise."

Other retailers are clearly hoping for the same kind of success. K mart, whose advertising reflects a diversity of ethnic and demographic groups, now uses people with disabilities in some of its ads. One new ad campaign includes disabled actress Colleen Stewart shopping in a wheelchair. Gordon is heartened by such initiative. "Those of us in the nonprofit world have tried for years to change the way disabled people are perceived," she says. Now, it seems the for-profit world is finally lending a hand.

SOURCE: From *Newsweek,* Feb. 24, 1992, © 1992, Newsweek Inc. All rights reserved. Reprinted by permission.

---

educational researchers to prove that students with disabilities can profit from the mainstream, when other students are allowed unrestricted access simply because they have no label. No one should have to pass anyone's test or prove anything in a research study to live and learn in the mainstream of school and community life. It is a basic right, not something one has to earn. (Stainback & Stainback, 1992, p. 31)

Arguments Against Full Inclusion

The notion of full inclusion has met with considerable resistance. There are at least five arguments that critics of full inclusion have forwarded: (1) Regular educators, special educators, and parents are largely satisfied with the current continuum of services; (2) regular educators are unwilling and/or unable to cope with all students with disabilities; (3) justifying full inclusion by asserting that people with disabilities are a minority is flawed; (4) full inclusion proponents' unwillingness to consider empirical evidence is professionally irresponsible; and (5) in the absence of data to support one service delivery model, special educators must preserve the continuum of services.

Satisfaction with the current continuum of services. Defenders of the full continuum of services point out that, for the most part, teachers and parents are satisfied with the degree of integration into regular education now experienced by children with disabilities. In a poll conducted by Louis Harris and Associates, Inc. (The ICD Survey III, 1989), for example, 77 percent of parents of students with disabilities were satisfied with the special education system. On the question of mainstreaming, most parents were satisfied with the current level of integration. In a survey of teachers, both general and special education teachers indicated their satisfaction with the current continuum of services (Semmel, Abernathy, Butera, & Lesar, 1991). Critics of full inclusion claim that the idea of full inclusion is being championed by only a few radical special educators.

Regular educators are unwilling and/or unable to cope. The notion that a few radical special educators are promoting full inclusion is closely linked to the argument that the full inclusion movement has not been embraced wholeheartedly by general education. Critics of full inclusion assert that general education teachers see the heterogeneity that characterizes the population of students with disabilities as overwhelming (Fuchs & Fuchs, 1991; Kauffman, Gerber, & Semmel, 1988; Walker & Bullis, 1991). They maintain that the reason special education came into being in the first place was that regular educators were unable to handle students with special needs. Critics believe that regular educators are in no better position today to accommodate the needs of these children. They point out that regular class teachers are already overburdened and that the current emphasis on producing higher academic achievement in their pupils is at odds with accepting more students with disabilities into their classes. As one critic of full inclusion has put it:

> Can [advocates of full inclusion]. . . possibly believe that children in regular classrooms are taught and educated in accordance with their individuality? Individualization in regular classrooms is quite a dead issue and has been for years. The barrage of curriculum materials, syllabi, grade-level expectations for performance, standardized tests, competency tests, and so on continue to overwhelm even the most flexible teachers. Individualization calls for child centeredness, and child centeredness has been on the run since the 1960s. (Lieberman, 1992, p. 15)
>
> Regular classroom teachers attempt to meet physical-motor, cognitive-intellectual, and social-emotional needs just as special educators do. Yet, their focus tends to be different. Regular class teachers are given an agenda called the curriculum. They are provided with it prior to seeing any student. They are told that this is what they have to teach, and sometimes what book to use and even how to use it. This more standardized approach to education for the masses generally succeeds . . . for the masses. It misses some individual children by a mile, who may be normal and a little bit different, or who may be disabled and a lot different. The greater the difference, the greater the chance that the student will fall through the cracks of any standard way of doing something. (Lieberman, 1992, pp. 21–22)

Not all may share such a jaundiced view of general education, but most critics of full inclusion sympathize with the regular class teacher's already arduous job. Although some critics blame regular education teachers for their unwillingness to accommodate more students with disabilities, many agree that their hesitation to do so is justified.

Justifying full inclusion by asserting that people with disabilities are a minority is flawed. Many critics of full inclusion do not deny that, in many ways, people with disabilities have been treated similarly to oppressed minority groups, such as African Americans, Hispanics, and women. They have suffered discrimination on the basis of their disability and, thus, can be considered an oppressed minority group. These critics, however, do not see that this minority group status translates into the same educational placement decisions as it does for African Americans, Hispanics, and women (Kauffman, 1989; Kauffman & Hallahan, 1993). They argue that for the latter groups, separation from the mainstream cannot be defended on educational grounds, but for students with disabilities, separation can. Students with disabilities are sometimes placed in special classes or resource rooms to accommodate their educational needs better. Placement in separate educational environments is inherently unequal, these critics maintain, when it is done for factors irrelevant to learning (e.g., skin color), but such placements may result in equality when done for instructionally relevant reasons (e.g., student's ability to learn, difficulty of material being presented, preparation of the teacher). Finally, critics of full inclusion argue that the most important civil right of the minority in question—students with disabilities and their parents—is the right to choose. That is, IDEA gives parents, and students themselves, when appropriate, the right to choose the environment *they,* not advocates of total inclusion, consider most appropriate and least restrictive.

Unwillingness to consider empirical evidence is professionally irresponsible. Some professionals see as folly the disregard of empirical evidence espoused by some proponents of full inclusion (Fuchs & Fuchs, 1991). These professionals believe that ethical actions are always of the utmost importance. They assert, however, that decisions of what is ethical should be informed by research. In the case of mainstreaming, they think it important to have as much data as possible on its advantages and disadvantages and how best to implement it before deciding if, and how, it should be put into practice. Some critics maintain that full inclusion proponents have gone too far in championing their cause, that they have resorted to rhetoric rather than reason. These critics assert that backers of full inclusion have traded in their credentials as scientific researchers in favor of becoming advocates and lobbyists.

Preserving the continuum of services.   Related to the last point concerning the use of data to support ethical decision-making, many professionals believe that research is mixed on the value of pull-out versus full inclusion models. In the absence of research supporting any one service delivery option, they think it wise to be cautious about changing the current configuration too quickly or dras-

*O*pponents of inclusion assert that large, competitive classrooms cannot provide the individualized teaching so important to students with special requirements.

tically. They admit that there are problems with the current special education system and that there may even be a need for more integration of students with disabilities, including the use of full inclusion. They are leery, however, about eliminating the range of service delivery options currently available to school personnel and parents. Fuchs and Fuchs (1991), for example, have stated:

> [Proponents of full inclusion] . . . seem fond of battle metaphors. We'll piggyback on their favored imagery by suggesting that, for many . . . [defenders of a continuum of services] regular education remains a foreign and hostile territory, neglecting many children with disabilities. PL 94–142, with its declaration of a free and appropriate education and its cascade of services and the LRE principle, represented in 1975 the capturing of a beachhead for children with disabilities. It is time to gather our energies and courage; validate comprehensive integration strategies; pressure mainstream administrators and teachers for greater accommodations; move inland! But as we mount this new offensive, we, like any general worthy of his rank, must make certain that the beachhead remains secure. It's the beachhead, after all, that provides supplies and, in a worst-case scenario, guarantees a safe retreat. The cascade of services is a source of strength and a safety net for the children we serve. Let's not lose it. (pp. 253–254)

Mainstreaming Practices

Whether or not one subscribes to full inclusion, the fact is that most special educators are in favor of some degree of mainstreaming—integration of students with disabilities with nondisabled students. Educators have devised a number of strategies for implementing mainstreaming. Most of these practices are still in the experimental stages; that is, we do not have a wealth of evidence indicating their effectiveness. Various authorities have recommended the following eight strategies:

1. Prereferral teams
2. Collaborative consultation
3. Cooperative teaching
4. Cooperative learning
5. Peer tutoring
6. Partial participation
7. Curriculum materials designed to change attitudes
8. Reverse mainstreaming

In the following sections we briefly describe each of these approaches.

Prereferral Teams

Prereferral teams (PRTs) work with regular classroom teachers to recommend different strategies for working with children exhibiting academic and/or behavioral problems. One of the primary goals is to establish "ownership" of these children by general and not special educators. In other words, PRTs try to keep referrals to special education down by stressing that general educators try as many alternative strategies as possible before deciding that difficult-to-teach students need to become the primary responsibility of special educators.

The makeup of PRTs varies from one place to another, sometimes including the school principal or a school psychologist, but almost always including a special educator and a general educator. In fact, because of the emphasis on general education's ownership, some have maintained that general educators are the most important team members (Chalfant, Pysh, & Moultrie, 1979; Gerber &

> ➤ **prereferral teams (PRT).** Made up of a variety of professionals, especially regular and special educators. These teams work with regular class teachers to come up with strategies for teaching difficult-to-teach children. Designed to influence regular educators to take ownership of difficult-to-teach students and to minimize inappropriate referrals to special education.

Semmel, 1985). A major justification for using classroom teachers to make decisions regarding referral to special education is that they may have information on individual children that is even more important than results of the usual standardized tests: "Teachers observe tens of thousands of discrete behavioral events during each school day. Formal tests of ability and achievement are based on analysis of only small samples of student behavior. Clearly teachers have available to them, if they choose to use it, a far richer and varied sample of student behavior than the typical 'test'" (Gerber & Semmel, 1984, p. 141).

There is very little research on the effectiveness of PRTs (Lloyd, Crowley, Kohler, & Strain, 1988). The few evaluations that have been done indicate two things: (1) they do cut down on the number of referrals to special education; and (2) team members and administrators report that they are effective (Schram et al., 1984).

Collaborative Consultation

In the late 1970s and early 1980s, the notion that teachers or school psychologists should provide consultation to regular class teachers became quite popular. In this model, the special education teacher or psychologist acts as an expert in providing advice to the regular class teacher. The special education teacher may see the child with disabilities in a resource room, or the student may receive all of his or her instruction in the regular class.

More recently, authorities have begun to advocate a variation of this approach that differs in two important ways. Referred to as **collaborative consultation**, this approach stresses mutuality and reciprocity: "Mutuality means shared ownership of a common issue or problem by professionals. Reciprocity means allowing these parties to have equal access to information and the opportunity to participate in problem identification, discussion, decision making, and all final outcomes" (West & Idol, 1990, p. 23). In collaborative consultation, then, the special educator and the regular class teacher assume equal responsibility for the student with disabilities, and neither one assumes more authority in making recommendations about how to teach the child.

Like PRTs, one can use collaborative consultation to keep regular class teachers from referring difficult-to-teach students to special education, or one can use it after the child has been identified for special education. Furthermore, one can use collaborative consultation in conjunction with PRTs. The PRTs deal with students before they are identified for special education; collaborative consultation is used with students once they have been identified as needing special education.

Research suggests that collaborative consultation is a promising approach to meeting the needs of many students with disabilities in general education settings. Nevertheless, much remains unknown about what makes consultation effective or ineffective in meeting students' needs.

Cooperative Teaching

Sometimes referred to as collaborative teaching, cooperative teaching takes the notions of mutuality and reciprocity in collaborative consultation one step further. In **cooperative teaching** regular class teachers and special educators jointly teach in the same general education classroom composed of students with and without disabilities. In other words, the special educator comes out of his or her separate classroom (sometimes permanently) to come into the regular class setting. In addition to promoting the notions of mutuality and reciprocity, one of the advantages that proponents of this model advance is that it helps the special

➤ **collaborative consultation.** A special educator and a general educator collaborate to come up with teaching strategies for a student with disabilities. The relationship between the two professionals is based on the premises of shared responsibility and equal authority.

➤ **cooperative teaching.** An approach in which regular class teachers and special educators teach together in the general classroom; it helps the special educator know the context of the regular classroom better.

educator know the everyday curricular demands faced by the student with disabilities. The special educator sees the context within which the student must function to succeed in the mainstream. As one teacher, when interviewed, put it:

> I have learned so much about the content itself which has helped me to teach English and math to students in my resource class . . . I certainly have gained insights into the students themselves. For instance, when I do observation for [re-evaluations] . . . I am able to go into a class on one day and that's what I see, how that particular child performed on that particular day. But to be able to see kids on a day-in and day-out basis, I really feel I have a much better sense of who tunes outs [sic] when and why and who plugs away every minute of the day and still has difficulty because he hasn't understood. I can see their interactions with their peers. I can see their interest in the subject matter. I have a much more complete view of each child. . . . (Nowacek, 1992, p. 275)

There are at least three different ways to implement cooperative teaching: (1) complementary instruction, (2) supportive learning activities, and (3) team teaching (Bauwens & Hourcade, 1991; Bauwens, Hourcade, & Friend, 1989). In complementary instruction, the regular class teacher assumes primary responsibility for teaching academic content, whereas the special educator teaches "academic survival skills (e.g., taking notes, identifying main ideas in reading or lectures, summarizing, and related study skills)" (Bauwens et al., 1989, p. 19). This model is especially appropriate at the secondary level because it is difficult for special educators to have expertise in all content areas (e.g., history, biology, chemistry, Spanish, French, and so forth).

Supportive learning activities involve both teachers concentrating on academic content. The general educator, however, is responsible for the core content, whereas the special educator provides supplementary instruction. For example, the special educator might lead a discussion with a group of students or assign and monitor a supplemental project.

In team teaching, most often practiced in elementary school, the regular class teacher and special education teacher jointly plan and teach all content to all the students. They take turns being responsible for different aspects of the curriculum. Under this model, a person walking into the classroom would have a difficult time distinguishing the general from the special educator.

Research on cooperative teaching is in its infancy. Researchers are consistently finding, however, that its success is dependent on at least two factors (Nowacek, 1992; Trent, 1992). First, enough time needs to be built into the general and special

Mainstreaming efforts require a combination of efforts from both regular and special education teachers.

educators' schedules for cooperative planning. Second, the two teachers' personalities and working styles need to be compatible. As one teacher has said:

> The biggest drawback I could see to using the collaborative model would be for the school system to say, "We're going to do this. We're going to train you teachers and you two are going to work together." That would not work at all. Carol and I have a relationship where it works. I'm sure there are other teachers that I couldn't work with. I think it's very person-specific . . . It does take a lot of adjustment for the classroom teacher because we're used to being in control—in charge—and all of a sudden, there's this other person in your room. (Nowacek, 1992, p. 274)

Because of the importance of interpersonal skills in making cooperative teaching and collaborative consultation successful, some researchers have cautioned teachers against neglecting the actual teaching of the *students* (Fuchs & Fuchs, 1992). In other words, teachers engaged in cooperative teaching or collaborative consultation need to work on getting along together, but not to the neglect of the students they are teaching.

Cooperative Learning

Much emphasis is placed on competition in the traditional regular class. This focus, some believe, is detrimental to the success of all students, especially those with disabilities or of lower ability (Johnson & Johnson, 1986; Slavin, 1988, 1991). The Johnsons have found that **cooperative learning**—involving students with disabilities and nondisabled peers in situations in which they must cooperate with one another—leads to better attitudes on the part of the nondisabled toward their peers with disabilities as well as to better attitudes of students with disabilities toward themselves.

The Johnsons believe that cooperative situations foster differentiated, dynamic, and realistic views of group members, especially when students with disabilities take part in the cooperative venture. By *differentiated*, they mean that a child is viewed as possessing more attributes than just the stereotypic ones that accompany his or her label. And by *dynamic*, they mean that a child's attributes

➤ **cooperative learning.** A teaching approach in which the teacher places students with heterogeneous abilities (for example, some might have disabilities) together to work on assignments.

*T*he canine character "Barkley" on "Sesame Street" serves as a "hearing dog" to character Linda, who has a hearing impairment.

may not be viewed by other group members as relevant to all aspects of the task at hand. Once the teacher places students in small, heterogeneous groups for the purpose of working toward a common goal, Johnson and Johnson state that a number of positive events will occur.

Although the Johnsons' use of cooperative learning has led to positive changes in attitudes, they have been less successful in affecting achievement. They have looked at achievement in only a few of their studies, and the results have been mixed. However, an investigator who has designed cooperative learning situations that have led to achievement gains is Robert Slavin.

Although only a few of Slavin's studies have included formally identified students with disabilities, he has used cooperative learning with low-ability students. To have positive effects on achievement, he concludes that cooperative learning must involve two elements: (1) there must be group incentives, and (2) there must be individual accountability. What should be avoided are situations in which the group's solution to a problem can be found by just one or two members. One way of avoiding this is to base rewards on the group's average so each individual's score contributes to the total score of the group.

Peer Tutoring

Yet another recommended method of integrating students with disabilities into the mainstream is **peer tutoring** (Jenkins & Jenkins, 1987), defined as one student who tutors another. Professionals have advocated using children with disabilities as tutors as well as tutees. When a child with a disability assumes the role of tutor, the tutee is usually a younger peer.

Research results on the effectiveness of peer tutoring are mixed (Scruggs & Richter, 1986). Evidence suggests that students with mild disabilities can benefit academically when serving as tutor or tutee. There are few empirical data, however, to show that it improves self-concept.

It is important to remember that, contrary to what some educators believe, peer tutoring does not save time (Gerber & Kauffman, 1981). A good peer-tutoring situation requires continuous organization and monitoring by the teacher.

➢ **peer tutoring.** A method that can be used to integrate students with disabilities in regular classrooms, based on the notion that students can effectively tutor one another. The role of learner or teacher may be assigned to either the student with a disability or the nondisabled student..

Partial Participation

Professionals concerned with mainstreaming students with relatively severe disabilities advocate the concept of partial participation (Giangreco & Putnam, 1991; Raynes, Snell, & Sailor, 1991). **Partial participation** means having students with disabilities participate, on a reduced basis, in virtually all activities experienced by all students in the regular classroom. Partial participation questions the assumption that it is a waste of time to include students with severe mental and physical limitations in certain activities because they cannot benefit from them in the same way that nondisabled students can. Instead of excluding anyone from these activities, advocates of partial participation recommend that the teacher accommodate the student with disabilities by such strategies as "providing assistance for more difficult parts of a task, changing the 'rules' of the game or activity to make it less difficult, or changing the way in which a task or activity is organized or presented" (Raynes et al., 1991, p. 329).

The objectives of partial participation are twofold. First, proponents maintain that it provides exposure to academic content that the student with disabilities might otherwise miss. Second, it helps students with disabilities achieve a greater degree of social interaction with nondisabled peers.

➢ **partial participation.** Students with disabilities, while in the regular classroom, engage in the same activities as nondisabled students but on a reduced basis; teacher makes adaptations in the activity to allow student to participate as much as possible.

Curriculum materials designed to change attitudes

Authors have developed curriculum materials to enlighten nondisabled students about students with disabilities. These materials often involve activities constructed to teach children about different aspects of disabilities, such as causes and characteristics, as well as to let students explore their feelings about children with disabilities. These materials range from full-blown curricula, such as *Accepting Individual Differences* (Cohen, 1977) and *What If You Couldn't? An Elementary School Program About Handicaps* (Children's Museum of Boston, 1978), to individual books, such as *Don't Feel Sorry for Paul* (Wolf, 1974). Many of these approaches involve a variety of media and activities. One especially creative approach is *Kids on the Block*, a puppet show with Muppet-like characters that have different kinds of disabilities (e.g., mental retardation, cerebral palsy, visual impairment, behavior disorders). The show comes with scripts designed to explain basic concepts about children with disabilities and has a variety of curriculum suggestions.

Another curricular approach to improving pupils' attitudes toward their peers who have disabilities is the use of simulations. Some professionals believe that teachers can promote understanding of disabilities by having nondisabled students simulate disabilities in and out of school (Wesson & Mandell, 1989). They believe walking through the school while blindfolded, wearing glasses smeared with petroleum jelly, or trying to button clothing with hands covered with thick socks, for example, may help students understand and appreciate the disabilities of their peers who have limited vision or mobility.

Although more and more schools are using materials designed to teach children in regular education about students with disabilities, very few efforts have been mounted to evaluate these curricular modifications systematically.

Reverse Mainstreaming

Traditionally, most people think of mainstreaming as placing a few students with disabilities in classes primarily made up of nondisabled students. Some professionals, however, have advocated what has come to be called **reverse mainstreaming**—that is, the placement for short periods of time of a few nondisabled students in classes primarily made up of children with disabilities. Authorities have attributed several benefits to reverse mainstreaming (McCann, Semmel, & Nevin, 1985). Because the students with disabilities are in the majority in a special education classroom, their feelings of being different are lessened. The onus of gaining social acceptance shifts from the students with disabilities to the nondisabled students. Also, the nondisabled children's fears and misconceptions about children with disabilities and what goes on in their special classes may diminish.

Although there is a well-articulated rationale for reverse mainstreaming, we need further research to answer certain questions. So far, there are few data on its effectiveness. We do not know, for example, the optimum length of time for integration or the optimum blend of child characteristics (e.g., age, gender, types of disabilities).

One fear raised is that nondisabled children will be harmed by reverse mainstreaming because it might expose them to inappropriate models. Available data, however, indicate that this is not the case. In one study, for example, researchers integrated nondisabled preschoolers with preschoolers with mild and moderate disabilities at a ratio of 1 to 2 (Odom, Deklyen, & Jenkins, 1984). They found no

➢ **reverse mainstreaming.** The practice of placing nondisabled students in classes predominately composed of persons with disabilities.

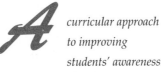

A curricular approach to improving students' awareness of disabilities is the use of simulations, wherein they experience various disabilities.

differences between the integrated group and a nonintegrated group on measures of intelligence, communication, and social development.

EARLY INTERVENTION

Many educators and social scientists believe that the earlier in life a disability is recognized and a program of education or treatment is started, the better the outcome for the child. Bricker (1986) states three basic arguments for early intervention: First, a child's early learning provides the foundation for later learning, so the sooner a special program of intervention is begun, the further the child is likely to go in learning more complex skills. Second, early intervention is likely to provide support for the child and family that will help prevent the child from developing additional problems or disabilities. Third, early intervention can help families adjust to having a child with disabilities; give parents the skills they need to handle the child effectively at home; and help families find the additional support services they may need, such as counseling, medical assistance, or financial aid.

Children whose disabilities are diagnosed at a very young age tend to be those with a specific syndrome (Down syndrome, for example) or an obvious physical disability. Many have severe and multiple disabilities. Typically, these young children's needs cannot be met by a single agency or intervention, so many professionals must work together closely if the child is to be served effectively. If the child's disabilities are recognized at an early age and intervention by all necessary professionals is well coordinated, the child's learning and development can often be greatly enhanced. The development of effective early intervention programs leads us to hope that we shall soon see dramatic decreases in the degree of disability that results from being born with a specific condition or acquiring a disability in early childhood. For example, we see the possibility of greatly reducing the disabilities—and enhancing the development—of children with Down syndrome, autism, cerebral palsy, and many other disabilities acquired through diseases or accidents.

Legislative History

A major reason to be encouraged about educational programming for infants and preschoolers with disabilities is that the federal government has been and continues to be committed to supporting research and educational efforts in this area.

More and more early intervention programs are springing up around the country. The federal government has made substantial inroads in providing monies and leadership in this most important area. Two crucial pieces of federal legislation for early intervention with children and families with disabilities are PL 90–538 and PL 99–457.

PL 90–538

➤ **PL 90–538.** Congressional legislation passed in 1968 that created the Handicapped Children's Early Education Program (HCEEP).

➤ **Handicapped Children's Early Education Program (HCEEP).** The first federal special education program aimed at young children with disabilities and their families. It has funded numerous demonstration and outreach projects.

In 1968 Congress passed **PL 90–538**, establishing the **Handicapped Children's Early Education Program (HCEEP)**, the first federal special education program aimed specifically at young children with disabilities and their families. HCEEP has funded model demonstration projects for delivering experimental educational programming for young children with disabilities. In addition, outreach projects have taken some of the best practices from the demonstration projects and transferred them to other sites. By 1981, HCEEP had funded 280 demonstration projects (at a cost of over $85 million) and 140 outreach projects (costing over $35 million) (Hebbeler, Smith, & Black, 1991).

Independent evaluations of HCEEP projects have designated them as highly successful. These projects have not only provided direct services to young children and their families, but they have also produced curriculum materials, assessment devices, and parent training materials.

PL 99–457

➤ **PL 99–457.** Extended the requirements of PL 94–142 to children aged three to five, with special incentive to states for instituting programs for ages birth to three years.

Passed in 1986, **PL 99–457** stipulates that states must provide preschool services to all children with disabilities, ages three to five years. In addition, it provides incentives to states to establish programs for infants and toddlers with disabilities, ages birth to three years, and their families. All states have elected to provide services for infants and toddlers (Turnbull & Turnbull, 1990). Today, we have many more early childhood programs for students with disabilities than were available 20 years ago.

Infants and toddlers ages birth to three years are eligible for services if they (a) are experiencing a developmental delay in cognitive, physical, language and speech, psycho-social, or self-help development; or (b) have a physical or mental condition with a high probability of resulting in a developmental delay.

Under PL 99–457, a variety of early intervention services, such as special education instruction, physical therapy, speech and language therapy, and medical diagnostic services, are available to help remediate the developmental delays of these infants and toddlers. In addition, this legislation involves the development of an **Individualized Family Service Plan (IFSP)**. Similar to an Individualized Education Program (IEP) for older children, the IFSP broadens the focus to include the family as well as the child. In fact, federal regulations stipulate that the family be involved in the development of the IFSP. Other important requirements are that the IFSP must contain statements of the

➤ **Individualized Family Service Plan (IFSP).** A plan for services for young children with disabilities (under 3 years of age) and their families; drawn up by professionals and parents; similar to an IEP for older children; mandated by PL 99–457.

- child's present levels of functioning in cognitive, physical, language and speech, psycho-social, and self-help development;
- family's resources, priorities, and concerns relating to the child's development;
- major expected outcomes for the child and family, including criteria, procedures, and time lines for assessing progress;
- specific early intervention services necessary to meet the child's and the family's needs, including frequency, intensity, location, and method of delivery;

Issues in Special Education **How Should MDA Use Telethon's $45M?**

CNN

The Jerry Lewis Labor Day Telethon to benefit individuals with muscular dystrophy has been a Labor Day tradition since its beginning in 1966. The telethon attracts up to 100 million TV viewers, an audience exceeded only by the Super Bowl and the Academy Awards. Money raised from the telethon aids medical research and pays for medical bills, wheelchairs, and summer camps for the more than one million people with muscular dystrophy, referred to as Jerry's "kids."

A counter-group which calls itself Jerry's Orphans is outraged at Lewis and his reference to adults with muscular dystrophy as his "kids." Founded by former telethon poster children, they are insulted by his views about people with disabilities, which they feel are condescending, paternalistic, and dated. The group is not against finding a cure, or an individual's wish to be cured. Their anger and concern surrounds the idea that persons with disabilities are dependent on Lewis's help and on the goodwill of society.

Some disability activists believe the message of telethons, in general, promotes the idea that people with disabilities only need a cure in order to lead whole and normal lives . . . a view they feel is demeaning and degrading and results in the forced stereotype of victimization.

However, some support for Lewis and the fundraiser is maintained among people with disabilities. Arnold D. Gale, a pediatric neurologist, who has muscular dystrophy, and whose life story was featured on the 1992 telethon, has spoken out against the removal of Lewis as master of ceremonies. There are also activists, who, while critical of the telethon's message, do not wish to undermine the financial success of the event, which generates millions of dollars every year. The 1991 telethon raised $45.1 million for the Muscular Dystrophy Association (MDA). Most of the proceeds are appropriated to aid in research for treatments and a cure, and to help families pay medical bills. About 24% of the funds are allocated to administrative expenses.

- Is it more important for people with disabilities to be healed or cured, or accepted as members of an educated and aware society?
- As the controversy over telethons continues, how can the funds be distributed within the goals and aims of the Americans with Disabilities Act?
- Some persons with disabilities feel that controversy over their needs has caused them to become fractured as a group. How might dissension affect their self-esteem and their unity and progress as a minority and political group?

- projected dates for initiating and ending the services;
- name of the case manager; and
- steps needed to ensure a smooth transition from the early intervention program into a preschool program.

Types of Programs

One common way of categorizing the variety of early intervention programs is to consider whether the primary location of the services is in a center, a home, or a combination of the two. A survey of early childhood intervention projects found that 52% of children were enrolled in centers, 27% received services at home, and 15% were served in a combination of the two (Karnes & Stayton, 1988). The survey also found that the typical attendance was for one to two hours per day for one to two days a week.

The earliest early intervention programs for children with disabilities were center-based. In center-based programs, the child and the family come to the center for training and/or counseling. One advantage to center-based programs is that center staff can see more children. Furthermore, some professionals believe that this program allows center staff to have more influence over what goes on in the interaction between parent and child.

In more recent years, authorities have advocated home-based programs or a combination of center- and home-based approaches. There are several advantages to approaches that take place in the home. A couple of the most important are that, (a) with the increase in mothers working outside the home and single-parent families, home-based programs are more convenient for more family members, and (b) skills and techniques learned by children and adults at the center need to be transferred to the home, but when these skills are learned in the natural environment, i.e., the home, this transfer is not necessary.

Issues

Compared to special education, in general, special education for infants, toddlers, and preschoolers has had few controversial issues. This is probably because so many professionals have fought for so long to get the needs of very young children recognized that they have not had time to engage in too many debates about specific details concerning early intervention. In a sense, early childhood special educators have been bound together by the common goal of securing legislation and programming for young children with disabilities. Nevertheless, there have been and continue to be some areas of disagreement among early childhood special education professionals. Some of the most compelling issues relate to (1) the appropriate role of the family in early intervention, (2) whether it is better to have a child- or a teacher-directed curriculum, and (3) the best way to achieve a successful transition from the early intervention program to the preschool program, and from the preschool program to the school program.

Appropriate Role of the Family

Shaping up as a significant issue is how the family should be involved in early intervention programming. One of the characteristics of recent early intervention programming (Guralnick, 1991), and indeed one of the hallmarks of the IFSP, has been the involvement of parents. The federal regulations, however, have not been directive in exactly how parents should be included in early intervention programming. Some are concerned that the notion of including parents may be being misinterpreted to mean that professionals should focus more on changing the family rather than on changing the child. Slentz and Bricker (1992), for example, have pointed out that federal regulations stipulate that any services provided for the family are for the purpose of meeting the needs of the child.

In particular, Slentz and Bricker are opposed to early childhood special educators' becoming heavily involved in assessment of family members. If they do, "parents may legitimately question why providing such information is necessary when they thought the purpose of the early intervention program was to help their child. Many families perceive this process as an invasion of privacy . . ." (Slentz & Bricker, 1992, p. 14). Instead, they believe that professionals should take a low-key approach to assessing families. Slentz and Bricker recommend that professionals briefly interview parents to find out the needs of the family and the child rather than administer a lengthy battery of tests. If parents indicate a need for it, they can be referred for further evaluation.

Closely related to the issue of assessment is the larger issue of who should be in control over decision-making for the family. Slentz and Bricker (1992) believe that "in large measure, families should decide on their goals and priorities with the early intervention staff assisting in the attainment of those goals" (pp. 17–18) As one expert has put it:

> Family decision making and control is clearly the approach policy makers wished to endorse in the current legislation. . . . The law intends to leave the final decision about children in the hands of their parents. The family is encouraged to seek professional advice on complex issues beyond its own expertise. Indeed, family members would not be performing their responsibilities if they did not do so. But the family is expected to maintain executive control over the important decisions and not cede that control to professionals, no matter how distinguished their credentials. (Gallagher, 1992, p. 8)

Child- Versus Teacher-Directed Programs

For some time, there has existed a tension between early childhood educators concerned with nondisabled populations and those focused on children with disabilities over the degree of teacher direction that is most appropriate. Heavily influenced by the theories of Piaget, most early childhood teachers are oriented toward a curriculum that allows children to explore their environment relatively freely. They advocate a developmental approach that assumes that children's development will unfold naturally with encouragement, guidance, and support from the teacher (Position Statement of National Association for the Education of

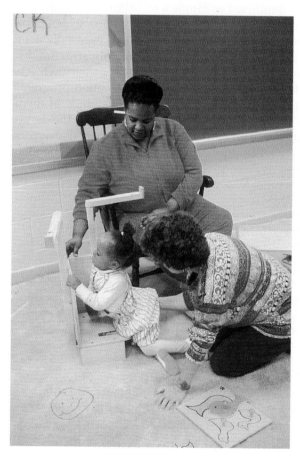

Recent legislation pertaining to early education for children with disabilities makes early detection even more important.

Young Children and National Association of Early Childhood Specialists in State Departments of Education, 1991).

Many early interventionists, on the other hand, come from a tradition that assumes children with disabilities need a heavy dose of direction from adults if they are to learn the skills they are lacking. As more and more special educators advocate that children with disabilities be integrated with nondisabled children, the issue of how much teacher-direction they need has come to the fore.

According to Wolery (1991), some of the relevant questions are:

- For what types of outcomes are child- and teacher-directed instruction best suited?
- What balance, if any should exist between the two types?
- Which children, if any, learn best from either type or given combinations of the two types?
- What phases of performance (acquisition, fluency, maintenance, generalization) are promoted by the two types? (Wolery, 1991, p. 130)

Transition From Early Intervention Programs to Preschool, and From Preschool to School

Closely related to the issue of child- versus teacher-direction is the issue of how best to help young children and their families make it through transition points in their lives. Transition points (e.g., a change in jobs, marital status, or residence) can be disruptive for families. For families of children with disabilities, one of the most stressful times can be the transition from one school situation to another. In the early childhood years, the stress may be especially acute because the child is moving from an environment that is heavily structured to one in which the child is provided more freedom to act on his or her own. The adult-child ratio, for example, is quite low in most early intervention programs. The child is surrounded by teachers, teacher aides, and various kinds of therapists. As he or she moves into a typical kindergarten setting, however, the degree of structure can change dramatically. Some authorities are worried that typical early intervention programs are making children with disabilities too dependent on adults. They believe that these programs are not fostering the kind of independence necessary to succeed in more integrated settings.

> The ecology of special education preschool classrooms may preclude opportunities for students to practice skills that foster independence. Students in special education preschools spend more time in small groups of individual instruction, and receive much more teacher prompting than do peers in typical preschool classes. Although these instructional arrangements may facilitate skill acquisition, they may inhibit the acquisition of the very academic support skills that facilitate a successful transition to the academic mainstream. Children in these special education classrooms have few opportunities to acquire or practice the independent skills that are important for success in kindergarten. (Fowler, Schwartz, & Atwater, 1991, p. 138)

Moving Toward the Twenty-First Century

As we move toward the twenty-first century, we are hopeful that early childhood education will continue to play an important role in eliminating and lessening the impact of disability on children and their families. We caution, however, not to assume that early intervention alone will mean fewer children with disabilities. Although we are devising more effective programs of early intervention, the number of children with disabilities is increasing. The reasons for this increase are many and complex and are related to changes in economic and social conditions in the United States during the 1980s and 1990s. Today, compared to a decade or two ago,

- More young children and their mothers are living in poverty, have poor nutrition, and are exposed to environmental conditions likely to cause disease and disability.
- More babies are born to teenage mothers.
- More babies are born to mothers who receive inadequate prenatal care, have poor nutrition during pregnancy, and abuse substances that can harm the fetus.
- More babies are born with a low birth weight.
- Environmental hazards, both chemical and social, are increasing.
- More children are subjected to abuse and an environment in which violence and substance abuse are pervasive.
- Cuts in social programs have widened the gap between needs and the availability of social services.

These facts prompted the President's Committee on Mental Retardation and the National Coalition on Prevention of Mental Retardation to speak of a new morbidity—a new set of disabilities (Baumeister, Kupstas, & Klindworth, 1990). The new morbidity includes a variety of behavioral, health, and school problems that affect a growing number of U.S. children and are caused by many of the preceding factors. Implementing and expanding the services provided under PL 99–457 and training the early childhood specialists necessary to provide effective early intervention are major challenges as we head toward the twenty-first century.

TRANSITION FROM SECONDARY SCHOOL TO ADULTHOOD

Preparing students for continued education, adult responsibilities, independence, and employment have always been goals of public secondary education. Most students complete high school and find jobs, enter a vocational training program, or go to college without experiencing major difficulties of adjustment. We know that dropout and unemployment rates are far too high for all youths, especially in economically depressed communities, but the outlook for students with disabilities may be even worse (Hendrick, MacMillan, & Balow, 1989; Wolman, Bruininks, & Thurlow, 1989). Published figures on dropout rates must be viewed with caution because there are many different ways of defining *dropout* and computing the statistics (MacMillan et al., 1992). Studies of what happens to students with disabilities during and after their high school years strongly suggest, however, that a higher percentage of them, compared to students without disabilities, have difficulty in making the transition from adolescence to adulthood and from school to work. Many drop out of school, experience great difficulty in finding and holding a job, do not find work suited to their capabilities, do not receive further training or education, or become dependent on their families or public assistance programs (Edgar, 1987; Neel, Meadows, Levine, & Edgar, 1988; Rusch, Szymanski, & Chadsey-Rusch, 1992).

Federal Initiatives

As was the case with early childhood, much of the impetus for programming for transition to adulthood came from the federal government. However, it took the federal government longer to take action in the case of transition to adulthood. By the early 1980s it recognized that there needed to be professional energy and federal dollars spent on students with disabilities as they entered adulthood.

The Transition Initiative

In the early 1980s, the federal government announced a new initiative referred to as "transition" (Will, 1984). The transition initiative called for more extensive services for students as they exited secondary schools and moved into employment. Several pieces of legislation were enacted to encourage transition programming. Although virtually all special educators were in favor of this type of programming, some were critical of the narrow focus on work as the definition of transition. As one authority explained:

> I argued (Halpern, 1985) that the goals of transition should never be confined to employment, but should encompass all appropriate dimensions of adult adjustment and involvement in the community. Now in the 1990s we no longer debate the appropriateness of a broader set of goals for transition. (Halpern, 1992, p. 203)

Based on analyses such as these, recent legislation of the 1990s has broadened the concept of transition. It has also put more teeth into the imperative of transition by providing more detail regarding how, when, and by whom transition must be provided.

The Transition Mandate

➤ **PL 101–476.** Enacted in 1990, stipulates that schools provide transition services from secondary school to adulthood for all children with disabilities; scope includes post-secondary education, vocational training, integrated employment, continuing and adult education, independent living, and community living; stipulates that a transition plan be included in the IEP no later than 16 years of age.

In 1990 Congress enacted legislation (**PL 101–476**) mandating that schools provide transition services for all students with disabilities. The federal government defines transition services as:

> a coordinated set of activities for a student, designed within an outcome-oriented process, which promotes movement from school to post-school activities, including post-secondary education, vocational training, integrated employment (including supported employment), continuing and adult education, adult services, independent living, or community participation.

To ensure proper planning for transition services, the federal government also requires that students with disabilities have a transition plan integrated into their Individualized Education Program (IEP). The IEP must contain a statement of needed transition services for students, beginning no later than 16 years of age and annually thereafter. (For students for whom it is appropriate, the statement is to be included in the IEP at a younger age.) In addition, the IEP must include a statement of the linkages and/or responsibilities of each participating agency before the student leaves the school setting.

In broadening the notion of transition to include more than transition to work, the federal definition stipulates a comprehensive program for students with disabilities. It also means that coordination of these various services is critical to the successful implementation of transition programming (DeStefano & Wermuth, 1992).

*I*ndividualized Family
Service Plans seek to involve
the family in available
services for young children with
disabilities.

Supported Employment

With the federal initiative and federal mandate for transition services has come an increase in the use of supported employment. In fact, it is cited in the federal definition of transition services as an example of integrated employment (see p. 78). **Supported employment**, designed to assist persons with disabilities who cannot function independently in competitive employment, is a method of ensuring that they are able to work in integrated work settings. Competitive employment is defined as working at least 20 hours per week. Integrated work settings are defined as:

> settings where (a) most workers are not handicapped and (b) individuals with handicaps are not part of a work group consisting only of others with handicaps, or are part of a small work group of not more than eight individuals with handicaps. Additionally, if there are no co-workers or the only co-workers are members of a small group of not more than eight individuals with handicaps, individuals with handicaps must have regular contact with nonhandicapped individuals, other than personnel who provide support services. Finally, these regulations require that supported employees be provided follow-up services at least twice monthly at the job site, except in the case of chronic mental illness. (Rusch & Hughes, 1990, p. 9)

According to Rusch and Hughes (1990), there are four models of supported employment:

- Individual placement
- Clustered or enclave placement
- Mobile work crew
- Entrepreneurial

In the individual placement model, an employment specialist (sometimes referred to as a job coach) places the individual with a business in the private

➤ **supported employment.** A method of integrating people with disabilities who cannot work independently into competitive employment; includes use of an employment specialist, or job coach, who helps person with disability function on the job.

sector. The employment specialist also provides on-site training that is gradually reduced as the worker is able to function on the job more independently.

The other three models involve groups of no more than eight people with disabilities and are designed for persons unable to assume as much independence as those under the individual placement model. All three involve on-going supervision by an employment specialist. In the clustered, or enclave, model, groups work together in a business or industrial setting. In the mobile work crew model, groups are organized around specific contract services, such as janitorial work. In the entrepreneurial model, groups provide a specific service product to businesses in the community.

Issues

Like early intervention programming, little controversy surrounds the basic premise of transition programming for students as they move from school to work. All special educators agree that transition programming is critical for successful adjustment of adults with disabilities. Some controversial areas, however, pertain to the specifics of transition. Many controversies have to do with trying to meet the diverse requirements of the federal mandate. Some professionals are debating how best to build a curriculum that covers education, employment, independent living, and community participation. This concern for meeting the diverse needs of students is manifested somewhat differently for students with more severe disabilities versus those with milder disabilities.

Students With Severe Disabilities

For students with severe disabilities, much of the concern focuses on the coordination and linkage of the many agencies outside of the school setting (DeStefano & Wermuth, 1992). Many special education personnel are unaccustomed to working with nonschool agencies. For example, the relationship between vocational and special education has traditionally been ambiguous. Federal regulations, however, now require that special education work with vocational education as well as with other agencies in the community.

For a number of years, special educators at the secondary level have been moving toward more involvement in the community, but the federal transition mandate has hastened the need for these outreach efforts. Approaches, such as supported employment, for example, require that special educators work with local employers in setting up and instituting training and working environments for students with disabilities. Not all special educators have been trained for this expanded role, however. We are still in the infancy stage of knowing how best to accomplish this interface between the school and community environments. There is a need for experimentation with approaches to educating special educators for this broader role.

Students With Mild Disabilities

For students with mild disabilities, much of the concern centers on attempting to meet their academic as well as their vocational needs. Teachers of secondary students are constantly faced with the decision of how much to stress academics versus vocational preparation. Because their disabilities are milder, many children with learning disabilities, for example, may be able to go on to

CASE STUDY: TOM ➤

Tom is average in height and slightly immature physically. He is relatively low-functioning with an attained IQ of 70, second-grade reading skills, and third-grade math skills. His behavior is noticeably inappropriate at times; he is very excitable and difficult to get along with. His speech tends to be disjointed, and he often uses clichés (which he generally misstates) to appear more knowledgeable and on top of things. He has only one friend, a slightly higher-functioning special education peer, whom he tries to dominate during social interactions. He drives and has his own car. He lives at home with his family and has no plans to move out.

He was adopted at birth; his parents were unaware of his disability until he was referred for testing in kindergarten. As he was growing up, they made every effort to provide a supportive and protective environment for him, although Tom thought they babied him too much.

Throughout high school, Tom saw himself as competent and intelligent. He never admitted to having a learning disability and dismissed any conversation suggesting such an idea. He felt he had been incorrectly placed in special classes that were below his ability and was anxious to graduate. He thought a lot about what he should do after graduation, and on one self-description survey indicated "need advice on what to do after high school." He talked about becoming an electrician, a contractor, a welder, and a forest ranger, but mostly he aspired to be a contractor (he had worked part time for a contractor, a family friend since ninth grade). Tom finally decided to enroll in a training program at the junior college to prepare him for a contractor's license. The summer after graduation, he began attending classes but again felt they were below his ability and he had been incorrectly placed (a college counselor had enrolled him in an Independent Living Skills class for disabled students). Tom dropped the course and took a leave of absence from school for a year so he could work full time with the contractor. Shortly afterward, the contractor's company went out of business and Tom lost his job. Tom's family arranged for him to work with an uncle who was also a contractor and welder (two of his cousins worked for Tom's uncle as well). After a few months, Tom lost that job, too.

At this point, no school, no job, Tom confided in the field researcher (whom he had known for over a year) of his fear that he might not have a "normal" future (he had confided in few people before about his learning problem). He acknowledged the extent of his learning disability and his concern about its impact on his plans for contractor's work. He seemed hopeless and his self-confidence had dropped markedly. He felt tremendous pressure "to decide about something" and asked the field researcher for help. Tom had one last hope, that perhaps he could enroll in a vocationally oriented junior college (i.e., trade technical college), and that maybe his uncle (the contractor) and the field researcher could help him check out the school. Tom seemed to be identifying with his uncle—Tom described him as "also learning disabled"—as though his uncle more than anyone could understand Tom's problem. It also seemed to reassure Tom to know he was not alone in the world with his learning disability.

Tom pursued admission to the contractor's program at the trade tech junior college and began attending classes during the spring semester. Within a few weeks of his starting the program, Tom's self-confidence and hopes for the future were restored. He boasted that going to trade tech is the best thing he has ever done.

SOURCE: From A. G. Zetlin and A. Hosseini, Six postschool case studies of mildly learning handicapped young adults, *Exceptional Children, 55*(5) (1989), 405–411. Copyright 1989 by The Council for Exceptional Children. Reprinted with permission.

post-secondary educational institutions, such as community colleges or universities. It is often difficult to tell as early as tenth grade, when such decisions need to be made, whether to steer students with learning disabilities toward a college preparatory or more vocationally oriented curriculum.

Some authorities believe that too many students with learning disabilities have been sold short on how much they can achieve academically. These authorities believe that such students are written off as academic failures who can never achieve at the college level. This diminished expectation for academic success translates into a curriculum that makes few academic demands on the students. For example, one study of learning disabilities classrooms at the secondary level found an "environmental press against academic content" (Zigmond & Miller, 1992, p. 25).

Other authorities maintain that an overemphasis on academics leaves many students with learning disabilities unprepared to enter the world of work upon leaving school. They believe that the learning problems of students with learning disabilities tend to be minimized. These authorities assert that just because students with learning disabilities are characterized as having mild disabilities, they do not necessarily have insignificant learning impairments.

Along these same lines, some professionals think there are far too few support services available to students with mild disabilities. Whereas transition services, such as supported employment, are available to persons with severe disabilities, individuals with milder disabilities are often left to fend for themselves once they graduate from secondary school. (See box on p. 81.)

America 2000 and transition programming for students with mild disabilities. Adding to the confusion over the debate about academics versus vocational preparation is the current emphasis placed on academics by the U.S. Department of Education. Beginning in the late 1980s and continuing into the 1990s, a number of national reports have criticized the general educational system in the United States. These reports, pointing to the low achievement levels of America's youth compared with those of other industrialized countries, have resulted in calls for higher standards in our nation's schools.

In response to these criticisms, President George Bush initiated America 2000, a plan to restructure and revitalize education in the United States. In the fall of 1989, Bush held the first Education Summit in Charlottesville, Virginia, attended by governors from all 50 states. Growing out of this historic meeting, were six national goals for the year 2000 agreed to by the governors (U.S. Department of Education, 1990):

- All children in America will start school ready to learn.
- The high school graduation rate will increase to at least 90 percent.
- American students will leave grades four, eight, and twelve having demonstrated competency in challenging subject matter including English, mathematics, science, history, and geography; and every school in America will ensure that all students learn to use their minds well, so they may be prepared for responsible citizenship, further learning, and productive employment in our modern economy.
- U.S. students will be first in the world in science and mathematics achievement.
- Every adult American will be literate and will possess the knowledge and skills necessary to compete in a global economy and exercise the rights and responsibilities of citizenship.
- Every school in America will be free of drugs and violence and will offer a disciplined environment conducive to learning.

Some assert that the national goals largely ignore the educational needs of students with disabilities. And some have maintained that the emphasis on higher standards has taken the focus away from the needs of students with disabilities who are unable to meet such high standards. As DeStefano and Wermuth (1992) have noted:

The idea of expanding secondary school programs to include more vocational training, preparation for independent living, and community experiences runs counter to
other national trends in education, which emphasize increased academic requirements, accountability expressed in terms of achievement in content area subjects, and
increased competition for dwindling educational resources. (p. 542)

As just one example, several states have moved to requiring minimum competency testing to receive a high school diploma. Many special educators have
expressed concerns about whether such requirements will be unfair to students
with disabilities (Halpern, 1992).

Moving Toward the Twenty-First Century

As we move toward the end of this century, despite some of the unresolved
issues, we can be encouraged by all the attention that special educators have
given to the area of transition. A variety of transition opportunities are available
now that were unavailable just a few years ago.

In considering transition issues, it is helpful to keep in mind that a smooth
and successful transition to adult life is difficult for any adolescent. Individuals
find many different routes to adulthood, and we would be foolish to prescribe a
single pattern of transition. Our goal must be to provide the special assistance
needed by adolescents and young adults with disabilities that will help them
achieve the most rewarding, productive, independent, and integrated adult life
possible. This goal cannot be achieved by assuming that all adolescents and
young adults with disabilities, or even all individuals falling into a given special
education category, will need the same special transition services or that all will
achieve the same level of independence and productivity. One of education's
great challenges is to devise an effective array of programs that will meet the
individual needs of students on their paths to adulthood.

SOME CONCLUDING THOUGHTS
REGARDING TRENDS AND ISSUES

If you are feeling a bit overwhelmed at the controversial nature of special education, then we have achieved our objective. We, too, are constantly amazed at the
number of unanswered questions our field faces. It seems that, just as we find
what we think are the right answers to a certain set of questions about how to
educate students with disabilities, another set of questions emerges. And each
new collection of questions is as complex and challenging as the last.

It would be easy to view this inability to reach definitive conclusions to
which everyone agrees as indicative of a field in chaos. We disagree. We prefer to
view this constant state of questioning as a sign of health and vigor. The controversial nature of special education is what makes it exciting and challenging. We
would be worried, and we believe people with disabilities and their families
would be worried, too, if the field were suddenly to decide that it had reached
complete agreement on most of the important issues. We should constantly be
striving to find better ways to provide education and related services for persons
with disabilities. In doing this, it is inevitable that there will be differences of
opinion.

*S*ummary

Special education has changed dramatically during its history, and the field appears poised for more changes. Three major trends are: integration, early intervention programming, and programming for transition from secondary school to adulthood. With an increase in these three areas have come a number of issues.

Integration, sometimes referred to as mainstreaming, involves the movement of people with disabilities from institutions to community living, from special schools to regular public schools, and from special classes to regular classes. Much of the philosophical rationale for integration comes from the principle of normalization. Normalization dictates that both the means and ends of education for people with disabilities should be as normal as possible. Controversies have surrounded implementation of the normalization principle. There is disagreement about whether it means the abolition of residential programs and special classes. Members of some groups, such as those who are deaf, have questioned whether normalization should mean integration for them. And some have cautioned that the overuse of technology may go against the concept of normalization.

Two important movements in the drive toward more integration have been deinstitutionalization and the regular education initiative. Started in the 1960s, deinstitutionalization is a trend to move people with disabilities into closer contact with the community and home. More and more people with disabilities are living in smaller group homes rather than large institutions. Some professionals believe there is no need for large residential institutions of any kind, whereas others believe they need to be a part of a continuum of services.

In the 1980s, the federal government began the regular education initiative (REI), a loosely defined movement to have regular class teachers assume more responsibility for children with special needs, such as those who are bilingual, economically disadvantaged, and/or those who have disabilities. Disagreement has raged over the REI, with some believing it means *full inclusion*—the practice of totally integrating *all* children with disabilities, no matter how severe, into regular classrooms in their home school. Others believe that, although there should be more mainstreaming than currently exists, there needs to be a continuum of services (e.g., residential institutions, special schools, special classes, resource rooms, regular classes) from which parents and professionals can choose.

Full inclusion is based on four premises: (1) labeling of people is harmful, (2) special education pull-out programs have been ineffective, (3) people with disabilities should be viewed as a minority group, and (4) ethics should take precedence over empiricism.

Anti-labeling arose out of fear that labeling students for special education stigmatizes them and makes them feel unworthy. Research on the effects of labeling is inconclusive. People do tend to view labeled individuals differently than they do those without labels. Some have maintained, however, that labels may provide an explanation for atypical behavior.

Over the past 30 years, more than 50 studies have compared outcomes for students with disabilities placed in special education versus regular classes, or resource rooms versus special classes. The results have not been very supportive of special education. Critics of this research, however, point out that virtually all of these studies have been methodologically flawed.

Advocates of full inclusion tend to view the problems people with disabilities face as being due to their being members of a minority group rather than the result of their disability. This view is consistent with that of the disability rights movement. Members of the disability rights movement have advocated for a variety of civil rights for persons with disabilities and have been influential in lobbying legislators and promoting more appropriate media portrayals of people with disabilities.

Some full-inclusion advocates do not care if full inclusion is more or less effective than pull-out special education programs; they believe in it because they think it is the ethical thing to do.

Opponents of full inclusion argue that (1) professionals and parents are largely satisfied with the current level of integration, (2) regular educators are unwilling and/or unable to cope with all students with disabilities, (3) although equating disabilities with minority group status is in many ways legitimate, it has limitations when it comes to translation into educational programming recommendations, (4) an unwillingness to consider empirical evidence is professionally irresponsible, and (5) in the absence of data to support one service delivery model, special educators must preserve the continuum of services.

Even those special educators who do not believe in full inclusion believe there needs to be more integration of students into regular classes and more research on better ways to implement mainstreaming. Some of the most popular mainstreaming practices are prereferral teams, collaborative consultation, cooperative teaching, cooperative learning, peer tutoring, partial participation, curriculum materials designed to change attitudes, and reverse mainstreaming. Prereferral teams are designed to come up with ways of accommodating difficult-to-teach students before they get referred for special education. In collaborative consultation, the special educator and general educator assume equal responsibility for making recommendations on how to teach the student. In cooperative teaching, the special educator and general educator teach jointly in the regular classroom for part or all of the day. In cooperative learning, teachers group students with and without disabilities in groups to work on tasks. Peer tutoring refers to the practice of nondisabled students' tutoring students with disabilities, and vice versa. Partial participation means having students with disabilities participate on a reduced basis in virtually all activities experienced by all students in the regular classroom. Curriculum materials designed to change attitudes include books, simulations, and puppets. Reverse mainstreaming is the placement, for short periods of time, of a few nondisabled students in classes composed primarily of students with disabilities.

Early intervention programs for children with disabilities and their families are now mandated by law. PL 99–457 stipulates that states must provide preschool services for all children with disabilities ages three to five years and provides incentives for programming from birth to three years. A cornerstone of PL 99–457 is the Individualized Family Service Plan (IFSP). The IFSP is like an IEP, but it broadens the focus to include the family.

There are several types of early intervention programs. A common way of categorizing them is according to whether they are center-based, home-based, or a combination of the two.

Three issues pertaining to early childhood intervention are (1) the appropriate role of the family, (2) whether the curriculum should be teacher- or child-centered, and (3) the best way to ensure a smooth transition from early intervention programs to preschools, and from preschools to schools.

Federal law now also stipulates programming for transition from secondary school to adulthood. Transition is defined as including a variety of post-school activities, including post-secondary education, vocational training, integrated employment, continuing and adult education, adult services, independent living, or community participation. The law mandates that students with disabilities have a transition plan incorporated into their IEP.

Supported employment is one of the ways we can integrate persons with disabilities into the workplace. Supported employment includes individual or group (clustered, mobile work crew, or entrepreneurial) models whereby people with disabilities engage in competitive employment with support from an employment specialist, or job coach.

Issues pertaining to implementing transition from secondary school to adulthood for people with severe disabilities focus largely on coordinating and linking the many agencies outside the school setting. For those with milder disabilities, many of the issues center on providing programming that balances their vocational and academic needs. Some are concerned that the recent press for more rigorous academic standards in the schools generally will result in the disregard of the needs of students with disabilities.

CARMELO C. GANNELLO

Carmelo C. Gannello has been a practicing artist since 1937. He became legally blind in 1956 as a result of an accident. His paintings currently hang in several major national galleries. He describes his work as being based on the circles and shapes that he sees in his eyes, using his unique "vision" to portray how a visually impaired person sees the world.

Remember and help America remember that the fellowship of human beings is more important than the fellowship of race and class and gender in a democratic society . . .

All children need [a] pride of heritage and sense of history of their own people and of all the people who make up the mosaic of this great nation. African-American and Latino and Asian American and Native American children should know about European history and cultures, and white children should know about the histories and cultures of diverse peoples of color with whom they share a city, a nation, and a world. I believe in integration. But that does not mean I become someone else or ignore or deny who I am. I learned the Negro National anthem, "Lift Every Voice and Sing," at the same time I learned "The Star Spangled Banner" and "America the Beautiful" and I love them all. I have raised you, my children, to respect other people's children, not to become their children but to become yourselves at your best. I hope others will raise their children to respect you.

➤ Marian Wright Edelman
The Measure of Our Success:
A Letter to My Children and Yours

Multicultural and Bilingual Aspects of Special Education

▲ ▲ ▲

*I*n the last decade of the twentieth century, many nations and regions have splintered into factions, clans, tribes, and gangs. In some cases, this splintering has been accompanied by extreme cruelty of individuals or groups toward others. Differences—especially those of religion, ethnic origin, color, custom, and social class—are too often the basis for viciousness toward other people. This has been the case throughout human history, and it remains a central problem of humankind. All cultures and ethnic groups of the world can take pride in much of their heritage, but most also bear a burden of shame because at some time in their history they have engaged in the ruthless treatment or literal enslavement of others. Sometimes this treatment has extended to certain members of their own group whose differences have been viewed as undesirable or intolerable.

In virtually every nation, society, religion, ethnic group, tribe, or clan, discrimination exists against those who are different in some dimension of human identity. The discrimination that we practice or experience stems from and perpetuates fear, hatred, and abusive relationships. If a group feels discriminated against or subjugated and sees no hope of becoming valued and being treated fairly, it inevitably seeks to become separate and autonomous, sometimes threatening or subjugating others in the process.

Our desire as a nation is to build a diverse but just society in which the personal freedom and pride of all cultural groups and respect for others' cultural heritage are the norm, a society in which fear, hate, and abuse are eliminated. Working toward this ideal demands a multicultural perspective, one from which we can simultaneously accomplish two tasks. First, as a nation of increasing cultural diversity, we must renew our efforts to achieve social justice and take specific steps to understand and appreciate one anothers' cultures. Second, in doing so we must pledge our first loyalty to common cultural values that make diversity a strength rather than a fatal flaw. We seek a commitment to our common humanity and to democratic ideals that bind people together for the common good and give all the freedom to revel in a pride of heritage. These two tasks of multicultural education in a multicultural nation are expressed in the words of Marian Wright Edelman in her letter to her children and others (see p. 87).

Since the civil rights movement of the 1960s, educators have become increasingly aware of the extent to which differences among cultural and ethnic groups affect children's schooling. Gradually, educators and others are coming to understand that the cultural diversity of our nation and the world demands multicultural education. Progress in constructing multicultural education has been slow, however, in part because of the way all cultural groups tend to view themselves as the standard against which others should be judged. Rogoff and Morelli (1989) note that in the United States this view has led to a focus on minority cultures.

> The United States, like many modern nations, is an aggregate of peoples of many cultural backgrounds. However, the role of culture is most noticeable when any of us views the practices of some other group than our own, and so the study of culture has generally focused on minorities in the United States and on people of other nations. It is easy for dominant cultural groups to consider themselves as standard and other groups as variations. (Think of the number of people who comment on other people's accents and insist that they themselves do not have one.) (p. 341)

Misconceptions about
MULTICULTURAL AND BILINGUAL ASPECTS OF SPECIAL EDUCATION

MYTH ➢ Multicultural education addresses the concerns of ethnic minorities who want their children to learn more about their history and the intellectual, social, and artistic contributions of their ancestors.

FACT ➢ This is a partial truth. In fact, multicultural education seeks to help the children of all ethnic groups appreciate their own and others' cultural heritage—plus our common American culture that sustains multiculturalism.

MYTH ➢ Everyone agrees that multicultural education is critical to our nation's future.

FACT ➢ Some people, including some who are members of ethnic minorities, believe that multicultural education is misguided and diverts attention from our integration in a distinctive, cohesive American culture.

MYTH ➢ Implementing multicultural education is a relatively simple matter of including information about all cultures in the curriculum and teaching respect for other cultures.

FACT ➢ Educators and others are struggling with how to construct a satisfactory multicultural curriculum and multicultural instructional methods. Nearly every aspect of the task is controversial—which cultures to include, how much attention to give to each, and what and how to teach about them.

MYTH ➢ Multiculturalism includes only the special features and contributions of clearly defined ethnic groups.

FACT ➢ Ethnicity is typically the focal point of discussions of multiculturalism, but ethnicity is sometimes a point of controversy if it is defined too broadly (for example, by lumping all Asians together). Besides ethnic groups, other groups and individuals, such as people identified by gender, sexual preference, religion, and disability, may want consideration in a multicultural curriculum.

MYTH ➢ Disproportionate representation of ethnic minorities in special education is no longer a problem.

FACT ➢ Some ethnic minorities are still underrepresented or overrepresented in certain special education categories. For example, African-American students, especially males, are overrepresented in programs for students with emotional or behavioral disorders and underrepresented in programs for gifted and talented students.

MYTH ➢ Disability is never related to ethnicity.

FACT ➢ Some disabilities are genetically linked and therefore are more prevalent in some ethnic groups. For example, sickle cell disease (a severe, chronic, hereditary blood disease) occurs disproportionately in children with ancestry from Africa, Mediterranean and Caribbean regions, Saudi Arabia, and India.

MYTH ➢ If students speak English, there is no need to be concerned about bilingual education.

FACT ➢ Conversational English is not the same as the more formal and sometimes technical language used in academic curriculum and classroom instruction. Educators must make sure that students understand the language used in teaching, not just informal conversation.

DIVERSITY TESTS SCHOOLS ➤

by Lisa Leff

Area educators struggle to balance curriculum

While pouring over the new, "multicultural" version of history the Prince George's County school system adopted for its students last year, a group of white parents detected a "slant" in some of the lessons.

In their view, the social studies curriculum on display at the local library favored black scholars whose theories that ancient Egypt was a purely black African civilization contradicted the work of classically trained historians.

The new lessons presented as "incontrovertible" the theory that Egyptians were black, said Claire Matte, a Bowie resident with two children in county schools who says the theory is much more open to debate.

No sooner had the guides received further editing, however, when a group of black parents offered its own 18-page critique.

The reworked material's writers, they said, displayed an "alarming" tendency to put qualifying language around the claims of Afrocentric researchers, but to present as "undisputed fact" traditional views such as whether Columbus was the first explorer to reach North America.

Such earnest disagreements—about whether history is an objective truth or a matter of interpretation— have been one by-product of the county's move toward a multicultural curriculum, an effort to give blacks, Hispanics, women, the elderly and other minority groups a more prominent place in increasingly diverse public school classrooms.

Although few have quarreled with the school system's goal, the word-for-word changes have kindled debate over whether they succeed in balancing previously lopsided lessons or fall into the realm of bias. Today, with another school year underway, the long-awaited curriculum has yet to find its way into the hands of teachers, and the initiative that put Prince George's at the forefront of the national multicultural movement has instead come to represent how difficult and politically charged such changes can be.

SOURCE: The Washington Post, November 28, 1992, pp. A1, A12.
© 1992, The Washington Post. Reprinted with permission.

Education that takes full advantage of the cultural diversity in our schools and the larger world requires much critical analysis and planning. The box above illustrates how difficult it may be for all cultural or ethnic groups to find common satisfaction in a curriculum, even if they are all seeking what they consider the multicultural ideal. Moreover, some argue that the multicultural ideal is misguided, that the more important goal is finding the common American culture and ensuring that our children have a common cultural literacy (Hirsch, 1987). Consider the perspective represented in the box on p. 91 (see also Rodriguez, 1982, 1992). Even the metaphors we use for dealing with cultural diversity and cultural unity are points of controversy. America has often been called a cultural melting pot, but some now reject the notion of total melding or amalgamation— they reject the metaphor of an alloy in which metals are dissolved in each other and fused into a new substance (Price, 1992). For example, one teacher in a videotaped case study of multicultural education comments about the American melting pot, "I have no desire to melt, but I would love to enrich. But I *do* not want to melt! . . . Back to my stew, if I'm going in as a carrot, I want to be tasted as a carrot and then still add to the flavor of the entire. . . . " (McNergney, 1992). To continue with the stew metaphor, there is controversy regarding how "chunky" our American culture should be.

That racism and discrimination remain serious problems in America and most other societies is obvious. These problems have no simple resolution, and they are found among virtually all ethnic groups. People of every cultural description struggle with the meaning of differences that may seem trivial or superficial to some but elicit powerful emotional responses and discrimination from others. Russell (1992), for example, describes color discrimination that is

SURPRISING ARGUMENT FOR AMERICAN CULTURE ➤ by Charles Trueheart

Richard Rodriguez makes the astonishing claim that America exists. "There is an America here. There is a culture here," he almost pleads.

This, of course, is not an original thought. What is original is its provenance—Rodriguez is a Mexican American, an intellectual, a prose poet—and its stinging repudiation of the prevailing ethnic ethos. Rodriguez calls it "that multiculturalism crap," or "Hispanic pseudo-nationalism."

He scoffs: "The notion that you can hold on to your culture—or lose it, for that matter—is an impossibility. Walt Disney is my culture! Howdy Doody is my culture!"

This resolute Americanism in the face of diversity worship may be why his celebrated first book, "Hunger of Memory" (1982), struck such a chord—a dulcet one to Americans fed up with ethnic special pleading, and a dissonant one to Americans passionately embracing their group identities. This onetime "poster child of affirmative action"—he sneers at the phrase—has become that creed's professional apostate.

Which may be why, among other honors that regularly come Rodriguez's way, last week he received one of the Charles Frankel humanities awards from President Bush. Had he lived to attend, academic scourge Allan Bloom would have been among the other recipients (as will Shelby Foote, Eudora Welty, and Harold K. Skramstad Jr., director of the Henry Ford Museum).

The award comes as Rodriguez, who lives in San Francisco, is touring the country to promote his latest, and only other, book, "Days of Obligation: An Argument With My Mexican Father." Like the autobiographical "Hunger of Memory," "Days" harvests the fruits of research Rodriguez conducted mainly in the vineyard of the self.

SOURCE: *The Washington Post*, November 28, 1992, p. F1. © 1992, The Washington Post. Reprinted with permission.

practiced not only between whites and African Americans, but also among African Americans of varied hue. Consider the hostilities and suffering associated with differences in color as well as in gender, religion, sexual orientation, abilities and disabilities, and political beliefs. The solution is not as simple as becoming sensitized to differences. Too often, Eurocentrism is met with Europhobia, Afrocentrism with Afrophobia, homocentrism with homophobia, sensitivity to difference with hypersensitivity about being different. Perhaps the solution must include both engendering sensitivity to differences and building confidence that one's own differences will not be threatened by others'.

Perhaps we *can* find a uniquely American culture, one that celebrates valued diversities within a framework of clearly defined common values. This perspective recognizes that not all diversity is valued, that tolerance has its limits, and that American culture is dynamic and continuously evolving.

> There are limits to cultural tolerance, a lesson the 20th century has repeatedly taught us. There are, among some cultures, deeply held convictions—about women and their bodies; about races; about children; about authority; about lawbreakers, the sick, the weak, the poor and the rich—that we absolutely deplore. The fact is, we need absolutes. Where a plurality of cultures exists, we need an overarching set of values cherished by all. Otherwise what begins as multicultural harmony inevitably descends into balkanization or chaos. . . .
>
> The simple truth, which is either denied or distorted by the prevailing orthodoxies, is that a thriving national culture does exist. It is neither a salad bowl nor static, received tradition, but an ever-evolving national process which selects, unrepresentatively, from the marketplace of raw, particular identities, those that everyone finds it useful and gratifying to embrace and transform into their own. (Patterson, 1993, p. C2)

We are optimistic about multicultural education because it is an opportunity to face our shared problems squarely and extract the best human qualities from each cultural heritage. Without denying any culture's inhumanity to others or to its own members, we have the opportunity to develop an appreciation of our individual and shared cultural treasures and engender tolerance, if not love, of all differences that are not destructive of the human spirit. We concur with Price (1992):

> The appropriate antidote for cultural insularity is a culture of inclusiveness that infuses every facet of our society . . . Were those who ardently preach American values truly to practice them, then perhaps our collective anxiety about the growing intolerance and insularity in America would, shall we say, melt away. (p. 213).

Multiculturalism is now a specialized field of study in education, and its full exploration is far beyond the scope of this chapter. Of particular concern to special educators is how exceptionalities are related to cultural diversity and the way in which special education fits within the broader general education context in a multicultural society. Cultural diversity presents particular challenges for special educators in three areas: assessment of abilities and disabilities, instruction, and socialization. Before discussing each of these challenges, we summarize some of the major concepts about education and cultural diversity that set the context for multicultural and bilingual special education.

EDUCATION AND CULTURAL DIVERSITY: CONCEPTS FOR SPECIAL EDUCATION

Culture has many definitions. As Banks (1988) points out, however, "most contemporary social scientists view culture as consisting primarily of the symbolic, ideational, and intangible aspects of human societies" (p. 73). Banks suggests six major components or elements of culture: values and behavioral styles, languages and dialects, nonverbal communication, awareness (of one's cultural distinctiveness), frames of reference (normative world views or perspectives), and identification (feeling part of the cultural group). These elements may together make up a national or shared culture, sometimes referred to as a **macroculture.** Within the larger macroculture are **microcultures**—smaller cultures that share the common characteristics of the macroculture but have their unique values, styles, languages and dialects, nonverbal communication, awareness, frames of reference, and identity. An individual may identify with the macroculture and also belong to many different microcultures, as shown in Figure 3–1. The variety of microcultures to which a person belongs affects his or her behavior.

➤ **macroculture.** A nation or other large social entity with a shared culture.

➤ **microculture.** A smaller group existing within a larger cultural group and having unique values, style, language, dialect, ways of communicating nonverbally, awareness, frame of reference, and identification.

Being from a culturally or linguistically diverse background does not in itself constitute a disability.

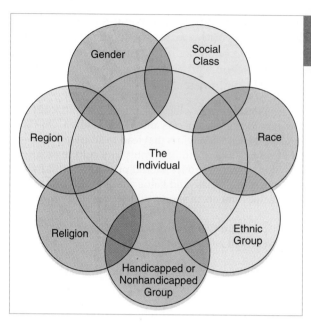

Figure 3-1

➤ *Individuals belong to many different microcultural groups.*

cultural diversity

- *values + behavioral styles*
- *language + dialects*
- *Nonverbal communication*
- *Awareness of ones own cultural distinctiveness*
- *frames of reference*
- *identification*

SOURCE: From J. A. Banks, *Multiethnic Education: Theory and Practice*, 2nd ed. p. 79 Copyright © 1988 by Allyn & Bacon. Reprinted with permission.

Macroculture in the United States consists of certain overarching values, symbols, and ideas, such as justice, equality, and human dignity. Microcultures within the U.S. macroculture may share these common values but differ among themselves in many additional ways. The number of microcultures represented in U.S. schools has increased in recent decades because of the variety of immigrants from other countries, particularly Southeast Asia. Duke (1990) notes that "these newcomers contribute to a diversity of cultures and languages that probably has not characterized American society since the turn of the century" (pp. 69–70). Students from some microcultures in U.S. society do extremely well in school, but others do not. The factors accounting for the school performance of microcultural minorities are complex, and social scientists are still searching for the attitudes, beliefs, behavioral styles, and opportunities that foster the success of specific microcultural groups (Jacob & Jordan, 1987).

Researchers have reported that Southeast Asian (Indochinese) refugee families adopting an orientation to certain American values—acquiring material possessions and seeking fun and excitement—have children whose academic performance is lower than that of children from families maintaining traditional Southeast Asian values—persistence, achievement, and family support (Caplan, Choy, & Whitmore, 1992). This finding suggests that schools and teachers may face an impossible task unless changes occur in students' home culture. "It is clear that the U. S. educational system can work—if the requisite familial and social supports are provided for the students outside school" (Caplan et al., 1992, p. 36). Ogbu (1992) also notes the critical role played by different minority communities in encouraging academic success among their children and youth. He differentiates between immigrant or voluntary minorities who have come to the United states primarily for their own economic and social benefit, and castelike or involuntary minorities who were originally brought to the United States against their will. Most Chinese and Punjabi Indians, for example, are voluntary minorities; African-American children and youth are, for the most part, members of an involuntary minority. Ogbu (1992) concludes that "minority children do not succeed or fail only because of what schools do or do not do, but also because of what the community does" (p. 12). He continues:

> At this point in my research I suggest four ways in which the involuntary minority community can encourage academic striving and success among its children. One is to teach the children to separate attitudes and behaviors that lead to academic success from attitudes and behaviors that lead to a loss of ethnic identity and culture or language . . . Second, the involuntary minority community should provide the children with concrete evidence that its members appreciate and value academic success as much as they appreciate and value achievements in sports, athletics, and entertainment.
>
> Third, the involuntary minority community must teach the children to recognize and accept the responsibility for their school adjustment and academic performance. . . .
>
> Finally, the involuntary minority middle class needs to reevaluate and change its role vis-a-vis the community. (p. 12)

Ogbu (1992) goes on to describe two ways in which minority individuals who have achieved middle-class status might interact with the minority community. For example, successful, educated, professional people might provide highly

*F*amily support, or lack thereof, is a key factor in all children's academic success.

visible role models for young people, demonstrating how they can achieve success in the wider society and retain their collective identity and bona fide membership in the minority community. This is the example typically provided by voluntary minorities.

> In contrast, involuntary minorities seem to have a model that probably does not have much positive influence on schooling. Members of involuntary minorities seem to view professional success as "a ticket" to leave their community both physically and socially, to get away from those who have not "made it." People seek education and professional success, as it were, in order to leave their minority community. (Ogbu, 1992, p. 13)

Although there is considerable evidence that various ethnic minority communities have a strong influence on students' achievement and school behavior, we offer three cautions. First, we need to guard against stereotypes—assumptions that one's cultural identity is sufficient to explain academic achievement or economic success. The Doonesbury cartoon below makes the point rather well, we feel. Second, the fact that minority communities may have a strong influence on school success does not relieve schools of the obligation to provide a multicultural education. All students need to feel that they and their cultural heritage are included in the mainstream of American culture and schooling. Third, unless teachers and other school personnel value minority students—see value and promise in them and act accordingly by setting demanding but not unreachable expectations—the support of families and the minority community may be insufficient to improve the academic success of minority students (Steele, 1992). Too often, minority students are devalued in school regardless of their achievement and behavior (Boutte, 1992; Steele, 1992).

The general purposes of multicultural education are to promote pride in one's own cultural heritage and understanding of microcultures different from one's own, and to foster positive attitudes toward cultural diversity. These purposes cannot be accomplished unless students develop an understanding and appreciation of their own cultural heritage, as well as an awareness and acceptance of cultures different from their own. Understanding and appreciation are not likely to develop automatically through unplanned contact with members of other microcultures. Rather, teachers must plan experiences that teach about

Doonesbury   BY GARRY TRUDEAU

ultural diversity can be reflected in families' attitudes toward disabilities.

culture and provide models of cultural awareness and acceptance and the appreciation of cultural diversity.

On the surface, teaching about cultures and engendering an acceptance and appreciation of cultural diversity appear to be simple tasks. However, two questions immediately complicate the matter when we get below the surface and address the actual practice of multiculturalism in education: (1) Which cultures shall we include? (2) What and how shall we teach about them? The first question demands that we consider all the microcultures that might be represented in the school and the difficulties inherent in including them all. The United States has more than 100 distinct microcultures based on national origin alone. In some urban school districts with large numbers of immigrant children, more than 20 different languages may be spoken in students' homes. But ethnic or national origin is only one dimension of cultural diversity, one branch of many in the multicultural program. Many advocates of multiculturalism consider gender, sexual orientation, religion, disability, and so on to be additional dimensions of cultural diversity that require explicit attention. Moreover, some microcultural groups find the traditions, ceremonies, values, holidays, and other characteristics of other microcultures unacceptable or even offensive. That is, when it comes to what and how to teach about other cultures, the stage may be set for conflict.

Issues in Special Education **School Guidance on Gays Has N.Y. Parents Divided**

CNN

New York—Neil Lodato, a construction worker in Queens, was waving his arms and shouting outside his daughter's school, P.S. 13. "They should stick to teaching these babies that 1+1=2, instead of what daddy and his boyfriend are doing in the bedroom.

"I learned about [gay couples] on the street, that's where she should, too," Lodato yelled, threatening to pull his 5-year-old daughter out of school if Schools Chancellor Joseph A. Fernandez gets his way. The superintendent wants all city children to be taught respect for homosexuals, as early as the first grade.

Diane Kristen, the mother of a second-grader, was one of the few parents not nodding in agreement with Lodato last week in the icy afternoon air outside one of the schools resisting Fernandez's plan. "It's fear and anger and homophobia like that," Kristen said, that is whipping New York into near hysteria.

More than a year after the 443-page multicultural curriculum guide called "Children of the Rainbow" was released, opposition to the three pages mentioning homosexuals continues to explode. In delis and dentist offices, in paneled Wall Street chambers and graffiti-sprayed subway cars, on television talk shows and at crowded PTA meetings, parents are fighting about the teaching guidelines that are paving the way for similar plans in school districts nationwide. . . .

Fernandez, mentioned as a possible candidate for secretary of education in the Clinton administration and well-regarded among urban school superintendents, has never shied from controversy. He led the way nationally in AIDS education for elementary schools and condom distribution in high schools. His autobiography, to be published next month, reveals that as a teenage dropout in Harlem he regularly snorted and injected heroin.

This latest battle, he says, is "emotional and draining" but he delved into it "because a lot of my kids come from gay relationships and lesbian relationships. . . . Everyone doesn't come from a traditional family structure."

In New York, there are certain minimum standards, he said, and the "Fourth R—Respect" for all people, including homosexuals, is among them.

Fernandez, who is picketed every day by opponents and cheered like a celebrity by supporters wherever he goes in the city, said he knows the issue is far from resolved.

He's right, judging from the conversation between Mayra Vasquez and Brunilda Perez, two nursing students from Brooklyn who were eating pizza before night classes.

I have nothing against gay people," said Vasquez. "I work with them, they are nice, better to talk to than straight people. But I'm not allowing my daughter in any school that teaches first-graders about them."

Perez could not disagree more: "There would be less gay-bashing, less discrimination against gays if the children were taught early."

SOURCE: Mary Jordan, *The Washington Post*, December 8, 1992, pp. A1, A12. © 1992, The Washington Post. Reprinted with permission.

Treating all cultures with equal attention and respect may present substantial or seemingly insurmountable logistical and interpersonal problems. The box above provides an example of the difficulty we may encounter in devising a multicultural curriculum that is not offensive to one cultural group because it gives specific attention to the orientation and values of another.

Given the multiplicity of microcultures, each wanting—if not demanding—its precise and fair inclusion in the curriculum, it is not surprising that educators sometimes feel caught in a spiral of factionalism and feuding. Furthermore, additional questions about cultural values inevitably must be addressed. Which cultural values and characteristics should we embrace? Which, if any, should we shun? Would we, if we could, fully sustain some cultures, alter some significantly, and eliminate others? Consider, for example, cultures in which women are treated

A purpose of special education is to ensure that children with disabilities are not further "disabled" by their cultural background.

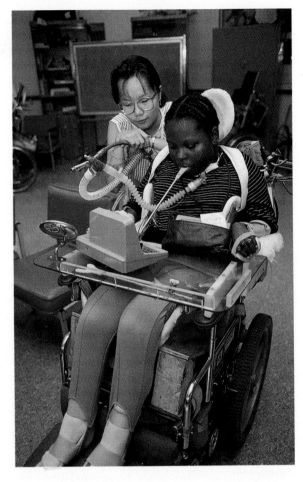

as chattel, the drug culture, the culture of street gangs, the culture of poverty. To what extent does every culture have a right to perpetuate itself? How should we respond to some members of the deaf culture, for example, who reject the prevention of deafness or procedures and devices that enable deaf children to hear, preferring deafness to hearing and wishing to sustain the deaf culture deliberately? Depending on how we define culture, the values of our own cultural heritage, and our role in multicultural education, we may find ourselves embroiled in serious cultural conflicts. No wonder that some describe the 1980s and 1990s as an era of culture wars (Hunter, 1991; Shor, 1986). To deal effectively with the multicultural challenge, we must focus on the challenges most pertinent to special education.

The microcultures of particular importance for special education are ethnic groups and exceptionality groups. Banks (1988) defines an ethnic group as "a group that shares a common ancestry, culture, history, tradition, and sense of peoplehood and that is a political and economic interest group" (p. 81). An ethnic group may be a majority or a minority of people in a given country or region. We define an exceptionality group as a group sharing a set of specific abilities or disabilities that are especially valued or that require special accommodation within

THNIC AND MULTICULTURAL CONCERNS: WHAT CEC IS DOING >

Over the years, CEC [The Council for Exceptional Children] has responded to the growing number of ethnic and multicultural issues and trends by creating a network of leaders to share information and promote the development of unit-sponsored ethnic and multicultural committees. These committees conduct activities designed to help members and other professionals serve students from diverse ethnic, cultural, and linguistic backgrounds.

The CEC *Ethnic and Multicultural Bulletin* is mailed three times a year to over 4,000 professionals, agencies, and organizations. It provides information on activities, projects, publications, resources, public policy, and professional meetings. In addition, it promotes the $500 annual Student CEC/FEC Ethnic and Minority Scholarship that is presented to a Student CEC member.

SOURCE: From Ethnic and multicultural concerns: What CEC is doing. *Teaching Exceptional Children,* Winter 1993, *Vol. 25* (2), 54. Copyright 1993 by The Council for Exceptional CHildren. Reprinted with permission.

a given microculture. Thus a person may be identified as exceptional in one ethnic group (or other microculture defined by gender, social class, religion, etc.) but not in another. Being unable to read or speak standard English, for example, may identify a student as having a disability in an Anglo-dominated microculture, although the same student is not considered disabled in a microculture in which English-language skills are unimportant. In certain cultures children avoid direct eye contact with adults in positions of authority. A child who does not look directly at the teacher may mistakenly be assumed to be inattentive or oppositional by adults from cultures in which eye contact between the teacher and pupil is expected. This child could be inappropriately identified as having a disability requiring special education.

Ethnicity and exceptionality are distinctly different concepts. In fact, multicultural special education must focus on two primary objectives that go beyond the general purposes of multicultural education:

1. Ensuring that ethnicity is not mistaken for educational exceptionality
2. Increasing understanding of the microculture of exceptionality and its relationship to other microcultures

Ethnicity may be mistaken for exceptionality when one's own ethnic group is viewed as setting the standard for all others. For example, patterns of eye contact, physical contact, use of language, and ways of responding to persons in positions of authority may vary greatly from one ethnic group to another. Members of each ethnic group must realize that what they see as deviant or unacceptable in their own group may be normal and adaptive in another ethnic group. That is, we must not mistakenly conclude that a student has a disability or is gifted just because he or she is different.

Members of minority ethnic groups are more apt to be identified as disabled because their differences are not well understood or valued by others. In part, this higher risk may be a result of prejudice—unreasonable or irrational negative attitudes, feelings, judgments, or behavior based on ignorance or misunderstanding. Prejudice may cause individuals to be judged as deviant or disabled on the basis of characteristics that are typical for their ethnic group or from stereotyping. That is, an individual's identity as a member of an ethnic group may result in the automatic assumption that he or she will behave in certain ways.

ACTIVITIES FOR IMPROVING UNDERSTANDING AND ACCEPTANCE BETWEEN HEARING STUDENTS AND STUDENTS WHO ARE DEAF ➤

1. Provide multiple opportunities for deaf and hearing students to interact on a regular basis, preferably on joint projects or activities.
2. Give deaf and hearing children the opportunity to discuss openly why they react positively or negatively toward each other.
3. Encourage children to express in what ways their own culture might appear strange to a person from the other group. For example, hearing children should imagine which aspects of spoken language might appear bizarre to a deaf person.
4. Discuss the fundamental ways in which *all* human groups are similar (kinship, division of tasks, language, prolonged childhood dependency, belief system, use of symbols, tool systems, etc.). Deaf and hearing people are equally "human" because each group has established its own specific responses to those *same* needs.
5. Teach children about the processes by which humans develop stereotypes, and have them list the ways in which they have seen themselves follow those processes in judging or misjudging deaf or hearing children.
6. Teach students that there is a wide variation of behavior *within* any culture; thus, stereotyping is bound to be false (e.g., some deaf people use sign language, while others do not).
7. Point out some nonstereotypic behaviors of both groups. For example, numerous deaf persons today have earned Ph.D.'s and teach in universities.
8. Teach about the positive contributions to human life by both groups. For example, focus on well-known deaf actors or athletes.
9. Help students to create and analyze a written description of a model culture in order to develop their thinking tools for understanding the deaf or hearing culture.

SOURCE: From Reducing ethnocentrism, by David S. Martin, *Teaching Exceptional Children*, Fall 1987, *Vol. 20*(1) 7–8. Copyright 1987 by The Council for Exceptional Children. Reprinted with permission.

People with certain exceptionalities can develop their own microcultures. Those with severe hearing impairments, for example, are described by some as belonging to a "deaf culture" that is not well understood by most normally hearing people and that results in feelings of isolation or separation from people with normal hearing (Martin, 1987; Padden & Humphries, 1988). An important aspect of multicultural special education is developing an increased awareness, understanding, and appreciation of cultural differences involving disabilities. The box above contains Martin's suggestions for reducing prejudice and stereotyping and increasing understanding among deaf and normally hearing students. Similar strategies may be needed to overcome prejudice and stereotyping involving other disability groups.

Multicultural special education is not merely a matter of overcoming students' prejudice and stereotyping. We must also educate ourselves as teachers to improve methods of assessment, provide effective instruction, and foster appropriate socialization. The box on page 99 notes how one professional organization is involved in educating teachers about cultural diversity. We now turn to specific problems in assessment, instruction, and socialization involving microcultural groups, including students with exceptionalities.

Assessment

Assessment is a process of collecting information about individuals or groups for the purpose of making decisions. In education, assessment ordinarily refers to testing, interviewing, and observing students. The results of assessment should help us decide whether problems exist in a student's education and, if problems are identified, what to do about them (Wallace, Larsen, & Elksnin, 1992).

Ysseldyke and Marston (1988) have discussed several characteristics of assessment that are important in the U.S. macroculture: "Assessment is a practice integral to making decisions about people. In our society there is a fundamental concern for accuracy, justice, and fairness in making decisions about individuals" (p. 21).

Unfortunately, the accuracy, justice, and fairness of many educational assessments, especially those involving special education, are open to question. Particularly when ethnic microcultures are involved, traditional assessment practices have frequently violated the U.S. ideals of fairness and equal opportunity regardless of ethnic origin, gender, or disability. That is, the assessment practices of educators and psychologists have frequently come under attack as (1) biased, resulting in misrepresentation of the abilities and disabilities of ethnic minorities and exceptional students, and (2) useless, resulting only in labeling or classification rather than improved educational programming (Council for Children with Behavioral Disorders, 1989; Reschly, 1987; Wallace et al., 1992).

The problems of assessment of students for special education are numerous and complex, and there are no simple solutions. Many of the problems are centered on traditional standardized testing approaches to assessment that have serious limitations: (1) They do not take cultural diversity into account, (2) they focus on deficits in the individual alone, and (3) they do not provide information useful in teaching. Although these problems have not been entirely overcome, awareness of them and the use of alternative assessment strategies are increasing.

Standardized tests may be biased because most of the test items draw on specific experiences that students from different microcultures may not have had. Tests may, for example, be biased toward the likely experiences of white middle-class students; be couched in language unfamiliar to members of a certain microculture; or be administered in a way that penalizes a student with impaired vision, hearing, or ability to answer in a standard way. Because test scores are often the basis for deciding that a student qualifies for special education, many scholars suspect that test bias accounts for the disproportionate representation of certain groups in special education, especially males and children of color (Chinn & Hughes, 1987).

Disproportional representation of male and black and Hispanic youths in special education is shown in Figures 3–2 and 3–3. These figures demonstrate that disproportional representation is much greater in some disability categories than in others among students in the 13–21 age range. Figure 3–2 on page 102 shows that males are especially overrepresented in the categories of serious emotional disturbance and specific learning disabilities. Females are not overrepresented in any category. Figure 3–3 on page 103 shows that for all categories combined, nearly 25 percent of youths age 13–21 who are receiving special education are black and about 8 percent are Hispanic. It is important to know that the percentage of high school students who are white is approximately 65 percent; approximately 12 percent are black about 8 percent are Hispanic. In commenting on the disproportionately high representation of black students in all categories, the U. S. Department of Education commented, "It is possible that black youth were more likely than their white counterparts to have experienced poor prenatal, perinatal, or postnatal health care and early childhood nutrition which may have resulted in actual disabilities" (1992, p. 15). Hispanic students are underrepresented in some disability categories (e.g., mental retardation and serious

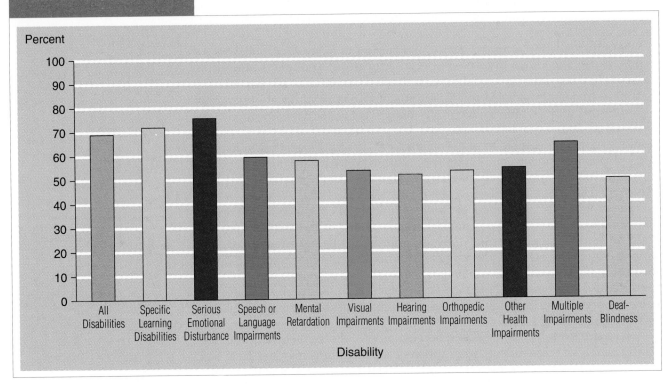

Figure 3-2 ➤ *Percentage of youth age 13–21 with disabilities who are male*

SOURCE: U. S. Department of Education. 1992, p. 12.

emotional disturbance) and overrepresented in others, especially orthopedic and other health impairments. The reasons for this overrepresentation are not clear. In any case, nonbiased assessment is a critical issue. The disproportionality should not be the result of biased testing or bias in other forms of assessment.

At best, test scores represent a sample of an individual's ability to respond to a standard set of questions or tasks; they do not tell us *all* the important things an individual has learned or how much a student *can* learn. Controversy over the biases inherent in standardized tests and the search for "culture-free" and "culture-fair" tests continue (McLoughlin & Lewis, 1990; Ysseldyke & Marston, 1988; Wallace et al., 1992). Three cautions are in order:

1. Tests give only clues about what a student has learned.
2. Test scores must be interpreted with recognition of the possible biases the test contains
3. Testing alone is an insufficient basis for classifying a student or planning an instructional program.

Traditional assessment procedures focus on the student, not on the environment in which the student is being taught. Critics of traditional assessment have decried the assumption that any deficit identified will be a deficit of the student.

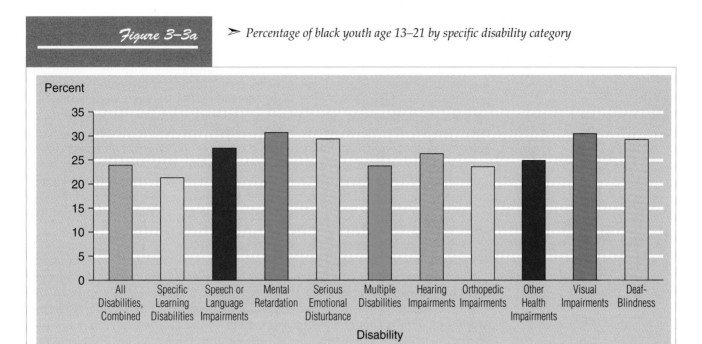

Figure 3–3a ➤ *Percentage of black youth age 13–21 by specific disability category*

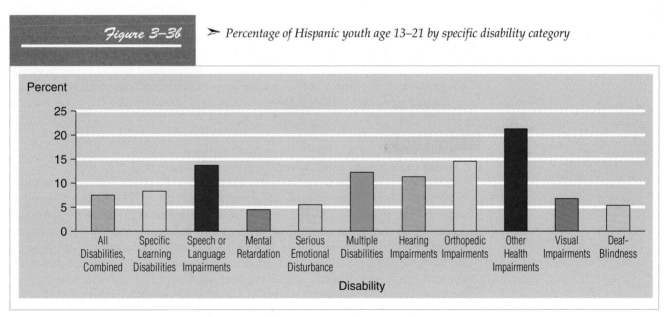

Figure 3–3b ➤ *Percentage of Hispanic youth age 13–21 by specific disability category*

SOURCE: U. S. Department of Education. 1992, p. 17.

In addition to assessing the student's behavior or performance, many educators are now suggesting an assessment of the instructional environment (Bender, 1988; Ysseldyke & Christenson, 1987). Assessment of the instructional environment may involve classroom observation and interviews with the student and teacher. It focuses on such items as whether instruction is presented clearly and effectively, the classroom is effectively controlled, the teacher's expectations are appropriate, appropriate curriculum modifications are made, thinking skills are being taught, effective motivational strategies are used, the student is actively engaged in academic responding and is given adequate practice and feedback on performance, and progress is directly and frequently evaluated. The purpose of assessment of the instructional environment is to make sure that the student is not mistakenly identified as the source of the learning problem. An underlying assumption is that this approach will decrease the likelihood that cultural differences will be mistaken for disabilities.

Traditional assessment procedures result in test scores that *may* be useful in helping to determine a student's eligibility for special education or other special services. These testing procedures do not, however, typically provide information that is useful in planning for instruction. An alternative approach that emerged in the 1980s is *curriculum-based assessment* (Deno, 1985; Howell & Morehead, 1987). This method of assessment contrasts sharply with traditional testing, in which students are tested infrequently and may never before have seen the specific items on the test. Curriculum-based assessment involves students' responses to their usual instructional materials; it entails direct and frequent samples of performance from the curriculum in which students are being instructed. (We discuss curriculum-based assessment in more detail in Chapter 5.) This form of assessment is thought to be more useful for teachers than traditional testing and to decrease the likelihood of cultural bias.

Finally, we note that fair and accurate assessment is an issue in identifying special gifts and talents as well as disabilities. Too often, the extraordinary abilities of students of color or other ethnic difference and those with disabilities are overlooked because of bias or ignorance on the part of those responsible for assessment. In Chapter 1, we emphasized the importance of identifying the abilities as well as the disabilities of students. To that we want to add the importance of being aware of culturally-relevant gifts and talents and recognizing and valuing the abilities of minority students (Patton, 1992; Steele, 1992).

Instruction

A major objective of multicultural education is ensuring that all students are instructed in ways that do not penalize them because of their cultural differences and that, in fact, capitalize on their cultural heritage. The methods used to achieve this objective are among the most controversial topics in education today. All advocates of multicultural education are concerned with the problem of finding instructional methods that help to equalize educational opportunity and achievement for all microcultural groups, methods that break down the inequities and discrimination that have been part of our public education system. But the question "What instructional methods are most effective in achieving this goal?" is highly debatable.

The controversy regarding instruction is generated by what Minow (1985) calls "the dilemma of difference." The dilemma is that either ignoring or recognizing

The teacher is one of the most significant variables in the success or failure of multicultural education.

students' linguistic or cultural differences can perpetuate them and maintain inequality of social power and opportunity among ethnic or other microcultural groups. If students' differences are ignored, the students will probably be given instruction that is not suited to their cultural styles or needs. They are then likely to fail to learn many skills, which in turn denies them power and opportunity in the dominant culture. For example, if we ignore non-English-speaking students' language and cultural heritage and force them to speak English, they may have great difficulty in school. "This story [of the harm children experience when their language and cultural differences are not recognized] manifests one half of the difference dilemma: nonacknowledgment of difference reiterates difference . . ." (p. 838).

However, the answer to this problem is not necessarily recognition of students' differences, for instruction geared to the students' cultural style may teach only skills valued by the students' microculture. Because the dominant culture does not value these skills, the students' difference is perpetuated. For example, if non-English-speaking students are taught in their native language and are not required to learn English, their progress in the English-speaking society will be slowed.

Here . . . is the other side of the dilemma; acknowledgment of difference can create barriers to important aspects of the school experience and delay or derail successful entry into the society that continues to make that difference matter. Both sides of the dilemma appear and reappear in the history of education for students who are not native English speakers. (Minow, 1985, p. 384)

Should a student who speaks no English be forced to give up his or her native language in school and learn to use only English (ignoring the cultural-linguistic difference)? Or should we use the student's native language as the primary vehicle of instruction, while teaching English as a second language (acknowledging the cultural-linguistic difference)? We could pose similar questions for students with severe hearing impairments: Should we teach them by using primarily sign language or spoken language? And the same dilemma of difference appears in providing instruction for students with other disabilities: To what extent should they be treated as different and provided with special accommodations, and to what extent should they be treated just like everyone else?

To a great extent, the controversy over the dilemma of difference has to do with how students fare in society after their school years, not just how they are treated in school. Delpit (1988) examines a variety of perspectives on the problem of multicultural education, including the following position:

> Children have the right to their own language, their own culture. We must fight cultural hegemony and fight the system by insisting that children be allowed to express themselves in their own language and style. It is not they, the children, who must change, but the schools. (p. 291)

Delpit's response to this perspective acknowledges both the benefit of recognizing and valuing different cultural styles and the necessity of accepting the realities of the society in which we live.

> I believe in diversity of style, and I believe the world will be diminished if cultural diversity is ever obliterated. Further, I believe strongly... that each cultural group should have the right to maintain its own language style. When I speak, therefore, of the culture of power, I don't speak of how I wish things to be but of how they are.
>
> I further believe that to act as if power does not exist is to ensure that the power status quo remains the same. To imply to children or adults... that it doesn't matter how you talk or how you write is to ensure their ultimate failure. I prefer to be honest with my students. Tell them that their language and cultural style is unique and wonderful but that there is a political power game that is also being played, and if they want to be in on that game there are certain games that they too must play.... They [my colleagues] seem to believe that if we accept and encourage diversity within classrooms of children, then diversity will automatically be accepted at gatekeeping points....
>
> I believe that will never happen. What will happen is that the students who reach the gatekeeping points ... will understand that they have been lied to and react accordingly. (1988, p. 292)

The gatekeeping points to which Delpit refers are admission to higher education and employment.

Hilliard (1989) also notes the necessity of taking students' cultural styles into account in teaching, and the equal necessity of good teaching that prepares students of all cultural groups for the demands of the larger society.

> There is something we can call style—a central tendency that is characteristic of both individuals and groups. This style is cultural—learned. It is meaningful in the teaching and learning interaction. Students' style is not, however, to be used as an excuse for poor teaching or as an index of low capacity. (p. 69)

Clearly, the problem of instruction in multicultural education is not easily resolved, especially for bilingual students in special education. Most authorities now agree, however, that accepting and fostering cultural diversity must not be used as an excuse for not teaching students the skills they need to survive and prosper in the larger context of American macroculture (Delpit, 1988; Hilliard, 1989; Ogbu, 1990, 1992).

Among the multicultural controversies of the 1990s are Afrocentric instruction and special African-American programs and schools. Afrocentric instruction is an alternative to the Eurocentrism of the prevailing curriculum and methods of instruction; it highlights African culture and seeks distinctively African modes of teaching and learning. Some suggest that Afrocentrism is a regressive practice that detaches students from the realities of their American social environment (Wortham, 1992). Others call for instructional practices that are culturally sensitive—attuned to the particular cultural characteristics of African-American learners (Franklin, 1992). The assumption underlying culturally sensitive instruction is that students with different cultural backgrounds need to be taught differently, that certain aspects of a student's cultural heritage determine to a significant extent how he or she learns best. For example, Franklin (1992) suggests that African-American students differ from others in the cultural values of their homes and families, their language and patterns of movement, their responses to variety and multiplicity of stimulation, and their preference for divergent thinking.

Perhaps it is understandable that when emphasis is placed on differences in the way students learn, there is also emphasis on devising special programs and schools that cater to these differences. Furthermore, the greater the diversity of cultural backgrounds of students in one class, the greater the difficulty in teaching all students effectively—if one assumes that cultural background determines how students are best taught. Of course, one might hypothesize that certain methods of instruction are equally effective for all students in a culturally diverse group. That is, one might argue that some instructional approaches (e.g., cooperative learning, peer tutoring, and cross-age grouping) allow teachers to provide culturally sensitive instruction to all members of a diverse group at once. Nevertheless, the notion that certain curricula and instructional practices are more appropriate for students of one ethnic origin than another may be used to justify distinctive programs, including African-American immersion schools in which all instruction is geared to the presumed particular learning characteristics of a single ethnic group (see Ascher, 1992; Leake & Leake, 1992). Such schools are often said to be segregationist in practice and intent, but Leake and Leake (1992) suggest that their philosophy opposes the concept of segregation.

> True integration occurs naturally when the differences between peers are minimal. Therefore, the bane of segregation is a culturally and ethnically diverse population of academically competent and self-confident individuals. The African-American immersion schools were designed to provide academically challenging and culturally appropriate experiences for their students. It was hoped that the anticipated increase in student achievement would work to vitiate the African-American students' feelings of inadequacy and impotence. (p. 784)

Do special programs designed with specific learning characteristics in mind help students learn more than they otherwise would and increase their self-esteem? This is a central controversy for both special education and multicultural general education, and research has not provided a clear answer for special programs of either type. Given that ethnicity and disability are two separate dimensions of human difference, however, special programming might be much more appropriate and effective for one dimension of difference than the other.

DIFFERENCE IN IDENTITY: THE STRUGGLE FOR ACCEPTANCE ➤

In the following passage from one of his autobiographical books, Ved Mehta describes his feelings—during his college years—of social isolation and contempt for his identity as a person who is blind and from an Eastern culture. How might his college classmates and instructors have enhanced his feelings of self-worth as a member of these two microcultural groups?

Mandy went home most weekends. At first, I worried that she never invited me to go with her and meet her family. She never even offered to give me her home address or telephone number. But here, again, far from condemning her behavior, I came to condone it, thinking I should be grateful to her for protecting me from her family's ire. Putting myself in her father's place, I reflected that if I had a daughter who had got herself involved with a handicapped person I would vigorously oppose the romance and try to persuade her not to consider throwing away her life on a handicapped person out of some misguided notion that she could make up for the magnitude of his problems. (Coming from a country with practically no tradition of romantic love, I assumed that dating was tantamount to marriage.)

Moreover, I told myself that I was not only handicapped but also a foreigner, who, no matter how superficially Westernized, could never have the same grasp of the English language and American customs that an American had. Just as living in a sighted society was making me contemptuous of everything to do with being blind, studying in America was making me contemptuous of everything to do with being Indian. As a freshman in college, I had taken courses in the history of Western civilization, the philosophy of Western civilization, and the classical music of Western civilization. In Berkeley, I was studying Western economics and American history. (Similar courses in Indian civilization were unheard of.) In the light of this Western education, everything Indian seemed backward and primitive. I remember once listening to a record of Mozart and being awed by the dozens of instruments magically playing in harmony, and then listening to a record of a sitar and being filled with scorn for the twang-twang of the gut.

SOURCE: From © Ved Mehta, *The Stolen Light*, first published by HarperCollins UK 1989 and WW Norton & Co 1989. p. 260. Reprinted with permission.

Hilliard (1992) posed the question of differential programming for students with disabilities as follows: "Can learning impediments be overcome or eliminated, allowing the formerly impaired student to perform significantly better than he or she would have without the services, or allowing the student to perform well in the mainstream academic program?" (p. 171). Research does not answer this question resoundingly—either affirmatively or negatively—for any model of delivering special education services. Whether making special education multicultural in its best sense will add to the weight of evidence regarding special education's effectiveness in improving disabled students' academic performance and success in the mainstream is an open question.

What is not an open question, however, is this: Must both special and general education adopt instructional programs that value all students and help all to be as successful as possible in American society, regardless of their specific cultural heritage? This question has been answered resoundingly in the affirmative, not by research but by our common commitment to the American values of equality of opportunity and fairness for all.

Socialization

Academic instruction is one of two primary purposes of education; the other is socialization. Socialization involves helping students to develop appropriate social perceptions and interactions with others and to learn how to work for desirable social change.

Destructive and stereotypic social perceptions and interactions among differing microcultural groups are long-standing problems in schools and communities in

*C*hildren from
different cultural
backgrounds can
benefit by working together to
foster independence.

the United States. The most obvious examples involve racial discrimination, although sex discrimination and discrimination against people of differing religions and disabilities are also common in our society. Teachers must become keenly aware of their own cultural heritage, identity, and biases before they can help their students deal with cultural diversity in ways that enhance democratic ideals, such as human dignity, justice, and equality (Banks, 1988). Becoming comfortable with one's own identity as a member of microcultural groups is an important objective for both teachers and students. Depending on the cultural context, accepting and valuing one's identity can be quite difficult. In the box on page 110, Ved Mehta (1989) describes his feelings of discomfort with his identity as a member of two microcultural groups—East Indians and persons who are blind.

Teaching about different cultures and their value may be important in reducing racial and ethnic conflict and promoting respect for human differences. Equally important, however, is structuring classroom interactions to promote the understanding and appreciation of others. One of the most effective ways of breaking down prejudice and encouraging appropriate interaction among students with different characteristics is cooperative learning (Johnson & Johnson, 1986; Slavin, 1988). In cooperative learning, students of different abilities and cul-

$\mathcal{C}$*omputers create new opportunities and alternatives for students from all backgrounds to succeed and gain confidence learning a new language.*

tural characteristics work together as a team, fostering interdependence. In *Among Schoolchildren*, Tracy Kidder describes this approach to socialization as it was used by a fifth-grade teacher, Chris Zajac:

> Then came fifteen minutes of study, during which teams of two children quizzed each other. Chris paired up good spellers with poor ones. She also made spelling an exercise in socialization, by putting together children who did not seem predisposed to like each other. She hoped that some would learn to get along with classmates they didn't think they liked. At least they'd be more apt to do some work than if she paired them up with friends. Her guesses were good. Alice raised her eyes to the florescent-lit ceiling at the news that she had Claude for a spelling partner. Later she wrote, "Today is the worst day of my life." Clarence scowled at the news that he had Ashley, who was shy and chubby and who didn't look happy either. A little smile collected in one corner of Chris's mouth as she observed the reactions. "Now, you're not permanently attached to that person for the rest of your life," she said to the class. (1989, pp. 28-29)

Teachers of exceptional children and youths must be aware of the variety of microcultural identities their students may be developing and struggling with. Review the multiple aspects of cultural identity suggested by Figure 3–1 (page 93) and reflect on the combinations of these and other subcultures that a given student might adopt. One of the microcultural identities not included in Figure 3–1 is sexual orientation. Yet many children and adolescents, including many with educational exceptionalities, experience serious difficulties with what some have called the "invisible culture" of gay and lesbian youth (McIntyre, 1992a). Students who are straight may struggle with their own prejudices against homosexuals, prejudices all too often fostered by both their peers and adults and sometimes given justification by identification with a religious or political microculture. Gay and lesbian students are often harassed and abused verbally and

CULTURAL DIFFERENCES IN DISCIPLINE ➢

The lack of knowledge that most educators possess regarding both child abuse (McIntyre, 1987) and culturally different childrearing (Garcia, 1978; McIntyre, 1992) creates fertile ground for misjudging the appropriateness of parental practices. Teachers who adhere to the disciplinary practices of the majority culture may find themselves viewing culturally different practices as being abusive. This would mean that use of culturally diverse childrearing practices places parents at greater risk for being reported to agencies in charge of handling abuse and neglect reports. A few of these practices and the reporting dilemmas they cause for concerned educators are addressed below.

➢ A novice teacher in a poor urban school district is distressed when, upon seeking advice from colleagues regarding discipline, he is told by them to use physical punishment. This coincides with the advice of the students in his class who tell him to "Hit 'em upside the head." In fact, physical punishment is more accepted in the low socio-economic classes (Gollnick & Chinn, 1990; Horton & Hunt, 1968; Persky, 1974; Spinetta & Rigler, 1972; Hanna, 1988), and educators who teach these students are more likely to approve of corporal punishment (McDowell & Friedman, 1979; Bauer, Dubanoski, Yamauchi & Honbo, 1990), perhaps believing that one must "use what they know."

➢A teacher phones a student's parents to inquire as to how that pupil came to have welts on his body. She is given a religious defense based on the biblical Book of Proverbs that promotes the use of "the rod." Indeed, Fundamentalists, Evangelists, and Baptists respond more punitively in disciplinary situations than people who are affiliated with other major religious orientations (Hyman, 1988). . . .

➢In the faculty lounge, a teacher hears that a student of hers has been locked out of his house. An Asian-American colleague mentions that this is a common disciplinary practice among Southeast Asian families. It is meant to shame "Americanized" children who have not met traditional familial expectations and obligations (Bempechat & Omori, 1990).

➢A newly certified teacher accepts a position at a school near an Indian reservation. She is appalled by the lack of guidance provided by a number of parents of her Native American students. Like many teachers from the mainstream culture (Swisher, 1990), she believes that the parents are neglectful and letting their children "run wild." She is unaware that among many tribes, non-interference, except in times of danger, is the guardians' policy (Devore & Schlesinger, 1987). . . . Additionally, many clans and tribes assign a great deal of the childraising responsibility to relatives, especially the grandparents (Devore & Schlesinger, 1987).

➢A teacher wrestles with the issue of whether to report a poor student's parents who are, in her mind, neglectful. She is aware that in low-income areas, early independence with limited guidance or training is the norm (Horton & Hunt, 1968; Miller, 1959), as is the use of inconsistent and harsh physical punishment whereby children are taught to obey rather than reason (Farrington, 1986; Hanna, 1988; Stack, 1974). However, these practices violate her beliefs regarding proper childrearing.

➢A teacher is told by the parents of a poor, urban black youth to "whup" (paddle) him if he misbehaves in class. The use of controlling and punitive child treatment is more likely to occur in the low-income black culture (Hanna, 1988; Stack, 1974) and may even be viewed by the child as a sign of caring and affection (Rosenfeld, 1971; Silverstein & Krate, 1975). The middle-class oriented behavior management techniques that avoid the expected swift physical punishment may actually cause anxiety for the youth (Hanna, 1988; Harrison-Ross & Wyden, 1973).

SOURCE: From T. McIntyre, & P. Silva, (1992). Culturally diverse childrearing practices: Abusive or just different? *Beyond Behavior*, 4(1), 8–9. Reprinted with permission.

physically in school and may suffer from serious depression or other psychological disorders as a result (McIntyre, 1992a; Uribe & Harbeck, 1992). Consider also that a student might be both homosexual and gifted, physically disabled, mentally retarded, or have any other educational exceptionality. Our point is that the task of socialization in a multicultural society demands attention to the multitude of identities that students may assume. It demands also an awareness that any of these identities may carry the consequence of social rejection, isolation, and alienation. Our task as educators is to promote understanding of cultural differences and acceptance of individuals whose identities are different from one's own.

One of the most difficult tasks of teaching is socializing students through classroom discipline (that is, through the management of classroom behavior). Managing classroom behavior presents a serious challenge for nearly all teachers and a particularly difficult challenge for most special education teachers (Kauffman, Mostert, Nuttycombe, Trent, & Hallahan, 1993). Two considerations are critical: (1) the relationship between the teacher's approach to classroom discipline and the parents' childrearing practices, and (2) the sensitivity of the teacher to cultural differences in responses to discipline.

Middle-class American teachers may have an approach to classroom discipline that they consider effective and humane but that differs radically from some cultures' accepted childrearing practices. As McIntyre and Silva (1992) point out, educators, like everyone else, are often ethnocentric, believing that their views are correct and others' are inferior. In the case of discipline involving students of culturally diverse backgrounds, the teacher may face difficult ethical decisions about child abuse or neglect. When do one's own beliefs about the treatment of children demand that a culturally condoned disciplinary practice be confronted as abuse? Answering this question is not easy, and you may want to reflect on the problems posed by McIntyre and Silva in the box on page 111.

McIntyre (1992b) summarizes some of the cultural differences we might find in expectations regarding classroom behavior. He also describes the cultural sensitivity demanded in managing behavior effectively and humanely. For example, students from different cultures may differ markedly in their pattern of eye contact with the teacher or another authority (especially when being corrected), interpretation of peer assistance on academic work, response to praise or external rewards, touching or being touched, response to deadlines, physical activity level during learning, response to explanations and questions, response to peer pressure, attitude toward corporal punishment, and so on. In selecting classroom management strategies, the teacher must be sensitive to such cultural differences but, at the same time, use an approach that is effective, fair, just, and ethically and legally defensible. This is, to say the least, a highly demanding task.

Finally, we note that education should not merely socialize students to fit into the existing social order. The goals of multicultural education include teaching students to work for social change (Banks, 1988), which entails helping students who are members of oppressed minorities to become advocates for themselves and other members of their microcultures.

Summary

Education for cultural diversity involves managing tension between microcultural diversity on the one hand and common macrocultural values on the other. Many microcultures are found in the U. S. macroculture, which values justice, equality, and human dignity. Progress in multicultural education is difficult because each microculture tends to see many of its own values as the standards against which others should be judged. Devising a multicultural curriculum that is satisfactory to all groups is difficult, and not everyone agrees that understanding cultural diversity is as important as building the common culture. Although multiculturalism is fraught with conflicts, it offers an opportunity to practice American values of tolerance, justice, equality, and individualism.

Communities and families contribute much to students' attitudes toward education and academic achievement. Minority communities can encourage academic success among students by highlighting values consistent with school achievement. However, we must guard against ethnic stereotypes of achievement or failure and understand that community and family attitudes toward schooling do not excuse educators from their responsibility to provide an effective and multicultural education for all students.

Multicultural education may at first seem to be a relatively simple matter, but it is complicated by questions about what cultures to include and what and how to teach about them. Many distinct microcultures exist, and some have values or customs that others find unacceptable or offensive. Microcultural groups may include not only gender and ethnicity, but also religious or political affiliation and sexual orientation. Finding a balance among cultural values and traditions that satisfies all groups is often quite difficult.

The types of cultural diversity most relevant to special education are ethnicity and disability or giftedness. We must remember, however, that students may be members of a variety of microcultural groups besides those designating educational exceptionality. Multicultural special education must give special attention to ensuring that ethnicity is not mistaken for educational exceptionality and to increasing the understanding of educational exceptionality and its relationship to other microcultures. Members of ethnic minority groups may be mistakenly identified as disabled or overlooked in attempts to identify special gifts and talents if their cultural practices and language are not understood by teachers. Individuals with certain exceptionalities (deafness, for example) may develop their own microcultures, and it is important to help others understand and appreciate these cultures.

Three specific problems in multicultural special education are assessment, instruction, and socialization. Assessment is a particularly critical issue because it forms the basis for decisions about instruction and placement; therefore, it is imperative that assessment be accurate, fair, and directly related to designing effective instruction. Traditional testing procedures are problematic for members of many ethnic minorities, and curriculum-based assessment is gaining wide acceptance as an alternative. Assessment of the learning environment may be as important as assessment of the student's skills.

Instruction presents many points of controversy for multicultural and bilingual special education. One of the great and pervasive problems of special education is the dilemma of difference—recognizing students' differences and providing special services of any kind may be helpful, but identification and special programming of any kind may also carry stigma and perpetuate the differences. Some leading scholars in multicultural education suggest that instruction should help students understand and preserve their own microculture while at the same time help students learn to function successfully in the American macroculture. Particularly controversial in the 1990s are Afrocentric instruction and special African-American schools or immersion programs. An open question is whether special programs—either for students with particular ethnic identities or those with disabilities—provide special benefits. Not open to question, however, is whether special and general education must adopt instructional programs that value all students and help all to be as successful as possible in American society, regardless of their cultural heritage.

Socialization is an aspect of education that some believe is as important as academic instruction. Multicultural special education seeks to improve students' understanding and acceptance of others' differences and to help all students, regardless of their differences from others, to feel valued and accepted. Teachers must be aware of the variety of multicultural identities their students may be adopting or struggling with; they must also be aware of the possible social consequences of these identities. Teachers may encounter particular multicultural problems in managing classroom behavior because of differences between their own views of discipline and childrearing and those of their students and students' parents.

*C*HAPTER FOUR

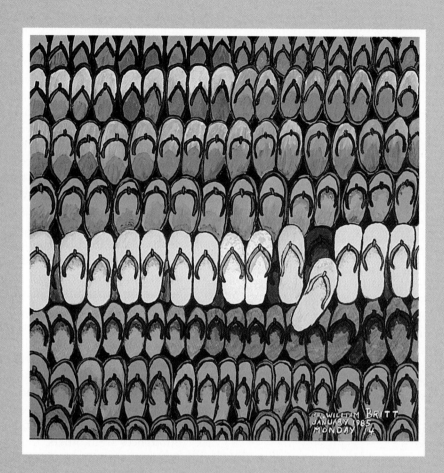

WILLIAM BRITT

William Britt, classified as mentally retarded, has been a practicing artist for many years. Initially self-taught, he refined his skills to an extraordinary level of professionalism at Westchester Community College in New York. Now in his late 50s, Britt's paintings have been shown in national exhibitions and are in private and public collections, including one painting hanging in The White House.

$\mathcal{E}$verywhere, however, we hear talk of sameness. "All men are created equal" it is declared. And at the ballot box and the subway rush, in Hiroshima and Coney Island it almost seems that way. Moreover, coming back from Staten Island on the ferry, as you see an unkempt bootblack lift his head to gaze at the Manhattan skyline—you know these words of Jefferson are not mere snares for votes and popularity. But standing on the same boat with the hand of your idiot son in one of yours—with mingled love and distaste placing a handkerchief against his drooling mouth—you know that Jefferson's words are not easy to understand.

There is a difference in sameness. Perhaps the days of our years are for the bootblack. But assuredly the nights are for our idiot son.

➤ Richard H. Hungerford
"On Locusts"

Mental
Retardation

*T*here is considerable danger in relying on Hungerford's portrayal (p. 115) for our only view of what it is like to have a child who is retarded. Such children may be heartbreakingly different from the children next door in some ways, but also like them in others. More and more research evidence indicates that retardation is quantitative rather than qualitative. In many areas, it seems, the retarded child functions like a nondisabled child—but a nondisabled child at a younger chronological age. Even the differences that do exist need not cause parents a lifetime of constant heartache. Hungerford's statement is valuable because it presents honest feelings. Unlike the romanticized portraits found in many TV dramas, movies, and books, children with retardation can evoke agony, hatred, sorrow, and frustration, as well as love, in their parents.

The Hungerford quote, published in 1950, points up something else as well. It reflects the once-popular stereotype of the person with retardation as a clumsy, drooling, helpless creature. Today we know this is simply not true. First, most children classified as mentally retarded are *mildly* retarded and look like the hypothetical average child living next door. Second, it can be misleading to characterize even the more severely retarded as helpless. With advanced methods of providing educational and vocational training, we are finding that people with retardation are capable of leading more independent lives than was previously thought possible. Given appropriate preparation, many are able to live and work with relatively little help from others.

The field of mental retardation has undergone a number of other exciting changes since the time Hungerford wrote. No longer is institutionalization the norm for persons who are severely retarded. More and more students with retardation are spending greater portions of their time in regular classrooms in their neighborhood schools. Terminology, too, is changing. Whereas the term, "idiot," which Hungerford uses, was once acceptable, today professionals try to come up with terms that are less stigmatizing.

Perhaps the most significant change since Hungerford wrote "On Locusts" is the fact that designating someone as mentally retarded has become much more difficult. Today, professionals are more reluctant to apply the label of mental retardation than they once were. At least three reasons account for this more cautious attitude toward identification of students as retarded. First, professionals became concerned about the misdiagnosis of children from ethnic minority groups as retarded. Twenty to 30 years ago, it was much more common for children from ethnic minorities, especially African-American and Hispanic students, to be labeled mentally retarded because they did not achieve well in school and they scored poorly on intelligence tests.

A second reason for using more stringent criteria for determining retardation is related to the fear that the stigma of such a diagnosis can have harmful consequences for the individual. Some believe that the label of mental retardation causes children to have poor self concepts and to be viewed by others negatively.

Third, some professionals now believe that, to a certain extent, mental retardation is a socially constructed condition. For example, the sociologist Jane Mercer (1973) holds that a person's social system determines whether he or she is retarded. She notes that most students labeled retarded, particularly those who

Misconceptions about PERSONS WITH MENTAL RETARDATION

MYTH ➤ Mental retardation is defined by how a person scores on an IQ test.

FACT ➤ The most commonly used definition specifies that, in order for a person to be considered mentally retarded, he or she must meet two criteria: (1) low intellectual functioning *and* (2) low adaptive skills.

MYTH ➤ Once diagnosed as mentally retarded, a person remains within this classification for life.

FACT ➤ A person's level of mental functioning does not necessarily remain stable, particularly for those who are mildly retarded. With intensive educational programming, some persons can improve to the point that they are no longer retarded.

MYTH ➤ In most cases, we can identify the cause of retardation.

FACT ➤ In most cases, especially of those who are mildly retarded or who require less intensive support, we cannot specify the cause. For many children who are mildly retarded, poor environment may be a causal factor, but it is extremely difficult to document.

MYTH ➤ Most mentally retarded children look different from nondisabled children.

FACT ➤ The majority of children with mental retardation are mildly retarded, or require less intensive support, and most of these look like nondisabled children.

MYTH ➤ We can identify most cases of mental retardation in infancy.

FACT ➤ Because most children with retardation are mildly retarded, because infant intelligence tests are not very reliable and valid, and because intellectual demands on the child increase greatly upon entrance to school, most children with retardation are not identified as retarded until they go to school.

MYTH ➤ Persons with mental retardation tend to be gentle people who have an easy time making friends.

FACT ➤ Because of a variety of behavioral characteristics and because they sometimes live and work in relatively isolated situations, some persons with mental retardation have difficulty making and holding friends.

MYTH ➤ The teaching of vocational skills to students with retardation is best reserved for secondary school and beyond.

FACT ➤ Many authorities now believe it appropriate to introduce vocational content in elementary school to students with mental retardation.

MYTH ➤ When workers with mental retardation fail on the job, it is usually because they do not have adequate job skills.

FACT ➤ When they fail on the job, it is more often because of poor job responsibility (poor attendance and lack of initiative) and social incompetence (interacting inappropriately with coworkers) than because of incompetence in task production.

MYTH ➤ Persons with mental retardation should not be expected to work in the competitive job market.

FACT ➤ More and more persons who are mentally retarded hold jobs in competitive employment. Many are helped through supportive employment situations in which a job coach helps them and their employer adapt to the work place.

are higher functioning, do not "officially" become retarded until they enter school. The school as a social system has a certain set of expectations some children do not meet.

DEFINITION

A more conservative approach to identifying students as mentally retarded is reflected in changes in definition that have occurred over the years. Since 1950, seven official definitions have been endorsed by the American Association on Mental Retardation (AAMR) (formerly the American Association on Mental Deficiency), the major professional organization dealing with persons with mental retardation. The current AAMR definition reads:

> *Mental retardation* refers to substantial limitations in present functioning. It is characterized by significantly subaverage intellectual functioning, existing concurrently with related limitations in two or more of the following applicable adaptive skill areas: communication, self-care, home living, social skills, community use, self-direction, health and safety, functional academics, leisure, and work. Mental retardation manifests before age 18. (AAMR Ad Hoc Committee on Terminology and Classification, 1992, p. 5)

*A*daptive behavior includes self-help skills, such as the ability to perform household tasks.

In making this definition operational, the professional is to rely on assessment of two areas: intellectual functioning and adaptive skills. **Intellectual functioning**, usually estimated by an IQ test, refers primarily to ability related to academic performance. **Adaptive skills**, usually estimated by adaptive behavior surveys, refers to abilities related to coping with one's environment.

This definition, as each of its predecessors, continues three trends consistent with a more cautious approach to diagnosing students as mentally retarded:

1. a broadening of the definition beyond the single criterion of an IQ score,
2. a lowering of the IQ score used as a cut-off for qualification as retarded, and
3. a conceptualization of retardation as a condition that can be improved and that is not necessarily permanent.

A Broadening of the Definition

At one time it was common practice to diagnose individuals as retarded solely on the basis of an IQ score. Today, we recognize that IQ tests are far from perfect and that they are but one indication of a person's ability to function. Professionals came to consider adaptive skills in addition to IQ in defining retardation because they began to recognize that some students might score poorly on an IQ test but still be "streetwise"—able to cope, for example, with the subway system, with an after-school job, with peers. Much of the current emphasis on adaptive skills can be traced to the 1970 report of the President's Committee on Mental Retardation entitled "The Six-Hour Retarded Child." It held that some students may function in the retarded range while they are in school for six hours of the day but behave just fine—adjust and adapt competently—once they return to their neighborhoods for the other eighteen hours.

Crafters of the current AAMR definition have been very specific in pointing to a broadening of the definition of mental retardation. They view intelligence as multi-faceted. In their rationale for the revised definition, they identify three types of intelligence: conceptual, practical, and social (AAMR Ad Hoc Committee on Terminology and Classification, 1992). **Conceptual intelligence** is primarily assessed in IQ tests. Practical and social intelligence are the bases for the adaptive skills aspect of the definition. **Practical intelligence** is defined as the "ability to maintain and sustain oneself as an independent person managing the ordinary activities of daily living" (p. 15). **Social intelligence** "refers to the ability to understand social expectations and the behavior of other persons and to judge appropriately how to conduct oneself in social situations" (p. 15).

Lowering of the IQ-Score Cut-Off

It was also common at one time for practitioners to use a cut-off score of 85 on an IQ test as an indicator of mental retardation. This cut-off score was endorsed by the AAMR until the mid-1970s, when they made it more difficult for people to be identified as retarded by establishing a cut-off score of 70 to 75. The current AAMR definition also sanctions this cut-off of 70 to 75. They established a 5-point spread of 70 to 75 to reinforce the notion that IQ scores should not be regarded as precise measurements, that professionals should use some clinical judgment in interpreting IQ scores.

➤ **intellectual functioning.** The ability to solve problems related to academics; usually estimated by an IQ test; one of two major components (the other is adaptive skills) of the AAMR definition.

➤ **adaptive skills.** Skills needed to adapt to one's living environment, e.g., communication, self-care, home living, social skills, community use, self-direction, health and safety, functional academics, leisure, and work; usually estimated by an adaptive behavior survey; one of two major components (the other is intellectual functioning) of the AAMR definition.

➤ **conceptual intelligence.** The traditional conceptualization of intelligence emphasizing problem solving related to academic material; what IQ tests primarily focus on assessing.

➤ **practical intelligence.** The ability to solve problems related to activities of daily living; an aspect of the adaptive skills component of the AAMR definition.

➤ **social intelligence.** The ability to understand social expectations and to cope in social situations; an aspect of the adaptive skills component of the AAMR definition.

Retardation as Improvable and Possibly Non-Permanent

At the time of the Hungerford quote, many authorities held little hope for enhancing significantly the functioning of people with retardation and essentially believed retardation to be incurable. Over the years, however, professionals have become more optimistic about the beneficial effects of educational programming. Not only do they believe that the functioning of virtually all persons with retardation can be improved, but they have forwarded the notion that some persons with retardation, especially those with mild retardation, can eventually improve to the point that they are no longer classified as retarded. In other words, many professionals now posit that retardation is not something an individual is automatically saddled with for the rest of his or her life. For example, although the current definition of the AAMR does not specifically address the issue of improvability, one of the assumptions stated in the manual in which the definition is presented states that: "With appropriate supports over a sustained period, the life functioning of the person with mental retardation will generally improve" (p. 5).

CLASSIFICATION

Professionals have typically classified persons with mental retardation according to the severity of their problems. For many years, the AAMR promoted the use of the terms **mild**, **moderate**, **severe**, and **profound retardation**, with each of these levels keyed to approximate IQ levels. For example, mild mental retardation is from 50–55 to approximately 70, and severe retardation is from 20–25 to 35–40. Most school systems now classify their students with mental retardation using these terms or a close approximation of them.

In 1992, however, the AAMR recommended a radical departure from this system of classification (AAMR Ad Hoc Committee on Terminology and Classification, 1992). Rather than categorize students based on their IQ scores, they recommended that professionals classify them according to how much support they need to function as competently as possible. Table 4–1 depicts these levels of support.

There are at least three reasons that the authors of the AAMR's new classification scheme believe it better than categorization based on intellectual functioning. First, the new classification gets away from reliance on a single IQ score for classification. Second, it implies that persons with retardation can achieve positive outcomes through appropriate support services. Third, when used in combination with consideration of adaptive skills, it results in descriptions that are more meaningful. Rather than saying, for example, that a person has severe retardation, one might say the person has retardation that requires extensive supports in self-care, home living, and work.

It is still too early to tell whether the new AAMR classification scheme will replace the old one in practice.

PREVALENCE

The average (mean) score on an IQ test is 100. Theoretically, we expect 2.27 percent of the population to fall two standard deviations (IQ = 70 on the WISC-R) or more below this average. This expectation is based on the assumption that intelli-

➤ **mild retardation.** A classification used to specify an individual whose IQ test score is between approximately 55 and 69.

➤ **moderate retardation.** A classification used to specify an individual whose IQ test score is between approximately 40 and 55.

➤ **severe retardation.** A classification used to specify an individual whose IQ test score is between approximately 25 and 40.

➤ **profound retardation.** A classification used to specify an individual whose IQ test score is below approximately 25.

𝒯able 4–1 ➤ AAMR Classification Scheme for Mental Retardation Based on Levels of Support

Intermittent	Supports on an "as needed basis." Characterized by episodic nature, person not always needing the support(s), or short-term supports needed during life-span transitions (e.g., job loss or an acute medical crisis). Intermittent supports may be high or low intensity when provided.
Limited	An intensity of supports characterized by consistency over time, time-limited but not of an intermittent nature, may require fewer staff members and less cost than more intense levels of support (e.g., time-limited employment training or transitional supports during the school-to-adult provided period).
Extensive	Supports characterized by regular involvement (e.g., daily) in at least some environments (such as work or home) and not time-limited (e.g., long-term home living support).
Pervasive	Supports characterized by their constancy, high intensity, provided across environments; potential life-sustaining nature. Pervasive supports typically involve more staff members and intrusiveness than do extensive or time-limited supports.

SOURCE: From AAMR AD HOC Committee on Terminology and Classification. (1992). *Mental retardation: Definition, classification, and systems of support.* Coptright © 1992 by American Association on Mental Retardation. Reprinted with permission.

gence, like so many other human traits, is distributed along a "normal curve." Figure 4–1 on page 122 shows the hypothetical normal curve of intelligence. This curve is split into eight areas by means of standard deviations. On the WISC-III, where one standard deviation equals 15 IQ points, 34.13 percent of the population scores between 85 and 100. Likewise, 2.14 percent scores between 55 and 70, and 0.13 percent scores below 55. Thus it would seem that 2.27 percent should fall between 0 and 70.

In keeping with the figure of 2.27 percent, the federal government for years had estimated the prevalence of retardation to be 2.3 percent. Since the federal government started requiring public schools to report actual counts of how many students they were officially identifying as mentally retarded, the prevalence figures have been much lower—somewhere around 1 to 1.5 percent. Authorities have pointed to three possible sources for the discrepancy. First, the fact that students who are mentally retarded must now meet the dual criteria of low IQ *and* low adaptive skills may have resulted in fewer identified children. Second, litigation focusing on the improper labeling of minority students as mentally retarded

Figure 4-1

➤ *Theoretical distribution of IQ scores based on normal curve.*

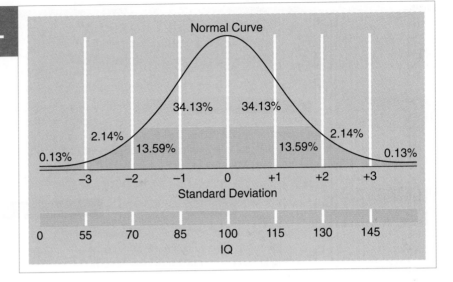

may have made school personnel more cautious about identifying these children as retarded. Third, in cases in which the IQ score is in the 70s, thus making identification as retarded a close call, parents and school officials may be more likely to label children as learning disabled than mentally retarded because learning disabled is perceived as a less stigmatizing label.

CAUSES

Many experts estimate that we are able to pinpoint the cause of mental retardation in only about 10 to 15 percent of the cases. Although some overlap is evident, for the most part causal factors for persons with mild retardation, requiring less intensive support services, differ from those for persons with more severe retardation, requiring more intensive support services.

Persons With Mild Retardation, or Those Requiring Less Intensive Support

Most individuals identified as retarded are classified as mildly retarded and need less intensive support to function. They typically do not differ in appearance from their nondisabled peers, and they are usually not diagnosed as retarded until they enter school and begin to fall behind in school work. In the majority of these cases, we are unable to specify the exact cause of the retardation. Although there are no definitive data, the estimate of 10 to 15 percent of identifiable causes of all retardation is undoubtedly even lower when considering only persons who are mildly retarded.

Professionals often refer to individuals with mild retardation as having **cultural-familial retardation.** Some use this term to refer to a person with a mild degree of retardation who has (1) no evidence of brain damage, (2) at least one parent who is retarded, and (3) at least one sibling who is retarded (if he or she has siblings) (Heber, 1959). The term was originally intended to indicate retardation that was caused by poor parenting (poor intellectual stimulation)

➤ **cultural-familial retardation.** Today, a term used to refer to mild retardation due to an unstimulating environment and/or genetic factors.

from parents who were retarded (Garber, Hodge, Rynders, Dever, & Velu, 1991). Today professionals use the term more broadly to indicate mild retardation that may be due to an unstimulating environment (possibly, but not necessarily specifically caused by poor parenting) and/or genetic factors. Just which factor is the culprit—environment or heredity—has been the subject of debate for years.

The Nature Versus Nurture Controversy

In the early part of this century, proponents of the viewpoint that genetics determines intellectual development largely held sway. The classic study of Skeels and Dye (1939), however, did much to strengthen the position of the environmentalists. Skeels and Dye investigated the effects of stimulation on the development of infants and young children, many of whom were classified as mentally retarded, in an orphanage. One group of children remained in the typical orphanage environment, while the other group was given stimulation. For the latter group, nurturance was provided by teenage girls who were retarded. The effects were clear-cut: Average IQs for members of the group given stimulation increased, whereas the other children's IQs decreased. Even more dramatic were the results of Skeels's follow-up study, done 21 years later:

> In the adult follow-up study, all cases were located and information obtained on them, after a lapse of 21 years. . . .
> All 13 children in the experimental group were self-supporting, and none was a ward of any institution. . . . In the contrast group of 12 children, one had died in adolescence following continued residence in a state institution for the mentally retarded,

*A*lthough it is difficult to pinpoint the environment as a cause of retardation, many authorities believe that poor social-environment conditions can lead to mild retardation.

and four were still wards of institutions, one in a mental hospital, and the other three in institutions for the mentally retarded.

In education, disparity between the two groups was striking. The contrast group completed a median of less than the third grade. The experimental group completed a median of the 12th grade. Four of the subjects had one or more years of college work, one received a B.A. degree and took some graduate training.

Marked differences in occupational levels were seen in the two groups. In the experimental group all were self-supporting or married and functioning as house-wives. The range was from professional and business occupations to domestic service, the latter the occupations of two girls who had never been placed in adoptive homes. In the contrast group, four (36 percent) of the subjects were institutionalized and unemployed. Those who were employed, with one exception, were characterized as "hewers of wood and drawers of water.". . .

Eleven of the 13 children in the experimental group were married: nine of the 11 had a total of 28 children, an average of three per family. On intelligence tests, these second generation children had IQs ranging from 86 to 125, with a mean of 104. In no instance was there any indication of mental retardation or demonstrable abnormality . . . .

In the contrast group, only two subjects had married. One had one child and subsequently was divorced. Psychological examination of the child revealed marked mental retardation. . . . Another male subject had a nice home and a family of four children, all of average intelligence. (Skeels, 1966, pp. 54–55)

By the 1960s there were many proponents of the nurture position. It was during this time, for example, that the federal government established the Head Start program. Head Start was based on the premise that the negative effects of poverty could be reduced through educational and medical services during the preschool years.

For many years theoreticians tended to view the nature-nurture issue from an either-or perspective—either you believed that heredity held the key to determining intellectual development or you held that the environment was the all-important factor. Today most authorities believe that both genetics and the environment are critical determinants of intelligence. They have arrived at this judgment on the basis of several studies, but perhaps the most convincing was that conducted by Capron and Duyme (1989), who compared the IQs of four groups of adopted children: (1) children whose biological and adoptive parents were both of high socioeconomic status (SES), (2) children whose biological parents were of high SES but whose adoptive parents were of low SES, (3) children whose biological and adoptive parents were both of low SES, and (4) children whose biological parents were of low SES but whose adoptive parents were of high SES. The average IQs of the four groups were 119.60, 107.50, 92.40, and 103.60, respectively. Confirming the importance of the environment, the average IQ of the adoptees was about 12 points higher (111.60 versus 99.95) when they were raised by parents of high SES (groups 1 and 4) rather than low SES (groups 2 and 3). Confirming the importance of heredity, the average IQ of the adoptees was about 16 points higher (113.55 versus 98.00) when their biological parents were of high SES (groups 1 and 2) compared to low SES (groups 3 and 4).

The more scientists study genetic and environmental determinants of intelligence, the more they realize how complex the influence of these factors is. For example, scientists are far from being able to specify the exact way in which the environment influences intellectual development. They do not know, for example, whether the effect of SES "is related to access to quality education, the variety and complexity of intellectual stimulation in the home, the parents' press for scholastic achievement, or some other factor that differentiates between high- and low-SES homes" (McGue, 1989, p. 507). Further complicating the issue, there is considerable evidence that the environment is far from static, even within families (Plomin, 1989; Rowe & Plomin, 1981). Traditionally, investigators viewed the environmental influence of being raised in a particular family as equally distributed across family members. Researchers now believe that different siblings in the same family experience different environments. The following scenario provides an example of how within-family variations can occur:

> Suppose a family with 16-year-old and 9-year-old boys visits the Space Center in Florida. The experience might have no effect whatsoever on the older child, who is heavily committed to basketball and dating. However, the younger boy, while showing aptitude in mathematics, has never really blossomed academically. He finds the Space Center fascinating. When he returns home he discovers his neighbor is a pilot, who shows the youngster about planes and takes him up for a ride. This ignites the child's interest in aviation. A unit on flight in a science class later that year reinforces it, and the child shows a marked increase in mental performance with this surge of motivation. (McCall, 1983, p. 414)

It should be obvious from the foregoing discussion that the study of the differential effects of heredity and environment on intellectual development has become more complex over the years. In other words, although we are now closer to an understanding of the potential effects of both environment and heredity, in individual cases we are far from knowing the exact contribution of each.

Persons With More Severe Retardation, or Those Requiring More Intensive Support

Determining causes of retardation is easier in persons whose retardation is more severe than in those who are mildly retarded. Unlike persons with mild retardation, individuals with more severe retardation often do look different from their nondisabled peers, and they are often diagnosed in infancy or before entering school. We can divide causes of retardation in persons with more severe retardation into two general categories—genetic factors and brain damage (MacMillan, 1982).

Genetic Factors

Mental retardation has a number of genetically related causes. These are, generally, of two types—those resulting from some damage to genetic material, such as chromosomal abnormalities, and those due to hereditary transmission. We discuss four conditions—Down syndrome, which results from chromosomal abnormality and Fragile X syndrome, PKU (phenylketonuria), and Tay-Sachs disease, all three of which are inherited.

Estimated to account for about 5 to 6 percent of all cases of retardation (Patton, Payne, & Beirne-Smith, 1990), **Down syndrome** is associated with a range of distinctive physical characteristics that vary considerably in number from one individual to another. Persons with Down syndrome may have thick epicanthal folds in the corners of the eyes, making them appear to slant upward slightly. Other common characteristics include small stature, decreased muscle

➤ **Down syndrome.** A condition resulting from a chromosomal abnormality; characterized by mental retardation and such physical signs as slanted-appearing eyes, flattened features, shortness, tendency toward obesity. The three major types of Down syndrome are *trisomy* 21, *mosaicism,* and *translocation.*

Persons with Down syndrome are usually identifiable by specific facial characteristics.

➢ **trisomy 21.** A type of Down syndrome in which the twenty-first chromosome is a triplet, making forty-seven, rather than the normal forty-six, chromosomes in all.

➢ **chromosome.** A rod-shaped entity in the nucleus of the cell; contains genes, which convey hereditary characteristics.

➢ **gene.** Responsible for hereditary characteristics; arranged at specific locations in the chromosomes within each cell.

➢ **amniocentesis.** A medical procedure that allows examination of the amniotic fluid around the fetus; sometimes recommended to determine the presence of abnormality.

➢ **chorionic villus sampling.** A method of testing the unborn fetus for a variety of chromosomal abnormalities, such as Down syndrome; a small amount of tissue from the chorion (a membrane that eventually helps form the placenta) is extracted and tested; can be done earlier than amniocentesis but risk of miscarriage is slightly higher.

➢ **sonography.** High-frequency sound waves are converted into a visual picture; used to detect major physical malformations in the unborn fetus.

tone (hypotonia), hyperflexibility of the joints, speckling of the iris in the eye, a small oral cavity that can result in a protruding tongue, short and broad hands with a single palmar crease, and a wide gap between the first and second toes (Batshaw & Perret, 1986; Blackman, 1984a).

Persons with Down syndrome frequently have a number of other physical problems. For example, they are at greater risk than nondisabled persons to have congenital heart defects and to develop visual impairments, upper respiratory infections, and leukemia, all of which reduce their life expectancy well below that of nondisabled persons (Patterson, 1987). Researchers have discovered an interesting link between Down syndrome and Alzheimer's disease, the meaning of which is still being investigated (Allore et al., 1988; Patterson, 1987). The neurons in the brains of individuals with Down syndrome over the age of 35 are characterized by the same abnormalities as those of people with Alzheimer's. In addition, people with Down syndrome are at greater than average risk of developing the behavioral symptoms of Alzheimer's disease. Researchers are coming closer and closer to discovering the gene or genes that cause Down syndrome.

The degree of retardation varies widely, most individuals falling in the moderate range. More children with Down syndrome than was once the case are achieving IQ scores in the mildly retarded range because of intensive preschool programming.

There are basically three types of Down syndrome. In children with the **trisomy 21** type (by far the most common) there is an extra chromosome.* In this

---

*The nucleus of a normal human cell contains 23 pairs of **chromosomes,** making a total of 46 chromosomes altogether. Chromosomes are composed of the essential genetic material—**genes.** Each gene within 22 of the chromosome pairs has a duplicate gene on the "matching" chromosome; the twenty-third pair is sex-linked, and its genes may be identical (XX for females) or different (XY for males).

RENATAL DIAGNOSIS OF BIRTH DEFECTS ➤

Beginning in the mid-1970s, there has been a dramatic increase in the availability of techniques for diagnosing defects in the unborn fetus. Three such methods are **amniocentesis**, **chorionic villus sampling (CVS)**, and **sonography.**

AMNIOCENTESIS

In amniocentesis, the physician inserts a needle through the abdominal wall and into the amniotic sac of the pregnant woman and withdraws about one ounce of amniotic fluid from around the fetus. Fetal cells are separated from the fluid and allowed to grow in a culture medium for two to three weeks. The cells are then analyzed for chromosomal abnormalities. Although a variety of genetic disorders can be detected through amniocentesis, it is most often used to detect Down syndrome. In addition, amniocentesis allows one to analyze the amniotic fluid itself. Such analysis can detect about 90 percent of cases of spina bifida, a condition in which the spinal column fails to close during fetal development. In the fetus with spina bifida, certain proteins leak out of the spinal fluid into the surrounding amniotic sac. The elevation of these proteins enables this defect to be detected (see Chapter 10 for further discussion of spina bifida). Physicians most often perform amniocentesis at 16 to 18 weeks after the woman's last menstrual period.

CHORIONIC VILLUS SAMPLING

In chorionic villus sampling (CVS), the physician inserts a catheter through the vagina and cervix and withdraws about 1/2000 of an ounce of villi, structures which will later become the placenta. Although first results are often available in two or three days, final verification takes two to three weeks. CVS can detect a variety of chromosomal abnormalities. The major advantage of CVS over amniocentesis is that it can be performed much earlier, between the ninth to eleventh week of pregnancy. If the woman then elects to have an abortion, she can have it with less risk. Some physicians are more hesitant to conduct CVS, however, because, being a newer procedure, less is known about it. In addition, although neither amniocentesis nor CVS is risky, the incidence of miscarriage after CVS is higher than it is after amniocentesis.

SONOGRAPHY

In sonography, high-frequency sound waves—ultrasound—are converted into a visual picture of the fetus. This technique can be used to detect some major physical malformations, such as spina bifida.

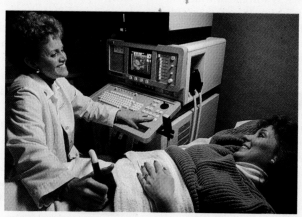

Sonography can be used to detect some major physical malfunctions, such as spina bifida, in the fetus.

KEEPING PRENATAL TESTING IN PERSPECTIVE

There is little doubt that rapid advances in the field of prenatal testing are now allowing people to detect a number of previously unavoidable birth defects. As amazing as this technology is, however, it in no way guarantees a perfect baby. Many disabilities cannot be detected by any available technique. In addition, as Pat Schnatterly, a genetic counselor in the University of Virginia's Department of Pediatrics, states,

Prenatal testing is most appropriate when you know ahead of time what it is you're looking for. Thus, it is offered to couples who have specific known risks. This would include, for example, women 35 years of age and over, who have a higher risk for giving birth to a baby with Down syndrome. It would also include couples (for example, those of Ashkenazi Jewish descent who would be at risk for having a child with Tay-Sachs) whose ethnic backgrounds indicated they were at risk.

SOURCES: From M. L. Batshaw and Y. M. Perret, *Children with Handicaps: A Medical Primer*, 2nd ed. Copyright © 1986. Paul H. Brookes and M. Chitwood, What's Past Is Prologue, *Helix*, 4 (2) 4–7. Copyright © 1986. Reprinted with permission. The interested reader is encouraged to consult these sources for further information.

➤ **mosaicism.** A type of Down syndrome in which some of the cells, owing to faulty development, have an extra chromosome and some do not.

➤ **translocation.** A type of Down syndrome in which the extra chromosome (the result of faulty development) in the twenty-first set breaks off and attaches itself to another of the chromosome pairs.

➤ **Fragile X syndrome.** Condition in which the bottom of the X chromosome in the twenty-third pair of chromosomes is pinched off; can result in a number of physical anomalies as well as mental retardation; occurs more often in males than females; thought to be the most common hereditary cause of mental retardation.

➤ **phenylketonuria (PKU).** A metabolic genetic disorder caused by the inability of the body to convert phenylalanine to tyrosine; an accumulation of phenylalanine results in abnormal brain development.

➤ **Tay-Sachs disease.** An inherited condition that can appear when both mother and father are carriers; results in brain damage and eventual death; it can be detected before birth through amniocentesis.

type, the twenty-first set of chromosomes is a triplet rather than a pair, causing a condition called *trisomy*. The second type, **mosaicism,** results when, because of faulty development, some of the individual's cells have this extra chromosome and others do not. In **translocation,** the third type, all or part of the extra chromosome of the twenty-first pair becomes attached to another of the chromosome pairs.

The likelihood of having a child with Down syndrome depends to a great extent on the age of the mother: More such children are born to women under 20 and, especially, over 40. For example, a woman between the ages of 20 and 30 has a 1 in 1,300 chance of having a Down syndrome baby, a woman between 30 and 34 has a 1 in 600 chance, a woman between 35 and 39 has a 1 in 300 chance, and a woman between 40 and 44 has a 1 in 80 chance (Hansen, 1978). There are tests available whereby Down syndrome and some other birth defects can be diagnosed in the fetus during pregnancy. (See the box on p. 127.) Physicians sometimes recommend such tests for older pregnant women because they are at higher risk of having a baby with Down syndrome.

Researchers are pointing to variables in addition to the age of the mother as possible causative factors in Down syndrome. Some of the factors being cited as potential causes are the age of the father, exposure to radiation, and exposure to some viruses (Patton et al., 1990).

Fragile X syndrome is thought to be the most common hereditary cause of mental retardation (Finucane, 1988). It is associated with the X chromosome in the twenty-third pair of "sex" chromosomes. In males, the twenty-third pair consists of an X and a Y chromosome; in females it consists of two X chromosomes. It is called *Fragile* X syndrome because, in affected individuals, the bottom of the X chromosome is pinched off in some of their blood cells. Fragile X occurs less often in females because they have an extra X chromosome, giving them better "protection" if one of their X chromosomes is damaged. Persons with Fragile X syndrome may have a number of physical features, such as large head; large, flat ears; long, narrow face; prominent forehead; broad nose; prominent, square chin; large testicles; large hands, with non-tapering fingers. In addition, they are more subject to having a heart murmur and repeated ear infections in childhood (Finucane, 1988).

Phenylketonuria (PKU) involves the inability of the body to convert a common dietary substance—phenylalanine—to tyrosine; the accumulation of phenylalanine results in abnormal brain development. Babies can undergo a screening test for PKU in the first few days after birth, and many states require this test be performed before an infant leaves the hospital. Unless a baby with PKU starts a special diet controlling the intake of phenylalanine in infancy and continues it into middle childhood, the child will usually develop severe retardation (Guthrie, 1984). Because some studies have shown that if the diet is stopped at middle childhood a decrease in IQ occurs, many authorities believe the diet should be maintained indefinitely (Batshaw & Perret, 1986). In addition to treating PKU once it has been detected, more and more emphasis is being placed on screening parents to determine if they are possible carriers of the PKU gene. Even though chances are slim (about 1 in 3,600) of two carriers marrying, if this does occur, genetic counseling is highly advised.

Tay-Sachs disease, like PKU, can appear when both mother and father are carriers. It results in progressive brain damage and eventual death. It occurs almost exclusively among Ashkenazi Jews—that is, those of East European extraction. Public health personnel have used genetic screening programs to identify carriers. The disease can also be detected *in utero*.

Brain Damage

Brain damage can result from a host of factors that fall into two general categories—infections and environmental hazards.

Infections. Infections that may lead to mental retardation can occur in the mother-to-be or the infant or young child after birth. Rubella (German measles), syphilis, and herpes simplex in the mother can all cause retardation in the child. Rubella is most dangerous during the first trimester (three months) of pregnancy. The veneral diseases, syphilis and herpes simplex, present a greater risk at later stages of fetal development (Hetherington & Parke, 1986). (Herpes simplex, which shows as cold sores or fever blisters, is not usually classified as a veneral disease unless it affects the genitals.)

Three examples of infections of the child that can affect mental development are meningitis, encephalitis, and pediatric AIDS. Meningitis is an infection of the covering of the brain that may be caused by a variety of bacterial or viral agents. Resulting more often in retardation and usually affecting intelligence more severely is encephalitis, an inflammation of the brain. Pediatric AIDS is the fastest growing infectious cause of mental retardation. In fact, researchers have projected that it may soon become the leading cause of mental retardation and brain damage (Diamond & Cohen, 1987). The majority of children with pediatric AIDS obtained their infection during birth from their mothers, who used intravenous drugs or were sexually active with infected men (Baumeister, Kupstas, & Klindworth, 1990).

Infections, as well as other causative factors, can also result in microcephalus or hydrocephalus. Microcephalus is a condition characterized by a small head with a sloping forehead. It can be caused by infections such as rubella or AIDS (Rubinstein, 1989) or by a genetic disorder. Retardation usually ranges from severe to profound. Hydrocephalus results from an accumulation of cerebrospinal fluid inside or outside the brain. Blockage of the circulation of the fluid, which results in a buildup of excessive pressure on the brain and enlargement of the skull, can occur for a variety of reasons—encephalitis, meningitis, malformation of the spine, or tumors. The degree of retardation depends on how early it is diagnosed and treated. Treatment consists of surgical implacement of a shunt (tube) that drains the excess fluid away from the brain and into a vein behind the ear or in the neck.

Environmental Hazards. Examples of environmental hazards that can result in mental retardation are a blow to the head, poisons, radiation, malnutrition, prematurity or postmaturity, and birth injury. Although we are discussing these potential causal agents in this section, which deals with the causes of more severe forms of retardation, there is considerable evidence that in their milder forms, each of these factors can result in mild retardation.

It should be obvious that a blow to a child's head can result in mental retardation. The obviousness of this connection, in fact, has served as an impetus for many of the mandatory laws pertaining to the use of child restraints in

---

➤ **rubella (German measles).** A serious viral disease, which, if it occurs during the first trimester of pregnancy, is likely to cause a deformity in the fetus.

➤ **syphilis.** A venereal disease that can cause mental subnormality in a child, especially if it is contracted by the mother-to-be during the latter stages of fetal development.

➤ **herpes simplex.** A type of veneral disease that can cause cold sores or fever blisters; if it affects the genitals and is contracted by the mother-to-be in the later stages of fetal development, it can cause mental subnormality in the child.

➤ **meningitis.** A bacterial or viral infection of the linings of the brain or spinal cord.

➤ **encephalitis.** An inflammation of the brain; can affect the child's mental development adversely.

➤ **pediatric AIDS.** Acquired immune deficiency syndrome that occurs in infants or young children; can be contracted by unborn fetuses from the blood of the mother through the placenta or through blood transfusions; an incurable virus that can result in a variety of physical and mental disorders; thought to be the fastest growing infectious cause of mental retardation.

➤ **microcephalus.** A condition causing development of a small head with a sloping forehead; proper development of the brain is prevented, resulting in mental retardation.

➤ **hydrocephalus.** A condition characterized by enlargement of the head because of excessive pressure of the cerebrospinal fluid.

*E*xpectant mothers who consume large amounts of alcohol are at risk of giving birth to infants with fetal alcohol syndrome, a condition characterized by physical and developmental disabilities.

automobiles. Besides the usual accidents that can lead to brain damage, more and more authorities are citing child abuse as a cause of brain damage that results in mental retardation and other disabilities (see Chapter 10).

Poisoning resulting in mental retardation can occur in the expectant mother or in the child. We are now much more aware of the harmful effects of a variety of substances, from obvious toxic agents, such as cocaine and heroin, to more subtle potential "poisons," such as tobacco, alcohol, caffeine, and even food additives. In particular, research has shown that pregnant women who smoke and/or consume alcohol have a greater risk of having babies with behavioral and physical problems. For example, women who are heavy smokers are more likely than nonsmokers to have premature babies (Hetherington & Parke, 1986). And premature babies are at risk for a variety of developmental disabilities.

Researchers have exposed **fetal alcohol syndrome (FAS)** as a significant health problem for expectant mothers who consume large quantities of alcohol and for their unborn children (Hetherington & Parke, 1986; F. R. Schultz, 1984; see also Chapter 10). Occurring in about one-third of the babies of pregnant alcoholic women, children with FAS are characterized by a variety of physical deformities as well as mental retardation.

Although pregnant women who drink moderately may not risk having children with FAS, evidence shows that even their infants will differ behaviorally from those born to women who do not drink during pregnancy. Among expectant mothers who drink moderately, there is evidence that the amount of alcohol they consume is related to their infants' arousal levels and central nervous system functioning (Streissguth, Barr, & Martin, 1983).

Some prescription drugs must also be avoided or used with caution by pregnant women. Research has linked some antibiotic, anticonvulsant, and anticancer medications to fetal malformations (Batshaw & Perret, 1986). Medication delivered to women during labor and delivery has also come under close scrutiny.

It is not always possible, of course, for expectant mothers to avoid using medication during pregnancy and labor. However, more and more authorities are questioning the high rates of drug ingestion by pregnant women; some studies have reported that expectant mothers in America ingest an average of six prescribed drugs and four over-the-counter drugs during their pregnancy. Given the

➢ **fetal alcohol syndrome (FAS).** Abnormalities associated with the mother's drinking alcohol during pregnancy. Defects range from mild to severe.

potential for some of these drugs to be **teratogens**—substances that cause malformations in the fetus—many authorities have expressed caution about their use.

Although its use is now prohibited, infants still become poisoned by eating lead-based paint chips, particularly in slum areas. Lead poisoning varies in its effect on children; high levels can result in death. The federal government now requires that automobile manufacturers produce cars that use only lead-free gasoline to lower the risk of inhaling lead particles from auto exhaust.

We have recognized the hazards of radiation to the unborn fetus for some time. Physicians, for example, are cautious not to expose pregnant women to X-rays unless absolutely necessary. Since the mid- to late-1970s, however, the public has become even more concerned over the potential dangers of radiation from improperly designed or supervised nuclear power plants.

Retardation caused by improper nutrition can occur because the expectant mother is malnourished or because the child, once born, does not have a proper diet (Cravioto & DeLicardie, 1975; Hallahan & Cruickshank, 1973).

Disorders due to an abnormal length of pregnancy—either too short (prematurity) or too long (postmaturity)—can also result in retardation. The latter is not as likely to cause retardation, although it is possible that the fetus will suffer from poor nutrition if it is long overdue (Robinson & Robinson, 1976). Prematurity is sometimes defined by the length of the pregnancy and sometimes by the weight of the infant at birth (5.5 pounds or lower is often used as an index of prematurity). Both premature and small infants are candidates for a variety of physical and behavioral abnormalities, including retardation (Blackman, 1984b). Prematurity itself is associated with a number of factors—poor nutrition, teenage pregnancy, drug abuse, and excessive cigarette smoking.

Brain injury can also occur during delivery if the child is not positioned properly in the uterus. One problem that sometimes occurs because of difficulty during delivery is **anoxia** (complete deprivation of oxygen).

> **teratogens.** Deformity-producing factors that interfere with normal fetal development.

> **anoxia.** Loss of oxygen; can cause brain injury.

ASSESSMENT

Professionals assess two major areas to determine whether persons are mentally retarded: intelligence and adaptive skills. To assess intelligence, the professional administers the test to the person. To assess adaptive skills, a parent or professional who is familiar with the person responds to a survey of different adaptive skills.

Intelligence Tests

There are many types of IQ tests. Because of their accuracy and predictive capabilities, practitioners prefer individually administered tests over group tests. Two of the most common individual IQ tests for children are the Stanford-Binet and the Wechsler Intelligence Scale for Children—Third Edition (WISC-III). Both of these tests are verbal, although the WISC-III is intended to assess both verbal and performance aspects of intelligence. It has a verbal and a performance scale with a number of subtests. The "full-scale IQ," a statistical composite of the verbal and performance IQ measures, is used when a single overall score for a child is desired.

Another relatively common IQ test is the Kaufman Assessment Battery for Children (K-ABC). Some psychologists recommend using the K-ABC with

> ➣ **mental age.** Refers to the IQ test score that specifies the age level at which an individual is functioning.

> ➣ **chronological age.** Refers to how old a person is; used in comparison with mental age to determine the IQ score of an individual.

$$IQ = \frac{MA}{CA} \times 100.$$

African-American students because they believe it is less culturally biased (Kamphaus & Reynolds, 1987).

Although not all IQ tests call for this method of calculation, you can get a rough approximation of a person's IQ by dividing **mental age** (the age level at which a person is functioning) by **chronological age** and multiplying by 100. For example, a ten-year-old student who performs on an IQ test as well as the *average* eight-year-old (and thus has a mental age of eight years) would have an IQ of 80.

Compared to most psychological tests, IQ tests such as the Stanford-Binet, WISC-III, and K-ABC are among the most reliable and valid. By *reliability*, we mean that a person will obtain relatively similar scores if given the test on two separate occasions that are not too close or far apart in time. *Validity* generally answers the question of whether the instrument measures what it is supposed to measure. A good indicator of the validity of an IQ test is the fact that it is generally considered the best single index of how well a student will do in school. It is wise to be wary, however, of placing too much faith in a single score from any IQ test. There are at least four reasons for caution:

1. Even on very reliable tests, an individual's IQ can change from one testing to another, and sometimes the change can be dramatic (McCall, Applebaum, & Hogarty, 1973).
2. All IQ tests are culturally biased to a certain extent. Children from minority groups, largely because of differences in language and experience, are sometimes at a disadvantage in taking such tests.
3. The younger the child, the less validity and reliability the test has. Infant intelligence tests are particularly questionable.
4. IQ tests are not the "be-all and end-all" when it comes to assessing a person's ability to function in society. A superior IQ does not guarantee a successful and happy life, nor does a low IQ doom a person to a miserable existence. Other variables are also important determiners of a person's coping skills in society. That is why, for example, professionals also assess adaptive skills, to which we now turn (see also the box on p. 133).

Adaptive Skills

Many adaptive skills measures are available. Three of the most commonly used are probably the Vineland Adaptive Behavior Scales (Sparrow, Balla, & Cicchetti, 1984), the AAMD Adaptive Behavior Scale-School Edition (Lambert & Windmiller, 1981), and the Adaptive Behavior Inventory for Children (Mercer & Lewis, 1977). The basic format of these instruments requires that a parent, teacher, or other professional answer questions related to the person's ability to perform adaptive skills. The particular skills assessed differ slightly from one measure to another, but they generally cover the adaptive skills stated in the AAMR definition: communication, self-care, home living, social skills, community use, self-direction, health and safety, functional academics, leisure, and work.

PSYCHOLOGICAL AND BEHAVIORAL CHARACTERISTICS

In considering the psychological and behavioral characteristics of persons with mental retardation, we hasten to point out that *individual* persons with mental retardation may not display all of the characteristics. There is great variability in

EEPING TESTS IN PERSPECTIVE ➢

Most professionals agree that tests, such as IQ tests and adaptive behavior instruments, are necessary. They can be helpful in making placement decisions and in evaluating program effectiveness. It is important to keep in mind, however, that they are far from perfect predictors about how a particular individual will function in the real world. The following excerpt from a case study of a woman with mental retardation makes this point nicely:

When I first saw her—clumsy, uncouth, all-of-a-fumble—I saw her merely, or wholly, as a casualty, a broken creature, whose neurological impairments I could pick out and dissect with precision. . . .

The next time I saw her, it was all very different. I didn't have her in a test situation, "evaluating" her in a clinic. I wandered outside, it was a lovely spring day, with a few minutes in hand before the clinic started, and there I saw Rebecca sitting on a bench, gazing at the April foliage quietly, with obvious delight. Her posture had none of the clumsiness which had so impressed me before. Sitting there, in a light dress, her face calm and slightly smiling, she suddenly brought to mind one of Chekov's young women—Irene, Anya, Sonya, Nina—seen against the backdrop of a Chekovian cherry orchard. She could have been any young woman enjoying a beautiful spring day. This was my human, as opposed to my neurological, vision . . . .

Why was she so de-composed before, how could she be so re-composed now? I had the strongest feeling of two wholly different modes of thought, or of organization, or of being. The first schematic—pattern-seeing, problem-solving—this is what had been tested, and where she had been found so defective, so disastrously wanting. But the tests had given no inkling of anything *but* the deficits, anything, so to speak, *beyond* her deficits.

They had given me no hint of her positive powers, her ability to perceive the real world—the world of nature, and perhaps of the imagination—as a coherent, intelligible, poetic whole: her ability to see this, think this, and (when she could) live this; they had given me no intimation of her inner world, which clearly *was* composed and coherent, and approached as something other than a set of problems or tasks. . . .

It was perhaps fortunate that I chanced to see Rebecca in her so-different modes—so damaged and incorrigible in the one, so full of promise and potential in the other—and that she was one of the first patients I saw in our clinic. For what I saw in her, what she showed me, I now saw in them all.

SOURCE: From O. Sacks, *The Man Who Mistook His Wife for a Hat: And Other Clinical Tales*, pp. 170–173. Copyright © 1970, by Oliver Sacks. Reprinted by permission of International Creative Management, Inc.

the behavior of persons who are retarded, and we must consider each person as unique. In this section, we discuss the following characteristics: attention, memory, self-regulation, language development, academic achievement, social development, and motivation.

Attention

The importance of attention for learning is critical. A person must be able to attend to the task at hand before he or she can learn it. For years researchers have posited that we can attribute many of the learning problems of persons with retardation to attention problems (e.g., Brooks & McCauley, 1984; Zeamon & House, 1963). Often attending to the wrong things, many people who are retarded have difficulty allocating their attention properly.

Memory

One of the most consistent research findings is that persons with mental retardation have difficulty remembering information. Many authorities have

*T*he self-concepts of
children with
retardation are
influenced by their relationships
with their peers.

conceptualized these memory problems within a theoretical framework that stresses the depth of processing that an individual must perform to remember certain material (Craik & Lockhart, 1972; Craik & Tulving, 1975). Researchers have found that memory tasks requiring deeper levels of processing—those that are more complicated—are even more likely to show disparities between persons with retardation and their nondisabled peers than are memory tasks requiring shallow levels of processing—those that are less complicated (E. E. Schultz, 1983).

Self-Regulation

➢ **self-regulation.** Referring generally to a person's ability to regulate his or her own behavior, e.g., to employ strategies to help in a problem-solving situation; an area of difficulty for persons who are mentally retarded.

➢ **metacognition.** A person's (1) awareness of what strategies are necessary to perform a task and (2) the ability to use self-regulation strategies.

One of the primary reasons that persons with mental retardation have problems with memory is that they have difficulties in self-regulation (Whitman, 1990). **Self-regulation** is a broad term referring to an individual's ability to regulate his or her own behavior. For example, when given a list of words to remember, most people rehearse the list aloud or to themselves in an attempt to "keep" the words in memory. In other words, they actively regulate their behavior by employing a strategy that will help them remember. People who are retarded are less likely than their nondisabled peers to use self-regulatory strategies such as rehearsal.

Closely connected to the ability to self-regulate is the concept of metacognition. **Metacognition** refers to a person's awareness of what strategies are needed to perform a task and "the ability to use self-regulatory mechanisms. . . such as planning one's moves, evaluating the effectiveness of one's ongoing activities, checking the outcomes of one's efforts. . . " (Baker, 1982, pp. 27–28). Self-regulation is, thus, a component of metacognition. Persons with mental retardation have difficulties in metacognition. (We discuss metacognition again in Chapter 5.)

Researchers are working on developing techniques to improve the metacognitive abilities of individuals with mental retardation (Whitman, 1990). More and more, teachers are emphasizing the teaching of metacognitive skills, including self-regulation, to students who are retarded.

Language Development

Delayed or deviant language development is evident in virtually all persons with mental retardation (Warren & Abbeduto, 1992). Speech problems—for example, articulation errors—also frequently accompany mental retardation. In general, the language of persons who are retarded, especially those who are less severely retarded, follows the same developmental course as that of nonretarded persons, but their language development progresses at a slower rate.

Poor language development and problems in self-regulation are connected (Whitman, 1990). Because many self-regulation strategies are linguistically based, individuals who have poor language skills are at a disadvantage in using self-regulation tactics.

Academic Achievement

Because of the strong relationship between intelligence and achievement, it is not surprising that students who are mentally retarded lag well behind their nonretarded peers in all areas of achievement. They also tend to be underachievers in relation to expectations based on their intellectual level (MacMillan, 1982).

Social Development

Some authorities have argued that retardation should be determined primarily by whether a person is able "to perform certain crucial social roles (e.g., worker, friend, neighbor) more than by the ability to master academic tasks" (Greenspan & Granfield, 1992, p. 443). They believe that what is important, ultimately, is the individual's ability to function in society.

People with mental retardation are candidates for a variety of social problems. They often have problems making friends (Luftig, 1988; Zetlin & Murtaugh, 1988) and have poor self-concepts (see box on p. 138 for a discussion of the importance of friendship) for at least two reasons. First, many do not seem to know how to strike up social interactions with others, and this difference is evident as early as preschool (Kopp, Baker, & Brown, 1992). Second, even when not attempting to interact with others, they exhibit behaviors that may "turn off" their peers. For example, they engage in higher rates of inattention and disruptive behavior than their nonretarded classmates.

Motivation

Many of the problems pertaining to attention, memory, self-regulation, language development, academic achievement, and social development place persons who are retarded at risk to develop problems of motivation. If they have experienced a long history of failure, they can be at risk to develop learned helplessness—the feeling that no matter how hard they try, they will still fail. Believing they have

> ➤ **learned helplessness.** A motivational term referring to a condition wherein a person believes that no matter how hard he or she tries, failure will result.

A Key to Success

BRUCE G. WOJICK

Middle school special education teacher, Niagara Falls (New York) Public Schools; B.S.Ed., Exceptional Education (Mental Retardation) State University College of New York at Buffalo; M.S. Ed., Niagara University

THEONE THOMAS HUG

Middle school home/career skills teacher; B.S.Ed., Home Economics Education, State University College of New York at Buffalo; M.S.Ed., Home Economics Education, State University College of New York at Buffalo.

➤ **Bruce** I see about seventy students daily, a few more boys than girls. They range in age from thirteen to sixteen; forty are white, twenty-eight are black, and two are Native American. Their disabling conditions include mental retardation, learning disabilities, and emotional disturbance. Their reading grade equivalents range from 1.5 to 3.8; math from 3.0 to 5.2.

➤ **Theone** I teach different groups of seventh- and eighth- grade students for ten weeks at a time. I see approximately 100 students daily and have four separate preparations per day just for the regular classes. My students range in age from twelve to sixteen. Classes include basic, average, and merited (gifted) abilities. I usually have one to three mainstreamed students per class who have mental retardation, learning disabilities, or behavioral disorders. For one ten-week

period per year, I teach a self-contained class of no more than twelve students who have mental retardation and behavioral disorders. My classes have about the same ethnic composition as Bruce's. As a teacher with very little background in exceptional education, most of my learning has come from actual experience and trial and error. I find it extremely important that special education teachers give me a background on each student. I'm eager for their suggestions and find good communication and mutual backup and support a necessity for the student's success.

➤ **Bruce** We've decided to describe our work with a student we'll call Cindy. Cindy was fourteen, an eighth-grader who was tall, was overweight, and had poor hygiene. She had poor gross motor coordination but adequate fine motor skills. Her reading and math were lower

than second-grade level. She had very poor social skills and was basically non-verbal. She started the school year with only one close friend, also nonverbal. She had a very limited attention span and a negative self-image, and she tended to daydream a lot. Her large stature, battle with adolescent skin problems, and unkempt hair contributed to the little effort her classmates made to befriend her. It was obvious she came from a poor background, where dress and neatness were unimportant.

➤ **Theone** Cindy was introverted in her speech and social skills. She wouldn't volunteer, and she'd never bring any attention to herself. She always sat alone in the cafeteria. But she was cooperative with adults. She really tried her best to complete assignments. She always tried to contribute when we called on her, even though she wasn't always correct. She was very helpful and seemed to like being in school. Her attendance was good. In terms of learning, she was very slow and required extremely clear and repetitive instructions. Her total lack of self-esteem and extremely quiet nature made it necessary for her teachers to recognize when she needed help, as she wouldn't solicit any.

➤ **Bruce** We immediately recognized that Cindy needed as much positive reinforcement as we could give her. She also needed to fit in with her peers in both our classes. So, as a team we decided that we would praise every effort she made, every response she gave. We made sure that we communicated about her work and efforts so that we could really just about double the positive reinforcement she would get.

➤ **Theone** As a regular classroom teacher I make a special effort with every mainstreamed child to make him or her feel comfortable—an important part of my class. I start out by carefully planning an assignment that I'm almost certain the student can complete successfully, and I give this assignment the first few days the special student is in my class. When Cindy came to my class, I gave the entire class instructions about a project. Then, while they were working, I went around the room and repeated the instructions to several students, spending extra time with Cindy. Once I got her started and she seemed comfortable, I reminded her frequently to keep working and keep up the good effort. Then, after she completed the project, I used hers as an example for the rest of the class of what we were trying to achieve. This encouraged other kids in the class to accept her—they recognized her personal success. Of course, this raised her self-esteem, too. And I told Bruce about her success so that he could give her additional praise. I felt it was really important to build up Cindy's confidence. Once she got some confidence, I felt we'd see improvement in her academic work.

➤ **Bruce** This kind of teamwork doesn't just happen. You see, once a student's schedule is completed by the special education department, I wait for at least a week to let the student get acquainted with each regular classroom teacher. Then I ask the student how he or she feels about each class and each teacher. It's really important that the student feel comfortable with the teacher I choose to team up with. The teachers who seem to show more interest in the students are the ones I always tend to work with on a closer basis. I want lots of positive reinforcement—praise, recognition for good behavior and achievement—to always be available from the regular teacher as well as from me. I believe that from the beginning Cindy felt fairly comfortable in both of our classes because of the positive reinforcement we agreed to give her. She got praise and encouragement from both of us, repeated over and over in and out of our classrooms.

➤ **Theone** Yes, we felt we could work well together as teachers. But we were really frustrated by the lack of concern on the part of Cindy's parents. They did come to parent conferences, but it seemed to us that otherwise they didn't seem to care very much how Cindy was doing.

➤ **Bruce** Any assignments or projects we gave Cindy to take home were always completed in school with our help. We're

not saying that Cindy's parents never helped her, but on the other hand there wasn't much evidence that they did. Cindy was the type of student who needed constant praise and attention to overcome her difficulties. And as far as we could tell the only place she got this was in school. Our working with Cindy during the school day just wasn't enough. Every new week with Cindy was a fresh start on building up her self-esteem—it seemed like it just disappeared every weekend and holiday.

➤ **Theone** Even so, we saw some really fantastic progress in Cindy in school. At the end of eight weeks in my class I gave an assignment to write a paper about a chosen career. Cindy chose babysitting. Students were supposed to find two pages worth of information, set it up in outline form, and eventu-

> *I want lots of positive reinforcement . . . to always be available from the regular teacher as well as from me.*

ally share it with the class as an oral report. This was a really, really big challenge for Cindy. Bruce and I both felt that our work had paid off when Cindy—well prepared, without hesitation—stood in front of the class and presented her report. She even looked at the class while she spoke! She had good information, and even showed pictures of babies and babysitters she had cut and mounted from magazines. Along with the pictures, she shared a photograph of herself as a baby with the rest of the class.

➤ **Bruce** The most rewarding aspect of working together as colleagues is being able to share the simple smiles and accomplishments of the student. Actually to see the results of our efforts is reward in itself. Sharing always makes the reward doubly nice.

➤ **Theone** I agree. And aside from the student-generated personal rewards is the professional reward. We both agree that being able to work with a colleague who is flexible, interested, and willing to communicate new ideas makes the work atmosphere more productive and enjoyable. Being able to work with a colleague who takes the time to listen, make suggestions, and honestly evaluate joint efforts promotes personal gratification through student successes. After years of teaching, this kind of cooperative experience renews your eagerness to be more effective.

➤ **Bruce** Right. But it isn't easy to make this happen. Finding time during the school day for teachers to get together is next to impossible The time the special student spends with the regular teacher is often the only break the special teacher has during the day. Theone and I agree that this problem of time or scheduling is the greatest barrier to working together.

➤ **Theone** As a regular classroom teacher, I find I am often forgotten when it comes to giving me information about a mainstreamed student. Unfortunately, in the past the lack of communication has set up situations in which I didn't even know that students were being mainstreamed until several weeks after they came into my class! The way a special education teacher can help me most is to take the time to identify and give me a quick background on each student he or she is mainstreaming into my class.

➤ **Bruce** I believe that it is my responsibility as the special education teacher to inform each receiving teacher of the student's potential, capabilities, idiosyncrasies, and so on. It's also my responsibility to acquaint myself with the mainstreamed class so that I can more realistically prepare an intelligent and rational IEP for the student.

➤ **Theone** Sometimes there is an unfortunate tendency for the special education teacher to claim "sole ownership" of students. This can impair effective, cooperative working relationships and build impenetrable barriers.

HE IMPORTANCE OF FRIENDSHIP ➤

Professionals often overlook the fundamental importance of friendship. The following extract highlights the critical role friendship can play in the lives of people who are mentally retarded.

A sense of belonging, of feeling accepted and of having personal worth are qualities that friendship brings to a person. Friendship creates an alliance and a sense of security. It is a vital human connection.

People who are mentally retarded want and need friendship like everyone else. Yet they typically have few opportunities to form relationships or to develop the skills necessary to interact socially with others. Their exposure to peers may be limited because they live and work in sheltered or isolated environments. They usually lack a history of socializing events like school clubs, parties, or sleepovers that help to develop or refine personal skills. They may not know how to give of themselves to other people and may be stuck in an egocentric perspective. Persons who are retarded may also respond inappropriately in social situations. Many people shun adults with retardation who freely hug or kiss strangers when greeting them . . . .

Because of their few contacts and opportunities, persons with retardation may attempt to befriend strangers or unwitting individuals. Many attempt to become social acquaintances with their professional contacts. In their effort to maintain the contacts and relationships they have developed, some individuals will overcompensate: calling their friend too many times, talking too long on the phone, demanding attention, and not being able to let up . . . .

Friends can play a vital role in the adjustment to community living of adults who are retarded by providing the emotional support and guidance through the exigencies of daily life. Certain organizations have begun to address the need for friendship by initiating social opportunities . . . [There are] social club[s] for adults with retardation in which members plan their own parties and projects. Some programs offer supervised dating; others establish one-to-one relationships between volunteers and clients for the purpose of aiding adjustment. (Patton, Payne, & Beirne-Smith, 1990)

With the increase in mainstreaming, many hope the problems that numerous persons with mental retardation have in obtaining and holding friendships will decrease. In the future, it will be interesting to see to what degree professionals will organize social clubs exclusively for persons with mental retardation versus having them socialize with nondisabled persons.

SOURCE: Reprinted with the permission of Merrill, an imprint of Macmillan Publishing Company from *Mental Retardation,* Third edition by James R.. Patton, Mary Beirne-Smith and James S. Payne. Copyright © 1990 by Merrill Publishing Company. (pp. 408–409)

little control over what happens to them and that they are primarily controlled by other people and events, some persons with retardation have a tendency to give up easily when faced with challenging tasks.

Professionals recognize the need to provide people with mental retardation with as much success as possible. (See, for example, the Collaboration Box on pp. 136–137, in which two teachers, Bruce Wojick and Theone Hug, work hard at making sure that the student, Cindy, achieves success.) In addition, they recognize that a good educational or vocational program for persons with mental retardation needs to contain a component focused on motivational problems.

EDUCATIONAL CONSIDERATIONS

Although there is some overlap, in general the focus of educational programs varies according to the degree of the students' retardation, or how much they require support services. For example, the lesser the degree of retardation, the more the teacher emphasizes academic skills, and the greater the degree of retardation, the more stress there is on self-help, community living, and vocational skills. You need to keep in mind, however, that this distinction is largely a matter

Issues in Special Education   Confronting the "NIMBY" Syndrome

CNN

*M*any view the trends toward deinstitutionalization of individuals with mental retardation as a positive step. After all, those with the potential capability to live independently should be allowed and encouraged to do so. The group home, or community residential facility (CRF), offers individuals with levels of retardation from mild to severe the opportunity to learn independent living skills in a non-institutional setting. It also provides a flexibility in living arrangements, or perhaps, something more akin to a "home" than any place called an "institution" possibly could.

The Lubin Center in Brooklyn provides 24 apartments to adults who are retarded living on their own. It is one of a small but growing number of dwellings in which the activities of the residents are unmonitored. All of the residents work and pay a percentage of their incomes for rent. Many cook, clean, care for themselves and handle their personal affairs as well as anyone else might.

While such ventures would be lauded by most in theory, when it comes to finding a "home" for group homes, individuals are often less welcoming. The "not-in-my-backyard" syndrome rears its head when residents are presented with the idea of sharing their neighborhoods with "the retarded."

Enlightened people who in theory feel compassion for the "developmentally delayed," at neighborhood site hearings express their fears of "imbeciles, maniacs, and perverts," not to mention plummeting property values.

- Imagine what your own reaction, or that of your parents, might be to the idea of a group home for individuals with retardation in your neighborhood.
- Describe efforts that could be made to overcome negative attitudes that might be held by those living in proximity to a group home.

SOURCE: From Neither Morons Nor Imbeciles Nor Idiots, by Sallie Tisdale, *Harper's,* June, 1990, pp. 47–56.

of emphasis; in practice, all students who are retarded, no matter the severity level, need academic, self-help, community living, and vocational skills.

We now discuss some of the major features of educational programs for students with mental retardation. We focus on the elementary school level here; we discuss preschool and secondary programming in later sections. Although the lines are sometimes blurred, we have divided our coverage into programming for students with mild retardation, or those requiring less intensive support, and students with more severe retardation, or those requiring more intensive support.

Students with Mild Retardation, or Those Requiring Less Intensive Support

Early elementary education is heavily oriented toward providing children who are retarded with **readiness skills,** abilities that are prerequisites for later learning. They include such things as the ability to

1. Sit still and attend to the teacher
2. Discriminate auditory and visual stimuli
3. Follow directions
4. Develop language

> **readiness skills.** Skills deemed necessary before academics can be learned (e. g. , attending skills, the ability to follow directions, knowledge of letter names).

5. Increase gross- and fine-motor coordination (e.g., hold a pencil or cut with a pair of scissors)
6. Develop self-help skills (e.g., tie shoes, button and unbutton, zip and unzip, use the toilet)
7. Interact with peers in a group situation

The teacher provides instruction in language and concept development. In addition, the teacher needs to help these children in the rudiments of socialization. Programs are available for training socially adaptive behaviors. An example is ACCEPTS (A Curriculum for Children's Effective Peer and Teacher Skills) (Walker et al., 1983), a tightly structured and sequenced set of activities designed to teach children to get along with their peers.

In the later elementary years, emphasis is greater on academics, usually on what are known as functional academics. Whereas the nonretarded child is taught academics, such as reading, in order to learn other academic content, such as history, the child with mental retardation is often taught reading in order to learn to function independently. In **functional academics,** the child learns academics in order to do such things as read a newspaper, read the telephone book, read labels on goods at the store, make change, and fill out job applications.

Although emphasized much more in high school, some children with mild retardation are taught the rudiments of community and vocational living skills in later elementary school (Hasazi & Clark, 1988). Many professionals believe that, because some students who are retarded take a relatively long time to learn particular skills, it is best to start acquainting them with these skills as early as elementary school.

➤ **functional academics.** Practical skills rather than academic learning.

Students with More Severe Retardation, Or Those Requiring More Intensive Support

Most authorities agree that the following features should characterize educational programs for students who are more severely retarded:

1. Age-appropriate curriculum and materials
2. Functional activities
3. Community-based instruction
4. Integrated therapy
5. Interaction with nondisabled students
6. Family involvement

Age-Appropriate Curriculum and Materials

The tendency in the past was to "baby" even older persons with severe retardation because of their intellectual limitations. Authorities now agree that this is not only demeaning but also educationally harmful (Bates, Renzaglia, & Wehman, 1981). Using infantile materials works against the goal of fostering as much independent behavior as possible.

Functional Activities

Because so much of educational programming for students with severe retardation is focused on preparing them to live as independently as possible, activities need to be practical (Wehman, Moon, Everson, Wood, & Barcus, 1988). Learning to dress oneself by practicing on a doll, for example, is not as effective as practice with one's own clothes. Some students with severe retardation can learn some academic skills. Because teaching them basic reading and math is very time-consuming, it is important to teach only what they will need and can learn (Snell, 1988).

Community-Based Instruction

In keeping with the notion of functional skills, educational programming needs to take place in the community as much as possible. Because many of the skills they learn are for use in settings outside the classroom, such as on public transportation or in the grocery store, instruction in such activities has proved more effective when done in those settings (Sailor et al., 1986). The teacher may want to use simulated experiences in the classroom, by creating a "mini-grocery store" with a couple of aisles of products and a cash register, for example, to prepare students before they go to a real store. But such simulations by themselves are not enough. Students need the experience of going into those settings in which they will need to use the skills they are learning.

Integrated Therapy

Many persons with severe retardation have multiple disabilities, necessitating the services of a variety of professionals, such as speech, physical, and occupational therapists. In keeping with the notion of functional activities, many authorities believe it better that these professionals integrate what they do with students into the overall educational program rather than meet with them alone in a therapy room. For example, they point out that it is better to teach students how to walk up and down the actual stairs in the school they attend than to use the specially made stairs that are traditionally placed in therapy rooms for this purpose (Snell, 1988).

Interaction with Nondisabled students

Professionals agree that students who are severely retarded and their nondisabled peers benefit from interaction. As we noted in Chapter 2, however, they do not always agree about how or how much interaction there should be. Some believe it is best to include students with severe retardation in regular classes alongside their nondisabled peers for the entire school day. Others believe the interaction should be on a more limited basis. For example, one method some schools use involves having nondisabled students act as tutors or classroom helpers in classes for students with severe retardation.

Family Involvement

As discussed in Chapter 12, family involvement is important for the success of educational programming for students with disabilities of all types and severity levels. Family involvement is particularly important for students who are severely retarded because many of the skills they are taught will be used in their homes (Bates, Renzaglia, & Wehman, 1981). The involvement can range from simply informing parents about the progress of their children to having parents act as classroom aides.

Appropriate vocational instruction for persons with mental retardation should take place in community settings.

➢ **applied behavior analysis.** The application and evaluation of principles of learning theory applied to teaching situations; used with all types of students with disabilities, but particularly appropriate for persons with severe and profound disabilities. It consists of six steps: identifying overall goals, accumulating further information through baseline measurement, specifying learning objectives, implementing the intervention, monitoring student performance, and evaluating the intervention.

➢ **baseline.** Used to assess the effects of an intervention. The therapist or teacher measures the client's or student's skill or behavior before instruction.

Using Applied Behavior Analysis to Teach Students with Mental Retardation

Although teachers use applied behavior analysis with all types of students with disabilities, it is particularly applicable with students who are mentally retarded, especially those with more severe learning problems. **Applied behavior analysis** is the application and evaluation of principles of learning theory in teaching situations. According to Wolery, Bailey, and Sugai (1988) it consists of six steps (see Table 4–2). First, the teacher identifies the overall goal. This usually consists of a skill area the student needs more work in or an inappropriate behavior that he or she needs to decrease. Second, further information is obtained on the identified skill area or behavior by taking a baseline measurement. The **baseline** measurement tells at what level the student is currently functioning; the teacher can later compare the student's performance after instruction with the original baseline performance. Third, the teacher decides on a specific learning objective; that is, he or she breaks down the overall goal into specific skills the child is to learn. Fourth, the teacher implements an intervention designed to increase needed skills or decrease inappropriate behavior, for example, a drill and practice routine for math problems or a reward system for good behavior. Fifth, the child's progress is monitored by measuring performance frequently, usually daily. Sixth, the teacher evaluates the effects of the intervention, usually by charting the student's performance during intervention and comparing it with the baseline performance. Based on this evaluation, the teacher decides whether to continue, modify, or end the intervention.

Table 4-2 ➤ Applied Behavior Analysis Teaching Model

STEP	PROCEDURES	EXAMPLE 1	EXAMPLE 2
1	Identify overall goals by using broad problem statements.	Laura is behind in her math skills.	Lorenzo has trouble staying in his chair.
2	Gather specific information about the problem.	Laura can add single-digit problems with sums to 10, but cannot carry.	Lorenzo gets out of his seat an average of 15 times per hour.
3	Specify learning objectives.	Laura will add numerals with sums to 30, at a rate of at least 5 correct solutions per minute.	Lorenzo will stay in his seat for at least 10 minutes before getting up.
4	Plan and implement an intervention program.	Drill and practice first on sums to 20, no carrying required; then teacher instruction and modeling for carrying procedure. Bonus free choice during recess for 90% correct or better on daily work sheets.	Lorenzo loses 5 minutes of recess each time he gets out of his seat without permission.
5	Monitor student performance.	Teacher keeps daily record of accuracy on worksheets. Every Friday teacher conducts a 1-minute timing to determine rate of performance.	Teacher counts Lorenzo's out-of-seat behavior during routinely selected periods, for a total of 20 minutes of observation per day.
6	Evaluate student performance.	Teacher charts accuracy and speed data weekly and uses information to decide whether or not a change is necessary.	Teacher keeps a daily chart of out-of-seat behavior. If Lorenzo goes 3 days without any improvement, she makes a change in consequences.

SOURCE: From M. Wolery, D. B. Bailey, & G. M. Sugai, Effective teaching: Principles and procedures of applied behavior analysis with exceptional students. p. 24. Copyright © 1988 by Allyn & Bacon, Inc. Reprinted with permission.

Service Delivery Models

Administrative placements for students with mental retardation range from regular classes to residential facilities. Although special classes for these students tend to be the norm, more and more students with retardation are being placed in more integrated settings. The degree of integration tends to be determined by the level of severity, with students who are less severely retarded being the most integrated. However, as we discussed in Chapter 2, some professionals believe that the degree of severity is relatively unimportant in decisions regarding placement. Some believe all students with retardation should be educated in the regular classroom and that schools should provide the necessary support services (e.g., a special aide or special education teacher) in the class.

It is too early to tell how successful the movement to place all students with retardation in regular classes will be. But the prevailing philosophy dictates that students with retardation should enjoy more integration with nondisabled students than is often the case. Virtually all special educators agree that placement in a self-contained classes with *no* opportunity for interaction with nondisabled students is inappropriate.

Although large residential facilities for persons with mental retardation are still in existence, they tend now to house a much higher percentage of residents who are more severely retarded and who have multiple disabilities than they once did (Cunningham & Mueller, 1991). As we discussed in Chapter 2, there is a distinct trend toward smaller, community-based facilities, referred to as community residential facilities. The **community residential facility (CRF)**, or group home, accommodates small groups (three to ten people) in houses under the direction of "house parents." The level of retardation in CRFs ranges from mild to severe. CRFs have been established for children, adolescents, and adults, with each home focused on a specific age range. Placement can be permanent or, with higher functioning individuals, it can serve as a temporary arrangement to prepare the person for independent living. In either case, the purpose of the CRF is to teach independent living skills in a more normal setting than a large institution offers.

➤ **community residential facility (CRF).** A place, usually a group home, in an urban or residential neighborhood where from about three to ten adults with retardation live under supervision.

EARLY INTERVENTION

We can categorize preschool programs for children with mental retardation as those whose purpose is to prevent retardation and those designed to further the development of children already identified as retarded. In general, the former address children who are at risk for mild retardation and the latter are for children who are more severely retarded.

Early Childhood Programs Designed for Prevention

The 1960s witnessed the birth of infant and preschool programs for at-risk children and their families. Since the late 1970s, when many of the young children placed in these programs were reaching their teenage years, we have been able to assess the effects of some of these programs. In 1984, for example, a follow-up study was done on the Perry Preschool Project (Berrueta-Clement, Schweinhart, Barnett, Epstein, & Weikart, 1984). Begun in the early 1960s, the Perry Preschool Project was designed to answer the question, "Can high-quality early childhood education help improve the lives of low-income children and their families and the quality of life of the community as a whole?" A sample of 123 three- and four-year-old African-American children, from impoverished backgrounds and having IQs between 60 and 90, was randomly assigned either to an experimental group that received two years of a cognitively oriented curriculum or to a control group that received no preschool program. When these students were studied again at 19 years of age, a number of differences favored those who had received the preschool program over those who had not:

- They scored significantly higher on a test designed to measure skills needed for educational and economic success.
- They were more likely to complete high school and almost twice as likely to attend college or receive other postsecondary training (38 versus 21 percent).
- They were less likely to have been classified as disabled, especially mentally retarded (15 versus 35 percent).

- They were more likely to be employed (50 versus 32 percent).
- They had a median annual income three times higher.
- They were more likely to report high levels of job satisfaction (42 versus 26 percent).
- They had a lower teenage pregnancy rate.
- They were less likely to be receiving welfare (19 versus 32 percent).

One of the best-known infant stimulation programs among those started more recently is the Abecedarian Project (Ramey & Campbell, 1987). Potential participants were identified before birth by selecting a pool of pregnant women living in poverty. For example, the typical child in this study came from a home headed by a single 20-year-old black woman who had less than a high school education and no earned income. After birth, half of the identified infants were randomly assigned to a day-care program and half were not. The program provided them with experiences to promote perceptual-motor, intellectual, language, and social development. The families were also given a number of social and medical services.

Once the children started kindergarten, a home/school resource teacher provided such things as tutoring, consultation with the regular classroom teacher, and consultation with the parents on the use of a set of home activities. Results reported through the end of first grade indicated an improvement in the IQ and achievement test scores compared with the group not receiving the program.

Project CARE, an offshoot of the Abecedarian Project, added a family component to the preschool program (Wasik, Ramey, Bryant, & Sparling, 1990). Among other things, the family component focused on helping parents foster the cognitive and social development of their children and on facilitating their contact with public agencies. Results reported through 54 months of age indicate the positive effects of this program on cognitive development.

Early Childhood Programs Designed to Further the Development of Children Who are Mentally Retarded

Unlike preschool programs for at-risk children, in which the goal is to prevent retardation from developing, programs for infants and preschoolers who are already identified as retarded are designed to help them achieve as high a cognitive level as possible. These programs place a great deal of emphasis on language and conceptual development. Because these children often have multiple disabilities, other professionals—for example, speech therapists and physical therapists—are frequently involved. Also, many of the better programs include opportunities for parent involvement. Parents can reinforce, through practice with their children, some of the skills that teachers are working on. For example, parents of infants with physical disabilities, such as cerebral palsy, can learn from physical therapists the appropriate ways of handling their children to further their physical development, and from speech therapists they can learn appropriate feeding techniques.

TRANSITION

Transition programming for individuals with mental retardation involves two related areas—community adjustment and employment. Most authorities agree

*P*rofessionals and students
recognize the importance of
transition programming,
preparing students to move from high
school to the workforce.

that although the degree of emphasis on transition programming should be greater for older than for younger students, such programming should begin in the elementary years. Table 4–3 depicts some examples of curriculum activities across the school years pertaining to domestic, community living, leisure, and vocational skills.

Community Adjustment

For persons with mental retardation to adjust to living in the community, they need to acquire a number of skills, many of which are in the area of self-help. Researchers have found, for example, that successful living in the community depends on such things as the ability to manage money, prepare meals, maintain a clean house, and keep one's clothing and oneself groomed (Schalock & Harper, 1978; Schalock, Harper, & Carver, 1981). In general, research has shown that attempts to train community survival skills can be successful, especially when the training occurs within the actual setting in which the individuals are to live.

One of the keys to being able to live in the community is ensuring that the citizenry is prepared to accept persons with retardation. Even those individuals who are able to live independently (i.e., not in a community residential facility) may require some special accommodations. Although not many data are available, one survey of landlords renting to individuals with mental retardation indicates that a substantial number of landlords do have some problems (Salend & Giek, 1988). Examples of these problems are independent living difficulties, such as failing in the upkeep of the property and overdependence on the landlord, and deviant behavior, such as playing the television too loudly. Fortunately,

look at examples

Table 4-3 ➢ Examples of Curriculum Activities Across the School Years for Domestic, Community Living, Leisure, and Vocational Skills

SKILL AREA

DOMESTIC	COMMUNITY	LEISURE	VOCATIONAL
Elementary School Student: Tim			
Picking up toys Washing dishes Making bed Dressing Grooming Eating skills Toileting skills Sorting clothes Vacuuming	Eating meals in a restaurant Using restroom in a local restaurant Putting trash into container Choosing correct change to ride city bus Giving the clerk money for an item he wants to purchase	Climbing on swing set Playing board games Playing tag with neighbors Tumbling activities Running Playing kickball	Picking up plate, silverware, and glass after a meal Returning toys to appropriate storage space Cleaning the room at the end of the day Working on a task for a designated period (15-20 minutes)
Junior High School Student: Mary			
Washing clothes Cooking a simple hot meal (soup, salad, and sandwich) Keeping bedroom clean Making snacks Mowing lawn Raking leaves Making a grocery list Purchasing items from a list Vacuuming and dusting living room	Crossing streets safely Purchasing an item from a department store Purchasing a meal at a restaurant Using local transportation system to get to and from recreational facilities Participating in local scout troop Going to neighbor's house for lunch on Saturday	Playing volleyball Taking aerobic classes Playing checkers with a friend Playing miniature golf Cycling Attending high school or local college basketball games Playing softball Swimming	Waxing floors Cleaning windows Filling lawn mower with gas Hanging and bagging clothes Bussing tables Working for 1-2 hours Operating machinery (such as dishwasher, buffer, etc.) Cleaning sinks, bathtubs, and fixtures Following a job sequence
High School Student: Sandy			
Cleaning all rooms in place of residence Developing a weekly budget Cooking meals Operating thermostat to regulate heat or air conditioning Doing yard maintenance Maintaining personal needs Caring for and maintaining clothing	Utilizing bus system to move about the community Depositing checks into bank account Using community department stores Using community grocery stores Using community health facilities (physician, pharmacist)	Jogging Archery Boating Watching college basketball Video games Card games (UNO) Athletic club swimming class Gardening Going on a vacation trip	Performing required janitorial duties at J.C. Penny Performing housekeeping duties at Days Inn Performing groundskeeping duties at VCU campus Performing food service at K St. Cafeteria Performing laundry duties at Moon's Laundromat Performing photography at Virginia National Bank Headquarters

SOURCE: Adapted from P. Wehman, M.S. Moon, J.M. Everson, W. Wood, & J.M. Barcus, *Transition from School to Work: New Challenges for Youth with Severe Disabilities* (Baltimore: Paul H. Brookes, 1988), pp. 140-142. Reprinted with permission.

In Their Own Words   CHRIS BURKE

When Chris Burke was born in 1965, doctors advised his parents to put him in an institution. Chris had been diagnosed with Down syndrome. Instead, Frank and Marian Burke decided to bring their new son home and make him a part of their family.

Today, Chris is the star of the hit television series "Life Goes On." He credits his family for providing the love and support that taught him to believe he could do whatever he wanted. In the following paragraphs from his autobiography, *A Special Kind of Hero,* coauthored with JoBeth McDaniel, he discusses his feelings about having Down syndrome as well as his early career aspirations.

Some people treat me differently because I have Down syndrome, but I just want to be treated like anyone else. And some people think that just because I have Down syndrome, I'm stupid or handicapped. I don't feel that way. My Down syndrome never kept me from doing anything I wanted to do. Everybody is born in different ways. I just happened to be born with an extra chromo-some, but it doesn't make me feel any different. I don't like it when people say I am a victim, or when they say I suffer from it. It's not a disease. I don't like it when they show the pictures of the little chromosomes, because it's personal to me. But I think it's great to have an extra chromosome and I like talking about it. It doesn't make me feel "down." Actually, I call it "Up syndrome" because I am happy and excited about my life. . . .

I have wanted to be an actor ever since I was a little munchkin, when I was five years old. That's when I got on the stage at school and everyone clapped. It was a lot of fun. It made me feel good and excited. . . .

I liked to watch television and imagine that I was a character on the shows. When I told people what I wanted to do, they didn't think it would happen. But I always thought it could. I believed in my dreams.

SOURCE: Chris Burke & JoBeth McDaniel, *A Special Kind of Hero,* (New York: Doubleday, 1991) pp.V, 247.

most of these kinds of problems could be avoided by providing landlords with a modest degree of information and assistance before they rent to a tenant who is retarded.

Employment

Traditionally, employment figures for adults with mental retardation have been appalling (Chadsey-Rusch, Rusch, & O'Reilly, 1991; Hasazi, Collins, & Cobb, 1988; Hasazi et al., 1985; Wehman et al., 1988). One statewide survey, for example, found that of students with mental retardation who had graduated from high school, only 41 percent were employed full or part time in the competitive job market (Hasazi et al., 1985).

Even though employment statistics for workers who are retarded have been pessimistic, most professionals working in this area are optimistic about the potential for providing training programs that will lead to meaningful employment for adults with retardation. Research indicates that, with appropriate training, persons with retardation can hold down jobs with a good deal of success measured by such things as attendance, employer satisfaction, and length of employment (Brown et al., 1986; Martin, Rusch, Tines, Brulle, & White, 1985; Rusch, Martin, & White, 1985; Stodden & Browder, 1986).

When persons with retardation do fail on the job, they may do so because they have problems related to job responsibility, task production competence, and/or social competence (Salzberg, Lignugaris/Kraft, & McCuller, 1988). Table 4–4 illustrates behaviors commonly associated with each of these areas. Contrary to popular opinion, considerable evidence suggests that job responsibility and social competence are more important than task production competence as reasons for job termination (Heal, Gonzalez, Rusch, Copher, & DeStefano, 1990; Salzberg et al., 1988).

A variety of vocational training and employment approaches for individuals with mental retardation are available. Most of these are subsumed under two very different kinds of arrangements—the sheltered workshop or nonsheltered work environment, or competitive employment.

Sheltered Workshops

The traditional job-training environment for adults with mental retardation, especially those classified as more severely retarded, has been the sheltered workshop. A **sheltered workshop** is a structured environment where a person receives training and works with other workers with disabilities on jobs requiring relatively low skills. This can be either a permanent placement or a transitional placement before a person obtains a job in the competitive job market.

Although sheltered workshops remain a relatively popular placement, more and more authorities are voicing dissatisfaction with them (Wehman, Moon, Everson, Wood, & Barcus, 1988). Among the criticisms are the following:

1. Clients make only between one and five dollars per day. Sheltered workshops rarely turn a profit. Usually managed by personnel with limited business management expertise, they rely heavily on charitable contributions.
2. There is no integration with nondisabled workers. This restricted setting makes it difficult to prepare workers who are mentally retarded for working side by side with nondisabled workers in the competitive work force.
3. They offer only limited job-training experiences. A good workshop should provide opportunities to learn a variety of new skills. All too often, however, the work is repetitive and does not make use of current industrial technology.

Competitive Employment

In contrast to sheltered employment, **competitive employment** is a job that provides at least the minimum wage in an integrated work setting in which most of the workers are not disabled. Although the ultimate goal for some adults with mental retardation may be competitive employment, many will need supported employment for a period of time or even permanently. In **supported competitive employment**, the person with retardation has a competitive employment position but receives ongoing assistance, often from a job coach. The major responsibilities of the **job coach**:

> may include job identification and development, vocational assessment and instruction, transportation planning, and interactions with parents, employers, Social Security, and other related service agencies. Job coaches provide on-site training to clients which addresses not only actual job tasks, but also social skill development and independent living skills. They monitor employee progress through performance observation and communication with employers and coworkers. (Berkell, 1988, pp. 164–165)

One potential problem with the supported competitive employment model is that the client can become too dependent on the support provided by the job coach (Lagomarcino, Hughes, & Rusch, 1989). If they are to move into a

> **sheltered workshop.** A facility that provides a structured environment for persons with disabilities in which they can learn skills; can be either a transitional placement or a permanent arrangement.

> **competitive employment.** A workplace that provides employment at at least minimum wage and one in which most workers are nondisabled.

> **supported competitive employment.** A workplace where adults who are disabled or retarded earn at least a minimum wage and receive ongoing assistance from a specialist or job coach, and where the majority of workers are nondisabled.

> **job coach.** A person who assists adult workers with retardation or disabilities, providing vocational assessment, instruction, overall planning and interaction assistance with employers, family, and related government and service agencies.

> # 𝒯*able 4-4* ➤ Summary of Behaviors Commonly Related to Involuntary Termination

SOCIAL-VOCATIONAL COMPETENCE

Job Responsibility	Task Production Competence	Task-related Social Competence	Personal-Social Competence
1. Poor attendance	1. Low rate of work	1. Not following and/or clarifying instructions	1. Bizarre, emotional, and aggressive behavior
2. Poor punctuality	2. Low quality of work	2. Not responding appropriately to criticism	2. Inappropriate conversation
3. Not attending consistently to job tasks	3. Lack of independent performance	3. Not interacting appropriately with co-workers and supervisors	3. Loud, vulgar, or sexually explicit behavior
4. Not calling in when late or absent	4. Inability to learn new tasks	4. Not requesting assistance when needed	4. Inappropriate dress, grooming, or eating
5. Stealing	5. Inability to perform diversity of tasks	5. Not requesting information when needed	5. Dirty appearance or excessive body odor
6. Lack of initiative		6. Not cooperating with co-workers	6. Absence of or excessive verbalizing
7. Lack of motivation			7. Emotional response to teasing or job pressure
8. Walking off the job			

SOURCE: From C.L. Salzberg, B. Lignugaris/Kraft, & G.L. McCuller, *Research in Developmental Disabilities*, 9 (1988), 168. Reprinted with permission.

➤ **picture cues.** Illustrations or photographs that provide a visual cue for completing a task; often used with workers who are mentally retarded to help them perform more independently on the job.

➤ **self-instruction.** A type of cognitive behavior modification technique that requires individuals to talk aloud and then to themselves as they solve problems.

➤ **self-monitoring.** A type of cognitive behavior modification technique that requires individuals to keep track of their own behavior.

➤ **self-reinforcement.** A type of behavior technique in which individuals reward themselves for job accomplishment and performance.

competitive employment setting, workers must learn to function independently, and even if they stay in a supported situation, it is important that they develop as much independence as possible.

To combat overdependence on the job coach, authorities have recommended that professionals teach employees who are retarded to use self-management techniques (Lagomarcino, Hughes, & Rusch, 1989; Rusch & Hughes, 1988; Rusch, Martin, & White, 1985; Wheeler, Bates, Marshall, & Miller, 1988). Rusch and his colleagues have noted that four self-management procedures are particularly effective in helping persons with mental retardation become more independent on the job: (1) picture cues, (2) self-instruction, (3) self-monitoring, and (4) self-reinforcement.

Picture cues provide a visual prompt to workers to help them perform work tasks. For example, on an assembly task the worker might prearrange the various parts on corresponding pictures in the order in which they are to be assembled.

Self-instruction involves workers' saying aloud what they are about to do. For example, the job coach might teach the worker to say aloud each major step in performing a task before he or she does it.

Self-monitoring involves workers' observing their own performance and then recording it. For example, they might observe and record the number of times they are late for work per week.

Self-reinforcement entails workers' rewarding themselves for appropriate performance. For example, a person might reward himself or herself with a night at the movies for having gone two consecutive weeks without being late for work.

Teachers have also successfully used self-instruction, self-monitoring, and self-reinforcement in classroom instruction with a variety of exceptional children. In particular, teachers have used them with children who are learning disabled (see Chapter 5).

Importance of the Family

More and more authorities are pointing to the family as a critical factor in whether persons with mental retardation will be successful in community adjustment and employment (Blacher & Baker, 1992). The majority of adults with mental retardation live with their families (Krauss, Seltzer, & Goodman, 1992). For those who live away from home, the family can still be a significant source of support for living in the community and finding and holding a job.

Prospects for the Future

Although current employment figures and living arrangements for adults with mental retardation may look bleak, there is reason to be optimistic about the future. Surveys indicate that although the sheltered workshop remains the most common work environment for adults who are retarded, placement in competitive employment is increasing (Schalock, McGaughey, & Kiernan, 1989). Evidence also shows that employers are taking a more favorable attitude toward hiring workers who are mentally retarded (Levy, Jessop, Rimmerman, & Levy, 1992). With the development of innovative transition programs, many persons with mental retardation are achieving levels of independence in community living and employment that were never thought possible.

SUGGESTIONS FOR TEACHING ➤ E. Jane Nowacek

Students with Mental Retardation in General Education Classrooms

WHAT TO LOOK FOR IN SCHOOL

Although children with more severe mental retardation are identified before entering school, students who are mildly retarded typically are identified during the first years of school. A primary indicator of mild mental retardation is the delayed development of motor, language, social and independent skills. Students with mild retardation are able to learn these skills, but their rate of learning is slow, and as a result, their level of development resembles that of younger children (Lewis & Doorlag, 1991). In addition, many students with mild mental retardation have short-term memory problems and do not know how to use learning strategies that nondisabled students seem to use spontaneously. Given these problems, it is not surprising that students with mild retardation have difficulty learning in all academic areas.

HOW TO GATHER INFORMATION

If you think one of your students may be mentally retarded, collect several examples of his or her work in arithmetic, reading, and writing. Share these samples—along with your observations of the student's motor, language, and social behaviors—with the special educator, counselor, or administrator in your building who manages the child-study committee. This committee considers persistent problems individual students experience in school and suggests modifications that may promote their learning and/or appropriate school behavior. If these modifications do not result in improvement, the committee may recommend that the student receive a full educational, medical, sociological, and psychological evaluation for special education. Student work samples, your records, and your observations will provide necessary information to the child-study committee.

Teaching Techniques to Try

To meet the needs of students with retardation, teachers emphasize instruction in functional academics and in daily living, social, and vocational skills (Polloway & Patton, 1992). To teach these skills, they use a variety of teacher-directed, student-directed, and peer-mediated approaches.

Teacher-directed methods

As you know from reading this chapter, we often use applied behavior analysis to teach students with mental retardation. Other approaches directed by teachers include task analysis and modeling. In the former method, teachers analyze a given task to determine what skills are needed before the student can be taught that skill (prerequisite skills) and what individual skills are needed to complete the task (component skills). To develop a task analysis, teachers often observe someone who is performing the task and record each step. Then, teachers perform the task using the steps they've noted to check for accuracy and completeness. Before beginning instruction, they teach any prerequisite skills students do not have. For a detailed description of how to construct a task analysis, see Moyer and Dardig's article (1978) "Practical task analysis for special educators."

A second teacher-directed approach is modeling, a method in which the teacher demonstrates or uses another individual who actively performs the behavior to be learned. After repeated demonstration, students imitate the model. To facilitate students' imitation and mastery of the modeled skill, teachers provide much practice, reinforcement, and feedback.

Teachers model both observable and nonobserverable behavior. By expressing their thoughts or thinking aloud as they complete a task, teachers model their thinking for students. Olson and Platt (1992) provide the following example of a think aloud used by Mr. Clarke as he taught reading:

> Today, I'd like to share with you a strategy I use when I come to a word that I don't know. . . . [Mr. Clarke reads the first sentence, "The weatherman said there will be snow flurries."] I know I've heard the word "flurries" before, but I don't know what it means. The word before "flurries" is "snow," so it has something to do with snow. . . I'll read on. The next sentence says, "When the little boy heard the weather report, he became angry, because he wanted to build a snowman." I think that can help me, because I know that you have to have a lot of snow to build a snowman. . . . Now, I may know what the word means. I'll bet it means light snow. Let me go back and check. . . . (p. 212).

Frequently teachers supplement think alouds by giving students a list of the steps involved in solving the problem. For example, in the think aloud described above, Mr. Clarke provided students with the following procedural steps:

1. Read the unknown word in the sentence.
2. See if any other words in the sentence can help you figure out the unknown word.
3. Use any background information you have to help you.
4. Read more of the sentences.
5. Repeat steps 2 and 3.
6. Substitute the new meaning.
7. Reread the sentences to see if the new meaning makes sense (Olson & Platt, 1992).

Cognitive modeling helps move students from teacher-directed to student-directed learning.

Student-directed procedures

Increasingly, educators are facilitating students' use of self-regulation procedures, such as self-monitoring, self-administering consequences, and self-instruction. These procedures are student-directed and promote student independence. Self-monitoring involves teaching students to record their own behaviors so they become aware of their behavior and regulate it. Self-administering requires students, not teachers, to give themselves predetermined consequences contingent on their own behavior. A recent review of self-management procedures used to teach persons with mental retardation reported that these two procedures typically are used to increase the occurrence of behaviors students already know how to perform, such as work and daily living skills (Harchik, Sherman, & Sheldon, 1992). Self-instruction, which involves students making directive verbal statements about their own behavior, is used to teach skills students have not yet mastered, such as academic skills (Harchik et al., 1992). See Chapter 5 for additional information about these procedures.

Peer-mediated procedures

Given the context of large, heterogeneous classes, teachers often use peer-mediated procedures to provide the additional practice and individual help students with mental retardation need. One such arrangement is peer tutoring, a technique that under certain conditions has been shown to benefit both tutor and tutee academically, behaviorally, and socially. In student tutoring programs, teachers typically provide instruction to all class members. Then students in the class (peer tutors) or older students (cross-age tutors) who have mastered the learning assist those individuals who require additional instruction and practice. Tutors can take on a variety of responsibilities, such as reviewing lessons, directing and monitoring the performance of newly learned skills, and providing feedback and reinforcement. Planning, supervising, and evaluating a peer tutoring program requires careful planning and supervision by the teacher. Several studies and reviews (Gerber & Kauffman, 1981; J. Jenkins, &

L. Jenkins, 1985; Knapczyk, 1989) indicate that the following conditions are necessary if peer-tutoring is to be effective:*

1. tutor training includes such skills as understanding the instructional objective(s), discrimination between correct and incorrect responses, delivery of corrective feedback and reinforcement, monitoring progress and record keeping, and appropriate interpersonal skills;
2. well-defined behavioral objectives reflect the regular education class curriculum;
3. instructional steps are carefully sequenced and clearly outlined in a lesson format that tutors can follow easily;
4. instruction continues in a single skill or concept until the tutee has mastered that learning;
5. easily identifiable tutee responses are required, which tutors can consistently recognize and correct or reinforce;
6. tutors monitor and record tutee performance on instructional objectives during each session;
7. teachers actively monitor both tutor and tutee performance frequently;
8. teachers deliver frequent reinforcement consistently to the tutor and the tutee contingent upon their appropriate performance;
9. tutorial sessions are scheduled at least two or three times each week with each meeting lasting approximately 15 to 30 minutes; and
10. tutors provide examples from all settings in which tutees are to use the learning.

*(Specific training information is available from Joseph Jenkins, Director of the Experimental Education Unit, Child Development and Mental Retardation Center, University of Washington, Seattle, WA.)

After teachers train tutors and tutorial sessions have begun, teachers should monitor the first lessons carefully and schedule debriefing sessions with the tutors to give them feedback on their performance. As the student-tutors become more proficient, teachers can reduce the frequency of the debriefing sessions. Scheduling additional brief weekly meetings in which tutors check on the assignments and the progress of their tutee provides them with needed information and an opportunity to ask for suggestions and to discuss problems. Offering this support to tutors along with personal attention not only improves the quality of the tutoring, but also helps maintain tutors' interest in the program. For information on class-wide student tutoring arrangement, see "Peer-mediated instruction: A promising approach to meet the diverse needs of LD adolescents" (Maheady, Harper, & Sacca, 1988).

The inclusion of students with severe retardation in general education classrooms has resulted in increased interest among educators in procedures that promote improvement in skills and enhance the social acceptance of these students. Recent reviews of methods for individualizing curriculum and instruction reported by Thousand and Villa (1990) suggest three approaches in addition to peer tutoring: mastery learning, computer-assisted instruction, and cooperative learning. To implement mastery learning, teachers conduct frequent, brief assessments of each student (e.g., curriculum-based assessment); develop individual objectives and establish specific preset mastery criteria; provide frequent feedback to students regarding their performance and progress toward mastery; and adjust or supplement instruction or practice of students who do not meet their mastery criteria. Individual goals include daily living, social, and vocational skills.

Teachers also use computer-assisted instruction (CAI) in several areas of instruction. For students with severe retardation, CAI may be used to introduce new information and to supplement teacher instruction (i.e., tutorials). CAI may also be used to provide the additional drill and practice these students require. Consult with a special educator in your school regarding appropriate software programs that meet the specific needs of your students.

Cooperative learning, an arrangement in which diverse students work in small groups to meet common goals, is a third approach teachers use to enhance learning in social and other skill areas. In Vermont, for example, specialists worked with classroom teachers to form cooperative learning groups that included intensively challenged students. To illustrate how these students were integrated into cooperative group activities, Thousand and Villa (1990) reported a seventh-grade biology lesson in which Bob, a 13-year-old with multiple disabilities was a participant. This lesson focused on dissecting a frog. Although Bob did not participate directly in the dissection, during this process he worked on his individual goals, which centered on structured communication. Group members helped Bob achieve his lesson objectives as they dissected the frog.

In preparing to integrate special students into general education classes and to promote the social acceptance of these students, Lewis and Doorlag(1991) recommend informing classmates about disabilities. Teachers often introduce this topic by discussing the concept of individual differences. Asking students to think about their own strengths and weaknesses promotes awareness of the fact that each person is unique and possesses different abilities and disabilities. Depending on the grade, teachers frequently follow-up this discussion with information about disabilities directly or with structured assignments and projects in which students conduct their own research. In addition, teachers provide experiences with people who have disabilities (Lewis & Doorlag, 1990). They invite adults with disabilities into the classroom, arrange visits to special education classes in the school, or use commercially developed materials, such as Kids on the Block, that includes puppets portraying children with disabilities. Once students with disabilities are mainstreamed, it is important that teachers provide structured interactions between nondisabled students and students with disabilities, using arrangements such as peer tutoring and cooperative learning.

HELPFUL RESOURCES

School Personnel

The special educator who also teaches students who are mentally retarded may provide additional instructional suggestions that have been successful in improving performance. This teacher also can recommend, and perhaps obtain, learning materials designed for special education students and suggest ways in which regular class materials can be adapted to students with retardation. In addition, he or she can recommend books on a variety of subjects that are of high interest to older students and written at lower reading levels. Finally, this teacher and the school psychologist are good resources for specific cognitive and behavioral information about your student.

Instructional Methods

Fowler, G. L., & Davis, M. (1985). The storyframe approach: A tool for improving reading comprehension. *Teaching Exceptional Children, 17,* 296–298.

Hamre-Nietupski, S., McDonald, J., & Nietupski, J. (1992). Integrating elementary students with multiple disabilities into supported regular classes. *Teaching Exceptional Children, 24,* 6–9.

Horton, S. (1983). Delivering industrial arts instruction to mildly handicapped learners. *Career Development for Exceptional Individuals, 6,* 85–92.

Isaacson, S. (1988). Teaching written expression; directed reading and writing; self-instructional strategy training; and computers and writing instruction, *Teaching Exceptional Children, 20,* 32–39.

Jenson, W. R., Sloane, H. N., & Young, K. R. (1988). *Applied behavior analysis in education: A structured teaching approach.* Englewood Cliffs, NJ: Prentice Hall.

Matson, J. L. (Ed.) (1990). *Handbook of behavior modification with the mentally retarded* (2nd ed.). New York: Plenum.

McDonnell, J., Wilcox, B., & Hardman, M. L. (1991). *Secondary programs for students with developmental disabilities.* Boston: Allyn & Bacon.

Olson, J., & Platt, J. (1992). *Teaching children and adolescents with special needs.* New York: Merrill, an imprint of Macmillan.

O'Shea, L., & O'Shea, D. (1988). Using repeated readings. *Teaching Exceptional Children, 20,* 26–29.

Polloway, E., & Patton, J. (1992). *Strategies for teaching learners with special needs* (5th ed.). New York: Merrill, an imprint of Macmillan.

Robinson, G. A., & Polloway, E. A. (Eds.). (1987). *Best practices in mental disabilities. Volume One.* Des Moines, IA: Iowa State Department of Education Bureau of Special Education.

Schloss, P. J., & Sedlak, R. A. (1982). Behavioral features of the mentally retarded adolescent: Implications for mainstreamed educators. *Psychology in the Schools, 19,* 98–105.

Schultz, J. B., Carpenter, C. D., & Turnbull, A. C. (1991). *Mainstreaming exceptional students: A guide for classroom teachers* (3rd ed.). Boston: Allyn & Bacon.

Curricula

Bender, M., & Valletutti, P. C. (1990). *Teaching function academics.* Austin, TX: Pro-Ed.

Carnine, D., Silbert, J., & Kameenui, E. J. (1990). *Direct instruction reading.* Columbus, OH: Merrill, an imprint of Macmillan.

Dixon, B., & Engelmann, S. (1979). *Corrective spelling through morographs.* Chicago, IL: Science Research Associates.

Engelmann, S., & Bruner, E. C. (1974). *DISTAR reading.* Chicago, IL: Science Research Associates.

Engelmann, S., & Bruner, E. C. (1983). *Reading mastery.* Chicago, IL: Science Research Associates.

Engelmann, S., Carnine, D., Johnson, G., & Meyers, L. (1989). *Corrective reading: Comprehension.* Chicago, IL: Science Research Associates.

Engelmann, S., Carnine, D., Johnson, G., & Meyers, L. (1988). *Corrective reading: Decoding.* Chicago, IL: Science Research Associates.

Silbert, J., & Carnine, D. (1981). *Direct instruction mathematics.* Columbus, OH: Merrill.

Wehman, P., & McLoughlin, P. J. (1990). Vocational curriculum for developmentally disabled persons. Austin, TX: Pro-Ed.

Literature about Individuals with Mental Retardation

ELEMENTARY

Carrick, C. (1985). *Stay away from Simon!* New York: Carion. (Ages 8–11) (Fiction=F)

Clifton, L. (1980). *My friend Jacob.* New York: E. P. Dutton. (Ages 6–10) (F)

Gillham, B. (1981). *My brother Barry.* London: A. Deutsch. (Ages 9–12) (F)

Hasler, E. (1981). *Martin is our friend.* Nashville, TN: Abingdon. (Ages 9–12) (F)

Rabe, B. (1988). *Where's Chimpy?* Berkeley, CA: Gray's Book Company. (Ages 4–7) (F)

Shyer, M. F. (1988). *Welcome home, Jellybean.* New York: Aladdin. (F)

Wright, B. R. (1981). *My sister is different.* Milwaukee, WI: Raintree. (Ages 4–7) (F)

SECONDARY

Bates, B. (1980). *Love is like peanuts.* New York, Holiday House. (Ages 13–15) (F)

Dougan, T., Isbell, L., & Vyas, P. (1983). *We have been there: A guidebook for families of people with mental retardation.* Nashville, TN: Abingdon. (Nonfiction=NF)

Hill, D. (1985). *First your penny*. New York: Atheneum. (F)

Hull, E. (1981). *Alice with golden hair*. New York: Atheneum. (F)

Kaufman, S. Z. (1988). *Retarded isn't stupid, Mom!* Baltimore, MD: Brookes. (NF)

Miner, J. C. (1982). *She's my sister*. Mankato, MN: Crestwood House. (Reading levels: Grade 3–4; Interest level: Grades 7–12) (F)

Slepian, J. (1980). *The Alfred summer*. New York: Macmillan. (F)

Slepian, J. (1981). *Lester's turn*. New York: Macmillan. (F) (A sequel to *The Alfred Summer*)

Computer Software

Alphabet Circus, DLM Teaching Resources, One DLM Park, Allen, TX 75002, (880) 527–5030. (Activities focus on letter recognition, alphabetical order, problem solving)

Animal Photo Farm, DLM Teaching Resources, One DLM Park, Allen, TX 75002, (880) 527–5030.

Bake and Take, Mindplay, 3130 North Dodge, Tucson, AZ 85716, (800) 221–7911. (Life skills)

Bobo's Park, Academic Technologies, Inc., (609) 778–4435. (Life skills)

Calendar Skills, Hartley Courseware, P.O. Box 431, Dimondale, MI 48821, (800) 247–1380.

Clock Works, MECC, 3490 Lexington Avenue, North, St. Paul, MN 55126, (800) 228–3504. (Time telling on digital and analog clocks)

Coins 'n Keys, Castle Special Computer Services, Inc. 9801 San Gabriel N.E., Albuquerque, NM 87111, (505) 293–8379. (Coin recognition and counting)

Comparative Buying Series, MCE, 157 S. Kalamazoo Mall, Suite 250, Kalamazoo, MI 49007.

Computer CUP, Amidon Publication, 1966 Benson Avenue, St. Paul, MN 56116, (880) 328–6502. (Nine discs teach basic concepts such as right-left, as many, beginning)

Counting Critters, MECC, 3490 Lexington Avenue, North, St. Paul, MN 55126, (800) 228–3504. (Basic number skills 1–20)

Daily Living Skills, Looking Glass Learning Products, 276 Howare Avenue, Des Plaines, IL 60018–1906, (800) 545–5457. (Reading prescriptions, medical product labels, classified ads, telephone directory, job applications, and paychecks)

Dinosaurs, Advanced Ideas, 680 Hawthorne Drive, Tiburon, CA 94920, (415) 425–5086. (Game format teaches matching, sorting, and counting)

Easy as ABE, Springboard/Spinnaker, Spinnaker Software, 201 Broadway, Sixth Floor, Cambridge, MA 02139, (800) 826–0706. (Games help young children identify and sequence alphabet letters and match upper and lower case letters.)

Financing a Car, MECC, 3490 Lexington Avenue, N., St. Paul, MN 55112.

First Day on the Job, MECC, 3490 Lexington Avenue, N., St. Paul, MN 55112.

Job Success Series, MCE, 157 S. Kalamazoo Mall, Suite 250, Kalamazoo, MI 49007.

Language L.A.B., Specialsoft, P.O. Box 1983, Santa Monica, CA 90406, (800) 421–6534.

Library and Media Skills, Educational Activities, P.O. Box 392, Freeport, Long Island, NY 11520, (800) 645–3777.

Library Skills, Micro Power & Light Company, 12820 Hillcrest Road, Suite 219, Dallas, TX 75230.

Reader Rabbit, Learning Company, 6493 Kaiser Drive, Fremont, CA 94555, (800) 852–2255.

Spell It!, Davidson & Associates, 19840 Pioneer Avenue, Torrance, CA 90503, (800) 545–7677.

Stickybear Town Builder, Optimum Resources, 10 Station Place, Norfolk, CT 06058, (800) 327–1473. (Map reading, planning, hypothesizing, problem solving)

Telling Time, Random House, 400 Hahn Road, Westminister, MN 21157.

Vocabulary Challenge, Learning Well, 2200 Marcus Avenue, New Hyde Park, NY 11040, (800) 646–6564.

Vocabulary Game, J & S Software, 140 Reid Avenue, Port Washington, NY 11050.

Ways to Read Words, Intellectual Software, 798 North Avenue, Bridgeport, CT 06606.

Whole Brain Spelling, SubLogic, 713 Edgebrook Drive, Champaign, IL 61820.

World of Work, Computer Age Education, 1442A Walnut Street, Suite 341, Berkeley, CA 94709.

Work Habits for Job Success, MEC, 1800 South 35th Street, Galesburg, MI 49078, (800) 421–4157.

Organizations

American Association on Mental Retardation, 1719 Kalorama Road, N.W., Washington, D.C. 20009, (202) 387–1968.

Association for Children with Retarded Mental Development, 162 Fifth Avenue, 11th floor, New York, NY 10010, (212) 741–0100.

Association for Retarded Citizens, P.O. Box 6109, Arlington, TX 76005, (817) 640–0204.

Mental Retardation Division of the Council for Exceptional Children, 1920 Association Drive, Reston, VA 22091, (703) 620–3660.

BIBLIOGRAPHY FOR TEACHING SUGGESTIONS

Gerber, M., & Kauffman, J. M. (1981). Peer tutoring in academic settings. In P.S. Strain (Ed.). *The utilization of classroom peers as behavior change agents* (pp. 155–187). New York: Plenum Press.

Harchik, A. E., Sherman, J. A., & Sheldon, A. B. (1992) The use of self-management procedures by people with developmental disabilities: A brief review. *Research in Developmental Disabilities*, 13, 211–227.

Jenkins, J., & Jenkins, L. (1985). Peer tutoring in elementary and secondary programs. *Focus on Exceptional Children*, 17, 1–12.

Knapczyk, D. R. (1989). Peer-mediated training of cooperative play between special and regular class students in integrated play settings. *Education and Training in Mental Retardation*, 24, 255–264.

Lewis, R. B., & Doorlag, D. H. (1991). *Teaching special students in the mainstream* (3rd ed.). New York: Merrill, an imprint of Macmillan.

Maheady, L., Harper, G. F., & Sacca, M. K. (1988). Peer-mediated instruction: A promising approach to meeting the diverse needs of LD adolescents. *Learning Disability Quarterly, 11*, 108–113.

McCann, S. K., Semmel, M. I., & Nevin, A. (1985). Reverse mainstreaming: Nonhandicapped students in special education classrooms. *Remedial and Special Education, 6*, 13–19.

Moyer, B., & Dardig, M. (1978). Practical task analysis for special educators. *Teaching Exceptional Children, 10*, 16–18.

Odom, S. L., Deklyen, M., & Jenkins, J. R. (1984). Integrating handicapped and nonhandicapped preschoolers: Developmental impact on nonhandicapped children. *Exceptional Children, 51*, 41–48.

Olson, J., & Platt, J. (1992). *Teaching children and adolescents with special needs*. New York: Merrill, an imprint of Macmillan.

Polloway, E., & Patton, J. (1992). *Strategies for teaching learners with special needs* (5th ed.). New York: Merrill, an imprint of Macmillan.

Poorman, C. (1980). Mainstreaming in reverse with a special friend. *Teaching Exceptional Children, 12*, 136–142.

Thousand, J. S., & Villa, R. A. (1990). Strategies for educating learners with severe disabilities within their local home schools and communities. *Focus on Exceptional Children, 23*(3), 1–24.

Summary

Professionals are generally more cautious about identifying students as retarded than they once were because (1) there has been a history of misidentifying students from minority groups, (2) the label of mental retardation may have harmful consequences for students, and (3) some believe that to a certain extent mental retardation is socially constructed. Changes in the definition of the American Association on Mental Retardation over the years reflect this cautious attitude toward identification. The current AAMR definition continues three trends: (1) a broadening of the definition beyond the single criterion of an IQ score (adaptive skills as well as conceptual intelligence are measured), (2) a lowering of the IQ score used as a cut-off, and (3) a view of retardation as a condition that can be improved.

The AAMR has traditionally classified persons as having *mild, moderate, severe*, and *profound* retardation based on their IQ scores. Currently, however, the AAMR is recommending classification based on how much support is needed: *intermittent, limited, extensive*, and *pervasive*.

From a purely statistical-theoretical perspective, 2.27 percent of the population should score low enough on an IQ test (below about 70) to qualify as retarded. Figures indicate, however, that about 1 to 1.5 percent of the population is identified as mentally retarded. The discrepancy may be due to three factors. First, both low adaptive skills and low conceptual intelligence are needed to consider a person retarded. Second, school personnel tend to be cautious about labeling minority children. Third, parents and professionals may prefer to have students labeled "learning disabled" rather than "mentally retarded" because they perceive it as less stigmatizing.

There are a variety of causes of mental retardation. Only in a few cases, especially among those with more mild retardation or those requiring less intensive support, can we actually specify the cause. Most people with mild retardation are considered culturally-familially retarded, a term used to include causes related to poor environmental and/or hereditary factors. Although the nature-nurture debate has raged for years, most authorities now believe that *both* heredity and the environment are important in determining intelligence. We can categorize causes of more severe retardation, or that requiring more intensive support, as due to genetic factors or brain damage. Down syndrome, Fragile X syndrome, PKU, and Tay-Sachs disease are all examples of genetic causes. Down syndrome results from a chromosomal abnormality but is not inherited as such. Fragile X syndrome, PKU, and Tay-Sachs are inherited. Authorities believe that Fragile X syndrome is the most common hereditary cause of retardation. Brain damage can result from infectious diseases—for example, meningitis, encephalitis, rubella, and pediatric AIDS—or environmental hazards, such as poisons (e.g., cocaine and alcohol) and excessive radiation. Premature birth can also result in mental retardation. With amniocentesis, chorionic villus sampling, or sonography, physicians are now able to detect a variety of defects in the unborn fetus.

Two of the most common IQ tests are the Stanford-Binet and the Wechsler Intelligence Scale for

Children—Third Edition (WISC-III). The latter has verbal and performance subscales. Some professionals recommend using the Kaufman Assessment Battery for Children (K-ABC) with African-American students because they believe it less culturally biased. There are several cautions in using and interpreting IQ tests: (1) An individual's IQ score can change; (2) all IQ tests are culturally biased to some extent; (3) the younger the child, the less reliable the results; and (4) a person's ability to live a successful and fulfilling life does not depend solely on his or her IQ. In addition to IQ tests, several adaptive behavior scales are available.

Persons with mental retardation have learning problems related to attention, memory, self-regulation, language development, academic achievement, social development, and motivation. An important concept related to self-regulation is metacognition—the awareness of what strategies are needed to perform a task and the ability to use self-regulatory mechanisms before, during, and after performing a task.

Educational goals for students with mild retardation emphasize readiness skills at younger ages and functional academics and vocational training at older ages. Functional academics are for the purpose of enabling the person to function independently. Educational programs for students with more severe retardation are characterized by (1) age-appropriate curriculum and materials, (2) functional activities, (3) community-based instruction, (4) integrated therapy, (5) interaction with nondisabled students, and (6) family involvement.

Depending to a large extent on the degree of retardation or the need for support, schools may place students in learning environments ranging from regular classrooms to residential institutions. Although residential institutions are still in existence and special classes in public schools are common, the trend is to include students who are mentally retarded in more integrated settings.

Preschool programming differs in its goals according to whether the program is aimed at preventing retardation or furthering the development of children already identified as retarded. For the most part, the former types of programs are aimed at children at risk of developing mild retardation, whereas the latter are for children with more severe retardation.

Transition programming for individuals with retardation includes goals related to domestic living, community living, leisure, and vocational skills. Although the emphasis on transition programming increases with age, authorities recommend that such efforts begin in elementary school. The employment picture for workers with retardation is changing. Although sheltered work environments remain popular, authorities have pointed out their weaknesses: (1) Wages are very low; (2) there is no integration with nondisabled workers; and (3) they offer only limited job-training experiences. Placement of workers who are retarded in supported competitive employment is becoming more prevalent. In supported competitive employment, the worker (1) receives at least a minimum wage, (2) works in a setting with mostly nondisabled workers, and (3) receives assistance from a job coach. Many authorities are advocating the use of self-management techniques (e.g., picture cues, self-instruction, self-monitoring, and self-reinforcement) to help workers with retardation to function more independently. Although employment figures are still discouraging, the growth in innovative programs gives reason to be hopeful about the future of community living and employment for adults with mental retardation.

GIOVANNI

Giovanni is a visual artist working in print lithography. After formal art training at Boston University School for the Arts and the Art Institute of Boston, he began to exhibit his work extensively. His learning disability has not precluded his ability to achieve success and recognition in the visual arts.

*A*nd report cards I was always afraid to show
Mama'd come to school
and as I'd sit there softly cryin'
Teacher'd say he's just not tryin'
Got a good head if he'd apply it
but you know yourself
it's always somewhere else

I'd build me a castle
with dragons and kings
and I'd ride off with them
As I stood by my window
and looked out on those
Brooklyn roads

➢ Neil Diamond
    "Brooklyn Roads"

Learning
Disabilities

▲   ▲   ▲

*N*eil Diamond's "Brooklyn Roads" (see page 159) expresses the frustrations often felt by children with learning disabilities. Such children have learning problems in school even though they may be no less intelligent than their nondisabled classmates. They have difficulties in one or more academic areas. Reading, in particular, often looms as a major stumbling block. Children with learning disabilities are also apt to be inattentive and hyperactive. In the early school years, their parents may see them as simply overenergetic. Later, this unconcern may turn to desperation when, unlike their playmates, these children fail to outgrow their poor school performance and ungovernable ways.

Professionals, too, have been frustrated by the problems presented by students with learning disabilities. Some of the most intense battles in all of special education have been waged over issues related to the education of students with learning disabilities. We can attribute much of the reason for this professional turmoil to two factors:

- The enigma of children who are not retarded but who have severe academic problems has often led parents of these children, as well as professionals, to seek quick-and-easy miracle cures. We now recognize that, in most cases, learning disability is a life-long condition with which a person must learn to cope.
- The field of learning disabilities is a relatively recent category of special education, having been recognized by the federal government in 1969. It is also now the largest category, constituting almost half of all students identified as eligible for special education. Much professional and popular media exposure has been focused on this rapidly expanding category, and this focus has created a hotbed wherein controversies can ferment.

Although the field of learning disabilities has had to struggle to overcome its penchant for questionable practices and to survive the intense scrutiny of professionals and the lay public, most who work within this area are happy to be a part of such a field. For them, controversy and ambiguity only add excitement to the already challenging task of educating students with learning disabilities. One controversy that has nagged the field for some time is that of definition, to which we now turn.

DEFINITIONS

At a parents' meeting in New York City in the early 1960s, Samuel Kirk proposed the term *learning disabilities* as a compromise because of the confusing variety of labels then used to describe the child with relatively normal intelligence who was having learning problems. Such a child was likely to be referred to as *minimally brain injured*, a *slow learner, dyslexic,** or *perceptually disabled*.

Many parents as well as teachers, however, believed the label *minimal brain injury* to be problematic. **Minimal brain injury** refers to individuals who show behavioral, but not neurological, signs of brain injury. They exhibit behaviors (e.g., distractibility, hyperactivity, and perceptual disturbances) similar to those

➤ **minimal brain injury.** A term used to describe a child who shows behavioral but not neurological signs of brain injury; the term is not as popular as it once was, primarily because of its lack of diagnostic utility—i. e., some children who learn normally show signs indicative of MBD.

*Dyslexia refers to a severe impairment of the ability to read.

MYTH ➤ All students with learning disabilities are brain damaged.

FACT ➤ Although more students with learning disabilities show evidence of damage to the central nervous system (CNS) than their nondisabled peers, many of them do not. Many authorities now refer to students with learning disabilities as having CNS dysfunction, which suggests a malfunctioning of the brain rather than actual tissue damage.

MYTH ➤ IQ-achievement discrepancies are easily calculated.

FACT ➤ A complicated formula determines a discrepancy between a student's IQ and his or her achievement.

MYTH ➤ Standardized achievement tests are the most useful kind of assessment device for teachers of students with learning disabilities.

FACT ➤ Standardized achievement tests do not provide much information about why a student has achievement difficulties. Informal reading inventories and formative evaluation measures give teachers a better idea of the particular problems a student is experiencing.

MYTH ➤ We need not be concerned about the social-emotional well-being of students with learning disabilities because their problems are in academics.

FACT ➤ Many students with learning disabilities do also develop problems in the social-emotional area.

MYTH ➤ The most serious problem of children who are hyperactive is their excessive motor activity.

FACT ➤ Although children who are hyperactive do exhibit excessive motor activity, most authorities now believe that their most fundamental problems lie in the area of inattention.

MYTH ➤ Medication for children with attention-deficit disorder is over-prescribed and presents a danger for many children.

FACT ➤ Some children receive medication who do not need it, but there is little evidence that vast numbers are inappropriately medicated. Medication can be an important part of a total treatment package for persons with attention-deficit disorder.

MYTH ➤ Most children with learning disabilities outgrow their disabilities as adults.

FACT ➤ Learning disabilities tend to endure into adulthood. Even most of those who are successful must learn to cope with their problems and show extraordinary perseverance.

with real brain injury, but their neurological examinations are indistinguishable from those of nondisabled individuals. The diagnosis of minimal brain injury was sometimes dubious because it was based on questionable behavioral evidence rather than on more solid neurological data. Moreover, it was not an educationally meaningful label because such a diagnosis offered little real help in planning and implementing treatment. The term *slow learner* described the child's performance in some areas but not in others—and besides, intelligence testing indicated that the *ability* to learn existed. *Dyslexic*, too, fell short as a definitive term because it described only reading disabilities, and many of these children had problems in other academic areas such as math. To describe a child as *perceptually disabled* just confused the issue further, for perceptual problems might be only part of a puzzling inability to learn. So it was finally around the educationally oriented term *learning disabilities* that the New York parents' group rallied to found the Association for Children with Learning Disabilities, now known as the Learning Disabilities Association of America. Following the lead of the parents, a few years later professionals and the federal government officially recognized the term.

The interest in learning disabilities evolved as a result of a growing awareness that a large number of children were not receiving needed educational services. Because they were within the normal range of intelligence, these children did not qualify for placement in classes for children with retardation. In addition, although many of them did show inappropriate behavior or personality disturbances, some of them did *not*. Thus it was felt that placement in classes for students with emotional disturbance was inappropriate. Parents of children who were not achieving at their expected potential—children who are *learning disabled* —wanted their children's *academic achievement* problems corrected.

Factors to Consider in Definitions of Learning Disabilities

Eleven different definitions of learning disabilities have enjoyed some degree of acceptance since the field's inception in the early 1960s (Hammill, 1990). Created by individual professionals and committees of professionals and lawmakers, each definition provides a slightly different slant. Four factors—each of which is included in some definitions, but not all—have historically caused considerable controversy:

1. IQ-achievement discrepancy
2. Presumption of central nervous system dysfunction
3. Psychological processing disorders
4. Learning problems not due to environmental disadvantage, mental retardation, or emotional disturbance

We discuss these factors briefly and then present the two most commonly used definitions.

➤ **IQ-achievement discrepancy.** Academic performance markedly lower than would be expected based on a student's intellectual ability.

IQ-Achievement Discrepancy

An **IQ-achievement discrepancy** means that the child is not achieving up to potential as usually measured by a standardized intelligence test. Professionals have used a number of methods to determine a discrepancy. For many years, professionals simply compared the mental age obtained from an intelligence test to the grade-age equivalent taken from a standardized achievement test. A difference of two years was often considered enough to indicate a learning disability, but two years below expected grade level is not equally serious at different grade levels. For example, a child who tests two years below grade eight has a less severe deficit than one who tests two years below grade four. So professionals have developed formulas that take into account the relative ages of the students.

Although some states and school divisions have adopted different formulas for identifying IQ-achievement discrepancies, many authorities have advised against their use. Some of the formulas are statistically flawed and lead to inaccurate judgments (McKinney, 1987b). Those that are statistically adequate are difficult and expensive to implement. Furthermore, they give a false sense of precision. That is, they tempt school personnel to reduce to a single score the complex and important decision of identifying a learning disability.

Because of these and other theoretical issues, some researchers have recommended abandoning the notion of an IQ-achievement discrepancy as a criterion for identifying learning disabilities (Fletcher, 1992; Siegel, 1989; Stanovich, 1991). Many, however, are unwilling to give up what they consider a fundamental aspect of defining learning disabilities. They believe that, with or without formulas, professionals can and should make judicious clinical judgments about whether a student is achieving up to his or her potential.

Central Nervous System Dysfunction

Many of the theoretical concepts and teaching methods associated with the field of learning disabilities grew out of work done in the 1930s and 1940s with children who were mentally retarded and brain injured (Werner & Strauss, 1941). When the field of learning disabilities was evolving, professionals noted that many of these children displayed behavioral characteristics similar to those exhibited by children known to have brain damage (distractibility, hyperactivity, perceptual disturbances). In the case of most children with learning disabilities, however, there is little neurological evidence of brain damage. Some professionals have been content to attribute brain damage to children with learning disabilities on the basis of behavioral characteristics alone. More recently, there has been a trend away from considering a child to be brain damaged unless the results from a neurological examination are unquestionable. The term *dysfunction* has come to replace *injury* or *damage*. Thus a child with learning disabilities is now more likely to be referred to as having brain dysfunction than brain injury. The change in terminology reflects the awareness of how hard it is to diagnose brain damage. *Dysfunction* does not necessarily mean tissue damage; it signifies a malfunctioning of the brain.

Psychological Processing Disorders

Authorities originally developed the field of learning disabilities on the assumption that children with learning disabilities have deficits in abilities to perceive and interpret stimuli—that is, they have psychological processing problems. Advocates of this viewpoint might assume, for example, that a child who is not learning to read has problems in perceiving and integrating visual information. Proponents of the psychological processing position believe that many children with learning disabilities need specific training in processing information to learn academic skills such as reading. Over the years, strong opposition has developed to the idea that children with learning disabilities exhibit psychological processing problems that can be remediated for the benefit of academic

CNN

*C*rack cocaine has been among the most prevalently used addictive drugs on the streets of the United States since around the mid-1980s. Children born to addicts have been entering the public education system for the past two to three years, and, with little sign of crack cocaine disappearing from use, will continue to do so for years to come.

Children born to addicts face a host of physical and environmental problems, some of which may be unidentified as yet. Congenital problems include damaged organs, organ systems, and limbs, irritability and discomfort, and sometimes permanent neurological damage. Environmental problems also prevail in situations where the mother remains addicted to cocaine and is incapable of coping with the needs of a new baby, much less one with special needs.

As for the specific learning problems these children will bring to school, time will have to tell the full story. However, some consistencies have been observed. For example, these children seem to react to the high level of stimulation which characterizes many of today's classrooms by either withdrawing completely, or the opposite, acting hyperactively or aggressively.

The most effective means of intervention in these cases must be early and intensive, occurring well before children enter elementary school. Programs which provide care for both children and parents, including medical care, nutritional counseling, parenting skills, and development follow-up seem to offer the most promise. However, such programs work best when the adult/child ratio is quite high and are therefore expensive—although probably not as expensive, financially and otherwise, than ignoring the problem until it is too late.

- How do you see children with learning problems related to parental drug abuse fitting into the special education system, if at all?
- What role can schools play in reducing the number of children who enter school with learning problems due to drug addiction?

performance. As we discuss later in the chapter, critics have noted the lack of solid evidence that psychological processing can be accurately measured and that training in processing information can lead to academic improvement.

Environmental Disadvantage, Mental Retardation, or Emotional Disturbance

Most definitions of learning disability exclude those children whose learning problems stem from environmental disadvantage, mental retardation, or emotional disturbance. The belief that such an exclusion clause is necessary attests to how difficult it can be sometimes to differentiate between some of these conditions. There is ample evidence, for example, that children from disadvantaged backgrounds are more apt to exhibit learning problems, and students who are mentally retarded or emotionally disturbed often display some of the same behavioral characteristics as pupils who are learning disabled (Hallahan & Kauffman, 1977). Most definitions assume that children with learning disabilities have intrinsic learning problems because of a central nervous system dysfunction, thus ruling out the environment as a causal factor. They state that learning disabilities can occur along with environmental disadvantage, mental retardation, or emotional disturbance, but for children to be considered learning disabled, their learning problems must be primarily the result of their learning disabilities.

We turn now to two of the most popular definitions.

The Federal Definition

Probably the most commonly accepted definition is that endorsed by the federal government:

> "Specific learning disability" means a disorder in one or more of the basic psychological processes involved in understanding or in using language, spoken or written, which may manifest itself in an imperfect ability to listen, think, speak, read, write, spell, or to do mathematical calculations. The term includes such conditions as perceptual handicaps, brain injury, minimal brain dysfunction, dyslexia, and developmental aphasia. The term does not include children who have learning problems which are primarily the result of visual, hearing, or motor handicaps, of mental retardation, of emotional disturbance, or of environmental, cultural, or economic disadvantage. (*Federal Register*, 1977, p. 65083)

The National Joint Committee for Learning Disabilities Definition

The National Joint Committee on Learning Disabilities (NJCLD), made up of representatives of several professional organizations, has issued an alternative definition:

> Learning disabilities is a general term that refers to a heterogeneous group of disorders manifested by significant difficulties in the acquisition and use of listening, speaking, reading, writing, reasoning, or mathematical abilities. These disorders are intrinsic to the individual, presumed to be due to central nervous system dysfunction, and may occur across the life span.
>
> Problems in self-regulatory behaviors, social perception and social interaction may exist with learning disabilities but do not by themselves constitute a learning disability.
>
> Although learning disabilities may occur concomitantly with other handicapping conditions (for example, sensory impairment, mental retardation, serious emotional disturbance) or with extrinsic influences (such as cultural differences, insufficient or inappropriate instruction), they are not the result of those conditions or influences. (National Joint Committee on Learning Disabilities, 1989, p.1)

Authors of the NJCLD definition believe it has several advantages over the federal definition (Hammill, Leigh, McNutt, & Larsen, 1981): (1) It is not concerned exclusively with children; (2) it avoids the phrase *basic psychological processes*, which has been so controversial; (3) spelling is not included because it is logically subsumed under writing; (4) it avoids mentioning ill-defined conditions (e.g., perceptual handicaps, dyslexia, minimal brain dysfunction) that have caused much confusion; and (5) it clearly states that learning disabilities may occur concomitantly with other disabling conditions.

PREVALENCE

According to figures kept by the federal government, the public schools have identified learning disabled somewhere between 4 to 5 percent of students six to seventeen years of age. Learning disabilities is by far the largest category of special education. Almost one-half of all students identified by the public schools as needing special education are learning disabled. The size of the learning disabilities category has more than doubled since 1976–1977, when prevalence figures first started being kept by the federal government.

Many authorities have maintained that the rapid expansion of the learning disabilities category reflects poor diagnostic practices. They believe that children are being overidentified, that teachers are too quick to label students with the slightest learning problem as learning disabled rather than entertain the possibility that their teaching practices are at fault. Others, however, have argued that the claim of overidentification has been exaggerated and that there are logical explanations for the increase in learning disabilities (see box on p. 167).

CAUSES

In most cases, the cause of a child's learning disabilities remains a mystery. Possible causes fall into three general categories—organic and biological, genetic, and environmental.

Organic and Biological Factors

For years, many professionals suspected that neurological factors were a major cause of learning disabilities. Not all agreed, however, because the evidence for a neurological cause was based on relatively crude neurological measures. In recent years, researchers have begun to harness advanced technology to assess brain activity more accurately. One research team, for example, has found that many students with learning disabilities have abnormal brain waves as measured by the digitally computerized recording and analysis of an **electroencephalogram (EEG)**. An EEG consists of electrical recordings obtained from electrodes placed at various sites on the head.

Researchers are also taking advantage of neuroimaging techniques to look at the underlying physiology of the brain. **Computerized tomographic scans (CT scans)** use a computer to assemble X-ray beams to produce an overall picture of the brain. **Magnetic resonance imaging (MRI)** uses radio waves instead of radiation to create cross-sectional images of the brain. CT scans and MRI data on the brains of persons with learning disabilities suggest a neurological cause for some cases of learning disabilities (Hynd, Marshall, & Gonzalez, 1991; Willis, Hooper, & Stone, 1992). These researchers suggest there is a disruption of neural cell formation during early fetal development.

Taken as a whole, these studies are not definitive evidence of a neurological basis of all students identified as learning disabled. Some have noted that, for the most part, the studies have been conducted on individuals with severe learning disabilities. The results, however, have turned many who were formerly skeptical into believers that central nervous system dysfunction may be a cause of many cases of learning disabilities.

Genetic Factors

Over the years, evidence has been accumulating that learning disabilities tend to "run in families" (Finucci & Childs, 1983; Owen, Adams, Forrest, Stoltz, & Fisher, 1971). Studies of twins (Hallgren, 1950; Olson, Wise, Conners, Rack, & Fulker, 1989) generally show that when one twin has a reading disability, the other is more likely also to have a reading disability if he or she is an identical (monozygotic—from the same egg) rather than a fraternal (dizygotic—two eggs) twin. Increasingly sophisticated methods have allowed genetic researchers to point to

➤ **electroencephalogram (EEG).** A graphic recording of the brain's electrical impulses.

➤ **computerized tomographic scans (CT scans).** A neuroimaging technique whereby X-rays of the brain are compiled by a computer to produce an overall picture of the brain.

➤ **magnetic resonance imaging (MRI).** A neuroimaging technique whereby radio waves are used to produce cross-sectional images of the brain; used to pinpoint areas of the brain that are dysfunctional.

*I*S THE INCREASE IN LEARNING DISABILITIES JUSTIFIED? ➤

In 1976–1977, about 23 percent of all students identified for special education were learning disabled. Today, that figure stands at about 50 percent. Many practitioners, researchers, and officials in the federal government have decried the expansion of the learning disabilities category. They believe that the increase represents the misidentification of many children as learning disabled.

Not all are convinced that the increase is completely unwarranted. Hallahan (1992), for example, asserts that much of the increase may represent bona fide cases of learning disabilities. He points to two factors that may have led to the doubling of the learning disabilities population. First, when figures started being kept in 1976–1977, the learning disabilities category had been in official existence for only a short time. Hallahan speculates that it may have taken professionals a few years to decide how to go about identifying children for this category of services. Indirect evidence for this comes from the fact that the increase in learning disabilities has slowed dramatically since the mid-1980s.

Second, Hallahan points to an abundance of social/cultural changes that he believes have raised children's vulnerability to develop learning disabilities. For example, an increase in poverty has placed children at greater risk for biomedical problems, including central nervous system dysfunction (Baumeister, Kupstas, & Klindworth, 1990). Furthermore, he states that even families not in poverty are under more stress than ever before, and this stress takes its toll on the time children have for concentrating on their school work and on their parents' ability to offer social support. In addition to being bombarded with a variety of attractive diversions (e.g., television, video games, videotape rentals), today's child of the suburbs spends an enormous number of hours each year being transported to and from school and numerous extracurricular activities (e.g., athletics, clubs, dance or music lessons). And parents have fewer hours in the day to devote to helping their children with school work. Hallahan cites a survey (Leete-Guy & Schor, 1992) showing that, since 1969, the amount of leisure time for families in the United States has declined dramatically. Those who hold jobs are working longer hours. Furthermore, in single-parent families and families in which both parents work, the time parents have to monitor their children's progress in school is reduced further.

Hallahan concludes:

Undoubtedly, some students are misidentified as learning disabled. The business of identification depends on clinical judgment, and clinical judgment always results in errors. But misdiagnosis may not account for all of the growth in the learning disabilities population. Exactly what proportion of the increase represents bogus cases of learning disabilities is open for speculation and future research. In the meantime, we should be open to the idea that at least some of the increase represents students who are in very real need of learning disabilities services. (p. 528)

heredity as a possible causal factor in learning disabilities, especially severe reading disabilities (Stevenson, 1992).

Environmental Factors

Environmental causes are difficult to document. There is much evidence showing that environmentally disadvantaged children are more prone to exhibit learning problems. It is still not certain if this is due strictly to inadequate learning experiences or to biological factors, such as brain damage or nutritional deprivation (Cravioto & DeLicardie, 1975; Hallahan & Cruickshank, 1973).

Another possible environmental cause of learning disabilities is poor teaching (Engelmann, 1977; Lovitt, 1977). Some believe that if teachers were better prepared to handle the special learning problems of children in the early school years, some learning disabilities could be avoided.

ASSESSMENT

Three types of tests are popular in the field of learning disabilities:

1. Standardized achievement tests

"Your feelings of insecurity seem to have started when Mary Lou Gurnblatt said, 'Maybe I don't have a learning disability—maybe you have a teaching disability.'"

SOURCE: J. H. Crouse and P. T. McFarlane, "Monopoly, myth, and convivial access" to the tools of learning, *Phi Delta Kappan,* 56(9)(1975), 593. Drawn by Tony Saltzman.

2. Informal reading inventories
3. Formative evaluation measures

Standardized Achievement Tests

Teachers and psychologists commonly use standardized achievement tests with students who are learning disabled because achievement deficits are the primary characteristic of these students. The fact that the test is standardized means that it has been administered to a large group so that any one score can be compared to the norm, or average. Several standardized achievement tests are currently in use. One of the most recent is the Wechsler Individual Achievement Test (WIAT), which assesses achievement in all of the areas pertaining to the federal definition of learning disabilities: basic reading, reading comprehension, spelling, written expression, mathematics reasoning, numerical operations, listening comprehension, and oral expression. The developers of the WIAT designed the test so it could be used in conjunction with the Wechsler Intelligence Scale for Children in order to look for discrepancies between achievement and ability.

One limitation to most standardized tests is that you cannot use them to gain much insight into the "whys" of a student's failure. Teachers and clinicians use them primarily to identify students with learning problems and to provide gross indicators of academic strengths and weaknesses.

The notion of using assessment data to help plan educational strategies has gained much of its popularity from professionals working in the area of learning disabilities. The other two methods of assessment we discuss—informal reading inventories and formative evaluation measures—are better suited to the philosophy that test scores are more useful for teachers if they can be translated into educational recommendations.

Informal Reading Inventories –made by teachers

A common method of assessment used by teachers in the area of reading is an informal reading inventory (IRI) which is

> a series of reading passages or word lists graded in order of difficulty. A student reads from the series of lists or passages, beginning with one that the teacher thinks is likely to be easy. As long as the reading does not become too difficult, the student continues to read from increasingly harder lists or passages. As the student reads, the teacher monitors performance and may record the kinds of reading errors a student makes (e.g., omitted word, mispronunciation, reversal). When an IRI is made up of passages, the teacher may ask questions after each one to help estimate the student's comprehension of the material. Depending on the student's accuracy in reading and answering questions, various levels of reading skill can be ascertained. . . . In general, the kind of material that a student can read with a certain degree of ease is considered to be at his or her *independent, instructional,* or *frustration level.* (Hallahan, Kauffman, & Lloyd, 1985, p. 210)

Because of the growing disenchantment with formal, or standardized, tests, there has been a trend toward the greater use of informal inventories. The major drawback to IRIs is that their reliability and validity depend on the skills of the teachers constructing them. In the hands of a skilled teacher, however, they can be invaluable for determining what level of reading material the student should be working on as well as for pinpointing specific reading deficits.

Formative Evaluation Methods

Formative evaluation methods directly measure a student's behavior to keep track of his or her progress (Deno, 1985; Fuchs, 1986; Fuchs & Fuchs, 1986; Germann & Tindal, 1985; Marston & Magnusson, 1985; White & Haring, 1980). Formative evaluation is less concerned with how the student compares with other students and more concerned with how the student compares with himself or herself. Although there are a variety of different formative evaluation models, at least five features are common to all of them:

1. The assessment is usually done by the child's teacher rather than a school psychologist or diagnostician.
2. The teacher assesses classroom behaviors directly. For instance, if the teacher is interested in measuring the child's pronunciation of the letter *l*, he or she looks at that particular behavior and records whether the child can pronounce that letter.
3. The teacher observes and records the child's behavior frequently and over a period of time. Most other kinds of tests are given once or twice a year at the most. In formative evaluation, performance is measured at least two or three times a week.
4. The teacher uses formative evaluation to assess the child's progress toward educational goals. After an initial testing, the teacher establishes goals for the child to reach in a given period of time. For example, if the child can orally read 25 words correctly in one minute out of a certain book, the teacher may set a goal, or criterion, of being able to read 100 words correctly per minute after one month. This aspect of formative evaluation is sometimes referred to as **criterion-referenced testing**.

> ➤ **formative evaluation methods.** Measurement procedures used to monitor an individual student's progress. They are used to compare an individual to himself or herself, in contrast to standardized tests, which are primarily used to compare an individual to other students.

> ➤ **criterion-referenced testing.** A procedure used to determine a child's level of achievement; when this level is established, a criterion, or goal, is set to fix a level at which the child should be achieving.

➤ **curriculum-based assessment (CBA).** This approach to assessment is a formative evaluation method designed to evaluate performance in the particular curriculum to which students are exposed. It usually involves giving students a small sample of items from the curriculum in use in their schools. Proponents of this assessment technique argue that it is preferable to comparing students with national norms or using tests that do not reflect the curriculum content learned by students.

5. The teacher uses formative evaluation to monitor the effectiveness of educational programming. For instance, in the preceding example, if after a few days the teacher realizes it is unlikely that the child will reach the goal of 100 words, the teacher can try a different educational intervention.

Curriculum-Based Assessment

Curriculum-based assessment (CBA) is a particular model of formative evaluation. Although drawing heavily on earlier research, CBA was largely developed by Deno and his colleagues (Deno, 1985; Fuchs, Deno, & Mirkin, 1984).

Because it is a type of formative evaluation, CBA has the five features just listed. In addition, it has two other distinguishing characteristics. First, it is designed to measure children's performance on the particular curriculum to which they are exposed. In spelling, for example, a typical CBA assessment strategy is to give children two-minute spelling samples, using dictation from a random selection of words from the basal spelling curriculum, the number of words or letter sequences correctly spelled serving as the performance measure. In math, the teacher may give the children two minutes to compute samples of problems from the basal text and record the number of digits computed correctly. Proponents of CBA state that this reliance on the curriculum is an advantage over commercially available standardized achievement tests, which are usually not keyed to the curriculum in any particular school.

Second, CBA compares performance of students with disabilities to that of their peers in their own school or school division. Deno and his colleagues advocate that the teacher take CBA measures on a random sample of nondisabled students so this comparison can be made. Comparison with a local reference group is seen as more relevant than comparison with national norming groups used in commercially developed standardized tests.

Researchers have found that CBA results in positive changes for both teachers and students with learning disabilities. Teachers who use CBA have more objective information for assessing whether students are meeting their goals and are more likely to modify their instruction if their students are not meeting those goals (Fuchs, Fuchs, & Strecker, 1989). Students also make more academic progress when CBA is in use (Fuchs, 1986).

PSYCHOLOGICAL AND BEHAVIORAL CHARACTERISTICS

Before discussing some of the most common characteristics of persons with learning disabilities, we point out two important features of this population. Persons with learning disabilities exhibit a great deal of *inter*-individual and *intra*-individual variation.

Inter-Individual Variation

In any classroom of students who are learning disabled, some will have problems in reading, some will have problems in math, some will have problems in spelling, some will be inattentive, and so on. One term for such inter-individual variation is *heterogeneity*. Although heterogeneity is a trademark of children from all of the categories of special education, the old adage, "no two are exactly alike," is particularly apropos for students with learning disabilities.

The broad range of disabilities has made it extremely difficult for teachers and researchers to work with and study students with learning disabilities. Teachers have found it difficult to plan educational programs for the diverse group of children they find in their classrooms. Researchers have been faced with the uncertainty of whether inconsistent results from study to study are indeed real or are caused by variations in children selected for one study versus another.

Teams of researchers have been tackling the problem of heterogeneity, attempting to find subgroups, or subtypes, of learning disabilities. Using sophisticated statistical techniques, these investigators have just begun to find suggestive evidence of subtypes (e.g., McKinney, 1987a, 1989; McKinney & Feagans, 1984; McKinney, Short, & Feagans, 1985; McKinney & Speece, 1986; Speece, McKinney, & Applebaum, 1985). It is still too early to tell whether the search for subtypes will yield information useful for teachers and researchers.

Intra-Individual Variation

In addition to varying from one to another, children with learning disabilities also have a tendency to exhibit variability within their own profile of abilities. For example, a child may be two or three years above grade level in reading but two or three years behind grade level in math. Such uneven profiles account for references to *specific* learning disabilities in the literature on learning disabilities. Some children have specific deficits in just one or a few areas of achievement or development.

Some of the pioneers in the field of learning disabilities alerted the field to intra-individual variation. Samuel Kirk was one of the most influential in advocating the notion of individual variation in students with learning disabilities. He developed the Illinois Test of Psycholinguistic Abilities, which purportedly measured variation in processes important for reading. Although researchers ultimately found that Kirk's test did not measure processes germane to reading (Hallahan & Cruickshank, 1973; Hammill & Larsen, 1974) and the test is rarely used today, most authorities still recognize intra-individual differences as a feature of many students with learning disabilities.

We now turn to a discussion of some of the most common characteristics of persons with learning disabilities.

Academic Achievement Problems

Academic deficits are the hallmark of learning disabilities. By definition, if there is no academic problem, a learning disability does not exist.

Reading

Reading poses the most difficulty for most students with learning disabilities. Most authorities believe that this problem is related to deficient language skills, especially **phonological skills**—the ability to understand the rules of how various sounds go with certain letters to make up words (Foorman & Liberman, 1989; Stanovich, 1991; Vellutino, 1987). It is easy to understand why problems with phonology would be at the heart of many reading difficulties. If a person has problems breaking words into their component sounds, he or she will have trouble learning to read.

➢ **phonological skills.** The ability to understand grapheme-phoneme correspondence, the rules by which sounds go with letters to make up words; generally thought to be the reason for the reading problems of many students with learning disabilities.

Even though phonological problems may be the cause of many reading problems, there is mounting evidence that a small proportion of reading problems may be due to difficulty in processing the orthographic, or visual, information from letters (Stanovich, 1991). It is still too early to tell how significant visual/orthographic problems are for persons with reading disabilities.

Written Language

People with learning disabilities often have problems in one or more of the following areas: handwriting, spelling, and composition (Newcomer & Barenbaum, 1991). Although even the best students can have less than perfect handwriting, the kinds of problems manifested by some students with learning disabilities are much more severe. Their written products are sometimes illegible, and the children are sometimes very slow writers. Spelling can be a significant problem because of the difficulty (noted in the previous section) in understanding the correspondence between sounds and letters.

In addition to the more mechanical areas of handwriting and spelling, students with learning disabilities also frequently have difficulties in the more creative aspects of composition (Englert, 1992; Englert et al., 1988; Montague & Graves, 1992; Montague, Graves, & Leavell, 1991; Thomas, Englert, & Gregg, 1987). Englert and her colleagues have identified three types of difficulties. First, these students are not aware of the basic purpose of writing as an act of communication; instead, they approach writing as a test-taking task. Second, their writing lacks fluency—they write shorter sentences and stories. For example, they have problems elaborating about the emotional and cognitive states of the characters in their stories (Montague & Graves, 1992). They are unable to "get inside the heads" of the characters about whom they write. Third, they do not spontaneously use writing strategies, such as planning, organizing, drafting, and editing.

Spoken Language

Many students with learning disabilities have problems with the *mechanical* (Mann, Cowin, & Schoenheimer, 1989; Vellutino, 1987) and *social uses of language* (Bryan & Bryan, 1986; Mathinos, 1988). Mechanically, they have trouble with **syntax** (grammar), **semantics** (word meanings), and as we have already noted, **phonology** (the ability to break down words into their component sounds and blend individual sounds together to make words).

With regard to social uses of language—commonly referred to as **pragmatics**—students with learning disabilities are often inept in the production and reception of discourse. In short, they are not very good conversationalists.

They are unable to engage in the mutual give and take that conversations require between individuals. When conversing with others, they are often agreeable and cooperative, but they tend to be unpersuasive and deferential. Their conversations are frequently marked by long silences because they do not use the relatively subtle strategies that their nondisabled peers do to keep conversations going. They are not skilled at responding to others' statements or questions and have a tendency to answer their own questions before their companion has a chance to respond. They tend to make task-irrelevant comments and make those with whom they are talking uncomfortable. In one often-cited study, for example, children with and without learning disabilities took turns playing the role of host in a simulated television talk show (Bryan, Donahue, Pearl, & Sturm, 1981).

≻ **syntax.** The way words are joined together to structure meaningful sentences.

≻ **semantics.** The study of the meanings attached to words and sentences.

≻ **phonology.** The study of how individual sounds make up words.

≻ **pragmatics.** The study within psycholinguistics of how one uses language in social situations; emphasizes functional use of language rather than its mechanics.

*P*ragmatics refers to the social uses of language. Many children with learning disabilities have problems with pragmatics which makes it difficult for them to carry on conversations.

Analysis of the verbal interactions revealed that in contrast to nondisabled children, children with learning disabilities playing the host role allowed their nondisabled guests to dominate the conversation. Also, their guests exhibited more signs of discomfort during the interview than did the guests of nondisabled hosts.

Math

Although disorders of reading, writing, and language have traditionally received more emphasis than problems of mathematics, the latter are now gaining a great deal of attention. Authorities now recognize that math problems are second only to reading disabilities as an academic problem area for students with learning disabilities. In one large-scale study of over 1,000 students with learning disabilities, for example, the *average* math percentile score was at about the 30th percentile (Kavale & Reese, 1992).

There is abundant evidence that students with learning disabilities who exhibit problems in math can have problems in computation of math facts (Mercer & Miller, 1992) and/or difficulties in math problem solving (Cawley & Parmar, 1992). In one study, the poor performance of students with learning disabilities on word problems was due to difficulties selecting and applying problem-solving strategies rather than to computational errors (Montague & Bos, 1990).

Perceptual, Perceptual-Motor, and General Coordination Problems

Studies indicate that some children with learning disabilities exhibit visual and/or auditory perceptual disabilities (see Hallahan, 1975, for a review). These problems are not the same as visual or auditory acuity problems evidenced in blindness or deafness. Rather, these are disturbances in organizing and interpreting visual and auditory stimuli. A child with visual perceptual problems might, for example, have trouble solving puzzles or seeing and remembering visual shapes. Or, he or she might have a tendency to reverse letters, e.g., mistake a *b* for a *d*. A child with auditory perceptual problems might have difficulty discriminating between two words that sound alike (e.g., *fit* and *fib*) or following orally presented directions.

Teachers and parents have also noted that some students with learning disabilities have difficulty with physical activities involving motor skills. They describe some of these children as having "two left feet" or "ten thumbs." The problems may involve both fine-motor (small motor muscles) and gross-motor (large motor muscles) skills. Fine-motor skills often involve the coordination of the visual and motor systems.

Several of the early theorists in the learning disabilities field believed a causal link exists between perceptual problems and learning disabilities, especially reading disabilities. Furthermore, they believed that by training visual perceptual skills in isolation from academic material, students with learning disabilities would read better. However, researchers have shown that such training does not improve reading ability (see Hallahan & Cruickshank, 1973, for a review).

Disorders of Attention and Hyperactivity

Students with attention problems display such characteristics as distractibility, impulsivity, and hyperactivity. Teachers and parents of these children often characterize them as being unable to stick with one task for very long, failing to listen to others, talking nonstop, blurting out the first thing on their mind, and being generally disorganized in planning their activities in and out of school.

At one time, *hyperactive*, was the term professionals used to describe such children. Although most of these children do display excessive motor activity,

nattention takes many forms, one of which is daydreaming.

xperts agree that attentional problems are at the heart of the hyperactivity among many children with learning disabilities.

authorities generally point to inattention as being the more critical problem and also believe that there are some children who exhibit attention problems without hyperactivity. The terms used now reflect this concern for attention problems. The psychiatric profession, for example, uses the classifications, *attention-deficit hyperactivity disorder* and *attention-deficit disorder without hyperactivity*, depending on whether there is hyperactivity present (Task Force on DSM-IV, 1991).

Numerous studies have documented the existence of attention problems in a large percentage of persons with learning disabilities. The best estimates available indicate that at least 33 percent of students with learning disabilities also have attentional problems (Shaywitz & Shaywitz, 1987). Similarly, although a child can have attention problems without also having a learning disability, the prevalence of learning disabilities is elevated significantly in children who are inattentive. The overlap between attention deficit disorders and learning disabilities has led to considerable controversy over whether the federal government should recognize attention deficit as a separate category (see box on p. 176).

Memory, Cognitive, and Metacognitive Problems

We discuss memory, cognitive, and metacognitive problems together because they are closely related. A person who has problems in one of these areas is likely to have problems in the other two as well. Parents and teachers are well aware that students with learning disabilities have problems remembering such things as assignments and appointments. In fact, they often exclaim in exasperation that they can't understand how a child so smart could forget things so easily. Numerous researchers have documented that many students with learning disabilities have a real deficit in memory (Hallahan, 1975; Hallahan, Kauffman, & Ball, 1973; Swanson, 1987; Torgesen, 1988; Torgesen & Kail, 1980).

Researchers have found that one of the major reasons that children with learning disabilities perform poorly on memory tasks is that, unlike their nondisabled peers, they do not use *strategies*. For example, most children, when presented with a list of words to memorize, will rehearse the names to themselves. They will also make use of categories by rehearsing words in groups that go together. Students with learning disabilities are not likely to use these strategies spontaneously.

...TENTION DEFICIT DISORDER BE A SEPARATE ...Y OF SPECIAL EDUCATION? ➤

...Disabilities Education Act (IDEA) does
...deficit disorder as a separate category
...the federal government and profes-
...the position that students with attention
...ty for special education unless they also
qualified for learning disabilities. Many parents and some
professionals, however, felt strongly that there should be a
separate category because some students did not meet criteria
set up for identification as learning disabled, but still exhibited
significant school problems because of inattention. Some also
maintained that, rather than keeping the best interests of the
children in mind, federal government and school officials were
more concerned about keeping the numbers of students in
special education down in order to save money.

In 1991, the U. S. Department of Education, after receiving
much pressure from parent groups, issued a memorandum to
state departments of education clarifying that students with
attention deficit disorders may be eligible for special education
under the category *other health impaired* "in instances where
the ADD is a chronic or acute health problem that results in
limited alertness, which adversely affects educational performance."

It is still too early to tell whether this policy will satisfy the
concerns of parents. Some believe that the other health
impaired category is too indirect a means of classifying these
children. They think that parents and professionals are not as
likely to recognize the special needs of students with attention
deficit disorders unless there is a separate category that identifies their needs. It is fair to say, however, that most professionals believe this memorandum has clarified the confusion and
there is no need for yet another category of special education.

➤ **cognition.** The ability to
solve problems and use
strategies; an area of difficulty
for many persons with
learning disabilities.

➤ **metacognition.** One's
understanding of the
strategies available for
learning a task and the
regulatory mechanisms to
complete the task.

The deficiency in the use of strategies on memory tasks is an indication of
children with learning disabilities' problems in cognition. **Cognition** is a broad
term covering many different aspects of thinking and problem solving. Students
with learning disabilities often exhibit disorganized thinking that results in problems with planning and organizing their lives at school and at home.

Closely related to children with learning disabilities' cognitive problems are
their problems in metacognition (Hallahan, Kneedler, & Lloyd, 1983; Kneedler &
Hallahan, 1984; Short & Weissberg-Benchell, 1989). **Metacognition** has two components:

(1) An awareness of what skills, strategies, and resources are needed to perform a
task effectively; and (2) the ability to use self-regulatory mechanisms to ensure the
successful completion of the task, such as planning one's moves, evaluating the effectiveness of one's ongoing activities, checking the outcomes of one's efforts, and reme-
diating whatever difficulties arise. (Baker, 1982, pp. 27–28)

An example of difficulties with the first component—awareness of skills,
strategies, and resources—was evident in a study in which the experimenter
asked children how they would go about remembering different things
(Torgesen, 1977). When asked such questions as "Suppose you lost your jacket
while you were at school, how would you go about finding it?" students with
learning disabilities could not produce as many strategies as could their nondisabled peers.

An example of the second component of metacognition—ability to self-regulate—is comprehension monitoring. **Comprehension monitoring** refers to abilities employed while one reads and attempts to comprehend textual material.
Investigators have found that many students with reading disabilities have problems, for example, in being able to sense when they are not understanding what
they are reading (Bos & Filip, 1982). Good readers are able to sense this and make
necessary adjustments, such as slowing down and/or rereading difficult passages. Students with reading problems are also likely to have problems picking

➤ **comprehension
monitoring.** The ability to
keep track of one's own
comprehension of reading
material and to make
adjustments to comprehend
better while one is reading;
often deficient in students
with learning disabilities.

out the main idea of a paragraph. Good readers spend more time and effort focusing on the major ideas contained in the text they read.

Social-Emotional Problems

Although by no means all, perhaps not even a majority of, children with learning disabilities have significant social-emotional problems, they do run a greater risk than their nondisabled peers of having these types of problems (Pearl, 1992). They have a tendency to be rejected by their peers and to have poor self-concepts.

One plausible reason for the social problems of some students with learning disabilities is that they have deficits in social cognition. They misread social cues and may misinterpret the feelings and emotions of others. Most children, for example, are able to tell when their behavior is bothering others. Students with learning disabilities sometimes act as if they are oblivious to the affect their behavior is having on their peers. They also have difficulty taking the perspective of others, of putting themselves in someone else's shoes.

It may also be that some of the behavioral characteristics of children with learning disabilities that we have already mentioned annoy others and/or make it more difficult for others to interact with them. For example, if the child with learning disabilities has problems with conversational skills, he or she may have difficulty acquiring and maintaining friendships. Or if the child has an attention deficit disorder that results in a propensity to intrude into other people's conversations, others may shun him or her.

Motivational Problems

Another source of problems for many students with learning disabilities is their motivation, or feelings about their own abilities to deal with life's many problems. (Deci & Chandler, 1986). They appear content to let events occur without attempting to take charge. They may demonstrate their motivational problems in three interrelated ways: (1) external locus of control, (2) negative attributions, and (3) learned helplessness.

External Locus of Control

Locus of control refers to one's view of being controlled by either internal or external factors. People with an internal locus of control believe that they are essentially in control of what happens to them, whereas those with an external locus of control believe that they are controlled by external factors, such as luck or fate. Individuals with learning disabilities are much more likely to exhibit an external rather than an internal locus of control (Hallahan, Gajar, Cohen, & Tarver, 1978; Short & Weissberg-Benchell, 1989). For example, when asked a question such as "Suppose you did a better than usual job in a subject at school. Would it probably happen (1) because you tried harder or (2) because someone helped you?" they are more likely to choose (2). In other words, these children view themselves as controlled by external rather than internal factors.

Negative Attributions

Closely related to the work on locus of control is research on **attributions**, which refer to what people think are the causes of their successes and failures. The findings on attributions of children who are learning disabled are consistent

> **locus of control.** A motivational term referring to how people attribute their successes or failures; people with an internal locus of control believe that they themselves are the reason for success or failure, whereas people with an external locus of control believe outside forces (e. g., other people) influence how they perform.

> **attributions.** Explanations given by people for their successes and failures. Attributions may be internal or external.

with what one would expect, given their propensity for an external locus of control. Bryan and Bryan (1986) provide the following summary of attribution research:

> Across ages, then, learning-disabled children and adolescents are unlikely to take pride in their successes and are particularly prone to minimize or discount whatever successes they achieve. They are not so reluctant, however, to minimize their responsibilities for failure. Further, they appear to be more pessimistic than nondisabled peers with regard to future success. (p. 203)

Learned Helplessness

Given the motivational profile of an external locus of control and pessimistic attributions, it is no wonder that authorities have also tagged children who are learning disabled as being at risk for developing **learned helplessness**, a person's belief that his or her efforts will not result in desired outcomes (Seligman, 1992). These people learn to expect failure no matter how hard they try; therefore, they tend to "give up" or to lose motivation. Children with learning disabilities tend to devalue effort, to believe that no amount of effort on their part will help them achieve. They tend to view themselves as helpless in the academic situation (Schunk, 1989).

Whether the learned helplessness causes the academic problems or vice versa is an unanswerable question at this point. It is logical to assume, however, that there is a kind of vicious circle: The child with learning disabilities who exhibits problems in certain areas learns to expect failure in any new situation. This expectancy of failure, or learned helplessness, may cause the child to give up readily in the face of a task that is not easily solvable. The result is more failure. A child who has experienced years of this kind of failure cycle including an accompanying expectancy of failure will probably need to be taught coping strategies for dealing with failure (Pearl, Bryan, & Donahue, 1980).

The Child with Learning Disabilities as an Inactive Learner with Strategy Deficits

Many of the psychological and behavioral characteristics we have described can be summed up by saying that the student who is learning disabled is an inactive learner lacking in strategies for attacking academic problems (Hallahan & Bryan, 1981; Hallahan & Reeve, 1980; Torgesen, 1977). Specifically, research describes the student with learning disabilities as someone who does not believe in his or her own abilities (learned helplessness), has an inadequate grasp of what strategies are available for problem solving (poor metacognitive skills), and has problems producing appropriate learning strategies spontaneously.

The practical implications of this constellation of characteristics is that students with learning disabilities may have difficulties working independently. They are not likely to be "self starters." Assignments or activities requiring them to work on their own may cause problems unless the teacher carefully provides an appropriate amount of support. Homework, for example, may pose particular problems (see box on p. 179). (Many of the cognitive training procedures we discuss later are designed to alleviate the passive learning style characterized by many students with learning disabilities.)

➤ **learned helplessness.** A motivational term referring to a condition wherein a person believes that no matter how hard he or she tries, failure will result.

OMEWORK AND THE STUDENT WITH LEARNING DISABILITIES ➤

The combination of calls for higher standards in the schools by general education reformers and for increased mainstreaming of students who are learning disabled by special education reformers has not mixed well in all respects. One of the problem areas is homework (Hallahan, 1992; Polloway, Foley, & Epstein, 1992).

In response to reformers' criticisms, teachers are increasing the amount of homework they assign their pupils (U.S. Department of Education, 1990). Unfortunately, the behavioral characteristics of many students with learning disabilities make them prime candidates for having homework problems. Their generally passive approach to learning and difficulty in working independently make it hard for many students with learning disabilities to tackle homework. Evidence of this comes from a survey of teachers and parents (Polloway et al., 1992).

Both groups rated students with learning disabilities as having overwhelmingly more problems with homework than their nondisabled peers. Their difficulties ranged from failing to bring home their homework, to being distracted while doing homework, to forgetting to bring their assignments back to class.

Many authorities on homework believe that teachers should use it primarily for having students practice proficiency in skills they already possess, rather than for learning new skills. This dictum would appear even more crucial for students with learning disabilities, who are so frequently characterized by their inability to work independently. Asking students to acquire new information during homework only puts students with learning disabilities further behind their peers and jeopardizes the goal of mainstreaming.

EDUCATIONAL CONSIDERATIONS

The following three categories reflect what most professionals recognize as the major approaches to the academic problems of students with learning disabilities:

- Process and multisensory training
- Cognitive training
- Direct instruction

And the following four categories are the major approaches for students who have attention deficit disorder:

- Structure and stimulus reduction
- Behavior modification
- Cognitive training
- Medication

In practice, one often finds a combination of two or more of these approaches.

Educational Methods for Academic Problems

Process and Multisensory Training

At one time, the most popular educational approach for students with learning disabilities involved the training of psychological processes, such as visual and auditory perception, presumed to be at the root of their academic problems (Frostig & Horne, 1964; Kephart, 1971, 1975; Kirk & Kirk, 1971; Minskoff, Wiseman, & Minskoff, 1974). For example, rather than working directly on academic materials, the teacher would have students engage in several visual perceptual exercises. One such exercise might be finding and tracing figures embedded within other lines and figures on a worksheet; another is connecting dots as they are drawn on a chalkboard by the teacher.

Closely related to process training are multisensory approaches, which include the use of multiple sensory modalities. A good example is Fernald's VAKT method (Fernald, 1943) wherein *V* stands for visual, *A* for auditory, *K* for kinesthetic, and *T* for tactual. In learning words, for instance, the child first sees the word (visual), then hears the teacher say the word (auditory). Next the child says the word (auditory), and finally, the child traces the word (kinesthetic and tactual). The assumption is that students will be more likely to learn if more than one sense is involved in the learning process.

Research has not been able to document the effectiveness of process and multisensory approaches, especially the former (see Hallahan & Cruickshank, 1973, for a review). For this reason, very few teachers use process training techniques today. One of the major criticisms of process training is that it is divorced too far from the academic material. That is, authorities have criticized the idea of having students work on visual and auditory perceptual exercises using worksheets that contain no academic content.

Cognitive Training

> ➤ **cognitive training.** Training procedures designed to change thoughts or thought patterns.

Cognitive training also concentrates on changing psychological processes, or thoughts, of persons with learning disabilities. It differs from process training in two important respects. First, most advocates of cognitive training recommend that it be carried out in conjunction with the academic material on which the student is having problems. Second, researchers have generally found it to be a successful approach (Borkowski, 1992; Pressley, Symons, Snyder, & Cariglia-Bull, 1989; Swanson, 1989).

Authorities give at least two reasons that cognitive training is particularly appropriate for students with learning disabilities. It is aimed at helping them overcome their:

1. cognitive and metacognitive problems by providing them with specific strategies for solving problems and
2. motivational problems of passivity and learned helplessness by stressing self-initiative and involving students as much as possible in their own treatment.

A variety of specific techniques falls under the heading of cognitive training. The box on p. 181 lists characteristics common to many successful cognitive training approaches. Here we present three techniques that are particularly useful for students with learning disabilities: self-instruction, mnemonic keyword method, and scaffolded instruction. (We discuss another cognitive training approach, the Learning Strategies Curriculum, in the section on secondary educational programming.) Keep in mind that these approaches can have a great deal of overlap.

> ➤ **self-instruction.** A type of cognitive behavior modification technique that requires individuals to talk aloud and then to themselves as they solve problems.

Self-Instruction. The idea of **self-instruction** is to bring to students' attention the various stages of problem-solving tasks while they are performing them and to bring behavior under verbal control (Meichenbaum, 1975; Meichenbaum & Goodman, 1971). All this is usually done gradually. Typically, the teacher first models the use of the verbal routine while solving the problem. Then he or she closely supervises the students' using the verbal routine while doing the task, and then the students do it on their own.

EIGHT PRINCIPLES OF EFFECTIVE COGNITIVE TRAINING PROGRAMS ➤

Many specific techniques fall under the rubric of cognitive training. Because of this diversity it is sometimes difficult for teachers to know which strategies are most likely to be successful. Pressley and colleagues, however, after examining several effective cognitive training programs, arrived at a list of eight common features (Pressley, Symons, Snyder, & Cariglia-Bull, 1989; Symons, Snyder, Cariglia-Bull, & Pressley, 1989). A teacher can use them as a guide when choosing among cognitive training options.

1. *Teach a few strategies at a time.* Rather than bombarding children with a number of strategies all at once, it is better to teach them just a few. In this way, there is a better chance that the students can learn the strategies in a comprehensive and not a superficial fashion.
2. *Teach self-monitoring.* It is helpful if students keep track of their own progress. When checking their own work, if they find an error, they should be encouraged to try to correct it on their own.
3. *Teach them when and where to use the strategies.* Many students with learning disabilities have problems with the metacognitive ability of knowing when and where they can use strategies that teachers have taught. Teachers must give them this information as well as extensive experience in using the strategies in a variety of different settings.
4. *Maintain the students' motivation.* Students need to know that the strategies work. Teachers can help motivation by consistently pointing out the benefits of the strategies,

explaining how strategies work, and charting students' progress.
5. *Teach in context.* Students should learn cognitive techniques as an integrated part of the curriculum. Rather than using cognitive training in an isolated manner, teachers should teach students to employ cognitive strategies during academic lessons.
6. *Do not neglect a nonstrategic knowledge base.* Sometimes those who use cognitive training become such avid proponents of cognitive strategies that they forget the importance of factual knowledge. The more facts children know about history, science, math, English, and so forth, the less they will need to rely on strategies.
7. *Engage in direct teaching.* Because the emphasis in cognitive training is on encouraging students to take more initiative in their own learning, teachers may feel that they are less necessary than is actually the case. Cognitive training does not give license to back off from directly teaching students. Students' reliance on teachers should gradually fade. In the early stages, teachers need to be directly in control of supervising the students' use of the cognitive strategies.
8. *Regard cognitive training as long term.* Because cognitive training often results in immediate improvement, there may be a temptation to view it as a panacea or a quick fix. To maintain improvements and have them generalize to other settings, however, students need extensive practice in applying the strategies they have learned.

An example of a study using self-instruction as an integral feature of instruction involved fifth and sixth grade students with learning disabilities solving math word problems (Case, Harris, & Graham, 1992). The five-step strategy the students learned to use involved saying the problem out loud, looking for important words and circling them, drawing pictures to help explain what was happening, writing the math sentence, and writing the answer. Furthermore, students were prompted to use the following self-instructions: (1) problem definition: What do I have to do? (2) planning: How can I solve this problem? (3) strategy use: "The five-step strategy will help me look for important words." (4) self-evaluation: "How am I doing?" (5) self-reinforcement: "Good job. I got it right."

An example of self-instruction used for spelling involved having a boy: (1) say the word out loud, (2) say the first syllable of the word, (3) name each of the letters in the syllable three times, (4) say each letter as he wrote it, and (5) repeat steps 2 through 4 for each succeeding syllable (Kosiewicz, Hallahan, Lloyd, & Graves, 1982).

Mnemonic Keyword Method. The **mnemonic keyword method** is designed to help students with memory problems remember information by presenting

> ➤ **mnemonic keyword method.** A cognitive training strategy used to help children with memory problems remember curriculum content. The teacher transforms abstract information into a concrete picture, which depicts the material in a more meaningful way.

A Key to Success

MYLA YOUNG BURGESS

Learning Disabilities Specialist; B. S., Communication Disorders, Hampton University; M. Ed., University of North Carolina at Greensboro

LAURA CLARK MILES

Fourth grade teacher; B. A., Music Education, Longwood College; Elementary certification; M. A., Educational Psychology, University of Virginia

> **Myla** Two years ago, Pat Parrot, Chesterfield County's collaborative teaching program facilitator, introduced me to collaborative teaching. She explained that collaborative teaching was an additional service delivery model that would help bridge the gap between special education and regular education.

As my students with learning disabilities experienced difficulties in mainstreaming, it became evident that I should try collaborative teaching. I began by attending a three-day workshop. My principal, Wes Hicks, attended on the day designated for administrators and teachers. After the workshop, he and I agreed we should try collaborative teaching on a small scale at the fourth grade level.

My first step was to select a co-teacher. I learned in the workshop that co-teachers should choose to work collaboratively and should share com-

mon beliefs and goals. With my manual in hand, I excitedly called Laura to ask her to be my co-teacher. She accepted with great enthusiasm. After telling our principal that Laura and I would be co-teaching, he immediately rearranged the fourth grade rolls so that the five students with learning disabilities we had chosen to participate in the program would all be in Laura's classroom. Having attended the workshop and believing in the philosophy of collaboration, he was more than willing to make these adjustments.

> **Laura** Before the school year started a couple of years ago, Myla called me to tell me about the collaborative teaching model. She had discussed it with our principal, and plans were underway to implement the program. I was excited by the prospect of participating in this new approach. As a classroom teacher for

thirteen years, I had often felt very inadequate in meeting the needs of students with learning disabilities who were mainstreamed into my regular classroom. I was anxious to learn new strategies and techniques to meet their needs.

That September was truly a new beginning for both of us. Our class consisted of five students with learning disabilities and twenty average-to above average-ability students. We began collaborative teaching using a complementary instruction approach, which allows the general classroom teacher to maintain the primary responsibility for teaching the academic curriculum while the special educator teaches organizational and study skills that students need to master the material. As the year progressed, we moved to a team teaching approach, which is when the general educator and special educator plan and teach the academic curriculum to all students within the classroom. Under this approach, we alternated presenting segments of lessons with whoever was not teaching being responsible for monitoring student performance and/or behavior. We continued using both approaches throughout the school year.

After Mr. Hicks had closely monitored our classroom the first year and reviewed the progress of all students, he was as committed to this program as we were. In planning our second year of collaborative teaching, we felt that an increase in collaboration time would better meet the needs of the upcoming fourth grade students with learning disabilities. To achieve this goal, our first priority was scheduling. Mr. Hicks played a vital role in creating the schedule and determining class size and student placement.

This class consisted of twenty-five students, including ten with learning disabilities, two with language impairment, and thirteen average-to above average-ability students. We used collaborative teaching for science/social studies, the majority of math, and 1 hour and 15 minutes of language arts. All students remained in the regular classroom all day with the exception of four students with learning disabilities who went to a resource room during language arts. These four students were two or more years below grade level in reading. During this year, we moved almost entirely to the team teaching approach, with Myla stressing independent learning strategies that benefited all students in the classroom.

> **Myla** We have found several advantages in using the collaborative teaching approach. First, there is more mastery of skills by all students. Two teachers in the classroom allow more individualized help, which enhances mastery of skills. With two teachers, we can give students more instruction, re-teaching, and enrichment when needed.

It is also helpful to have two judgments on assessments, classroom objectives, and lesson presentations. For example, it is good to have two points of view regarding the appropriateness of the format and validity of written tests as well as the appropriateness of alternative assessments for students with disabilities. Sometimes our presentations are not received by students as we had expected. The second teacher can sometimes interpret from a student's point of view what went wrong with the lesson.

We gain from each other's experiences. Each of us is continually attending workshops or classes in our fields. This brings more and more ideas and resources to the classroom. We each learn from each other, and the class receives instruction based on the strengths of each of us.

> **Laura** We also have more time to address emotional needs. Students with learning disabilities often have emotional needs which interfere with their academics. With the support of the guidance counselor, school psychologist, and teacher of students with emotional disturbance, individual needs are better met with two teachers in the classroom. For example, while one of us is teaching academics, the other is free to address emotional or attention problems that might interfere, without instruction being interrupted.

> **Myla** Students seem to gain a sense of self-worth and confidence in their own ability by displaying strengths and improving on their weaknesses in a regular classroom environment. They also have a better sense of belonging because they are with the same students all day and have the same schedule.

> **Laura** Collaborative teaching with flexible groups makes it possible to provide enrichment, practice, re-teaching, and teaching at all levels of instruction. Flexible groups means having different groups, determined daily, based on specific instructional and social objectives for a particular day. These groups are set up for cooperative learning activities or station teaching, which is instructional content divided into two parts. Half the group is taught topics such as vocabulary expansion or comprehension. We then switch groups so that all students receive the same instruction. Because it is rare that both of us are absent on the same day, collaborative teaching allows for stability of classroom instruction. Stability of classroom instruction is also increased because there is less time wasted with students traveling to and from the resource room.

We also think that this approach facilitates modeling and the teaching of strategies. We find we draw on each other's strengths to model certain strategies. Myla, because of her training in special education, is familiar with many more strategies. For example, we teach them strategies for paragraph writing, test taking, and a variety of mnemonic strategies.

It has been our experience that this program increases the expectations for students with disabilities. Students performances have often exceeded our initial expectations. We find it appropriate to allow students to go as far and as fast as they can. Students with learning disabilities must know that his or her expectations are the same as those for the regular student.

Collaborative teaching also lowers the pupil-teacher ratio. It is very important

that the classroom size does not exceed twenty-five students. Too many students create obstacles for a successful program. We believe that students with learning disabilities should not comprise more than half the class and that at least one-half of the class should be average or above average in ability.

> **Myla** I'd like to describe just one student, who is probably our greatest success story. Mary is a determined and motivated young lady who functions in the low average range of intellectual ability with skill deficits in visual perception, non-verbal reasoning, and visual-motor integration. She has been in the learning disabilities program since kindergarten. Mary has difficulty with word recognition, word attack, reading comprehension, written language, math concepts, recalling math facts, comprehension of social studies and science concepts, and copying from the board.

As a fourth grader, Mary's schedule in the morning included science/social studies, which alternated every nine weeks, and math. We taught all of these collaboratively. After lunch, she went to the learning disabilities resource room for the remainder of the day for instruction in reading and written language.

We began the school year with many doubts and concerns as to how and to what extent we would be able to meet Mary's needs. Most important, we did not lower our expectations for Mary's performance. Our philosophy was to improve Mary's self-esteem, increase her independence, and have her achieve the highest level of success possible.

Mary far exceeded our original expectations. We worked very closely with her parents, who were very supportive, and the combined effort contributed greatly to her success. Using all of the techniques and modifications of the program allowed her to function in the regular classroom learning the required skills and concepts.

them with pictorial representations of abstract concepts (Mastropieri & Scruggs, 1988; Scruggs & Mastropieri, 1992). By making abstract information more concrete, students are better able to remember content in a variety of subjects, such as English, history, science, and foreign languages. For example,

> to teach that "radial symmetry" refers to structurally similar body parts that extend out from the center of organisms, such as starfish, an acoustically similar keyword, ("radio cemetery") was constructed from the unfamiliar term, radial symmetry. In the picture, radio cemetery was shown in the shape of a star, with radios as headstones, and skeletons dancing to the music from the radios. Each arm of the star is shown to be similar in appearance to each other arm, to enforce the concept... (Scruggs & Mastropieri, 1992, p. 222)

➤ **scaffolded instruction.** A cognitive approach to instruction whereby the teacher provides temporary structure or support while students are learning a task; the support is gradually removed as the students are able to perform the task independently.

➤ **reciprocal teaching.** A teaching method in which students and teachers are involved in a dialogue to facilitate reading comprehension.

Scaffolded Instruction. **Scaffolded instruction** provides assistance to students when they are first learning a task and then gradually the help is reduced so that eventually the students are doing the task independently. Scaffolded instruction is supported by the Russian psychologist Vygotsky's theory that states that children learn from their elders in ways that are similar to apprentices who learn their craft from masters. Several investigators have recommended that teachers provide this kind of temporary support to students with learning disabilities (Englert, Raphael, Anderson, Anthony, & Stevens, 1991; Palincsar, 1986).

The types of supports, or scaffolds, that teachers can use vary. One approach that uses scaffolded instruction is called **reciprocal teaching** because the teacher and students take turns "teaching" the content to one another. In this method, students (a) see cognitive strategies modeled by the teacher and (b) try out those cognitive strategies while being monitored by the teacher. The idea is for the teacher's monitoring to become less vigilant as the students become more adept at learning. Here is an example of reciprocal teaching in action:

> The adult teacher assigned a segment of the passage (usually a paragraph) to be read and either indicated that it was her turn to be the teacher or assigned one of the students to teach the segment. The adult teacher and the students then read the assigned segment silently. After reading the text, the teacher (student or adult) for that segment summarized (reviewed) the content, discussed and clarified any difficulties, asked a question that a teacher or test might ask on the segment, and finally, made a prediction about future content. All of these activities were embedded in as natural a dialogue as possible, with the teacher and other students giving feedback to one another. (Brown & Campione, 1984, p. 174)

Direct Instruction

➤ **direct instruction.** A method of teaching academics, especially reading and math. It emphasizes drill and practice and immediate feedback. The lessons are precisely sequenced, fast-paced, and well-rehearsed by the teacher.

Direct instruction differs from process training even more than cognitive training in its emphasis on instruction using academic materials. It focuses specifically on the instructional process. Advocates of direct instruction stress a systematic analysis of the concept to be taught, rather than of the characteristics of the student. A variety of direct instruction programs is available for reading, math, and language. These programs consist of precisely sequenced, fast-paced lessons taught to small groups of four to ten. There is a heavy emphasis on drill and practice. The teacher teaches from a well-rehearsed script and pupils follow the lead of the teacher, who often uses hand signals to prompt participation. The teacher offers immediate corrective feedback for errors and praise for correct responses.

Two of the most popular direct instruction programs are *Corrective Reading: Decoding* and *Corrective Reading: Comprehension* (Englemann, Carnine, Johnson, &

Meyers, 1988, 1989). A wealth of research evidence supports the effectiveness of direct instruction programs. Not only do they result in immediate academic gains, but there are also indications that they lead to long-term academic gains (see Lloyd, 1988, for a review of this research).

Educational Methods for Attention Deficit Disorders

Structure and Stimulus Reduction

William Cruickshank developed an educational program for students with learning disabilities based on earlier work with children who were mentally retarded (Strauss & Kephart, 1955; Strauss & Lehtinen, 1947). Cruickshank's approach (Cruickshank, Bentzen, Ratzeburg, & Tannhauser, 1961) included three principles:

1. Structure
2. Reduction of environmental stimulation
3. Enhancement of intensity of teaching materials

Basically, a **structured program** is heavily teacher directed—that is, the teacher determines most of the activities for the student. The rationale for this approach is that children with attention problems cannot make their own decisions until carefully educated to do so.

Because of the assumption that children with attention problems are susceptible to distraction, irrelevant stimuli are reduced. What the teacher wants the child to attend to is increased in intensity (often through the use of bright colors). **Stimulus reduction** is achieved by some of the following modifications:

- Soundproofed walls and ceilings
- Carpeting
- Opaque windows
- Enclosed bookcases and cupboards
- Limited use of colorful bulletin boards
- Use of cubicles and three-sided work areas

It is rare today to see teachers using all of the components of Cruickshank's program. Most authorities now believe that a structured program may be important in the early stages of working with some students with attention deficit disorders, but that these students gradually need to become more independent in their learning. They also believe that not all children with attention deficit disorders are distracted by things in their environment. For those who are distractible, however, some authorities recommend the use of such things as cubicles to reduce extraneous stimulation.

Behavior Modification

Many authorities point to behavior modification as a way of controlling inattentive behavior. The use of reinforcement (e.g., verbal praise, extra time on the computer) to increase attentive behaviors, and punishment (e.g., reduced time for recess) can have powerful effects on behavior. A good example of a behavior modification program used to increase attentive behavior is the classic study of a disruptive first-grader named Levi (Hall, Lund, & Jackson, 1968). In this study, the teacher's attention to the student served as a reinforcer. Levi's attention increased dramatically when the teacher ignored Levi when he was not attending and responded to him only when he was on-task.

> **structured program.** A concept largely forwarded by Cruickshank; emphasizes a teacher-directed approach in which activities and environment are structured for children who are distractible and hyperactive.

> **stimulus reduction.** A concept largely forwarded by Cruickshank; an approach to teaching distractible and hyperactive children that emphasizes reducing extraneous (nonrelevant to learning) material.

Some teachers are hesitant to use behavior modification because they believe it is too manipulative and controlling. They also cite the difficulty of applying it in regular classrooms where most of the students do not need a behavior modification program. Other teachers, especially those who work in special settings, are staunch advocates of behavior modification for students with attention problems.

Cognitive Training

Many authorities recommend cognitive training techniques as a way of getting students with attention deficit disorders to take control over their own behavior. These authorities believe that, by thinking about their behavior more carefully, students can regulate their impulsive and inattentive behavior. An example of a cognitive training technique that teachers have used to help students with attention problems is self-monitoring (Hallahan, Lloyd, Kosiewicz, Kauffman, & Graves, 1979; Lloyd, Hallahan, Kosiewicz, & Kneedler, 1980). **Self-monitoring** refers to procedures that require the person to keep track of his or her behavior. In self-monitoring of attention, students monitor whether they are paying or not paying attention while engaged in academic work. The procedure is simple. The teacher places a tape recorder near the child. While the child is engaged in some kind of academic activity, a tape containing tones (the time between tones varies randomly) is played. Whenever he or she hears a tone, the child is to stop work and ask, "Was I paying attention?" He or she then records on a separate score sheet a "Yes" or "No" depending on his or her own assessment of attentional behavior. Here is a set of sample instructions:

> "Johnny, you know how paying attention to your work has been a problem for you. You've heard teachers tell you, 'Pay attention,' 'Get to work,' 'What are you supposed to be doing' and things like that. Well, today we're going to start something that will help you help yourself pay attention better. First we need to make sure that you know what paying attention means. This is what I mean by paying attention." (Teacher models immediate and sustained attention to task.) "And this is what I mean by not paying attention." (Teacher models inattentive behaviors such as glancing around and playing with objects.)
>
> "Now you tell me if I was paying attention." (Teacher models attentive and inattentive behaviors and requires the student to categorize them.) "Okay, now let me show you what we're going to do. While you're working, this tape recorder will be turned on. Every once in a while, you'll hear a little sound like this:" (Teacher plays tone on tape.) "And when you hear that sound quietly ask yourself, 'Was I paying attention?' If you answer 'yes,' put a check in this box. If you answer 'no,' put a check in this box. Then go right back to work. When you hear the sound again, ask the question, answer it, mark your answer, and go back to work. Now, let me show you how it works." (Teacher models entire procedure.) "Now, Johnny, I bet you can do this. Tell me what you're going to do every time you hear a tone. Let's try it. I'll start the tape and you work on these papers." (Teacher observes student's implementation of the entire procedure, praises its correct use, and gradually withdraws her presence.) (Hallahan, Lloyd, & Stoller, 1982, p. 12)

Researchers have documented the effectiveness of self-monitoring with students ranging in age from elementary (Hallahan et al., 1979, 1980) to the secondary grades (Prater, Joy, Chilman, Temple, & Miller, 1991). And some investigators have shown that adding a component in which the students graph their own assessments of their on-task behavior is also effective (DiGangi, Maag, & Rutherford, 1991). One explanation for the effects of self-monitoring is that it helps students with attention problems become more aware of and in control of their own attention processes.

➤ **self-monitoring.** A type of cognitive behavior modification technique that requires individuals to keep track of their own behavior.

Medication

For years, physicians have been prescribing medication for children with attention deficit disorders. Although antidepressants are sometimes used, psychostimulants, such as Ritalin, are the most common. In the past, the use of drugs has been controversial. Some, for example, have claimed that the use of drugs represents a conspiracy of the middle class to keep the lower class docile and oppressed, and that the use of these drugs in childhood leads to drug abuse in the teenage years. Today, however, most authorities recognize that drugs can be a very important part of a total treatment package for many students with attention deficit disorders.

Research on the effectiveness of psychostimulants for helping children attend better is plentiful. (See Henker & Whalen, 1989; Kauffman & Hallahan, 1979; Pelham & Murphy, 1986; Shaywitz & Shaywitz, 1987 for reviews). The major organization of parents of children with attention deficit disorders, Children with Attention Deficit Disorders (Ch.A.D.D., 1992), has also endorsed the use of medication as an effective treatment approach for many persons with attention deficit disorders.

Even though medication helps many children with attention deficit disorder, and some are now recommending it for use with adults (Ch.A.D.D., 1992), there are some important cautions to keep in mind:

- Although most children respond favorably to medication, for a few it is not effective.
- There are some relatively common side effects that go along with the psychostimulants, e.g., insomnia and loss of appetite.
- Parents and teachers need to monitor closely the behavior of the student while on medication. The best dosage level can sometimes be difficult to establish.
- Teachers and parents need to be careful not to give children the message that the drug is the only answer to their problems. Children should not become so dependent on the drug that they give up attempting to take responsibility for their behavior.
- These drugs are relatively powerful substances. They should not be prescribed at the least hint of inattention or poor school work. Physicians, parents, and teachers need to communicate effectively before making the decision to use drugs.

With these cautions in mind, medication can be an indispensable aspect of treatment for many students with attention deficit disorder.

Service Delivery Models

Although students with learning disabilities sometimes attend residential programs or special classes, the resource room is the most common form of service delivery. Because students with learning disabilities, as usually defined, have at least near-average intelligence and may have deficits in only a few areas of academic achievement, they are often seen as good candidates for such placement. The amount of time an individual student spends in the resource room varies considerably, depending on the student's characteristics and the philosophy of the particular school. Some students may spend an hour or two per day in a resource room, whereas others may receive special services only an hour or two per week.

The most accurate predictors of later academic problems are preacademic skills, such as counting and identification of letters, numbers, shapes, and colors.

As we discussed in Chapter 2, more and more schools are moving toward some kind of cooperative teaching arrangement where regular and special education teachers work together in the regular classroom. Some believe this model is particularly appropriate for students with learning disabilities because it allows them to stay in the regular classroom for all, or almost all, of their instruction.

EARLY INTERVENTION

There is very little preschool programming for children with learning disabilities because of the difficulties in identifying them at such a young age. When we talk about testing the preschool child for learning disabilities, we are really talking about prediction rather than identification (Keogh & Glover, 1980). In other words, because preschool children do not ordinarily engage in academics, it is not possible, strictly speaking, to say that they are behind academically. Unfortunately, all other things being equal, prediction is always less precise than identification.

At least two factors make prediction at preschool ages of later learning disabilities particularly difficult:

1. In many cases of learning disabilities, we are talking about relatively mild problems. Many of these children seem bright and competent until faced with a particular academic task, such as reading or spelling. Unlike many

other children with disabilities, children with learning disabilities are not so immediately noticeable.

2. It is often difficult to determine what is a true developmental delay and what is merely a maturational slowness. Many nondisabled children show slow developmental progress at this young age, but they soon catch up with their peers.

Although most professionals hesitate to program for children with learning disabilities at the preschool level, ideally it would be good to do so. We have a great need for research on better predictive tests at the preschool level. At present we know that the most accurate predictors are preacademic skills (Mercer, Algozzine, & Trifiletti, 1979). **Preacademic skills** are behaviors that are needed before formal instruction can begin, such as identification of letters, numbers, shapes, and colors.

TRANSITION

Until the late 1970s and early 1980s, there was relatively little educational programming for learning disabilities that extended beyond the elementary school years. This attitude of benign neglect probably emanated from the mistaken impression that children with learning disabilities would outgrow their disabilities. Although more positive than for children with some other disabilities (e.g., behavior disorders), the long-term prognosis for some individuals with learning disabilities is not rosy. There is a danger, for example, that students with learning disabilities will drop out of school in their teenage years. Also, some run the risk of engaging in delinquent behaviors (see box on p. 190).

Even for the vast majority of students with learning disabilities who do not engage in delinquent behaviors and who do not drop out of school, the future can be uncertain. Several studies of adults with learning disabilities document that many persons with learning disabilities have persistent problems in learning, socializing, holding a job, and performing daily living skills (Gerber & Reiff, 1991; Gerber, Ginsberg, & Reiff, 1992; Kavale, 1988; Reiff & Gerber, 1992; Spekman, Goldberg, & Herman, 1992). Even those who are relatively successful in their transition to adulthood often must devote considerable energy to coping with daily living situations. For example, in an intensive study of adults with learning disabilities, one of the subjects (S3), an assistant dean of students at a large urban university, found it:

> essential that organization and routines remain constant. For example, she recounted that her kitchen is arranged in a specific fashion. Most implements are visible rather than put away because she would not be able to remember where to find them. Once, when her roommate changed the kitchen setup, S3 had great difficulty finding anything, and when she did, she couldn't remember where to return it. She had to reorganize the kitchen to her original plan. When she moved from her home state to the New Orleans area, she kept her kitchen set up in exactly the same way as previously. "I don't know if that's just because I'm stubborn or because it's comfortable."
>
> The need for organization and structure seems to pervade her daily living. She mentioned that she imposes structure on everything from the arrangement of her medicine cabinet to her professional life. She has her work day carefully organized and keeps close track of all her appointments. She has trouble coping with unannounced appointments, meetings or activities. She said that if her work routine is interrupted in such a fashion, "I can't get it together." (Gerber & Reiff, 1991, p. 113)

➤ **preacademic skills.** Behaviors that are needed before formal academic instruction can begin (e. g., ability to identify letters, numbers, shapes, and colors).

*L*EARNING DISABILITIES AND JUVENILE DELINQUENCY: IS THERE A CAUSAL CONNECTION? ➤

There is a higher prevalence of learning disabilities among juvenile delinquents than is ordinarily found in the general population. A review of prevalence studies (Murphy, 1986) found that although the particular prevalence rates vary widely from a low of 9 percent to a high of 36.5 percent, even the most conservative figures contrast sharply with what is usually found in the population at large.

The reason for the high rate of learning disabilities among juvenile delinquents has been a topic of debate for years. There are several feasible explanations for the association between the two categories, some of which specify a direct causal link between the two and some of which do not. In a review of this literature funded by the U.S. Department of Justice's Office of Juvenile Justice and Delinquency Prevention, Keilitz and Dunivant (1986) found five theoretical explanations. The first three theories are causal; the last two are not:

CAUSAL THEORIES

1. *School failure theory:* This theory posits that learning disabilities directly result in school failure, which then results in juvenile delinquency. There are five hypothesized ways in which this can happen. These students may
   a. Become angry at their inability to learn and "strike back at society in anger and retaliation" (p. 19)
   b. Be influenced by other delinquency-prone students with whom they are grouped in school, for example, behavior-disordered children
   c. Because of their school failure become disenchanted with teachers and other symbols of the school as an institution, and this disenchantment may diminish their commitment to socially accepted behavior
   d. Perceive that their academic failure will prohibit them from obtaining a job leading to adequate financial resources and prestige, and this, in turn, leads them to try to obtain money and prestige through illegal means
   e. Because of their lack of success in school blame others rather than themselves for negative events
2. *Susceptibility theory:* According to this theory, children with learning disabilities have certain personality and cognitive attributes that make them susceptible to delinquent behavior. These characteristics include such things as poor impulse control, problems in reading social cues, and suggestibility.
3. *Differential treatment theory:* This theory posits that there may not actually be any difference in how often students with or without learning disabilities commit delinquent acts. Instead, there is a difference in whether they are caught for their delinquent acts and/or how they are

treated by the juvenile justice system. This theory has three hypotheses:
   a. *Differential arrest hypothesis:* This hypothesis holds that students with learning disabilities are more likely than nondisabled students to be apprehended by the police for the same activities. Differential arrest rates may occur for a variety of reasons—for example, students with learning disabilities may have an inability to use strategies for not being caught or to talk their way out of arrest.
   b. *Differential adjudication hypothesis:* This hypothesis posits that youths with learning disabilities, after being arrested, are more likely to have their cases settled judicially. A variety of explanations for this higher incidence of adjudication have been forwarded—for example, their lack of self-control and social ineptness may cause the authorities to bring them to trial.
   c. *Differential disposition hypothesis:* For some of the same reasons noted under a and b, this hypothesis holds that youths with learning disabilities receive harsher treatment by the juvenile court.

NONCAUSAL THEORIES

4. *Sociodemographic characteristics theory:* This theory holds that learning disabilities and juvenile delinquency frequently occur together because they are both caused by social factors, such as parents' education level and socioeconomic status.
5. *Response bias theory:* This theory holds that adolescents who are learning disabled do not commit more delinquent acts than their nondisabled peers. However, when asked in surveys or questionnaires to reveal their delinquent behaviors, they are less likely to conceal them.

If we look at these five theories and some of the subtheories, it should be apparent just how complicated the relationship between learning disabilities and juvenile delinquency is. No wonder there has been so much debate about whether there is a causal connection. Although we need more research on this issue, Keilitz and Dunivant (1986) have conducted two large-scale studies that support the three preceding causal theories. From these results, they have concluded:

> Generally, the data are consistent with causal theories that describe the contribution learning disabilities makes to delinquent behavior. Of course, LD is only one among many causes of delinquency. Only a relatively small proportion of the youth population is affected by LD. Within this group, however, learning disabilities appear to be one of the important causes of delinquency (p. 24).

Factors Related to Successful Transition

How any particular adult with learning disabilities will fare depends on a variety of factors and is difficult to predict. Several researchers have been addressing the topic of what contributes to successful adjustment of adults with learning disabilities (Gerber & Reiff, 1991; Gerber et al., 1992; Kavale, 1988; Murphy, 1992; Reiff & Gerber, 1992; Spekman et al., 1992). Their results have consistently pointed to at least five factors that distinguish those who are successful from those who are not. First, and perhaps most important, those who succeed have shown an extraordinary degree of perseverance. The following quotes from successful adults with learning disabilities are typical:

"I've always had a kind of burning feeling . . . kind of like being on fire to be successful."

"You fight until you can't fight anymore, and then you fight some more . . . you take the hurt and turn it inward and it becomes part of the burn . . . it has to burn."

"If the fires of your drive go out, you will lose your self-respect." (Gerber et al., 1992, p. 480)

Second, successful adults with learning disabilities set goals for themselves. As one highly successful individual explained, "'Successful people have a plan. You have to have a plan, goals, strategy; otherwise you are flying through the clouds and then you hit the mountain'" (Gerber et al., 1992, p. 480).

Third, they have a realistic acceptance of their weaknesses coupled with an attitude of building on their strengths. They do not wallow in self-pity. As one team of researchers concluded, "They seemed to compartmentalize their learning disability and saw it as only one aspect of their identity rather than define themselves entirely by it" (Spekman et al., 1992, p. 167). And one way some of them build on their strengths is by selecting occupations that match their abilities and minimize their difficulties.

Fourth, those who succeed tend to have access to a strong informal network of social support. They have been able to draw upon help from parents, husbands, friends, and so forth at various stages during and after transition to adulthood.

Finally, adults with learning disabilities are more likely to succeed if they have had intensive and long-term educational intervention (Kavale, 1988). Fortunately, we now have numerous secondary programs for students with learning disabilities, and there has been a blossoming of programs at the college level.

Secondary Programming

There are a variety of approaches to educating students with learning disabilities at the secondary level. Zigmond and Sansone (1986) note that these models differ in (1) how much time students spend with the special versus general education teachers and (2) the degree to which their curriculum is "special," or different from the general curriculum. Models can differ on each of these two dimensions. At the one extreme are those approaches, used with students with relatively mild learning disabilities, in which the student spends little or no time with special educators and does not have a special curriculum. For example, the special education teacher may consult with the general education teachers to help them adjust their teaching to accommodate students, or the special education teacher may tutor students on subjects in which they are having difficulties.

➤ **functional academics.**
Practical skills rather than academic learning.

➤ **work-study program.**
Designed to introduce students to a variety of vocational opportunities while still in school. On-the-job training is provided, and the student's performance is evaluated.

At the other extreme of the two dimensions are approaches designed for students with severe learning disabilities. They require intensive involvement with special educators and a different type of curriculum. For example, similar to what we often use with students with mild retardation (see Chapter 4), these programs may combine a **functional academics** curriculum with a **work-study program**. Functional academics refers to the teaching of academics, such as reading to gain practical, independent living skills (e.g., reading newspapers, job applications, telephone books, and so forth) rather than to attain other academic content. Work-study programs involve on-the-job training. These more intensive approaches are oriented more toward preparing students for the job market than toward achieving higher levels of academic preparation.

Many adolescents' problems are neither so mild nor so severe that the preceding approaches are appropriate. We can best serve these students with programs having a modest amount of special educator involvement and some use of different curricula. An example is the Learning Strategies Curriculum.

Learning Strategies Curriculum. Donald Deshler, Jean Schumaker, and their colleagues have developed a curriculum for secondary students with learning disabilities called the Learning Strategies Curriculum (Deshler & Schumaker, 1986; Ellis, Deshler, & Schumaker, 1989). The idea behind this approach is that adolescents with learning disabilities need strategies to learn how to learn more than they need specific subject content.

The organization of the Learning Strategies Curriculum is determined by the major demands of the secondary curriculum. It therefore comprises three strands. One is devoted to helping students acquire information from written materials. A second strand helps students remember important information and facts. A third strand helps to improve written expression, complete assignments on time, and take tests.

Multipass is an example of one set of the strategies used in the strand designed for getting information from written materials (Schumaker, Deshler, Alley, Warner, & Denton, 1982). Based on the SQ3R method (Robinson, 1946), Multipass has the student make many "passes" (hence the name) through the reading material. The three major passes are the Survey, the Size-Up, and the Sort-Out. These three passes are embedded in a context of highly individualized programming and a heavy reliance on ensuring that the student achieves certain performance goals before moving on to the next stage. Here is a description of Multipass:

The purpose of the Survey Pass was to familiarize the student with main ideas and organization of the chapter. Thus, this previewing pass required the student to: (a) read the chapter title, (b) read the introductory paragraph, (c) review the chapter's relationship to other adjacent chapters by perusing the table of contents, (d) read the major subtitles of the chapter and notice how the chapter is organized, (e) look at illustrations and read their captions, (f) read the summary paragraph, and (g) paraphrase all the information gained in the process.

The Size-Up Pass was designed to help students gain specific information and facts from a chapter without reading it from beginning to end. This pass required the student to first read each of the questions at the end of the chapter to determine what facts appeared to be the most important to learn. If the student was already able to answer a given question as a result of the Survey Pass, a check mark (√) was placed next to the question. The student now progressed through the entire chapter following these steps: (a) look for a textual cue (e.g., bold-face print, subtitle, colored print, italics); (b) make the cue into a question (e.g., if the cue was the italicized vocabulary word *conqueror*, the student asked, "What does conqueror mean?"; if the cue was the subtitle "The Election of 1848," the student might ask, "Who won the election of 1848?" or "Why was the election of 1848 important?"; (c) skim through the surrounding text to find the answer to the question; and (d) paraphrase the answer to yourself without looking in the book. When the student reached the end of the chapter using these four steps for each textual cue, he/she was required to paraphrase all the facts and ideas he/she could remember about the chapter.

The Sort-Out Pass was included to get students to test themselves over the material presented in the chapter. In this final pass, the student read and answered each question at the end of the chapter. If the student could answer a question immediately, he/she placed a checkmark next to it. If the student was unable to answer a question, however, the answer was sought by (a) thinking in which section of the chapter the answer would most likely be located, (b) skimming through that section for the answer, (c) if the answer was not located, thinking of another relevant section, and (d) skimming that section, and so on until the student could answer the question. A checkmark was then placed next to the question, and the student moved on to answer the next question. (Schumaker, Deshler, Alley, Warner, & Denton, 1982, pp. 298–299)

Postsecondary Programming

Postsecondary programs include vocational and technical programs as well as community colleges and four-year colleges and universities. More and more individuals with learning disabilities are enrolling in colleges and universities, and more and more universities are establishing special programs and services for these students. One of the major difficulties for the student who is learning disabled in the transition from high school to college is the decrease in the amount of guidance provided by adults (Siperstein, 1988). Many students find this greater emphasis on self-discipline particularly difficult. The greater demands on writing skills (Gajar, 1989) and note-taking also present major problems for many college students with learning disabilities.

> For many LD [learning-disabled] adults, the task of taking notes in lectures is overwhelming, nor is it any wonder. Note-taking requires simultaneous listening, comprehending, and synthesizing and/or extracting main ideas while retaining them long enough to formulate a synopsis and write it down. The writing act, in turn, requires automaticity and speed in letter formation and sufficient legibility and spelling ability to decipher what has been written at a later time. (Vogel, 1987, p. 523)

Siperstein (1988), believing in a long-range view of programming for college-bound students with learning disabilities, has conceptualized service delivery as consisting of three transitions: (1) high school to college, (2) during college, and (3) college to employment. During the first stage, high school to college, a major goal is to foster awareness of what college options are available. Because of their frequent experiences with failure, many students with learning disabilities do not aspire to education beyond high school. The emphasis should be preparing students to make the right choice of colleges as well as on delineating what accommodations they will need in their programs. Parents and students need to consider the unique characteristics of the student as well as those of different colleges and their programs in matching the student with the appropriate institution (McGuire & Shaw, 1987). During this stage, pupils and their families may take advantage of published guides to college programs for students with learning disabilities—for example, *A Guide to Colleges for Learning-Disabled Students* (Liscio, 1986) and Lovejoy's *Four-Year College Guide for Learning-Disabled Students* (1985). Also students can be made aware of the special accommodations available for students who are learning disabled taking the Scholastic Aptitude Test (SAT) and the American College Test (ACT).

Notetaking during lectures poses problems for many college students with learning disabilities.

In Their Own Words EILEEN SIMPSON

Eileen Simpson is a widely published author of novels and short stories. Like Woodrow Wilson, Nelson Rockefeller, Thomas Edison, Gustave Flaubert, W. B. Yeats, and Hans Christian Andersen, she also grew up with dyslexia (a reading disability).

Her autobiography, *Reversals: A Personal Account of Victory over Dyslexia,* describes in vivid detail her battle to become literate against what was then, to her, an unknown enemy. Her struggles also placed her in conflict with those around her—her teachers and guardians who did not have an inkling about the perplexing affliction called dyslexia.

The following passage describes one of the many anguished "reading lessons" conducted between a helpless student and an angry, frustrated teacher.

Miss Henderson and now Auntie: There seemed to be nothing I could do to please either of them. How, in the past, had it been so easy, so effortless to be a favorite? With a feeling of impending doom I would begin. I might get halfway through the first sentence before Auntie would say in a dry, controlled voice, "In the context the word cannot possibly be 'saw.' 'The man saw going home.' Does that make sense to you? It must be 'was.'"

I'd repeat, "The man was going home." In the next sentence, or the one after, meeting the word again, I'd hesitate. Had I said 'was' before and had Auntie corrected it to 'saw,' or vice versa? My brain ached.

"Don't tell me you don't recognize that word. *I just told it to you.* You're *not trying.*"

Both my teachers accused me of not trying. They had no idea what an effort I was making. Was, saw, was, saw. How were they so sure which it was? Rattled by Auntie's foot tapping, I decided for "saw."

"No, no, NO. How *can* you be so stupid? The word is 'was.' WASWASWAS. And for heaven's sake *stop sniveling.* If those nuns hadn't fallen for your tears, you'd be able to read by now and we wouldn't be going through this. . ."

SOURCE: Eileen Simpson, *Reversals: A Personal Account of Victory over Dyslexia* (Boston: Houghton Mifflin Company, 1979) pp. 19–20.

The second stage, which covers the time during college, focuses on enhancing the chances of successfully earning a degree. It includes support services for both academic and social functioning. For example, in addition to tutoring, the college can provide such services as note-taking, transcription of taped lectures, and study skills workshops. The administration can modify program standards by waiving certain requirements (e.g., a foreign language) (Vogel, 1987), and the faculty can alter their usual teaching and evaluation activities for example, by making themselves more available for student consultation and allowing untimed tests. An important resource in programming are the college students themselves who are learning disabled. Third- and fourth-year students with learning disabilities can help establish peer support systems.

The third stage, transition from college to employment, is important because even if they survive the rigors of college, many individuals with learning disabilities have difficulties obtaining appropriate employment in the competitive job market. Possible strategies are workshops for career awareness, job-search strategies, and job-maintenance skills (Siperstein, 1988).

There is little doubt that much of what we need to know to program effectively students with learning disabilities at the postsecondary level remains to be learned. However, the field has made great strides in opening windows of opportunity for these young adults. Authorities have noted that many college applicants with learning disabilities attempt to hide their disability for fear they will not be admitted (Shaywitz & Shaw, 1988). If the burgeoning interest in postsecondary programming for individuals who are learning disabled continues, we may in the near future see the day when students and colleges routinely collaborate to use information concerning the students' learning disability in planning their programs.

Students with Learning Disabilities in General Education Classrooms

WHAT TO LOOK FOR IN SCHOOL

All persons with learning disabilities, by definition, have near average, average, or above average intelligence. They may learn some academic skills easily, while they acquire other skills with difficulty. In addition to underachievement in some school subjects, these students exhibit other behaviors that may help you identify them in your classrooms. In primary grades, they may appear to be delayed in language, motor, and readiness skills. They may experience general coordination problems, appear clumsy, or have difficulties with specific fine motor skills, such as buttoning clothes, lacing shoes, cutting with scissors, coloring within lines, and writing. Their use of language also may lag behind that of their classmates. They may speak in an immature or "babyish" way and have difficulty expressing themselves in conversation and group discussions. Sometimes children with learning disabilities do not demonstrate reading readiness skills, such as right-left and up-down orientations, spatial relationships, and eye-hand coordination.

In intermediate grades, students with learning disabilities may have difficulty following directions. They may have problems reading written materials and understanding abstract concepts and inferences. In addition, they may be ineffective learners who do not know how to plan their work or how to remember information from one day to the next.

Many students with learning disabilities in middle and high school appear to be unmotivated. They often need extra prodding to work independently in class and to complete homework assignments. In addition, acting before thinking may result in their turning in "careless," incomplete papers, and getting in trouble for interacting impulsively with other students. Individuals with learning disabilities also may be disorganized. They often lose or misplace books, pencils, and homework. Furthermore, they may be easily frustrated with tasks that are too difficult and mask this problem by saying they "had better things to do" or "didn't feel like it." The social problems that many of these students experience at all ages may be increasingly apparent as they mature. Frequently they say and do the wrong thing unknowingly and misread social situations.

The wide range of academic and social problems persons with learning disabilities experience complicates identification. You can be instrumental in helping to identify students with learning disabilities by collecting achievement information, by recording observations of their social-emotional behaviors, and by sharing this information with the special education teacher or counselor in your school. In fact, classroom teachers usually are the first to recognize signs of learning disabilities and to refer students to child-study teams.

HOW TO GATHER INFORMATION

You can use a variety of materials and procedures to gather information about your students' achievement. Reading a student's cumulative folder provides information about past school performance that may indicate whether the problems you are observing are new or part of a pattern exhibited across several grades. This folder also contains attendance and retention data and group achievement test results that provide a comparison of your student's achievement with that of other students of the same grade. Talking with former teachers may provide additional information about your student's ability to meet regular class demands, necessary instructional modifications, and his or her social adjustment.

To gather current information, you can conduct any of several informal assessment procedures, such as informal inventories (see p. 169) and criterion-referenced tests (see p. 169), or analyze samples of your student's work for error patterns and inconsistent use of skills. Another effective procedure you can use is curriculum-based assessment (CBA) (see p. 170). In addition to providing guidelines for grouping students and for placing them in curricular materials that are appropriate to their skill level, CBA measures identify specific skills students have not yet mastered. These measures, coupled with your observation of the student's behaviors, may suggest a learning disability. For detailed instructions on how to construct curriculum-based assessment, read Blankenship's (1985) article, "Using Curriculum-Based Assessment Data to Make Instructional Decisions."

TEACHING TECHNIQUES TO TRY

Self-Regulatory Strategies

Once identified as having a learning disability, students must learn to manage a wide range of learning problems. One of the most common difficulties they face is not knowing how to plan, monitor, and check their work or how to remediate the problems they experience in learning. Teachers can help them to learn needed strategies, such as self-monitoring (see p. 186) and self-instruction (see p. 180).

Academic Strategies

Students with learning disabilities also need to learn strategies in academic areas. You will notice that most of the following strategies include components designed to teach specific skills and the self-regulation procedures students need to use them successfully.

COMPOSITION

One strategy teachers use to improve written expression is the PLEASE strategy, which was designed to address problems related to prewriting, planning, composition, and paragraph revision (Welch, 1992). The six steps in this strategy cue students to:

P = **Pick** a topic.
L = **List** your ideas about the topic.
E = **Evaluate** your list.
A = **Activate** the paragraph with a
    topic sentence.
S = **Supply** supporting sentences.
E = **End** with a concluding sentence and
    Evaluate your work.

In the first step, students are taught not only to pick a topic, but also to define the audience for whom they are writing, and to select a format, such as compare/contrast or cause/effect. In step two, teachers explain techniques of listing information (e.g., outlines and semantic maps). Next, students are taught how to evaluate the completeness of their list and how to organize the ideas they will use in writing supporting sentences. During step four, teachers instruct students to write a short, declarative topic sentence that "activates" the main idea for the reader. Then, students select ideas from their lists and write them as sentences in support of the main idea. In the sixth step, they are taught to write a concluding sentence by paraphrasing their topic sentence. Finally, students are reminded to evaluate their written work for capitalization, appearance, punctuation, and spelling.

Graham and his associates (1992) have created a planning and writing strategy to improve essay writing that includes several steps similar to the PLEASE strategy. This other strategy instructs students to:

Step 1 Do PLANS (Pick goals, List ways to meet the goals, And make Notes, Sequence notes);
Step 2 Write and say more;
Step 3 Test goals.

The first step consists of a series of prewriting activities that involve students in setting product goals (i.e. purpose, structure, and length) and process goals, noting the ideas they generated to use in their essays, and sequencing their notes by numbering them. Step 2 is a reminder to students to continue planning after they have begun writing and to explain their ideas fully. The final step cues students to evaluate whether they met the goals they set in Step 1. If they have not reached a goal, teachers instruct them to think about how they can accomplish it the next time they write.

For a discussion of additional planning. organizing, drafting, and editing/revising strategies, see Englert's (1992) article entitled "Writing Instruction from a Sociocultural Perspective: The Holistic, Dialogic, and Social Enterprise of Writing."

READING COMPREHENSION

To facilitate students' understanding of text, educators have developed several self-questioning strategies. In general, these strategies promote learning by activating students' prior knowledge, establishing a purpose for reading, directing attention to important features of the text and vocabulary, and checking for problems in comprehension.

Chan (1991) developed a self-questioning strategy that involves five topics related to understanding text that are problematic for many students with learning disabilities: (1) deleting redundant information; (2) deleting trivial information; (3) rating sentences in order of importance; (4) identifying explicit main ideas; and (5) identifying implicit main ideas. For each topic, teachers instruct students to ask themselves a set of questions while reading. These self-questions are:

Deleting redundant information:
a. Does this sentence repeat what has already been said?
b. Shall I leave it out?
c. What is the paragraph mainly about?

Deleting trivial information:
a. Does this sentence tell me anything new or more important?
b. Shall I leave it out?
c. What is the paragraph mainly about?

Locating topic sentences:
a. What does the paragraph seem to be about?
b. Does this sentence tell me anything new or more important than the main ideas?
c. Is my guess right?
d. Which sentence gives the main idea?
e. Which answer gives the main idea of the passage?

Identifying implicit main ideas:
a. What does the paragraph seem to be about?
b. Does this sentence just tell me more about the main idea?
c. Which answer gives the main idea?
d. Which answer gives the main idea of the passage?

ARITHMETIC

Research indicates that many students with learning disabilities experience problems not only in reading and written expression, but also in mathematics. These difficulties begin early in school and continue throughout high school (Mercer, 1992). DRAW is a strategy designed to help students solve problems. Each letter of DRAW reminds students to perform a specific step:

D = **Discover** the sign (e.g. +, - x)
R = **Read** the problem
A = **Answer** or DRAW a representation of the problem using lines, and tallies and checks
W = **Write** the answer

TEACHING STRATEGIES

We know that in order for students to use any strategy independently, teachers must provide extensive instruction in the use of the strategy (Ellis, Deshler, Lenz, Schumaker, & Clark, 1991). Educators recommend following these principles (Ellis et al., 1991):

1. Teach prerequisite skills (i.e., those required in the strategy) before beginning strategy instruction.
2. Teach each strategy regularly and intensively to facilitate students' fluent use of the strategy.
3. Emphasize personal effort by students as an important factor in the successful application of strategies.
4. Require students to master strategies by requiring them to use strategies correctly and fluently.
5. Integrate instruction throughout these eight steps of strategy instruction:

Step 1 Pretest and ask students to make a commitment to learn the strategy.
Step 2 Describe the strategy.
Step 3 Model the strategy.
Step 4 Provide many opportunities for verbal practice of the strategy.
Step 5 Provide practice and feedback in materials at students' own level.
Step 6 Provide advanced practice and feedback.
Step 7 Post-test and ask students to make a commitment to generalize their use of strategies.
Step 8 Promote use of strategies in different learning and content settings by helping students discriminate when to use each strategy; to remember the strategy steps; to experiment with using the strategy in different situations; to develop a plan to improve strategy performance; and to adapt each strategy to meet additional problems.

6. Emphasize the processes involved in using strategies, such as paraphrasing, setting priorities, setting goals, and self-monitoring.
7. Emphasize the generalized use of strategies in a variety of learning situations and settings.

HELPFUL RESOURCES

School Personnel

As discussed in the other chapters, several people in your school system can help you identify and manage the special education students in your classroom. The resource teacher who also teaches your mainstreamed students has information about individual learning problems that you may find helpful. This teacher also may be able to suggest specific materials, additional learning strategies, and methods that will help your students learn. Arranging regularly scheduled meetings with the resource teacher may facilitate the exchange of information about your students' progress, about planning, and about coordination of the instructional programs you both are implementing.

Instructional Methods

Bley, N. S., & Thornton, C. A. (1989). *Teaching mathematics to the learning disabled* (2nd ed.). Austin, TX: Pro-Ed.

Bos, C. S., & Vaughn, S. (1991). *Strategies for teaching students with learning and behavior problems* (2nd ed.). Boston: Allyn & Bacon.

Ekwall, E. E. (1989). *Locating and correcting reading difficulties* (5th ed.). Columbus, OH: Merrill.

Hammill, D. D., & Bartel, N. R. (1990). *Teaching students with learning and behavior problems* (5th ed.). Boston: Allyn & Bacon.

Mercer, C. (1991). *Teaching students with learning problems* (4th ed.). New York: Merrill (Macmillan).

Meltzer, L. J. (Ed.) (1992). *Strategy assessment and instruction for students with learning disabilities*. Austin, TX: Pro-Ed.

Olson, J., & Platt, J. (1992). *Teaching children and adolescents with special needs*. New York: Merrill (Macmillan).

Palincsar, A. S., & Brown, A. L. (1984). Reciprocal teaching of comprehension-fostering and monitoring activities. *Cognition and Instruction. 1*, 117–175.

Polloway, E. A., & Patton, J. R. (1992). *Strategies for teaching learners with special needs* (5th ed.). New York: Merrill (Macmillan).

Polloway, E. A., & Smith, T. E. C. (1992). *Language instruction for students with disabilities* (2nd ed.). Denver, CO: Love.

Pressley, M. & Associates (1990). *Cognitive strategy instruction that really improves children's academic performance*. Cambridge, MA: Brookline Books.

Scheid, K. (1990). *Cognitive-based methods for teaching mathematics to students with learning problems*. Columbus, OH: LINC Resources.

Smith, T. E. C., Finn, D. M., & Dowdy, C. A. (1992). *Teaching students with mild disabilities*. Fort Worth, TX: Harcourt Brace Jovanovich.

Wallace, G., & Kauffman, J. M. (1986). *Teaching students with learning and behavior problems*. Columbus, OH: Merrill (Macmillan).

Wood, J. W. (1992). *Adapting instruction for mainstreamed and at-risk students*. New York: Merrill (Macmillan).

Curricula and Instructional Materials

Ashlock, R. B. (1986). *Error patterns in computation: A semi-programmed approach* (4th ed.). Columbus, OH: Merrill/Macmillan.

Brigance, A. H. (1991). *Victory!* East Moline, IL: LinguiSystem, Inc.

Carnine, D., & Kameenui, E. J. (1992). *Higher order thinking: Designing curriculum for mainstreamed students.* Austin, TX: Pro-Ed.

Carnine, D., Silbert, J., & Kameenui, E. J. (1990). *Direct instruction reading* (2nd ed.). Columbus, OH: Merrill/Macmillan.

Cawley, J. F., Fitzmaurice-Hayes, A., & Shaw, R. (1988). *Mathematics for the mildly handicapped: Guide to curriculum and instruction.* Boston: Allyn & Bacon.

Dixon, R., & Engelmann, S. (1979). *Corrective spelling through morographs.* Chicago: Science Research Associates.

Dixon, R., Engelmann, S., Meier, M., Steely, D., & Wells, T. (1989) *Spelling mastery.* Chicago: Science Research Associates.

Engelmann, S., & Bruner, E. C. (1983). *Reading mastery.* Chicago: Science Research Associates.

Engelmann, S., & Carnine, D. (1982). *Corrective mathematics program.* Chicago: Science Research Associates.

Engelmann, S., Carnine, D., Johnson, G., & Meyers, L. (1988). *Corrective reading: Decoding.* Chicago: Science Research Associates.

Engelmann, S., Carnine, D., Johnson, G., & Meyers, L. (1989). *Corrective reading: Comprehension.* Chicago: Science Research Associates.

Lloyd, J., & Keller, C. E. (1989). Effective mathematics instruction: Development, instruction, and programs. *Focus on Exceptional Children. 21,* 1–10.

Mercer, C. D., & Miller, S. P. (1991). *Strategic math series:* Multiplications facts 0–81. Lawrence, KS: Edge Enterprises.

Silbert, J., & Carnine, D. (1981). *Direct instruction mathematics.* Columbus, OH: Merrill/Macmillan.

Walker, H. M., Todis, B., Holmes, D., & Horton, G. (1988). *The Walker social skills curriculum: The ACCESS Program.* Austin, TX: Pro-Ed.

Welch, M., & Link, D. P. (1989) Write, PLEASE: A strategy for efficient learning and functioning in written expression (video cassette). Salt Lake City: University of Utah, Department of Special Education, Educational Tele-Communications.

University of Kansas, Institute for Research on Learning Disabilities. P.O. Box 972, Lawrence, KS. (The Kansas IRLD has several strategy packages available that concentrate primarily on study skills, reading comprehension and written language skills.)

Literature about Individuals with Learning Disabilities

ELEMENTARY

Aiello, B., & Shulman, J. (1988). *Secrets aren't (always) for keeps.* Frederick, MD: Kids on the Block. (Fiction=F)

Cassedy, S. (1987). *M.E. and Morton.* New York: Crowell. (F)

Fisher, G., & Cummings, R. (1990). *The survival guide for kids with LD.* Minneapolis, MN: Free Spirit. (Ages 9–12) (Nonfiction=NF)

Greenwald, S. (1983). *Will the real Gertrude Hollings please stand up?* New York: Little, Brown & Company.

Griff, P. R. (1984). *The beast in Ms. Rooney's room.* New York: Dell. (Ages 6–9) (F)

Hall, L. (1988). *Just one friend.* New York: Collier Books. (F)

Lasker, J. (1980). *Nick joins in.* Chicago: Albert Whitman. (Ages 5–8) (F)

Levinson, M. (1985). *And don't bring Jeremy.* New York: Holt, Rinehart, and Winston. (F)

Shreve, S. (1984). *The flunking of Joshua T. Bates.* New York: Knopf. (Ages 9–12) (F)

Wolff, V. E. (1988). *Probably still Nick Swansen.* New York: Holt. (F)

SECONDARY/ADULT

Hampshire, S. (1982). *Susan's story: An autobiographical account of my struggle with dyslexia.* New York, NY: St. Martin's Press. (NF)

Computer Software

Ace Detective, Mindplay, 3130 North Dodge, Tucson, AZ 85716, (800) 221–7911.

Bank Street Speller, Computer Aids, 20417 Nordhoff Street, #M5, Chatsworth, CA 91311.

Beamer, Data Command, P.O. Box 548, Kankakee, IL 60901, (800) 528–7390.

Captain's Log: Cognitive Training System Network Services, 1915 Huguenot Road., Richmond, VA 23235, (804) 379–2253.

Core Reading and Vocabulary Development, Educational Activities Inc. P.O. Box 392, Freeport, NY 11520, (800) 645–3739.

Create-Spell It, Hartley Courseware, Inc., P.O. Box 431, Dimondale, MI 48821, (800) 247–1380.

Decisions, Decisions, Tom Snyder Productions, 90 Sherman Street, Cambridge, MA 02140, (617) 876–4433. (Promotes decision-making for secondary students through simulations.)

Disney Comic Strip Maker, Mindscape, 1345 West Diversey Parkway, Chicago, IL 60614, (312) 525–1500.

DLM Math Fluency Program, DLM Teaching Resources, One DLM Park, Allen, TX: 75002, (800) 527–5030.

Fast-Track Fractions, DLM Teaching Resources, One DLM Park, Allen, TX: 75002, (800) 527–5030. (Compare, add, subtract, multiply, divide fractions)

Explore-a-Story, D.C. Heath & Company, 125 Spring Street, Lexington, MA 02173, (617) 860–1847.

Explore-a-Science, D.C. Heath & Company, 125 Spring Street, Lexington, MA 02173, (617) 860–1847.

Following Directions, Laureate Learning Systems, Inc., 110 E. Spring Street, Winooski, VT 05404, (802) 562–6801.

Keyboarding Primer, MECC, 3490 Lexington Avenue, North, St. Paul, MN 55126, (800) 228–3504.

Multiply with Balancing Bear, Sunburst Communications, 39 Washington Avenue, Pleasantville, NY 10570, (800) 628–8897.

Newsroom, Scholastic Software, 730 Broadway, Department J S., New York, New York, 10003, (800) 541–5513.

Outliner, MECC, 3490 Lexington Avenue, North, St. Paul, MN 55126, (800) 228–3504.

Reader Rabbit, Learning Company, 6493 Kaiser Drive, Fremont, CA 94555, (800) 852–2255. (Basic reading and spelling skills)

Special Education Collection, Humanities Software, P.O. Box 950, Hood River, OR 97031, (800) 245–6737.

Type to Learn, Sunburst Communications, 39 Washington Avenue, Pleasantville, NY 10570, (800) 628–8897.

Typing Tutor, Scholastic Software, 730 Broadway, Department J S., New York, NY 10003, (800) 541–5513.

Writing Workshop, Milliken, P.O. Box 21579, St. Louis, MO 63132, (314) 991–4220.

Word Processing Programs:
No graphics:
Bank Street Writer III, Scholastic Software 730 Broadway, Department JS, New York, NY 10003, (800) 541–5513.
Bank Street Writer Plus, Broderbund Software, 500 Redwood, P.O. Box 6121, Novato, CA 94948–6121, (800) 521–6263.
Children's Writing and Publishing Center, Learning Company, 6493 Kaiser Drive, Fremont, CA 94555, (800) 852–2255.
Dr. Peet's Talking Text Writer, Hartley Courseware, Inc. P.O. Box 431, Dimondale, MI 48821, (880) 247–1380.
Magic Slate II, Sunburst Communications, Inc., 39 Washington Avenue, Pleasantville, NY 10570, (800) 628–8897.
Talking Textwriter, Scholastic Software, 730 Broadway, Department JS, New York, NY 10003, (800) 541–5513.

Graphics:
Bank Street Story Book, Mindscape, 1345 West Diversey Parkway, Chicago, IL 60614, (312) 525–1500.
Story Board, Data Command, Inc., P.O. Box 548, Kankakee, IL 60901, (800) 528–7390.

Videodiscs

Earth Science, Systems Impact, Inc., 200 Girard Street, Suite 214, Gaithersburg, MD 20877, (301) 869–0400.

Interactive Mathematics, Ferranti Educational Systems.

Mastering Decimals and Percents, Systems Impact, Inc.

Mastering Equations, Roots, and Exponents, Systems Impact, Inc.

Mastering Fractions, Systems Impact, Inc.

Mastering Ratios and Word Problem Strategies, Systems Impact, Inc.

Principles of Alphabet Learning Systems (PALS), IBM.

Understanding Chemistry and Energy, Systems Impact, Inc.

Videodisc Compendium for education and training (1989). St. Paul, MN: Emerging Technology Consultants, Inc. (Lists describe more than 400 instructional videodiscs.)

Organizations

Council for Exceptional Children, Division of Learning Disabilities, 1920 Association Drive, Reston, VA 22091, (703) 620–3660.

Council for Learning Disabilities, P.O. Box 40303, Overland Park, KS 66204, (913) 492–8755.

Learning Disabilities Association of America, 4156 Library Road, Pittsburgh, PA 15234, (412) 341–1515.

National Center for Learning Disabilities, 99 Park Avenue, Sixth Floor, New York, NY 10016, (212) 687–7211.

Orton Dyslexia Society, 724 York Road, Baltimore, MD 21204, (301) 296–0232.

BIBLIOGRAPHY FOR TEACHING SUGGESTIONS

Blankenship, C. S. (1985). Using curriculum-based assessment data to make instructional decisions. *Exceptional Children*, 52, 233–238.

Chan, L. K. S. (1991). Promoting strategy generalization through self-instructional training in students with reading disabilities, *Journal of Learning Disabilities*, 4, 427–433.

Ellis, E. S., Deshler, D. D., Lenz, B. K., Schumaker, J. B., & Clark, F. (1991). An instructional model for teaching learning strategies. *Focus on Exceptional Children*, 23, 1–23.

Englert, C. S. (1992). Writing instruction from a sociocultural perspective: The holistic, dialogic, and social enterprise of writing. *Journal of Learning Disabilities*, 25, 153–172.

Graham, S., Macarthur, C., Schwartz, S., & Page-Voth, V. (1992). Improving the compositions of students with learning disabilities using a strategy involving product and process goal setting. *Journal of Learning Disabilities*, 58, 322–334.

Mercer, C. D., & Miller, A. R. (1991). *Strategic math series: Multiplication facts 0-81*. Lawrence, KS: Edge Enterprises.

Mercer, C. D., & Miller, S. P. (1992). Teaching students with learning problems in math to acquire, understand, and apply basic math facts. *Remedial and Special Education*, 13, 19–35, 61.

Videodisc compendium for education and training (1989). St. Paul, MN: Emerging Technology Consultants, Inc.

Welch, M. (1992). The PLEASE strategy: A metacognitive learning strategy for improving the paragraph writing of students with mild learning disabilities. *Learning Disability Quarterly*, 15, 119–128.

Summary

In the early 1960s, parents and professionals advocated a new category of special education—learning disabilities—to describe individuals who, in spite of normal or near-normal intelligence, have a puzzling array of learning problems. What prompted the creation of this area was the realization that many children with learning problems were not receiving needed educational services.

The four most common factors in definitions of learning disabilities are IQ-achievement discrepancy, presumption of central nervous system (CNS) dysfunction, psychological processing problems, and learning problems not due to environmental disadvantage, mental retardation, or emotional disturbance. The most commonly used definition is the federal government's, which includes all four factors. Another popular definition, that of the National Joint Committee for Learning Disabilities, does not include psychological processing problems.

The prevalence of students identified as learning disabled has increased dramatically, more than doubling since 1976–1977. Some believe this growth indicates that teachers are too quick to label students as learning disabled; others argue that social-cultural factors (e.g., increased poverty, increased stress on families) have contributed to the growth of learning disabilities.

Causal factors for learning disabilities fall into organic and biological, genetic, and environmental categories. More and more evidence is accumulating that many persons with learning disabilities have CNS dysfunction. Also, evidence is accruing that some cases of learning disabilities are attributable to genetic factors. Environmental causes have been more difficult to pinpoint, although some professionals believe that poor teaching can lead to learning disabilities.

Practitioners use tests of three general types to assess students with learning disabilities: standardized achievement tests, informal reading inventories, and formative evaluation measures. Growing in popularity are formative evaluation methods, which have five features: (1) The teacher usually does the assessment; (2) the teacher assesses classroom behaviors directly; (3) the measures are taken frequently and over a period of time; (4) the assessment is done in conjunction with the setting of educational goals; and (5) the teacher uses the assessment information to decide whether the educational program for an individual student is effective.

Curriculum-based assessment is a type of formative evaluation.

Persons with learning disabilities exhibit a great deal of inter- and intra-individual variation in their psychological and behavioral characteristics. The inter-individual variation is reflected in the heterogeneity of this population. Intra-individual variation means that persons with learning disabilities often have uneven profiles of abilities.

Academic deficits are the hallmarks of learning disabilities. Reading disabilities are often related to poor phonological skills. Students with learning disabilities can also have problems in written or spoken language and math.

Some persons with learning disabilities have problems in perceptual, perceptual-motor, or general coordination. Research has not documented the claim of early theorists that training these skills would help reading problems.

Children with learning disabilities have a higher prevalence of attention-deficit disorders. There has been considerable controversy over whether the federal government should recognize attention deficit as a separate category or whether the needs of students with attention problems who have educational problems are met by existing categories such as learning disabilities.

Many individuals with learning disabilities demonstrate memory deficits. They have cognitive problems that lead to disorganization, and metacognitive problems interfere with their awareness of learning strategies and the ability to regulate their use.

Persons with learning disabilities have a tendency to be rejected by their peers and to have poor self-concepts. In addition, they can have motivational problems as demonstrated by an external locus of control, negative attributions, and learned helplessness.

Some authorities believe that a composite of many of the preceding characteristics indicates that many students with learning disabilities are passive rather than active learners. Many of their problems, such as a propensity to have problems with homework, may be due to this inactive approach to learning.

Educational methods for the academic problems of students with learning disabilities are process training, cognitive training, and direct instruction. In process training, psychological processes such as visual and/or auditory perception—rather than academics—are the focus of instruction. Although once quite popular, process training is not used much today. Multisensory training assumes that students are more likely to learn if more than one sense is involved in the learning process.

Cognitive training also focuses on psychological processes by emphasizing the changing of thought processes, but it differs from process training in two ways. First, it is usually done in conjunction with academic material. Second, researchers have found it more successful than process training perhaps because it concentrates on helping students overcome their cognitive, metacognitive, and motivational problems. Self-instruction, mnemonic keyword method, and scaffolded instruction are all examples of cognitive training techniques.

Direct instruction focuses even more directly on academics than does cognitive training. It concentrates on instructional processes and a systematic analysis of the concept to be taught, rather than on characteristics of the student.

Methods for the attention problems of students with learning disabilities are structure and stimulus reduction, behavior modification, cognitive training, and medication. A structured and stimulus reduction approach emphasizes a highly teacher-directed approach combined with a reduction in extraneous simulation.

In behavior modification, the student's attention is rewarded and his or her inattention is ignored or punished.

Cognitive training for attention problems assumes that students can regulate their impulsive and inattentive behavior by thinking about their behavior more carefully. An example of a cognitive training technique for attention problems is self-monitoring, the self-evaluation and self-recording of on- and off-task behavior.

Medication, usually in the form of psychostimulants, can be highly effective for increasing the concentration of many, but not all, persons with attention problems. Because the medication is powerful, with some possible side effects, teachers, parents, and physicians need to work together to monitor its effects.

The resource room is the most common placement for students with learning disabilities. Cooperative teaching, in which regular and special education teachers work together in the regular classroom, is gaining in popularity.

Most professionals are cautious about establishing programs for children with learning disabilities at the preschool level because it is so hard to predict at that age which children will develop later academic problems. We do know that certain preacademic skills, such as letter, shape, and color recognition, are the best predictors of later academic learning.

The importance of educational programming at the secondary level and beyond is underscored by evidence that persons with learning disabilities do not automatically outgrow their problems as adults. Students with learning disabilities are at risk to drop out of school, and evidence suggests a higher prevalence of learning disabilities among juvenile delinquents. The majority who stay in school and do not engage in delinquent behaviors are still at risk of having problems in learning, socializing, holding a job, and performing daily living skills. Factors related to successful transition to adulthood are (1) perseverance, (2) goal setting, (3) realistic acceptance of weaknesses coupled with building on strengths, (4) a supportive social network, and (5) intensive and long-term educational intervention.

Educational programming at the secondary level varies according to (1) how much time students spend with the special versus general education teacher, and (2) the degree to which the curriculum is "special," or different from the general curriculum.

Postsecondary programs include vocational and technical schools as well as community colleges and four-year colleges. More and more universities and colleges are establishing programs and services for students with learning disabilities.

C HAPTER SIX

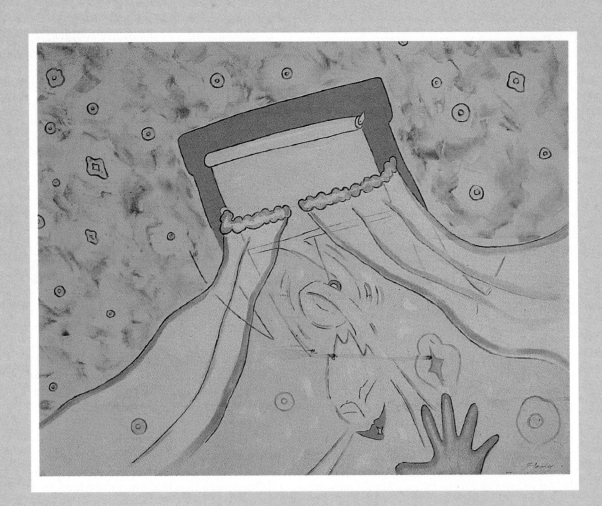

HENRY HAAS

Henry Haas has a brother, John Andrew, diagnosed with schizophrenia, with whom he collaborates on his paintings and poetry. His work has been featured widely, including one painting that appeared on the cover of the invitation to "America in Concert," held in Washington, DC, in 1993.

$\mathcal{Y}$oung child with dreams
Dream every dream on your own.
When children play,
Seems like you end up alone.
Papa says he'd love to be with you,
If he had the time,
So you turn to the only friend
You can find,
There in your mind.

➤ Neil Diamond
"Shilo"

Emotional or Behavioral Disorders

▲ ▲ ▲

$\mathbf{C}$hildren and youths who have emotional or behavioral disorders are not ▲ ▲ ▲ typically good at making friends. In fact, their most obvious problem is failure to establish close and satisfying emotional ties with other people. As Neil Diamond's song suggests (see p. 203), the only friends they may be able to find are imaginary ones. Typically, their peers are not attracted to them, and most adults do not find them pleasant to be around.

Some of these children are withdrawn. Other children or adults may try to reach them, but their efforts are usually met with fear or disinterest. In many cases, this kind of quiet rejection continues until those who are trying to make friends give up. Because close emotional ties are built around reciprocal social responses, people naturally lose interest in someone who does not respond to social overtures.

Many other children with emotional or behavioral disorders are isolated from others not because they withdraw from friendly advances but because they strike out with hostility and aggression. They are abusive, destructive, unpredictable, irresponsible, bossy, quarrelsome, irritable, jealous, defiant—anything but pleasant to be with. Naturally, other children and adults choose not to spend time with this kind of child unless they have to, and others tend to strike back at a youngster who shows these characteristics. It is no wonder, then, that these children and youths seem to be embroiled in a continuous battle with everyone.

Where does the problem start? Does it begin with behavior that frustrates, angers, or irritates other people? Or does it begin with a social environment so uncomfortable or inappropriate that the only reasonable response of the child is withdrawal or attack? These questions cannot be answered fully on the basis of current research. The best thinking today is that the problem is not just in the child's behavior or just in the environment. The problem arises because *the social interactions and transactions between the child and the social environment are inappropriate.* This is an *ecological* perspective—an interpretation of the problem as a negative aspect of the child *and* of the environment in which he or she lives.

Special education for these students is in many ways both confused and confusing. The terminology of the field is inconsistent, and there is much misunderstanding of definitions. Reliable classifications of children's behavior problems have only recently emerged from research. The large number of theories regarding the causes and the best treatments of emotional and behavioral disorders makes it difficult to sort out the most useful concepts. Thus the study of this area of special education demands more than the usual amount of perseverance and critical thinking.

TERMINOLOGY

Many different terms have been used to designate children who have extreme social-interpersonal and/or intrapersonal problems, including emotionally handicapped, emotionally impaired, behaviorally impaired, socially/emotionally handicapped, emotionally conflicted, having personal and social adjustment problems, and seriously behaviorally disabled. These terms do not designate distinctly different types of disorders; that is, they do not refer to clearly different types of children and youths. Rather, the different labels appear to represent

MYTH ➤ Most children and youths with emotional or behavioral disorders escape the notice of people around them.

FACT ➤ Although it is difficult to identify the types and causes of problems, most children and youths with emotional or behavioral disorders, whether aggressive or withdrawn, are quite easy to spot.

MYTH ➤ Students with emotional or behavioral disorders are usually very bright.

FACT ➤ Relatively few students with emotional or behavioral disorders have high intelligence; in fact, most have a low-normal IQ.

MYTH ➤ Youngsters who exhibit shy, anxious behavior are more seriously impaired than those whose behavior is hyperaggressive.

FACT ➤ Youngsters with aggressive, acting-out behavior patterns have less chance for social adjustment and mental health in adulthood. Neurotic, shy, anxious children and youths have a better chance of getting and holding jobs, overcoming their problems, and staying out of jails and mental hospitals unless their withdrawal is extreme. This is especially true for boys.

MYTH ➤ Most students with emotional or behavioral disorders need a permissive environment in which they feel accepted and can accept themselves for what they are.

FACT ➤ Research shows that a firmly structured and highly predictable environment is of greatest benefit for most students.

MYTH ➤ Only psychiatrists, psychologists, and social workers are able to help children and youths with emotional or behavioral disorders overcome their problems.

FACT ➤ Most teachers and parents can learn to be highly effective in helping youngsters with emotional or behavioral disorders, often without extensive training or professional certification. Many of these children and youths do require services of highly trained professionals as well.

MYTH ➤ Undesirable behaviors are only symptoms; the real problems are hidden deep in the psyche.

FACT ➤ There is no sound scientific basis for belief in hidden causes; the behavior and its social context are the problems. Causes may involve thoughts, feelings, and perceptions.

personal preferences for terms and perhaps slightly different theoretical orientations. The terminology of the field is so variable and confused that you can pick a label of choice simply by matching words from Column A with words from Column B below (and if it seems appropriate, adding other qualifiers such as "seriously" or "severely").

Column A	Column B
Emotional	Disturbance
Social	Disorder
Behavioral	Maladjusment
Personal	Handicap
	Impairment

"Seriously emotionally disturbed" was the term used when PL 94–142 (IDEA) was enacted; today, that term is criticized as inappropriate. "Behaviorally disordered" is consistent with the name of the Council for Children with Behavioral Disorders (CCBD, a division of the Council for Exceptional Children) and has the advantage of focusing attention on the clearly observable aspect of these children's problems—disordered behavior (Huntze, 1985). Many authorities favor terminology indicating that these children may have emotional *or* behavioral problems *or both*.

In 1990, the National Mental Health and Special Education Coalition, representing over 30 professional and advocacy groups, proposed the new terminology "emotional or behavioral disorder" to replace "serious emotional disturbance" in federal laws and regulations (Forness & Knitzer, 1992). It now appears that "emotional or behavioral disorder" may become the generally accepted terminology of the field, although changes in federal and state laws and regulations may be slow in coming.

DEFINITION

Defining emotional and behavioral disorders has always been problematic. Professional groups and experts have felt free to construct individual working definitions to fit their own professional purposes. For practical reasons, we might say that someone has had an emotional or behavioral disorder whenever an adult authority said so. Until very recently, no one has come up with a definition that is understandable and acceptable to a majority of professionals.

Definitional Problems

There are valid reasons for the lack of consensus regarding definition (Kauffman, 1993). Defining emotional and behavioral disorders is somewhat like defining a familiar experience—anger, loneliness, or happiness, for example. We all have an intuitive grasp of what these experiences are, but their objective definition is far from simple. The factors that make it particularly difficult to arrive at a good definition of emotional and behavioral disorders are these:

- Lack of precise definitions of mental health and normal behavior
- Differences among conceptual models
- Difficulties in measuring emotions and behavior

Children with emotional or behavioral disorders frequently behave in ways that frustrate and anger adults.

- Relationships between emotional and behavioral disorders and other disabilities
- Differences in the professionals who categorize and serve children and youths

Consider each of these problems in turn. Mental health and normal behavior have been hard to define precisely. It is no wonder, then, that the definition of emotional or behavioral disorder presents a special challenge. Professionals who work with youngsters who have emotional or behavioral disorders have been guided by a variety of conceptual models, as we will discuss further. These conceptual models—assumptions or theories about why people behave as they do and what we should do about it—may offer conflicting ideas about just what the problem is. Thus people who adopt different conceptual models may define emotional or behavioral disorder in very different terms. Measurement is basic to any definition, and emotions and behavior—the things disordered in this case—are notoriously difficult to measure in ways that make a precise definition possible. Ultimately, subjective judgment is called for, even with the best measurements available of emotions and behavior. Emotional and behavioral disorders tend to overlap a great deal with other disabilities, especially learning disabilities and mental retardation. It is therefore hard to define emotional or behavioral disorder as a disability clearly distinct from all others. Finally, each professional group has its own reasons for serving individuals with emotional or behavioral disorders. For example, clinical psychologists, school psychologists, social workers, teachers, and juvenile justice authorities all have their particular concerns

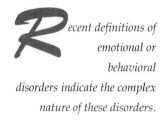

*R*ecent definitions of emotional or behavioral disorders indicate the complex nature of these disorders.

and language. Differences in the focus of different professions tend to produce differences in definition.

Current Definitions

Although the terminology used and the relative emphasis given to certain points vary considerably from one definition to another, it is possible to extract several common features of current definitions. There is general agreement that emotional or behavioral disorder refers to

- Behavior that goes to an extreme—behavior that is not just slightly different from the usual
- A problem that is chronic—one that does not quickly disappear
- Behavior that is unacceptable because of social or cultural expectations

One definition that must be considered is included in the federal rules and regulations governing the implementation of IDEA. In federal laws and regulations, "seriously emotionally disturbed" has been defined as follows:

(i) The term means a condition exhibiting one or more of the following characteristics over a long period of time and to a marked extent, which adversely affects educational performance:
   (A) An inability to learn that cannot be explained by intellectual, sensory, or health factors;
   (B) An inability to build or maintain satisfactory relationships with peers and teachers;
   (C) Inappropriate types of behavior or feelings under normal circumstances;
   (D) A general pervasive mood of unhappiness or depression; or
   (E) A tendency to develop physical symptoms or fears associated with personal or school problems.
(ii) The term includes children who are schizophrenic or autistic.* The term does not include children who are socially maladjusted unless it is determined that they are seriously emotionally disturbed.

*The U.S. Department of Education later decided that autism will no longer be included under the category of seriously emotionally disturbed. See Bower (1982) for comment on this change. In 1990, autism became a separate category under IDEA.

The federal definition is modeled after one proposed by Bower (1981). Bower's definition, however, does not include the statements found in part (ii) of the federal definition. These inclusions and exclusions are, as Bower (1982) and Kauffman (1986, 1993) have pointed out, unnecessary; common sense tells us that Bower's five criteria for emotional disturbance indicate that "autistic" and "schizophrenic" children *must be included* and that "socially maladjusted" children *cannot be excluded*. Furthermore, the clause "which adversely affects educational performance" makes interpretation of the definition impossible unless the meaning of "educational performance" is clarified. Does "educational performance" refer only to academic achievement? If so, then children with other characteristics who achieve on grade level are excluded.

In recent years the federal definition has been widely criticized, and the federal government has more than once mandated a study of it. One of the most widely criticized and controversial aspects of the definition is its exclusion of children who are socially maladjusted but not emotionally disturbed. Strong moves have been made in some states and localities to interpret social maladjustment as **conduct disorder**—aggressive, disruptive, antisocial behavior and the most common type of problem exhibited by students who have been identified as having emotional or behavioral disorders. Cline (1990) has noted that excluding students with conduct disorder is inconsistent with the history of IDEA. Moreover, the American Psychological Association and the Council for Children with Behavioral Disorders have condemned this practice. Lawyers have defended the exclusion. The controversy continues (e.g., Forness, 1992; Nelson, Rutherford, Center, and Walker, 1991; Skiba & Grizzle, 1992; Slenkovich, 1992a, 1992b).

A second definition that must be considered is the one proposed in 1990 by the National Mental Health and Special Education Coalition. The coalition's proposed definition is:

(i) The term emotional or behavioral disorder means a disability characterized by behavioral or emotional responses in school so different from appropriate age, cultural, or ethnic norms that they adversely affect educational performance. Educational performance includes academic, social, vocational, and personal skills. Such a disability

    (A) is more than a temporary, expected response to stressful events in the environment;

    (B) is consistently exhibited in two different settings, at least one of which is school-related; and

    (C) is unresponsive to direct intervention in general education, or the child's condition is such that general education interventions would be insufficient.

(ii) Emotional and behavioral disorders can co-exist with other disabilities.

(iii) This category may include children or youths with **schizophrenic** disorders, **affective disorders**, **anxiety disorder**, or other sustained disorders of conduct or adjustment when they adversely affect educational performance in accordance with section (i). (Forness & Knitzer, 1992, p. 13)

The coalition is working to have the proposed definition and terminology adopted in federal laws and regulations, with the hope that the states will adopt

➤ **conduct disorder.** A disorder characterized by overt, aggressive, disruptive behavior or covert antisocial acts such as stealing, lying, and fire setting; may include both overt and covert acts.

➤ **schizophrenic.** Characterized by psychotic behavior manifested by loss of contact with reality, bizarre thought processes, and inappropriate actions.

➤ **affective disorder.** A disorder of mood or emotional tone characterized by depression or elation.

➤ **anxiety disorder.** A disorder characterized by anxiety, fearfulness, and avoidance of ordinary activities because of anxiety or fear.

them as well. Advantages of the proposed definition over the federal definition include the following:

- It uses terminology reflecting current professional preferences and concern for minimizing stigma.
- It includes both disorders of emotions and disorders of behavior and recognizes that they may occur either separately or in combination.
- It is school-centered but acknowledges that disorders exhibited outside the school setting are also important.
- It is sensitive to ethnic and cultural differences.
- It does not include minor or transient problems or ordinary responses to stress.
- It acknowledges the importance of prereferral interventions but does not require slavish implementation of them in extreme cases.
- It acknowledges that children and youths can have multiple disabilities.
- It includes the full range of emotional or behavioral disorders of concern to mental health and special education professionals without arbitrary exclusions.

CLASSIFICATION

Since there are many ways to have an emotional or behavioral disorder, it seems reasonable to expect that individuals could be grouped into subcategories according to the types of problems they have. Still, there is no universally accepted system for classifying emotional or behavioral disorders for special education.

Psychiatric classification systems have been widely criticized. Hobbs (1975) commented, "It is important to note that competent clinicians would seldom use for treatment purposes the categories provided by diagnostic manuals; their judgment would be more finely modulated than the classification schemes, and more sensitive than any formal system can be to temporal, situational, and developmental changes" (pp. 58–59). Clearly, the usual diagnostic categories—for example, those found in publications of the American Psychiatric Association—have little meaning for teachers. Some psychologists and educators have recommended relying more on individual assessment of the child's behavior and situational factors than on traditional diagnostic classification (Kerr & Nelson, 1989; Morse, 1985).

An alternative to traditional psychiatric classifications is the use of statistical analyses of behavioral characteristics to establish clusters or *dimensions* of disordered behavior. Using sophisticated statistical procedures, researchers look for patterns of behavior that characterize children who have emotional or behavioral disorders. By using these methods, researchers have been able to derive descriptive categories that are less susceptible to bias and unreliability than the traditional psychiatric classifications (Achenbach, 1985).

Achenbach and others (Achenbach, Howell, Quay, & Conners, 1991; Quay, 1986; Walker & Severson, 1990) have identified two broad, pervasive dimensions of disordered behavior: **externalizing** and **internalizing**. Externalizing behavior involves striking out against others. Internalizing behavior involves mental or emotional conflicts such as depression and anxiety. A variety of more specific dimensions has been found by several researchers. Quay and Peterson (1987), for example, describe six dimensions characterized by the following kinds of behavior:

➤ **externalizing.** Acting-out behavior; aggressive or disruptive behavior that is observable as behavior directed toward others.

➤ **internalizing.** Acting-in behavior; anxiety, fearfulness, withdrawal, and other indications of an individual's mood or internal state.

- *Conduct disorder*—seeks attention, shows off, is disruptive, annoys others, fights, has temper tantrums
- *Socialized aggression*—steals in company with others, is loyal to delinquent friends, is truant from school with others, has "bad" companions, freely admits disrespect for moral values and laws
- *Attention problems-immaturity*—has short attention span, has poor concentration, is distractible, is easily diverted from task at hand, answers without thinking, is sluggish, is slow-moving, is lethargic   ADD
- *Anxiety-withdrawal*—is self-conscious, is easily embarrassed, is hypersensitive, feelings are easily hurt, is generally fearful, is anxious, is depressed, is always sad
- *Psychotic behavior*—expresses far-fetched ideas, has repetitive speech, shows bizarre behavior   Schizophrenia
- *Motor excess*—is restless, is unable to sit still, is tense, is unable to relax, is overtalkative

Individuals may show behaviors characteristic of more than one dimension; that is, the dimensions are not mutually exclusive. A child or youth might exhibit several of the behaviors associated with the attention problems-immaturity dimension (short attention span, poor concentration) and perhaps several of those defining conduct disorders as well (fighting, disruptive behavior, annoying others).

Children may exhibit characteristic types of behavior with varying degrees of intensity or severity. That is, all dimensions of behavior may be exhibited to a greater or lesser extent; the range may be from normal to severely disordered. For example, an individual might have a severe conduct disorder. The classification of the severe disorders typically called **childhood psychosis** or **pervasive developmental disorders,** presents particular problems. Children with these disorders exhibit behavior that is qualitatively as well as quantitatively different from that of others (Wenar, Ruttenberg, Kalish-Weiss, & Wolf, 1986). They are often described as inaccessible to others, unreachable, out of touch with reality, or mentally retarded. Prior and Werry (1986) have said of children with childhood psychosis that "[Their] interpretation of [themselves], of the world, and of [their] place in it is so seriously at variance with the actual facts of the matter as to interfere with everyday adaptation and to strike the impartial observer as incomprehensible" (p. 156).

Two types of severe childhood disorders are distinguished by most researchers: **autism** and **schizophrenia.** Children with autism are characterized by a lack of responsiveness to other people, major problems in communication (many do not have any useful language), peculiar speech patterns (such as parroting what they hear), and bizarre responses (e.g., peculiar interests in or attachment to objects). They often engage in repetitive, stereotyped behavior. Children with schizophrenia have a severe disorder of thinking. They may believe they are controlled by alien forces or have other delusions or hallucinations. Typically, their emotions are inappropriate for the actual circumstances, and they tend to withdraw into a private world.

One major difference between autism and schizophrenia is that a child with autism is typically recognized as having a disorder before the age of thirty months. Childhood schizophrenia is a disorder that typically begins after a normal period of development, usually longer than thirty months. Autism and

> **psychosis.** A major mental disorder exhibited in seriously disturbed behavior and lack of contact with reality; *schizophrenia* is a form of psychosis.

> **pervasive developmental disorder.** Severe disorder characterized by abnormal social relations, including bizarre mannerisms, inappropriate social behavior, and unusual or delayed speech and language.

> **autism.** A disorder   Before 30 months
characterized by extreme withdrawal, self-stimulation, cognitive deficits, language disorders, and onset before the age of thirty months.

> **schizophrenia.** Psychotic behavior manifested by loss of contact with reality, bizarre thought processes, and inappropriate actions.

schizophrenia in children, then, are differentiated partly on the basis of the child's age at the first appearance of symptoms. There are other differences between the two conditions, especially these: (1) Children with schizophrenia usually have delusions (bizarre ideas) and hallucinations (seeing or hearing imaginary things), whereas children with autism usually do not; (2) children with schizophrenia tend to have psychotic episodes interspersed with periods of near normal behavior, whereas children with autism tend to have persistent symptoms; (3) about 25 percent of children with autism have epileptic seizures, whereas children with schizophrenia seldom have seizures (Rutter & Schopler, 1987).

As mentioned in the discussion of the definition, autism is no longer considered by the U.S. Department of Education under the category "seriously emotionally disturbed," the category described in this chapter as emotional or behavioral disorders. The reasons for this reclassification are likely these: (1) the parents of children with autism objected—and with good reason—to the blame implied by the term "emotional disturbance," particularly the explicit blame heaped upon them by prominent psychoanalytical thinking (e.g., Bettelheim, 1950, 1967), and (2) autism seems clearly to be caused primarily by a neurological or biochemical dysfunction. Autism is discussed in this chapter and Chapter 7 (Communication Disorders) because of the implications of having autism, e. g., (1) the child exhibits highly problematic emotional and behavioral responses to everyday circumstances; and (2) the child's problems are often centered on difficulty in communicating. Autism is not discussed at length in Chapter 10 (Physical Disabilities) because the nature of the physical problem in autism remains essentially unknown, and the most successful interventions in autism involve behavior modification and adaptive communication.

In summary, the most useful classifications of emotional or behavioral disorders describe behavioral dimensions. The dimensions described in the literature involve a wide range of problems, including conduct disorder, socialized aggression, attention problems and immaturity, anxiety and withdrawal, excessive movement, and psychotic behavior. These dimensions include a variety of antisocial conduct, delinquent behavior, substance abuse, depression, and autism and schizophrenia. Nevertheless, because of ambiguity in the federal definition of "serious emotional disturbance," controversy persists regarding the classifications that should be included for special education purposes.

PREVALENCE

Estimates of the prevalence of emotional or behavioral disorders in children and youths have varied tremendously because there has been no standard and reliable definition or screening instrument. For decades, the federal government estimated that 2 percent of the school-age population was "seriously emotionally disturbed." The government's estimate was *extremely* conservative. Rather consistently, credible studies in the United States and many other countries of the world have indicated that at least 6 to 10 percent of children and youths of school age exhibit serious and persistent emotional/behavioral problems (Brandenburg, Friedman, & Silver, 1990; Kauffman, 1993; Kazdin, 1989). Data published by the U.S. Department of Education (1992), however, show that only about 1 percent of schoolchildren in the United States are identified as "seriously emotionally disturbed." The Department of Education now recognizes that this is an underserved category of special education students whose needs are particularly complex.

The most common types of problems exhibited by students in special education for emotional or behavioral disorders are externalizing (aggressive, acting-out disruptive behavior). Most of the students identified as having such disorders are not psychotic. Boys outnumber girls by a ratio of 5 to 1 or more. Overall, boys tend to exhibit more aggression and conduct disorder than girls do (Achenbach et al., 1991).

Juvenile delinquency and the antisocial behavior known as conduct disorder present particular problems in estimating prevalence. Delinquent youths constitute a considerable percentage of the population. About 3 percent of U.S. youths are referred to a juvenile court in any given year. Many others engage in serious antisocial behavior but are not referred to the courts. One point of view is that *all* delinquent and antisocial youths should be thought of as having emotional or behavioral disorders. Some argue, however, that most delinquents and others who commit frequent antisocial acts are "socially maladjusted," not "seriously emotionally disturbed" for special education purposes. Clearly, disabling conditions of various kinds are much more common among juvenile delinquents than among the general population (Henggeler, 1989; Murphy, 1986). Just as clearly, the social and economic costs of delinquency and antisocial behavior are enormous. Adolescent males account for a disproportionately high percentage of serious and violent crime in our society (Henggeler, 1989). Those who exhibit serious antisocial behavior are at high risk for school failure as well as other negative outcomes (Kazdin, 1987; Patterson, DeBeryshe, & Ramsey, 1989; Walker, Steiber, & O'Neill, 1990). If schools are to address the educational problems of delinquent and antisocial children and youths, the number served by special education will have to be increased dramatically.

CAUSES

The causes of emotional or behavioral disorders have been attributed to four major factors: biological disorders and diseases, pathological family relationships, negative cultural influences, and undesirable experiences at school. Although in the majority of cases there is no conclusive empirical evidence that any of these factors is directly responsible for the disorder, some may give a child a predisposition to exhibit problem behavior, and others may precipitate or trigger it. That is, some factors, such as genetics, influence behavior over a long time and increase the likelihood that a given set of circumstances will trigger maladaptive responses. Other factors (e.g., observing one parent beating the other) may have a more immediate effect and may trigger maladaptive responses in an individual who is already predisposed to problem behavior.

Another concept important in all theories is the idea of *contributing factors*. It is extremely unusual to find a single cause that has led directly to a disorder. Usually, several factors together contribute to the development of a problem. In almost all cases, the question of what specifically has caused the disorder cannot be answered because no one really knows.

Biological Factors

Behavior and emotions may be influenced by genetic, neurological, or biochemical factors, or by combinations of these. Certainly there is a relationship between body and behavior, and it would therefore seem reasonable to look for a biological causal factor of some kind for certain emotional or behavioral disorders. But

*N*ot all rebellious or defiant juvenile behavior is delinquent, nor is all such behavior known to juvenile authorities.

➤ **temperament.** Inborn behavioral style, including general level of activity, regularity or predictability, approach or withdrawal, adaptability, intensity of reaction, responsiveness, mood, distractibility, and persistence. The temperament is present at birth but may be modified by parental management.

only rarely is it possible to demonstrate a relationship between a specific biological factor and an emotional or behavioral disorder. Many children with emotional or behavioral disorders have no detectable biological flaws that could account for their actions, and many behaviorally normal children have serious biological defects. For most children with emotional or behavioral disorders, there simply is no real evidence that biological factors alone are at the root of the problem. For those with severe and profound disorders, however, there is evidence to suggest that biological factors may contribute to the condition (Prior & Werry, 1986).

All children are born with a biologically determined behavioral style, or temperament. Although children's inborn temperaments may be changed by the way they are reared, some believe that children with "difficult" temperaments are predisposed to develop emotional or behavioral disorders (Thomas & Chess, 1984). There is no one-to-one relationship between temperament and disorders, however. A "difficult" child may be handled so well or a child with an "easy" temperament so poorly that the outcome is quite different from what one might predict on the basis of initial behavioral style. Other biological factors besides temperament—disease, malnutrition, and brain trauma, for example—may predispose children to develop emotional or behavioral problems (Baumeister, Kupstas, & Klindworth, 1990; Lozoff, 1989). Substance abuse also may contribute to serious emotional and behavioral problems (Newcomb & Bentler, 1989). Except in rare instances it is not possible to determine that these factors are direct causes of problem behavior.

As is the case in mental retardation, there is more often evidence of a biological cause among children with severe or profound disabilities. Children with autism or schizophrenia frequently, but not always, show signs of neurological defects (Prior & Werry, 1986). There is convincing evidence that genetic factors contribute to schizophrenia (Gottesman, 1991; Plomin, 1989), although even when there is severe and profound disorder, the role of specific biological factors often remains a mystery (Kauffman, 1993; Prior & Werry, 1986). It is now generally accepted that autism is a neurological disorder, but the nature and causes of the neurological defect are unknown.

As biological and psychological research becomes more sophisticated, it is apparent that biological factors cause or set the stage for many disorders that formerly were widely assumed to be caused mostly or entirely by social interactions. Schizophrenia and autism are the foremost examples. Another example is **Tourette's disorder**, which is characterized by multiple motor tics (repetitive, stereotyped movements) and verbal tics (i.e., the individual makes strange noises or says inappropriate words or phrases). Although we now understand autism, schizophrenia, Tourette's disorder, attention deficit hyperactivity disorder (ADHD), some forms of depression, and many other disorders to be caused wholly or partly by brain or biochemical dysfunctions, these biological causal factors remain poorly understood. That is, exactly how genetic, neurological, and other biochemical factors contribute to these disorders is not known, nor do we know how to correct the biological problems involved in these disorders.

> **Tourette's disorder.** A neurological disorder beginning in childhood (about 3 times more prevalent in boys than in girls) in which stereotyped motor movements (tics) are accompanied by multiple vocal outbursts that may include grunting or barking noises or socially inappropriate words or statements.

It is clear that traumatic brain injury, now a separate category of disability under IDEA, may cause psychosocial problems. Depending on what part of the brain is injured and when the injury occurs during development, the individual may experience serious difficulty in psychosocial behavior—responding appropriately to social circumstances, controlling rage reactions or aggression, showing appropriate affect, and so on.

Four points are important to remember about biological causes. First, the fact that disorders have biological causes does not mean that they are not emotional or behavioral disorders. An emotional or behavioral disorder can have a physical cause; the biological malfunction is a problem because of the disorder it creates in the individual's emotions or behavior. Second, causes are seldom exclusively biological or psychological. Once a biological disorder occurs, it nearly always creates psychosocial problems that then also contribute to the emotional or behavioral disorder as well. Third, biological or medical treatment of the disorder is seldom sufficient to resolve the problem. Medication may be of great benefit, but it is seldom the only intervention that is needed. The psychological and social aspects of the disorder must also be addressed. Fourth, medical or biological approaches are sometimes of little or no benefit and the primary interventions are psychological or behavioral, even though the disorder is known to have primarily a biological cause. Medications do not work equally well for all cases, and for some disorders no generally effective medications are known.

Family Factors

Mental health specialists have been tempted to blame behavioral difficulties primarily on parent-child relationships because the nuclear family—father, mother, and children—has a profound influence on early development. In fact, some advocates of psychoanalysis believe that almost all severe problems of children stem from early negative interactions between mother and child. However, empirical research on family relationships indicates that the influence of parents on their children is no simple matter, and that children with emotional or behavioral disorders may influence their parents as much as the parents influence them. It is increasingly clear that family influences are interactional and transactional and that the effects of parents and children on one another are reciprocal (Patterson, DeBaryshe, & Ramsey, 1989; Patterson, Reid, & Dishion, 1992). Even in cases of severe and profound emotional or behavioral disorders, it is not possible to find consistent and valid research findings that allow the blame for the children's problem behavior to be placed primarily on their parents (Gottesman, 1991; Sameroff, Steifer, & Zax, 1982).

The outcome of parental discipline depends not only on the particular techniques used but also on the characteristics of the child (Rutter, 1985). Generalizations about the effects of parental discipline are difficult to make, for as Becker (1964) commented long ago, "There are probably many routes to becoming a 'good parent' which vary with the personality of both the parents and children and with the pressure in the environment with which one must learn to cope" (p. 202). Nevertheless, sensitivity to children's needs, love-oriented methods of dealing with misbehavior, and reinforcement (attention and praise) for appropriate behavior unquestionably tend to promote desirable behavior in children. Parents who are generally lax in disciplining their children but are hostile, rejecting, cruel, and inconsistent in dealing with misbehavior are likely to have aggressive, delinquent children. Broken, disorganized homes in which the parents themselves have arrest records or are violent are particularly likely to foster delinquency and lack of social competence.

In discussing the combined effects of genetics and environment on behavioral development, Plomin (1989) warns against assuming that the family environment will make siblings similar. "Environmental influences do not operate on a family-by-family basis but rather on an individual-by-individual basis. They are specific to each child rather than general for an entire family" (p. 109). Thus, although we know that some types of family environments (abusive, neglectful, rejecting, and inconsistent, for example) are destructive, we must also remember that each child will experience and react to family relationships in his or her unique way.

Educators must be aware that most parents of youngsters with emotional or behavioral disorders want their children to behave more appropriately and will do anything they can to help them. These parents need support resources—not blame or criticism—for dealing with very difficult family circumstances. The Federation of Families for Children's Mental Health was organized in 1989 to help provide such support and resources, and parents are organizing in many localities to assist each other in finding additional resources (Jordan, Goldberg, & Goldberg, 1991). In the box on page 218, one of the founding members shares her perspective on why parents are so often blamed for their children's emotional or behavioral disorders.

School Factors

Some children already have emotional or behavioral disorders when they begin school; others develop behavioral or emotional disorders during their school years, perhaps in part because of damaging experiences in the classroom itself. Children who exhibit disorders when they enter school may become better or worse according to how they are managed in the classroom. School experiences are no doubt of great importance to children; but like biological and family factors, we cannot justify many statements regarding how such experiences contribute to the child's behavioral difficulties. A child's temperament and social competence may interact with classmates' and teachers' behavior in contributing to emotional or behavioral problems. When a child with an already difficult temperament enters school lacking the skills for academic and social success, he or she is likely to get negative responses from peers and teachers (Martin, 1992).

There is a very real danger that such a child will become trapped in a spiral of negative interactions in which he or she becomes increasingly irritating to and irritated by teachers and peers. The school can contribute to the development of emotional problems in several rather specific ways. Teachers may be insensitive to children's individuality; they may require a mindless conformity to the rules and routines. Educators and parents alike may hold too high or too low expectations for the child's achievement or conduct, and they may communicate to the child who disappoints them that he or she is inadequate or undesirable.

Discipline in the school may be too lax, too rigid, or inconsistent. Instruction may be offered in skills for which the child has no real or imagined use. The school environment may be such that the misbehaving child is rewarded with recognition and special attention (even if that attention is criticism or punishment), whereas the child who behaves is ignored. Finally, teachers and peers may be models of misconduct—the child may misbehave by imitating them (Kauffman, 1993).

In considering how they may be contributing to disordered behavior, teachers must ask themselves questions about their expectations, instruction, and approach to behavior management (Kauffman, Mostert, Nuttycombe, Trent, & Hallahan, 1993). Teachers must not assume blame for disordered behavior to which they are not contributing, yet it is equally important that teachers eliminate whatever contributions they may be making to their students' misconduct.

Cultural Factors

Children, their families, and schools are embedded in a culture that influences them (Rogoff & Morelli, 1989). Aside from family and school, many environmental conditions affect adults' expectations of children and children's expectations for themselves and their peers. Values and behavioral standards are communicated to children through a variety of cultural conditions, demands, prohibitions, and models. Several specific cultural influences leap to mind: the level of violence in the media (especially television and motion pictures), the use of terror as a means of coercion, the availability of recreational drugs and the level of drug abuse, changing standards for sexual conduct, religious demands and restrictions on behavior, and the threat of nuclear accidents or war.

Undoubtedly, the culture in which children are reared exerts an influence on their emotional, social, and behavioral development. Case studies of rapidly changing cultures bear this out. Other studies suggest cultural influences on anxiety, depression, and aggression (Goldstein, 1983; Hawton, 1986). The level of violence depicted on television and in movies is almost certainly a contributing factor in the increasing level of violence in our society.

Garmezy (1987) and Baumeister, Kupstas, & Klindworth (1990) also note the changing cultural conditions in the United States during the 1980s that predisposed children to develop emotional or behavioral disorders and a variety of

ＰERSONAL REFLECTIONS ➤

Family Factors

Dixie Jordan is the parent of a 19-year-old son with an emotional and behavioral disorder, Coordinator of the EBD Project at the PACER Center in Minneapolis (a resource center for parents of children with disabilities), and a founding member of the Federation of Families for Children's Mental Health.

Why do you think there is such a strong tendency to hold parents responsible for their children's emotional or behavioral disorders?

I am the parent of two children, the younger of which has emotional and behavioral problems. When my firstborn and I were out in public, strangers often commented on what a "good" mother I was, to have such an obedient, well-behaved, and compliant child. Frankly, I enjoyed the comments, and really believed that those parents whose children were throwing tantrums and generally demolishing their environments were simply not very skilled in child-rearing. I recall casting my share of reproachful glances in those days, and thinking with some arrogance that raising children should be left to those of us who knew how to do it well. Several years later, my second child and I were on the business end of such disdain, and it was a lesson in humility that I shall never forget. Very little that I had learned in the previous 3 years as a parent worked with this child; he was neurologically different, hyperactive, inattentive, and noncompliant even when discipline was consistently applied. His doctors, his neurologist, and finally his teachers referred me to "parenting classes," as though the experiences I had had with my older child were nonexistent; his elementary principal even said that there was nothing wrong that a good spanking wouldn't cure. I expected understanding that this was a very difficult child to raise, but the unspoken message was that I lacked competence in basic parenting skills, the same message that I sent to similarly situated parents just a few years earlier.

Most of us in the world today are parents. The majority of us have children who do not have emotional or behavioral problems. Everything in our experience suggests that when our children are successful and obedient, it is because of our parenting. We are reinforced socially for having a well-behaved child from friends, grandparents, even strangers. It makes

sense, then, to attribute less desirable behaviors in children to the failure of their parents to provide appropriate guidance or to set firm limits. Many parents have internalized that sense of responsibility or blame for causing their child's emotional problems, even when they are not able to identify what they might have done wrong. It is a very difficult attitude to shake, especially when experts themselves cannot seem to agree on causation. With most children, the "cause" of an emotional or behavioral disorder is more likely a complex interplay of multiple factors than "parenting styles," "biology," or "environmental influences" as discrete entities, but it is human nature to latch onto a simple explanation—and inadequate parenting is, indeed, a simple explanation. When systems blame parents for causing their child's emotional or behavioral disorders, the focus is no longer on services to help the child learn better adaptive skills or appropriate behaviors, but on rationalizing why such services may not work. When parents feel blamed, their energies shift from focusing on the needs of their child to defending themselves. In either instance, the child is less well served.

Another reason that people hold parents responsible for their children's emotional or behavioral disorders is that parents may be under such unrelenting stress from trying to manage their child's behavior that they may resort to inappropriate techniques because of the failure of more conventional methods. A parent whose 8-year-old hyperactive child smashes out his bedroom window while being timed out for another problem may know that tying the child to a chair is not a good way to handle the crisis, but may be out of alternatives. It may not have been the "right" thing for the parent to do, but is hardly responsible for causing the child's problems in the first place. It would be a mistake to attribute the incidence of abuse or neglect as "causing" most emotional or behavioral disorders without consideration that difficult children are perhaps more likely to be abused due to their noncompliant or otherwise difficult behaviors.

SOURCE: Reprinted with the permission of Macmillan Publishing Company from *Characteristics of emotional and behavioral disorders of children and youth* (5th ed) by James M. Kauffman. Copyright © 1993 By Macmillan Publishing Company. PP. 220–221.

other disabling conditions. Among these are dramatic increases in the number of children living in poverty. There have also been substantial increases in the number of children born to teenage mothers and to mothers who have abused crack cocaine and other substances. At the same time, medical and social services available to poor children and their families have been cut substantially. In short, the Reagan era was a period of enormous affluence for some Americans but also a period in which poverty and related problems grew rapidly. Neglect of the problems of poor children and their families have led some to question the importance of the health and welfare of children in U.S. culture (see also Rogoff & Morelli, 1989).

Clearly, our "culture" affects the way children behave in school. But even when culture is considered as a cause, we must be aware of interactive effects. Schools and families influence our culture; they are not simply products of it. Finally, refer back to Chapter 3 and the importance of a multicultural perspective. Consideration of cultural factors in causing emotional or behavioral disorders requires that culturally normative behavior not be construed as "disordered."

IDENTIFICATION

It is much easier to identify disordered *behaviors* than it is to define and classify types and causes of emotional or behavioral disorders. Most students with emotional or behavioral disorders do not escape the notice of their teachers. Occasionally a student will not be a bother to anyone and thus be "invisible," but it is usually easy for experienced teachers to tell when a student needs help. The most common type of emotional or behavioral disorder—conduct disorder—attracts immediate attention, so there is seldom any real problem in identification. Immature students and those with personality problems may be less obvious, but they are not difficult to recognize. Students with emotional or behavioral disorders are so readily identified by school personnel, in fact, that few schools bother to use systematic screening procedures. Also, special services for those with emotional or behavioral disorders lag far behind the need. There is not much point in screening for problems when there are no services available to treat them.

Children with pervasive developmental disorders are easily recognized. In fact, the parents of children with autism frequently report that, soon after their child's birth, they noticed that he or she was strange or different from most children—unresponsive, rigid, or emotionally detached, for example. Children with schizophrenia are seldom mistaken for those who are developing normally. Their unusual language, mannerisms, and ways of relating to others soon become matters of concern to parents, teachers, and even many casual observers. But children with these disorders are a small percentage of those with emotional or behavioral disorders, and problems in their identification are not usually encountered.

However, it should not be thought that there is never any question about whether a student has an emotional or behavioral disorder. The younger the child, the more difficult it is to judge whether that child's behavior signifies a serious problem. And some children with emotional or behavioral disorders are undetected because teachers are not sensitive to their problems or because they do not stand out sharply from other children in the environment who may have even more serious problems. Furthermore, even sensitive teachers sometimes make errors of judgment. Finally, some students with emotional or behavioral disorders do not exhibit problems at school.

Formal screening and accurate early identification for the purpose of planning educational intervention are complicated by the problems of definition already discussed. In general, however, teachers' informal judgment has served as a fairly valid and reliable means of screening students for emotional or behavioral problems (as compared with judgments of psychologists and psychiatrists). When more formal procedures are used, teachers' ratings of behavior have turned out to be quite accurate (Edelbrock & Achenbach, 1984). Children's ratings of their peers and their own behavior have also proved helpful (Bower, 1981).

Walker and his colleagues have devised a screening system for use in elementary schools based on the assumption that a teacher's judgment is a valid and cost-effective though greatly underused method of identifying children with emotional or behavioral disorders (Walker & Severson, 1990). Although teachers tend to overrefer students who exhibit externalizing behavior problems (those with conduct disorders), they tend to underrefer students with internalizing problems (those who are characterized by anxiety-withdrawal). To make certain that children are not overlooked in screening, but that time and effort are not wasted, a three-step process is used.

First, the teacher lists and rank-orders students with externalizing and internalizing problems. Those who best fit descriptions of students with externalizing problems and those who best fit descriptions of those with internalizing problems are listed. Then they are rank-ordered from most like to least like the descriptions. Second, the teacher completes two checklists for the three highest-ranked pupils on each list. One checklist asks the teacher to indicate whether or not each pupil exhibited specific behaviors during the past month (such as "steals," "has tantrums," "uses obscene language or swears"). The other checklist requires the teacher to judge how often (never, sometimes, frequently) each pupil shows certain characteristics (e.g., "follows established classroom rules," or "cooperates with peers in group activities or situations"). Third, pupils whose scores on these checklists exceed established norms are observed in the classroom and on the playground by a school professional other than the classroom teacher (a school psychologist, counselor, or resource teacher).

Classroom observations indicate the extent to which the pupil meets academic expectations; playground observations assess the quality and nature of social behavior. These direct observations of behavior, in addition to teachers' ratings, are then used to decide whether or not the child has problems that warrant classification for special education. Such carefully researched screening systems may lead to improved services for children with emotional or behavioral disorders. Systematic efforts to base identification on teachers' judgment *and* careful observation should result in services being directed to those most clearly in need.

PSYCHOLOGICAL AND BEHAVIORAL CHARACTERISTICS

Describing the characteristics of children and youths with emotional or behavioral disorders is an extraordinary challenge because disorders of emotions and behavior are extremely varied. We provide a general picture of these children; individuals may vary markedly in intelligence, achievement, life circumstances, and emotional and behavioral characteristics.

Intelligence and Achievement

The idea that children and youths with emotional or behavioral disorders tend to be particularly bright is a myth. Research clearly shows that the average student

*E*xperts are looking *differently at intelligence* *as expressed in the* *context of some emotional or* *behavioral disorders. One of these* *children has a severe emotional or* *behavioral disorder.*

with an emotional or behavioral disorder has an IQ in the dull-normal range (around 90) and that relatively few score above the bright-normal range. Compared to the normal distribution of intelligence, more children with emotional or behavioral disorders fall into the ranges of slow-learner and mild mental retardation. Although children with autism are often untestable, those who can be tested are likely to have IQs in the retarded range; the average for these children is about 50. On the basis of a review of the research on the intelligence of students with emotional or behavioral disorders, Kauffman (1993) hypothesized distributions of intelligence as shown in Figure 6–1. Of course, we have been referring to children with emotional or behavioral disorders as a group. Some children who have emotional or behavioral disorders are extremely bright and score very high on intelligence tests.

The cognitive deficits of many individuals with severe disorders such as autism appear to be both real and permanent. We caution, however, that intensive early behavioral intervention may reveal cognitive abilities that have not been apparent. That is, some individuals have cognitive deficits that early intensive intervention can largely overcome; these individuals may be mistakenly assumed to have permanent cognitive deficits. Further research may challenge the way the intelligence of individuals with autism is viewed and assessed. Lovaas and his research group (e.g., Lovaas, 1987) have shown that with very early and very intensive behavioral intervention a substantial proportion of children with autism recover and have intelligence within the range considered normal (i. e., between 70 and about 130). The curve Kauffman hypothesized for students with autism (Figure 6–1 on p. 222) may need to be revised upward, at least for a subgroup of children.

There are pitfalls in assessing the intellectual characteristics of a group of children by examining the distribution of the IQs. Intelligence tests are not perfect instruments for measuring what we mean by "intelligence," and it can be argued that emotional or behavioral difficulties may prevent children from

➤ *Hypothetical frequency distributions of IQ for most students with emotional or behavioral disorders and students with autism as compared to a normal frequency distribution.*

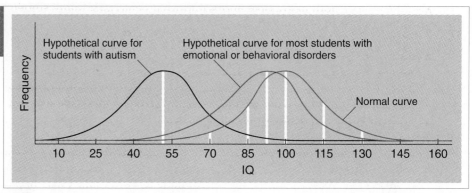

SOURCE: Reprinted with the permission of Macmillan Publishing Company from *Characteristics of emotional and behavioral disorders of children and youth* (5th ed.) by James. M. Kauffman. Copyright © 1993 by Macmillan Publishing Company, p. 227.

scoring as high as they could. That is, it might be argued that intelligence tests are biased against children with emotional or behavioral disorders and that their "true" intelligence is higher than the test scores indicate. Still, the lower-than-normal IQs for these students do indicate lower ability to perform tasks other students can perform successfully, and the lower scores are consistent with impairment in other areas of functioning (academic achievement and social skills, for example). IQ is a relatively good predictor of how far a student will progress academically and socially, even in cases of severe and profound disorders.

Most students with emotional or behavioral disorders are also underachievers at school, as measured by standardized tests (Kauffman, 1993). A student with an emotional or behavioral disorder does not usually achieve at the level expected for his or her mental age; seldom does one find such a student to be academically advanced. Many students with severe disorders lack even the most basic reading and arithmetic skills, and the few who seem to be competent in reading or math are often unable to apply their skills to everyday problems. Some children with severe disorders do not even possess basic self-care or daily living skills, such as using the toilet, grooming, dressing, and feeding.

Social and Emotional Characteristics

Previously, we described two major dimensions of disordered behavior based on analyses of behavior ratings: externalizing and internalizing. The externalizing dimension is characterized by aggressive, acting-out behavior; the internalizing dimension is characterized by anxious, withdrawn behavior. Our discussion here will focus on the aggressive and withdrawn types of behavior typically exhibited by students with emotional or behavioral disorders.

Although both aggressive and withdrawn behaviors are commonly seen in most children with emotional or behavioral disorders, we will discuss the characteristics of severe and profound disorders in a separate section. These children may be qualitatively as well as quantitatively different from others, for certain behavioral features set them apart. Remember, too, that a given student might, at different times, show both aggressive and withdrawn behaviors. Many students with emotional or behavioral disorders have multiple problems.

At the beginning of this chapter, we said that most students with emotional or behavioral disorders are not well-liked by their peers. Studies of the social status of students in regular elementary and secondary classrooms have indicated that those who are identified as having emotional or behavioral disorders are seldom socially accepted. Given what we know about the behavioral characteristics of these students and the behavioral characteristics that support social acceptance, this should come as no surprise: "The research indicates that children—whether normal or exceptional—who are in frequent conflict with authority, who fight or bother others a great deal, and who demonstrate verbal aggression are rarely the objects of social acceptance" (Drabman & Patterson, 1981, p. 53). Students who show these characteristics are actively rejected, not just neglected, by their peers.

Aggressive, Acting-Out Behavior (Externalizing)

As noted earlier, conduct disorders are the most common problems exhibited by students with emotional or behavioral disorders. Hitting, fighting, teasing, yelling, refusing to comply with requests, crying, destructiveness, vandalism, extortion—these behaviors, if exhibited often, are very likely to earn a child or youth the label "disturbed." Normal children cry, scream, hit, fight, become negative, and do almost everything else children with emotional or behavioral disorders do, only not so impulsively and so often. Youngsters of the type we are discussing here drive adults to distraction. They are not popular with their peers either, unless they are socialized delinquents who do not offend their delinquent friends. They typically do not respond quickly and positively to well-meaning adults who care about them and try to be helpful.

Some of these students are considered to have attention deficit hyperactivity disorder or brain-injury; some are called **sociopathic** because they appear to hurt others deliberately and without any sense of doing wrong. Their behavior is not only extremely troublesome, but also appears to be resistant to change through typical discipline. Often they are so frequently scolded and punished that punishment means little or nothing to them. Because of adult exasperation and their own deviousness, they get away with misbehavior a lot of the time. We are talking about children who behave horribly not once in a while, but so often that the people they must live with or be with cannot stand them. Of course, aggressive, acting-out children typically cannot stand the people they have to live and be with either, and often for good reason. Such children are screamed at, criticized, and punished a lot. The problem, then, is not just the child's behavior. What must be examined if the child or anyone else is to be helped is the *interaction between the child's behavior and the behavior of other people in his or her environment.*

Aggression has been analyzed from many viewpoints. The analyses that have the strongest support in empirical research are those of social learning theorists, such as Bandura (1973), and behavioral psychologists, such as Patterson (Patterson, Reid, & Dishion, 1992). Their studies take into account the child's experience and his or her motivation, based on the anticipated consequences of aggression. In brief, they view aggression as *learned* behavior, and they assume that it is possible to identify the conditions under which it will be learned. The following statements about learned aggression are supported by research.

➤ **sociopathic.** Behavior characteristic of a sociopath; someone whose behavior is aggressively antisocial and who shows no remorse or guilt for misdeeds.

➤ **aggression.** Behavior that intentionally causes others harm or that elicits escape or avoidance responses from others.

Children learn many aggressive behaviors by observing parents, siblings, playmates, and people portrayed on television and in movies. Individuals who model aggression are more likely to be imitated if they are high in social status and are observed to receive rewards and escape punishment for their aggression, especially if they experience no unpleasant consequences or obtain rewards by overcoming their victims. If children are placed in an unpleasant situation and they cannot escape from the unpleasantness or obtain rewards except by aggression, they are more likely to be aggressive, especially if this behavior is tolerated or encouraged by others.

Aggression is encouraged by external rewards (social status, power, suffering of the victim, obtaining desired items), vicarious rewards (seeing others obtain desirable consequences for their aggression), and self-reinforcement (self-congratulation or enhancement of self-image). If children can justify aggression in their own minds (by comparison to the behavior of others or by dehumanizing their victims), they are more likely to be aggressive. Punishment may actually increase aggression under some circumstances: when it is inconsistent or delayed, when there is no positive alternative to the punished behavior, when it provides an example of aggression, or when counterattack against the punisher seems likely to be successful.

Teaching aggressive children to be less obnoxious is no simple matter, but social learning theory and behavioral research do provide some general guidelines. In general, research does not support the notion that it is wise to let children "act out" their aggression freely. The most helpful techniques include providing examples (models) of nonaggressive responses to aggression-provoking circumstances, helping the child rehearse or role-play nonaggressive behavior, providing reinforcement for nonaggressive behavior, preventing the child from obtaining positive consequences for aggression, and punishing aggression

*A*ggressive children are frequently in conflict with others.

in ways that involve as little counteraggression as possible (using "time-out" or brief social isolation rather than spanking or yelling).

The seriousness of children's aggressive, acting-out behavior should not be underestimated. A popular idea for decades was that although these children cause a lot of trouble, they are not as seriously disturbed or disabled as are children who are shy, anxious, or neurotic. Research has exploded this myth. When combined with school failure, aggressive, antisocial behavior in childhood generally means a gloomy future in terms of social adjustment and mental health, especially for boys. Neurotic, shy, anxious children are much more likely to be able to get and hold a job, overcome their emotional problems, and stay out of jails and mental hospitals than are adults who had conduct problems and were delinquent as children (see Kazdin, 1987).

Of course, there are exceptions to the rule. But there is a high probability that the aggressive child who is a failure in school will become more of a social misfit as an adult than will the withdrawn child. When we consider that conduct disorders and delinquency are highly correlated with school failure, the importance of meeting the needs of acting-out and underachieving children is obvious (Kauffman, 1993).

Immature, Withdrawn Behavior (Internalizing)

In noting the seriousness of aggressive, acting-out behavior, we do not intend to downplay the disabling nature of immaturity and withdrawal. In their extreme forms, withdrawal and immaturity may be characteristics of the disorders known as schizophrenia and autism. Such disorders not only have serious consequences for individuals in their childhood years, but also carry a very poor prognosis for adult mental health. The child whose behavior fits a pattern of extreme immaturity and withdrawal cannot develop the close and satisfying human relationships that characterize normal development. Such a child will find it difficult to meet the pressures and demands of everyday life.

All children exhibit immature behavior and act withdrawn once in a while. Children who fit the withdrawn, immature description, however, are typically infantile in their ways or reluctant to interact with other people. They are social isolates who have few friends, seldom play with children their own age, and lack the social skills necessary to have fun. Some retreat into fantasy or daydreaming; some develop fears that are completely out of proportion to the circumstances; some complain constantly of little aches and pains and let their "illness" keep them from participating in normal activities; some regress to earlier stages of development and demand constant help and attention; and some become depressed for no apparent reason (see Klein & Last, 1989; Kovacs, 1989).

As in the case of aggressive, acting-out behavior, withdrawal and immaturity may be interpreted in many different ways. Proponents of the psychoanalytic approach are likely to see internal conflicts and unconscious motivations as the underlying causes. Behavioral psychologists tend to interpret such problems in terms of failures in social learning. This view is supported by more empirical research data than other views (Kauffman, 1993). A social learning analysis attributes withdrawal and immaturity to an inadequate environment. Causal factors may include overrestrictive parental discipline, punishment for appropriate social responses, reward for isolate behavior, lack of opportunity to learn and practice social skills, and models (examples) of inappropriate behavior. Immature or withdrawn children can be taught the skills they lack by arranging

Issues in Special Education   Eating Disorders: The Perfect Child

Eating Disorders are not the type of behavior disorder that would necessarily be recognized by a teacher. In fact, they often pose no classroom or learning problems at all. They are not characterized by behavior that is disruptive to the classroom teacher. Indeed, eating disorders occur most commonly among "perfect" children, specifically, teenage girls whose great motivation is to please others. However, serious health problems and even death can be the result.

Anorexia nervosa is a condition in which a person, who is usually only slightly overweight or has no weight problem at all, begins a diet to lose weight and stays on it long after any excess weight is lost. Anorectics lose the ability to perceive their bodies realistically, seeing themselves as grotesquely overweight even if they're actually emaciated. Cessation of menstruation, loss of hair, dehydration, and eventually deadly symptoms can result. At this point, professional intervention and/or hospitalization is required.

Bulimia is a condition in which a person binges, eating enormous amounts of food, and then purges by way of either forced vomiting or through the use of diuretics, laxatives, or excessive exercise. Many bulimics show similar symptoms to anorexia, and are in danger of suffering similar health consequences.

At the root of these disorders are usually feelings of low self-esteem and an intense drive to be perfect and pleasing to all others: parents, teachers, and peers. Medical treatment would most likely be a part of a larger program aimed at the root causes of these potentially deadly diseases.

• Why is it difficult to define emotional disorders, such as bulimia and anorexia, as disabilities?

• Should school guidance and/or counseling departments have more opportunities to present mental health issues to students and parents?

opportunities for them to learn and practice appropriate responses, showing models engaging in appropriate behavior, and providing rewards for improved behavior.

A particularly important aspect of immature, withdrawn behavior is depression. Only recently have mental health workers and special educators begun to realize that depression is a widespread and serious problem among children and adolescents (Forness, 1988; Guetzloe, 1991; Klein & Last, 1989). Today the consensus of psychologists is that the nature of depression in children and youths is quite similar in many respects to that of depression in adults. The indications of depression include disturbances of mood or feelings, inability to think or concentrate, lack of motivation, and decreased physical well-being. A depressed child or youth may act sad, lonely, and apathetic; exhibit low self-esteem, excessive guilt, and pervasive pessimism; avoid tasks and social experiences; and/or have physical complaints or problems in sleeping, eating, or eliminating. Sometimes depression is accompanied by such problems as bed-wetting (nocturnal enuresis), fecal soiling (encopresis), extreme fear of or refusal to go to school, failure in school, or talk of suicide or suicide attempts.

Suicide has increased dramatically during the past decade among those between the ages of 15 and 24; it is now among the leading causes of death in this age group (Guetzloe, 1991; Hawton, 1986). Depression, especially when severe and accompanied by a sense of hopelessness, is linked to suicide and suicide attempts. Therefore, it is important for all those who work with young people to be able to recognize the signs (Poland, 1989). Substance abuse is also now a major problem among children and teenagers and may be related to depression (Newcomb & Bentler, 1989).

Depression sometimes has a biological cause, and antidepressant medications have at times been successful in helping depressed children and youths overcome their problems. In many cases, however, no biological cause can be found. Depression can also be caused by environmental or psychological factors, such as the death of a loved one, separation of one's parents, school failure, rejection by one's peers, or a chaotic and punitive home environment. Interventions based on social learning theory—instructing children and youths in social interaction skills and self-control techniques and teaching them to view themselves more positively, for example—have often been successful in such cases.

Characteristics Associated with Autism, Schizophrenia, and Other Pervasive Developmental Disorders

The characteristics of autism, schizophrenia, and other pervasive developmental disorders are not entirely distinct (Durand & Carr, 1988; Prior & Werry, 1986; Rutter & Schopler, 1987). Differentiating among these conditions is often difficult, especially in young children. Although autism and schizophrenia are typically distinguished by certain characteristics, particularly age of onset (see page 211), some types of behavior are common among children with a variety of severe disorders. These behaviors, if exhibited to a marked extent and over a long period of time, typically carry a poor prognosis; even with early, intensive intervention, a significant percentage of children are unlikely to recover completely (Lovaas, 1987; Petty, Ornitz, Michelman, & Zimmerman, 1984). Not every individual with autism, schizophrenia, or another pervasive developmental disorder exhibits all of these characteristics:

- *Absent or distorted relationships with people*—inability to relate to people except as to objects, inability to express affection, or ability to build and maintain only distant, suspicious, or bizarre relationships.
- *Extreme or peculiar problems in communication*—absence of verbal language or language that is not functional, such as **echolalia** (parroting what one hears), misuse of pronouns (e.g., *he* for *you* or *I* for *her*), **neologisms** (made-up, meaningless words or sentences), talk that bears little or no resemblance to reality.
- *Self-stimulation*—repetitive, stereotyped behavior that seems to have no purpose other than providing sensory stimulation (this may take a wide variety of forms, such as swishing saliva, twirling objects, patting one's cheeks, flapping one's hands, staring, etc.).
- *Self-injury*—repeated physical self-abuse, such as biting, scratching, or poking oneself, head banging, etc.
- *Perceptual anomalies*—unusual responses or absence of response to stimuli that seems to indicate sensory impairment or unusual sensitivity.

> **echolalia.** The meaningless repetition (echoing) of what has been heard.

> **neologism.** A coined word that is meaningless to others; meaningless words used in the speech of a person with a mental disorder.

- *Apparent cognitive deficits*—inability to respond adequately to intelligence and achievement tests or inability to apply apparent intelligence to everyday tasks.
- *Aggression toward others*—severe tantrums or calculated physical attack that threatens or injures others.
- *Lack in daily living skills*—absence or significant impairment of ability to take care of one's basic needs, such as dressing, feeding, or toileting.

EDUCATIONAL CONSIDERATIONS

If you ask special educators and mental health professionals how students with emotional or behavioral disorders should be educated, you will get many different answers—partly because the general category embraces so many different problems, ranging from aggression to withdrawal, and degrees of disability, ranging from mild to profound. But the major reason for differing views goes back to something first mentioned in our discussion of definition—the problem of different conceptual models or theories.

Contrasts and Similarities in Conceptual Models

Conceptual models are just theories until they are used to guide educational practices; then the essential differences among models can be tested empirically. The differences among recommended practices and their outcomes, therefore, should provide the basis for evaluation of conceptual models. Although it would seem relatively simple to compare them, the job is actually quite difficult because it is not always apparent whether a difference between practices is a real one or just a matter of terms. For example, is the difference between the "planned ignoring" technique (a practice associated with the psychoeducational model) and "extinction" (a practice associated with the behavioral model) a real one? Does the teacher actually do different things? In reading the statements of those who propose different theoretical models, one gets the impression that the differences are often more words than deeds.

Of course, there are some real differences between conceptual models. For example, the proponents of a psychoanalytic model purposely encourage acting-out behavior in some circumstances, on the assumption that the child must work through underlying conflicts before more desirable behavior can be expected. In contrast, behaviorists discourage misbehavior because they believe it only makes the problem worse. They consistently try to suppress inappropriate behavior and reward desirable responses. The real differences between some conceptual models may make them incompatible, for under some circumstances they suggest directly opposite actions and cannot be used in combination.

Our purpose here is merely to point out that there are many different views regarding the education of students with emotional and behavioral disorders and to provide brief sketches of the major features of several different approaches (see Table 6–1). McDowell, Adamson, and Wood (1982) provide a more detailed analysis of various approaches and their theoretical underpinnings. Some concepts are common to several approaches, and in practice we seldom find a really "pure" single viewpoint. But as pointed out, the ideas of one model can be incompatible with those of another. There is a limit to the extent to

Can mix & match approaches

	Psycho-Analytic Approach	Psycho-Educational Approach	Humanistic Approach	Ecological Approach	Behavioral Approach
The Problem	A pathological imbalance among the dynamic parts of the mind (id, superego, ego)	Involves both underlying psychiatric disorders and readily observable misbehavior and underachievement	Belief that the student is out of touch with his or her own feelings and can't find fulfillment in traditional educational settings	Belief that the student interacts poorly with the environment; student and environment affect each other reciprocally and negatively	Belief that the student has learned inappropriate responses and failed to learn appropriate ones
Purpose of Educational Practices	Use of psychoanalytic principles to help uncover underlying mental pathology	Concern for unconscious motivation/underlying conflicts and academic achievement/positive surface behavior	Emphasis on enhancing self-direction, self-evaluation, and emotional involvement in learning	Attempts to alter entire social system so it will support desirable behavior when intervention is withdrawn	Manipulates student's immediate environment and the consequences of behavior
Characteristics of Teaching Methods	Reliance on individual psychotherapy for student and parents; little emphasis on academic achievement; highly permissive atmosphere	Emphasis on meeting individual needs of the students; reliance on projects and creative arts	Use of nontraditional educational settings in which the teacher serves as resource and catalyst rather than as director of activities; nonauthoritarian, open, affective, personal atmosphere	Involves all aspects of a student's life, including classroom, family, neighborhood, and community, in teaching useful life and educational skills	Involves measurement of responses and subsequent analyses of behaviors to change them; emphasis on reward for appropriate behavior

Table 6–1 ➤ Approaches to Educating Students with Emotional or Behavioral Disorders

which a teacher can pick and choose techniques without their becoming self-defeating (Kauffman, 1993).

Current Syntheses of Conceptual Models

Within the past decade, psychologists of all theoretical persuasions have placed new emphasis on the self. Morse (1985) describes a "metamorphosis" in psychologists' thinking about why individuals behave and perceive things as they do: "This metamorphosis is a result of the blending of developmental and learning psychology with a balanced attention to both the affective and cognitive aspects, which is sometimes called social cognition" (p. 4). The synthesis of developmental

Collaboration

A Key to Success

JAY SHIPMAN

Teacher of students with behavioral disorders, grades K-6, Coolidge School, Neenah, Wisconsin; B.A. History, St. Norbert College; M.Ed., Special Education, University of Wisconsin-Oshkosh

BOB RABOIN

Fifth-grade teacher; B.S.Ed., University of Wisconsin-Superior

➢ **Jay** We'll describe our work with Todd, a fifth-grader. Todd was small but strong, and a good runner. He had dark hair, somewhat protruding blue eyes, and enough braces on his teeth to rechrome a '58 Buick. He rarely spoke to anyone, and when he did it was almost impossible to hear him. He typically did not respond to adults or children who talked to him, and he didn't look at them either. Todd was capable of above-average academic work in all areas, but he did so little that it took a long time to figure out what he knew. If I asked him to correct a mistake, no matter how gently I phrased it, he would deny he had made a mistake and call me a liar. Then he might sneer and swear, turn over his desk, throw his books, and make loud noises or bark like a dog for two or three hours. This scenario was repeated three or four days a week. Todd acted this way anytime he was asked to do something he didn't care

to do at the moment. His tantrums could take place anytime I asked him to sit down or use a pencil instead of a pen. He would hit me or punch other students and teachers when things didn't go his way. For example, once he got his book bag tangled up with another boy's as they were getting on the bus. Todd was instantly furious, thrashing like a wild animal caught in a net. When he was free, he slugged a boy—who just happened to be standing in front of him—in the back of the head. He threw his tray at the woman who served the school lunches and called her a "fucking bitch" because she wouldn't give him a second helping. He seemed to have missed the fact that there wasn't any food left. The first three months of the year Todd rarely left my room. He had no friends and was still trying to see if we would let him be the person in charge. I saw him as fearful, withdrawn, and furious.

➢ **Bob** You get the idea we weren't dealing with a typical fifth-grader here!

➢ **Jay** My first job as the special education teacher was to reduce Todd's aggression and increase his compliance. I talked with Todd's parents and concluded that the major factors contributing to Todd's behavior were manipulative behaviors he had learned in the family. His mother seemed concerned but helpless. Todd could manipulate her easily. His father appeared unconcerned and condescending, as though I had a problem. It wasn't hard to see why Todd was used to getting his own way and felt that others should do his bidding or there was something wrong with them. I started very early to make sure that he knew I was in charge. I set up a program with his parents: We would make rules and stick to them. Todd could throw tantrums all he wanted—we really couldn't stop him—but that wouldn't change the consequences. We wanted to show him that he had the power to choose how he reacted to the rules, but he did not have the power to change or make the rules. Home and school tried to accentuate the positive and withhold what he liked when he made poor choices. We tried to keep the consequences logical: You don't go out for recess when you don't work; you don't go to the movies when you swear at your mother. The point with Todd wasn't to punish him—that only would have made things worse. He simply needed to know that eleven-year-olds don't tell adults what to do. My job was to ride out his tantrums calmly so he would be left with the consequences of his choices. If I got upset, then he would get more reinforcement for being manipulative and aggressive.

➢ **Bob** My first contact with Todd was when Jay introduced me to him in the hall. I tried to make casual conversation. This wasn't easy because Todd didn't talk to me, but I kept it up. I ran into Todd on the playground, usually to pry his hands off some other kid's throat. I don't think this made him a big fan of mine, but I'm not sure it did much damage either. Todd was so turned in on himself that I don't think he even remembered me when he came to my class in December. He came to my special project class at first. We do string art and woodworking and macramé, among other things. Todd came as a reward for doing well in the special education class. By December Todd would have done anything to get away from Jay, and he liked the stuff we did. My job was to be as aware as possible of what Jay and Todd had gone through so far. Jay and I do not teach the same way; we don't need to be alike. I did need to make sure that the consequences were the same for Todd, even if our rules and personal styles were different. Jay sends me a rating slip for every class. I teach the way I normally do, and Todd takes the rating slip back to Jay after every class. Todd gets the same consistent consequences; I don't have to design an individual reward system, and the changes are kept to a minimum for Todd. My part of the bargain is to teach fifth grade, and I need to provide the best possible environment for Todd to see and practice appropriate social behavior. I talk a lot with my students about the individual needs of various students. We learn to tolerate differences and eventually respect them. Jay and I talk when we need to, sometimes three times a day and sometimes not for a week. Todd gradually participated in more and more classes. We had minor problems but nothing major. Jay's job is to get the kid to the point of being able to handle a class in my room. He should show up in my room with the right materials and follow the rules. I make individual adjustments for most of my students when I can. If the students cannot meet my minimum standards over a period of time, they go back to Jay's room for awhile. Jay's never questioned that. Good teachers do what's best for a student, but we all have limits. Knowing your limits isn't a sign of weakness; it shows insight and respect for others.

➤ **Jay** The most challenging aspect of teamwork is the communication. This is hard when you have a violent student in your room that you cannot leave alone. Talking confidentially about a mainstreamed student is hard when you're holding onto one of them. The major challenge I faced with Todd was a private issue for me. I had to find reasons to want to work with and for Todd. He insulted me verbally, lashed out at me physically, and was the most rude and cruel student I had worked with in years. I wasn't sure Todd would last five days in Bob's class. I told Bob I had this boy who was usually extremely withdrawn but could, without apparent provocation, jump on some kid and start crushing his windpipe. Bob said that Todd sounded fine and he anticipated no major problems. I knew that meant that Todd was welcome and we would take it one day at a time, one class at a time. I think Todd saved most of his major acting out for times when he wasn't in Bob's room. He couldn't break the habits of ten years in three months, but he had lots of respect for Bob and worked very hard to do well and not "let him down." We want-

> *. . . we would take it one day at a time, one class at a time.*

ed not to shield Todd from consequences and gradually to transfer the responsibility for applying those consequences to Bob.

➤ **Bob** My challenges as a fifth-grade teacher were different. I had to get to know Todd. I had to get accurate information from Jay on what I could reasonably expect academically and behaviorally. I also had to try to predict how Todd was going to affect and be affected by the other students in my class. I had to make sure I filled out the rating slips after every class so Jay could apply the proper consequences and help Todd get any late work done. This seems like a small thing, but with about thirty students it isn't always easy to remember to do it. I had one more person to teach, one more batch of papers to correct, and one more child to show that I cared about him and respected him. These are things I think any student should take for granted. My point is that they take time.

➤ **Jay** Any of the students we work with have been badly damaged through the malice or ignorance of others. It is extremely gratifying to see a student who was chronically depressed or angry finally become happy much of the time. Most people have given up on our students. We get a chance to experience the joy of watching a boy discover that life can be a gift as well as a burden. This is what makes teaching a wonderful profession.

➤ **Bob** I think collaboration is primarily a product of the desire to work together and the amount of time and resources available.

➤ **Jay** I think my primary responsibility is to make sure that the situation is productive and successful for the student and the regular teacher. A big part of my time is devoted to establishing and maintaining good working relationships with other teachers. I have to earn the respect of secretaries, custodians, teachers, bus drivers, and the principal. If you do not find it easy to get along with a wide variety of people, being a teacher of disturbed children will be very difficult. You have to be aware of personal and classroom stress and plan accordingly. You think about who has the time and the personality that will work for a given child. The most common mistake in mainstreaming is placing a student who isn't ready or picking a poor placement.

➤ **Bob** My teaching doesn't change much when I have a student with an emotional/behavioral disorder. I've been told what to expect, but I've never been told to change what I do. Jay has asked me to make adjustments for a given child, and we've always at least worked out a compromise. I have the hardest time when I don't think I have the resources that a student needs. There are times when the numbers or group chemistry just make it impossible to give a student the attention he or she may need.

➤ **individual psychology.**
An approach to understanding human behavior that blends psychological and behavioral principles with understanding of individual experience.

➤ **cognitive-behavior modification.** A training approach that emphasizes teaching individuals to control their own thought processes; often used with learning-disabled children who are in need of an educational approach that stresses self-initiative and learning strategies.

and learning perspectives is called **individual psychology** by Morse and other writers. **Cognitive-behavior modification** is not exactly the same as individual psychology, but it is also an attempt to blend learning theory with concern for the individual's thoughts, feelings, and perceptions (Harris, Wong, & Keogh, 1985; Meichenbaum, 1977; see also Chapter 5).

People change their behavior, most psychologists now agree, for multiple reasons. They do not change simply because they obtain new understandings about themselves or because they resolve their troubled feelings. Neither do they change simply because someone arranges different consequences for their behavior or shows them appropriate behavioral models. The most effective methods of changing behavior typically require attention to the child as a thinking, feeling person *and* to the consequences of the child's behavior. Attempts to blend learning and developmental theories often result in involving the child in self-management. This may mean self-monitoring (keeping track of one's own behavior), self-instruction (talking one's way through a problem), self-evaluation (judging one's own performance), self-reinforcement (complimenting oneself or allowing oneself a reward for good performance), and so on.

Setting goals for oneself is an example of an intervention involving self-control. Lyman (1984) worked with six boys, aged 11 to 13, who were considered emotionally disturbed and attended a school in a residential treatment facility. The boys exhibited conduct disorders, including such problem behaviors as noncompliance with teachers' directions, aggression, truancy, and destruction of property. All of them were considerably behind their age-mates academically and had difficulty staying on task in the classroom. Lyman experimented with the effects of private and public goal setting. In the private goal-setting phase, each student was called to the teacher's desk and given the following instructions individually:

> We're going to try something to help you work better in class. I want you to pick a goal for yourself for a percentage of time you're going to work for the next hour. Working means looking at your workbook or response sheet, asking a question about your work, or listening to the teacher. This should be a level that you can try for and that you think is a fair goal for yourself. Try to challenge yourself but don't set a goal that would be unfair to you. Now I want you to pick a percent of time for your goal. I'll write it down on this card and give it to you to remind you of your goal. (p. 398)

In the public goal-setting phase, the teacher gave students the same individual instructions, but instead of saying "'I'll write it [the goal] down on this card and give it to you to remind you of your goal,' the teacher said, 'I'll write it down on this card and put it up here on this chart to remind you of your goal'" (p. 398). The student's card was then placed beside his or her name on a bulletin board at the front of the class under the heading "Work Goals." The students all performed better (i.e., spent more time on task) when their goal setting was public than when it was private.

Another intervention that gets students cognitively and affectively involved in changing their behavior is showing them videotape replays of their classroom conduct. Watching the replays is typically accompanied by feedback from the teacher, self-evaluation, and perhaps explicit reinforcement (e.g., with praise and tokens or points, which can later be exchanged for other rewards) for behavioral improvement. Osborne, Kiburz, and Miller (1986) used this approach to decrease the self-injurious behavior of a 15-year-old boy in a resource class and in English and math classes. Walther and Beare (1991) used a similar strategy to increase the on-task behavior of a 10-year-old student in a special class for children with emotional or behavioral disorders. Kern-Dunlap et al. (1992) worked with five boys, ranging in age from 11 to 13 (fourth, fifth, and sixth graders), who were enrolled in special self-contained classes for students with "serious emotional disturbance" in two different schools. In their study they used a "package" consisting of three principal components: (1) students' observation of replays of their interactions with their peers during a videotaped activity period, (2) students' self-evaluation of the peer interactions observed in the replays, and (3) delayed feedback and reinforcement for desirable peer interactions.

The work by Kern-Dunlap et al. (1992) provides not only an illustration of the intervention, but also examples of student behavior that often results in their being identified for special education, and the opposite—behavior that characterizes skilled social interaction. The difficulty experienced by students with emotional or behavioral disorders often involves negative peer interactions. Moreover, their problematic interactions often erupt when they are engaged in relatively loosely structured activities that are not closely supervised. In working with these students, it is extremely important to know precisely what behavior will be encouraged and what behavior is unacceptable. Kern-Dunlap et al. (1992, p. 357) described desirable and undesirable behavior as follows:

Desirable peer interactions were defined as any verbal or nonverbal interaction that was positive or neutral and appropriate to the context of a school environment. Desirable verbal interactions included validating statements such as praise statements (e.g., "Good job," "You're going to win," "Good try"), statements intended to help a peer successfully complete his or her turn in the game being played (e.g., "You get another turn," "Move three more spaces"), and neutral statements or questions (e.g., "How many cards do you have left?," "I want to buy Boardwalk," "I like this game, do you?"). Desirable nonverbal interactions included validating gestures (e.g., thumbs up signal) or supportive touches (e.g., high fives, patting a peer on the shoulder.). Undesirable interactions were defined as any verbal or nonverbal interactions that were inappropriate in the school context. Undesirable verbal interactions included statements that were derogatory or insulting (e.g., "You're stupid," "You don't know how to play this game"), statements that ordered a peer to do something (e.g., "Pay attention!" "Gimme that," "Put that down") in a demeaning or demanding manner and/or with a volume noticeably louder and harsher than normal, or statements inappropriate to the context (e.g., sexual in content). Undesirable peer interactions also included insulting or derogatory gestures (e.g., sticking one's tongue out, "shooting the bird") or aggressive behavior (e.g., grabbing materials from a peer, hitting, slapping, or kicking a peer, striking out at another).

The frequency of desirable and undesirable peer interactions was recorded each day for each student for a 20-minute activity period during which students in the class (ranging in number from three to eight) played board games or card games. Figure 6–2 (on page 234) shows the frequency of desirable and undesirable behavior of two of the five boys from one of the schools. On baseline days (days 1 to 9 and 21 to 24 for Sam, days 6 to 17 for Dave), the activity periods were videotaped but no feedback was given. On the days labeled video feedback in Figure 6–2, an adult spent 10 to 20 minutes individually with each of the participants—replaying parts of the previous day's tape, asking the student to describe and give examples of desirable and undesirable peer interactions, giving the student examples, asking the student to evaluate his or her own behavior, and providing feedback and reinforcement (points that could be exchanged for a variety of small rewards). As shown in Figure 6–2, when this procedure was used, both

Figure 6-2   ➤ *Frequency of desirable (dashed lines) and undesirable (solid lines) peer interactions during 20-minute activity sessions for the 2 students in School 1.*

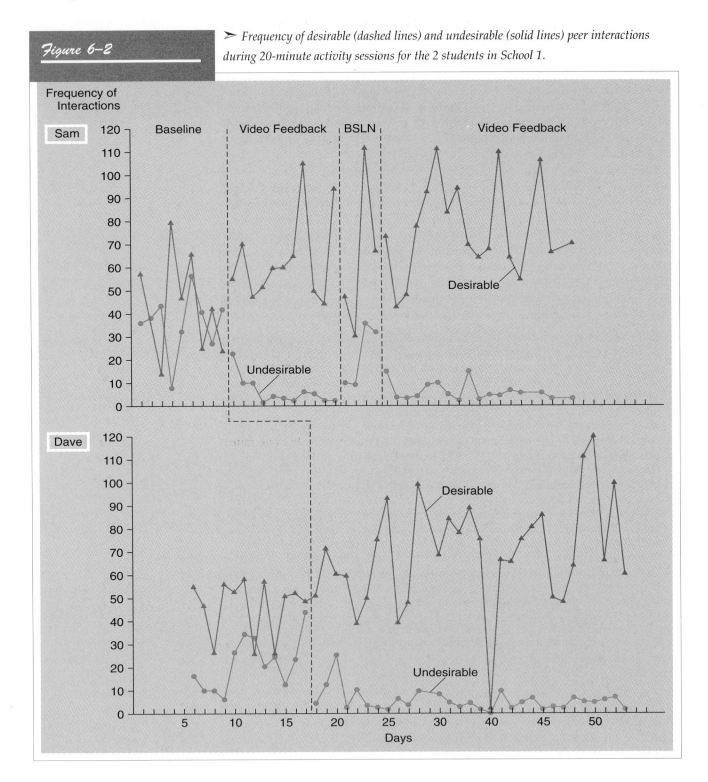

SOURCE: L. Kern-Dunlap, G. Dunlap, S. Clarke, K. E. Childs, R. L. White, & M.P. Stewart. Effects of a videotape feedback package on the peer interactions of children with serious behavioral and emotional challenges. *Journal of Applied Behavior Analysis, 25,* p. 360. Copyright © 1992 by Journal of Applied Behavior Analysis. Reprinted with permission.

boys increased their desirable behavior and decreased their undesirable behavior. Similar changes were seen in the other three boys in the study as well.

Balancing Behavioral Control with Academic and Social Learning

Some writers have observed that the quality of educational programs for students with emotional or behavioral disorders is often dismal, regardless of the conceptual model underlying practice. The focus is often on rigid external control of students' behavior, and academic instruction and social learning are often secondary or almost entirely neglected (Knitzer, Steinberg, & Fleisch, 1990). Although the quality of instruction is undoubtedly low in too many programs, examples can be found of effective academic and social instruction for students at all levels (Peacock Hill Working Group, 1991). Behavioral control strategies are an essential part of educational programs for students with externalizing problems. Without effective means of controlling disruptive behavior, academic and social learning are extremely unlikely. Excellent academic instruction will, certainly, reduce many behavior problems (Kauffman et al., 1993). Nevertheless, even the best instructional programs will not eliminate the disruptive behavior of all students. Teachers of students with emotional or behavioral disorders must have effective control strategies, preferably those involving students as much as possible in self-control. In addition, teachers must offer effective instruction in academic and social skills that will allow their students to live, learn, and work with others.

Importance of Integrated Services

Children and youths with emotional or behavioral disorders tend to have multiple and complex needs (Mattison, & Gamble, 1992; Mattison, Morales, & Bauer, 1992). For most, life is coming apart in more ways than one. In addition to their problems in school, they typically have family problems and a variety of difficulties in the community (e.g., engaging in illegal activities, an absence of desirable relationships with peers and adults, substance abuse, difficulty finding and maintaining employment). Thus a child or youth with emotional or behavioral disorders may need, in addition to special education, a variety of family-oriented services, psychotherapy or counseling, community supervision, training related to employment, and so on.

Numerous writers have observed that no single service agency can meet the needs of most of these children and youths, and that the needed services are typically offered in a fragmented, uncoordinated, and ineffective fashion (Knitzer, 1982; Knitzer et al., 1990; Leone, 1990; Nelson & Pearson, 1991; Peacock Hill Working Group, 1991). Integrating the needed services into a more coordinated and effective effort is now seen as essential. As progress is made in providing more integrated services, teachers will be expected to work more closely with other professionals.

Strategies that Work

Regardless of the conceptual model that guides education, we can point to several effective strategies. Most of these strategies are incorporated in the behavioral model, but other models may include them as well. Successful strategies at all levels, from early intervention through transition, balance concern for academic and social skills and provide integrated services. These strategies include the following elements (Peacock Hill Working Group, 1991):

- *Systematic, data-based interventions*—interventions that are applied systematically and consistently and that are based on reliable research data, not unsubstantiated theory;
- *Continuous assessment and monitoring of progress*—direct, daily assessment of performance, with planning based on this monitoring;
- *Provision for practice of new skills*—skills are not taught in isolation but are applied directly in everyday situations through modeling, rehearsal, and guided practice;
- *Treatment matched to the problem*—interventions that are designed to meet the needs of individual students and their particular life circumstances, not general "formulas" that ignore the nature, complexity, and severity of the problem;
- *Multi-component treatment*—as many different interventions as are necessary to meet the multiple needs of the students (e.g., social skills training, academic remediation, medication, counselling or psychotherapy, family treatment or parent training, etc.);
- *Programming for transfer and maintenance*—interventions designed to promote transfer of learning to new situations, recognizing that quick fixes nearly always fail to produce generalized change;
- *Commitment to sustained intervention*—interventions designed with the realization that many emotional or behavioral disorders are developmental disabilities and will not be eliminated entirely or "cured."

Must have parents permission to videotape child. They have to know ahead of time. And specify if they can show show it to another person.

◦Goal setting

Service Delivery Models

A relatively small percentage of children and youths with emotional or behavioral disorders are officially identified and receive any special education or mental health services at all (Institute of Medicine, 1989). Consequently, those who do receive special education tend to be those with very serious problems, although most (along with those who have mild mental retardation or learning disabilities) have typically been assumed to have only "mild" disabilities. That is, the problems of the typical student with an emotional or behavioral disorder who is identified for special education may be more serious than many people have assumed. "Severe" does not apply only to the disorders of autism and schizophrenia; a child can have a severe conduct disorder, for example, and its disabling effects can be extremely serious and persistent (Kazdin, 1987; Patterson et al., 1992; Wolf, Braukmann, & Ramp, 1987).

A higher percentage of students with emotional or behavioral disorders than of students with most other disabilities are educated outside regular classrooms and schools, probably in part because students with these disorders tend to have more serious problems before they are identified. Because emotional or behavioral disorders include so many different types of behavioral and emotional problems, it is hard to make generalizations about the way programs are administered. Programs for students with autism or schizophrenia and for juvenile delinquents tend to be administered differently from those for students with other types of problems, so we shall discuss them under different headings.

Programs for Students with Autism or Schizophrenia

Many children with autism must be taught individually at first. They simply do not learn in a group without having had intensive individual instruction first because of their great difficulty in paying attention, responding, and behaving appropriately in a group. After they have learned some of the basic skills required for instruction, they may be taught in small groups. If intensive early intervention is provided, large-group instruction may be feasible and many children can be integrated into regular schools and classrooms.

Teachers of children with autism must have more than empathy and a desire to help. Unless teachers are equipped with specific teaching skills, the time they spend with these children will amount to little more than custodial care. A permissive environment maintained under the fiction of "therapy" is not likely to be effective and may in fact be detrimental to the child's progress. Empathy and humanistic concern are to be encouraged, but skill in using behavior modification techniques is essential for teachers who work with such children.

The curriculum for some children with autism must be basic in the early stages of education—a lot like curriculum for most children with severe mental retardation. It may involve teaching daily living skills, language, and preacademic skills. Teachers who work with these children must be willing to spend countless hours of patient labor to achieve small gains. Moreover, they must be ready to persist in working with children whose behavior is extremely unpleasant and who will often reject efforts to help them (Bower, 1989; Durand & Carr, 1988; Koegel, Rincover, & Egel, 1982).

Views of autism and its treatment are in a stage of transition. Recent studies indicate that some children with autism may learn without the highly structured and intensive instruction that has characterized the most effective interventions to date, suggesting that current views of autism may need to be revised (Rogers & DiLalla, 1991). Alternative means of communication suggest that some children and youths with autism are much more intellectually capable than previously thought (Biklen & Schubert, 1991). Early intervention and commitment to the least restrictive environment are resulting in the placement of many more students with autism in regular schools and classes. It is difficult to predict how autism will be viewed by the year 2000, and where most students with autism will be taught.

Students with schizophrenia vary widely in the behavior they exhibit and the learning problems they have. Some may need hospitalization and intensive treatment. Others may remain at home and attend regular public schools. The trend today is away from placement in institutions or special schools and toward inclusion in regular public schools. In some cases, children with schizophrenia who attend regular schools are enrolled in special classes.

Programs for Juvenile Delinquents

Educational arrangements for juvenile delinquents are hard to describe in general terms because delinquency is a legal term, not an educational distinction, and because programs for extremely troubling youths are so varied from state to state and among localities. Special classes or schools are sometimes provided for youths who have a history of threatening, violent, or disruptive behavior. Some of these classes and schools are administered under special education law, but others are not because the pupils assigned to them are not considered "seriously emotionally disturbed." In jails, reform schools, and other detention facilities housing children and adolescents, wide variation is found in educational practices (Nelson, Rutherford, & Wolford, 1987). Education of incarcerated children and youths with learning disabilities is governed by the same laws that apply to those who are not incarcerated, but the laws are not always carefully implemented. Many incarcerated children do not receive assessment and education appropriate for their needs because of lack of resources, poor cooperation among agencies, and the attitude that delinquents and criminals are not entitled to the same educational opportunities as law-abiding citizens (Leone, 1990; Leone, Rutherford, & Nelson, 1991; Nelson, Rutherford, & Wolford, 1987).

Programs for Students with Other Disorders

The trend in programs for students with other types of disorders is toward integration into regular schools and classrooms. When children are placed in separate schools and classes, educators hope for reintegration into the mainstream. Integration of these students is typically difficult and requires intensive work on a case-by-case basis (Fuchs, Fuchs, Fernstrom, & Hohn, 1991; Lloyd, Kauffman, & Kupersmidt, 1990; Walker & Bullis, 1991).

The academic curriculum for most students with emotional or behavioral disorders parallels the curriculum for most students. The basic academic skills have a great deal of survival value for any individual in our society who is capable of learning them; failure to teach a student to read, write, and perform basic arithmetic deprives him or her of any reasonable chance for successful adjustment to the everyday demands of life. Students who do not acquire academic skills that allow them to compete with their peers are likely to be socially rejected (Kauffman, 1993; Patterson, Kupersmidt, & Griesler, 1989). Students with emotional or behavioral disorders may need specific instruction in social skills as well. We emphasize two points: First, effective methods are needed to teach basic academic skills; second, social skills and affective experiences are as crucial as academic skills. How to manage one's feelings and behavior and how to get along with other people are essential features of the curriculum for many students with emotional or behavioral disorders. These children cannot be expected to learn such skills without instruction, for the ordinary processes of socialization obviously have failed.

Teachers of students with emotional or behavioral disorders must be able to tolerate a great deal of unpleasantness and rejection without becoming counter-aggressive or withdrawing. Most of the students they teach are rejected by others. If kindness and concern were the only things required to help these students, they probably would not be considered to have disabilities. The teacher cannot expect caring and decency always to be returned. Teachers must be sure of their own values and confident of their teaching and living skills. They must be able and willing to make wise choices for students when the children choose to behave unwisely. (Kauffman, 1993; Kauffman et al., 1993).

EARLY INTERVENTION

Early identification and prevention are basic goals of intervention programs for any category of disability. For students with emotional or behavioral disorders, these goals present particular difficulties—yet they hold particular promise. The difficulties are related to definition and measurement of emotional or behavioral disorders, especially in young children; the particular promise is that young children's social-emotional behavior is quite flexible, so preventive efforts seem to have a good chance of success.

As mentioned previously, defining emotional or behavioral disorders in such a way that children can be reliably identified is a difficult task. Definition and identification involving preschool children are complicated by several additional factors. First, the developmental tasks that young children are expected to achieve are much simpler than those expected of older children, so the range of normal behaviors to be used for comparison is quite restricted. Infants and toddlers are expected to eat, sleep, perform relatively simple motor skills, and respond socially to their parents. School-age children must learn much more varied and complex motor and cognitive skills and develop social relations with a variety of peers and adults. Second, there is wide variation in the child-rearing practices of good parents and in family expectations for preschool children's behavior in different cultures, so we must guard against inappropriate norms used for comparison. "Immature," "withdrawn," or "aggressive" behavior in one family may not be perceived as such in another. Third, in the preschool years children's development is rapid and often uneven, making it difficult to judge what spontaneous improvements might occur.

Fourth, the most severe types of emotional or behavioral disorders often are first observed in the preschool years. But it is frequently difficult to tell the difference between emotional or behavioral disorders and other conditions, like mental retardation or deafness. Often the first signs are difficulty with basic biological functions (e.g., eating, sleeping, eliminating) or social responses (e.g., responding positively to a parent's attempts to offer comfort or "molding" to the parent's body when being held). Difficulty with these basic areas or in achieving developmental milestones like walking and talking indicate that the child may have an emotional or behavioral disability. But these difficulties may also be indicators of other conditions, such as mental retardation, sensory impairment, or physical disability.

The patterns of behavior that signal problems for the preschool child are those that bring them into frequent conflict with or keep them aloof from their parents or caretakers and their siblings or peers. Many children who were referred to clinics for disruptive behavior when they were 7 to 12 years of age showed clear signs of behavior problems by the time they were 3 or 4 years old—or even younger (Loeber, Green, Lahey, Christ, & Frick, 1992). Infants or toddlers who exhibit a very "difficult temperament"—who are irritable; have irregular patterns of sleeping, eating, and eliminating; have highly intense responses to many stimuli and negative reactions toward new situations are at risk for developing serious behavior problems unless their parents are particularly skillful at handling them. Children of preschool age are likely to elicit negative responses from adults and playmates if they are much more aggressive or much more withdrawn than most children their age. (Remember the critical importance of same-age comparisons. Toddlers frequently grab what they want, push other children down and throw things and kick and scream when they don't get their way; toddlers normally do not have much finesse at social interaction and often hide from strangers.)

Because children's behavior is quite responsive to conditions in the social environment and can be shaped by adults, the potential for *primary prevention*—

preventing serious behavior problems from occurring in the first place—would seem to be great. If parents and teachers could be taught effective child management skills, perhaps many or most cases could be prevented. Furthermore, one could imagine that if parents and teachers had such skills, children who already have emotional or behavioral disorders could be prevented from getting worse (*secondary prevention*). But as Bower (1981) notes, the task of primary prevention is not that simple. For one thing, the tremendous amount of money and personnel needed for training in child management are not available. For another, even if the money and personnel could be found, professionals would not always agree on what patterns of behavior should be prevented or on how undesirable behavior could be prevented from developing (Kazdin, 1987).

If overly aggressive or withdrawn behavior has been identified in a preschooler, what kind of intervention program is most desirable? Our experience and reading of the literature lead us to the conclusion that behavioral interventions are highly effective (see also Peacock Hill Working Group, 1991; Strain et al., 1992). A behavioral approach implies defining and measuring the child's behaviors and rearranging the environment (especially adults' and other children's responses to the problem child) to teach and support more appropriate conduct. In the case of aggressive children, social rewards for aggression should be prevented. For example, hitting another child or throwing a temper tantrum might result in brief social isolation or time out instead of adult attention or getting one's own way.

Researchers are constantly seeking less punitive ways of dealing with problem behavior, including aggression. The best way of handling violent or aggressive play or play themes, for example, would be one that effectively reduces the frequency of aggressive play yet requires minimum punishment. In one study with children between the ages of three and five, violent or aggressive theme play (talk or imitation of weapons, destruction, injury, etc.) was restricted to a small area of the classroom defined by a carpet sample (Sherburne, Utley, McConnell, & Gannon, 1988). Children engaging in imaginative play involving guns, for example, were merely told by the teacher, using a pleasant tone of voice, "If you want to play guns, go over on the rug" (p. 169). If violent theme play continued for more than ten seconds after the teacher's warning, the child or children were physically assisted to the rug. They were not required to stay on the rug for a specific length of time, merely to go there if they wanted to engage in aggressive play. This simple procedure was quite effective in reducing violent and aggressive themes in the children's play.

In all cases of aggression, attention and other rewards for desirable, nonaggresive behavior must be provided. Sometimes prompts for appropriate behavior and models of good conduct are also needed. Socially withdrawn preschoolers have responded well to several behavioral techniques: providing peer models (either live or filmed) of social interaction, training peers to initiate social interactions, and encouraging preschoolers to play games in which affectionate behaviors are shown (Strain & Fox, 1981). Early intervention with preschoolers, whether they are aggressive or withdrawn, has the potential to improve their behavior substantially and to make some children with severe disorders "normal"—that is, indistinguishable from their peers—by the time they are in the elementary grades (Lovaas, 1987; Strain, 1987; Strain, Steele, Ellis, & Timm, 1982). Nevertheless, "the long-term effectiveness of behavioral therapy for autism

All young children must be taught socially appropriate ways of interacting with their peers and adults.

remains much in question, at times sparking intense debate even among investigators using it" (Bower, 1989, p. 312).

TRANSITION

The programs designed for adolescents with emotional or behavioral disorders have varied widely in aims and structure (Kerr, Nelson, & Lambert, 1987). Nelson and Kauffman (1977) described the following types, which remain the basic options today: regular public high school classes, consultant teachers who work with the regular teacher to provide individualized academic work and behavior management, resource rooms and special self-contained classes to which students may be assigned for part or all of the school day, work-study programs in which vocational education and job experience are combined with academic study, special private or public schools that offer the regular high school curriculum in a different setting, alternative schools that offer highly individualized programs that are nontraditional in both setting and content, and private or public residential schools.

Incarcerated youths with emotional or behavioral disorders are an especially neglected group in special education (Nelson, Rutherford, & Wolford, 1987). One suspects that the special educational needs of many (or most) of these teenagers who are in prisons are neglected because incarcerated youths are defined as "socially maladjusted" rather than "seriously emotionally disturbed." The current federal definition appears to allow the denial of special education to a large number of young people who exhibit extremely serious misbehavior and have a long history of school failure.

reative expression can help young people communicate their feelings and understand the world.

One of the reasons it is difficult to design special education programs for students with emotional or behavioral disorders at the secondary level is that this category of youths is so varied. Adolescents categorized for special education purposes as "seriously emotionally disturbed" may have behavioral characteristics ranging from autistically withdrawn to aggressively delinquent, intelligence ranging from severely retarded to highly gifted, and academic skills ranging from preschool to college level. Therefore it is hardly realistic to suggest that any single type of program or model will be appropriate for all such youths. In fact, youths with emotional or behavioral disorders, perhaps more than any other category of exceptionality, need a highly individualized, creative, and flexible education. Programs may range from teaching daily living skills in a sheltered environment to advanced placement in college, from regular class placement to hospitalization, and from the traditional curriculum to unusual and specialized vocational training.

Transition from school to work and adult life is particularly difficult for adolescents with emotional or behavioral disorders. Many of them lack basic academic skills necessary for successful employment. In addition, they often behave in ways that prevent them from being accepted, liked, and helped by employers, co-workers, and neighbors. It is not surprising that they are among the students most likely to drop out of school and among the most difficult individuals to train in transition programs (Edgar, 1987; Frank, Sitlington & Carson, 1991; Neel, Meadows, Levine, & Edgar, 1988; Wagner & Shaver, 1989).

Many children and youths with emotional or behavioral disorders grow up to be adults who have real difficulties leading independent, productive lives. The outlook is especially grim for children and adolescents who have conduct disor-

In Their Own Words JANET FRAME

Janet Frame was born in New Zealand in 1924. She is a gifted and prolific writer and author of nine novels, several collections of short stories, and a book of poetry. Her struggle to become a writer is also the harrowing story of her struggle with mental illness. Judged at one point to be "schizophrenic and permanently insane," she endured the frightening conditions of early 20th century mental institutions. When a book of her short stories, *The Lagoon*, received a literary award, she narrowly escaped a scheduled lobotomy.

The following excerpt from her autobiography, *An Angel at My Table*, recalls her suicide attempt as a student, and the finesse with which she concealed her turmoil from those around her.

"You're so thoughtful," Mrs. T. said. "I'm lucky to have such a quiet student. You wouldn't even know you were in the house, you're so quiet!"

(A lovely girl, no trouble at all.)

At the end of my third week when school again loomed before me I was forced to realize that suicide was my only escape. I had woven so carefully, with such close texture, my visible layer of 'no trouble at all, a quiet student, always ready with a smile (if the decayed teeth could be hidden), always happy,' that even I could not break the thread of the material of my deceit. I felt completely isolated. I knew no-one to confide in, to get advice from; and there was nowhere I could go. What, in all the world, could I do to earn my living and still live as myself, as I knew myself to be. Temporary masks, I knew, had their place; everyone was wearing them, they were the human rage; but not masks cemented in place until the wearer could not breathe and was eventually suffocated.

On Saturday evening I tidied my room, arranged my possessions, and swallowing a packet of aspros, I lay down in bed to die, certain that I would die. My desperation was extreme.

The next morning, near noon, I woke with a roaring in my ears and my nose bleeding. My first thought was not even a thought, it was a feeling of wonder and delight and thankfulness that I was alive. I staggered from my bed and looked at myself in the mirror; my face was a dusky red. I began to vomit, again and again. At last my nose stopped bleeding but the roaring in my ears continued. I returned to bed and slept, waking at about ten o'clock that evening. My head still throbbed, my ears rang. I hurried to the bathroom, turned on the tap, and vomited again. Mrs. T., who had spent the weekend at Kathleen's and had been home about two hours, came to the door of her bedroom.

"Is everything all right?" she asked.

"Oh yes," I called. "Everything's fine. I've had a busy day." (No trouble, no trouble at all.)

SOURCE: Janet Frame, *An Angel at My Table*, (New York: George Braziller, 1984), p. 65.

ders. Contrary to popular opinion, the child or youth who is shy, anxious, or neurotic is not the most likely to have psychiatric problems as an adult. It is, rather, the conduct-disordered (hyperaggressive) child or youth whose adulthood is most likely to be characterized by socially intolerable behavior (Kazdin, 1987). About half the children who are hyperaggressive will have problems that require legal intervention or psychiatric care when they are adults.

Successful transition to adult life is often complicated by neglectful, abusive, or inadequate family relationships. They characterize a high percentage of adolescents with conduct disorders.

Examples of relatively successful high school and transition programs are available, most of which employ a behavioral approach (Peacock Hill Working Group, 1991). However, it is important to stress *relatively* because many adolescents and young adults with severe conduct disorders appear to have a true developmental disability that requires intervention throughout their life span (Wolf, Braukmann, & Ramp, 1987).

Students with Emotional or Behavioral Disorders in General Education Classrooms

WHAT TO LOOK FOR IN SCHOOL

Recognizing students with emotional or behavioral disorders is sometimes easy and sometimes complex. Some children and adolescents with these disorders are aggressive. They act out in ways that are obviously inappropriate for school. For example, they may physically provoke others to frequent fights, or they may verbally annoy others by constantly criticizing or teasing. Their aggressive, overt behavior quickly suggests potentially serious behavior problems.

On the other hand, some students with emotional or behavioral disorders are withdrawn. They exhibit more subtle behaviors, which in the context of a busy classroom may be difficult to identify. In the early elementary grades, they may whine or cry in situations that usually don't cause such responses. They also may be dependent, asking others for help to complete work they can do on their own. They may be alone, without friends, or sad or depressed much of the time.

The key to identifying both the aggressive and the withdrawn types of emotional or behavioral disorders is the persistence and severity of the behaviors. To be considered serious, students must show these behaviors to a marked degree over a long period of time in a variety of settings.

HOW TO GATHER INFORMATION

If you suspect any of your students may have serious emotional or behavioral problems, you can help identify them in several ways. Record the specific behaviors you observe, the approximate time of the day and the date, the context in which the behavior occurred, and the consequences. For example, you might note, Alan slapped and kicked Sam after a softball game during recess on Monday, November 2 and describe the circumstances provoking the incident as well as the consequences for Alan.

Noting the exact times for more subtle behavior problems may be difficult. Recording your observations at the end of the day or during a planning period is helpful. For example, you might report that Laura was alone while other students talked together before school in class, during lunch in the cafeteria, and at recess outdoors on Tuesday, October 30. This log will provide an important record of the frequency, severity, and circumstances surrounding the behaviors, which may help you and the school psychologist, counselor, or special education teacher identify the exact nature of the problem.

Describing particularly serious events in greater detail is also helpful. The student's comments regarding these events and the consequences of the behavior provide valuable information. For example, one teacher reported:

David started a fire in the art storage area adjacent to the art room after school on Friday, December 11. He said he did it to get back at the art teacher, who sent him to the principal's office during class that day for splattering paint on another student's holiday project for parents. His parents were called and came to school immediately. Following a discussion of the seriousness of his behavior and the potential legal ramifications, David was suspended for 10 days. No charges were filed.

Noting relevant information from parents, such as descriptions of the student's behavior at home or treatment he or she is receiving outside of school, is also important.

TEACHING TECHNIQUES TO TRY

Although there are several approaches to the treatment of children and adolescents with emotional or behavioral disorders, one that teachers often use identifies the factors in school that contribute to the students' inappropriate behaviors and the factors in school that can be altered to change those behaviors. Interventions include helping students to increase appropriate behaviors, decrease inappropriate ones, and learn behaviors they do not know already.

To manage students' behaviors Lewis and Doorlag (1990) suggest teachers follow a step-by-step process:

1. Stating the behavioral expectations for all students in the class
2. Determining whether students who meet these expectations are receiving reinforcement so they will continue to meet the expectations
3. If there are students who do not meet the expectations, determining whether they understand the expectations and whether they have the needed skills to perform the behaviors
4. For students who use inappropriate behaviors, identifying a behavior to change
5. Deciding how you will observe and gather information on this behavior
6. After reviewing the information you have collected, determining whether the behavior needs to be increased, decreased, or learned

7. Choosing a strategy that is positive rather than punishing
8. While using the strategy, collecting information on the student's behavior
9. Reviewing this information to decide whether this strategy should be continued, modified, or stopped
10. When the student performs the behavior at the desired level, continuing to monitor and return to Step 4 if the student has other behaviors that require intervention

Selecting Approaches

An important consideration in choosing a behavior management approach is the degree of intrusiveness and restrictiveness it involves. Intrusiveness refers to the extent to which interventions impinge on students' rights and/or bodies and the degree to which they interrupt educational activities (Kerr & Nelson, 1989). Less intrusive procedures, for example, do not result in restriction of student movement or in the interruption of typical, ongoing educational activities. "Restrictiveness refers to the extent to which an intervention inhibits students' freedom to be treated like all other pupils" (Kerr & Nelson, 1989, p.107). Although most experts agree it is preferable to begin managing behavior by selecting the least intrusive and restrictive procedure appropriate to the behavior you want to change, they do not agree on the rank order of these procedures. Kerr and Nelson (1989, p. 107) suggest the following hierarchy listing from less to more restrictive or intrusive:

Enhancement Procedures:	Reductive Procedures:
Self-regulation	Differential reinforcement
Social reinforcement	Extinction
Modeling	Verbal aversives
Contracting	Response cost
Activity reinforcement	Time-out
Token reinforcement	Overcorrection
Tangible reinforcement	Physical aversives
Edibile reinforcement	
Tactile and sensory reinforcement	

It is important to note that some of the procedures listed under Enhancement Procedures may be used both to increase and decrease behaviors. For example, teachers use models to strengthen, weaken, or maintain behavior (Bandura, 1969). However, those listed under Reductive Procedures are used only to decrease behaviors. The remainder of the section will discuss the less intrusive and restrictive procedures listed above.

Increasing Appropriate School Behaviors

One strategy teachers use to increase a student's appropriate behavior involves rewarding, or reinforcing, that behavior each time the student exhibits it. The reward can take many forms. It may be a point or token exchangeable at a later time for a special privilege. Because social reinforcement is less intrusive and restrictive than other types of reinforcement, teachers typically select it first. Verbal praise, such as "Good work, Tony. I liked the way you worked by yourself on the math problems," is an example of social reinforcement. Smiles, handshakes, nods, gentle pats on the back are other examples. However, not all students like the same rewards. You will want to find the one that works with a particular student or groups of students.

Activity reinforcement follows the application of the Premack Principle, which also is called "grandma's law" because it is based on the same idea that prompted grandma to say, "If you eat your vegetables, then you can have your dessert" (Polloway & Patton, 1993.). The Premack Principle makes high frequency behaviors, such as talking with a friend or playing computer games, contingent on the performance of low-frequency behaviors, such as completing assignments or responding appropriately to adults (Premack, 1959). Some activities that teachers find are reinforcing for their students include being a team leader, receiving extra story time, listening to music, and looking at magazines.

Like social and activity reinforcement, token reinforcement is contingent upon the performance of a specific desired behavior. In a token system, or token economy, students receive tokens, such as points or chips, which they can trade at a later time for activity reinforcers, tangible reinforcers (e.g., stickers, certificates, magnets, markers) or edible reinforcers (e.g., pretzels, popcorn). Polloway and Patton (1993) point out that in token reinforcement systems, students earn tokens for appropriate behavior just as adults receive money for their job performance.

The timing of the reinforcer is key to its impact. It is important to reward students as soon as you observe them demonstrating the appropriate behaviors. For example, if you are trying to increase the number of assignments a student completes, reward the student at the time he or she turns in a completed paper. Waiting until you have graded and returned the assignment will not be as effective.

Once the student exhibits the desirable behavior regularly, then you can begin gradually to decrease the frequency of the reward until the student continues to use the behavior at the specified level with less frequent rewards. The following example illustrates how one teacher used positive reinforcement to increase her student's assignment completion:

Sara is a thirteen-year-old student of average intelligence with behavior disorders who rarely turns in her class assignments. Her teacher, Mrs. Ellenon, wanted to increase to 80 percent the percentage of class assignments she handed in daily, after noting that Sara completed only one out of five assignments (20 percent) each day for a week. Mrs. Ellenon also observed that during seat work,

Sara often became very upset and then cried. When this happened Mrs. Ellenon immediately comforted her by talking individually with her until the crying stopped. In reviewing these observations, Mrs. Ellenon suspected her individual attention to Sara was reinforcing the crying, and she decided to use that attention to reward Sara each time she turned in an assignment. The first day she used the reward strategy, Sara completed three out of five assignments (60 percent), and Mrs. Ellenon talked privately with her after she handed in each paper. Sara did so well that on the third day, with Sara's consent, Mrs. Ellenon reduced the reward to one individual talk after Sara completed two assignments and then only after she finished three assignments. By the eleventh day Sara reached the 80 percent criterion level Mrs. Ellenon established.

In addition to reinforcement procedures, teachers can increase appropriate behaviors by using a behavioral contract, which systematizes the use of reinforcement. This written agreement between adult(s) and the student specifies what rewards and consequences will be contingent on the student's performance of a specific behavior. Like any contract, its contents are negotiated and all participants must agree to its terms. A contract states:

- the behavior to be performed
- the conditions under which the behavior will be performed
- the criterion for successful performance of the behavior
- the reward for performing the behavior
- the consequences for failing to perform the behavior
- the signatures of the contract participants
- the date (teachers who plan to use several contracts to improve a student's behaviors also often include the number of the contract).

The following is an example of a contract negotiated by Mrs. Randolph, Bill and Bill's parents to decrease his arguing and fighting.

BEHAVIORAL CONTRACT

Mrs. Randolph will check a Good Play card for Bill each time he plays during recess without fighting or arguing with any student. When Bill has earned 10 checks from Mrs. Randolph and has had his card signed by his parents, he may use the computer for 15 minutes.

Signed: _____ (Student)

_____ (Teacher)

_____ (Parents)

written on (date) _____

To increase specific behaviors, teachers also may provide a model of the behavior for students to imitate. Students imi-

tate more readily the behavior of models who are similar to themselves in some way, who have high status, and who have been reinforced (Kerr & Nelson, 1989). Both live and vicarious models, such as those shown in videotapes or films, have been effective in altering behavior in public school classrooms. Kerr and Nelson point out that although behavioral procedures, such as reinforcement and modeling, are often discussed separately in textbooks, in practice they often are used in combination. For example, teachers may model a behavior, such as expressing anger appropriately, then have students practice this skill in role-plays and reinforce their performance.

Decreasing Inappropriate School Behaviors

Just as some students need help increasing appropriate behaviors, others require help in reducing behaviors that are not appropriate for school. Frequently teachers select differential reinforcement of incompatible behaviors (DRI) which involves reinforcing a behavior that is incompatible with the one the teacher wants to decrease. A related positive approach teachers frequently use is differential reinforcement of alternate behaviors (DRA). During this procedure, teachers reinforce alternatives to the specific behavior targeted for change. For example, if you want to promote a student raising his or her hand instead of talking out in class, you would reinforce hand raising.

Although several techniques are effective in decreasing behaviors, many of them involve using types of punishment. Punishment is defined as "consequences that reduce the future probability of a behavior" (Kauffman, 1993, p. 505). When using any form of punishment, teachers should:

1. Combine punishment with positive reinforcement of alternative behaviors;
2. Manage punishment procedures carefully and use them consistently and immediately as suggested by the 10-step process discussed previously (see pp. 244–245);
3. Use punishment only after positive procedures have been unsuccessful.

The more restrictive procedures, such as time-out, overcorrection, and physical aversives should only be used by trained professionals.

Less intrusive punishment procedures include purposeful ignoring of a student's behavior, withholding other rewards, and public postings. Teachers, for example, have used public posting to improve behaviors such as disruptions in the halls (Staub, 1987, cited in Kerr & Nelson, 1989) by recording the daily performance of the class and "best record to date" on a large poster displayed at both ends of a school corridor. One of the most frequently used forms of punishment is reprimands. When using reprimands, make them privately, not publicly; stand near the student while reprimanding; and give the student direct eye contact before scolding (Kerr & Nelson, 1989).

Prevention of Inappropriate Behaviors

Because using even mild forms of punishment is less desirable than using positive strategies, teachers may reduce the need to use punishing techniques by preventing many behavior problems. Kerr and Nelson suggest that the notion of structuring is helpful in prevention. They recommend teachers carefully consider the antecedents of inappropriate behavior to include the use of physical space, daily scheduling, and rules and routines to influence or structure student behavior. As you think about using classroom rules and routines, reflect on the following suggestions made by Lewis and Doorlag (1987):

1. Make rules and routines positive, concrete, and functional, relating them to the accomplishments of learning and order in the classroom (e.g., "work quietly at the learning centers" rather than "don't talk when working").

2. Design rules and routines to anticipate potential classroom problems and to manage these situations. For example, teachers may want students to raise their hands when they need help rather than calling out or leaving their seat to locate the teacher.

3. Establish classroom rules and routines at the beginning of the school year by introducing them the first day.

4. Demonstrate or model the rules and routines and continue to provide opportunities for students to practice them until they have mastered them.

5. Associate rules and routines with simple signals that tell students when they are to carry out or stop specific activities and behaviors.

6. Monitor how students follow rules and routines, rewarding students for appropriate behaviors.

Although many behavioral management strategies, as those just discussed, are teacher-directed, other effective strategies are managed by the student (see p. 186) or, in part, by other students. One peer-mediated intervention used frequently is cooperative learning (see p. 66).

HELPFUL RESOURCES

School Personnel

In addition to the school personnel listed in previous chapters, school psychologists may be helpful in understanding and managing students with serious emotional or behavioral disorders. They can provide specific information about student's problems based on their individual evaluations, recommend procedures teachers can use in their classrooms, and offer individual or group counseling for students with emotional or behavioral disorders.

School counselors are valuable in-building resources. They may help when students have behavioral crises. In addition, they are an important link between the classroom teacher and parents. They can provide frequent reports of student progress and coordinate home-school plans to improve students' behavior and performance.

Instructional Methods

Cartledge, G. & Milburn, J. F. (1986). *Teaching social skills to children*. New York: Pergamon Press.

Center, D. B. (1989). *Curriculum and teaching strategies for students with behavioral disorders*. Englewood Cliffs, NJ: Prentice Hall.

Erickson, M. T. (1992). *Behavior disorders of children and adolescents: Assessment, etiology, and intervention*. Englewood Cliffs, NJ: Prentice-Hall.

Grossman, H. (1990) *Trouble-free teaching: Solutions to behavior problems in the classroom*. Mountain View, CA: Mayfield.

Kaplan, J. S., & Drainville, B. (1991). *Beyond behavior modification* (2nd ed.). Austin, TX: Pro-Ed.

Kerr, M. M. & Nelson, C. M. (1989). *Strategies for managing behavior problems in the classroom* (2nd ed.).. Columbus, OH: Merrill.

Macht, J. (1990). *Managing classroom behavior*. New York: Longman.

Morgan, D. P., & Jenson, W. R. (1988). *Teaching behaviorally disordered students: Preferred practices*. New York: Merrill/Macmillan.

Morgan, S. R., Reinhart, J. A. (1991). *Interventions with students with emotional disorders*. Austin, TX: Pro-Ed.

Nelson, C. M., & Pearson, C. (1991). *Integrating services for children and youth with emotional and behavioral disorders*. Reston, VA: Council for Exceptional Children.

Rosenberg, M. S., Wilson, R., Maheady, L., & Sindelar, P. (1992). *Educating students with behavior disorders*. Boston: Allyn & Bacon.

Schroeder, C. S., & Gordon, B. N., (1991). *Assessment and treatment of childhood problems*. New York: The Guilford Press.

Smith, D. D. (1984). *Effective discipline*. Austin, TX: Pro-Ed.

Walker, H. M., & Walker, J. E. (1991). *Coping with noncompliance in the classroom*. Austin, TX: Pro-Ed.

Walker, J. E., & Shea, T. M. (1991). *Behavior management: A practical approach for educators*. (5th ed.). New York: Merrill/Macmillan.

Curricula and Instructional Materials

Goldstein, A. P., Sprafkin, R. P., Greshaw, N. J., & Klein, P. (1980). *Skillstreaming the adolescent: A structural learning approach to teaching prosocial skills*. Champaign, IL: Research Press.

Hazel, J. S., Shumaker, J. B., Sherman, J. A. & Sheldon-Wildgen, J. (1981). *ASSET: A social program for adolescents*. Champaign, IL: Research Press.

Jackson, N. F., Jackson, D. A., & Monroe, C. (1983). *Getting along with others*. Champaign, IL: Research Press.

Mannix, D. (1990). *I can behave*. Austin, TX: Pro-Ed.

McGinnis, E., Goldstein, A. P., Sprafkin, R. P., & Gershaw, N. J. (1984). *Skillstreaming the elementary school child: A guide for teaching prosocial skills*. Champaign, IL: Research Press.

Stokes, T. F. & Baer, D. M. (1988). *The Social Skills Curriculum.* Circle Pines, MN: American Guidance Service.

Walker, H., McConnell, S., Holms, D., Todis, B., Walker, J., & Golden, N. (1983) *The Walker social skills curriculum: The ACCEPTS program.* Austin, TX: Pro-Ed.

Weisgerber, R., Appleby, J., & Fong, S. (1984). *Social solution curriculum.* Developed at American Institute for Research, Palo Alto, CA, Burlingame, CA: Professional Associated Resources.

Literature About Individuals with Behavioral Disorders

ELEMENTARY

Berger, T. (1979). *I have feelings, too.* New York: Human Sciences Press. (Fiction=F)

Sheehan, C. (1981). *The colors that I am.* New York: Human Science Press. (F)

Simon, N. (1974). *I was so mad!* Chicago: A. Whitman. (Middle School) (F)

Hamilton, V. (1971). *The planet of Junior Brown.* New York: Macmillan. (F)

Patternson, K. (1978). *The great Gilly Hopkins.* New York: Cromwell. (F)

Platt, K. (1968). *The boy who could make himself disappear.* Dell. (F)

SECONDARY/ADULT

Berger, G. (1981). *Mental illness.* New York: Franklin Watts. (Nonfiction=NF)

Greenfeld, J. (1978). *A place for Noah.* New York: Washington Square Press. (NF)

Greenfeld, J. (1986). *A client called Noah.* San Diego: Harcourt Brace Jovanovich. (NF)

Hayden, T. L. (1980). *One child.* New York: Putnam. (NF)

Hyde, M. O. (1983). *Is this kid "crazy"?: Understanding unusual behavior.* Philadelphia: Westminister. (NF)

Computer Software

Little Computer People, Triton Products Company, P. O. Box 8123, San Francisco, CA 94128, (800)227–6900.

Videodisc

Interactive Videodisc Social Skills (IVSS) Program, Ron Thorkildsen, Department of Special Education, Utah State University, Logan, UT, 84322–6500, (801)750–1999.

Organizations

Council for Children with Behavioral Disorders, 1920 Association Dr., Reston, VA 22091.

BIBLIOGRAPHY FOR TEACHING SUGGESTIONS

Bandura, A. (1969). *Principles of behavior modification.* New York: Holt, Rinehart, & Winston.

Kauffman, J. M. (1993). *Characteristics of emotional and behavioral disorders of children and youth* (5th ed.). Columbus, OH: Merrill/Macmillan.

Kerr, M. M. , & Nelson, C. M. (1989). *Strategies for managing behavior problems in the classroom* (2nd ed.). Columbus, OH: Merrill.

Lewis, R. B. & Doorlag, D. H. (1990). *Teaching special students in the mainstream* (3rd ed.). New York: Merrill/Macmillan.

Polloway, E. A., & Patton, J. S. (1993). *Strategies for teaching learners with special needs* (5th ed.). New York: Merrill/Macmillan.

Premack, D., (1959). Toward empirical behavior laws: I. Positive reinforcement. *Psychological Review*, 66, 219–233.

Summary

Emotional or behavioral disorders are not simply a matter of undesirable or inappropriate behavior. They involve inappropriate social interactions and transactions between the child or youth and the social environment. Most youngsters with emotional or behavioral disorders are isolated from others, either because they withdraw from social contact or because they behave in an aggressive, hostile way and other people withdraw from them.

Many different terms have been used for children's emotional or behavioral disorders. In the language of the Individuals with Disabilities Education Act, they are "seriously emotionally disturbed." The term "emotional or behavioral disorder" is becoming widely accepted, due primarily to the work of the National Mental Health and Special Education Coalition, which proposed a new definition and terminology in 1990.

The definition of emotional or behavioral disorder is particularly difficult. Features common to nearly all definitions are statements that the behavior goes to an extreme, that it is unacceptable because of social or cultural expectations, and that the problem is chronic, not transient. The current federal definition lists five characteristics, one or more of which may indicate that the child is "seriously emotionally disturbed" if it is exhibited to a marked extent, persists over a long time, and adversely affects educational performance: (1) inability to learn that cannot be explained by intellectual, sensory, or health factors, (2) inability to build or maintain satisfactory relationships with peers and teachers, (3) inappropriate behavior or feelings under normal conditions, (4) a pervasive mood of unhappiness or depression, and (5) physical symptoms, pains, or fears associated with personal or school problems. These characteristics obviously include children with autism or schizophrenia, although children with autism have been excluded from the category in federal regulations, and children with schizophrenia have been explicitly included. Children who are "socially maladjusted but not seriously emotionally disturbed" are also excluded by the current federal definition. This exclusion presents great problems in determining who is eligible for special education, and some professional organizations have condemned the practice of excluding children who are "socially maladjusted."

The National Mental Health and Special Education Coalition's proposed definition defines emotional or behavioral disorder as a disability characterized by behavioral or emotional responses to school so different from appropriate age, cultural, or ethnic norms that they adversely affect educational performance. Educational performance is defined as more than academic performance; it includes academic, social, vocational, and personal skills. An emotional or behavioral disorder is more than a temporary or expected response to stressful events. It is exhibited in more than one setting, and it is unresponsive to direct intervention in general education. Finally, the proposed definition notes that the term emotional or behavioral disorders covers a wide variety of diagnostic groups, including sustained disorders of conduct or adjustment that adversely affect educational performance and can co-exist with other disabilities.

Determining subcategories of emotional or behavioral disorders is difficult. Most authorities today agree that psychiatric categories have been of little value for educational purposes and recommend reliance on individual assessment of each student's behavior and social situation. Dimensional classification describes clusters of interrelated behaviors. Two broad, pervasive dimensions are externalizing (aggressive, acting out) and internalizing (anxiety, withdrawal). Narrower, more

specific dimensions, such as conduct disorder (antisocial behavior, which may be overt or covert), attention problems, anxiety, depression, socialized delinquency, psychotic behavior, and so on, have also been identified. All children may exhibit some of the behaviors characteristic of these dimensions of disorder, but children and youths with emotional or behavioral disorders exhibit some behaviors to an extreme degree; for most subcategories, disordered behavior differs from normal behavior primarily in quantity. The disorders labeled by these dimensions are not mutually exclusive. That is, individuals may exhibit extreme behaviors characterizing more than one dimension; it is possible for a child to exhibit both conduct disorder and depression. Children and youths with severe emotional or behavioral disorders tend to have problems along multiple dimensions.

The severe disorders called pervasive developmental disorders describe children who appear to be qualitatively as well as quantitatively different from children without disabilities. Two such disorders are autism and childhood schizophrenia. Autism is a severe developmental disorder that begins before the child is 30 months old and is characterized by lack of responsiveness to people, problems in communication, peculiar speech, peculiar interests, and stereotyped behavior. Schizophrenia is a disorder of thinking characterized by delusions and hallucinations.

Estimates of the prevalence of emotional or behavioral disorders vary greatly, in part because the definition is not precise. Most researchers estimate that 6 to 10 percent of the child population is affected, but only about 1 percent of the school-aged population is currently identified as having emotional or behavioral disorders and is receiving special education services. Most children and youths who are identified for special education purposes are boys, and most exhibit externalizing behavior. About 3 percent of U.S. youths are referred to juvenile court in any given year. Relatively few of these receive special education services for emotional or behavioral disorders.

A single, specific cause of an emotional or behavioral disorder can seldom be identified. In most cases, it is possible only to identify causal factors that contribute to the likelihood that a child will develop a disorder or that predispose a child to developing a disorder. Major contributing factors are found in biological conditions, family relationships, school experiences, and cultural influences. Possible biological factors include genetics, temperament (an inborn behavioral style), malnutrition, brain trauma, and substance abuse. Most biological causes are poorly understood, and social as well as medical intervention is almost always necessary. Family disorganization, parental abuse, and inconsistent discipline are among the most important family factors contributing to emotional or behavioral disorders. However, poor parenting is not always or solely the cause. Furthermore, family factors appear to affect each family member in a different way. School factors that may contribute to emotional or behavioral disorders are insensitivity to students' individuality, inappropriate expectations, inconsistent or inappropriate discipline, unintentional rewards for misbehavior, and undesirable models of conduct. Cultural factors include the influences of the media, values and standards of the community and peer group, and social services available to children and their families. Family, school, and the wider culture create a complex web of cultural causal factors.

Efforts to prevent emotional or behavioral disorders are concentrated on identifying and teaching the social skills that help children make and keep friends and get along with adults. Prevention also involves reducing risk factors, such as neglect, abuse, family conflict, and school failure.

Most children and youths with emotional or behavioral disorders—especially those with serious conduct disorder or autism—are easily recognized. Few schools use systematic screening procedures, partly because services would be unavailable for the many students likely to be identified. The most effective identification procedures use a combination of teachers' rankings and ratings and direct observation of students' behavior. Peer rankings or ratings are often used as well.

The typical student with an emotional or behavioral disorder has an IQ in the dull-normal range. The range of intelligence is enormous: a few are brilliant, and more than in the general population have mental retardation. Most children with autism test in the moderate to severe range of mental retardation, but new views of autism suggest that some of these children may have considerably higher intelligence than previously thought. Most children and youths with emotional or behavioral disorders lack, in varying degrees, the ability to apply their knowledge and skills to the demands of everyday living.

Students who express their problems in aggressive, acting-out behavior are involved in a vicious cycle.

Their behavior alienates others so that positive interactions with adults and peers become less likely. Children and youths whose behavior is consistently antisocial have less chance of learning to make social adjustments and of achieving mental health in adulthood than do those who are shy, anxious, or neurotic.

Students with autism or other pervasive developmental disorders often lack basic self-care skills, may appear to be perceptually disabled, and appear to have serious cognitive limitations. Especially evident and important is their inability to relate to other people. In addition, deviations in speech and language abilities, self-stimulation or self-injury, and the tendency to injure others deliberately combine to give these students a poor prognosis. Some of them function permanently at a level of mental retardation and require sustained supervision and care. Recent research brings hope that many may make remarkable progress with early intensive intervention. Some may learn an alternative means of communication.

Good descriptions of special education programs for students with emotional or behavioral disorders are seldom found, and there are many different views of what programs should offer. Traditional conceptual models are giving way to a synthesis of ideas in which attention is given both to changing behavior and dealing with what the individual thinks and feels. Newer approaches to intervention emphasize enhancing the student's self-control through such means as self-monitoring, self-assessment, goal-setting, and videotape feedback. It is important to balance behavioral control with concern for academic and social learning and to provide integrated services—to see that students receive all the different services they need in a coordinated fashion. Regardless of the conceptual model guiding intervention or the characteristics of the students involved, the following strategies work: using systematic, data-based interventions; assessing and monitoring progress continuously; providing opportunities to practice new skills; providing treatment matched to the student's problem; offering multi-component treatment to meet all the student's needs; programming for transfer and maintenance of learning; and sustaining intervention as long as it is needed.

A relatively small percentage of children and youths with emotional or behavioral disorders receive special education and related services. Only those with the most severe problems are likely to be identified, and one consequence is that many are educated outside regular classrooms and schools. The trend, however, is toward greater integration in regular schools and classes.

Early identification and prevention are goals of early intervention programs. The problem behavior of many children later referred to clinics for emotional or behavioral disorders is evident early in life. These problems bring them into frequent conflict with their caretakers or peers. With early, intensive intervention, great improvements can be seen in nearly all cases.

Programs of special education for adolescents and young adults with emotional or behavioral disorders are extremely varied and must be highly individualized because of the wide differences in intelligence, behavioral characteristics, achievements, and circumstances of the students. Transition from school to work and adult life is particularly difficult for students with emotional or behavioral disorders, and they are among those most likely to drop out of school. The outlook for adulthood is particularly poor for youths with severe conduct disorder; many may require intervention throughout their lives.

CHAPTER SEVEN

JOHN ANDREW HAAS

John Andrew Haas has been diagnosed with schizophrenia, and considers his paintings to be partly a reflection of his disorder. His painting "Going" is dedicated to Peter Townshend of The Who, on behalf of Very Special Arts. John Andrew Haas works as a painter and poet, in collaboration with his brother Henry Haas, the featured artist in Chapter 6.

I said goodbye and turned to go, but she wrapped her purple-green arms around my neck, kissed my cheek, and said, "I love you, Jeremy."

"I'll miss you so much."

"I really, truly love you with all my soul," she said.

"My Dad's waiting. I better go."

She took her arms off me and stepped back, straightened her smock. Then she said, "I've already told you I love you, Jeremy. Can't you say, 'I love you, Faith'?"

"I love you," I said.

"I love you, *Faith*," she insisted.

This little scene in the garage occurred only a few months after my futile attempt to say *Philadelphia* in the living room. Stutterers have a tendency to generalize their fear of one word that begins with a particular sound to a fear of all words that begin with the same sound. In the space of the summer I'd effectively eliminated every *F* from my vocabulary, with the exception of the preposition, "for," which for the time being was too small to incite terror. A few weeks later, my fear of *F* ended when another letter—I think it was *L*—suddenly loomed large. But at the moment, early October 1962, in Faith's garage, I was terrified of *F*s. I simply wasn't saying them. I hadn't called Faith by her first name for nearly a month and had, instead, taken to calling her Carlisle, as if her patronymic had become a term of jocular endearment.

"I can't," I said. "I can't say that."

➤ David Shields
   Dead Languages

Communication Disorders

▲ ▲ ▲

➢ **speech disorders.** Oral communication that involves abnormal use of the vocal apparatus, is unintelligible, or so inferior that it draws attention to itself and causes anxiety, feelings of inadequacy, or inappropriate behavior in the speaker.

➢ **stuttering.** Speech characterized by abnormal hesitations, prolongations, and repetitions; may be accompanied by grimaces, gestures, or other bodily movements indicative of a struggle to speak, anxiety, blocking of speech, or avoidance of speech.

➢ **communication disorders.** An impairment in the ability to use speech or language to communicate.

Communication is such a natural part of our everyday lives that we seldom stop to think about it. Social conversation with families, friends, and casual acquaintances is normally so effortless and pleasant that it is hard to imagine anyone having difficulty with it. Most of us have feelings of uncertainty about the adequacy of our speech or language only in stressful or unusual social situations, such as talking to a large audience or being interviewed for a job. If we always had to worry about communicating, we would worry about every social interaction we had.

Not all communication disorders involve disorders of speech. Some **speech disorders** are not so handicapping in social interactions as **stuttering,** nor is stuttering the most common disorder of speech. The problem Shields describes (see p. 253) affects only about one person in a hundred, and then usually just during childhood. But stuttering is a mystery, a phenomenon about which theories continue to surface (Perkins, Kent, & Curlee, 1991). Its causes and cures remain largely unknown, although for many years it captured a large share of speech-language pathologists' attention. In one sense, then, stuttering is a poor example to use in introducing a chapter on communication disorders. It is not the most representative disorder, it is difficult to define precisely, its causes are not fully understood, and few suggestions about how to overcome it can be made with confidence. But in another sense stuttering is the best example. When people think of speech and language disorders, they tend to think first of stuttering (Owens, 1986). It is a disorder we all have heard and recognized (if not experienced) at one time or another, the social consequences are obvious, and although it *appears* to be a simple problem with obvious "logical" solutions ("Just slow down"; "Relax, don't worry"; "Think about how to say it"), these seemingly common sense approaches do not work.

Today, difficulty such as the one described by Shields (p. 253) is viewed within the broad context of **communication disorders** because of the obstacle it presents to social interaction, a major purpose of language. Jeremy's stuttering was an inability to convey his thoughts and feelings to Faith, not just a problem of being fearful and not being able to say certain words. In thinking about communication disorders, the context in which communication occurs must be considered in addition to people's reasons for communicating, and the rules that govern the "games" of discourse and dialogue (Nelson, 1993).

Our points here are simply these: First, all communication disorders carry social penalties; second, communication is among the most complex human functions, and disorders of this function do not always yield to intuitive or common sense "solutions."

DEFINITIONS

Speech and language are tools used for communication. Communication requires *encoding* (sending in understandable form) and *decoding* (receiving and understanding) messages. Communication always involves a sender and a receiver of messages, but it does not always involve language. Animals communicate through movements and noises, for example, but their communication does not qualify as a true language. We are concerned here only with communication through language.

▶ *Misconceptions about*
▶ PERSONS WITH COMMUNICATION DISORDERS

MYTH ➤ Children with language disorders always have speech difficulties as well.

FACT ➤ It is possible for a child to have good speech and yet not make any sense when he or she talks; however, most children with language disorders have speech disorders as well.

MYTH ➤ Individuals with communication disorders always have emotional or behavioral disorders or mental retardation.

FACT ➤ Some children with communication disorders are normal in cognitive, social, and emotional development.

MYTH ➤ How children learn language is now well understood.

FACT ➤ Although recent research has revealed quite a lot about the sequence of language acquisition and has led to theories of language development, exactly how children learn language is still unknown.

MYTH ➤ Stuttering is primarily a disorder of people with extremely high IQs. Children who stutter become stuttering adults.

FACT ➤ Stuttering can affect individuals at any level of intellectual ability. Some children who stutter continue stuttering as adults; most, however, stop stuttering before or during adolescence with help from a speech-language pathologist. Stuttering is primarily a childhood disorder, found much more often in boys than in girls.

MYTH ➤ Disorders of phonology (or articulation) are never very serious and are always easy to correct.

FACT ➤ Disorders of phonology can make speech unintelligible; it is sometimes very difficult to correct phonological or articulation problems, especially if the individual has cerebral palsy, mental retardation, or emotional or behavioral disorders.

MYTH ➤ A child with a cleft palate always has defective speech.

FACT ➤ The child born with a cleft palate may or may not have a speech disorder, depending on the nature of the cleft, the medical treatment given, and other factors such as psychological characteristics and speech training.

MYTH ➤ There is no relationship between intelligence and disorders of communication.

FACT ➤ Communication disorders tend to occur more frequently among individuals of lower intellectual ability, although these disorders may occur in individuals who are extremely intelligent.

MYTH ➤ There is not much overlap between language disorders and learning disabilities.

FACT ➤ Problems with verbal skills—listening, reading, writing, speaking—are often a central feature of a learning disability. The definitions of language disorders and several other disabilities are overlapping.

DEFINITIONS OF THE AMERICAN SPEECH-LANGUAGE-HEARING ASSOCIATION ➤

COMMUNICATIVE DISORDERS

A. A SPEECH DISORDER is an impairment of voice, articulation of speech sounds, and/or fluency. These impairments are observed in the transmission and use of the oral symbol system.

　1. A VOICE DISORDER is defined as the absence or abnormal production of voice quality, pitch, loudness, resonance, and/or duration.

　2. An ARTICULATION DISORDER is defined as the abnormal production of speech sounds.

　3. A FLUENCY DISORDER is defined as the abnormal flow of verbal expression, characterized by impaired rate and rhythm that may be accompanied by struggle behavior.

B. A LANGUAGE DISORDER is the impairment or deviant development of comprehension and/or use of a spoken, written, and/or other symbol system. The disorder may involve (1) the form of language (phonologic, morphologic, and syntactic systems), (2) the content of language (semantic system), and/or (3) the function of language in communication (pragmatic system) in any combination.

　1. Form of Language

　　a. PHONOLOGY is the sound system of a language and the linguistic rules that govern the sound combinations.

　　b. MORPHOLOGY is the linguistic rule system that governs the structure of words and the construction of word forms from the basic elements of meaning.

　　c. SYNTAX is the linguistic rule governing the order and combination of words to form sentences, and the relationships among the elements within a sentence.

　2. Content of Language

　　a. SEMANTICS is the psycholinguistic system that patterns the content of an utterance—the intent and meanings of words and sentences.

　3. Function of Language

　　a. PRAGMATICS is the sociolinguistic system that patterns the use of language in communication, which may be expressed motorically, vocally, or verbally.

COMMUNICATIVE VARIATIONS

A. COMMUNICATIVE DIFFERENCE/DIALECT is a variation of a symbol system used by a group of individuals that reflects and is determined by shared regional, social, or cultural/ethnic factors. Variations or alterations in the use of a symbol system may be indicative of primary language interferences. A regional, social, or cultural/ethnic variation of a symbol system should not be considered a disorder of speech or language.

B. AUGMENTATIVE COMMUNICATION is a system used to supplement the communicative skills of individuals for whom speech is temporarily or permanently inadequate to meet communicative needs. Both prosthetic devices and/or nonprosthetic techniques may be designed for individual use as an augmentative communication system.

SOURCE: American Speech-Language-Hearing Association, *Definitions: Communicative disorders and variations, ASHA, 24,* (1982) 949–950. Reprinted with permission.

➤ **language.** An arbitrary code or system of symbols to communicate meaning.

➤ **speech.** Forming and sequencing oral language sounds during communication.

➤ **augmentative communication.** Alternative forms of communication that do not use the oral sounds of speech.

Language is the communication of ideas through an arbitrary system of symbols used according to certain rules that determine meaning. When people think of language, they typically think of the oral language most of us use. **Speech**—the behavior of forming and sequencing the sounds of oral language—is the most common symbol system used in communication between humans. Some languages, however, are not based on speech. For example, American Sign Language does not involve speech sounds; it is a manual language used by many people who cannot hear speech. **Augmentative communication** for people with disabilities involving the physical movements of speech may consist of alternatives to the speech sounds of oral language.

The American Speech-Language-Hearing Association provides definitions of disorders of communication, including **speech disorders, language disorders,** and variations in communication (differences or dialects and augmentative systems) that are not disorders (see the box on above). Note that language disorders include problems in the comprehension and use of language for communication, regardless of the symbol system used (spoken, written, or other). The *form, content,* and/or *function* of language may be involved. The form of language includes sound combinations **(phonology),** construction of word forms such as plurals and verb tenses **(morphology),** and construction of sentences **(syntax).** The content of language refers to the intentions and meanings people attach to words and sentences **(semantics).** Language function is the use to which language is put in communication, and it includes nonverbal behavior as well as vocalizations that form the pattern of language use **(pragmatics).**

Speech disorders are impairments in the production and use of oral language. They include disabilities in producing voice, making speech sounds **(articulation),** and producing speech with a normal flow **(fluency).**

Differences in speech or language that are shared by people in a given region, social group, or cultural/ethnic group should not be considered disorders. For example, black English (Ebonics or Black English Vernacular), Appalachian English, and the New York dialect are varieties of English, not disorders of speech or language (ASHA, 1983). Augmentative communication systems do not imply that a person has a language disorder. Rather, such systems are used by those who have a temporary or permanent inability to use speech satisfactorily for communication. Those who use augmentative communication systems may or may not have a language disorder in addition to their inability to use speech.

PREVALENCE

Establishing the prevalence of communication disorders is difficult because they are extremely varied, are sometimes difficult to identify, and often occur as part of another disability (e.g., mental retardation, traumatic head injury, learning disability, or autism; see Nelson, 1993). Federal data indicate that over a million children—about one-fourth of all children identified for special education—receive services primarily for language or speech disorders (U.S. Department of Education, 1992). Moreover, speech-language therapy is also one of the most frequently provided related services for children with other primary disabilities (e.g., mental retardation or learning disability). The box on page 258 outlines the other categories associated with language disorders of children and youths. The outline suggests the multiple, interrelated causes of language disorders and other disabilities. *Central factors* refer to causes associated with central nervous system (i.e., brain) damage or dysfunction. *Peripheral factors* refer to sensory or physical impairments that are not caused by brain injury or dysfunction but that, nevertheless, contribute to language disorders. *Environmental and emotional factors* refer to language disorders that have their primary origin in the child's physical or psychological environment. *Mixed factors* are included because language disorders often have multiple causes—combinations of central, peripheral, and environmental or emotional factors. Thus, "when one considers the total number of handicapped students receiving some form of service (e.g., primary handicap or related service) for their communication disorders, the provision of speech-language pathology and audiology services is the largest aspect of mandatory special education" (Casby, 1989, p. 29).

Casby points out that many children with communication disorders are not receiving an appropriate amount of services from speech-language pathologists

> **speech disorders.** Oral communication that involves abnormal use of the vocal apparatus, is unintelligible, or so inferior that it draws attention to itself and causes anxiety, feelings of inadequacy, or innappropriate behavior in the speaker.

> **language disorders.** A lag in the ability to understand and express ideas that puts linguistic skill behind an individual's development in other areas, such as motor, cognitive, or social development.

> **phonology.** The study of how individual sounds make up words.

> **morphology.** The study within psycholinguistics of word formation; of how adding or deleting parts of words changes their meaning.

> **syntax.** The way words are joined together to structure meaningful sentences.

> **semantics.** The study of the meanings attached to words and sentences.

> **pragmatics.** The study within psycholinguistics of how one uses language in social situations; emphasizes functional use of language rather than its mechanics.

> **articulation.** Refers to the movements the vocal tract makes during production of speech sounds; enunciation of words and vocal sounds.

> **fluency.** The flow with which oral language is produced.

ATEGORICAL FACTORS ASSOCIATED WITH CHILDHOOD LANGUAGE DISORDERS ➤

I. Central factors

   A. Specific language disability

   B. Mental retardation

   C. Autism

   D. Attention-deficit hyperactivity disorder

   E. Acquired brain injury

   F. Others

II. Peripheral factors

   A. Hearing impairment

   B. Visual impairment

   C. Physical impairment

III. Environmental and emotional factors

   A. Neglect and abuse

   B. Behavioral and emotional development problems

IV. Mixed factors

SOURCE: Reprinted with the permission of Macmillan Publishing Company from *Childhood language disorders in context: Infancy through adolescence.* by Nicola Wolf Nelson. Copyright © 1993 by Macmillan Publishing Company, p. 84.

and audiologists. There is a need for more speech-language pathologists in the schools, as well as for greater knowledge of communication disorders by special and general education teachers and greater involvement of teachers in helping students learn to communicate effectively.

Before discussing the disorders of language and speech, we provide a brief description of normal language development. Communication disorders cannot be understood and corrected without knowledge of normal language development. A discussion of language disorders is presented first and more extensively than speech disorders. Language disorders are emphasized because the primary focus of speech-language pathologists and other specialists in communicative disorders has shifted from speech to language during the evolution of special education and related services.

LANGUAGE DEVELOPMENT

The newborn makes few sounds other than cries. The fact that within a few years the human child can form the many complex sounds of speech, understand spoken and written language, and express meaning verbally is one of nature's great miracles. The major milestones in this "miraculous" ability to use language are fairly well known by child development specialists. The underlying mechanisms that control the development of language are still not well understood, however. What parts of the process of learning language are innate, and what parts are controlled by the environment? What is the relationship between cognitive development and language development? These and many other questions about the origins and uses of language cannot yet be answered definitively.

Sequence of Development

Research has demonstrated that infants are much more adept at communication than was previously thought. They receive and give messages to their caretakers in ways that were not formerly understood. Mothers and other caretakers approach babies as if they can communicate. This is significant in understanding early language learning because it highlights the social nature of the process.

Interaction of infants and care givers includes joint reference to objects (e.g., "Oh, look!"), joint action (e.g., games such as peek-a-boo), turn taking (often during joint action), and situational variations (e.g., games played during bathing or diaper changing, but not when the infant is being put to sleep in the crib). It is the need to communicate—to exchange meanings involving social interactions—that sets the stage for the development of language. Recognition of this principle has led to intense interest in the social contexts and uses of language. As you read the description of the emergence of oral language, you should keep in mind the social use of language for children at various stages of development.

At about two to three months of age, babies begin "gooing," and by four to six months they are babbling. That is, they make some of the vowel and consonant sounds and other noises over and over, often apparently just to explore their vocal apparatus and to entertain themselves. Sometimes they babble when they are alone and will stop abruptly if an adult attends to them. Sometimes babbling occurs when they are being cared for or played with. These vocalizations may be social—used to communicate with their caretakers.

Babbling soon turns into vocal play. The sounds children are able to make gradually increase in variety. They begin to string sounds together (da-da-da) and, toward the end of the first year, to put different syllables together (duh-buh). They make vocal sounds more frequently and seem to take delight in their own performance. But they also begin to take an interest in listening to the speech of adults and to carry on "conversations" by "answering" when spoken to. Now they begin to use intonations, changing the pitch and intensity of their vocal productions to make them sound like adults' commands, questions, or exclamations. They experiment with rhythm and intonation patterns.

What they are "saying" is still meaningless gibberish if taken out of its social context—but it sounds as if they are talking. Their vocalizations, facial expressions, and gestures may be a form of effective communication with adults who know them well. Mother and child may make their desires and intentions mutually understood even though other adults may be unable to interpret the child's "speech." Children play delightedly (and delightfully) with vocalizations and may continue this kind of vocal play for a few years, even though by that age they have acquired a vocabulary of several hundred words and may be putting two and three words together in simple sentences. An important thing to note here is that at more advanced stages of normal language development, there is greater variation in the age at which milestones are reached. For example, there is greater variation in the age at which children usually speak their first words than there is in the age at which children normally begin to babble.

At about the same time children learn to walk and to feed themselves—roughly between ten and eighteen months—they normally say their first words. Actually, it is not at all easy to pinpoint when a child starts to use words because approximations of words often occur in an infant's vocalizations, and it is often impossible to judge their communicative intent. Even before they have started to say what everyone would agree are words, babies have begun to exhibit an understanding of simple questions and commands. During the second year vocal play continues. Children may utter unintelligible strings of syllables with occasional understandable words mixed in. They may sometimes be *echolalic* (i.e., repeat what they have heard without understanding it or being able to use it appropriately in conversation). Many of their words are idiosyncratic or poorly articulated. They may use a single word in place of an entire phrase or sentence

*C*hildren with speech
disorders often
need explicit
instruction to learn intelligible
speech.

(*sue* to indicate "Put on my shoe"). The listener has to rely on intonations, facial expression, gestures, and the social context to interpret the meaning of these single-word expressions. Children may also use one word to indicate a single, undifferentiated class of objects (*doggie* to indicate all animals).

After age two, children's language develops rapidly (Bloom, 1991). Their single-word utterances are replaced by speech more closely approximating the syntax used by adults when they speak to each other. At the age of two years, children ordinarily use expressions that average about two words in length; by the time they are five years old, their average sentence is up to about six words in length. At age two, they may have a vocabulary of several hundred words; by the age of five, they know many more, and their vocabulary continues to increase at a rapid rate. By the time they are about five, their speech is readily understandable by anyone. By the time they begin school, they are fluent speakers and have mastered most of the basic *morphological* characteristics of language (they can construct word forms such as plurals, verb tenses, and compound words correctly). By the time they are eight or nine years old, they have mastered all the *phonemic* components of language (their articulation of the speech sounds is correct).

We repeat: There is a great variability in the age at which children will demonstrate a particular level of speech or language performance (Bernstein & Tiegerman, 1989; Owens, 1986; Stoel-Gammon, 1991). The statements we have made may be used as guidelines for judging the adequacy of an individual's language development, but only as very general guidelines. For example, one should not jump to the conclusion that an eight-year-old who still makes a few errors in articulation and constructs a few incorrect plurals is significantly slow in speech or language development (See Nelson, 1993).

Theories of Development

Although no one knows exactly how or why children learn language, we do know that language development is related in a general way to physical maturation, cognitive development, and socialization. But the details of the process—the particulars of what happens physiologically, cognitively, and socially in the learning of language—are still being debated.

Carrow-Woolfolk (1988) and Nelson (1993) discuss six theories of language that have dominated the study of human communication at various times. Although all six theories have made significant contributions to our understanding of language and its disorders, not all are now equally popular among communication scientists. Neuropsychological theories were dominant in the 1950s, behavioral and information-processing theories dominated in the 1960s, and linguistic and cognitive organization theories were popular in the 1970s. In the 1980s and 1990s, pragmatic, social interactional theories have received the most attention.

Pragmatic theories emphasize that language is taught and learned through social interactions and that comprehending and producing language are equally important. The social and cultural contexts of language determine what language will be learned, how it will be learned, and how it will be used for communication (Hoffnung, 1989; Shiefelbusch & McCormick, 1981). The pragmatic view of language makes it extremely difficult, if not impossible, to separate language development from cognitive and social development (McCormick & Shiefelbusch, 1984; Nelson, 1993). Indeed, one of the limitations or criticisms of pragmatic theories is that "pragmatics is so broad that it moves into boundaries of all learning" (Carrow-Woolfolk, 1988, p. 83).

Theories of language development and research based on them have established the following:

- Language learning depends on brain development and proper brain functioning; language disorders are sometimes a result of brain dysfunction, and ways to compensate for the dysfunction can sometimes be taught.
- Language learning is affected by the consequences of language behavior; language disorders can be a result of inappropriate learning, and consequences can sometimes be arranged to correct disordered language.
- Language can be analyzed as inputs and outputs related to the way information is processed; faulty processing may account for some language disorders, and more effective processing skills can sometimes be taught.
- Language is based on linguistic rules; language disorders can be described as failure to employ appropriate rules for encoding and decoding messages, and sometimes these disorders can be overcome by teaching the use of linguistic rules.
- Language is one of many cognitive skills; language disorders reflect basic problems in thinking and learning, and sometimes these disorders can be addressed effectively by teaching specific cognitive skills.
- Language arises from the need to communicate in social interactions; language disorders are a breakdown in ability to relate effectively to one's environment, and the natural environment can sometimes be arranged to teach and support more effective interaction.

All of these theories contain elements of scientific truth as we know it, but none is able to explain the development and disorders of language completely.

All six theories have advantages and disadvantages for assessing language disorders and devising effective interventions. Pragmatic or social interactional theory is widely viewed as having the most direct implications for speech-language pathologists and teachers. We now turn to the disorders of speech and language.

LANGUAGE DISORDERS

As discussed earlier, speech-language pathologists have shifted their concern away from speech disorders. Much more interest is now shown in the disorders of language. The primary reason for the shift in focus from speech to language is the recognition that disorders of language are much more debilitating—they are much more at the center of difficulties in communication. The distinction between speech and language disorders is significant. It is possible for a child to have normal speech— to have acceptable voice, articulation, and fluency—yet not make sense when talking or misinterpret the meaning of what is heard or read. Speech has to do with intelligible vocal encoding of messages; language has to do with the formulation and interpretation of meaning. Language involves listening and speaking, reading and writing, technical discourse, and social interaction. Language problems are basic to many of the disabilities discussed in this text, especially hearing impairment, mental retardation, learning disability, traumatic head injury, and autism.

Classification of Language Disorders

Language disorders can be classified according to several criteria. The ASHA definitions on page 257 provide a classification scheme involving five subsystems of language; *phonology* (sounds), *morphology* (word forms), *syntax* (word order and sentence structure), *semantics* (word and sentence meanings), and *pragmatics* (social use of language). Difficulty with one of these dimensions of language is virtually certain to be accompanied by difficulty with one or more of the others. However, children with language disorders often have particular difficulty with one dimension. Language disorders involving these subsystems are illustrated in the box on pages 263–264.

A second scheme for classifying language disorders is by comparison to the normal developmental schedule and sequence (Leonard, 1986). The child with a language disorder may follow the same sequence of development as most children but achieve each skill or milestone at a later age. Some children whose language development is delayed will catch up and achieve all the language characteristics of nondisabled children, but at a later age. Others reach a final level of development significantly below that of their peers who do not have disabilities. Still other children are generally delayed in language development but show great discrepancies in the rate at which they acquire certain features of language. Differences in the development of a child with a language disorder and a normally developing child are outlined in Table 7–1. Notice that, in general, the sequence of development is similar for the two children, but the child with the language disorder shows slower development. Careful examination of the table reveals that the children show different relationships among certain linguistic features. For example, the normally developing child uses indirect requests when the mean length of her sentences is 4.10 words, but the child with the language disorder does not use them until her average sentences are 4.50 words.

ISORDERS OF THE FIVE SUBSYSTEMS OF LANGUAGE ➤

Oral language involves communication through a system of sound symbols. Disorders may occur in one or more of five subsystems of oral language: *phonology* (sounds and sound combinations), *morphology* (words and meaningful word parts), *syntax* (sequences and combinations of words), *semantics* (meanings or content), and *pragmatics* (use for communication). The following interactions illustrate disorders in each of these subsystems. Note that a given illustration may involve more than a single subsystem.

PHONOLOGY

Alvin has just turned 6. He is in kindergarten, but has been receiving speech therapy for 2 years. At 4, his parents sought assistance when his speech and language remained unintelligible and he did not appear to be "growing out" of his problem. He has two older siblings whose speech and language are well within the normal range. Alvin substitutes and omits a number of speech sounds, and in addition, he has difficulty with other subsystems of language as shown in the example below:

Clinician: I'd like you to tell me about some words. Here's something that you may have for breakfast: orange juice. What's orange juice?

Alvin: I doh noh. [I don't know.]

Clinician: See if you can guess. What color is orange juice?

Alvin: Ahnge. N you dink i. [Orange. And you drink it.]

Clinician: That's good. Tell me some more about orange juice.

Alvin: Doh noh.

Clinician: Let's try another. What's sugar? Tell me what sugar is.

Alvin: Yukky.

Clinician: Yukky? Why?

Alvin: Cah i wahtuns yer tee. ['Cause it rottens your teeth.]

MORPHOLOGY

Children with language disorders in the morphological realm will exhibit difficulty in either understanding or producing morphological inflections. These include the ability to add -s to change a word from singular to plural; to include 's to make a word a possessive; -ed to change the tense of a word from present to past; or to use other inflectional endings to differentiate comparatives and superlatives, among others.

Children with morphological difficulties will use inappropriate suffixes. . . . Here are a few . . . examples, taken from the test protocols of school-age children:

Examiner: Anna, say this after me: *cow*.

Anna: (age 6) Cow.

Examiner: Good. Now say *boy*.

Anna: Boy.

Examiner: Now put them together. Say *cowboy*.

Anna: Boy.

Examiner: Frank, find two little words in this big word: *outside*.

Frank: (age 7) Outside.

Examiner: Not quite right. We need *two* words.

Frank: (Shrugs and looks around the room)

Examiner: Well, if one word is *side*, the other would be . . . ?

Frank: Be?

Examiner: Jamie, can you tell me a story?

Jamie: (age 8) I can't think of none.

Examiner: What if the story began, "One night I walked into a dark haunted house . . . and . . .

Jamie: I met a ghost. He wanted to kill me. But he couldn't. I ran very, very fastest. And all of a sudden I saw a coffin. I hides in there. And all of a sudden there a ghostes inside there. And I sent out of the coffin. And then there weres a guy named Count. And then he tried to suck my blood. And then he couldn't find me because I hided. And then I met a mummy. And then he wanted to tie me up . . . and . . . that's all.

SYNTAX

Marie is 8 years old and in a special first-grade class. Her syntactical difficulties are demonstrated in the following storytelling event:

Clinician: Marie, I want you to listen carefully. I am going to tell you a story; listen, and when I'm done, I want you to tell me the story.

Marie: (interrupting) I don't know.

Clinician: I haven't told you the story yet. Remember, listen carefully to my story. When I'm done, you are to tell me everything you can remember about the story. One day Mr. Mouse went for a walk. As he was walking, he saw a cat lying in the road. The cat had a stone in his paw so he couldn't walk. Mr. Mouse pulled the stone out of the cat's paw. The cat thanked Mr. Mouse for helping him. They shook hands and walked down the road together.

Marie: Uh, uh, uh . . . Cat was on the road and Mr. Mouse taken out the stone his paw, and then they walked down together the hill and they said thanks, and they walk on the hill, and the mouse chase him.

This task of retelling a story reveals that Marie has difficulty not only in syntax but in the ordering of events and in accurate recall. Indeed, Marie seems unaware that she has modified the story considerably, including giving the story a new ending.

SEMANTICS

Clinician: Burt, tell me about birthday parties.

Burt: (age 6) Sing "Happy Birthday," blow away candles, eat a birthday cake, open your presents.

Clinician: All right. Now listen to this story and then say it back to me . . . tell me the whole story: "One day, a little boy went to school. He went up the steps of the school and opened the door. The boy went into his classroom and started playing with his friends. The teacher said, 'Time to come to circle.' The boy put away his toys and sat down on the rug."

Burt: A teacher . . . a boy played with a teacher's toys . . . time for us to come to circle . . . and it's the end.

You will note that Burt does not "blow out" candles; rather, his retrieval of information from semantic memory provides the response "blow away." In addition, it is clear that even the immediate retelling of a story, which in reality represents a string of events well within Burt's everyday experience, is very difficult for Burt. The pauses noted reflect the period of time during which Burt attempted to recall the necessary information.

PRAGMATICS

. . . Greg, age 7, interacts with his special education teacher. Greg is in a self-contained classroom for mentally retarded children and is one of the more verbal children in the class. Assessment by the speech-language pathologist indicates difficulties in phonology, syntax, morphology, and semantics. He has been identified as suffering from a significant language delay. On most language tests, he functions between 2:7 and 3:6 years of age. His teacher, who has visited his home many times, notes that there are no toys, no books, no playthings, and that there appears to be little communication between Greg and his mother, a single parent. The teacher is eager to draw Greg into conversation and story-telling, and has arranged a "talking and telling time" as part of the daily activities with the seven children who comprise her class.

Teacher: Greg, I'd like you to tell me a story. It can be about anything you like.

Greg: No me.

Teacher: Go ahead, it's your turn.

Greg: (having had previous instruction on "taking turns") No, s'yer turn.

Teacher: You do it. It's your turn.

Greg: I can't. I forget.

Teacher: I bet you can tell me a story about school.

Greg: You eat snack. What we have for snack?

Greg's teacher praises his contribution to the conversation and moves on to another student. She grins to herself; she and Greg have had a running joke about "turns." She feels that Greg tends to use "it's your turn" (when it is inappropriate) to delay the necessity to respond. This time she has enticed him into contributing to the conversation by requesting that he recall something that happens frequently within the school context. Greg attempts to comply, recalling from memory a favored episodic event—a small victory for both Greg and his teacher.

SOURCE: K. G. Butler, *Language disorders in children* (Austin, TX: Pro-Ed, 1986), pp. 13–14, 16–17, 19, 23, 28–29. Reprinted with permission.

A third way of classifying language disorders is based on the presumed cause or related conditions. Leonard (1986) notes that during the previous 20 years, efforts have been made to describe the language characteristics of children with mental retardation, autism, hearing impairments, and various other conditions. This classification scheme has not worked very well because the language problems of children with different diagnostic labels are often similar, and the problems of those in a given diagnostic category are often extremely varied.

Although a discussion of language disorders could be organized around the categorical factors shown in the box on page 258, it is important to note that for these categories "The real world does not often offer 'textbook examples' " (Nelson, 1993, p. 84).

Table 7-1 ➤ Pattern of Development Shown by a Child with a Language Disorder and a Nondisabled Child

CHILD WITH LANGUAGE DISORDER			NONDISABLED CHILD		
Age	Attainment	Example	Age	Attainment	Example
27 months	First words	this, mama, bye bye, doggie	13 months	First words	here, mama, bye bye, kitty
28 months	50-word vocabulary		17 months	50-word vocabulary	
40 months	First two-word combinations	this doggie more apple this mama more play	18 months	First two-word combinations	more juice here ball more T.V. here kitty
48 months	Later two-word combinations	Mimi purse Daddy coat block chair dolly table	22 months	Later two-word combinations	Andy shoe Mommy ring cup floor keys chair
52 months	Mean sentence length of 2.00 words		24 months	Mean sentence length of 2.00 words	
55 months	First appearance of -ing	Mommy eating		First appearance of -ing	Andy sleeping
63 months	Mean sentence length of 3.10 words		30 months	Mean sentence length 3.10 words	
				First appearance of is	My car's gone!
66 months	First appearance of is	The doggie's mad			
73 months	Mean sentence length of 4.10 words		37 months	Mean sentence length of 4.10 words	Can I have some cookies?
				First appearance of indirect requests	
79 months	Mean sentence length of 4.50 words	Can I get the ball?	40 months	Mean sentence length of 4.50 words	
	First appearance of indirect requests				

SOURCE: Reprinted with the permission of Merrill, an imprint of Macmillan Publishing Company from *Human communication disorders*, 2nd ed. by George H. Shames and Elizabeth H. Wiig. Copyright © 1986 by Merrill Publishing Company.

➣ specific language disability. Language disorders not attributable to impairments of hearing, intelligence, or the physical mechanisms of speech; language disorder of unknown origin.

➣ prelinguistic communication. Communication through gestures and noises before the child has learned oral language.

Among the categories listed by Nelson (1993; box, p. 258) is **specific language disability**, the term used for language impairments that are not attributable to impairments of hearing, intelligence, or the physical structures necessary to produce speech (e.g., oral cavity, tongue, larynx, diaphragm). Specific language disability means that the individual's language is impaired but we don't know why; we know only that it is *not* due to certain factors (e.g., hearing impairment) that are known to be causes in other cases. Nelson (1993) notes that specific language disability has been called by a variety of names, including *specific learning disability, minimal brain injury, developmental language disorder*, and so on. The definition has been a controversial issue and, much like the definition of learning disability, has been based on the exclusion of plausible causes. The cause of specific language disability is assumed to be a neurological dysfunction, although the exact nature of the dysfunction is unknown—again, a parallel of the learning disability category. Little wonder, perhaps, that professionals working in the fields of learning disabilities and language disorders have much in common when they consider definition, assessment, and intervention (compare our discussion here with our discussion of learning disabilities in Chapter 5).

Yet another classification scheme has been suggested by Naremore (1980), who relies on description of the language and related behaviors of a child. It is important to know (1) what language and nonlanguage behaviors the child imitates because much language learning is based on imitation, (2) what the child comprehends because receptive language is important in early learning, and (3) what language the child produces spontaneously because communication is the ultimate goal. With this in mind, we discuss four general types of language disorders: Absence of verbal language, qualitatively different language, delayed language, and interrupted language development.

Absence of Verbal Language

Some children three years of age or older show no signs that they understand language and do not use language spontaneously. They may make noises, but they use these for communication in ways that may characterize the communication of infants and toddlers before they have learned speech (i.e., they may use **prelinguistic communication**). For example, they may use gestures or vocal noises to request objects or actions from others, to protest, to request a social routine (e.g., reading), or as a greeting (Ogletree, Wetherby, & Westling, 1992). Some nonverbal individuals are extremely effective communicators. A case in point is "Genie," a 13-year-old girl whose absence of verbal language was likely the result of her being kept a prisoner in one room in her own home by her father, almost totally isolated from human contact from infancy (Curtiss, 1977; Rymer, 1992). Susan Curtiss, a psycholinguist who worked with Genie, described Genie's ability to communicate nonverbally as follows:

> "Genie was the most powerful nonverbal communicator I've ever come across," Curtiss told me. "The most extreme example of this that comes to mind: Because of her obsession [with plastic, likely due to the fact that there were plastic items in the room to which she was confined by her father], she would notice and covet anything plastic that anyone had. One day, we were walking—I think we were in Hollywood. I would act like an idiot, sing operatically, to get her to release some of that tension she always had. We reached the corner of this very busy intersection, and the light turned red, and we stopped. Suddenly, I heard the sound—it's a sound you can't mistake—of a purse being spilled. A woman in a car that had stopped at the intersection was

emptying her purse, and she got out of the car and ran over and gave it to Genie and then ran back to the car. A plastic purse. Genie hadn't said a word." (Rymer, 1992, April 13, p. 81).

Many nonverbal children are clearly disabled in other ways besides their lack of language. Some of them are known to be deaf or deaf and blind; some are developmentally disabled in obvious ways (i.e., profoundly retarded or brain damaged and physically disabled); some show bizarre patterns of behavior and may be diagnosed as autistic. A few of the children who fall into this category are normal in physical development, relate to other people in normal ways except for lack of language, and are alert to visual stimuli. These children seem to have a problem in processing or making sense of auditory stimuli. Usually, the reason for their disability is not clear, but the suspicion is that they have suffered neurological damage.

Children who have little or no useful language by the time they are three years old are usually considered to have severe mental retardation or severe emotional disturbance (unless they are deaf). Teaching these children to speak is one of the first goals in their education. Without functional language, they cannot become truly social beings (Lane, 1976; Warren & Abbeduto, 1992). Because nonverbal children often have severe retardation or autism, teachers of these children must have a working knowledge of how speech and language skills can be taught. The task is not the sole responsibility of the speech-language pathologist.

In the 1960s and 1970s, systematic efforts to teach language to nonverbal children consisted of the use of operant conditioning methods. That is, a step-by-step sequence of behaviors approximating functional language was established, and the child's responses at each step in the sequence were rewarded. The rewards typically consisted of praise, hugs, and food given by the teacher immediately following the child's performance of the desired behavior. At the earliest step in the sequence the child might be reinforced for establishing eye contact with the teacher. The next step might be making any vocalization while looking at the teacher, next making a vocalization approximating a sound made by the teacher, then imitating words spoken by the teacher, and finally replying to the teacher's questions. Of course, this description is a simplification of the procedures that were employed, but through such methods, nonverbal children were taught basic oral language skills (Devany, Rincover, & Lovaas, 1981; Koegel, Rincover, & Egel, 1982).

A major problem of early research on these methods was that few of the children acquired truly functional language, even after intensive and prolonged training. Their speech tended to have a stereotyped, mechanical quality and often was used for a restricted range of purposes. A current trend in language training for nonverbal children is to try to make their language *functional*. The goal is to give the child a tool for communication—a means of influencing and interacting with the environment. Instead of training the child to imitate words in isolation or to use syntactically and grammatically correct forms, we might train him or her to use a language structure to obtain a desired result. For example, the child might be taught to say, "I want juice" (or a simplified form: "juice" or "want juice") in order to get a drink of juice. The goal is to train the child to use language in a functional way in social contexts—to train *communicative competence* (McCormick & Schiefelbusch, 1984). Evaluations of the long-term effectiveness of early, intensive operant conditioning in which functional language is emphasized have shown that it produces dramatic improvement in the language of many children with autism (Lovaas, 1987).

The first consideration in such training is the arrangement of an environment that will give the child many opportunities to use language and that will provide immediate reinforcement for steps toward communication. This requires parents and teachers to work closely with a communication specialist. A second consideration in training is how to combine structure, content, and function—what is said and what is talked about or intended.

Today, efforts to teach nonverbal children to speak emphasize building natural acts of communication. Earlier intervention programs depended primarily on the use by an adult of highly structured, tightly controlled lessons in which the child was taken through a developmental sequence analogous to that of normal language development. Differences between the analogue and natural teaching methods used by Koegel, O'Dell, and Koegel (1987) are summarized in Table 7–2. Note that under the natural language paradigm (NLP) conditions, the emphasis is on pragmatics—using language in social interactions.

A recent development in teaching nonverbal individuals to communicate is **facilitated communication,** a strategy discussed further under augmentative and alternative communication (see pages 280–282). Facilitated communication has been used with individuals who have cerebral palsy and those with autism (e.g., Biklen, 1990, 1992b; Crossley & MacDonald, 1984). Facilitated communication is a controversial and as yet largely untested approach that may be suggested as an alternative to the systematic training that Lovaas, Koegel, and others have found to be successful with many children who have autism. As one advocate for children with autism has commented:

> I believe that the hype about facilitated communication and autism could lead to autistic children being denied access to the intensive systematic education interventions that are available for autism. The efficacy of these procedures has been well documented in the research literature. (Bettison, 1991, p. 563)

Qualitatively Different Language

Some children can make speech sounds with no difficulty and acquire an extensive oral vocabulary. The way they use words, however, is very different from normal speech. These children do not use speech effectively in communication. We give a few examples of qualitative differences in language that impair its value for communication.

Some children are echolalic (they repeat, parrotlike, what they've heard). An attempted conversation with an echolalic child might go like this:

Adult: Are you Johnny?
Child: Johnny?
Adult: Yes.
Child: Yes.
Adult: I'm Jim.
Child: Jim.
Adult: Right.
Child: Right.
Adult: What's your name?
Child: Your name?
Adult: No, *your* name.
Child: *Your* name.

➤ **facilitated communication.** A type of augmentative communication in which someone helps the communicator type by holding or touching the communicator's hand or arm.

Table 7-2 ➤ Differences Between the Analogue and the Natural Language Paradigm Conditions

	ANALOGUE CONDITION	NATURAL LANGUAGE PARADIGM (NLP) CONDITION
Stimulus items	a. Chosen by clinician b. Repeated until criterion is met c. Phonologically easy to produce irrespective of whether they were functional in the natural environment	a. Chosen by child b. Varied every few trials c. Age appropriate items that can be found in child's natural environment
Prompts	a. Manual (e.g., touch tip of tongue, or hold lips together)	a. Clinician repeats item
Interaction	a. Clinician holds up stimulus item; stimulus item not functional within interaction	a. Clinician and child play with stimulus item (i.e., stimulus item is functional within interaction)
Response	a. Correct responses or successive approximations reinforced	a. Looser shaping contingency so that attempts to respond verbally (except self-stimulation) are also reinforced
Consequences	a. Edible reinforcers paired with social reinforcers	a. Natural reinforcer (e.g., opportunity to play with the item) paired with social reinforcers

SOURCE: From R. L. Koegel, M. C. O'Dell and L. C. Koegel, A Natural language teaching paradigm for nonverbal autistic children, *Journal of Autism and Developmental Disorders, 17* (1987). p. 191. Copyright © 1987 by Plenum. Reprinted with permission.

Adult: Johnny.
Child: Johnny.
Adult: I'm Jim.
Child: I'm Jim.
Adult: No, *I'm* Jim.
Child: *I'm* Jim.
Adult: . . . Forget it.
Child: Forget it.

Other children may speak jargon or nonsense words that fail to meet the demands of social situations. Sometimes we find that a child understands what is said to him or her but almost never imitates speech or spontaneously produces it. Or when asked to imitate a sentence, a child may not be able to convey its meaning, as most children could. Naremore (1980, p. 156) gives this example: "'When asked to repeat the sentence, 'The little boy's dump truck is broken,' a nondisabled two-year-old said, 'Dump truck broke,' whereas a six-year-old with a language disability responded with, 'Boy is break.'" The child without a language disability did not imitate the adult precisely but chose words that preserved the meaning of the sentence. The child with a language disability could not convey the meaning of the sentence.

The qualitative differences we have mentioned so far are most frequently associated with severe emotional or behavioral disorders, mental retardation, or autism. Recently there has been interest in the language disorders of children with learning disabilities (see Chapter 5). The research to date has not pinpointed the ways in which the language of children with learning disabilities is different from other children's language, but it appears that these children are less capable than nondisabled children of making themselves understood (Hallahan, Kauffman, & Lloyd, 1985). They do not seem to comprehend language well or be able to adapt their language usage to the social context so that meaning is communicated. In talking to younger children, for example, they may fail to make their language appropriately simple. They may not understand instructions or the meaning of another person's statements. They may say things in social situations that most children would know are inappropriate. Finally, they may fail to understand or produce written language, even though their oral language skills are adequate (see Butler, 1986a; Wallace et al., 1992).

Language is always embedded in a social context. Its meanings and nuances can easily be lost by the producer or interpreter so that no communication takes place. Qualitative differences in language can seriously distort or obscure meaning or pragmatic value. These differences often occur in the language abilities of children whose social behavior and academic achievement are impaired. In fact, language disabilities appear to be closely connected with learning disabilities of all types. The implications of qualitative differences in language for remediation strategies are not presently clear. However, it is likely that an emphasis on the *functions* of language and *strategies* for comprehension and production will be most helpful in this area (Lahey, 1988; Nelson, 1993).

Delayed Language

A child may progress through the stages of language development with one principal exception: He or she does so at a significantly later age than most children. Many of the children whose language development is delayed show a pervasive developmental lag. Frequently they are diagnosed as having mental retardation or another developmental disability. Sometimes they come from environments where they have been deprived of many experiences, including language stimulation from adults, required for normal development.

It may be difficult in some cases to tell the difference between delayed and qualitatively different language because not much is known about the normal development of language and because qualitative differences may be very subtle (Nelson, 1993). Usually, children with delayed language learn language in the same way most children do, and their level of language learning approximates their level of general intellectual ability.

Interrupted Language Development

Children can *acquire* a language disorder after a period of normal development if their hearing or brain functioning is seriously damaged. Deprivation of oxygen, accident, or infection, for example, can result in damage to the mechanisms of hearing or to the brain (see Chapters 8 and 10). The specific effects of acquired hearing loss or brain injury depend not only on the nature and extent of the loss or injury, but also on the age of the child when the loss or injury occurs. A child deafened before he or she learns oral language will not learn language as easily as one who learned language before the deafness was acquired; and the more language experience a child has acquired before being deafened, the better his or her communication skills are likely to be. On the other hand, damage to the brain generally has more serious consequences when it occurs later in the development of language. The younger child's nervous system is generally more "plastic"—it compensates more easily for loss of or damage to its tissues.

Children whose language development has been interrupted by an illness or accident that damaged the brain are sometimes said to have **acquired aphasia** (Nelson, 1993). The terms *severely language impaired* and *severe language disability* are also used to designate the disabilities of children who have extreme difficulties in acquiring or using language, especially when the disabilities are known or thought to be the result of brain damage. Head injury is an increasingly common cause of language disorders, and language disorders resulting from head injury frequently complicate a student's return to school following physical recuperation (Blosser & DePompei, 1989).

> ➤ **acquired aphasia.** Loss or impairment of the ability to understand or formulate language because of accident or illness.

Strategies for Assessment and Intervention

We have already mentioned some of the considerations for assessing and correcting various types of language disorders. Here we provide a thumbnail sketch of the general features of language assessment and intervention. Only a brief sketch is possible because the assessment, classification, and treatment of language disorders are complex and changing rapidly. Although much research is under way, relatively little is understood about the disorders of this most complex of all human activities.

Two general strategies of language assessment are to determine in as much detail as possible what the child's current language abilities are and to observe the ease and speed with which the child learns new language skills. The first strategy typically involves standardized testing, nonstandardized testing, use of developmental scales, and behavioral observations (Wallace et al., 1992). Standardized testing has many dangers and is not always useful in planning an intervention program. But it can sometimes be helpful in making crude comparisons of the child's abilities in certain areas. Development scales are ratings or observations that may be completed by direct observation or based on memory or records of developmental milestones. Nonstandardized tests and behavioral observations are nonnormative in nature, but they may yield the most important assessment information. As Schiefelbusch and McCormick (1981) point out, the subjective judgment of an experienced clinician based on observation of the child's language in a variety of environments and circumstances may provide the most useful basis for intervention. Because language disorders vary widely in nature and are seen in individuals ranging from early childhood through old age, assessment and intervention are never simple and are always idiosyncratic (Nelson, 1993).

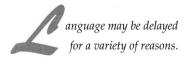

*L*anguage may be delayed
for a variety of reasons.

An intervention plan must take into consideration the content, form, and use of language (Fey, 1986). That is, one must consider (1) what the child talks about and should be taught to talk about, (2) how the child talks about things and how he or she could be taught to speak of those things more intelligibly, and (3) how the child uses language and how his or her use of it could be made to serve the purposes of communication and socialization more effectively. In arranging a training sequence, one might base instruction on the normal sequence of language development. Other sequences of instruction might be more effective, however, since children with language disorders obviously have not learned in the normal way and since research suggests that different sequences of learning may be more effective (Devany, Rincover, & Lovaas, 1981). It is more and more apparent that effective language intervention must occur in the child's natural environment and involve parents and classroom teachers, not just the speech-language pathologist (Bernstein & Tiegerman, 1989; Lahey, 1988; Nelson, 1993).

Educational Considerations

Helping children overcome speech and language disorders is not the responsibility of any single profession. Identification is the joint responsibility of the classroom teacher, the speech-language pathologist, and the parents. The teacher can carry out specific suggestions for individual cases. By listening attentively and empathetically when children speak, providing appropriate models of speech and language for children to imitate, and encouraging children to use their communication skills appropriately, the classroom teacher can help not only to improve speech and language but also to prevent disorders from developing in the first place.

Role of the Teacher in Language Use *(Pragmatics)*

The primary role of the classroom teacher is to facilitate the *social use of language*. Phonology, morphology, syntax, and semantics are certainly important. Yet the fact that a student has a language disorder does not necessarily mean the teacher or clinician must intensify efforts to teach the student about the form, structure, or content of language. Rather, language must be taught as a way of solving problems by making oneself understood and making sense of what other people say.

The classroom offers many possibilities for language learning. It should be a place in which there are almost continuous opportunities for students and teachers to employ language and obtain feedback in constructive relationships. Language is the basic medium through which most academic and social learning takes place in school. Nevertheless, the language of schools, in both classrooms and textbooks, is often a problem for students and teachers (Butler, 1986b; Nelson, 1993; Wallach & Miller, 1988).

School language is more formal than the language many children use at home and with playmates. It is structured discourse in which listeners and speakers or readers and writers must learn to be clear and expressive, to convey and interpret essential information quickly and easily. Without skill in using the language of school, a child is certain to fail academically and virtually certain to be socially unsuccessful as well.

The box on page 274 illustrates a problem in using language in school. Helping students like Tom learn to use language as a tool for academic learning and social relations is particularly difficult, because their language disorders seem to reflect basic problems in cognition—understanding or thinking. Teachers must use their own cognitive and language skills to devise ways to help such children learn more effective use of language.

Teachers need the assistance of speech-language specialists in assessing their students' language disabilities and in devising interventions. Part of the assessment and intervention strategy must also examine the language of the teacher. Problems in classroom discourse involve how teachers talk to students as well as how students use language. Learning how to be clear, relevant, and informative and how to hold listeners' attention are not only problems for students with language disorders, but also problems for their teachers.

One example of the role of the teacher's language in classroom discourse is asking questions. Blank and White (1986) note that teachers often ask students questions in areas of their identified weakness. For example, a teacher might ask a preschooler who does not know colors to identify colors repeatedly. Unfortunately, teachers may not know how to modify their questions to teach a concept effectively, so their questions merely add to the child's confusion.

The following exchange between a teacher and a child diagnosed as having difficulties with problem solving and causal reasoning illustrates this point.

Teacher: How could grass in a jungle get on fire?
  Child: 'Cause they (*referring to animals*) have to stay in the jungle.
Teacher: (*in an incredulous tone*) You mean the grass gets on fire because the animals stay in the jungle?
  Child: Yeah.
Teacher: I don't think so. What if there was a fire in somebody's house—
  Child: (*interrupting*) Then they're dead, or hurt.

LANGUAGE LEARNING IN THE CLASSROOM ➤

Observing group instruction within the later elementary classrooms can be most instructive. In the classroom described below, children's linguistic understanding is tested, and misunderstandings are resolved. (Note the importance of context. A different response might have been anticipated if the request had occurred in an obstetrician's office.)

Teacher: Okay, Tom. What's a contraction?

Tom: It's like when . . . a contraction . . . you contract stuff.

Teacher: Yes, but what does *contraction* mean?

Tom: (No response.)

Several students: (overlapping comments) I know! I know!

Teacher: (shifting her gaze to another student) Okay, Susan.

Susan: It's when you make something smaller.

Tom: Yeah. When the road contracts, it gets broken up. Our driveway got contracts and broken up.

Lisa: You mean "cracks up."

Teacher: But what about the kind of contraction we learned about yesterday?

Robert: Oh, a "word contraction."

Teacher: Yes. What is a word contraction?

Susan: It's when you make a word smaller.

Tom: The word . . . it gets broken up.

Teacher: Right. Excellent.

A commendation is also in order for this teacher, who skillfully manipulates the questioning so that Tom, who initially appears to be having considerable difficulty, is able to semantically map the correct meaning of the word and to not only gain insight, but share that insight with the remainder of the group. This interactive sequence of mutual discovery is an important step on the way to language success and truly literate students.

SOURCE: K. G. Butler, *Language disorders in children* (Austin, TX: Pro-Ed, 1986), pp. 40–41. Reprinted with permission.

Teacher: Yeah, they'd be hurt. But how would a fire start in somebody's house?

Child: By starting something with matches.

Teacher: A match, okay. Now do you think this could have started with a match?

Child: Yeah.

Teacher: This fire in the jungle? Who would have a match in the jungle? The animals?

Child: A monkey.

Teacher: A monkey would have a match in the jungle?

Child: (*nodding*) I saw that on TV. . . .

After seventeen more exchanges, the teacher gave up (Blank & White, 1986, p. 4.).

Alternative question-asking strategies can be used to help students think through problems successfully. When students fail to answer a higher-order question because it is beyond their level of information or skill, the teacher should reformulate the problem at a simpler level. After the intermediate steps are solved, the teacher can return to the question that was too difficult at first, as illustrated by the following dialogue:

Adult: Why do we use tape for hanging pictures?

Child: 'Cause it's shiny.

Adult: Here's a shiny piece of paper and here's a shiny piece of tape. Let's try them both. Try hanging the picture with the shiny paper.

Child: (*does it*)

Adult: Does it work?

Child:　No, it's falling.
Adult:　Now, try the tape.
Child:　(*does it*)
Adult:　Does it work?
Child:　Yeah, it's not falling.
Adult:　So, why do we use the tape for hanging pictures?
Child:　It won't fall. (Blank & White, 1986, p. 5)

Teachers sometimes do not clearly express their intent in questioning students or fail explicitly to delimit the topic of their questions. Consequently, students become confused. Teachers must learn to clarify the problem under such circumstances. As Blank and White (1986) have noted, "Teachers do not establish psychological comfort and eagerness to learn by making students spend as much, if not more, energy deciphering the intent than the content of their questions" (p. 8).

Teachers must also give unambiguous feedback to students' responses to their questions. Too often, teachers do not tell students explicitly that their answers are wrong, for fear of showing nonacceptance. Lack of accurate, explicit feedback, however, prevents students from learning the concepts involved in instruction.

Our points here are these: First, the teacher's role is not merely to instruct students *about* language but also to teach them *how to use it*. More specifically, the teacher must help students learn *how to use language in the context of the classroom*. Second, the teacher's own use of language is a key factor in helping students learn effectively, especially if students have language disorders.

Written language is a special problem for many students with language disorders. In fact, as students progress through the grades, written language takes on increasing importance. Students are expected to read increasingly complex and difficult material and understand its meaning. In addition, they are expected to express themselves more clearly in writing. The interactions teachers have with students about their writing—the questions they ask to help students understand how to write for their readers—are critical to overcoming disabilities in written language (Wong, Wong, Darlington, & Jones, 1991).

Finally, we note that intervention in language disorders employs many of the same strategies used in learning disabilities. As discussed earlier, the definitions of specific language disability and specific learning disability are parallel, if not nearly synonymous. Metacognitive training, strategy training, and other approaches that we discuss in Chapter 5 are typically appropriate for use with students who have language disorders.

AUGMENTATIVE AND ALTERNATIVE COMMUNICATION

For some individuals, oral language is out of the question; they have physical or cognitive disabilities in ways that preclude their learning to communicate through normal speech. A system of augmentative or alternative communication (AAC) must be designed for them. Franklin and Beukelman (1991) define augmentative communication as follows:

> Augmentative communication refers to the variety of communication approaches that are used to assist persons who are limited in their ability to communicate messages through natural modes of communication. These approaches may be unaided,

Collaboration

A Key to Success

ARDELL FITZGERALD

Speech-language pathologist, Montezuma Elementary School, Albuquerque Public Schools; B.A., Speech Pathology, University of Colorado; M.A., Speech Pathology, University of Colorado; Certificate of Clinical Competence in Speech-Language Pathology, American Speech-Language-Hearing Association

ELLEN BRUNO

Special education early development (SEED) kindergarten teacher, Rio Rancho Elementary School, Albuquerque Public Schools; B.S., Speech and Hearing, Indiana State University; M.Ed., Deaf Education, University of Miami

➢ **Ardell** My caseload includes twenty-nine children from kindergarten to fifth grade, both in regular education and a special education classroom. The speech and language disorders I work with include articulation, stuttering, voice, language/learning disabilities, developmental apraxia, and hearing impairment. I'm responsible for evaluation, diagnosis, and remediation. I also team-teach four days a week in a special education kindergarten class (eight children with a teacher and an aide) and pull out children in small groups who have been identified as having communication disorders from fifteen regular classrooms. I also meet with the school support team weekly to discuss interventions for children who are having problems in regular classrooms. I screen children referred by teachers, parents, and the support team and help make decisions about the necessity for diagnostic testing.

➢ **Ellen** Before assuming my present position as a special education kindergarten teacher, I taught children with hearing impairments for seven years, kids with behavior disorder for four years, and students with communication disorders for five years. Now I'm teaching five- to seven-year-olds who are more than two years below age level in at least one of the following developmental areas: cognitive, psychomotor, speech/language, or social/emotional. The SEED classroom has a maximum of eight children with special needs who are integrated with a group of sixteen "normal" children in a morning kindergarten program. An early childhood educator, two educational aids, and I team-teach all twenty-four children.

➢ **Ardell** We'll describe our work with Sara, a seven-year-old.

➢ **Ellen** I met Sara at the very beginning of the school year. I was pleased to have a second-grade girl in my all-boy class and excitedly asked about her summer. She beamed and rambled on and on. I had no idea what she was saying but politely nodded and commented, "Gee, that sounds like fun!"

➢ **Ardell** Sara's severely disordered articulation and language interfered with communication. Because of her developmental apraxia (difficulty planning and sequencing motor movements), she was almost 90 percent unintelligible to the unfamiliar listener. She produced many of her sounds in the back of her mouth, substituting /k/ and /g/ for the tongue-tip sounds. Not only her speech sounds but also her sentence structure was disordered.

➢ **Ellen** In the classroom, Sara was especially slow to tune into instructions. She needed to be alerted before she could take in information. Because of her low muscle tone and trunk support, she was unable to sit at her desk or on the floor for an activity longer than ten minutes. She was weak in understanding basic concepts. She had difficulty sequencing, retelling a simple story, following directions, predicting, and telling why. These problems were common to many of my communication-disordered students. Academically, Sara was on a readiness level in reading and on a first-grade level in math.

➢ **Ardell** Sara had many strengths. Her intelligence was normal. Her ability to understand language was better than her expressive ability. She was pleasant, cooperative, and willing to try a task several times. In spite of her communication problems, she readily initiated conversation with peers and teachers. At the beginning of the school year, Ellen and I discussed what we had learned about Sara from reports, individual assessments, and classroom observation. I shared information about Sara's speech patterns and disordered language structures. We decided that I could best address these areas in individual sessions in my room but that I would keep Ellen and others informed about Sara's progress so they could reinforce phonological skills in the classroom. For example, during reading sessions Ellen would know which words Sara could pronounce correctly. We also involved Sara's parents. I set up a weekly time for her mother to join our therapy session; she was very conscientious about participating in the sessions. Sara's father had severe cerebral palsy and was unable to model correct speech, but he often lent emotional support for Sara just by his presence.

➤ **Ellen** My job was to address many of the language concerns within the classroom. Ardell and I have similar philosophies about language intervention. We believe it doesn't stop when the speech-language pathologist (SLP) leaves the classroom or the child leaves the SLP's room. It goes on during math, art, and science, and throughout the day. One of our goals was to present information on a level that Sara could understand and respond to successfully. It was our job to make sure our "teacher talk" matched Sara's level. We were able to help one another analyze our own language and its effect on the children by giving one another feedback. Occasionally we video-taped lessons. Many times we had to adapt reading questions or directions on commercially made materials so Sara would understand the materials.

➤ **Ardell** Ellen and I wrote individualized instructional plans for all our students, including Sara. Ellen was responsible for the academic goals and I developed speech goals. We collaborated on the language goals because both of us would be implementing them. Many of the students in Ellen's classroom had communication disorders, so we set up a weekly forty-five minute period when we would team-teach a language lesson. Because we worked so closely together, we held parent conferences together.

➤ **Ellen** At the beginning of the semester, Ardell and I set aside a long planning time to map out the units we wanted to team-teach during the next few months. We used curriculum guides to help us choose themes in science, social studies, and literature. We also met weekly to write objectives for each unit. During our meetings, we would decide who was to make or bring the necessary materials to do the lesson. Sometimes we would take turns writing a script for the lesson.

➤ **Ardell** Another member of our team was the occupational therapist (OT). She was able to answer our "what-to-do" questions about Sara's sensory-motor integration problems. The OT worked with us during the weekly classroom language lesson and came to our weekly planning sessions.

➤ **Ellen** One of the most challenging aspects of teaming was keeping communication going when both of us had busy

> *. . . teaming requires a commitment . . . to set aside sufficient time to communicate about students.*

schedules. Many times we had planning sessions over a brown-bag lunch. We often didn't have enough time to plan our classroom activities and talk about needs of specific children like Sara. We sometimes talked during recess and sent quick notes back and forth about Sara, but we needed to develop a better system.

➤ **Ardell** We juggled our schedules, and toward the middle of the year we began meeting for team planning when Ellen's class was having PE. We started a "traveling notebook" for Sara in which parents, teachers, and specialists wrote daily or almost daily progress notes, questions, comments, and home and school activity suggestions for carryover of skills. The notebook gave us a way to communicate that included the parents. One of the most rewarding aspects of

working as a team was seeing positive changes in Sara and her classmates. We saw less fragmenting of learning and more generalization of skills. Sara's end-of-the-year evaluation showed substantial gains. Her receptive language skills were on her age level. Although Sara's speech was still difficult to understand at times, she began to generalize new articulation skills to her reading and spontaneous speech. Her reading level increased to first grade, and her math increased to second-grade level. Ellen and I shared Sara's triumphs—they made it worth giving up our lunch times! As a result of teaming, we became friends as well as colleagues.

➤ **Ellen** Students benefited from our teaming, and so did I. My positive experience made it very comfortable to step into a different teaming program this year at a new school. I'm now teaching a special kindergarten class with eight children and teaming with a regular kindergarten teacher with sixteen children. We have two aides. Our children are in the same classroom all morning. After the half-day morning session ends, my special education children remain in school and receive an additional hour of instruction from the special education team, including the SLP, OT, and me. Planning time and home visits are built into the program after 1:30 P.M. dismissal.

➤ **Ardell** One barrier to teaming is time. Especially in the beginning, teaming requires a commitment by the team to set aside sufficient time to talk about students. Another barrier is lack of clarity in sharing assignments and responsibilities. One team member can feel she or he is carrying most of the responsibility for planning and be resentful. Expectations have to be clearly defined.

➤ **Ellen** Another barrier is differences in philosophies and teaching styles. This can be overcome if there is a willingness to listen and learn from one another. The specialist may be uncomfortable in a classroom and prefer to do therapy in a private setting. Or the classroom teacher may feel threatened by the expertise of the specialist.

as in manual sign and adapted gestures, or aided, with utilization of communication boards or electronic devices. Regardless of the communication mode employed, the goals of augmented communicators are similar to those of natural speakers, that is, to express wants and needs, to share information, to engage in social closeness, and to manage social etiquette. . . . (p. 321)

Those for whom AAC must be designed range in intelligence from highly gifted to profoundly retarded, but they all have one characteristic in common—inability to communicate effectively through speech because of a physical impairment. Some may be unable to make any speech sounds at all; others need a system to augment their speech when they cannot make themselves understood because of environmental noise, difficulty in producing certain words or sounds, or unfamiliarity with the person with whom they want to communicate.

As Franklin and Beukelman (1991) note, manual signs or gestures may be useful for some individuals. But many individuals with severe physical limitations are unable to use their hands to communicate through gestures or signs; they must use another means of communication, usually involving special equipment. The problems to be solved in helping these individuals communicate include selecting a vocabulary and giving them an effective, efficient means of indicating elements in their vocabularies. Although the basic ideas behind AAC are quite simple, selecting the best vocabulary and devising an efficient means of indication for many individuals with severe disabilities are extraordinarily challenging. Since its founding in 1983, the International Society for Augmentative and Alternative Communication (ISAAC) has challenged experts from a variety of disciplines to devise better AAC systems (Schlosser & Lloyd, 1991).

A variety of approaches to AAC have been developed, some involving relatively simple or "low technology" solutions and some requiring complex or "high technology" solutions.

There are many different ways to provide an individual with a means to indicate the elements of his message, all of which are elaborations on combinations of two fundamental approaches: direct selection and scanning. With direct selection, the individual points directly to his selection in some fashion. With scanning, someone or something points to the items for the individual one at a time. When the item the individual desires is indicated, he or she gives some type of signal. The game "Twenty Questions" is an example of the scanning approach. Another example is a rotating arrow that the individual could stop. A person pointing to items one at a time until signaled by the handicapped individual would be another example of scanning. (Vanderheiden, 1984, p. 41)

An extremely wide variety of direct-selection and scanning methods have been devised for AAC, depending on the capabilities of the individual. The system used may involve pointing with the hand or a headstick, eye movements, or operation of a microswitch by foot, tongue, head movement, or breath control. Sometimes the individual can use a typewriter or computer terminal fitted with a key guard so that keys are not likely to be pressed accidentally or use an alternative means for selecting key strokes. Often communication boards are used. A communication board is an array of pictures, words, or other symbols that can be operated either with a direct-selection or scanning strategy. The content and arrangement of the board will vary, depending on the person's capabilities, preferences, and communication needs.

Speed, reliability, portability, cost, and overall effectiveness in helping a person communicate independently are factors to be considered in designing and

ndividuals whose motor disabilities preclude them from communicating orally can use augmentative communicating systems.

evaluating AAC (Beukelman, 1991; Nelson, 1992). Some systems of AAC are very slow, unreliable (either because of the equipment or a poor match with the abilities of the user), cumbersome, or useful only in very restricted settings. Beukelman (1991) notes that people typically think of the equipment and material costs involved in AAC, but that the real costs must include instruction and learning. A communication board will not necessarily be useful just because it is available. And the most sophisticated technological solution to communication is not always the one that will be most useful in the long run.

Today, increasingly innovative and creative technological solutions to the problem of nonvocal communication are being found. At the same time, the importance of making decisions on a highly individual basis is recognized (Bull, Cochran, & Snell, 1988; Calculator & Jorgensen, 1991). Until rather recently, AAC was seen primarily as a means of allowing users to demonstrate the language skills they have already acquired. Today, there is increasing emphasis on how AAC is used as a tool for teaching language—for helping AAC users not only to give voice to what they feel and know about specific tasks, but also to acquire increasingly sophisticated language skills (Nelson, 1992).

Users of AAC encounter three particular challenges not faced by natural communicators. First, AAC is much slower than natural communication—perhaps one-twentieth the typical rate of speech. This can result in great frustration for both the AAC user and natural communicators. Second, users of AAC who are not literate must rely on a vocabulary and symbols that are selected by others. If the vocabulary and symbols as well as other features of the system are not well chosen, AAC will be quite limited in the learning and personal relationships it allows. Third, AAC must be constructed to be useful in a variety of social contexts, allow accurate and efficient communication without undue fatigue, and support the individual's learning of language and academic skills (Franklin &

Beukelman, 1991). Progress in the field of AAC requires that all of these challenges be addressed simultaneously.

The need for AAC is increasing as more people with severe disabilities are surviving and taking their places in the community. As Franklin and Beukelman (1991) observe,

> a relatively large number of individuals communicate entirely or in part using an augmentative mode as they attempt to participate in their homes, schools, recreational activities, and employment settings. The number of augmented communicators is growing rapidly (p. 334).

As more students with severe disabilities are integrated into regular educational programs at all levels, the availability and appropriate use of AAC in regular classrooms become more critical issues (Calculator & Jorgensen, 1991). Although relatively few AAC users were found in higher education in the late 1980s, Huer (1991) noted that "access to technology for improved communication (both spoken and written) is a service that will become increasingly important to disabled university students" (p. 236).

The remarkable increase in the power and availability of microcomputers is radically changing our ability to provide AAC. New applications of microcomputers may lead to breakthroughs that will allow people with severe disabilities to communicate more effectively, even if they have extremely limited muscle control (see "Brain Speak" in the box on page 281). Furthermore, existing microcomputer software suggests ways of encouraging children to use their existing language skills (see "Special Effects" in the box on page 281). Technological developments will no doubt revolutionize AAC by the time we enter the twenty-first century.

Facilitated Communication

One type of AAC that emerged in the late 1980s and became very controversial in the early 1990s is called facilitated communication. This technique was first employed in Australia with students with cerebral palsy (Crossley & MacDonald, 1984; Crossley & Remington-Gurney, 1992). In brief, it involves physically assisting someone who is unable to type or point to vocabulary elements.

Facilitated communication was brought to the United States and used with people with autism by Biklen (1990, 1992b; Biklen & Schubert, 1991). Biklen's approach to facilitation has been primarily through keyboard devices; the user of facilitated communication is taught to type out messages one letter at a time using the index finger.

> The facilitator does not assist the communication user in making a selection of letters or other targets but may help the student to isolate the index finger and stabilize the student at the hand, wrists, or arm during typing, while generally pulling the student's arm back after each selection. (Biklen, 1992b, p. 16)

According to Biklen (1992b) and Biklen and Schubert (1991), the facilitator also provides initial training, maintains focus on the communication task, and avoids testing the competence of the student ("It is important to treat the person being facilitated as competent" [p. 46]). Eventually, if possible, the physical support is faded. For many students, continued physical support appears to be necessary.

AUGMENTING AND ENCOURAGING COMMUNICATION: MICROCOMPUTERS OFFER NEW POSSIBILITIES ➤

BRAIN SPEAK

Imagine a three-dimensional object rotating in space. Now relax and think of a landscape. Finally multiply two numbers in your head. You've just spelled out a three-letter word in a language that engineers at Colorado State University are developing to allow severely disabled people to communicate with computers.

The pattern of electrical activity in the brain can vary slightly with different mental tasks. "If an EEG is able to distinguish between these patterns," says Jorge Aunon, head of the electrical engineering department at Colorado State, "you immediately have the beginnings of an alphabet." If each pattern associated with a particular task represents a letter, a person can spell out a word in "brain-wave language" simply by thinking of a series of tasks.

Aunon tested the idea by taping electrodes to the scalps of five subjects and recording their brain-wave patterns while they performed five different mental tasks. A computer was able to identify the tasks from the patterns 95 percent of the time.

Nevertheless, when the experiment was repeated two weeks later the features of each person's EEG had changed, and the computer could not read them. But Aunon thinks this problem might be overcome by developing computer software that a user could "train" each morning to recognize his particular cerebral alphabet for that day.

SOURCE: From Brain speak by Andrew Revkin *Discover, 10* (6), (1989), 14. Copyright © 1989 Discover Publications. Reprinted with permission.

SPECIAL EFFECTS

Client: A five-year-old male with an unknown cognitive level but suspected moderate mental retardation was placed in a preschool program for children with multiple disabilities. He had no previous computer experience.

Communication characteristics: Mostly single word with occasional two-word utterances previously observed by his teachers and clinician. Attention to task during most school activities was reported to be poor, with minimal successful interaction with peers or adults.

Computer application: Muppet Learning Keys (Koala Technologies, 1984) is an alternative keyboard for children, which plugs into the gameport of the host computer. It consists of a large (18" by 18") tablet covered with colorful touch-sensitive control pads. The control pads, or "keys," represent the alphabet, primary colors, numbers from 0 to 9, and some specialized keys including a STOP key and a GO key. Accompanying software makes use of this special keyboard. During the Discovery Stage activity, for example, pressing the C causes a camel to appear on the screen. Pressing number 6 causes six camels to appear. Pressing the GO key causes the camels to prance on the screen (along with music), and pressing STOP will freeze this action. There is no prescribed order or directions to follow. If no keys are pressed, nothing happens. However, if *any* key is pressed, something happens.

Results: Much to the clinician's surprise, this child quickly assumed control of the *Muppet Keys* and maintained a high level of interest and attention to task throughout even his first 15-20-minute session with this program. He was able to shift his attention between the screen, the clinician, and the keys appropriately. Spontaneous two-word utterances and appropriate verbal imitations related to the activity were frequently observed, including appropriate verbal and nonverbal interaction with the clinician. He systematically explored the consequences of pressing the keys, quickly learning functions such as which ones would stop and start activity on the screen or change the color and number of items shown. His interaction with the clinician and the computer during this activity suggested better learning and adaptation skills than he had previously demonstrated during evaluations or instruction. Using this computer-based activity as a shared context, the clinician had a rich opportunity to address receptive and expressive language goals across several sessions.

SOURCE: From G. L. Bull, P. S. Cochran, and M. E. Snell, Beyond CAI: Computers, language, and persons with mental retardation, *Topics in Language Disorders, 8*(4) (1988), 68–69. Copyright © 1988 Aspen Publishers, Inc. Reprinted with permission.

Facilitated communication immediately generated controversy in the United States (Biklen, 1992a, 1992b; Calculator, 1992; McLean, 1992; Cummins & Prior, 1992) for two primary reasons: First, there are questions in many cases about just who is actually communicating; is the person with a disability really communicating, or is the facilitator subtly cueing or guiding the selection of letters or words? Some students will communicate only with certain facilitators. Little research has been done that tests the reliability of the method, and there is so far no satisfactory explanation for how or why the method works. Initial studies suggest that the facilitators often determine what is communicated (Cummins & Prior, 1992; Thompson, 1993; Wheeler, Jacobson, Paglieri, & Schwartz, 1993). Second, some people with disabilities who use facilitated communication have made claims that family members or caretakers have abused them—claims that have had serious consequences for the accused but have in some cases been difficult or impossible to verify (Seligman, 1992; Shapiro, 1992).

At this point, it appears that facilitated communication does allow some individuals to communicate rather well; for others, it has been of little benefit. It also appears that some advocates may have made exaggerated claims of the value of facilitated communication. Research and evaluation of clinical practice during the next decade will reveal the extent to which facilitated communication is useful and, perhaps, something about how and why it works when it does (McLean, 1992).

COMMUNICATIVE DIFFERENCES

An increasing concern of classroom teachers and speech-language clinicians is encouraging the communication of children whose cultural heritage or language patterns are not those of the professional's microculture (see Chapter 3 for a discussion of microculture). On the one hand, care must be taken not to mistake a cultural or ethnic difference with disorder; on the other hand, disorders existing in the context of a language difference must not be overlooked (Langdon, 1989; Nelson, 1993). When assessing children's language, the professional must be aware of the limitations of normative tests.

> Children who score below norms, not because they have speech or language impairments but because they have language experiences that do not match those measured by most evaluation tools, must not be labeled as handicapped. On the other hand, children from diverse cultural communities who *have* true language disorders must be identifiable (Bernstein & Tiegerman, 1989, p. 426).

A child may not have a language disorder yet have a communicative difference that demands special teaching. Delpit (1988) and Foster (1986) have discussed the need for teaching children of nondominant cultures the rules for effective communication in the dominant culture while understanding and accepting the effectiveness of the children's "home" language in its cultural context. Failure to teach children the skills they need to communicate effectively according to the rules of the dominant culture will deny them many opportunities.

Nelson (1993) notes that many students for whom language difference is an issue do not speak an entirely different language, but a variation peculiar to a group of speakers—a dialect. For example, one dialect that is different from standard English but not a language disorder is Black English Vernacular (BEV). BEV has certain features not shared by other English dialects because it originated from features of West African languages. Teachers must understand—and help their students understand—that BEV and other dialects are not inferior or limited language systems (Franklin, 1992). As we have already noted, however, students must understand the value of learning and using the language rules of the dominant culture (Delpit, 1988). Furthermore, it is critical that communication specialists and teachers keep recognition of language difference and language disorder in perspective.

> Difficult questions arise for language disorders specialists when they attempt to differentiate language disorder from language difference. Professionals may either "undercompensate" for language difference—and run the risk of identifying children as disabled when they are merely using language skills different from those tapped by most testing methods—or they may "overcompensate" for language difference, and assume that any child from a sociolinguist community that differs from the mainstream must not have a language disorder.... Both practices are discriminatory and must be avoided. (Nelson, 1993, p. 34)

A major concern in both special and general education today is teaching the child who is learning English as a second language (ESL), who is non-English proficient (NEP), or who has limited English proficiency (LEP). Bilingual education is a field of concern and controversy because of the rapidly changing demographics in many American communities (see Crawford, 1992). Spanish-speaking children are a rapidly growing percentage of many school districts (Fradd, Figueroa, & Correa, 1989). Moreover, a large number of Asian/Pacific children have immigrated to the United States during the past decade (Cheng, 1989). Many of these children have no proficiency or limited proficiency in English. Some of them have disabilities as well. Bilingual special education is "an emerging discipline with a brief history" (Baca & Amato, 1989, p. 168). Finding the best way to teach children to become proficient in English, particularly when they have disabilities as well as language differences, is a special challenge for the 1990s (Baca & Amato, 1989; Baca & Cervantes, 1989; Ortix, Yates, & Garcia, 1990).

SPEECH DISORDERS

As we noted at the beginning of the chapter, speech disorders include disorders of voice, articulation, and fluency. Remember that an individual may have more than one disorder of speech and that speech and language disorders sometimes occur together.

Voice Disorders

People's voices are perceived as having pitch, loudness, and quality. Changes in pitch and loudness are part of the stress patterns of speech. Vocal quality is related not only to production of speech sounds but also to the nonlinguistic aspects of speech. Together, the three dimensions of voice are sufficient to reveal a person's identity, and often a good deal about the individual's physical and emotional status as well. *Voice disorders,* though difficult to define precisely, are characteristics of pitch, loudness, and/or quality that are abusive of the **larynx;** hamper communication; or are perceived as markedly different from what is customary for someone of a given age, sex, and cultural background. Voice disorders that involve a dysfunction within the larynx are referred to as *disorders of phonation.* Disorders having to do with the dysfunction of the oral and nasal air passageways are called *disorders of* **resonance.**

Voice disorders can result from a variety of biological and nonbiological causes. Growths in the larynx (such as nodules, polyps, or cancerous tissue), infections of the larynx (laryngitis), damage to the nerves supplying the larynx,

> **larynx.** The structure in the throat containing the vocal apparatus (vocal cords); laryngitis is a temporary loss of voice caused by inflammation of the larynx.

> **resonance.** Refers to the quality of the sound imparted by the size, shape, and texture of the organs in the vocal tract.

*T*he voice must be
modulated
according to the
demands of a given situation. Some
disorders involve inappropriate use
of the voice, speaking too loudly or
softly for the requirements of the
situation.

➤ **cleft palate.** Condition in which there is a rift or split in the upper part of the oral cavity or the upper lip (cleft lip).

or accidental bruises or scratches on the larynx can cause disorders (Love, 1992). Misuse or abuse of the voice also can lead to a voice that is temporarily abnormal. High school cheerleaders, for example, frequently develop temporary voice disorders (Campbell, Reich, Klockars, & McHenry, 1988). Disorders resulting from misuse or abuse can damage the tissues of the larynx. Sometimes a person has psychological problems that lead to a complete loss of voice (aphonia) or to severe voice abnormalities. Voice disorders having to do with resonance may be caused by physical abnormalities of the oral cavity (such as **cleft palate**) or damage to the brain or nerves controlling the oral cavity. Infections of the tonsils, adenoids, or sinuses can also influence how the voice is resonated. Most people who have a severe hearing loss typically have problems in achieving a normal or pleasingly resonant voice. Finally, sometimes a person simply has not learned to speak with an appropriately resonant voice. There are no biological or deep-seated psychological reasons for the problem; rather, it appears that the person has learned faulty habits of positioning the organs of speech (Moore, 1986; Starkweather, 1983).

When children are screened for speech and language disorders, the speech-language pathologist is on the lookout for problems in voice quality, resonance, pitch, and loudness. If a problem is found, referral to a physician is indicated. A medical report may indicate that surgery or other treatment is needed because of a growth or infection. Aside from the medical evaluation, the speech-language pathologist will evaluate when the problem began and how the individual uses his or her voice in everyday situations and under stressful circumstances. Besides looking for how voice is produced and structural or functional problems, the pathologist looks for signs of infection or disease that may be contributing to the disorder and for signs of serious illness.

A speech-language pathologist is a highly trained professional capable of assuming a variety of roles in assisting persons who have speech and language disorders. Entering the profession requires rigorous training and demonstration of clinical skills under close supervision. Certification requires completion of a master's degree in a program approved by the American Speech-Language-Hearing Association (ASHA). You may want to write to ASHA, 10801 Rockville Pike, Rockville, MD 20852 for a free booklet, *Careers in Speech-Language Pathology and Audiology.*

Because of the emphasis on *least restrictive environment* or mainstreaming (see Chapters 1 and 2), speech-language pathologists are doing more of their work in regular classrooms and are spending more time consulting with classroom teachers than they have in the past. The speech-language pathologist of the future will need more knowledge of classroom procedures and the academic curriculum, especially in reading, writing, and spelling, and will be more involved in the overall education of children with communication disorders. More emphasis will be placed on working as a team member in the schools to see that children with disabilities obtain an appropriate education. Because of legislation and changing population demographics, speech-language pathologists of the future will also probably be more involved with preschool children and those with learning disabilities and severe, multiple disabilities. There will be broader concern for the entire range of communication disorders, including both oral and written communication.

Articulation Disorders

Distinctions between articulation disorders and phonological disorders are sometimes difficult to make. *Phonology* refers to the study of the rules for using the sounds of language. When a person has difficulty communicating because he or she does not use speech sounds according to standard rules, the disorder is phonological. *Articulation* refers to the "movements of the articulators in production of the speech sounds that make up words of our language" (McReynolds, 1986, p. 142). The distinction between articulation and phonological disorders is a technical one, and even speech-language pathologists may disagree about how a given individual's problem should be classified.

Articulation and phonological disorders involve errors in producing words. Word sounds may be omitted, substituted, distorted, or added. Lisping, for example, involves a substitution or distortion of the [s] sound (e.g., *thunthine* or *shunshine* for *sunshine*). Missing, substituted, added, or poorly produced word sounds may make a speaker difficult to understand or even unintelligible. Such errors in speech production may also carry heavy social penalties, subjecting the speaker to teasing or ridicule.

When are articulation or phonological errors a disorder? Deciding that errors represent a disorder depends on a clinician's subjective judgment. That judgment will be influenced by the clinician's experience, the number and types of errors, the consistency of these errors, the age and developmental characteristics of the speaker, and the intelligibility of the person's speech.

Young children make many errors in speech sounds when they are learning to talk. Many children do not master all the phonological rules of the language and learn to produce all the speech sounds correctly until they are eight or nine years old. Furthermore, most children make frequent errors until after they enter school. The age of the child is thus a major consideration in judging the adequacy of articulation. Another major consideration is the phonological characteristics of the child's community because children learn speech largely through imitation.

A child reared in the deep South may have speech that sounds peculiar to residents of Long Island, but that does not mean that the child has a speech disorder.

The number of children having difficulty in producing word sounds decreases markedly during the first three or four years of elementary school. Among children with other disabilities, especially mental retardation and neurological disorders like cerebral palsy, the prevalence of articulation disorders is higher than in the general population.

Lack of ability to articulate speech sounds correctly can be caused by biological factors. For example, brain damage or damage to the nerves controlling the muscles used in speech may make it difficult or impossible to articulate sounds (Love, 1992). Furthermore, abnormalities of the oral structures, such as a cleft palate, may make normal speech difficult or impossible. Relatively minor structural changes, such as loss of teeth, may produce temporary errors. Delayed phonological development may also result from a hearing loss. But most children's articulation disorders are not the result of biological factors. Nor can one say with confidence that they are the result of perceptual-motor problems or psychosocial factors. There simply is no satisfactory explanation for the fact that some children whose development appears to be normal in every other way persist in making articulation errors (McReynolds, 1986).

Parents of preschool children may refer their child for assessment if he or she has speech that is really difficult to understand. Most schools screen all new pupils for speech and language problems, and in most cases a child who still makes many articulation errors in the third or fourth grade will be referred for evaluation. Older children and adults sometimes seek help for themselves when their speech draws negative attention. A speech-language pathologist will assess not only phonological characteristics, but also social and developmental history, hearing, general language ability, and speech mechanism. Although speech-language pathologists' interest in phonological disorders has appeared to wane in recent years, with more attention being given to language, persistent phonological disorders may have serious long-term consequences. A follow-up study found that children with moderate phonological disorders persisting through at least first grade were different—28 years later—from a comparison group. Compared to those without phonological disorders, they tested lower in articulation, expressive language ability, and receptive language; however, they did not appear to have lower nonverbal reasoning ability or to have more personality problems than the comparison group (Felsenfeld, Broen, & McGue, 1992).

The decision about whether to include the child in an intervention program will depend on the child's age, other developmental characteristics, and the type and consistency of the articulatory errors. Phonological disorders are often accompanied by other disorders of speech or language; the child may need intervention in multiple aspects of communication (Ruscello, St. Louis, & Mason, 1991). The decision will also depend on the pathologist's assessment of the likelihood that the child will self-correct the errors and of the social penalties, such as teasing and shyness, the child is experiencing. If the child misarticulates only a few sounds but does so consistently and suffers social embarrassment or rejection as a consequence, an intervention program is usually called for.

Fluency Disorders

Normal speech is characterized by some interruptions in speech flow. All of us occasionally get speech sounds in the wrong order (*revalent* for *relevant*), speak too fast to be understood, pause at the wrong place in a sentence, use an inappropriate pattern of stress, or become *disfluent*—that is, stumble and backtrack, repeating syllables or words, and fill in pauses with *uh* while trying to think of how to finish what we have to say. It is only when the speaker's efforts are so intense or the interruptions in the flow of speech are so frequent or pervasive that they keep the speaker from being understood or draw extraordinary attention that they are considered disorders. Besides, listeners have a greater tolerance for some types of disfluencies than others. Most of us will more readily accept speech-flow disruptions we perceive as necessary corrections of what the speaker has said or is planning to say than disruptions that appear to reflect the speaker's inability to proceed with the articulation of what he or she has decided to say.

The most frequent type of fluency disorder is stuttering. About 1 percent of children and adults are considered stutterers. More boys than girls stutter. Most stutterers are identified by at least age five (Andrews et al., 1983). However, parents sometimes perceive their child as stuttering as early as twenty to thirty months of age (Yairi, 1983). The majority of stutterers begin to show an abnormal speech pattern between two and five years of age. Many children quickly outgrow their childhood disfluencies. These children generally use regular and effortless disfluencies, appear to be unaware of their hesitancies, and have parents and teachers who are unconcerned about their speech patterns (Shames & Rubin, 1986). Those who stutter for more than a year and a half or two appear to be at risk for becoming chronic stutterers (Yairi & Ambrose, 1992).

A child who is thought to stutter should be evaluated by a speech-language pathologist. Early diagnosis is important if the development of chronic stuttering is to be avoided. Unfortunately, many educators and physicians do not refer potential stutterers for in-depth assessment because they are aware that disfluencies are a normal part of speech-language development. But nonreferral is extremely detrimental to children who are at risk to stutter. If their persistent stuttering goes untreated, it may result in a lifelong disorder that affects their ability to communicate, develop positive feelings about self, and pursue certain educational and employment opportunities (Meyers, 1986; Shames & Rubin, 1986). "It is now recognized that early intervention is a crucial component of adequate health care provision for stuttering" (Onslow, 1992, p. 983).

Speech Disorders Associated with Orofacial Defects

A wide variety of abnormalities of the mouth and face can interfere with speech and language (McWilliams, 1986). Nearly all of these defects are present at birth. A few are acquired through accident or disease in which part of the facial tissues must be removed surgically. The defects can involve the tongue, lips, nasal passages, ears, teeth and gums, and **palate.** Any defect in the mechanisms of hearing and speaking can affect the development and use of speech and language. By far the most common orofacial defect in children is an orofacial cleft—a rift or split in the upper part of the oral cavity or the upper lip. (Cleft lip is sometimes referred to inappropriately by uninformed or insensitive individuals as "harelip.")

The prevalence of clefts varies from one racial group to another. It is about 1 in 750 to 1,000 births for Caucasians, but about 1 in 500 for Asians and about 1 in 2,000 or 3,000 for persons of African descent. More boys than girls are born with clefts (McWilliams, 1986). Orofacial clefts may result from genetic inheritance, mutant genes, abnormalities in chromosomes, or damage to the embryo during

> ➤ **palate.** The roof of the mouth.

development. Regarding causes and characteristics, Shprintzen (1988) notes that children with cleft palates are "a hodgepodge of children who have their clefts in common but little else" (p. 147). Therefore careful individualized assessment is crucial.

Assessment of orofacial defects and their implications for speech and language requires an interdisciplinary team of specialists. Intervention, too, must be an interdisciplinary effort. A pediatrician and a plastic surgeon are typically involved from the beginning. Frequently a child with an orofacial defect has health problems requiring consultation with other medical specialists. Dentists, audiologists, psychologists, and speech-language pathologists are part of the team required for adequate assessment and intervention.

Speech Disorders Associated with Neurological Damage

> **dysarthria.** A condition in which brain damage causes impaired control of the muscles used in articulation.

> **apraxia.** The inability to move the muscles involved in speech or other voluntary acts.

The muscles that make speech possible are under voluntary control. When there is damage to areas of the brain controlling these muscles or to the nerves leading to them, there is a disturbance in the ability to speak normally. These disorders may involve articulation of speech sounds (**dysarthria**) or selecting and sequencing speech (**apraxia**). Difficulties in speaking happen because the muscles controlling breathing, the larynx, the throat, the tongue, the jaw, and/or the lips cannot be controlled precisely. Depending on the nature of the injury to the brain, perceptual and cognitive functions may also be affected; the individual may have a language disorder in addition to a speech disorder (Blosser & DePompei, 1989; LaPointe, 1986; Love, 1992; Mysak, 1986).

In Chapter 10 we discuss the many possible causes of brain injury. Among them are physical trauma, oxygen deprivation, poisoning, diseases, and strokes. Any of these can be the cause of dysarthria or apraxia. Probably the condition that most frequently accounts for dysarthria and apraxia in children is *cerebral palsy*—brain injury before, during, or after birth that results in muscular weakness or paralysis. Vehicular accidents are a frequent cause of brain injury in adolescence and young adulthood.

The speech-language pathologist will assess the ability of the person with neurological impairment to control breathing, phonation, resonation, and articulatory movements by listening to the person's speech and inspecting the speech mechanism (Love, 1992). Medical, surgical, and rehabilitative specialists in the treatment of neurological disorders also must evaluate the person's problem and plan a management strategy. In cases in which the neurological impairment makes the person's speech unintelligible, alternative communication systems may be required.

EARLY INTERVENTION

Preschoolers who require intervention for a speech or language disorder typically have multiple disabilities that are sometimes severe or profound. Language is closely tied to cognitive development, so impairment of general intellectual ability is likely to have a retarding influence on language development. Conversely, lack of language may hamper cognitive development. Because speech is dependent on neurological and motor development, any neurological or motor problem might impair ability to speak. Normal social development in the preschool years depends on the emergence of language, so a child with language impairment is at a disadvantage in social learning. Therefore, it is seldom that the preschool child's language is the only target of intervention (Ensher, 1989; Nelson, 1993).

Researchers have become increasingly aware that language development has its beginning in the earliest mother-child interactions. Concern for the child's development of the ability to communicate cannot be separated from concerns for development in other areas (Ensher, 1989). Therefore, speech-language pathologists are a vital part of the multidisciplinary team that evaluates an infant or young child with disabilities and develops an Individualized Family Service Plan (IFSP). Early intervention programs involve extending the role of the parent. This means a lot of simple play with accompanying verbalizations. It means talking to the child about objects and activities in the way most mothers talk to their babies. But it also means choosing objects, activities, words, and consequences for the child's vocalizations with great care so the chances that the child will learn functional language are enhanced (McKnight-Taylor, 1989; McMorrow, Foxx, Faw, & Bittle, 1986).

Early childhood specialists now realize that *prelinguistic* intervention is critical for language development—intervention should begin *before* the child's language emerges. The first few months of life are a critical period during which the foundations for language are laid in the nonverbal "dialogues" infants have with their mothers and other caretakers (Nelson, 1993).

In the early years of implementing IFSPs, emphasis was placed on assessment of families' strengths and needs and training parents how to teach and manage their children. More recently, professionals have come to understand that assessing families in the belief that professionals know best is often misguided (Crais, 1991; Slentz & Bricker, 1992). Parents can, indeed, be helped by professionals to play an important role in their children's language development (Alpert & Kaiser, 1992). But the emphasis today is on working with parents as knowledgeable and competent partners whose preferences and decisions are respected (see also discussion in Chapter 12).

Intervention in early childhood is likely to be based on assessment of the child's behavior related to the content, form, and especially the use of language in social interaction. For the child who has not yet learned language, assessment and intervention will focus on imitation, ritualized and make-believe play, play with objects, and functional use of objects. At the earliest stages in which the content and form of language are interactive, it is important to evaluate the extent to which the child looks at or picks up an object when it is referred to, does something with an object when directed by an adult, and uses sounds to request or refuse things and call attention to objects. When the child's use of language is considered, the earliest objectives involve the child's looking at the adult during interactions; taking turns in and trying to prolong pleasurable activities and games; following the gaze of an adult and directing the behavior of adults; and persisting in or modifying gestures, sounds, or words when an adult does not respond.

In the preschool, teaching **discourse** (conversation skills) is a critical focus of language intervention. In particular, emphasis is placed on teaching children to use the discourse that is essential for success in school. Children must learn, for example, to report their experiences in detail and to explain why something happened, not just add to their vocabulary. They must learn not only word forms and meanings but also how to take turns in conversations and maintain the topic of a conversation or change it in an appropriate way. Preschool programs in

> **discourse.** Conversation; skills used in conversation, such as turn-taking and staying on the topic.

which such language teaching is the focus may include teachers' daily individualized conversations with children, daily reading to individual children or small groups, and frequent classroom discussions. In a program described by Roberts et al. (1989), "teachers were taught to use a high quality of interaction by modeling talk that was informative, reflective, and problem solving, and by responding to children in such a way as to acknowledge, comment on, question, and extend what they said" (p. 776).

Current trends are directed toward providing speech and language interventions in the typical environments of young children (Ensher, 1989). This means that classroom teachers and speech-language pathologists must develop a close working relationship, the specialist working directly with children in the classroom and advising the teacher about the intervention that he or she can carry out as part of the regular classroom activities (Wilcox, Kouri, and Caswell, 1991). It is also likely to mean involving the child's peers in intervention strategies. Because language is essentially a social activity, its facilitation requires involvement of others in the child's social environment, peers as well as adults. Normally developing peers have been taught to assist in the language development of children with disabilities by doing the following during playtimes: establishing eye contact; describing their own or others' play; and repeating, expanding, or requesting clarification of what the child with disabilities says (Goldstein & Strain, 1989). Another intervention strategy involving peers is sociodramatic play. Children are taught in groups of three, including a child with disabilities, to act out social roles such as those people might take in various settings (e.g., a restaurant or shoe store). The training includes scripts that specify what each child is to do and say, which may be modified by the children in creative ways. Goldstein and Strain (1989) reviewed research showing that such interventions have resulted in significant improvements in the quality of normally developing children's playtime interactions as well as in advances in language development of children with disabilities.

In summary, early intervention in speech and language disorders emphasizes the development of functional communication, not isolated skills. Communication is so intertwined with all areas of the child's development that intervention strategies must be made an integral part of the child's everyday world. Speech and language interventions for young children seldom involve activities that are best carried out in a clinic or separate setting. Rather, they are almost always interactions that must be programmed as part of the child's daily routines and typical interactions with peers and adults.

TRANSITION

In the past, adolescents and adults in speech and language intervention programs generally fell into three categories: the self-referred, those with other health problems, and those with severe disabilities. Adolescents or adults may refer themselves to a speech-language pathologist because their phonology, voice, or stuttering is causing them social embarrassment and/or interfering with occupational pursuits. These are generally persons with problems of long standing who are highly motivated to change their speech and obtain relief from the social penalties their differences impose.

Those with other health problems have suffered damage to speech or language capacities as a result of disease or injury. They may have lost part of their

**Facilitated Communication:
Who's Doing the Talking?**

*M*any individuals have remained frustratingly trapped in silence for most of their lives by problems related to autism, cerebral palsy, motor impairments, and various other disorders disrupting communication skills. In many cases, intellectual capabilities have been assessed incorrectly, with tragic long-term results, due to an intelligent person's inability to communicate.

With the recent development of a technique known as facilitated communication, a method of keyboard communication developed by educator Douglas Biklen, working with autistic children, poignant stories abound of individuals set free after years of imposed silence. The method seems fairly simple. Individuals type out messages on a keyboard using the assistance of trained facilitators whose role is simply to manually support their hands and wrists as they type.

However, not everyone in the special education field has been won over by this putative breakthrough. Wariness is perhaps part of the basis for their skepticism, particularly those working with autism cases who have seen their share of "fad" cures.

But the heart of the controversy over facilited communication is the question of who is actually doing the communicating, the individual or the facilitator. How can one be sure that the facilitator is not manipulating the client's responses in some subtle way, whether intentionally or not. For example, it seems reasonable that a facilitator anxious for a client to succeed might unintentionally become his or her "ghost writer."

- What kinds of controls might be effective to ensure that a trained facilitor's assistance is truly benign?
- In this age of electronic advancement, can you conceive of other methods of communication that may become available to those unable to speak?

speech mechanism through injury or surgical removal. Treatment of these individuals always demands an interdisciplinary effort. In some cases of progressive disease, severe neurological damage, or loss of tissues of the speech mechanism, the outlook for functional speech is not good. However, surgical procedures, medication, and prosthetic devices are making it possible for more people to speak normally. Loss of ability to use language is typically more disabling than loss of the ability to speak. Head injury may leave the individual with a seriously diminished capacity for self-awareness, goal setting, planning, self-directing or initiating actions, inhibiting impulses, monitoring or evaluating one's own performance, or problem solving (Ylvisaker & Szekeres, 1989). Recovering these vital language-based skills is a critical aspect of transition of the adolescent or young adult from hospital to school and from school to independent living.

Individuals with severe disabilities may need the services of a speech-language pathologist to help them achieve more intelligible speech. They may also need to be taught an alternative to oral language or given a system of augmented communication. One of the major problems in working with adolescents and adults who have severe disabilities is setting realistic goals for speech and language learning. Teaching simple, functional language such as social greetings, naming objects, and making simple requests may be realistic goals for some adolescents and adults (McMorrow et al., 1986). A major concern of transition programming is ensuring that the training and support provided during the school

*T*he classroom environment can provide students with many opportunities to sharpen their communication skills.

years are carried over into adult life (Falvey, McLean, & Rosenberg, 1988). To be successful, the transition must include speech-language services that are part of the natural environment. That is, the services must be community based and be integrated into vocational, domestic, recreational, consumer, and mobility training activities. Speech-language interventions for adolescents and young adults with severe disabilities must emphasize functional communication—understanding and making oneself understood in the social circumstances most likely to be encountered in everyday life. For example, Lord (1988) identified two primary goals for the communication of adolescents with autism: participating in age-appropriate social relationships outside the family and developing the ability to use language to pursue one's interests. Developing appropriate conversation skills (e.g., establishing eye contact, using greetings, taking turns, and identifying and staying on the topic), reading, writing, following instructions related to recreational activities, using public transportation, and performing a job are examples of the kinds of functional speech-language activities that may be emphasized.

Today, much more emphasis is being placed on the language disorders of adolescents and young adults who do not fit into any of the categories just described. Many of these individuals were formerly seen as having primarily academic and social problems that were not language related, but now it is understood that underlying many or most of the school and social difficulties of adolescents and adults are basic disorders of language (Wallach & Miller, 1988). These language disorders are a continuation of difficulties experienced earlier in the person's development.

• **Failure to understand instructions.** When a person has difficulty performing essential job or daily living tasks, consider the possibility that the person may not understand the language of instructions and may not have sufficient communicative skill to ask for repetition or clarification.

• **Inability to use language to meet daily living needs.** When individuals can produce enough words to formulate a variety of utterances, including questions, then they can travel independently, shop independently, use the telephone when they need to, and ask for assistance in getting out of problem situations when they arise. If persons cannot function in a variety of working, shopping, and social contexts, consider that communicative impairments may be limiting their independence.

• **Violation of rules of politeness and other rules of social transaction.** The ability to function well in a variety of contexts with friends, acquaintances, and one-time contacts depends on sensitivity to the unspoken rules of social interaction. One of the most frequently cited reasons for failure of workers with disabilities to "fit in" with fellow workers is their inability to engage in small-talk during work breaks. Examples that might cause difficulty are failure to take communicative turns when offered, or conversely, interrupting the turns of others; saying things that are irrelevant to the topic; not using politeness markers or showing interest in what the other person says; making blunt requests owing to lack of linguistic skill for softening them; failing to shift style of commu-

nication for different audiences (e.g., talking the same way to the boss as to co-workers); and any other communicative behavior that is perceived as odd or bizarre. If people seem to avoid interacting with the target person, referral may be justified.

• **Lack of functional ability to read signs and other symbols and to perform functional writing tasks.** The ability to recognize the communicative symbols of the culture enables people to know how to use public transportation, to find their way around buildings, to comply with legal and safety expectations, and to fill out forms or use bank accounts. Communicative specialists may be able to assist in identifying the best strategies for teaching functional reading and writing skills and encouraging the development of other symbol-recognition and -use skills.

• **Problems articulating speech clearly enough to be understood, stuttering, or using an inaudible or inappropriate voice.** Other speech and voice disorders may interfere with the person's ability to communicate. When such problems are noted, refer the individual to a speech-language pathologist.

SOURCE: Reprinted with the permission of Macmillan Publishing Company from *Childhood language disorders in context: Infancy through adolescence* by Nicola Wolf Nelson. Copyright © 1993 by Macmillan Publishing Company. p. 401.

> There is strong evidence now . . . that many young language impaired children will continue to encounter difficulties in acquiring more advanced language skills in later years and that these problems will be manifested in both social and academic realms. Thus children's understanding of figurative language affects both their ability to use slang correctly with peers and their ability to recognize metaphors that appear in language arts or English literature texts. (Stephens, 1985, p. v)

Classroom teachers are in a particularly good position to identify possible language-related problems and request help from a communication specialist. The box above describes for teachers several characteristics exhibited by older children and adolescents that may indicate a need for intervention. Addressing problems like these as early and effectively as possible is important in helping youngsters make successful transitions to more complex and socially demanding environments.

Some adolescents and adults with language disorders are excellent candidates for *strategy training,* which teaches them how to select, store, retrieve, and process information (see Hallahan et al., 1985, and Chapter 5). Others, however,

In Their Own Words JOHN UPDIKE

John Updike is one of the foremost literary figures of this century. Born in Pennsylvania in 1932, he has written over 36 novels, numerous short stories, essays, and magazine articles, as well as considerable contributions to literary criticism.

His autobiography, *Self-Consciousness*, describes many of the formative experiences of his life up to age 35, including his struggles with stuttering. The following passage describes the author's memories of his first experience with stuttering.

. . . . My first memory of the sensation is associated with our Shillington neighbor Eddie Pritchard, a somewhat larger boy than I whom I was trying, on the sidewalk in front of our houses, to reason into submission. I think he was calling me "Ostrich," a nickname I did not think I deserved, and a fear of being misunderstood or mistaken for somebody else has accompanied the impediment ever since. There seems to be so much about me to explain—all of it subsumable under the heading of "I am not an ostrich"—that when freshly encountering,

say, a bored and hurried electrician over the telephone, my voice tends to seize up. If the electrician has already been to the house, the seizing up is less dramatic, and if I encounter not his voice but that of his maternal-sounding secretary, I become quite vocal—indeed, something of a minor virtuoso of the spoken language. For there is no doubt that I have lots of words inside me; but at moments, like rush-hour traffic at the mouth of a tunnel, they jam.

It happens when I feel myself in a false position. My worst recent public collapse, that I can bear to remember, came at a May meeting of the august American Academy and Institute of Arts and Letters, when I tried to read a number of award citations—hedgy and bloated, as citations tend to be—that I had not written. I could scarcely push and batter my way through the politic words, and a woman in the audience loudly laughed, as if I were doing an "act."

SOURCE: John Updike, *Self-Consciousness*, (New York: Alfred A. Knopf, 1989), pp. 79–80.

do not have the required reading skills, symbolic abilities, or intelligence to benefit from the usual training in cognitive strategies.

Whatever techniques are chosen for adolescents and older students, the teacher or speech-language pathologist should be aware of the principles that apply to intervention with these individuals. Larson and McKinley (1985) note the importance of understanding the theoretical basis of intervention and summarize several additional principles as follows:

Clinicians must treat their adolescent clients like the maturing adults they are, engaging them as full partners committed to the intervention enterprise. Clinicians should recognize that many adolescents will need and will benefit from counseling regarding the impact of their language disorders on academic progress, personal and social growth, and the achievement of vocational goals. Finally, adolescents seem to function best in natural group settings, in which peers talk to peers and learn from each other. (p. 77)

Students with Communication Disorders in General Education Classrooms

WHAT TO LOOK FOR IN SCHOOL

As you know from reading the chapter, the term communication disorders encompasses a wide variety of speech and language disabilities. This section will focus on the communication problems experienced by students of near-average or above-average intelligence who do not have sensory or orthopedic disabilities. For information about modifications for students with sensory impairments and physical disabilities, see Chapters 8, 9 , and 10. Mild and moderate speech disorders may be easy to identify because they affect speech sounds. Common indicators of articulation problems include (Cantwell & Baker, 1987):

1. Omission of certain sounds from speech (e.g., "ca" for "cat")
2. Substitution of certain sounds for other sounds (e.g., "wabbit" for "rabbit")
3. Reversal of the order of sounds within words (e.g., "aminal" for "animal")
4. Difficulty in saying certain speech sounds (e.g., sh/r/th)
5. Frequent nonspeech vocalizations (e.g., clicks tongue, hums)
6. Difficulty performing oral movements (e.g., chewing, yawning)

Signals of fluency and voice impairments include (Cantwell & Baker, 1987):

1. Constant congestion or nasality
2. Constantly harsh-sounding or breathy-sounding voice
3. Continual hoarseness
4. Speaking in too-soft voice
5. Speaking in sing-song voice
6. Speaking in monotone
7. Unusually high or low voice pitch
8. Unusual pattern of stressing words in sentences
9. Struggling to say words (e.g. grimaces, blinks eyes, clenches fists)

In contrast to speech disorders, many language disabilities remain undiagnosed until children are in school. Listen for indicators of language problems such as (Shore, 1986; Wiig & Semel, 1984):

- Primary grades: Difficulty in following verbal directions; problems with preacademic skills (e.g., recognizing sound differences), phonics, word attack, and structural analysis; limited vocabulary
- Intermediate grades: Word substitutions; frequent confusion of language concepts such as "on" and "in"; confusion with verb tenses; inappropriate use of pronouns; difficulty in recalling the names of familiar objects and people
- Middle and high school: Inability to understand abstract concepts and multiple word meanings; difficulty in using grammatically correct and complex sentences; difficulty communicating information to others and in varying communication to accommodate listener differences

In addition, poor speech and language skills may affect children's social interactions and interpersonal relationships at all grade levels. Nowacek and McShane (1992) emphasize the importance of using language in social interactions and identify the following skills as essential:

- focusing attention on the speaker
- giving feedback to the speaker
- requesting clarification
- initiating and concluding conversations
- communicating in appropriate ways in different contexts
- giving information and making requests
- maintaining the topic of conversation and turn taking
- repairing breakdowns in communication

TEACHING TECHNIQUES TO TRY

Language problems such as those listed above can adversely affect students academically and socially. Teachers play an important role in assisting their students with communication disorders by providing appropriate language models and opportunities for communication and by using mediated learning strategies.

Providing Appropriate Models

Because students imitate the language they hear, it is important that classroom teachers model correct language usage, grammar, and articulation in their own communication. Teachers also can provide appropriate language models by reading fiction and nonfiction to students; making audiotapes of content area material available; and showing selected television programs on videotapes (Gearheart, Weishahn, & Gearheart, 1992). In addition, some teachers elect to model specific language forms. For example, during language arts, Mrs. Allison worked with a small group of students who were having difficulty with the format: *subject is verb + ing*. She showed them a picture of a child running and said, "The boy is running." After demonstrating this language format several times, she instructed the students to follow her model as they described additional pictures. She reinforced their correct responses and provided corrective feedback as they practiced in group and throughout the day.

Providing Communication Opportunities

In another approach to language instruction, teachers plan learning experiences in which students can actively use language. Increasingly they are selecting and implementing cooperative learning. In cooperative learning, students work together in small groups to reach a common goal. They are accountable not only for their own achievement, but also for the learning of other group members. This interdependence makes cooperative learning an especially effective technique for integrating students with disabilities into mainstream classes because it promotes communication and positive attitudes among diverse students.

To begin using cooperative learning in the classroom, teachers form groups of four or five students that are heterogeneous in gender, race, disabling condition, and academic skills. Then, they organize their classrooms by arranging the desks so group members can talk together and share materials easily. Several educators recommend discussing the concept of cooperation and other social skills, such as expressing opposition, in advance of using this approach to teach specific school subjects. Typically students work together for a marking period so they have sufficient time to develop and use cooperative skills with other members of their group.

To ensure all students have opportunities to use listening and speaking skills, teachers may implement number heads together (Kagan, 1990). In this form of cooperative learning, each student in a four-person group receives a number, 1 through 4. After posing a question, the teacher asks students to put their heads together to be certain each person in the groups knows the answer and can explain it. The teacher then calls one number, indicating that only students with that number may raise their hands to answer. This structure facilitates the participation of all students and does not allow a few individuals to answer most of the discussion questions.

Another type of cooperative learning is the three-step interview. Like numbered heads together, this structure provides an alternative to whole-class discussion. It includes the following steps (Kagan, 1990):

1. Within each four-person cooperative group, teachers form pairs and students conduct a one-way interview about the discussion topic;
2. Next, students reverse roles and the interviewers become the interviewees;
3. Finally, all students take turns sharing information they learned during the interview in a roundrobin fashion.

According to Kagan, this approach "is far better (than group discussion) for developing language and listening

skills as well as promoting equal participation" (p. 13). For additional information on cooperative learning methods, see *Circles of Learning: Cooperation in the Classroom; Cooperative Learning ; Learning to Cooperate, Cooperating to Learn;* and, *The Jigsaw Classroom.*

Mediated Learning Strategies

A third method of language instruction assists students to formulate more complex and specific messages and involves the teacher's using mediated or scaffolding strategies. In this approach, the teacher's role is to facilitate language use both by providing opportunities for language to be produced and by offering scaffolds to assist students to be active participants (Feuerstein, 1980). These scaffolds consist of procedures such as prompts, questions, and restatements (Norris & Hoffman, 1990). For example, during a class discussion on the revolutionary war, Mrs. Miller made language as it occurred naturally during discussion manageable for students with communication disorders by posing questions and providing prompts. These prompts indicated more information was needed and cued students about the type of information that was required. Some prompts teachers use include (Norris & Hoffman, 1990):

- Additive (and. . .)
- Temporal (and then, first, after, next, when)
- Causal (because, since, in order to)
- Adversative (but, except, however)
- Conditional (if, unless, if-then)
- Spatial (in, next to, which was on)

Norris and Damico (1990) point out that teachers also use mediated strategies to establish the content. Pointing to relevant cues in pictures, asking specific questions to help students formulate their ideas, giving students an opportunity to express their understanding of information, and helping students to relate ideas to their own experience are examples of strategies teachers typically use. For additional strategies see Norris and Hoffman's (1990) article "Language Intervention within Naturalistic Environments."

HELPFUL RESOURCES

School Personnel

Speech-language pathologists are responsible for providing therapy to students with communication disorders. For a discussion of the roles they play in the education of students, see p. 285.

Instructional Methods

Bashir, A. (1989). Language intervention and the curriculum. *Seminars in Speech and Language, 10,* 181–191.

Bernstein, D. K., & Tiegerman, E. (1989). *Language and communications disorders in children* (2nd ed.), Columbus, OH: Merrill.

Butler, K. G. (Ed.). (1991). *Communicating for learning.* Gaithersburg, MD: Aspen.

Buttrill, J., Niizawa, J., Biemer, C., Takahashi, C., & Hearn, S. (1989). Serving the language learning disabled adolescent: A strategies-based model. *Language, Speech, and Hearing Services in Schools, 20*, 185–204.

Cantwell, D. P., & Baker, L. (1987). *Developmental speech and language disorders.* New York: The Guilford Press.

Cheng, L. L. (1989). Intervention strategies: A multicultural approach. *Topics in Language Disorders, 9*(3), 84–91.

Christensen, S. S., & Luckett, C. H. (1990). Getting into the classroom and making it work. *Language, Speech, and Hearing Services in Schools, 21*, 110–113.

Creaghead, N. A., Newman, P. W., & Secord, W. A. (1989). *Assessment and remediation of articulatory and phonological disorders* (2nd ed.). Columbus, OH: Merrill/Macmillan.

Fey, M. E. (1986). *Language intervention with young children.* San Diego, CA: College-Hill Press.

Gruenewalk, L. J., & Pollak, S. A. (1990). *Language interaction in curriculum and instruction* (2nd ed.). Austin, TX: Pro–Ed.

Lovinger, S. L. (1991). Language learning disabilities: *A new and practical approach for those who work with children and their families.* New York: Continuum.

Haynes, W. O., Moran, M. J., & Pindzola, R. H. (1990). *Communication disorders in the classroom.* Dubuque, IA: Kendall/Hunt.

Hurvitz, J. A., Pickert, S. M., & Rilla, D. C. (1987). Promoting children's language intervention. *Teaching Exceptional Children, 19*, 12–15.

Larson, V. L., & McKinley, N. L. (1987). *Communication assessment and intervention strategies for adolescents.* Eau Claire, WI: Thinking Publications.

Lindsfors, J. W. (1987). *Children's language and learning* (2nd ed.). Englewood-Cliffs, NJ: Prentice-Hall.

Mannix, D. (1987). *Oral language activities for special children.* West Nyack, NY: The Center for Applied Research in Education.

McCormick, L. & Schiefelbusch, R. L. (1990). *Early language intervention* (2nd ed.). Columbus, OH: Merrill/Macmillan.

Nelson, D. C. (1991). *Practical procedures for children with language disorders: Preschool-adolescence.* Austin, TX: Pro-ed.

Norris, J. A. (1989). Providing language remediation in the classroom: An integrated language-to-reading intervention model. *Language, Speech, and Hearing Services in Schools. 20*, 205–217.

Norris, J. A., & Hoffman, P. R. (1990). Language intervention within naturalistic environments. *Language, Speech, and Hearing Services in Schools, 21*, 72–84.

Owens, R. E. (1991). *Language disorders: A functional approach to assessment and intervention.* New York: Merrill/Macmillan.

Oyer, H. J., Crowe, B. J., Haas, W. H. (1987). *Speech, language, and hearing disorders: A guide for the teacher.* Boston: Little, Brown & Company.

Schiefelbusch, R. L., & Lloyd L. L. (Eds.). (1988). *Language perspectives: Acquisition, retardation, and intervention.* Austin, TX: Pro-Ed.

Silliman, E. R., & Wilkinson, L. C. (1991). *Communicating for learning: Classroom observation and collaboration.* Gaithersburg, MD: Aspen.

Wiig, E. H. (1990). Linguistic transitions and learning disabilities: A strategic learning perspective. *Learning Disability Quarterly, 13*, 128–140.

Wiig, E. H. (1984). *Language assessment and intervention for the learning disabled* (2nd ed.). Columbus, OH: Merrill/Macmillan.

Curricular and Instructional Materials

Auslin, M. S. (1989). *Idiom Workbook Series,* Austin, TX: Pro-Ed.

Bloomin' series provides activities to improve pragmatics by focusing on such areas as holidays, recipes, experiments, and language arts. LinguiSystems, 3100 Fourth Avenue, P. O. Box 747, East Moline, IL.

Flowers, A. M. (1986). *The big book of language through sounds* (3rd ed.), Austin, TX: Pro-Ed.

Frimmer, B. (1986). *Sounds and language: A work/play approach.* Danville, IL: Interstate Printers and Publishers.

Help Series includes exercises in areas such as language processing, concepts, paraphrasing, problem-solving, and pragmatics, LinguiSystems, 3100 Fourth Avenue, P. O. Box 747, East Moline, IL.

Holloway, J. A. (1987). *Aunt Amanda: On cloud nine and other idioms and expressions.* Danville, IL: Interstate Printers and Publishers.

Johnston, E. B., Weinrich, B. D., & Johnson, A. R. (1984). *A sourcebook of pragmatic activities: Theory and intervention for language therapy (PK-6).* Tucson, AZ: Communication Skill Builders.

Kagan, A. (1981). *"Teach 'n' reach" communicatively handicapped: Hearing impaired, language impaired* (Book 2 out of 4). La Mesa, CA: La Mesa-Spring Valley School District, Special Programs Department, 4750 Date Avenue, La Mesa, CA 92041.

McKinley, N. L., & Lord-Larson, V. (1985). Neglected language-disordered adolescent: A delivery model. *Language, Speech, and Hearing Services in Schools, 16*, 2–15.

Weinrich, B. D., Glaser, A. J., & Johnston, E. B. (1986). *A sourcebook of adolescent pragmatic activities: Theory and intervention for language therapy (Grades 7–12 and ESL).* Tucson, AZ: Communication Skill Builders.

Wiig, E. H., & Bray, C. W. (1983). *Let's talk for children.* San Antonio, TX: The Psychological Corporation.

Wiig, E. H. (1985). *Words, expression and contexts: A figurative language program.* San Antonio, TX: The Psychological Corporation.

Literature about Individuals with Communication Disorders

ELEMENTARY

Arthur, R. (1985). *The three investigators in the mystery of the stuttering parrot.* New York: Random House. (Ages 9–12) (Fiction=F)

Brown, A., & Forsberg, G. (1989). *Lost boys never say die.* New York: Delacorte Press. (Ages 9–12) (F)

Bunting, E. (1980). *Blackbird singing*. New York: Macmillan. (Ages 9–12) (F)

Corrigan, K. (1984). *Emily, Emily*. Toronto: Annick Press. (Elementary)(Stuttering) (F)

Cosgrove, S. (1983). *Creole*. Los Angeles: Price Stern Sloan. (Elementary) (Stuttering) (F)

Hague, K. (1985). *The legend of the veery bird*. New York: Harcourt, Brace, Jovanovich. (Elementary) (Stuttering) (F)

Knopp, P. (1980). *Wilted*. New York: Coward, McCann & Geoghegan. (Ages 9–12) (F)

SECONDARY

Berger, G. (1981). *Speech and language disorders*. New York: Franklin-Watts. (Ages 13–18) (Nonfiction=NF).

Evans , J. (1983). *An uncommon gift*. Philadelphia, PA: Westminister. (Ages 13–18) (NF).

Computer Software

Alphabet Sounds, Data Command, P. O. Box 548, Kankakee, IL 60901, (800) 528–7390.

Basic Vocabulary Builder on Computer, Ballard & Tighe, Inc., 480 Atlas Street, Brea, CA 92621, (714) 321–4332.

Drills in Language Concepts, College–Hill Press, 4284 41st Street, San Diego, CA, (800) 854–2541.

Fish Scales, DLM Teaching Resources, One DLM Park, Allen, TX, 75002, (800) 527–5030. (Weight, length, and distance measurement)

Grammar Grelims, Davidson & Associates, 19840 Pioneer Ave., Torrance, CA 90505, (800) 545–7677.

I Can Talk, Soft Cole, 1804 Mississippi, Lawrence, KS 66044, (913) 842–6044.

Idioms in America, Communication Skill Builders, P. O. Box 42050, Tucson, AZ 85733, (602) 323–7500.

Language L.A.B., Specialsoft, P. O. Box 1983, Santa Monica, CA 90406, (800) 421–6534.

New Talking Sitckybear Opposites, Optimum Resources, Inc., 10 Station Pl, Norfolk, CT 06058, (800) 327–1473.

Paint with Words, MECC, 3490 Lexington Avenue North, St. Paul, MN 55126, (800) 228–3504.

Reading Around Words Program, Instructional/ Communications Technology, Inc. 10 Stepar Place, Huntington Station, NY 11746, (800) CALL-ICT.

Sight Word Spelling, Exceptional Children's Software, P. O. Box 487, Hays, KS 67601, (913) 625–9281.

Soft Text: Word Study, Continental Press, Inc, 520 East Bainbridge Street, Elizabethtown, PA 17022, (800) 233–0759.

Study Buddy, Access Unlimited-Speech Enterprises, 3535 Briarpark Drive Ste. 102, Houston, TX 77024, (800) 848–0311.

Talk About a Walk. College-Hill Press, 4284 41st Street, San Diego, CA 92105, (800) 854–2541.

Talking Textwriter, Scholastic Software, 730 Broadway, Dept. JS, New York, NY 10003, (800) 541–5513.

Understanding Questions I and II, Sunset Software, 9277 East Corrine Drive, Scottsdale, AZ 85260, (602) 451–0753.

Understanding Sentences II: Abstract Meanings, Sunset Software, 9277 East Corrine Drive, Scottsdale, AZ 85260, (602) 451–0753.

Organizations

American Speech-Language-Hearing Association, 10801 Rockville Pike, Rockville, MD 20852, (301) 897–5700.

Division for Children with Communication Disorders, Council for Exceptional Children, 1920 Association Drive, Reston, VA 22091.

BIBLIOGRAPHY FOR TEACHING SUGGESTIONS

Aronson, E., Blaney, N., Stephan, C., Skies, J., & Snapp, M. (1978). *The jigsaw classroom*. Beverly Hills, CA: Sage.

Cantwell, D. P., & Baker, L. (1987). *Developmental speech and language disorders*. New York: The Guilford Press.

Feuerstein, R. (1980). *Instrumental enrichment: An intervention program for cognitive modifiability*. Baltimore, MD: University Park Press.

Gearheart, B. R., Weishahn, M. W., & Gearheart, C. J. (1992). *The exceptional student in the regular classroom* (5th ed.). New York: Merrill.

Johnson, D. W. & Johnson, R. T., Holubes, E. J., & Roy, P. (1984). *Circles of learning: Cooperation in the classroom*. Washington, D. C.: Association for Supervision and Curriculum Development.

Kagan. S.(1985). Dimension of cooperative classroom structures. In R. Slavin, S. Sharan, S. Kagan, R. Hertz Lazowitz, C. Webb, & R. Schmuck (Eds.), *Learning to cooperate, cooperating to learn*. New York: Plenum.

Kagan, S. (1990). The structured approach to cooperative learning. *Educational Leadership, 47*, 12–15.

Norris, J., & Damico, J. S. (1990). Whole language in theory and practice: Implications for language intervention. *Language, Speech, and Hearing Services in Schools, 21*, 212–220.

Norris, J., & Hoffman, P. R. (1990). Language intervention within naturalistic environments. *Language, Speech, and Hearing Services in Schools, 21*, 72–84.

Nowacek, E. J., & McShane, E. (1992). Oral language. In E. Polloway and J. Patton (Eds.), *Strategies for teaching learners with special needs* (5th ed.). New York: Merrill.

Shore, K. (1986). *The special education handbook*. New York: Teachers College Press.

Slavin, R. E. (1990). *Cooperative learning: Theory, research and practice*. Englewood Cliffs, NJ: Prentice-Hall.

Wiig, E. H., & Semel, E. (1984). *Language assessment and intervention for the learning disabled* (2nd ed.), Columbus, OH: Merrill.Wiig, E. H., & Semel, E. (1984). Language assessment and intervention for the learning disabled (2nd ed.), Columbus, OH: Merrill.

Summary

Communication requires sending and receiving meaningful messages. Language is the communication of ideas through an arbitrary system of symbols that are used according to rules. Speech is the behavior of forming and sequencing the sounds of oral language. Communication disorders may involve language or speech or both. The prevalence of communication disorders is difficult to determine, but disorders of speech and language are among the most common disabilities of children.

Language development begins with first mother-child interactions. The sequence of language development is fairly well understood, but relatively little is known about how and why children learn language. Some theories of language development include the following major ideas: Language learning depends on brain development and proper brain functioning; language learning is affected by the consequences of language behavior; language is learned from inputs and outputs related to information processing; language learning is based on linguistic rules; language is one of many cognitive (thinking) skills; language arises from the need to communicate in social interactions. Research supports some aspects of all theories, but social interactional or pragmatic theory is now accepted as having the most important implications for speech-language pathologists and teachers.

Today, more attention is given to language disorders because they are more debilitating. They may be classified in several ways. One classification is based on the five subsystems of language: phonology, morphology, syntax, semantics, and pragmatics. Other classifications are based on comparisons between normal and delayed language or on the presumed causes of disorders or related conditions. Another type of classification includes: the child has not developed any verbal language; the child's language qualitatively differs from normal language; follows the normal pattern of development but is delayed; development is interrupted.

Assessment and intervention in language disorders require standardized testing and more informal clinical judgments. An intervention plan must consider what the child talks about and should talk about, how the child talks and should speak to become more intelligible, and how the child uses language for communication and socialization. Helping children learn to use language effectively is not the task of any single professional group. Speech-language pathologists now regularly work with classroom teachers to make language learning an integral part of classroom teaching.

Augmentative or alternative communications systems are needed for those whose physical or cognitive disabilities preclude oral language. These systems create a way to select or scan an array of pictures, words, or other symbols. Microcomputers have radically changed augmentative communication. Facilitated communication, a recent and controversial approach to augmented communication that has not been fully tested.

Dialect or native language differences must not be mistaken for language disorders. However, the language disorders of children with communicative differences must not be overlooked. Bilingual special education is an emerging discipline as more children have little or no proficiency in English.

Children may have more than one type of speech disorder, and disorders of speech may occur along with language disorders. Voice disorders may involve pitch, loudness, and quality of phonation, which may be unpleasant to the listener, interfere with communication, or abuse the larynx. Articulation or phonological disorders involve omission, substitution, distortion, or addition of word sounds, making speech difficult to understand. The most common fluency disorder is stuttering. Speech disorders associated with orofacial clefts (cleft palate or cleft lip) typically involve articulation and voice problems. Neurological damage can affect people's speech by making it difficult for them to make the voluntary movements required.

Children requiring early intervention for speech and language disorders typically have severe or multiple disabilities. A young child's ability to communicate cannot be separated from other areas of development. Consequently, early language intervention involves all social interactions between a child and his or her caretakers and peers, and emphasizes functional communication in the child's natural environment.

Adolescents and young adults with speech and language disorders may be self-referred, have health problems, or have multiple and severe disabilities. Transition programming has provided for the carryover of training and support during the school years into adult life. Emphasis today is on functional communication skills taught in naturalistic settings. Language disorders among young children are the basis for academic and social learning problems in later years.

MARY THORNLEY

Mary Thornley, a nationally recognized visual artist who is hearing impaired (see also Chapters 1 and 12), had her work exhibited in "Art Across America" which had its opening in Washington, DC as part of the Presidential Inaugural festivities in January 1993.

*N*o deaf child who has earnestly tried to speak the words which he has never heard—to come out of the prison of silence, where no tone of love, no song of bird, no strain of music ever pierces the stillness—can forget the thrill of surprise, the joy of discovery which came over him when he uttered his first word. Only such a one can appreciate the eagerness with which I talked to my toys, to stones, trees, birds and dumb animals, or the delight I felt when at my call Mildred ran to me or my dogs obeyed my commands. It is an unspeakable boon to me to be able to speak in winged words that need no interpretation.

➤ Helen Keller
The Story of My Life

Hearing Impairment

▲ ▲ ▲

*A*lthough Helen Keller's achievements were unique in the truest sense of the word, the emotions she conveys here are not (see page 301). The child who is deaf who does acquire the ability to speak must certainly experience a "joy of discovery" similar to Keller's. Hearing impairment is a great barrier to the normal development of the English language. As we will see, even if the impairment is not severe enough for the child to be classified as "deaf," but rather as "hard of hearing," the child with a hearing impairment is at a distinct disadvantage in virtually all aspects of English language development. The importance of the English language in our society, particularly in school-related activities, is obvious. A significantly large group of educators believe that many of the problems of people with hearing impairment related to social and intellectual development are primarily due to their deficiencies in English. We will explore this issue in some depth in this chapter.

Another related controversy inherent in Keller's words is the debate concerning whether the child who is deaf should be educated to communicate orally or through manual **sign language**. Keller's opinion is that the ability to speak offers a richer means of communication. But she was extraordinary; extremely few individuals who are deaf have attained her level of fluency. Furthermore, because for many years educators exclusively emphasized teaching children who are deaf to speak and actively discouraged their use of sign language, they unwittingly denied these children access to communication. Equal to the poignancy of Keller's breakthrough with verbal language was Lynn Spradley's discovery of communication through sign language after years of frustration with trying to speak:

> "Tom! Bruce! Come quick!" . . .
> I jumped up. In an instant we were in Lynn's room.
> "Watch!" Louise said, tears streaming down her face. "She said it two times!" Lynn, legs crossed in front of her, sat at the head of her bed. Louise, sitting on the edge, turned back to Lynn.
> "I—love—you," her voice came through the tears as she signed. She hugged Lynn, then sat back and waited.
> Lynn, beaming, held up two tiny fists, crossed them tightly against her heart, then pointed knowingly at Louise. Without hesitating, she reached out and hugged Louise tightly. The room was blurred; fighting back tears, I picked up Lynn, pulled her close in a long embrace, then sat back on the edge of her bed.
> "I—love—you," I signed slowly, my voice quivering as I spoke. I dropped my hands and waited.
> "Love you," Lynn signed clearly, confidently, then reached out to hug me. I looked at Louise. There were tears in our eyes.
> Bruce hugged his little sister. "I love you," he signed perfectly, a broad smile on his face.
> "Love you," Lynn signed back, this time in a more definite exaggerated rhythm. She had found her voice! (Spradley & Spradley, 1978, pp. 245-246)

The oral versus manual debate has raged for a long time. For many years there was no middle ground. Although some still debate the merits of each, many educators now have begun to use a method of "total communication," which involves a combination of both of these orientations.

➣ **sign language.** A manual language used by people who are deaf to communicate a true language with its own grammar.

PERSONS WITH HEARING IMPAIRMENT

MYTH ➤ Deafness is not as severe a disability as blindness.

FACT ➤ Although it is impossible to predict the exact consequences of a disability on a person's functioning, in general, deafness poses more difficulties in adjustment than does blindness. This is largely due to the effects hearing loss can have on the ability to understand and speak oral language.

MYTH ➤ It is unhealthy for people who are deaf to socialize almost exclusively with others who are deaf.

FACT ➤ Many authorities now recognize that the phenomenon of a Deaf culture is natural and should be encouraged. In fact, some are worried that too much mainstreaming will diminish the influence of the Deaf culture.

MYTH ➤ In learning to understand what is being said to them, people with hearing impairment concentrate on reading lips.

FACT ➤ *Lipreading* refers only to visual cues arising from movement of the lips. Some people who are hearing impaired not only read lips, but also take advantage of a number of other visual cues, such as facial expressions and movements of the jaw and tongue. They are engaging in what is referred to as *speechreading*.

MYTH ➤ Speechreading is relatively easy to learn and is used by the majority of people with hearing impairment.

FACT ➤ Speechreading is extremely difficult to learn, and very few people who are hearing impaired actually become proficient speechreaders.

MYTH ➤ American Sign Language (ASL) is a loosely structured group of gestures.

FACT ➤ ASL is a true language in its own right with its own set of grammatical rules.

MYTH ➤ ASL can convey only concrete ideas.

FACT ➤ ASL can convey any level of abstraction.

MYTH ➤ People within the Deaf community are in favor of mainstreaming students who are deaf into regular classes.

FACT ➤ Some within the Deaf community have voiced the opinion that regular classes are not appropriate for many students who are deaf. They point to a need for a critical mass of students who are deaf in order to have effective educational programs.

MYTH ➤ Families in which both the child and the parents are deaf are at a distinct disadvantage compared to families in which the parents are hearing.

FACT ➤ Research has demonstrated that children who are deaf who have parents who are also deaf fare better in a number of academic and social areas. Authorities point to the parents' ability to communicate with their children in ASL as a major reason for this advantage.

DEFINITION AND CLASSIFICATION

There are many definitions and classification systems of hearing impairment. By far the most common division is between deaf and hard of hearing. This would seem simple enough, except that the two categories are defined differently by different professionals. The extreme points of view are represented by those with a physiological orientation and those with an educational orientation. Those maintaining a strictly physiological viewpoint are interested primarily in the *measurable degree* of hearing loss. Children who cannot hear sounds at or above a certain intensity (loudness) level are classified as deaf; others with a hearing loss are considered hard of hearing. Hearing sensitivity is measured in **decibels** (units of relative loudness of sounds). Zero decibels (0 dB) designates the point at which the average person with normal hearing can detect the faintest sound. Each succeeding number of decibels indicates a certain degree of hearing loss. Those who maintain a physiological viewpoint generally consider those with hearing losses of about 90 dB or greater to be deaf, those with less to be hard of hearing.

People with an educational viewpoint are concerned with how much the hearing loss is likely to affect the child's ability to speak and develop language. Because of the close causal link between hearing loss and delay in language development, these professionals categorize primarily on the basis of spoken language abilities. Following is the most commonly accepted set of definitions reflecting this educational orientation:

- *Hearing impairment*: A generic term indicating a hearing disability that may range in severity from mild to profound: it includes the subsets of *deaf* and *hard of hearing*.
- A *deaf* person is one whose hearing disability precludes successful processing of linguistic information through audition, with or without a hearing aid.
- A *hard of hearing* person is one who, generally with the use of a hearing aid, has residual hearing sufficient to enable successful processing of linguistic information through audition (Brill, MacNeil, & Newman, 1986, p. 67)

Educators are extremely concerned about the *age of onset* of the hearing impairment. Again, the close relationship between hearing loss and language delay is the key here. The earlier the hearing loss manifests itself in a child's life, the more difficulty he or she will have in developing the language of the hearing society, e.g., English. For this reason, professionals frequently use the terms **congenitally deaf** (those who were born deaf) and **adventitiously deaf** (those who acquire deafness at some time after birth). Two other frequently used terms are even more specific in pinpointing language acquisition as critical: **Prelingual deafness** is "deafness present at birth, or occurring early in life at an age prior to the development of speech or language"; **postlingual deafness** is "deafness occurring at any age following the development of speech and language" (Brill, MacNeil, & Newman, 1986, p. 67). Experts differ regarding the dividing point between prelingual and postlingual deafness. Some believe it should be at about eighteen months, whereas others think it should be lower, at about twelve months or even six months (Meadow-Orlans, 1987).

The following hearing threshold classifications are common: mild (26-54 dB), moderate (55-69 dB), severe (70-89 dB), and profound (90 dB and above). These

➤ **decibels.** Units of relative loudness of sounds; zero decibels (0 dB) designates the point at which people with normal hearing can just detect sound.

➤ **congenitally deaf.** Deafness that is present at birth; can be caused by genetic factors, by injuries during fetal development, or by injury incurred at birth.

➤ **adventitiously deaf.** Deafness that occurs through illness or accident in an individual who was born with normal hearing.

➤ **prelingual deafness.** Deafness that occurs before the development of spoken language, usually at birth.

➤ **postlingual deafness.** Deafness occurring after the development of speech and language.

levels of severity according to loss of hearing sensitivity cut across the broad classifications of "deaf" and "hard of hearing." The broader classifications are not directly dependent on hearing sensitivity. Instead, they stress the degree to which speech and language are affected.

Some authorities object to following any of the various classification systems too strictly. These definitions, because they deal with events that are difficult to measure and that occur in variable organisms, are not precise. It is best not to form any hard-and-fast opinions about an individual's ability to hear and speak solely on the basis of a classification of his or her hearing disability.

PREVALENCE

Estimates of the numbers of children with hearing impairment vary considerably. Such things as differences in definition, populations studied, and accuracy of testing contribute to the varying figures. The U.S. Department of Education's statistics indicate that about .13 percent of the population from six to seventeen years of age is identified as deaf or hard of hearing by the public schools. Although the U.S. Department of Education does not report separate figures for the categories of deaf and hard of hearing, some authorities believe that many children who are hard-of-hearing who could benefit from special education are not being served.

ANATOMY AND PHYSIOLOGY OF THE EAR

The ear is one of the most complex organs of the body. The many elements that make up the hearing mechanism are divided into three major sections: the outer, middle, and inner ear. The outer ear is the least complex and least important for hearing; the inner ear is the most complex and most important for hearing. Figure 8–1 shows these major parts of the ear.

The Outer Ear

The outer ear consists of the auricle and the external auditory canal. The canal ends with the **tympanic membrane** (eardrum), which is the boundary between the outer and middle ear. The **auricle** is the part of the ear that protrudes from the side of the head. Although the auricle is the one part of the ear visible to all, it is the least important in terms of hearing (Martin, 1986). The part that the outer ear plays in the transmission of sound is relatively minor. Sound is "collected" by the auricle and is funneled through the external auditory canal on to the eardrum, which vibrates, sending the sound waves on to the middle ear.

The Middle Ear

The middle ear comprises the eardrum and three very tiny bones (**ossicles**) called the **malleus** (hammer), **incus** (anvil), and **stapes** (stirrup) contained within an air-filled space. The chain of the malleus, incus, and stapes conducts the vibrations of the eardrum along to the **oval window,** which is the connecting link between the middle and inner ear. To prevent a significant loss of energy between the vibration of the eardrum and the vibration of the oval window, the chain of bones is constructed in a way that takes advantage of the physical laws

➤ **tympanic membrane (eardrum).** The anatomical boundary between the outer and middle ear; the sound gathered in the outer ear vibrates here.

➤ **auricle.** The visible part of the ear, composed of cartilage; collects the sounds and funnels them via the external auditory canal to the eardrum.

➤ **ossicles.** Three tiny bones (malleus, incus, and stapes) that together make possible an efficient transfer of sound waves from the eardrum to the oval window, which connects the middle ear to the inner ear.

➤ **malleus.** Hammer-shaped bone in the ossicular chain of the middle ear.

➤ **incus.** Anvil-shaped bone in the ossicular chain of the middle ear.

➤ **stapes.** Stirrup-shaped bone in the ossicular chain of the middle ear.

➤ **oval window.** Connects the middle and inner ear.

Figure 8–1

➤ *Illustration of the outer, middle, and inner ear*

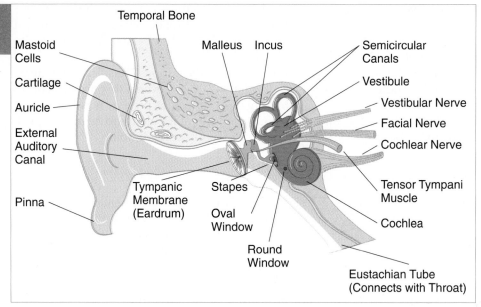

SOURCE: Adapted from H. L. Davis and S. R. Silverman (Eds.), *Hearing and Deafness,* 4th ed. Copyright © 1978 by Holt, Rinehart & Winston, Inc. Reprinted by permission.

of leverage. Because of this, there is an efficient transfer of energy from the air-filled cavity of the middle ear to the dense, fluid-filled inner ear (Davis, 1978a; Martin, 1986).

The Inner Ear

About the size of a pea, the inner ear is an intricate mechanism of thousands of moving parts. Because it looks like a maze of passageways and because of its complexity, this part of the ear is often called a *labyrinth.* The inner ear is divided into two sections according to function: the **vestibular mechanism** and the **cochlea.** These sections, however, do not function totally independently of each other.

The vestibular mechanism, located in the upper portion of the inner ear, is responsible for the sense of balance. It is extremely sensitive to such things as acceleration, head movement, and head position. Information regarding movement is fed to the brain through the vestibular nerve.

By far the most important organ for hearing is the cochlea. Lying below the vestibular mechanism, this snail-shaped organ contains the parts necessary to convert the mechanical action of the middle ear into an electrical signal in the inner ear that is transmitted to the brain. In the normally functioning ear, sound causes the malleus, incus, and stapes of the middle ear to move. When the stapes moves, it pushes the oval window in and out, causing the fluid in the cochlea of the inner ear to flow. The movement of the fluid in turn causes a complex chain of events in the cochlea ultimately resulting in excitation of the cochlear nerve. With stimulation of the cochlear nerve, an electrical impulse is sent to the brain, and the sound is heard.

➤ **vestibular mechanism.** Located in the upper portion of the inner ear; consists of three soft, semicircular canals filled with a fluid that is sensitive to head movement, acceleration, and other movements related to balance.

➤ **cochlea.** A snail-shaped organ that lies below the vestibular mechanism; its parts convert the sound coming from the middle ear into an electrical signal in the inner ear, which is transmitted to the brain.

MEASUREMENT OF HEARING ABILITY

There are three general types of hearing tests: pure-tone audiometry, speech audiometry, and specialized tests for very young children. Depending on the characteristics of the examinee and the use to which the results will be put, the **audiologist** may choose to give any number of tests from any one or a combination of these three categories.

Pure-Tone Audiometry

Pure-tone audiometry is designed to establish the individual's threshold for hearing at a variety of different frequencies. (Frequency, measured in **Hertz (Hz) units,** has to do with the number of vibrations per unit of time of a sound wave; the pitch is higher with *more* vibrations, lower with *fewer*.) A person's threshold for hearing is simply the level at which he or she can first detect a sound; it refers to how *intense* a sound must be before the person can detect it. Intensity is measured in units known as decibels (dB).

Pure-tone audiometers present tones of various intensities (dB levels) at various frequencies (Hz). Audiologists are usually concerned with measuring sensitivity to sounds ranging from 0 to about 110 dB. A person with average-normal hearing is barely able to hear sounds at a sound-pressure level of 0 dB. The zero-decibel level is frequently called the zero hearing-threshold level (HTL) or **audiometric zero.**

Hertz are usually measured from 125 Hz ("low" sounds) to 8,000 Hz ("high" sounds). Sounds below 125 Hz or above 8,000 Hz are not measured because most speech does not fall outside this range. (The whistle designed to call dogs, for example, has a frequency too high to be heard by human beings.) Frequencies contained in speech range from 80 to 8,000 Hz, but most speech sounds have energy in the 500 to 2,000 Hz range.

The procedure for testing a person's sensitivity to pure tones is relatively simple. Each ear is tested separately. The audiologist presents a variety of tones within the range of 0 to about 110 dB and 125 to 8,000 Hz until he or she establishes at what level of intensity (dB) the individual can detect the tone at a number of frequencies—125 Hz, 250 Hz, 500 Hz, 1,000 Hz, 2,000 Hz, 4,000 Hz, and 8,000 Hz. For each of these frequencies there is a measure of degree of hearing impairment. A 50-dB hearing loss at 500 Hz, for example means the individual is able to detect the 500-Hz sound when it is given at an intensity level of 50 dB, whereas the average person would have heard it at 0 dB.

Speech Audiometry

Because the ability to detect and understand speech is of prime importance, a technique called **speech audiometry** has been developed to test a person's detection and understanding of speech. Speech detection is defined as the lowest level (in dB) at which the individual can detect speech without understanding. More important is the determination of the dB level at which one is able to *understand* speech. This is known as the **speech reception threshold (SRT).** One way to measure SRT is to present the person with a list of two-syllable words, testing each ear separately. The dB level at which he or she can understand half the words is often used as an estimate of SRT level.

> **audiologist.** An individual trained in audiology, a science dealing with hearing impairments, their detection, and remediation.

> **pure-tone audiometry.** A system whereby tones of various intensities and frequencies are presented to determine a person's hearing loss.

> **Hertz (Hz) unit.** A measurement of the frequency of sound; refers to highness or lowness of a sound.

> **audiometric zero (zero decibel level).** Lowest level at which people with normal hearing can hear.

> **speech audiometry.** A technique that tests a person's detection and understanding of speech rather than using pure tones to detect hearing loss.

> **speech reception threshold (SRT).** The decibel level at which a person can understand speech.

standard method for testing children's hearing is through the use of the pure tone audiometer.

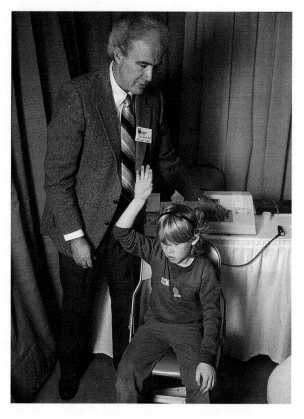

Tests for Young and Hard-to-Test Children

A basic assumption for pure-tone and speech audiometry is that the person being tested understands what is expected of him or her. The individual must be able to comprehend the instructions and to show with a head nod or raised hand that he or she has heard the tone or word. He or she must also be cooperative. None of this may be possible for very young children (under about four years of age) or for children with other disabilities.

Play Audiometry

This technique establishes rapport with the child and motivates him or her to respond. The examiner sets up the testing situation as a game. Using pure tones or speech, the examiner teaches the child to do various activities whenever he or she hears a signal. The activities are designed to be attractive to the young child. For example, the child may be required to pick up a block, squeeze a toy, or open a book.

Reflex Audiometry

➤ **reflex audiometry.** The testing of responses to sounds by observation of such reflex actions as the orienting response and the Moro reflex.

Infants normally possess some reflexive behaviors to loud sounds, which are useful for the testing of hearing by **reflex audiometry.** Present at birth is the *Moro reflex*, which is defined as a movement of the face, body, arms, and legs and a blinking of the eyes. Another response that may be used to determine hearing ability is the *orienting response*. This response is evident when the infant turns his or her head and body toward the source of a sound.

Evoked-Response Audiometry

Another method of measuring hearing in a person unable to make voluntary responses is **evoked-response audiometry.** This technique involves measuring changes in brain-wave activity by using an electroencephalograph (EEG). All sounds heard by an individual result in electrical signals within the brain, so this method has become more popular with the development of sophisticated computers. Although very expensive and difficult to interpret, evoked-response audiometry has certain advantages. It can be used during sleep, and the child can be sedated and thus not be aware that he or she is being tested.

School Screening

Virtually all children who have severe hearing losses are identified before they reach school, but this is not always the case for children with mild hearing impairments. Many schools, therefore, have routine hearing screening programs. Hearing screening tests are administered either individually or in a group. Hearing screening tests, especially those that are group administered, are less accurate than those administered in an audiologist's office. Children detected as having a possible problem through screening are referred for more extensive evaluation.

CAUSES

Conductive, Sensorineural, and Mixed Impairments

Professionals classify causes of hearing loss on the basis of the location of the problem within the hearing mechanism. There are three major classifications: conductive, sensorineural, and mixed hearing losses. A **conductive hearing impairment** refers to an impairment that interferes with the transfer of sound along the conductive pathway of the middle or outer ear. A **sensorineural hearing impairment** involves problems in the inner ear. A **mixed hearing impairment** is a combination of the two.

Audiologists attempt to determine the location of malfunctioning. The first clue may be the severity of the loss. A general rule of thumb is that hearing losses greater than 60 or 70 dB involve some inner-ear problem. Audiologists use the results of pure-tone testing to help determine the location of hearing impairments, converting the results to an audiogram—a graphic representation of the weakest (lowest dB) sound the individual can hear at each of several frequency levels. The profile of the audiogram helps determine whether the loss is conductive, sensorineural, or mixed.

Impairments of the Outer Ear

Although impairments of the outer ear are not as serious as those to the middle and inner ear, several conditions of the outer ear can cause a person to be hard of hearing. In some children, for example, the external auditory canal does not

➤ **evoked-response audiometry.** A technique involving electroencephalograph measurement of changes in brain-wave activity in response to sounds.

➤ **conductive hearing impairment.** A hearing loss, usually mild, resulting from malfunctioning along the conductive pathway of the ear, i.e., the outer or middle ear.

➤ **sensorineural hearing impairment.** A hearing loss, usually severe, resulting from malfunctioning of the inner ear.

➤ **mixed hearing impairment.** A hearing loss resulting from a combination of conductive and sensorineural hearing impairment.

form, resulting in a condition known as atresia. Children may also develop **external otitis,** or "swimmer's ear," an infection of the skin of the external auditory canal. Tumors of the external auditory canal are another source of impairment.

Impairments of the Middle Ear

Although abnormalities of the middle ear are generally more serious than problems of the outer ear, they too usually result in a person's being classified as hard of hearing rather than deaf. Most middle-ear hearing losses occur because the mechanical action of the ossicles is interfered with in some way. Most middle-ear impairments, unlike inner-ear impairments, are correctable with medical or surgical treatment.

The most common problem of the middle ear is **otitis media**—an infection of the middle-ear space caused by viral and bacterial factors, among others. It is primarily a disease of childhood not easy to detect, especially in infancy when it often occurs with no symptoms (Giebink, 1990). Otitis media is linked to abnormal functioning of the eustachian tubes. If the eustachian tube malfunctions because of a respiratory viral infection, for example, it cannot do its job of ventilating, draining, and protecting the middle ear from infection (Giebink, 1990). The prevalence of otitis media is much higher in children with Down syndrome or cleft palate because these conditions often result in malformed eustachian tubes. Otitis media can result in temporary conductive hearing loss, and, if untreated, can lead to rupture of the tympanic membrane.

More subtle in its effects, but still a childhood middle-ear problem of some significance, is **nonsupperative otitis media.** This condition, which can occur without infection, also usually results from a disruption of the functioning of the eustachian tube. It is generally preceded by a bout with infectious otitis media. In addition, some authorities hold that allergies, by leading to eustachian tube malfunctioning, can cause nonsupperative otitis media (Castiglia, Aquilina, & Kemsley, 1983).

Impairments of the Inner Ear

The most severe hearing impairments are associated with the inner ear. Unfortunately, inner-ear hearing losses present the greatest problems for both education and medicine. Troubles other than those related to loss of threshold sensitivity are frequent. For example, sound distortion often occurs. Disorders of the inner ear can result in problems of balance and vertigo along with hearing loss. Also, some individuals with inner-ear impairments may hear roaring or ringing noises.

Causes of inner-ear disorders can be hereditary or acquired. The most frequent cause of childhood deafness is heredity (Schildroth, Rawlings, & Allen, 1989). Acquired hearing losses of the inner ear include those due to bacterial infections (such as meningitis, the second most frequent cause of childhood deafness), prematurity, viral infections (such as mumps and measles), anoxia (deprivation of oxygen) at birth, prenatal infections of the mother (such as maternal rubella, congenital syphilis, and cytomegalovirus), Rh incompatibility (which can now usually be prevented with proper prenatal care of the mother), blows to the head, unwanted side effects of some antibiotics, and excessive noise levels.

Congenital cytomegalovirus (CMV) is the most frequently occurring virus among newborns. It is difficult to know precisely how many cases of deafness

CMV causes because it is difficult to diagnose, but authorities are now paying more attention to it as a causal agent of deafness (Schildroth & Hotto, 1992) as well as of other disabling conditions.

PSYCHOLOGICAL AND BEHAVIORAL CHARACTERISTICS

Hearing loss can have profound consequences for some aspects of a person's behavior and little or no effect on other characteristics. Everyone knows the question "If you were forced to choose, which would you rather be—blind or deaf?" On first impulse most of us choose deafness, probably because we rely on sight for mobility and because many of the beauties of nature are visual. But in terms of functioning in an English language-oriented society, the person who is deaf is at a much greater disadvantage.

English Language and Speech Development

By far the most severely affected areas of development in the person who is hearing-impaired in the United States are the comprehension and production of the *English* language. We stress here the fact that it is the English language because that is the predominant language in the United States of those who can hear. In other words, people who are hearing-impaired are generally deficient in the language used by most people of the "hearing" society in which they live. The distinction is important because people who are hearing-impaired can be expert in their own form of language. The current opinion is that individuals who use American Sign Language are taking part in the production and comprehension of a true language. We return to this point later in this chapter.

Regarding English, however, it is an undeniable fact that individuals with hearing impairment are at a distinct disadvantage. This is true in terms of language comprehension, language production, and speech. With regard to speech, for example, teachers have reported that 23 percent of students with hearing impairment have speech that is not intelligible, 22 percent have speech that is barely intelligible, and 10 percent are unwilling to speak in public. Speech intelligibility is linked to degree of hearing loss, with 75 percent of children who are profoundly deaf having nonintelligible speech but only 14 percent of children with less than severe hearing loss having nonintelligible speech (Wolk & Schildroth, 1986). In addition, it is much more difficult for children who are prelingually deaf to learn to speak than for those who have acquired their deafness, mainly because they do not receive auditory feedback from the sounds they make. In addition, they have not heard an adult language model. An interesting research finding is that infants born deaf enter the babbling stage at the same time as hearing infants but soon abandon it (Ling & Ling, 1978; Schow & Nerbonne, 1980; Stoel-Gammon & Otomo, 1986). By as early as eight months of age, and possibly earlier, babies who are hearing-impaired babble less than hearing infants. And the babbling they do is of a qualitatively different nature (Stoel-Gammon & Otomo, 1986). It is thought that these differences occur because hearing infants are reinforced by hearing their own babbling and by hearing the verbal responses of adults. Children, unable to hear either themselves or others, are not reinforced.

The lack of feedback has also been named as a primary cause of poor speech production in children who are deaf. As Fry (1966) states, hearing children learn to associate the sensations they receive when they move their jaws, mouth, and tongue with the auditory sounds these movements produce. Children with hearing impairment are obviously handicapped in this process. In addition, they have a difficult time hearing the sounds of adult speech, which other children hear and imitate, so they do not have an adequate adult English speaking model.

Table 8–1 gives general examples of the effects various degrees of hearing loss may have on English language development. This is only a general statement of these relationships since many factors interact to influence language development in the child with hearing impairment.

Intellectual Ability

The intellectual ability of children with hearing impairment has been a subject of much controversy over the years. For many years, professionals believed that the conceptual ability of individuals who are deaf was deficient because of their deficient spoken language. This belief was erroneous for two reasons. First, the assumption that language can be equated with cognitive abilities, popularized by the famous Russian psychologist, Vygotsky (1962), has been largely debunked. Vygotsky assumed that the early speech of children becomes interiorized as inner speech, and inner speech becomes the equivalent of thought. Most psychologists now believe that Vygostky's notions of the primary role of language in the development of cognition were misguided. Second, researchers have warned that we should not assume that persons who cannot speak because they are deaf have no language. They may not have a spoken language, such as *English*, but if they use American Sign Language, they are using a true language with its own rules of grammar. We will return to this point later.

Another reason that hearing professionals may have assumed that children who are deaf are cognitively deficient is that they have had so much trouble communicating with them. Even if these children use sign language, divided attention is a problem (Wood, 1991). In any teaching situation, the child who is being signed to must attend to the signs as well as to any instructional materials. Some adults, not allowing for the extra cognitive load placed on the child who is deaf, may become frustrated with the child's seemingly slow absorption of the lesson being taught.

Any intelligence testing done with people who are hearing impaired must take into account their English language deficiency. Performance tests, rather than verbal tests, especially if they are administered in sign, offer a much fairer assessment of the IQ of a person with a hearing impairment. The Wechsler performance scales are most often used with persons who are deaf (Blennerhassett, 1990).

Academic Achievement

Unfortunately, most children with hearing impairment have extreme deficits in academic achievement. Reading ability, which relies heavily on English language skills and is probably the most important area of academic achievement, is most affected. Numerous studies have painted a bleak picture for the reading achievement of students with hearing impairment (Allen, 1986; Trybus & Karchmer, 1977; Wolk & Allen, 1984). Representative findings are that the growth in reading achievement of students with hearing impairment is about one-third that for hearing students. It is not at all unusual for students who are deaf, upon gradua-

Table 8–1 ➤ Relationship of Degree of Impairment* to Understanding of Language and Speech		
	AVERAGE OF THE SPEECH FREQUENCIES IN BETTER EAR	**EFFECT OF HEARING LOSS ON UNDERSTANDING OF LANGUAGE AND SPEECH**
Slight	27–40 dB (ISO)	May have difficulty hearing faint or distant speech. May experience some difficulty with language arts subjects.
Mild	41–55 dB (ISO)	Understands conversational speech at a distance of 3–5 feet (face to face). May miss as much as 50 percent of class discussions if voices are faint or not in line of vision. May exhibit limited vocabulary and speech anomalies.
Marked	56–70 dB (ISO)	Conversation must be loud to be understood. Will have increased difficulty in group discussions. Is likely to have defective speech. Is likely to be deficient in language usage and comprehension. Will have limited vocabulary.
Severe	71–90 dB (ISO)	May hear loud voices about 1 foot from the ear. May be able to identify environmental sounds. May be able to discriminate vowels but not all consonants. Speech and language defective and likely to deteriorate.
Extreme	91 dB or MORE (ISO)	May hear some loud sounds but is aware of vibrations more than tonal patterns. Relies on vision rather than hearing as primary avenue for communication. Speech and language defective and likely to deteriorate.

SOURCE: Adapted from Report of a Committee for a Comprehensive Plan for Hearing-Impaired Children, May 1968, Office of the Superintendent of Public Instruction, Title VI, Elementary and Secondary Education Act, and the University of Illinois, Division of Services for Crippled Children.
* Medically irreversible conditions and those requiring prolonged medical care.

tion from high school, to be able to read at no more than a fourth grade level, barely at newspaper literacy level. Even in math, their best academic subject, they trail their hearing peers by substantial margins.

Several studies have demonstrated that children who are deaf who have parents who are deaf have higher reading achievement than do those who have hearing parents (Kampfe & Turecheck, 1987). Authorities speculate that this is due to two factors:

- Parents who are deaf are able to communicate better with their children through the use of ASL, providing the children with needed support.
- Children who are deaf who have parents who are deaf are more likely to be proficient in ASL, and ASL aids these children in learning written English and reading (Lane, 1992).

Social Adjustment

Social and personality development in the hearing population depend heavily on communication. And the situation is no different for those who are deaf. The hearing person has little difficulty finding people with whom to communicate. The person who is deaf, however, may face problems in finding others with whom he or she can converse. Studies have demonstrated that many students who are deaf are at risk for loneliness (Charlson, Strong, & Gold, 1992; Loeb & Sarigiani, 1986). Two factors are important in considering the possible isolation of students who are deaf: mainstreaming and hearing status of the parents.

Researchers have shown that in mainstream settings, typically very little interaction occurs between students who are deaf and those who are not (Gaustad & Kluwin, 1992). Furthermore, in mainstream settings students who are deaf feel more emotionally secure if they have other students who are deaf with whom they can communicate (Stinson & Whitmire, 1992). This is not always possible, however, because of the low prevalence of hearing impairment. Some authorities believe that students who attend residential schools are less likely to experience isolation because they have other students with whom they can easily communicate. At the same time, children in residential schools are prone to feel alienated from their families.

Some authorities believe that the child who is deaf who has hearing parents runs a greater risk of being unhappy than if he or she has parents who are deaf. This is because many hearing parents do not become proficient in ASL and are unable to communicate with their child easily. Given that over 90 percent of children who are deaf have hearing parents, this problem in communication may be critical.

Probably the need for social interaction is most influential in leading many persons with hearing impairment to associate primarily with others with hearing impairment. If their parents are deaf, children who are deaf are usually exposed to other deaf families from an early age. Even if they have hearing parents, and even if they do not come into contact as children with many other children who are deaf, many persons who are deaf end up, as adults, socializing predominantly with others who are deaf. This phenomenon of socializing with others who are deaf is attributable to the influence of the Deaf culture.

The Deaf Culture

In the past, most professionals viewed isolation from the hearing community on the part of many people who are deaf as a sign of social pathology. More and more professionals, however, are agreeing with the many people who are deaf who believe in the value of having their own Deaf culture. They view this culture as a natural condition emanating from the common bond of sign language.

Because communication is so key to social interaction, people with hearing impairments often socialize together.

The unifying influence of sign language is the first of six factors noted by Reagan (1990) as demarcating the Deaf community as a true culture: (1) linguistic differentiation, (2) attitudinal deafness, (3) behavioral norms, (4) endogamous marital patterns, (5) historical awareness, and (6) voluntary organizational networks. Regarding *linguistic differentiation*, Reagan states that the Deaf community can most accurately be described as bilingual, with individuals possessing varying degrees of fluency in ASL and English. *Attitudinal deafness* refers to whether a person thinks of himself or herself as deaf. It may not have anything to do with a person's hearing acuity. For example, a person with a relatively mild hearing loss may think of himself or herself as deaf more readily than does someone with a profound hearing loss. The Deaf community has its own set of *behavioral norms* with regard to such things as eye contact and physical touching. *Endogamous marriage patterns* are evident from surveys showing rates of in-group marriage as high as 90 percent. The Deaf community has a long oral history that has contributed to its *historical awareness* of significant people and events pertaining to people who are deaf. Finally, there is an abundance of *voluntary organizational networks* for the Deaf community, e.g., the National Association of the Deaf, World Games for the Deaf (Deaf Olympics), and the National Theatre of the Deaf.

These six factors help us understand the Deaf culture from a theoretical perspective. The following statement portrays just how strong the Deaf culture is from a practical perspective:

> Although deaf people comprise a minority group that reflects the larger society, they have devised their own codes of behavior. For example, it's all right to drop in

*I*ndividuals with hearing
impairments have
become a particularly
strong advocacy group for
themselves.

unannounced, because many people don't have the special TTY telephone hookups. How else could they contact their friends to let them know they're coming? If a deaf person has a job that needs to be done—from electrical wiring to accounting—he's expected to go to a deaf person first. The assumption is that deaf people won't take advantage of each other and that they need to support their own kind. . . . The deaf world has its own heroes, and its own humor, some of which relies on visual puns made in sign language, and much of which is quite corny. Because deafness is a disability that cuts across all races and social backgrounds, the deaf world is incredibly heterogeneous. Still, deafness seems to take precedence over almost everything else in a person's life. A deaf person raised a Catholic will more likely attend a Baptist deaf service than a hearing mass. (Walker, 1986, p. 22).

Many within the Deaf community, and some within professional ranks, are concerned that the cultural status of children who are deaf is in peril (Gaustad & Kluwin, 1992; Janesick & Moores, 1992). They believe that the increase in mainstreaming is eroding the cultural values of the Deaf culture. In the past, much of Deaf culture was passed down from generation to generation through contacts made at residential schools, but today's children who are deaf may have little contact with other children who are deaf if they attend their local schools. Some authorities have recommended that schools provide classes in Deaf history and culture for students who are deaf who attend local schools.

Issues in Special Education   Media's Portrayal of Persons with Hearing Impairment

*T*he Columbia Pictures film, *Calendar Girl,* has been a hot topic within the Deaf community ever since the producers, Penny Marshall and Elliott Abott, announced the choice of a hearing actor to portray a deaf character.

The Deaf Coalition, an alliance of Deaf Theater organizations, and other organizations related to deafness, organized a letter-writing and petition campaign to try to influence the producers to find a deaf actor for the role.

There are about 15 million persons with hearing impairment in the U.S., which is not a small minority. However, the Deaf community considers itself a cultural minority, distinguished from the majority by its language (American Sign Language). The Deaf Coalition believes a hearing person could never pass for a native signer even after years of practice. The Coalition feels that, for the Deaf community, seeing a hearing actor playing a native signer is demeaning in the same way seeing a white actor in blackface would be to an African American.

Historically, the portrayal of deafness in American film and television has not been positive. For most members of the hearing society, the success of a character who is deaf is measured by the attainment of audible speech. Many films show characters who are deaf with unrealistic lip-reading abilities. Lip-reading is difficult to learn and not completely accepted as a means of communication. Quite often in the visual media, people who are deaf have been portrayed as victims. The Deaf Coalition is concerned that because of the biased and limiting depiction of deafness in visual media, they have been subjected to a distorted public perspective.

Recent films, like *Children of a Lesser God* (1986), have helped to change this perspective. The film suggests that the Deaf community has its own inner strengths as well as problems of assimilation in a world dominated by sight and sound. The National Theater of the Deaf has benefited and broadened the world of theater by performing productions with actors who are deaf who sign the text and interpreters who speak their lines.

- Currently, privately produced media works of Hollywood and television networks are not required to comply with the goals of the Americans with Disabilities Act. Should Hollywood and TV networks be required to caption media productions?
- Some actors who are deaf feel that many producers and directors see an actor's deafness as being his/her only defining characteristic. What can be done to educate them about hiring actors who are deaf and deafness in the visual media?

Some within the Deaf community have been aggressive in their attacks on what they consider an oppressive medical and educational establishment. Lane (1992), for example, has declared that people who are deaf should not be considered disabled or in need of special education as it is currently defined. Instead, he argues, people who are deaf should be considered a linguistic minority, and their education should be the equivalent of bilingual education.

An example of just how much this segment of the Deaf community is at odds with many professionals is contained in its response to the value of the medical procedure referred to as cochlear implantation. After several years of experimentation, the Food and Drug Administration approved, in 1990, the use of cochlear implants for children. Cochlear implants consist of an internal electromagnetic coil, with an electrode that runs into the cochlea of the inner ear, and an external coil. The surgeon implants the internal coil into the bone behind the ear and fits an external coil on the skin over the internal coil. A microphone worn on a person's clothing picks up sound and carries it to the external coil, which transmits it to the internal coil, which transmits it to the electrode implanted in the cochlea. Cochlear implants are far from allowing a person who is deaf to hear sound normally.

Generally recommended for children who have virtually no hearing (Moog & Geers, 1991), some professionals report that cochlear implants allow such children to hear some environmental sounds that they could not hear previously (e.g., car horns and ringing phones) and make it somewhat easier for them to acquire intelligible speech. Authorities predict that more and more implants will be done and that the procedure will be perfected so that someday it will lead to significant improvements in hearing. Although hailed as a medical breakthrough by some professionals, other advocates of the Deaf community see the implants as overly zealous medical tinkering. They do not think the benefits, which thus far have been rather limited, warrant the invasive medical procedures (Lane, 1992). And at least one authority has argued that, even if the procedure were perfected, it should not be used if one truly believes that children who are deaf are a cultural minority group and not disabled:

> I expect most Americans would agree that our society should not seek the scientific tools or use them, if available, to change a child biologically so he or she will belong to the majority rather than the minority—even if we believe that this biological engineering might reduce the burdens the child will bear as a member of a minority. Even if we could take children destined to be members of the African-American, or Hispanic-American, or Native American, or Deaf American communities and convert them with bio-power into white, Caucasian, hearing males—even if we could, we should not. We should likewise refuse cochlear implants for young deaf children even if the devices were perfect (Lane, 1992, p. 237)

Many professionals would consider this position too radical and scientifically constraining, but it typifies how deep feelings about the Deaf community can run.

EDUCATIONAL CONSIDERATIONS

The problems facing the educator working with students with hearing impairments are formidable. As one would expect, one major problem is communication. Dating back to the sixteenth century, there has been a raging debate concerning how individuals who are deaf should converse (Lane, 1984). This controversy is sometimes referred to as the oralism-manualism debate to represent two very different points of view—one of which advocates teaching people who are deaf to speak and the other, the use of some kind of manual communication. Manualism was the preferred method until the middle of the nineteenth century, when oralism began to gain predominance. Currently, most educators advocate the use of both oral and manual methods in what is referred to as a **total communication approach.**

We first discuss the major techniques that make up the oral approach and the oral portion of the total communication approach, then we take up total communication, and then we discuss the controversy surrounding the use of ASL in classrooms.

Oral Techniques: Auditory Training and Speechreading

Auditory Training

Auditory training is a procedure for teaching the child who is hearing impaired to make use of what hearing he or she possesses. Advocates claim that

➢ **total communication approach.** An approach for teaching students with hearing impairment that blends oral and manual techniques.

➢ **auditory training.** The procedure of teaching children who are deaf or hard-of-hearing to make full use of their residual hearing ability.

all but a very few children who are totally deaf are able to benefit from auditory training. Hearing aids, discussed in more detail later, are a major part of auditory training.

The three major goals of many auditory training programs are the development of (1) an awareness of sound, (2) the ability to make gross discriminations among environmental sounds, and (3) the ability to discriminate among speech sounds. Regarding the first goal, it is sometimes difficult for children, especially those who have not worn a hearing aid from infancy on, to know that there is such a thing as "sound." Advocates of auditory training, thus, stress the importance of introducing hearing aids as soon as possible.

Once the teacher is sure that the child is aware of sound, then he or she can begin to teach what sounds go with which things in the environment. This is sometimes done by requiring children to match prerecorded sounds with their corresponding pictures.

Once gross environmental sound discriminations are learned, the teacher concentrates on teaching the child to discriminate speech sounds. Two environmental factors that make the discrimination of speech sounds complicated are high reverberation and a low signal-to-noise ratio. **Reverberation** refers to the amount of echo in a room. In technical terms, it is the time it takes for a sound to decrease 60 dB after it has been turned off (Hawkins, 1990). A room with surfaces that absorb sound (e.g., acoustical tiles, carpeting, drapes) have lower reverberation times than those with reflective surfaces (e.g., tile floors, blackboards, desks). The **signal-to-noise ratio** refers to the dB level of the speaker divided by the dB level of the rest of the noise in a room.

> ➤ **reverberation.** The amount of echo in a room; technically, the amount of time it takes for sound to decrease to 60 dB (decibels) after it is turned off; affects the difficulty with which people, especially those with hearing impairment, can understand speech.

> ➤ **signal-to-noise ratio.** The dB level of the speaker divided by the dB level of the rest of the room; affects the ability of a person, especially one who is hearing impaired, to understand speech.

A total communication approach is a blend of oral and manual methods.

$\mathcal{C}$ollaboration

A Key to Success

KEN ALEXANDER

Teacher of students who are deaf/hard-of-hearing, total communication, Special District of St. Louis County; B.A., Education and Psychology, Webster University; M.Ed., Education of the Deaf, Western Maryland College

LYNN POTT

Fifth-grade teacher, Bellerive Elementary School, and instructor, Washington University; B.S., Elementary Education, University of Missouri; M.Ed., Maryville College; doctoral student, St. Louis University

➤ **Ken** The eight students I currently teach range in age from eight to eleven. They have severe to profound bilateral sensorineural hearing losses and are placed in my total communication class at Bellerive Elementary. (Total communication, which utilizes the simultaneous methods of speech, lip-reading, amplification, and sign language, is one of two types of programs offered by our special district; the other is auditory/oral, which emphasizes understanding and using spoken language.) Two of my students have parents who are deaf, and three have one or more siblings who are deaf. Although all the students are encouraged to use their best speech, only two of the eight have good to excellent conversational speech. The other six are generally unintelligible to those unfamiliar with the speech of persons who are deaf. Three of these students have transferred from oral programs at age eight or older. Seven of the eight have excellent signed communication skills. Five of the eight have good written English-language skills (this means they have generally good written English for children who are deaf: For instance, the structure of the language may be correct, but they may have problems in verb conjugation). The other three have concepts and ideas to express in writing but have great difficulty with basic English patterns.

➤ **Lynn** My fifth-grade class of twenty-eight is a heterogeneous group. The average academic level is above national norms, but my students have a wide range of ability—third-grade to seventh-grade reading levels. I teach all subject areas.

➤ **Ken** We'll describe our work with Beth, a twelve-year-old. Her father is a fluent signer and knowledgeable of deaf culture. Her mother is also a skilled com-

municator in sign language. Picture an artistic, creative student who is continuously struggling with perfection. She is eager to learn English and its relationship to American Sign Language. She is equally enthusiastic about reading and expressing herself in written English. She is above average in intelligence, a charming student with an amiable manner, but one whose emotions are usually kept in check. She's a visual-manual learner who relies on an interpreter to facilitate communication in the mainstream. A child who is profoundly deaf, she has a good sense of communication and languages, and therefore is remarkable in her communicative skills, although her speech intelligibility is only fair. She's a student who feels responsible for her own destiny. In short, you can see that she's the cat's pajamas!

➤ **Lynn** Beth is an achiever. She wants to be sure her assignments are completed correctly and neatly. During her first month in my class she didn't ask any questions, but she answered questions through the interpreter. Beth is a listener and an observer. She watches everything that goes on in the classroom. Because she is so attentive, she has become a leader among her three classmates who are hearing-impaired. She knows what's going on and clarifies concepts for the other students with hearing impairments. Sometimes she gets frustrated with them. I've learned to watch her facial expressions and the forcefulness in her signing. I can tell when she's frustrated. At first, she didn't want to call attention to herself, so she'd save her questions and ask for Ken's help when she returned to his classroom. By the second semester she'd lost much of her shyness and would ask questions. As she grew more confident in my classroom, she began to speak as she signed. Some of her speech could be understood, but with difficulty.

➤ **Ken** Beth was mainstreamed for science, social studies, and language at the fifth-grade level. As the teacher for students who are deaf, I was responsible for any preteaching, reviewing, and additional explanations to ensure success.

Sometimes, specific vocabulary for science and social studies needed to be invented, based on concepts of American Sign Language and consistent with signs already in existence. I taught these in my classroom to facilitate speedy and appropriate interpreting while Beth was in hearing classes.

➤ **Lynn** As a classroom teacher I was responsible for presenting the curriculum content, giving the assignments, and testing for understanding. At the beginning of the year I needed to understand Beth's capabilities and what I could expect of her.

➤ **Ken** I recall one instance that was a particular problem—beginning note taking. Fifth grade introduces note taking as part of beginning outline skills and conceptualization of content. I had decided not to use a note taker and the usual paper. I knew that outlining skills were more important. I took the time to explain to Beth that in sixth grade note takers would be used, but that in the fifth grade it was more important to write a simple outline. She needed to learn specialized techniques to develop memory skills. I helped her learn techniques to use at home during independent study. Her parents were also involved in the various study techniques. All this helped her learn to discriminate important information from what was less important. Another challenging aspect of our teamwork, unrelated to her academic skills, was her overall social development—as a person who is deaf with a peer group that is deaf coexisting within a larger hearing society. Another matter requiring immediate attention was parental denial. One of her parents felt that her academic successes meant that she was ready to be totally mainstreamed with the necessary support. This was a denial of her deafness. The fact is that Beth's hearing peers could never know her as a person, although they could admire her for her abilities or academic skills. She didn't seek out deep, meaningful communication with hearing peers; therefore, they had virtually no sense of her as a person. Through discussion in our classroom, as well as guided discussion

groups led by a counselor for students who are deaf, we were able to help Beth come to grips with this issue. She came to accept these realities as she saw them: She was deaf; she enjoyed socializing primarily with her peers who are deaf or within the deaf community; she could learn more content being mainstreamed with an interpreter and be more challenged intellectually within a larger, hearing-student classroom. In the final analysis, she had a strong self-identity as a person who is deaf existing within a larger hearing society.

➤ **Lynn** I definitely needed Ken's help. I had never had students with hearing impairment in my classroom before, and I had twenty-eight other students. Ken kept me informed of any concerns or problems that Beth was having. He was similar to a private tutor to Beth. Rather than burden

> *A rewarding outcome . . . was that we saw Beth came to accept herself better within the larger mainstream.*

me with reteaching, he would clarify concepts and strategies so Beth would have confidence in the regular classroom. It worked. As the year progressed, Beth began volunteering on a regular basis. He was the link that helped connect the integrated classroom to the comfortable, but isolated, deaf/hard-of-hearing classroom.

➤ **Ken** During the course of Beth's fifth-grade year I saw attitude changes because of the way Lynn and I worked as a team. In the beginning of the year, Beth was concerned about how she would be perceived by her hearing peers. She was afraid they would reject her because of her speech skills or that they might equate her poor speech production with lower IQ. Instead, her hearing peers began to see her as a well-functioning fifth-grader.

We worked within a framework that facilitated relaxed integration in academic areas as well as nonacademic areas. This allowed her hearing peers to see her during work and play, and it also helped her to develop more self-confidence about her abilities compared to those of her hearing peers. Consequently, she acquired a strong, healthy self-concept outside of her small group of peers who are deaf. A rewarding outcome of my collaboration with Lynn was that we saw Beth come to accept herself better within the larger mainstream.

➤ **Lynn** There were other rewards, too. As the students in my classroom began to understand Beth's feelings, they grew to respect and admire her for her abilities. She became their classmate and friend. I also grew as a teacher. I learned from Ken and Beth to watch people so that I can understand them—all people, not just those with handicaps. I remember Ken saying how significant facial expressions and body language are to his students. As a class, we talked about this. We all became more aware of the different aspects of communication. My students began to learn sign language so they could communicate with Beth.

➤ **Ken** I guess the major barrier that keeps special and general education teachers from working together are the intense and often acrimonious feelings associated with ethnocentric identity. These attitudes often include an "us-them" mentality, denigration of American Sign Language, the feeling that speech is all important, low expectations of people with disabilities, and a focus on disability rather than ability.

➤ **Lynn** Classroom teachers need to be aware of their own feelings and the feelings that students who are deaf experience. It is so important to have a teacher of children with hearing impairment who truly understands the frustrations of the students and is patient with the classroom teacher. If that special teacher doesn't provide input, a barrier could materialize. Perhaps this is why some mainstreaming programs are not successful.

Studies have shown that reverberation and signal-to-noise ratio can have a significant effect on how well children, especially those with hearing impairments, are able to understand speech (Hawkins, 1990). Studies have also shown that some classrooms, especially those in older buildings having high ceilings and no carpets, and those in open classroom situations, have reverberation times and signal-to-noise ratios that would make the understanding of speech very difficult for many students with hearing impairment (Hawkins, 1990). At the same time, some authorities have noted the importance of gradually preparing students with hearing impairment for coping with discriminating speech under less than optimal conditions (Sanders, 1982).

Speechreading

Speechreading, sometimes inappropriately called lipreading, involves teaching children who are hearing impaired to use visual information to understand what is being said to them. *Speechreading* is a more accurate term than *lipreading* because the goal is to teach students to attend to a variety of stimuli in addition to specific movements of the lips. For example, proficient speechreaders "read" contextual stimuli so they can anticipate certain types of messages in certain types of situations. They are able to use facial expressions to help them interpret what is being said to them. Even the ability to discriminate the various speech sounds that flow from a person's mouth involves attending to visual cues from the tongue and jaw as well as the lips. For example, to learn to discriminate among vowels, the speechreader concentrates on cues related to the degree of jaw opening and lip shaping (see Figure 8–2).

Cued speech is a method of augmenting speechreading. In cued speech, the individual uses hand shapes to represent specific sounds while speaking. Although it has some devoted advocates, cued speech is not used widely in the United States.

Unfortunately, speechreading is extremely difficult, and good speechreaders are rare. It is easy for those of us who have hearing to overlook some of the factors that make speechreading difficult. For one thing, speakers produce many sounds with little obvious movement of the mouth. There are many **homophenes**, different sounds that are visually identical. For example, the speechreader cannot distinguish among the pronunciation of [p], [b], or [m]. There is variability among speakers in how they produce sounds. And such things as poor lighting, rapid speaking, and talking with one's head turned are further examples of why good speechreading is a rare skill (Menchel, 1988).

Total Communication

As noted previously, most schools have adopted the total communication approach, a combination of oral and manual methods. The shift from oral-only instruction to total communication that occurred in the 1970s was primarily because researchers found that children who were deaf fared better academically and socially if they had parents who were deaf than if they had hearing parents (Moores & Maestas y Moores, 1981). Investigators attributed this difference to the greater likelihood of signing in families in which children and parents were both deaf.

Signing English Systems

Signing English systems are the type of manualism most often used in the total communication approach. **Signing English systems** refer to approaches

➤ **speechreading.** A method that involves teaching children to use visual information from a number of sources to understand what is being said to them; more than just lipreading, which uses only visual clues arising from the movement of the mouth in speaking.

➤ **cued speech.** A method to aid speechreading in those with hearing impairment; the speaker uses hand shapes to represent sounds.

➤ **homophenes.** Sounds identical in terms of revealing movements (visible articulatory patterns).

➤ **signing English systems.** Used simultaneously with oral methods in the total communication approach to teaching students who are deaf; different from American Sign Language because it maintains the same word order as spoken English.

Figure 8-2

➤ *Differentiation among vowels is made on the basis of jaw opening and lip shaping. The contrast between /à/ (as in* father*) and /ē/ (as in* he*) is shown here.*

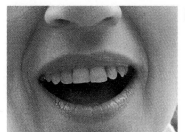 **[ȧ]**

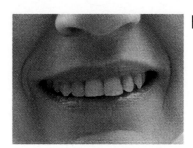 **[ē]**

that professionals have devised for teaching people who are deaf to communicate. There are several such systems, for example, Signing Exact English (Gustason, Pftezing, & Zawolkow, 1972) and Signed English (Bornstein, Hamilton, & Saulnier, 1983). The fact that teachers use signing English systems instead of ASL has sparked heated debate. **Fingerspelling**, the representation of letters of the English alphabet by finger positions, is also used occasionally to spell out certain words (see Figure 8–3 on page 324).

➤ **fingerspelling.** Spelling the English alphabet by various finger positions on one hand.

The Controversy Over Using ASL in the Classroom

Many within the Deaf community have championed the use of ASL in the classroom (Lane, 1987, 1992; Padden & Humphries, 1988; Sacks, 1989). This small but growing group of advocates asserts that ASL is the natural language of people who are deaf and that it should be fostered because it is the most natural and efficient way for students to learn about the world. Signing English systems are not true languages, such as ASL (see box on p. 325). Signing English systems have been invented by one or a few people in a short period of time, whereas true sign languages, such as ASL, have evolved over several generations of users.

One of the most important differences between the two is that signing English systems follow the same word order as spoken English, thus making it possible to sign and speak at the same time; ASL has a different word order, making the simultaneous use of spoken English and ASL extremely difficult. Defenders of signing English systems state that the correspondence in word order between signing English systems and English helps students learn English better. Advocates of ASL assert that the use of signing English systems is too slow and awkward to be of much benefit in learning English. They argue that word order is not the critical element in teaching a person to use and comprehend English. Furthermore, they believe that fluency in ASL provides students with a rich background of information that readies them for the learning of English:

Sound waves, movements of lips, printed words, or signs play only a small role in leading us to understand a sentence. The meaning of each word and its grammatical

Figure 8–3

➤ *Fingerspelling alphabet*

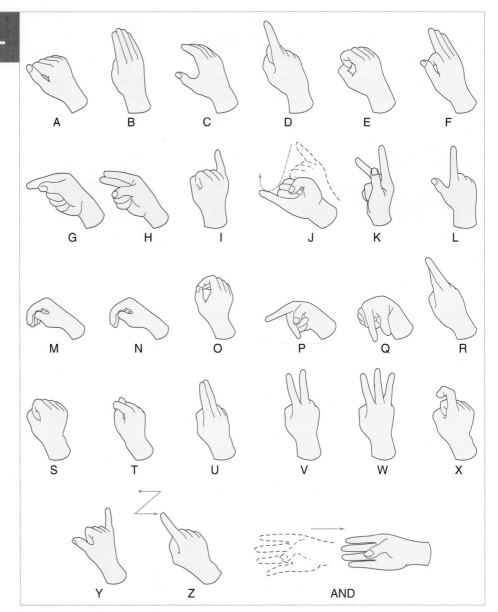

SOURCE: Adapted from L. J. Fant, Jr., *Say it with hands.* Copyright © 1971 from National Association for the Deaf, 1971, Silver Spring, MD. pp. 1–2. Reprinted with permission.

class are likewise not the basis of comprehension. In interpreting a sentence, in arriving at its sense, we rely unconsciously, and thus much more than we realize, on our knowledge of life, knowledge that is not specific to the particular language in which the sentence is communicated, knowledge that comes from general acculturation. Would a person commit an action like the one I understood? Can it be done in principle? Would the subject of the sentence be likely to do it? Acculturation is also the key to composing good sentences; children who know a lot about life have a lot to talk about, and they know which words and structures tend to come together. Thus, stu-

MERICAN SIGN LANGUAGE IS A TRUE LANGUAGE ➤

Many people, even some of those working in the area of deaf education, have the misconception that ASL and other sign languages are not true languages. (There is no universal sign language; ASL is only one among many. Most of them are nearly as different from each other as the spoken languages of the world.) Some believe ASL is merely a loosely constructed system of gestures, and some believe that the signs are so highly pictorial in nature that they limit ASL to the representation of concrete rather than abstract concepts. Research has demonstrated that ASL's detractors are wrong on both counts.

ASL HAS ITS OWN GRAMMAR

Far from a disorganized system, ASL has its own, very complicated grammar. It was the linguist William Stokoe who first submitted that analogous to the phonemes of spoken English, each sign in ASL consists of three parts: handshape, location, and movement (Stokoe, 1960; Stokoe, Casterline & Croneberg, 1976). He proposed that there are 19 different handshapes, 12 locations, and 24 types of movements. Scoffed at by his colleagues when he first advanced his theory, Stokoe has come to be regarded as a genius for his pioneering work on the structure of ASL (Sacks, 1989; Wolkomir, 1992).

ASL CAN BE USED TO CONVEY ABSTRACT IDEAS

The misconception that ASL transmits primarily concrete ideas probably comes from the belief held by many that signs are made up mostly of pictorial, or iconic, cues. Actually, the origin of some signs is iconic. But over time, even many of these iconic signs have lost their pictorial qualities (Klima & Bellugi, 1979). Sacks (1989) notes that it is the duality of sign—the use of the abstract and the concrete—that contributes to its vividness and aliveness. The following description captures the beauty of sign:

> The creativity can be remarkable. A person can sculpt exactly what he's saying. To sign "flower growing," you delicately place the fingertips at each side of the nose as if sniffing the flower, then you push the fingertips of one hand up through the thumb and first finger of the other. The flower can bloom fast and fade, or, with several quick bursts, it can be a whole field of daffodils. In spoken English, most people would seem silly if they talked as poetically as some supposedly illiterate deaf people sign. With one handshape—the thumb and little finger stretched out, the first finger pointing forward—you can make a plane take off, encounter engine trouble and turbulence, circle an airport, then come in for a bumpy landing. That entire signed sentence takes a fraction of the time that saying it aloud would. (Walker, 1986, p. 48)

dent-centered education conducted in the child's most fluent language is actually fostering his literacy in English even without a single word of English spoken. Of course, English must also be taught explicitly, with the aid of the child's most fluent language. (Lane, 1992, p. 182)

As yet, the use of ASL in public school classes is rare (Kluwin, 1992). However, a few schools are beginning to experiment with its use (Stewart, 1990).

Service Delivery Models

We find students with hearing impairment in settings ranging from general education classes to residential institutions. Since the passage of PL 94-142 in the mid-1970s, more and more of these students are attending local schools in self-contained classes, resource rooms, and regular classes (Schildroth & Hotto, 1991).

Many within the Deaf community, however, have been critical of the degree of mainstreaming that is occurring (Lane, 1987, 1992; Padden & Humphries, 1988). They argue that residential schools, and to a lesser extent day schools, have been a major influence in fostering the concept of a Deaf culture and ASL. Mainstreaming, they believe, forces students who are deaf to lose their Deaf identity and places them in a hearing and speaking environment in which it is almost impossible to succeed.

This researcher attaches diodes to her fingertips to trace the graceful and complex patterns created by fluent sign language, which many feel is the superior method of communication for individuals with hearing impairments.

Even some professionals who advocate mainstreaming of some sort point to the need for what they term a critical mass of students who are deaf (Higgins, 1992; Kluwin, 1992). As one investigator has put it:

> A critical mass enables educators to group deaf children appropriately (in self-contained classes as needed) and to provide the necessary staff, services, and equipment. It also increases the potential for deaf and hearing students to develop successful relations and for deaf youth to become part of a signing community should they choose to do so. (Higgins, 1992, p. 109)

In order to achieve the critical mass necessary to provide what they consider effective programs, more school districts may move toward centralization of their programs. Some have already begun to place many of the students who are deaf in one building. Although the majority of the students in the building are hearing, students who are deaf can be placed in self-contained classes, resource rooms, and/or regular classes. In addition to consolidating services and fostering a Deaf culture, some have noted that, given the possibility that a child will need a variety of placements over several years, such an arrangement lessens the need for frequent school changes (Moores, Cerney, & Garcia, 1990).

Officials of the United States Department of Education have become concerned that too much mainstreaming of students who are deaf is occurring (Viadero, 1992). They have advanced the position that the intent of PL 94-142 was not to place all students who are deaf in regular classrooms. In other words, they are promoting the notion of a full continuum of services that was discussed in Chapter 2.

Technological Advances

A number of technological advances have made it easier for persons with hearing impairment to communicate with and/or have access to information from the hearing world. This technological explosion has taken place primarily in four areas: hearing aids, computer-assisted instruction, television, and the telephone.

Hearing Aids

The two main types of hearing aids are those that fit in the ear and those that are worn behind the ear. The behind-the-ear hearing aid is the one recommended for children because it can be used with FM systems available in some class-rooms (Hawkins, 1990). Whether a student will be able to benefit from a hearing aid by itself depends a great deal on the acoustic qualities of the classroom. Most classrooms have so much reverberation and such a low signal-to-noise ratio that an FM system is needed to really help the child (Hawkins, 1990). In an FM sys-tem, the teacher wears a wireless lapel microphone and the student wears an FM receiver (about the size of a cigarette package). The student hears the amplified sound either through a hearing aid that comes attached to the FM receiver or by attaching a behind-the-ear hearing aid to the FM receiver. (More and more per-sonal behind-the-ear hearing aids are being manufactured with this capability.)

Although hearing aids are an integral part of educational programming for students with hearing impairment, some children who are deaf cannot benefit from them because of the severity and/or kind of their hearing impairment. Generally, hearing aids make sounds louder, not clearer, so if a person's hearing is distorted, a hearing aid will merely amplify the distorted sound.

For those who can benefit from hearing aids, it is critical for the student, par-ents, and teachers to work together to ensure the maximum effectiveness of the aid. This means that the teacher should be familiar with the operation and main-tenance of the instrument. Research has generally shown a high degree of mal-function in personal hearing aids and FM systems used in schools (Hawkins, 1990).

Computer-Assisted Instruction

Professionals are using microcomputers to teach reading, writing, and sign language to students with hearing impairment (Prinz, Pemberton, & Nelson, 1985). Experimental microcomputer programs that show visual displays of

*H*earing aids come in a variety of designs, and teachers should be familiar with the workings of as many styles as possible.

The availability of captions makes television accessible to people with hearing impairments.

speech are seen as a possible way of improving speech (Boothroyd, 1987). And investigators are developing interactive videodiscs to help hearing people learn sign language (Slike, Chiavacci, & Hobbis, 1989).

Television Captioning and Teletext

Numerous television programs are now captioned for use by people with hearing impairment, and many videotapes available from video rental stores are captioned. A special decoder attached to the television allows the viewer to see captions for live (e.g., sporting events and news shows) and taped programs. Teletext provides access to such information as news, cultural calendars, and community announcements.

Telephone Adaptations

Persons with hearing impairment have traditionally had problems using telephones either because their hearing loss was too great or because of acoustic feedback—noise caused by closeness of the telephone receiver to their hearing aids. The development of the **teletypewriter (TTY)** has allowed them access to the telephone. A person can use a TTY connected to a telephone to type a message to anyone else who has a TTY. A special phone adaptation allows people without a TTY to use the pushbuttons on their phone to "type" messages to persons with TTYs.

EARLY INTERVENTION

Researchers and practitioners have espoused the importance of education for infants and preschoolers with hearing impairments. Because language development is such an issue with children who are hearing impaired and because early childhood is such an important time for the development of language, it is not surprising that many of the most controversial issues surrounding early intervention in the area of deafness focus on language. As indicated in the earlier discussion of oralism versus manualism, some people maintain that English language should be the focus of intervention efforts, and some people hold that ASL

➣ **teletypewriter (TTY).** A device connected to a telephone by a special adapter; allows communication between persons who are hearing impaired and the hearing over the telephone.

should be used starting in infancy. Among English language advocates there are professionals who recommend a total communication approach combining spoken English and some kind of signed English system.

Research comparing children who are deaf who have parents who are deaf versus those with parents who are hearing has consistently found that the latter are at a greater risk of having a variety of problems (Meadow-Orlans, 1990). For example, infants who are deaf who have parents who are deaf develop ASL at a rate similar to the rate at which hearing infants of hearing parents develop English. Infants who are deaf who have hearing parents do not develop either English or ASL at as fast a rate. And in the social arena, children who are deaf who have hearing parents tend to be more immature and dependent on the teacher. The fact that over 90 percent of children who are deaf have parents who are hearing underscores the importance of intervention for many infants who are deaf.

Authorities point to the use of ASL by parents who are deaf as a major factor in the developmental differences found between deaf children who have deaf parents and those who do not. They also note that while hearing parents are likely to be taken by surprise with their baby's "handicap," parents who are themselves deaf are more likely to view the deafness as "normal" and to be better prepared to care for their infant's needs:

> For deaf parents, deafness is a familiar condition. They have a wide circle of deaf friends. . . . They know the educational opportunities available for deaf children, and the vocational possibilities that lie ahead. They can anticipate rearing their deaf child as they themselves were reared, or perhaps with modifications based on experiences they want to avoid. For parents with normal hearing, all these areas provide unknown vistas. . . .
>
> For most parents with normal hearing, the diagnosis of deafness in a young child comes as a profound shock. Often, the diagnosis confuses deafness with other kinds of impairments, such as mental retardation or emotional disturbance. The struggle to achieve a firm medical opinion about the child's condition may be debilitating for parents, and this concern and confusion interferes with early childrearing practices. (Meadow-Orlans, 1990, p. 286)

Some of this interference in childrearing practices apparently involves the day-to-day interactions between the parent and the infant. Researchers have found, for example, that interactions between mothers and infants are more facilitative and natural when both the infant and parents are deaf than when the infant is deaf and the parents are hearing. Hearing mothers of infants who are deaf tend to be more directive in their interactions with their infants, more likely to start an interaction that is unrelated to the child's activity or expressed interest (Spencer & Gutfreund, 1990). Researchers have also suggested that too much maternal directiveness leads to slower language development.

Hearing mothers, especially if they desire to teach their infants sign language, may need help in understanding the importance of the visual modality in communicating with their infants (Koester & Meadow-Orlans, 1990). They need to understand, for example, that the eye gaze of the infant who is deaf is extremely important because it is his or her way of expressing interest and motivation. They also need to be aware that, just as hearing babies babble vocally, babies who are deaf engage in "babbling" with their hands as they begin to acquire sign language (Wolkomir, 1992).

In Their Own Words   LOU ANN WALKER

Lou Ann Walker is the hearing daughter of two deaf parents. From the time she was a toddler she served as liaison between her parents and an outside world that did not always understand or welcome people with such "afflictions." Her unusual situation, and a deep love and respect for her parents, gives her a unique vision, enabling her to enter the sometimes impenetrable world of deafness.

Ms. Walker currently lives in New York City, and is a professional writer contributing to several national publications. She also teaches classes in sign language in her spare time, and is the recipient of a Rockefeller Foundation Humanities grant to research the subject of hearing children of deaf parents.

The following exercpts from her autobiography, *A Loss For Words: The Story of Deafness in a Family,* describe both the author's memories of having to shield her parents from the callousness of others, and the strength of the bond shared between them.

Curled up in the seat, chin dug into my chest, I noticed there was a lull in the conversation. Dad was a confident driver, but Mom was smoking more than usual.

"Something happened? That gas station?" Mom signed to me.

"No, nothing," I lied.

"Are you sure?"

"Yes. Everything is fine." Dad and I had gone in to pay and get directions. The man behind the counter had looked up, seen me signing and grunted, "Huh, I didn't think mutes were allowed to have driver's licenses." Long ago I'd gotten used to hearing those kinds of comments. But I never could get used to the way they made me churn inside. . . .

As I sat in the living room, I realized that if all my parents had to endure—and all my sisters and I ever had to hear—was a little name-calling, life would have been much easier. On the face of it, deafness seems to be a simple affliction. If you can't hear, people assume you can make up for that lack by writing notes, that you can pass your spare time reading books, that you can converse by talking and reading lips. Unfortunately, things are always more complicated than they seem.

Until they're about the age of two, babies are tape recorders, taking in everything that is being said around them. The brain uses these recordings as the basis of language. If for any reason a baby is deprived of those years of language, he can never make up the loss. For those who become completely deaf—"profoundly" is the term audiologists apply—during infancy, using the basics of English becomes a task as difficult as building a house without benefit of drawings or experience in carpentry. Writing a grammatically correct sentence is a struggle. Reading a book is a Herculean effort. . . .

Dad led Mom to the dance floor. They stole a couple of glances at the dancers around them to make sure the beat hadn't changed—or the music stopped. After a few cautious steps they danced to whatever beat they felt like, wrapped in each other's arms. Dad twirled Mom around and held her as they dipped.

SOURCE: Lou Ann Walker, *A Loss for Words: The Story of Deafness in a Family,* (New York: Harper and Row Publishers, 1986), pp. 9, 19, 20.

TRANSITION

Before the mid-1960s, the only institution established specifically for the postsecondary education of students with hearing impairment was Gallaudet College (now Gallaudet University). Except for this one institution, these students were left with no choice but to attend traditional colleges and universities. Traditional post-secondary education was generally not equipped to handle the special needs of students with hearing impairment, so it is little wonder that a study by Quigley, Jenne, and Phillips (1968) was able to identify only 224 graduates with hearing impairment of regular colleges and universities in the United States between 1910 and 1965.

Findings such as these led to the expansion of postsecondary programs. The federal government has now funded a wide variety of postsecondary programs for students with hearing impairment. In 1965, the National Technical Institute

he Deaf West Theatre has been hugely successful as an enterprise run exclusively by individuals with hearing impairment.

for the Deaf (NTID) (established at the Rochester Institute of Technology) was founded. The NTID program, emphasizing training in technical fields, complements the liberal arts orientation of Gallaudet University. At NTID some students with hearing impairment also attend classes with hearing students at the Rochester Institute of Technology. Research has indicated that this mainstreaming is related to better academic achievement and future career adjustment (Saur, Coggiola, Long, & Simonson, 1986).

Following the establishment of NTID, an explosion of postsecondary programs occurred. There are now well over 100 postsecondary programs in the United States and Canada for students with hearing impairment. By law, Gallaudet and NTID are responsible for serving students from all 50 states and territories. Others serve students from several states, from one state only, or from a specific district only.

There has also been an increase in transition programming for students who are deaf who are not going on to postsecondary educational institutions. Unfortunately, some of this programming is not yet very well articulated, especially in local public schools (Bull & Bullis, 1991). Because they have a much longer history of dealing with transition issues, residential schools have better transition plans than do local school districts. Transition programs in local schools for students who are hearing impaired should improve in quality as they become more accustomed to delivering such services.

For students who are hearing impaired, much progress has been made in the availability of postsecondary education opportunities and transition programs for those not going to college, but there is still considerable room for improvement. The unemployment rate and the number of persons who are over-qualified for jobs are still too high. As Lane (1992) notes, there is a long tradition of preparing students who are deaf for manual trades. Since unskilled and semi-skilled trades are fast disappearing from the workforce in favor of jobs requiring higher level skills, adults who are deaf face even greater obstacles as they enter the job market. Professionals involved in transition programming for students who are hearing impaired have myriad challenges facing them as we move toward the 21st century.

SUGGESTIONS FOR TEACHING ➤

E. Jane Nowacek

Students with Hearing Impairment in General Education Classrooms

WHAT TO LOOK FOR IN SCHOOL

Children with mild hearing losses can attend school for several years before their impairments are identified. Although they may have learned to compensate for their hearing difficulties in many school situations, they are at a disadvantage when compared academically to their nondisabled classmates and at risk to become frustrated learners and socially isolated from other students. For these reasons, it is important that you are aware of the following indicators of a possible hearing loss:

1. difficulties in understanding spoken language and/or speaking
2. frequent absences due to earaches, sinus congestion, allergies, and related conditions
3. inattention and daydreaming
4. disorientation and/or confusion, especially when noise levels are high
5. difficulties in following directions
6. frequent imitation of other students' behaviors in the classroom

HOW TO GATHER INFORMATION

If these signs occur consistently, contact the speech and language specialist assigned to your school who can administer tests to determine whether or not there is a hearing loss. If your student is found eligible for special education, support will be available to you. The type of assistance will depend on the student's specific needs and the services provided by your school system. It is important that you understand both the services your student will receive and the complete educational plan he or she will follow. For example, you may want to ask the special education teacher the following questions (White, 1981):

- Do I have the information I need to plan an effective educational program in all subjects I teach? Do I have appropriate materials to carry out this program?
- How should I schedule and group students to maximize educational and social opportunities?
- What amplification equipment will be used by the student? By me?
- Who is responsible for demonstrating the use of this equipment and for maintaining it?
- Whom do I contact and what procedures do I follow to request assistance if a problem arises?

If a student with hearing impairments is to be mainstreamed into your class, Jaussi (1991) recommends preparing classmates in several ways. Lead class discussions about hearing losses, hearing aids, and other amplification devices. Encourage students to talk about their own feelings about deafness. Introduce them to persons with hearing impairments by arranging classroom visits with children or adults who are deaf or who have hearing losses. Read accounts of persons with hearing impairments. (See *Literature* at the end of the chapter for specific references for fictional and nonfictional books on persons with hearing losses.)

TEACHING TECHNIQUES TO TRY

Students who are mainstreamed can be expected to follow the regular curriculum if they have the prerequisite skills (Ross, Brackett, & Maxon, 1991). Students with hearing losses, however, may require modifications of the physical, instructional, and social environments to benefit fully from education in the mainstream. Modifications of the physical environment may involve simple changes in seating, such as moving students away from sources of background noise such as open windows and doors and noisy heating and cooling systems (Ross, 1982). Adapting seating arrangements so students are located in the front of the room with their chair or desk turned slightly so they can see the faces of all the other students, permitting free movement around the classroom to reduce the distance between themselves and the speakers, and using flexible seating arrangements that allow students to change seats as activities change promote understanding and participation in class activities (Ross, 1982). In addition, arranging desks in a staggered pattern rather than in straight rows enables the bodies of students to further reduce reflected sound and improves the acoustics of the classroom (Gerheart, Weishahn, & Gearheart, 1992).

Kampfe (1984) summarizes other adaptations to the physical environment that require more extensive planning and expense. These modifications include reducing classroom noise by carpeting floors, draping windows, and covering walls with materials that absorb extraneous noise such as corkboard or Styrofoam sheets; locating the classroom away from high traffic and noise areas as gyms, cafeterias, and playgrounds; and minimizing class activities in large echoing rooms.

Instructional modifications also can enhance the learning of your students who are hearing impaired. Using teaching formats that include exhibits, demonstrations, experiments, and simulations provide hands-on experiences that tend to promote understanding and are easier to follow than lectures and whole-class discussions. Writing directions in short, simple sentences and using pictures to illustrate the procedure or process supplements the oral explanations you give during demonstrations (Waldron, Diebold, & Rose, 1985).

When you do use lecture and discussion formats, you can promote understanding (Kampfe, 1984; Palmer, 1988; Ross et al., 1991) by:

- Positioning yourself so your face is illuminated even when the room is darkened to show slides or videotapes;

- Using an overhead projector to note important points, key words, directions, and assignments so you can face students while speaking;
- Providing lecture notes or outlines;
- Avoiding moving around the room and turning your back to students when speaking so they can see your face;
- Shortening and simplifying verbalizations;
- Repeating main points or paraphrasing them into a simpler form;
- Repeating questions and answers given by other students;
- Providing summaries throughout the lecture or discussion;
- Using nonverbal cues, such as facial expressions, body movements, and gestures;
- Signaling changes in topic within a lecture or discussion;
- Calling speakers' names to reduce time spent in locating the source of speech;
- Requiring students to raise hands to reduce the noise and confusion that results when several people are talking at once;
- Checking student comprehension of instruction often.

In addition to modifying oral communication, educators also emphasize the importance of adapting written materials because the "best instructional format with deaf students. . . is predominantly pictorial with some. . . verbal information" (Waldron, Diebold, & Rose, 1985, p. 40). Adapting materials by using visual displays, such as diagrams, pictures, graphs, and flow charts reduces language and reading demands.

Regardless of the teaching format you use, it is advisable to follow a preview, teach, and review cycle (Ross et al., 1991). Flatley and Gittinger (1990) recommend three preview strategies for students with hearing impairment. The first strategy, pinpointing facts and fallacies, helps identify and clarify misconceptions before students integrate new information with their prior knowledge. Teachers can develop an anticipation guide, which directs students to agree or disagree with statements of key concepts, as one type of preview strategy. Student responses to the guide allow teachers to pinpoint existing misconceptions informally. A second preview strategy involves representing information in a graphic organizer, a visual display of informational components and their relationship to one another. The selection of a specific type of organizer depends on the content (e.g., compare and contrast matrices, problem/solution outlines, and cycle graphic organizers). Fishbone maps (See Figure 8–4) illustrate the causal relationships of a complex event such as an election. For specific information on types and construction of graphic representations see Jones, Pierce and Hunter (1989). A third strategy involves categorizing ideas. Like the other preview strategies, it activates prior knowledge, here

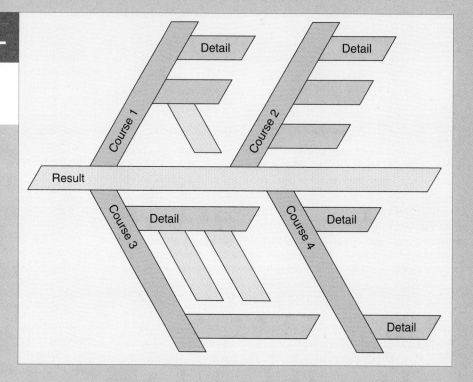

Figure 8-4

➤ *An example of a fishbone map*

by asking students to brainstorm a list of words they associate with the concept or topic under study. Once the list is complete, students and teacher define the words, group by category, and then label the categories. Like graphic organizers, categorization provides a framework for students to organize information. In fact, many teachers arrange the words on a large chart to create a graphic organizer of the concept or topic.

Just as previewing helps students access prior knowledge, organize new information, and integrate it with existing knowledge, so reviewing reinforces new vocabulary and concepts. Clues and questions are one example of an effective review strategy (Flatley & Gittinger, 1990). To implement this strategy, teachers select vocabulary words and write each word on a separate index card. Next, they write a question on the reverse side of the card for which the word is the correct answer. Teachers then give several cards to cooperative groups, instructing them to take turns answering questions until they identify the words.

Student tutors can assist in the review process as well, and pupils with hearing impairment may benefit socially as well as academically from tutoring by a classmate. Tutors can provide additional examples, practice, and clarification, as needed. Also, tutors can help prepare students with hearing impairment for quizzes and coach them in test-taking strategies. For additional information about peer tutoring, see the Suggestions for Teaching section in Chapter 4.

Teachers can create additional opportunities for social and academic interactions by using the buddy system. In this arrangement, a normally hearing student sits next to a student who has a hearing loss to clarify explanations, directions, page numbers, and other oral communications (Robinson, 1984). Buddies may share class notes so that students with hearing impairment can concentrate on the speaker. And Buddies can also alert students to warning signals, such as fire alarms.

In addition to these classroom arrangements that promote social interactions among students with hearing impairment and hearing students, some schools are offering American Sign Language (ASL) as a foreign language alternative. It is hoped that increasing the modes of communication that all students have in common will expand the social interactions that occur among students.

Helpful Resources

School Personnel

In many school systems, special education services are provided to students with hearing impairment by specialists who work in several schools (sometimes called deaf educators). Typically, they work with students in each building one day or one-half day a week on such skills as communication, auditory training, listening, and reading (Dilka, 1984).

These educators are good resources for information about hearing impairment, amplification equipment, and instructional modifications. They also may adapt instructional materials for use in a mainstream class.

Recently, school systems have begun to employ educational interpreters to facilitate communication among students with hearing impairment, teachers, and others in the classroom and school. A report of the National Task Force on Educational Interpreting (Stuckless, Avery, & Harwitz, 1989) outlines the appropriate roles for these interpreters within mainstream classes as follows:

1. The primary responsibility of educational interpreters is to facilitate communication between deaf persons and others in schools.
2. This role may include interpreting during out-of-class activities, such as field trips, club meetings, and sporting events.
3. In addition, educational interpreters can be expected to participate in planning meetings with the classroom teacher. During these meetings, they coordinate plans for the student with hearing impairment by discussing course content, lesson plans, and upcoming tests. Educational interpreters also need preparation time to preview instructional materials and to become oriented to the content and vocabulary.
4. Expanded responsibilities of tutoring, sign language instruction, and general classroom assistance may be provided by educational interpreters.

The Task Force report reminds teachers that "educational interpreters should not be asked to assume responsibilities for duties for which they do not have the needed training and/or background knowledge" (p. 9). With this recommendation in mind, teachers should not ask educational interpreters to provide formal instruction or classroom supervision. Tutoring and other expanded duties should be conducted under the direct supervision of the teacher.

Many educators strongly recommend that the specialist trained in hearing impairment, the classroom teacher, the educational interpreter, and the student meet at the beginning of the semester to discuss their roles and responsibilities in detail (LeBuffe, 1988). LeBuffe says that in such a meeting,

. . . students will learn that it is their responsibility, not the interpreter's, to ask questions, take part in class discussions, and keep track of homework assignments. The interpreter will be reminded that he or she is there only to interpret, not to be a disciplinarian or teacher. Teachers will be assured that they are in charge of the entire class, including the mainstreamed students, and will be given helpful information on hearing loss and support services. The role of the deaf education teacher will be described and details concerning punctuality, discipline, classwork, homework, class participation, notetaking, and the use of hearing aids will be explained. (p.5)

For a complete list of the responsibilities of each of the participants in the meeting see Le Buffe (1988).

Instructional Methods

Berg, F. S. (1987). *Facilitating classroom listening: A handbook for teachers of normal and hard of hearing students.* San Diego, CA: College Hill; Little, Brown & Co.

Berry, V. (1988). Classroom intervention strategies and resource materials for the auditorily handicapped child. In R. J. Roeser & M. P. Downs (Eds.), *Auditory disorders in school children* (2nd ed.) (pp. 325-349). New York: Thieme Medical.

Berry, V. (1992). Communication priorities and strategeis for the mainstreamed child with hearing loss. *The Volta Review, 94* (1), 29-36.

Bolte, A. (1987). Our language routine: Reading together and loving it. *Perspectives for teachers of the hearing impaired.* 5, 3-5.

Brackett, D. (1990). Communication management of the mainstreamed hearing impaired student. In M. Ross (Ed.), *Hearing impaired children in the mainstream* (pp. 119-130). Parkton, MD: York Press.

Conway, L. (1990). Issues relating to classroom management. In M. Ross (Ed.), *Hearing impaired children in the mainstream* (pp. 131-157). Parkton, MD: Aork Press.

Dreher, B., & Duell, E. (1987). Videotapes make storybooks come alive. *Perspectives for teachers of the hearing impaired*, 5, 18-20.

Ewoldt, C., & Hammermeister, F. (1986). The language experience approach to facilitating reading and writing for hearing-impaired students. *American Annals of the Deaf*, 13, 271-274.

Gelzer, L. (1988). Developing reading appreciation in young deaf children. *Perspectives for teachers of the hearing impaired*, 6, 13-16.

Gearheart, B. R., Weishahn, M. W., & Gearheart, C. J. (1992). *The exceptional student in the regular classroom* (5th ed.). New York: Merrill/Macmillan.

Gjerdingen, D., & Manning, F. D. (1991). Adolescents with profound hearing impairments in mainstreamed education: The Clarke Model. *The Volta Review*, 93, 139-148.

Heathman, M. D., & LeBuffe, J. R. (1988). Three steps in developing high school students' notetaking skills. *Perspectives for teachers of the hearing impaired*, 7, 9-12.

Lewis, R. B., & Doorlag, D. (1991). *Teaching special students in the mainstream* (3rd ed.) (pp. 356-380). New York: Merrill.

Lucker, J. L. (1987). Strategies for building your students' self-esteem. *Perspectives for teachers of the hearing impaired*, 6, 9-11.

Martin, F. M. (Ed.). (1987). *Hearing disorders in children.* Austin, TX: Pro-ed.

Nussbaum, D. (1988). *There's a hearing impaired child in my class.* Washington, D. C.: Gallaudet University Press.

Ross, M., Brackett, D., & Maxon, A. B. (1991). *Assessment and management of mainstreamed hearing-impaired children: Principles and practices.* Austin, TX: Pro-ed.

Stern, R. C. (1980). Adapting media to meet your students' needs. *American Annals of the Deaf, 12,* 861-865.

Sunal, D. W., & Burch, P. E. (1982). School science programs for hearing impaired students. *American Annals of the Deaf, 127,* 411-417.

Wray, D., Hazlett, J., & Flexer, C. (1988). Strategies for teaching writing skills to hearing-impaired students. *Language, Speech, and Hearing Services in Schools, 19,* 182-190.

Curricular Materials

Captioned films that address subjects such as business, English, Mathematics, and Career Education are available from: Modern Talking Picture Service, Captioned Films Division, 500 Park Street, St. Petersburg, FL 33709, (800) 237-6213.

Cowen, N. (1986). *Preparing for work.* Washington, D. C.: Gallaudet University Press.

Curricular guides and materials designed for hearing impaired students are available for several areas from the bookstore at Gallaudet University. For a free catalogue of current offerings, write or call: Gallaudet Bookstore, Kendall Green, P. O. Box 103, Washington, DC 20002, (202) 651-5380.

Fitz-Gerald, M. (1986). *Information on sexuality for young people and their families.* Washington, DC: Gallaudet College. (ERIC Document Reproduction Service No. ED 294 407)

Gillespie, S. (1988). *Science Curriculum Guide: Kendall Demonstration Elementary School,* (2nd ed.), Washington, DC: Gallaudet College. (ERIC Document Reproduction Service No. ED 298 741)

Introduction to communication (1986). Washington, DC: Outreach, Pre-College Programs, Gallaudet College. (ERIC Document Reproduction Service No. ED 298 746)

Kurlychek, K. (1991). *Software to go.* Washington D. C.: Gallaudet University Press. (This catalogue lists and describes commercial software that may be borrowed by educators of students with hearing impairement.)

Lane, L. G. (1990). *Gallaudet survival guide to signing* (2nd ed.). Washington D. C.: Gallaudet University Press.

Lists of captioned videotapes are available from the bookstore at Gallaudet University.

Pucciarelli, C. S. (Ed.), (1987). *Curriculum for mainstreamed preschool children who are hearing impaired.* Westbury, NY: Nassau County Board of Cooperative Educational Services. (ERIC Document Reproduction Service No. ED 299 778)

Sunal, D. W. & Sunal, C. S. (1981). *Teachers guide for science-adapted for the hearing impaired: Introduction and Levels 3-7.* Morgantown, WV: West Virginia University. (ERIC Document Reproduction Service No. ED JUNRIE)

Literature about Individuals with Hearing Impairment

ELEMENTARY

Andrews, J. F. (1992). *Hasta luego, San Diego.* Washington, D. C.: Gallaudet University Press. (Ages 9-12) (Fiction=F)

Aseltine, L., & Mueller, E. (1986). *I'm deaf and it's okay.* New York: Albert Whitman. (Ages 5-8) (F)

Bove, L. (1980). *Sesame Street sign language fun.* New York: Random House. (Ages 5-8) (Nonfiction=NF)

Bridges, C. (1980). *The hero.* Northridge, CA: Joyce Media, Inc. (F)

Crowley, J. (1981). *The silent one.* New York: Knopf. (Ages 9-12) (F)

Curtis, P. (1981). *Cindy a hearing ear dog.* New York: E. P. Dutton. (NF)

Guccione, L. D. (1989). *Tell me how the wind sounds.* New York: Scholastic. (Ages 9-12) (F)

Hess, L. (1985). *The good luck dog.* New York: Chas. Scribner's. (F)

Hilbok, B. (1981). *Silent dancer.* New York: Messner. (Ages 9-12) (NF)

Levi, D. H. (1989). *A very special friend.* Washington, DC: Kendall Green Publications. (F)

Peterson, J. W. (1977). *I have a sister. My sister is deaf.* New York: Harper & Row. (NF)

Pollock, P. (1982). *Keeping it secret.* New York: Putnam. (Ages 9-12) (F)

Riskind, M. (1981). *Apple is my sign.* Boston: Houghton, Mifflin. (Ages 9-12).(F)

SECONDARY

Albronda, M. (1980). *Douglas Tilden: Portrait of a deaf sculptor.* Silver Springs, MD: T. J. Publications. (Ages 16-18) (NF)

Carroll, C. (1992). *Clerc: The story of his early years.* Washington, D. C.: Gallaudet University Press. (Ages 13-15) (NF)

Clark, M. G. (1980). *Who stole Kathy Young?* New York: Dodd, Mead. (Ages 13-15) (F)

Glick, F. P., & Pellman, D. R. (1982). *Breaking silence: A family grows with deafness.* (Ages 13-18) (NF)

Levinson, N. S. (1981). *World of her own.* New York: Harvey House. (Ages 13-15) (F)

Morganroth, B. (1981). *Will the real Renie Lake please stand up?* New York: Atheneum. (Ages 13-15) (F)

Neisser, A. (1983). *The other side of silence: Sign language and the deaf community.* New York: Knopf. (Ages 16-18) (NF)

Quinn, P. (1991). *Matthew Pinkowski's special summer.* Washington, D. C.: Gallaudet University Press.

Ray, N. L. (1981). *There was this man running.* New York: Macmillan. (Ages 13-15) (F)

Rosen, L. (1984). *Just like everyone else.* New York: Harcourt Brace Jovanovich. (Ages 13-15) (F)

Schein, J. D. (1989). *A home among strangers: Exploring the deaf community in the United States.* Washington, D. C.: Gallaudet University Press.

Spradley, T. S., & Spradley, J. P. (1978). *Deaf like me.* New York: Random House. (Ages 16-18) (NF)

Computer Software

Academic Skills and Drill Builder Program in Language Arts, Developmental Learning Materials, One DLM Park, Allen, TX 75002, (800) 527-5030.

Adventures of Jimmy Jumper: Prepositions, Exceptional Children's Software, P. O. Box 487, Fort Hays, KS 67601, (913) 625-9281.

Blackout! A Capitalization Game, Gamco Industries, P. O. Box 1911, Big Spring, TX 79721, (800) 351-1404. (Grades 4-10)

Create with Garfield, Developmental Learning Materials, One DLM Park, Allen, TX 75002, (800) 527-5030.

Figurative Language, Hartley Courseware, P.O. Box 419, Diamondale, MI 48821, (800) 247-1380.

Grammar Gremlins, Davidson Associates, 3135 Kashiwa St., Torrance, CA 90505, (800) 545-7667. (Grades 3-6)

Grammar Toy Shop, MECC, 6160 Summit Drive North, Minneapolis, MN 55430-4003, (800) 685-6322.

Homonyms, Hartley Courseware, P.O. Box 419, Diamondale, MI 48821, (800) 247-1380. (Grades 2-5)

Idea Invasion, DLM, One DLM Park, P. O. Box 4000, Allen, TX 75002, (800) 527-5030. (Language arts, basic skills)

Kidwriter, Spinnaker Software, 201 Broadway, Cambridge, MA 02139, (800) 323-8088. (Grades 1-5)

Lessons in Syntax, Dormac, Inc., P.O. Box 270459, San Diego, CA 921228-099983, (800) 547-8032.

Micro Labs, Laureate Learning Systems, 110 East Spring Street, Winoski, VT 05404, (800) 562-6801.

Spell It!, Davidson Associates, 3135 Kashiwa St., Torrence, CA 90505, (800) 545-7667. (Grades 3-9)

Spellicopter, DesignWare, 185 Berry Street, San Francisco, CA 94107.

Stickybear Reading, Weekly Reader Family Software, 245 Long Hill Road, Middletown, CT 05457.

Spelling Tutor, Nibble, P.O. Box 325, Lincoln, MA 01773.

Those Amazing Reading Machines series, MECC, 6160 Summit Drive North, Minneapolis, MN 55430-4003, (800) 685-6322.

Walt Disney Comic Strip Maker, Apple Scribe, DMP, 666 Fifth Avenue, New York, NY 10103.

Where is Puff? UCLA Intervention Program for Handicapped Children, 1000 Vetern Ave., Room 23-10, Los Angeles, CA 90024, (301) 825-4821. (Requires Echo Speech synthesizer, color monitor)

Who, What, Where, Why? Hartley Courseware, P.O. Box 419, Diamondale, MI 48821, (800) 247-1380. (Grades 1-4)

Word Invasion, Developmental Learning Materials, One DLM Park, Allen, TX 75002, (800) 527-5030.

Word Master, Developmental Learning Materials, One DLM Park, Allen, TX 75002, (800) 527-5030.

Services

Schools and programs for deaf students in the United States (1992). *American Annals of the Deaf, 137*, 102-167.

Postsecondary programs for deaf students in the United States (1992). *American Annals of the Deaf, 137*, 182-191.

Supportive and rehabilitative programs for the deaf in the United States (1992). *American Annals of the Deaf, 137*, 214-239.

Organizations

National Association for the Deaf, 814 Thayer Avenue, Silver Spring, MD 20910, (301) 587-1788.

National Foundation for Children's Hearing Education and Research, 928 McLean Avenue, Yonkers, NY 10704, (914) 237-2676.

Self-Help for Hard of Hearing People, 7800 Wisconsin Avenue, Bethesda, MD 20814, (301) 657-2248.

BIBLIOGRAPHY FOR TEACHING SUGGESTIONS

Dilka, K. L. (1984). The professions and others who work with the hearing-impaired child in school. In R. H. Hull & K. L. Dilka (Eds.), *The hearing-impaired child in school* (pp. 69-82). Orlando, FL: Grune & Stratton.

Flatley, J. K., & Gittinger, D. J. (1990). Teaching abstract concepts: Keys to the world of ideas. *Perspectives for teachers of the hearing impaired, 8*, 7-9.

Gearheart, B. R., Weishahn, M.W., & Gearheart, C. J. (1992). *The exceptional student in the regular classroom* (5th ed.). New York: Merrill/Macmillan.

Jaussi, K. R. (1991). Drawing the outsiders in: Deaf students in the mainstream. *Perspectives for teachers of the hearing impaired, 9*, 12-15.

Jones, B. F., Pierce, J., & Hunter, B. (1989). Teaching students to construct graphic representations. *Educational Leadership, 46*, 20-25.

Kampfe, C. M. (1984). Mainstreaming: Some practical suggestions for teachers and administrators. In R. H. Hull & K. L. Dilka (Eds.), *The hearing-impaired child in school* (pp. 99-112). Orlando, FL: Grune & Stratton.

LeBuffe, A. R. (1988). A clarification of the roles and responsibilities of teachers, students, and interpreters in a mainstream setting. *Perspectives for Teachers of the Hearing Impaired, 6*, 5-7.

Palmer, L. (1988). Speechreading as communication. *The Volta Review, 90*, 33-42.

Robinson, E. B. (1984). Hamilton P. S.: An alternative that's working, *Perspectives for teachers of the hearing impaired, 3*, 11-12.

Ross, M. (1982). *Hard of hearing children in regular schools.* Englewood Cliffs, NJ: Prentice-Hall.

Ross, M., Brackett, D., & Maxon, A. B. (1991). *Assessment and management of mainstreamed hearing-impaired children.* Austin, TX: Pro-ed.

Stuckless, E. R., Avery, J. C., & Hurwitz, T. A. (Eds.). (1989). *Educational interpreting for deaf students: Report of the National Task Force on Educational Interpreting.* Rochester, NY: National Technical Institute for the Deaf.

Waldron, M. B., Diebold, T. J., & Rose, S. (1985). Hearing impaired students in regular classrooms: A cognitive model for educational services. *Exceptional Children, 52*, 39-43.

White, N. A. (1981). The role of the regular classroom teacher. In V. J. Froehlinger (Ed.), *Today's hearing-impaired child: Into the mainstream of education* (pp.108-127). Washington, DC: Alexander Graham Bell Association for the Deaf.

Summary

In defining hearing impairment, educators are concerned primarily with the extent to which the hearing loss affects the ability to speak and understand spoken language. They refer to people with hearing impairment who cannot process linguistic information as *deaf* and those who can as *hard of hearing.* In addition, those who are deaf at birth or before language develops are referred to as having *prelingual deafness,* and those who acquire their deafness after spoken language starts to develop are referred to as having *postlingual deafness.* Professionals favoring a physiological viewpoint define deaf children as those who cannot hear sounds at or above a certain intensity level; they call others with hearing impairment *hard of hearing.*

The three most commonly used types of tests for hearing acuity are pure-tone audiometry, speech audiometry, and specialized tests for very young and hard-to-test children. The examiner uses pure tones or speech to find the intensity of sound (measured in decibels) the person can hear at different frequency levels (measured in Hertz). Audiologists must often test very young children, as well as those who may have difficulty understanding what is expected of them, using play, reflex, or evoked-response audiometry.

Professionals often classify causes of hearing loss according to the location of the problem within the hearing mechanism. *Conductive* losses are impairments that interfere with transferral of sound along the conductive pathway of the ear. *Sensorineural* problems are confined to the complex inner ear and are apt to be more severe and harder to treat.

Impairments of the outer ear are caused by such things as infections of the external canal or tumors. Middle-ear troubles usually occur because of some malfunction of one or more of the three tiny bones called ossicles in the middle ear. Otitis media, a condition stemming from eustachian tube malfunctioning, is the most common problem of the middle ear. The most common inner-ear troubles are linked to hereditary factors. Acquired hearing losses of the inner ear include those due to bacterial infections (such as meningitis), viral infections (such as mumps and measles), prenatal infections of the mother (such as cytomegalovirus, maternal rubella, and syphilis), and deprivation of oxygen at birth.

Impairment of hearing ability can have a profound effect on people, largely because of the emphasis on spoken language in our society. In the past, because they held to the notion that language is the equivalent of thought, professionals believed that deafness led to intellectual inferiority. Researchers now question the theory that thought is dependent on language. Furthermore, authorities now recognize that sign language is as true a language as spoken language. They recommend that people who are deaf be tested in sign language and/or with nonverbal tests of intelligence.

In general, the academic achievement of students with hearing impairment is very low. Even in math, their best academic area, they demonstrate severe underachievement. Several studies have shown that children who are deaf who have parents who are deaf have higher reading achievement than children who are deaf who have hearing parents. This is probably because parents who are deaf are able to communicate more easily with their children through sign language.

Because of problems finding people with whom to communicate, students who are deaf are at risk for loneliness. This problem is particularly acute in mainstream settings in which there are few students with hearing impairment with whom to communicate. Some authorities also believe that students who are deaf who have hearing parents may experience more unhappiness because of the difficulty they have in communicating with their parents.

Because of these problems in communicating with the larger society, many people who are deaf socialize almost exclusively with others who have hearing impairment. At one time, many professionals viewed this tendency toward isolation as negative. More and more authorities are pointing out the potential benefits of a Deaf culture. The Deaf culture is built on six features: linguistic differentiation, attitudinal deafness, behavioral norms, endogamous marriage patterns, historical awareness, and voluntary organizational networks. Some believe that the cultural status of students who are deaf is vulnerable because of the current emphasis on mainstreaming in the schools.

For many years there were two basic approaches to teaching students with hearing impairment: oralism and manualism. Today, most educators of students who are deaf favor *total communication,* a blend of oralism and manualism. Most educators who use total communication stress auditory training and speechreading and employ signing English systems, which are different from American Sign Language. Signing English systems are not true languages and follow the same word order of spoken English. There is controversy over whether teachers should use ASL instead of signing English systems.

Students with hearing impairment can be found in a variety of settings, ranging from general education classrooms to residential settings. Although there has been an increase in mainstreaming, not all within the Deaf community have viewed this increase positively. Some professionals believe that there needs to be a critical mass of students who are deaf in order for programming to be effective.

Numerous technological advances are helping persons with hearing loss. These innovations are occurring primarily in the areas of hearing aids, computer-assisted instruction, television, and telephones.

There are now many programs for infants and preschoolers with hearing impairment. Research indicates that the families of children who are deaf who have hearing parents may be in greater need of intervention than are families of children who are deaf who have parents who are also deaf.

Until the mid-1960s, there was very little special provision for the postsecondary education of students with hearing impairment. In addition to Gallaudet University and the National Technical Institute for the Deaf, which focus on the education of students who are hearing impaired, there are now several postsecondary programs for students with hearing impairment. Transition programming for students who do not intend to take part in postsecondary programs is also expanding. Unemployment and the number of persons who are overqualified for their jobs among people who are hearing impaired are still exceedingly high.

DON PEARSON

Already a professional artist when his vision began to deteriorate at age 24, Don Pearson had trouble convincing many of his doctors that his impending blindness would not have a devastating effect on his career. Having devised working systems to compensate for his loss of vision, he hopes that his work demonstrates his ability to overcome his visual impairment.

JILL: God, I can't find anything in my place. The ketchup usually winds up in my stocking drawer and my stockings are in the oven. If you really want to see chaos, come and look at... (She catches herself, self-consciously), I mean... I meant...

DON: I know what you mean. Relax. I'm no different from anyone else except that I don't see. The blindness is nothing. The thing I find hard to live with is other people's reactions to my blindness. If they'd only behave naturally. Some people want to assume guilt—which they can't because my mother has that market cornered—or they treat me as though I were living in some Greek tragedy, which I assure you I'm not. Just be yourself.

JILL: I'll try... but I've never met a blind person before.

DON: That's because we're a small, very select group—
        like Eskimos. How many Eskimos do you know?

JILL: I never thought blind people would be like you.

DON: They're not all like me. We're all different.

JILL: I mean... I always thought blind people were kind
        of... you know... spooky.

DON: (In a mock-sinister voice) But, of course. We sleep all day hanging upside-down from the shower rod. As soon as it's dark, we wake up and fly into people's windows. That's why they say, "Blind as a bat."

> Leonard Gershe
"Butterflies Are Free"

Visual
Impairment

*J*ill's discomfort with Don's blindness in the opening dialogue (see p. 341) is not that unusual. Visual impairments seem to evoke more awkwardness than most other disabilities. Why are we so uncomfortably aware of blindness? For one thing, blindness is *visible*. We often do not realize that a person has impaired hearing, for example, until we actually talk to that person. The person with visual impairment, however, usually has a variety of symbols—cane, thick or darkened glasses, a guide dog.

Another possible reason for being self-conscious around people who are blind is the role that eyes play in social interaction. Poets, playwrights, and songwriters have long recognized how emotionally expressive the eyes can be for the sighted. We all know how uncomfortable it can be to talk with someone who does not make eye contact with us. Think how often we have heard someone say, or have ourselves said, that we prefer to talk "face to face" on an important matter rather than over the telephone. We seem to rely a great deal on the expressiveness of people's eyes to judge how they are responding to what we are saying.

Also, research has shown that most of us have a special fear of blindness (Conant & Budoff, 1982). It is reportedly the third most feared condition, with only cancer and AIDS outranking it (Jernigan, 1992). One reason we may be so frightened of becoming blind is that our eyes seem so vulnerable. Our ears feel safely tucked away; eyes seem dangerously exposed. Another reason we fear loss of vision is that the sense of sight is linked so closely with the traditional concept of beauty. We derive great pleasure from our sight. Our feelings about others are often based largely on physical appearances that are visually perceived.

So, despite the fact that blindness is the least prevalent of all disabilities, people dread it. With a bit of reflection, however, it becomes obvious that our anxieties about blindness are irrational. Most of our apprehension about blindness can be attributed to our lack of experience in interacting with individuals with visual impairment. It is not until we talk to people with visual impairment or read about their appreciation of sounds, smells, and touch that we begin to realize that sight is not the only sense that enables us to enjoy beauty or interact socially with other people.

Like anyone with a disability, the person who is blind wants to be treated like everyone else. Most people who are blind do not seek pity or unnecessary help. In fact, they can be fiercely protective of their independence. As Don says in the introductory dialogue, "We're all different." In this chapter, we hope to change the idea that children with visual impairment are all alike in some odd way. We start by presenting a fact that most sighted people do not know: The majority of people who are blind can actually see.

DEFINITION AND CLASSIFICATION

The two most common ways of describing visual impairment are the legal and educational definitions. The former is the one laypeople and those in the medical professions use; the latter is the one educators favor.

► ► PERSONS WITH VISUAL IMPAIRMENT

MYTH ➤ People who are legally blind have no sight at all.

FACT ➤ Only a small percentage of those who are legally blind have absolutely no vision. Many have a useful amount of functional vision.

MYTH ➤ People who are blind have an extra sense that enables them to detect obstacles.

FACT ➤ People who are blind do not have an extra sense. Some can develop an "obstacle sense" by noting the change in pitch of echoes as they move toward objects.

MYTH ➤ People who are blind automatically develop better acuity in their other senses.

FACT ➤ Through concentration and attention, individuals who are blind can learn to make very fine discriminations in the sensations they obtain. This is not automatic but rather represents a better use of received sensations.

MYTH ➤ People who are blind have superior musical ability.

FACT ➤ The musical ability of people who are blind is not necessarily better than that of sighted people but many people who are blind pursue musical careers as one way in which they can achieve success.

MYTH ➤ Braille is not very useful for the vast majority of people who are blind; it should only be tried as a last resort.

FACT ➤ Very few people who are blind have learned Braille, primarily due to fear that using Braille is a sign of failure and to an historical professional bias against Braille. Authorities acknowledge the utility of Braille for people who are blind.

MYTH ➤ Braille is of no value for those who have low vision.

FACT ➤ Some individuals with low vision have conditions that will eventually result in blindness. More and more, authorities think that these individuals should learn Braille to be prepared for when they cannot read print effectively.

MYTH ➤ If people with low vision use their eyes too much, their sight will deteriorate.

FACT ➤ Only rarely is this true. Visual efficiency can actually be improved through training and use. Wearing strong lenses, holding books close to the eyes, and using the eyes often cannot harm vision.

MYTH ➤ Mobility instruction should be delayed until elementary or secondary school.

FACT ➤ Many authorities now recognize that even preschoolers can take advantage of mobility instruction, including the use of a cane.

MYTH ➤ The long cane is a simply constructed, easy to use device.

FACT ➤ The National Academy of Sciences has drawn up specifications for the manufacture of the long cane and using it properly.

MYTH ➤ Guide dogs take people where they want to go.

FACT ➤ The guide dog does not "take" the person anywhere; the person must first know where he or she is going. The dog is primarily a protection against unsafe areas or obstacles.

Legal Definition

The legal definition involves assessment of visual acuity and field of vision. A person who is **legally blind** has visual acuity of 20/200 or less in the better eye even with correction (e.g., eyeglasses) or has a field of vision so narrow that its widest diameter subtends an angular distance no greater than 20 degrees. The fraction 20/200 means that the person sees at 20 feet what a person with normal vision sees at 200 feet. (Normal visual acuity is thus 20/20.) The inclusion of a narrowed field of vision in the legal definition means that a person may have 20/20 vision in the central field but severely restricted peripheral vision. Legal blindness qualifies a person for certain legal benefits, such as tax advantages and money for special materials.

In addition to this medical classification of blindness, there is also a category referred to as partially sighted. According to the legal classification system, persons who are partially sighted have visual acuity falling between 20/70 and 20/200 in the better eye with correction.

Educational Definition

Many professionals, particularly educators, have found the legal classification scheme inadequate. They have observed that visual acuity is not a very accurate predictor of how people will function or use whatever remaining sight they have. Although a small percentage of individuals who are legally blind have absolutely no vision, the majority are able to see. For example, an extensive study of students who are legally blind found that only 18 percent were totally blind (Willis, 1976).

Many of those who recognize the limitations of the legal definition of blindness and partial sightedness favor the educational definition, which stresses the method of reading instruction. For educational purposes, individuals who are blind are so severely impaired they must learn to read Braille or use aural methods (audiotapes and records). (**Braille,** a system of raised dots by which blind people "read" with their fingertips, consists of quadrangular cells containing from one to six dots whose arrangement denotes different letters and symbols.) Educators often refer to those individuals with visual impairment who can read print, even if they need magnifying devices or large-print books, as having **low vision.**

PREVALENCE

Blindness is primarily an adult disability. Most estimates indicate that blindness is approximately one-tenth as prevalent in school-age children as in adults. Less than .10 percent of the population ranging from 6 to 17 years of age is classified by the federal government as visually impaired. This makes visual impairment one of the least prevalent disabilities in children.

ANATOMY AND PHYSIOLOGY OF THE EYE

The anatomy of the visual system is extremely complex, so our discussion here will focus just on basic characteristics. Figure 9–1 shows the functioning of the eye. The physical object being seen becomes an electrical impulse sent through

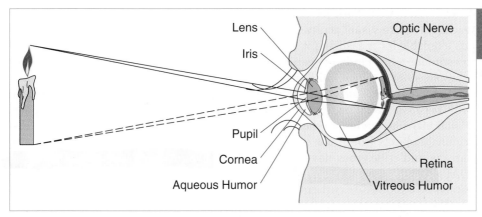

SOURCE: Adapted from National Society for the Prevention of Blindness, *Pub. V-7*, 1964. Copyright 1964. Reprinted with permission.

the optic nerve to the visual center of the brain, the occipital lobes. Before reaching the optic nerve, light rays reflecting off the object being seen pass through several structures within the eye. The light rays:

1. Pass through the **cornea** (a transparent cover in front of the iris and pupil), which performs the major part of the bending (refraction) of the light ray so that the image will be focused
2. Pass through the **aqueous humor** (a watery substance)
3. Pass through the **pupil** (the contractile opening in the middle of the **iris,** the colored portion of the eye that contracts or expands depending on the amount of light striking it)
4. Pass through the **lens,** which refines and changes the focus of the light rays before they pass through the **vitreous humor** (a transparent gelatinous substance)
5. Come to a focus on the **retina** (the back portion of the eye containing nerve fibers connected to the optic nerve)

MEASUREMENT OF VISUAL ABILITY

Visual acuity is most often measured with the **Snellen chart,** which consists of rows of letters (for individuals who know the alphabet) or *E*s (for the very young and for those who cannot read). In the latter case, the *E*s are arranged in various positions, and the person's task is to indicate in what direction the "legs" of the *E*s are facing. Each row corresponds to the distance at which a person with normal vision can discriminate the direction of the *E*s. (There are eight rows, one corresponding to each of the following distances: 15, 20, 30, 40, 50, 70, 100, and 200 feet.) People are normally tested at the 20-foot distance. If they can distinguish the direction of the letters in the 20-foot row, they are said to have 20/20 central visual acuity for far distances. If they can distinguish only the much larger letters in the 70-foot row, they are said to have 20/70 central visual acuity for far distances.

There are at least two reasons why the Snellen chart is not very useful for predicting the ability to read print. First, it measures visual acuity for distant, but not near, objects—which is why it is necessary to report the results in terms of central visual acuity for *far* distances. Many educational activities, particularly reading, require visual acuity at close distances, and there are a variety of methods available for measuring it. The results of some of these methods can be used to estimate what kinds of reading material the person will be able to read, for example, store catalogs, children's books, or high school texts.

Second, the Snellen chart is not very appropriate for predicting ability to read print because visual acuity does not always correspond with visual efficiency. **Visual efficiency** refers to the ability, for example, to control eye movement, discriminate objects from their background, and pay attention to important details. Barraga and colleagues have developed the Diagnostic Assessment Procedure (DAP) to assess visual efficiency (Barraga, 1983; Barraga & Collins, 1979) accompanied by a 150-lesson curriculum.

There are screening procedures less time-consuming than the DAP but more thorough then the Snellen (Rathgeber, 1981). Using these screening tests, teachers can identify children in need of a more complete eye exam. Unfortunately, some schools use only the Snellen chart as a screening procedure. Because it does not pick up all possible types of visual problems, teachers should be alert to other signs that a child might have a visual impairment. The National Society for the Prevention of Blindness (1972) has listed a number of signs of possible eye problems (see the box on page 347).

CAUSES

The most common visual problems are the result of errors of refraction. **Myopia** (nearsightedness), **hyperopia** (farsightedness), and **astigmatism** (blurred vision) are all examples of refraction errors that affect central visual acuity. Although each can be serious enough to cause significant impairment (myopia and hyperopia are the most common impairments of low vision), usually glasses or contact lenses can bring vision within normal limits.

Myopia results when the eyeball is too long. In this case, the light rays from the object in Figure 9–1 would be in focus in front of rather than on the retina. Myopia affects vision for distant objects, but close vision may be unaffected. When the eyeball is too short, *hyperopia* (farsightedness) results. In this case, the light rays from the object in the diagram would be in focus behind rather than on the retina. Hyperopia affects vision for close objects, but far vision may be unaffected. If the cornea or lens of the eye is irregular, the person is said to have *astigmatism*. In this case, the light rays from the object in the figure would be blurred or distorted.

Among the more serious impairments are those caused by glaucoma, cataracts, and diabetes. They occur primarily in adults, but each of them, particularly the latter two, can occur in children. **Glaucoma** is a condition in which there is excessive pressure in the eyeball. Left untreated, the condition progresses to the point at which the blood supply to the optic nerve is cut off and blindness results.

The cause of glaucoma is presently unknown (although it can be caused secondarily by other eye diseases), and its onset can be sudden or very gradual. Because its incidence increases dramatically after age thirty-five and because it can be prevented if detected early, it is often strongly recommended that *all* adults have periodic eye examinations after age thirty-five. A common complaint during early stages of glaucoma is that lights appear to have halos around them

---

➣ **visual efficiency.** A term used to refer to how well one uses one's vision, including such things as control of eye movements, attention to visual detail, and discrimination of figure from background. It is believed by some to be more important than visual acuity alone in predicting a person's ability to function visually.

➣ **myopia.** Nearsightedness; usually results when the eyeball is too long.

➣ **hyperopia.** Farsightedness; usually results when the eyeball is too short.

➣ **astigmatism.** Blurred vision caused by an irregular cornea or lens.

➣ **glaucoma.** A condition of excessive pressure in the eyeball; the cause is unknown but if untreated, blindness results.

SIGNS INDICATING POSSIBLE EYE PROBLEMS ➤

BEHAVIOR
- Rubs eyes excessively
- Shuts or covers one eye, tilts head, or thrusts head forward
- Has difficulty in reading or in other work requiring close use of the eyes
- Blinks more than usual or is irritable when doing close work
- Holds books close to eyes
- Is unable to see distant things clearly
- Squints eyelids together or frowns

APPEARANCE
- Crossed eyes
- Red-rimmed, encrusted, or swollen eyelids
- Inflamed or watery eyes
- Recurring styes

COMPLAINTS
- Eyes itch, burn, or feel scratchy
- Cannot see well
- Dizziness, headaches, or nausea following close eye work
- Blurred or double vision

(Thomas, 1985). **Cataracts** are caused by a clouding of the lens of the eye, which results in blurred vision. In children the condition is called *congenital cataracts,* and distance and color vision are seriously affected. Surgery can usually correct the problems caused by cataracts. Diabetes can cause **diabetic retinopathy,** a condition resulting from interference with the blood supply to the retina.

Several other visual impairments primarily affect children. Visual impairments of school-age children are often due to prenatal causes, many of which are hereditary. We have already discussed congenital (meaning present at birth) cataracts and glaucoma. Another congenital condition is **coloboma,** a degenerative disease in which the central and/or peripheral areas of the retina are not completely formed, resulting in impairment of the visual field and/or central visual acuity. Another prenatal condition is **retinitis pigmentosa,** a hereditary disease resulting in degeneration of the retina. Retinitis pigmentosa causes the person's field of vision to narrow. Also included in the prenatal category are infectious diseases that affect the unborn child, such as syphilis and rubella.

One of the most dramatic medical discoveries in the causes of blindness involved a condition now referred to as **retinopathy of prematurity (ROP)** (previously called *retrolental fibroplasia).* ROP, which results in scar tissue forming behind the lens of the eye, began to appear in the 1940s in premature infants. In the 1950s, researchers determined that excessive concentrations of oxygen often administered to premature infants was causing blindness. The oxygen was necessary to prevent brain damage, but it was often given at too high a level. Since then, hospitals have been careful to monitor the amount of oxygen administered to premature infants. When the cause of ROP was discovered, some authorities thought its occurrence would be drastically reduced, but this has not happened. In fact, there appears to be a resurgence of ROP (Bishop, 1991; Ferrell et al., 1990). With medical advances many more premature babies are surviving, but they need very high levels of oxygen.

We can group together two other conditions resulting in visual problems because both are caused by improper muscle functioning. **Strabismus** is a condition in which the eye(s) is (are) directed inward (crossed eyes) or outward. Left untreated, strabismus can result in permanent blindness because the brain will eventually reject signals from a deviating eye. Fortunately, most cases of

➤ **cataracts.** A condition caused by a clouding of the lens of the eye; affects color vision and distance vision.

➤ **diabetic retinopathy.** A condition resulting from interference of the blood supply to the retina; the fastest-growing cause of blindness.

➤ **coloboma.** A degenerative disease in which the central and/or peripheral areas of the retina are incompletely formed, resulting in impairment of the visual field and/or central visual acuity.

➤ **retinitis pigmentosa.** A hereditary condition resulting in degeneration of the retina; causes a narrowing of the field of vision.

➤ **retinopathy of prematurity (ROP).** Formerly referred to as retrolental fibroplasia, a condition resulting from administration of an excessive concentration of oxygen at birth; causes scar tissue to form behind the lens of the eye.

➤ **strabismus.** A condition in which the eyes are directed inward (crossed eyes) or outward.

Retinitis pigmentosa, a hereditary disease, causes a narrowing of the field of vision (a). Cataracts create a haziness over the entire field of vision, causing images to appear out of focus (b).

(a)

(b)

➤ **nystagmus.** Condition in which there are rapid involuntary movements of the eyes; sometimes indicates a brain malfunction and/or inner ear problems.

strabismus are correctable with eye exercises or surgery. **Nystagmus** is a condition in which there are rapid involuntary movements of the eyes, usually resulting in dizziness and nausea. Nystagmus is sometimes a sign of brain malfunctioning and/or inner ear problems.

PSYCHOLOGICAL AND BEHAVIORAL CHARACTERISTICS

Language Development

Most authorities believe that lack of vision does not alter very significantly the ability to understand and use language. They point to the many studies that show that students who are visually impaired do not differ from sighted students on verbal intelligence tests. They also note that studies comparing the two groups have found no differences with regard to major aspects of language (McGinnis, 1981; Matsuda, 1984). Because auditory more than visual perception is the sensory modality through which we learn language, it is not surprising that studies have found people who are blind to be unimpaired in language functioning. The child who is blind is still able to hear language and may even be more motivated than the sighted child to use language because it is the main channel through which he or she communicates with others.

However, there are a few subtle differences in the way in which language usually develops in children who are visually impaired compared to sighted children (Andersen, Dunlea, & Kekelis, 1984; Warren, 1984). Their early language tends to be somewhat restricted by lack of visual experiences. For example, whereas their language tends to be more self-centered, sighted children use language more readily to refer to activities involving other people and objects. Although such differences are relatively subtle and do not indicate that children with blindness will lead a linguistically deficient existence, it is a good idea to provide children who are blind with as rich an exposure to language as possible at as young an age as possible (Warren, 1984).

Intellectual Ability

Performance on Standardized Intelligence Tests

Samuel P. Hayes was the pioneer in the intelligence testing of people who are blind (Hayes, 1942, 1950). He took verbal items from a commonly used IQ test of his time—the Stanford-Binet—to assess individuals with blindness. His rationale was that people without sight would not be disadvantaged by a test that relied on verbal items, and therefore this kind of test would be a more accurate measure of intelligence than tests that contained items of a visual nature.

Since the work of Hayes, professionals have continued to use verbal IQ tests with individuals with visual impairment, but they have also emphasized the importance of measuring areas of intelligence related to spatial and tactual abilities. Many professionals advocate the use of intelligence tests that assess spatial and tactual skills because these abilities have a direct bearing on how well persons with visual impairment can traverse their environment and read Braille. Several intelligence tests that emphasize these nonverbal areas are now available in a few countries, e.g., Blind Learning Aptitude Test (Newland, 1979) and Intelligence Test for Visually Impaired Children (Dekker, Drenth, Zaal, 1991; Dekker, Drenth, Zaal, & Koole, 1990).

At one time it was popular for researchers to compare the intelligence of sighted persons with that of persons with blindness. Most authorities now believe that such comparisons are virtually impossible because finding comparable tests is so difficult (Warren, 1984). Using verbal tests is not entirely satisfactory because they exclude important performance areas. Some have used performance tests with individuals with visual impairment and sighted individuals while requiring the latter to wear blindfolds, but this is problematic because sighted individuals are unaccustomed to doing performance tasks without using their vision. From what we do know, however, there is no reason to believe that blindness results in lower intelligence.

Conceptual Abilities

The same problems have also hindered research involving laboratory-type tasks of conceptual ability. Many researchers, using conceptual tasks originally developed by the noted psychologist, Jean Piaget, have concluded that children who are blind lag behind their sighted peers (e.g., Davidson, Dunn, Wiles-Kettenmann, & Appelle, 1981; Stephens & Grube, 1982). But these comparisons are questionable because, like comparisons on IQ tests, it is virtually impossible to find equivalent tasks for those with and without sight.

Nevertheless, some important differences exist between how those with and without sight perceive the world, most of which are due to the difference between tactual and visual experiences. Persons who are blind rely much more on tactual and auditory information to learn about the world than do the sighted, who obtain a great deal of information through sight. As one person who is blind described it, he "sees" with his fingers (Hull, 1990).

An important difference between those with and without sight is that the latter need to be much more vigilant in order to pick up information from their environment:

> For the sighted child, the world meets him halfway. What he sees encourages him to move further out into his environment and to explore it. He learns literally hundreds of thousands of things from observation, imitation, and identification, without any effort on his part or on the part of his parents or teachers. (Scott, 1982, p. 34)

Children with visual impairment need to take much more initiative in order to learn what they can from their environment. In addition, they apparently become adept at being able to obtain concepts through what they hear from others (Groenveld & Jan, 1992).

Little is known about the tactual sense of children who are blind and how best to develop it. But we do know that good tactual perception, like good visual perception, relies on being able to use a variety of strategies (Berlá, 1982; Griffin & Gerber, 1982). The child with blindness who compares a pencil and ruler, for example, by using such strategies as comparing the length of each to body parts and listening to differences in pitch when each is banged against a table will have an advantage in understanding the differences and similarities between these two objects. Research has shown that the earlier the child with visual impairment is trained to use such strategies, the more beneficial the training will be for tactual development (Berlá, 1981).

We also know that degree of visual impairment and the age of its onset are important determinants of how the child will explore his or her environment. Children whose blindness was present at birth will generally rely more on their tactual sense to learn about the world than will those who acquire their blindness later. Likewise, children who are totally blind will depend more on the tactual sense for concept development than will those with low vision.

Mobility

➤ **cognitive mapping.** A nonsequential way of conceptualizing the spatial environment that allows a person who is visually impaired to know where several points in the environment are simultaneously; allows for better mobility than does a strictly sequential conceptualization of the environment.

A very important ability for the successful adjustment of many people with visual impairment is their mobility—their skill in moving about in their environment. Mobility skills depend to a great extent on spatial ability. Authorities have delineated two ways in which the person with visual impairment processes spatial information—as a sequential route or as a map depicting the general relation of various points in the environment (Bigelow, 1991; Herman, Chatman, & Roth, 1983; Rieser, Guth, & Hill, 1982). The latter method, referred to as cognitive mapping, is preferable because it offers more flexibility in navigating. Consider three sequential points—A, B, and C. A sequential mode of processing spatial information restricts a person's movement so he or she can move from A to C only by way of B. But a person with a cognitive map of points A, B, and C can go from A to C directly without going through B.

Mobility skills vary greatly among people with visual impairment. (And even the best of travelers who are blind occasionally run into problems in navigating. See box on p. 351 for an account of how not to help someone who is blind when he or she is lost.) It is surprisingly difficult to predict which individuals will be the best travelers. For example, common sense seems to tell us that mobility would be better among those who have more residual vision and those who lose their vision later in life, but this is not always the case (McLinden, 1988; Warren & Kocon, 1974). A critical variable appears to be *motivation*, and some authorities have noted that those who have more residual vision and those who become visually impaired later in life may have a tendency to become more frustrated by their loss of vision and less motivated to acquire mobility skills.

"Obstacle Sense"

For some persons who are blind, the ability to detect physical obstructions in the environment is a large part of their mobility skills. Walking along the street,

HOW NOT TO HELP A PERSON WHO IS BLIND AND LOST ➢

When the sighted encounter someone who is lost, their natural inclination is to ask the person where he or she is headed. As the following entry in the diary of John M. Hull (1990) indicates, this question can lead to confusion when the person lost happens to be blind.

GETTING LOST   8 November

I think it is David Scott Blackhall, in his autobiography *The Way I See Things* (London, Baker, 1971), who remarks how annoying he found it when people refused to answer his question about where he was and insisted on asking him where he was trying to get to. I share this experience.

Going home the other night I was turned out of my way by some construction work on one of the footpaths. By mistake I turned along a side street, and after a block or so, when I realized I had made a mistake somewhere, I was not sure exactly where I was. There were some chaps working on a car parked on the roadside. 'Excuse me', I said. 'Could you tell me please where I am? What is the name of this street?'

The chap replied, 'Where are you trying to get to?'

With what I hoped was a good-humored laugh, I said, 'Never mind about that, just tell me, please, what street this is?'

'This is Alton Road, You usually go up Bournbrook Road, don't you? It's just a block further along.'

I thanked him, and explained that I needed now to know exactly whereabouts on Alton Road I was so that I could get to Bournbrook Road. 'Which side of Alton Road am I on? If I face that way, am I looking towards Bristol Road or is it the other way?'

'You live high up Bournbrook Road, don't you? Well, if you take the next road to the left you'll be OK.'

But which way is 'left'? Does he mean me to cross the road or to stay on this side? At this point, the blind and sighted enter into mutual bafflement.

When a sighted person is lost, what matters to him or her is not where he is, but where he is going. When he is told that the building he is looking for lies in a certain direction, he is no longer lost. A sighted person is lost in the sense that he does not know where the building he is looking for is. He is never lost with respect to what street he is actually on; he just looks at the street sign on the corner of the block. It is his direction he has lost, rather than his position. The blind person lost has neither direction nor position. He needs position in order to discover direction. This is such a profound lostness that most sighted people find it difficult to imagine.

SOURCE: From Touching the rock *by John M. Hull. Copyright © 1990 by John M. Hull. Reprinted by permission of Pantheon Books, a division of Random House, Inc., pp. 144–145.*

they often seem able to "sense" an object in their path. This ability has come to be known as the **obstacle sense**—an unfortunate term in some ways because many laypeople have taken it to mean that people who are blind somehow develop an extra sense. It is easy to see why this misconception has existed. Even people who are blind have had a very difficult time explaining the phenomenon (Hull, 1990). A number of experiments have shown that, with experience, people who are blind come to be able to detect subtle changes in the pitch of high-frequency echoes as they move toward objects. Actually, they are taking advantage of the **Doppler effect**, a physical principle that says the pitch of a sound rises as a person moves toward its source.

Although the obstacle sense can be important for the mobility of someone without sight, by itself it will not make its user a highly proficient traveler. It is merely an aid. Extraneous noises (traffic, speech, rain, wind) can render the obstacle sense unusable. Also, it requires walking at a fairly slow speed to be able to react in time.

The Myth of Sensory Acuteness

Along with the myth that people with blindness have an extra sense is the general misconception that they automatically develop better acuity in their other senses. This is not true. They do not, for example, have lowered thresholds

➢ **obstacle sense.** A skill possessed by some people who are blind whereby they can detect the presence of obstacles in their environment. Research has shown that it is not an indication of an extra sense, as popularly thought; it is the result of being able to detect subtle changes in the pitch of high frequency echoes.

➢ **Doppler effect.** Term used to describe the phenomenon of the pitch of a sound rising as the listener moves toward the source of that sound.

AMERICA'S BOSWELL DRIVES INTO THE DARK ➤

DUDLEY DOUST ON A REMARKABLE PLAYER

After he had stooped to feel the texture of the grass, and finger the edge of the cup, Charley Boswell paced with his caddie across the green to his ball. He counted as he went . . . 48, 49, 50 feet. "It's mostly downhill," said his caddie, crouching to line up the face of Boswell's putter. "Take off about 10 feet, and putt it like a 40-footer."

Boswell stroked the ball. It sped across the green, climbed and fell, curved, slowed down and dropped with a rattle into the hole. Boswell grinned: "Did you see that one?" Yes, I had seen it. But he hadn't. Charley Boswell is blind. In fact, he is one of the most remarkable blind sportsmen in the world and playing off a handicap as low as 12, he has won the United States Blind Golfers' Association Championship 17 times.

Putting, oddly enough, is one of Boswell's strong departments. Given, of course, the fact that his caddie reads the putt, his execution is immaculate. "A tip that we blind golfers can pass on to the sighted player," he said, "I don't worry about the breaks on a green. Don't try to curb your putt because, as Bobby Jones always said, every putt is a straight putt and let the slopes do the work."

A few weeks ago I met Boswell in California, where he was playing a benefit match for the Braille Institute of America. He had come up from Alabama, where he is the State Commissioner in the Department of Revenue, a remarkable enough job, and now he was walking to the second tee on a course in the lush Coachelle Valley. A wind blew down from the mountains. "Funny thing," he said, "wind is really the only thing that bothers me. It affects my hearing, and that ruins my sense of direction."

On the second tee his caddie, who is his home professional back in Alabama, lined up the face of Boswell's driver and stepped away. Boswell, careful not to lose this alignment, did not waggle his clubhead. He paused, setting up some inner rhythm, and swung with the certainty of a sighted player. He groaned as the ball tailed off into a slice.

"There are two ways I can tell if I hit a good shot," he said, frowning. "I can feel it through the clubhead and, more important, I finish up high on my follow-through. Come on, let's walk. I can't stand golf carts—they bother my judgment of distance."

Boswell has been walking down darkened fairways since shortly after the Second World War. Blinded when a German antitank gun scored a direct hit on his vehicle in the Ruhr, he was sent back to an American hospital for rehabilitation. A former gridiron footballer and baseball player, Boswell did not take easily to pampered, supervised sport.

"I tried swimming, and it bored me. I tried horseback riding until I rode under a tree and got knocked off. I tried ten-pin bowling, and that wasn't any good either—I fell over the ball-track." He laughed, idly swinging his club as he walked. "Then one day this corporal came in and suggested we play golf. I told him to get the hell out of my room."

Boswell had never swung a golf club in his life but, a few days later, aged 28, he gave it a try: "He handed me a brassie. I took six practice swings, and then he teed one up and I hit it dead centre, right out of the sweet spot. I tell you, I was lucky. If I'd missed the ball that first time I would have quit golf." There are no false heroics about Boswell.

Some holes later he, or rather we, found his ball in a bunker. The bunker shot was clearly the most difficult shot in Boswell's bag. Playing it required him to break two Rules of Golf: he not only needed his usual help from someone to line up his club but, to avoid topping the ball, or missing it altogether, he had to ground his club in the sand. "Also, I can't get fancy and cut across the ball," he said. "I have to swing square to the line of flight. I have to play it like an ordinary pitch."

These handicaps, he later pointed out, were in part counterbalanced by the actual advantages of being blind on a golf course. Boswell, for instance, is never tempted to play a nine-iron when a seven-iron will do the job. "In a match blind players play the course, not their opponents, because we can't see what they're doing anyway," he said, on the way to a score of 91 which, for him, was neat but not gaudy. "You know, I was once playing with Bob Hope, and he said: 'Charley, if you could see all the trouble on this golf course, you wouldn't be playing it.' And I suppose he was right."

SOURCE: Dudley Doust, *Sunday Times,* London, February 6, 1977. Reprinted by permission.

for sensation in touch or hearing. What they are able to do is make better use of the sensations they obtain. Through concentration and attention, they learn to make very fine discriminations. Another common belief is that people who are blind automatically have superior musical talent. Some do follow musical careers, but this is because music is an area in which they can achieve success.

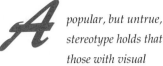 *A popular, but untrue, stereotype holds that those with visual impairments necessarily have superior musical ability.*

Academic Achievement

Most professionals agree that direct comparisons of the academic achievement of students who are blind with sighted students must be interpreted cautiously because the two groups must be tested under different conditions. There are, however, Braille and large-print forms of some achievement tests. The few studies that have been done suggest that both children with low vision and those who are blind are behind their sighted peers (Suppes, 1974; Rapp & Rapp, 1992). Their academic achievement, however, is not as adversely affected as that of students who are hearing impaired. Hearing is evidently more important for school learning than seeing.

Social Adjustment

At one time, the prevailing opinion of professionals was that people with visual impairment were at-risk to exhibit personality disturbances. Most authorities now agree that personality problems are not an inherent condition of blindness. Social difficulties that may arise are more likely due to society's inappropriate reaction to blindness than to personality flaws of those without sight.

Much of this inappropriateness may be caused by our unfamiliarity with people who are blind. Because we do not have many acquaintances who are blind, we are not used to their usual patterns of social interaction. Social skills that come naturally to the sighted may be very difficult for some people with visual impairment. One good example is smiling. Smiling is a strong *visual* cue used by two sighted people to provide feedback to one another. For some people with visual impairment, however, smiling is not as spontaneous a social response as it is for the sighted. John M. Hull, whose eyesight deteriorated gradually over several years, kept a diary of his experiences. The following two entries pertain to smiling:

> Nearly every time I smile, I am conscious of it. I am aware of the muscular effort; not that my smiles have become forced, as if I were pretending, but it has become a more or less conscious effort. Why is this? It must be because there is no reinforcement.

It is faulty to assume that those with visual problems necessarily have social problems as well.

There is no returning smile....Most smiling is responsive. You smile spontaneously when you receive a smile. For me it is like sending dead letters. Have they been received, acknowledged? Was I even smiling in the right direction? (Hull, 1990, p. 34)

Yesterday morning I was kneeling on the floor, helping Lizzie to get dressed. When she was finished, I stood her up in front of me and said, 'Now! Let's have a look at you.' I held her face lightly between my hands while she stood there, and gave her a big smile.

We remained like that for a moment and then she said, 'Daddy, how can you smile between you and me when I smile and when you smile because you're blind?'...

'You mean, how do I know when to smile at you?'...

'Yes', she said, 'when you're blind.'

'It's true, darling', I said, 'that blind people often don't know when to smile at people, and I often don't know when to smile at you, do I?'

She agreed.

'But today I knew you were smiling, darling, because you were standing there, and I was smiling at you, and I thought you were probably smiling at me. Were you?'

Happily she replied, 'Yes!'

So this little child, having just had her fourth birthday, is able to articulate the breakdown which blindness causes in the language of smiles. I noticed the fine distinction she made by implication between smiling at someone and the smiling which takes place between people. (Hull, 1990, pp. 202-203)

In addition to smiling, sighted people usually use a number of other subtle visual cues when communicating with one another that may be missing from the normal repertoire of people who are blind. Sighted people use a variety of facial expressions, hand gestures, and body movements to convey their feelings during social interaction.

An important point to keep in mind is that even though people with visual impairment differ from the sighted in how they interact socially, this does not mean that they are socially maladjusted. It does mean, however, that *initial* interactions between the sighted and those without sight may be strained. We emphasize "initial" because once sighted individuals and those without sight become acquainted, these problems in communication largely disappear (Fichten, Judd, Tagalakis, Amsel, & Robillard, 1991).

Another important point is that it should not only be up to those who are visually impaired to change their ways of interacting socially. Sighted people are also responsible for instances of faulty communication with people who are blind:

> For instance, a sighted professor was overheard telling a student who was blind, "OK. Just grab those (he pointed to a bunch of papers) and we can go." In another instance, while giving a lift to an acquaintance who was blind, the driver remarked, "We're at the junction you specified. Which house is it—the one with the brown or yellow balconies?" The response to this innocent, but inappropriate query was delivered with a chuckle, "I don't know about brown or yellow balconies; take me to the building on the right." (Fichten, Judd, Tagalakis, Amsel, & Robillard, 1991, p. 371)

Not only may some people with visual impairment profit from instruction in using appropriate visually-based cues, such as facial expressions, head nods, and gestures, but sighted people also can learn to use their natural "telephone skills" when communicating with persons who are blind. Two sighted people talking on the telephone use a variety of auditorially-based cues (e.g., assenting with "uh hum" or "yeah," asking for more information, adjusting tone of voice) to help them communicate even though they cannot see each other (Fichten et al., 1991). If sighted individuals consciously try to use these strategies when interacting with people who are blind, communication may be smoother.

Stereotypic Behaviors

An impediment to good social adjustment for some students with visual impairment is **stereotypic behaviors**. These are repetitive, stereotyped movements such as body rocking, poking or rubbing the eyes, repetitive hand or finger movements, and grimacing. For many years, the term **blindisms** was used to refer to these behaviors because it was thought that they were manifested only in those who are blind, but they are also sometimes characteristic of children with normal sight who are severely retarded or disturbed.

Several competing theories concern the causes of stereotypic behaviors. Most of them involve the notion that these behaviors are a physiological attempt to stabilize one's level of arousal (Baumeister, 1978). For example, one position holds that children with low levels of sensory stimulation, such as those without sight, make up for this deprivation by stimulating themselves in other ways (Thurrell & Rice, 1970). Another theory holds that, even with adequate sensory

> **stereotypic behaviors.**
Any of a variety of repetitive behaviors (e. g., eye rubbing) that are sometimes found in individuals who are blind, severely retarded, or psychotic. Sometimes referred to as stereotypies or blindisms.

> **blindisms.** Repetitive, stereotyped movements such as rocking or eye rubbing; also characteristic of some persons who are blind, severely retarded or psychotic; more appropriately referred to as stereotypic behaviors.

RICKI CURRY

Itinerant teacher for students with visual impairment, Piedmont Regional Education Program; A.B., Experimental Psychology, Brown University; M.Ed., Special Education (Visual Impairment) University of Virginia

PATTY UPDIKE FOSTER

Third-grade teacher, Hollymead Elementary School, Charlottesville, Virginia; B.S.Elem.Ed., Radford University; graduate work in early childhood education, University of Virginia

➢ **Ricki** My caseload varies from year to year as children move into the area served by the regional program. During the year Pat and I worked together, my caseload included sixteen children over a four-county area. Of these, three were totally blind and the others had varying degrees of visual impairment. Most of my students who were partially sighted were in regular classes receiving weekly itinerant services. They ranged from preschool through high school. Two of my students who were blind were in self-contained classes for children with moderate disabilities, and one (John) was based in a class for students with learning disabilities and mainstreamed into Pat's class for a large part of the school day.

➢ **Pat** I teach twenty-six students ranging from two mainstreamed special education students who read on a first-grade level to gifted children who read on a

fifth- or sixth-grade level. They're nine- and ten-year-olds. We'll describe our work with nine-year-old John.

➢ **Ricki** John has been blind from birth. He functions very independently and learns quickly. He never needs coaxing to work or to learn and has an amazingly long attention span for academic work. He is socially aware and has a really on-target sense of humor. He doesn't work or move very quickly, though, and we're always trying to "hurry him up." Someone who observed him described him as a "little tank"—he keeps plugging away and gets where he's going but his pace is steady, not speedy.

➢ **Pat** I see John as a generally cheerful boy who likes meeting and getting to know people. He's usually cooperative and eager to learn new things. He shares his experiences willingly, always expect-

ing to be accepted by his peers and teachers. He has a great sense of humor and uses that to play jokes on others. At first, he didn't understand that we could see certain actions. For instance, he would sneak a snack out of his desk before it was snack time and not realize that I could see him eating it. He has a terrific memory and easily identifies his associates by voice. He's very flexible and trusting, which enables him to work well with anyone, and he's willing to try new things. For example, he often opts to have a "new" person as his sighted guide because, as he puts it, "I haven't gotten to know them yet." Sometimes he's moody—very silent. Sometimes he's lazy, pretending he can't find his place in his Brailled text.

➢ **Ricki** Pat and I worked together to integrate John into her class. John moved to our region the summer before he entered third grade, and it was decided that for his first year in the school system he would be best served with a "home base" in a special education class so that we could assess his skills and needs in a protected environment. John's previous placement had been in a special class for students with visual impairments in a university lab school, so he really had no experience in a typical public school setting. At the same time, we wanted to give him the opportunity to learn to function socially and academically in the mainstream, so he had reading and math in the special class and other things in Pat's class.

➢ **Pat** I had John in my class for science, social studies, P.E., snack, silent reading time, and lunch. My primary responsibility was John's socialization and academic development in science and social studies. I chose and planned activities and decided when they would need adaptation for John. When this was necessary I asked Ricki to come up with methods and materials—usually a visual aid, but certainly not limited to that. I evaluated the content of his work and gave grades. Sometimes I had Ricki evaluate the Brailling skills John used and help me grade the work from a language arts perspective. I chose sighted guides for John and generally helped integrate him socially. I also helped John communicate daily assignments to his parents.

➤ **Ricki** Pat took complete responsibility for John while he was with her class. I was not in the building during these times. Before the school year started Pat and I discussed the adaptations that John would need and the materials and services I could provide. Throughout the year, Pat gave me print handouts to Braille for John, and I provided him with his science and social studies books in Braille. I spent the first week of school following John around so that I could identify times during the day when he needed help and orient him to various routines and locations. Ricki and I problem-solved getting him through the lunch line independently, out to recess, through a P.E. class with a sighted buddy. Pat and I worked out a rotating group of student sighted guides from her class. At the beginning of a month, Pat would give me a list of four or five students who would be John's sighted guides for that month. I took them out of class for a short training session and then Pat assigned John a sighted guide each day. His sighted guide was responsible for being his lunch companion (John sometimes needed help finding his seat after going through the line) and his P.E. buddy (to guide him out to the playground for recess and back into the building after recess, but not to spend recess playing with him).

➤ **Pat** For me, the most demanding part of all this was the need for advance planning so that materials could be obtained or made on time. Scheduling was a problem because Ricki was not full time at our school and therefore not always there when I needed Brailling or advice. John's parents were very cooperative and undemanding, but I felt that perhaps special education parents are accustomed to more regular feedback than they usually get in a regular education classroom. We lacked materials on certain topics, especially local interest units. Sometimes there was a lapse

between assignments being completed in Braille and encoded back into print because Ricki's an itinerant teacher.

➤ **Ricki** Finding enough common time in our schedules to discuss programming and materials was the most difficult and frustrating thing for me. As an itinerant teacher, I was always on the run; as a classroom teacher, Pat was always involved with a group of students. After school we both often had meetings. So we managed by "catching" each other and talking in snips of time. I often felt that I wasn't providing Pat with what she needed because of this lack of shared planning time.

➤ **Pat** The most rewarding aspect was the challenge of adapting the classroom routine to meet John's need without altering it so that the other students suffered. It

> *It was very exciting to have a colleague to share John's triumphs with.*

was very exciting to have a colleague to share John's triumphs with. Ricki was extremely willing to help in any way needed and there were many materials available in Braille. Ricki was quite willing to research any availability and order what we needed. One of the most heartwarming results was the effect on the other students. Because of John's very pleasant personality he made many friends, and all the students liked and admired him. They learned compassion and that true friendships could be formed with a student with disabilities. We also had students with other mild disabilities in our class. One student had always been quite uncoordinated. As a result she had problems relating socially and was very shy. John's presence helped the students recognize in a very real way that we all have the same needs for friendship and understanding regardless of our capabilities or disabilities. I saw a lot of growth in

compassion toward this student, and I attribute this to their friendship with John. This helped to put other disabilities into perspective also.

➤ **Ricki** For me, seeing how a master teacher can integrate a child who is blind into her classroom without major adaptations was a real inspiration. Pat's classroom was a "real world" situation, and with very little help from me, she and John and the other students established the necessary routines and relationships that made it possible for him to be part of the class. Because this kind of integration is always the goal of a special education teacher, I felt lucky to be involved in such a success. It made me more hopeful for integration of my other students who may not yet be as capable as John. Pat also gave me a model to refer to when trying to identify other mainstreaming teachers.

➤ **Pat** The greatest barrier to working together is lack of extra planning time to address the child's special needs. Classrooms sometimes have to be physically rearranged to accommodate a special needs student. The teacher may also be fearful of what she might expect from the student emotionally and physically and how that might affect her classroom. Classroom teachers feel already burdened and are reluctant to take on another, somewhat demanding student. Another hindrance is the unclear definition of responsibilities of resource and classroom teacher. Also, the two personalities of the teachers must be compatible, and there must be a workable trust level between the two.

➤ **Ricki** I think our different perspectives and responsibilities cause many misunderstandings and a lack of appreciation for each other's problems. I have the luxury of zeroing in on one student at a time, but a classroom teacher has to look at the big picture and be responsible for many individuals at once. Asking a classroom teacher to give one special student a larger slice of time is definitely an imposition—one that some classroom teachers can tolerate better than others.

stimulation, social isolation can cause individuals to seek added stimulation through stereotypic behaviors (Warren, 1981, 1984).

Stereotypic behaviors can be manifested as early as a few months of age. Researchers have found that eye poking and body rocking are among the most prevalent types of stereotypic behaviors and the most difficult to eliminate (Bambring & Troster, 1992). Most authorities agree that it is important to eliminate stereotypic behaviors. In addition to being socially stigmatizing and possibly physically damaging, they can interfere with the child's ability to learn (Bambring & Troster, 1992). Engaging in such behaviors means less time for active learning. Although their reduction can be very difficult, researchers are constantly attempting to find successful treatments for decreasing the frequency of stereotypic behaviors. One team of researchers, for example, was successful in dramatically reducing the frequency of head rocking in an 11-year-old student by instructing him to place his hand on his cheek or chin whenever he was rocking his head (Ross & Koening, 1991). They theorized that this treatment was effective for this student because it provided him with cognitive control over his stereotypic behavior.

EDUCATIONAL CONSIDERATIONS

Lack of sight can severely limit a person's experiences because a primary means of obtaining information from the environment is not available. What makes the situation even more difficult is that educational experiences in the typical classroom are frequently visual. Nevertheless, most experts agree that we should educate students who are visually impaired in the same general way as we do sighted children. Teachers need to make some modifications, but they can apply the same general educational principles. The important difference is that students with visual impairment will have to rely on other sensory modalities to acquire information.

The student with little or no sight will possibly require special modifications in four major areas: (1) Braille, (2) use of remaining sight, (3) listening skills, and (4) mobility training. The first three pertain directly to academic education, particularly reading; the last refers to skills needed for everyday living.

Braille

In nineteenth-century France, Louis Braille, who was blind, introduced the basic system of writing for people who are blind. This system is still used today. Braille was based on a military system of writing messages that could be read at night. The Braille method was to replace the use of raised-line letters. In the 1930s, Standard English Braille was established as the standard code, making it possible for all Braille readers to read, no matter who had trained them.

The basic unit of Braille is a quadrangular "cell" containing anywhere from one to six dots (see Figure 9–2). Two means of writing in Braille are the Perkins Brailler and the slate and stylus. The **Perkins Brailler** (Figure 9–3, p. 360) has six keys, one for each of the six dots of the cell. The keys, when depressed simultaneously, leave an embossed print on the paper. More portable than the Perkins Brailler, is the **slate and stylus** (Figure 9–4, p. 361). The stylus is pressed through the openings of the slate, which holds the paper between its two halves.

Perhaps the most hotly debated topic in the field of visual impairment concerns whether we should teach students who are blind to use Braille or one of the

➤ **Perkins Brailler.** A system making it possible to write in Braille; has six keys, one for each of the six dots of the cell, which leave an embossed print on paper.

➤ **slate and stylus.** A method of writing in Braille in which the paper is held in a slate while the stylus is pressed through openings to make indentations in the paper. With this method the Braille cells are written in reverse order, and thus it is more difficult to use than the Perkins Brailler. It is more portable than the Perkins Brailler, however.

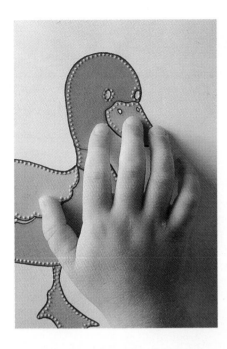

*B*raille makes numerous activities possible for people with visual problems.

other methods of communication, such as tape recorders or voice-activated computers. At one time it was fairly common for students with blindness to use Braille, but over the past several years Braille usage has declined dramatically. For example, the percentage of students who are blind who use Braille has steadily declined since the mid-1960s, when nearly half used Braille, to the most recent statistics indicating that only 10.1 percent use Braille (Pierce, 1991).

Many within the community of blind people are alarmed at the reduced availability of Braille and assert that it has led to a distressing rate of illiteracy (Ianuzzi, 1992; Mauer, 1991; Nicely, 1991; Raeder, 1991; Schroeder, 1990, 1992). They charge that too few sighted teachers are proficient in Braille and that they do little to discourage the notion held by some children that using Braille indicates inferiority. As the Executive Director of the National Braille Press has put it:

> *There is an institutionalized prejudice against blindness and Braille.* Braille for the blind student is sometimes shunned by the teacher, administrator, or even the parent or

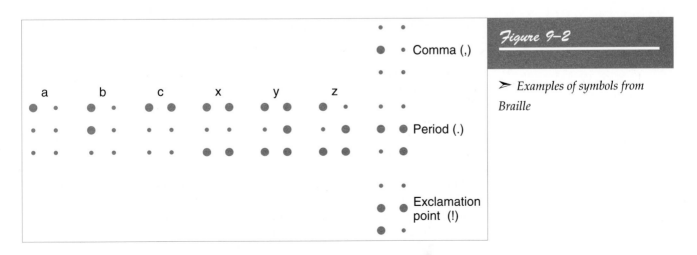

Figure 9-2

➣ *Examples of symbols from Braille*

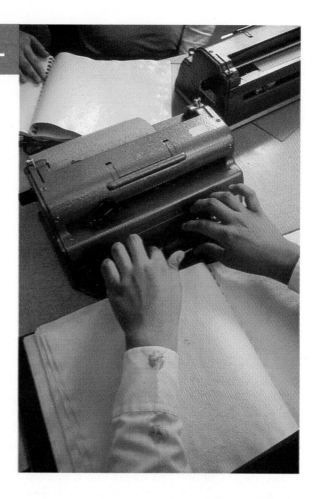

Figure 9-3

➤ *A Perkins Brailler in use*

student because it further identifies the student as being blind; and, in all too many minds, albeit oftentimes subconsciously, there is a stigma attached to blindness and a damaging attitude of unduly diminished expectations of blind students. (Raeder, 1991, p. 36)

Advocates of Braille point out that it is essential for most students who are legally blind to learn Braille in order to lead independent lives. They argue that, although tape recorders, computers, and other technological devices can contribute much to reading and acquiring information, these devices cannot replace Braille. For example, finding a specific section of a text or "skimming" (using a tape recorder) are difficult, but these kinds of activities are possible when using Braille. Taking notes for class, reading a speech, or looking up words in a dictionary are easier when using Braille than when using a tape recorder (Maurer, 1991). Braille proponents are especially concerned that the slate and stylus be preserved as a viable method of taking notes. They point out that just as computers have not replaced the pen and pencil for the sighted, neither can they take the place of the slate and stylus for people who are blind.

Many authorities now recommend that some students with low vision who are able to read large print or print with magnification should also be taught Braille (Holbrook & Koenig, 1992), similar to the way some Hispanic students are taught both Spanish and English. There are many students with low vision whose

Figure 9-4

➤ *A slate and stylus in use*

condition dictates that their visual acuity will worsen over the years. Learning Braille at an early age will prepare them for when their eyesight no longer allows them to read print. The vignette in the box on page 362 demonstrates how important Braille instruction can be for these students and how social stigma can get in the way of learning Braille.

As a way of ensuring that Braille becomes more readily available, advocates have lobbied for **Braille bills**. Although the specific provisions of these bills vary from state to state, the National Federation of the Blind, a major proponent of Braille bills, has drafted a model bill that specifies two important components. The Federation's prototype bill states that (1) Braille must be available for students if any members of the IEP team, including parents, indicate that it is needed, and (2) teachers of students with visual impairment need to be proficient in Braille.

In addition to the passage of Braille bills, there are other indications that the current low usage of Braille may turn around in the next few years. For example, a committee of the American Printing House for the Blind has published guidelines for selecting learning media. The committee reinforced the notion of Braille as a logical choice for many students with visual impairment. The following are some of the guidelines the committee proposed:

> Special attention should be given to the time in a student's educational career when instruction in the use of both media is begun. The following facts must be considered in making this decision:
>
> a. Some young students may not demonstrate a preference for either visual or tactile pre-school readiness materials. It is extremely important that these children receive early instruction with all types of media in order to determine later which will be the most appropriate learning medium/media for them.
>
> b. Because the reading load in higher grades is heavier, this is not a good time for students to begin instruction in a new medium. Students who are going to use both print and braille should be introduced to both media as early as possible and in the primary grades.

➤ **Braille bills.** Legislation passed in several states making Braille more available to students with visual impairment. Specific provisions vary from state to state, but major advocates have lobbied for (a) making Braille available if parents want it, and for (b) ensuring that teachers of students with visual impairment are proficient in Braille.

BRAILLE IS NOT JUST FOR THOSE WHO ARE BLIND >

There are many individuals whose visual impairment is not severe enough in childhood to require Braille but whose condition will worsen in time to the point where using Braille will be a desirable option. For these students, it makes sense to start Braille instruction before they actually need to rely on it extensively. Unfortunately, as the following vignette shows, one of the barriers to beginning Braille instruction with these students is the social stigma attached to using Braille.

When I was seven years old, I became legally blind from a condition known as Stephens-Johnson's Syndrome. This left me with visual acuity in the neighborhood of 20/400. Prior to this time I was fully sighted and had completed first, and one-half of second, grade receiving ordinary print reading instruction.

Because of associated health problems, I remained at home for two and one-half years, receiving home teaching services from the local school district. At that time, there were no special education services available for low vision children, and the concept of "sight saving" was generally held by practicing opthalmologists. For this reason, all of my lessons were conducted orally—two to three times a week for an hour at a time. At the age of ten, I returned to public school, participating in a regular fifth grade class. While I was not aware that I would eventually lose the remainder of my sight, my mother must have been informed and began searching for someone to teach me braille. Since I had some sight, I did not regard myself as a blind person, and therefore, had no interest in learning braille. Additionally, my poor eyesight mostly represented a source of embarrassment for me, resulting in an aversion to learning braille. I would much rather have hidden my eye problem, rather that making it public through braille reading.

While the home teacher was diligent, I never practiced between lessons, and read the braille visually rather than by touch. He was using the Illinois Series, which used single-sided braille for the first two books, allowing me to read it visually without too much problem. When I got to the third book, which was inter-point braille, I could no longer read the material with my eyes, causing frustration by me and my teacher, with the end result of braille instruction being dropped.

Throughout school, I was exempt from any assignment which I could not see well enough to complete. As can be imagined, my education was limited primarily to what I could pick up from sitting in class.

Toward the end of junior high school, my vision began deteriorating further. A long series of eye surgeries ensued, resulting in total blindness at the age of sixteen. At this point, I was in the Fall semester of my senior year of high school and was again receiving home instruction, since my many eye surgeries prevented me from attending school. A home teacher again provided me with the Illinois Braille Series which I used to teach myself braille. After completing the Illinois Series, I read my first novel—Animal Farm. When I began, I was reading a page in forty-eight minutes. One hundred fifty-five pages later, when I finished the book, I was reading a page in sixteen minutes. My slow reading rate was due to poor braille reading techniques associated with being self-taught, coupled with a lack of reading experience, overall. I read with the index finger of my right had only-scrubbing up and down, and backtracking frequently. My general lack of literacy was a major impediment to acquiring any reasonable proficiency in braille. I can remember puzzling over the word "neighbor", which seemed incomprehensible with my limited knowledge of phonics.

I wish to stress that my experience with print and braille reading must not be viewed simply as an example of poor training. As a young child, blindness represented inferiority to me and a constant source of feelings of inadequacy. I believed that I was less capable than others, and believed it was due to my poor vision. I could not imagine that techniques used by the blind could allow me to function competitively. Some training was available to me, but my own attitudes about blindness caused me to reject braille at the cost of self-confidence and basic literacy.

Frederic K. Schroeder
Santa Fe, New Mexico

SOURCE: Caton, H. (Ed.) (1991). *Print and Braille literacy: Selecting appropriate learning media.* Louisville, KY: American Printing House for the Blind. Reprinted with permission.

c. Some students may have trouble moving from one learning medium to another and may need specific instruction to learn to use each medium most efficiently.

The following principles related to classroom performance of visually impaired students are of critical importance:

a. Expectations related to academic achievement should be the same for visually impaired students and normally sighted students.

b. It is possible that diminishing classroom or homework assignments or accepting poorer quality in work may camouflage the need to change the medium. However, the nature of the eye disorders of some children may cause extreme fatigue, extremely restricted fields may result in very slow reading, etc. In these cases, teachers and other decision makers may have to make some adjustments in the amount of time or work required of the visually impaired student.

c. Students who have trouble keeping up with sighted classmates academically should be helped to understand that the problem may be caused by the presentation of the material rather that their blindness or the learning medium they are using. (Caton, 1991, pp. 6-7)

Use of Remaining Sight

For many years, there was a great deal of resistance to having children with visual impairment use their sight in reading and some other activities. There have been many myths about this issue. Among the most common are these: (1) Holding books close to the eyes harms the eyes, (2) strong lenses hurt the eyes, and (3) using the eyes too much injures them (Hanninen, 1975). At one time classes for students with low vision were called "sight conservation" or "sight-saving" classes, reflecting the popular assumption that using the eyes too much causes them to deteriorate. It is now recognized that only in very rare conditions is this true. In fact, studies have shown that teachers can actually train students to use what visual abilities they do have to better advantage (Barraga & Collins, 1979; Collins & Barraga, 1980).

The two general methods of aiding children with visual impairment to read print are large-print books and magnifying devices. Large-print books are simply books printed in larger-size type. This text, printed primarily for sighted readers, is printed in 10-point type. Figure 9–5 on page 364 shows print in 18-point type. Type sizes for readers with visual impairment range up to 30-point type, but 18-point is one of the most popular.

The major difficulty with large-type books is that a great deal of space is required to store them. In addition, they are of limited availability, although, along with the American Printing House for the Blind, a number of commercial publishers are now publishing and marketing large-print books.

Magnifying devices range from glasses and hand-held lenses to closed-circuit television scanners that present enlarged images on a TV screen. These devices can be used with normal-size type or large-type books.

Listening Skills

The importance of listening skills for children who are blind cannot be overemphasized. The less a child is able to rely on sight for gaining information from the environment, the more crucial it is that he or she become a good listener. Some professionals still assume that good listening skills will develop automatically in children who are blind. This belief is unfortunate, for it is now evident that children do not spontaneously compensate for poor vision by magically developing superior powers of concentration. In most cases, they must be taught how to listen. A variety of curriculum materials and programs are available to teach children listening skills (e.g., Bischoff, 1979; Swallow & Conner, 1982).

Listening skills are becoming more important than ever because of the increasing accessibility of recorded material. The American Printing House for

Figure 9–5

This is an example of 18-point type.

the Blind and the Library of Congress are major sources for these materials. One can simply play the material at normal speed or use a compressed speech device that allows one to read at about 250 to 275 words per minute. The idea behind this method is to discard very small segments of the speech. Some of the more sophisticated compressed speech devices use a computer to eliminate those speech sounds that are least necessary for comprehension.

Mobility Training

How well individuals cope with a visual disability depends to a great extent on how well they are able to move about. Whether a person withdraws from the social environment or becomes independent depends greatly on mobility skills. There are four general methods available to aid the mobility of people with visual impairment: (1) the long cane, (2) a guide dog, (3) human guides, and (4) electronic devices.

The Long Cane

Professionals most often recommend the long cane for those individuals with visual impairments in need of a mobility aid. The traveler sweeps the **long cane** in an arc, lightly touching the ground in front. Although it does not provide very

➤ **long cane.** A mobility aid used by individuals with visual impairment who sweep it in a wide arc in front of them; proper use requires considerable training. It is the mobility aid of choice for most travelers who are blind.

*C*omputers can help accommodate the needs of some individuals with visual impairment.

7he long cane has proved to be the most useful travel aid for most people with visual impairment.

good protection to the upper part of the body, the long cane has many other advantages:

> The long cane is the most effective and efficient mobility aid yet devised for safe, independent travel by the majority of visually impaired people. The scanning system in which the user operates the cane supplies echo-ranging cues and force-impact data that give vital information about the immediate environment. It informs the traveler about the nature and condition of the surface underfoot, gives sufficient forewarning of downsteps or dropoffs to prevent falls or injury, and protects the lower part of the body from collision. The cane informs the user about various ground-surface textures which can be related to specific areas and destinations. It is a highly maneuverable aid that allows investigation of the environment without actual hand contact. The long cane is reliable, long lasting, and somewhat unaffected by unfavorable weather and temperature conditions. Most require no accessories, and virtually no maintenance except occasional replacement of a worn tip. The cane can be accommodated to most users' physical specifications and, in some instances, their disabilities. (Farmer, 1980, p. 359)

Although the long cane looks like a simple device, scientists, mobility specialists, and others working under the auspices of the National Academy of Sciences have drawn up specifications for its construction. In addition, although watching a skilled user of the long cane may give the impression that it is easy to manipulate, extensive training in its proper use is often required.

At one time, orientation and mobility teachers thought that young children were too young to be taught mobility skills. Before 1980, it was very difficult for parents to find a cane for their preschooler with visual impairment (Cheadle,

1991). Today, however, more and more preschoolers are being taught cane techniques. Many professionals recommend that cane training be initiated as soon as the child is walking independently with only minor irregularities in balance and gait (Skellenger & Hill, 1991).

Instead of using canes with preschoolers, some professionals encourage the use of other devices, such as a push-toy or hula-hoop that the child pushes along the ground in front of himself or herself. Researchers have also invented the Connecticut Pre-cane, which is shaped generally like the long cane but with a much wider base (Foy, Von Scheden, & Waiculonis, 1992).

A Guide Dog

Contrary to popular notions, a **guide dog** is not recommended very often for people with visual impairment. Extensive training is required to learn how to use a guide dog properly. The extended training—as well as the facts that guide dogs are large, walk relatively fast, and need to be cared for—make them particularly questionable for children. For some adults, however, the guide dog has proven to be a valuable aide and companion. Contrary to what most people think, the dog does not "take" the person who is blind anywhere. The person must first know where he or she is going; the dog is primarily a safeguard against walking into

➢ **guide dog.** A dog specially trained to help guide a person who is blind; not recommended for children and not used by very many adults who are blind because the user needs special training in how to use the dog properly; contrary to popular opinion, the dog does not "take" the person anywhere but serves primarily as a safeguard against walking into dangerous areas.

While less common than the long cane, the guide dog is used by some individuals with vision problems as an aid for getting around.

dangerous areas. Some users of guide dogs point out that dogs are able to alert their owners to important things in their environment, such as stairways, entrances, exits, and elevators, sooner than can be detected by a cane (Gabias, 1992).

Human Guides

The human guide undoubtedly enables a person to have the greatest freedom in moving about safely, but this arrangement is not practical in most cases. Furthermore, too much reliance on another person causes a dependency that can be harmful. Even people who are blind who are highly proficient travelers have noted that a certain degree of independence is sacrificed when walking accompanied by a sighted person (Hull, 1990). In order to converse with the companion, the person without sight can be distracted from paying attention to the cues he or she needs to travel efficiently and comes to rely on the sighted companion. This also can give the sighted individual the false impression that the person who is blind does not have good mobility skills.

Most people who travel unaccompanied do not need help from those around them. However, if we see a person with visual impairment who looks like he or she needs assistance, we should first ask if help is wanted. If physical guidance is required, we should allow the person to hold onto our arm above the elbow and walk a half-step behind us. Sighted people have a tendency to grasp the arm of persons without sight and "push" them in the direction they are heading.

Electronic Devices

Researchers are working on a number of sophisticated electronic devices for sensing objects in the environment. Most of them are still experimental, and most

While many individuals with visual impairment are quite independent, it is rarely "wrong" to offer assistance if it seems to be needed.

are expensive. Representative examples that have been under development for some time are the Laser cane and the Sonicguide. These devices operate on the principle that human beings can learn to locate objects by means of echoes, much as bats do.

The Laser cane can be used in the same way as the long cane or as a sensing device that emits three beams of infrared light (one up, one down, and one straight ahead), which are converted into sound after they strike objects in the path of the traveler (Farmer, 1975).

The Sonicguide is for use with individuals ranging in age from infancy to adulthood (Bower, 1977; Kay, 1973; Strelow & Boys, 1979). Worn on the head, the device emits ultrasound and converts reflections from objects into audible sound. Depending on characteristics of the sound, such as its pitch, clarity, and direction, the Sonicguide wearer can learn about such things as the distance, texture, and direction of objects. Because it is still experimental, a number of unresolved issues relate to the use of the Sonicguide. With the infant model, for example, issues pertain to optimum age of introduction (Aitkin & Bower, 1982; Ferrell, 1980; Harris, Humphrey, Muir, & Dodwell, 1985; Sampaio, 1989; Strelow, 1983). Another issue concerns whether the Sonicguide might delay language development. Some have speculated that the sound from the aid might interfere with perception of speech sounds.

A word of caution is in order in considering electronic mobility devices. Because of their amazing technology, it is easy to be too optimistic about these devices. There are at least five things to keep in mind in this regard. Electronic devices are:

1. still experimental, we need to know a lot more about them;
2. still very expensive; they are not available to everyone;
3. not a substitute for more conventional techniques such as the long cane;
4. not easily used; they require extensive training;
5. not a substitute for spatial concepts, the device may aid in the perception of objects, but the person who is blind must use the perceptual information gained to form spatial concepts, or cognitive maps, of his or her environment. (Warren, 1989)

Technological Aids

In recent years, a technological explosion has resulted in new electronic devices for the use of people with visual impairment (see the box on p. 370). Among the first was the **Optacon**, a hand-held scanner that converts print to tactile letters that are felt on the index finger. There is also an Optacon II for scanning computer screens. A major advantage of the Optacon and Optacon II is portability; major disadvantages are expense and the slow rate of reading they allow.

The **Kurzweil Reading Machine** and the **Kurzweil Personal Reader**, especially the former, are less portable than the Optacon, but they allow a reading rate as fast as human speech. They convert print with practically any typeface into synthesized speech. The user places the material on a scanner which "reads" the material with an electronic voice. Because of expense, The Kurzweil Reading Machine is limited mainly to libraries and institutions. One can purchase the much smaller Kurzweil Personal Reader for about $10,000. In addition, there is a PC/Kurzweil Personal Reader, starting at about $4,000, that can be used with an IBM or Apple personal computer to convert print to speech.

➢ **Optacon.** A device used to enable persons who are blind to "read"; consists of a camera that converts print into an image of letters, which are then produced by way of vibration onto the finger.

➢ **Kurzweil Reading Machine.** A computerized device that converts print into speech for persons with visual impairment. The user places the printed material over a scanner that then "reads" the material aloud by means of an electronic voice.

➢ **Kurzweil Personal Reader.** A version of the Kurzweil Reading Machine that can be used with an IBM or Apple computer.

For the user of Braille, **VersaBraille** saves time and space. The user records Braille onto tape cassettes and plays them back on the machine's reading board. The VersaBraille II Plus converts letters on a personal computer screen into Braille.

For low vision students, some investigators have been experimenting for several years with closed circuit television systems (Miller-Wood, Efron, & Wood, 1990). These allow the student to see an enlarged image on the screen of what the teacher is presenting.

Similar to captioning for people with hearing impairment, a service is now available for making television more accessible to people with visual impairment (Cronin & King, 1990). The **Descriptive Video Service**, developed by National Public Radio Station WGBH in Boston, is available for several public television programs. A narrated description of key visual features of the program is inserted in between lapses in the dialogue.

Some experts have stressed that many of these technological aids are not very useful without proper training in how to use them (Halliday, 1992). As with some sighted people, people who are blind can sometimes be intimidated by computers unless they are introduced to the computer's capabilities appropriately.

➤ **VersaBraille.** A device used to record Braille onto tape cassettes that are played back on a reading board; the VersaBraille II Plus is a laptop computer on which a person can type Braille that can be converted into print copies.

➤ **Descriptive Video Service.** Provides audio narrative of key visual elements; available for several public television programs; for use of people with visual impairment.

Service Delivery Models

There are four major educational placements for the child with visual impairment. From most to least segregated, they are the residential school, the special class, resource room, and the itinerant teacher. Most states operate residential institutions for this population. Given the very low prevalence of this category of exceptionality, one advantage of residential institutions is that they allow for the concentration of a number of specialized services in one place (Warren, 1981). If these services were to be provided by the schools, they would need to be spread out geographically. Today, although some still argue for a full continuum of services (Erwin, 1991), this kind of placement is much less popular than it once was. Virtually all children with visual impairment were educated in residential institutions in the early 1900s, but now almost all receive their education in public schools. Much of this migration out of residential institutions occurred in the years following the passage of PL 94-142 (IDEA) in 1975. Very few children who are blind are now placed in residential schools unless they have additional disabilities, such as mental retardation or deafness.

Also in support of the prevailing philosophy of integrating children with visual impairments with the sighted is the fact that many residential facilities have established cooperative arrangements with local public schools (Cronin, 1992; McIntire, 1985; Stewart, Van Hasselt, Simon, & Thompson, 1985). The staff of the residential facility usually concentrates on training independent living skills, such as mobility, personal grooming, and home management, while local school personnel emphasize academics. Also, support services, such as speech and physical therapy, are sometimes better delivered by personnel from institutions because they have had more experience working with children who are blind. And some point out that, given the low prevalence of blindness, having these children come to a residential site periodically affords them an opportunity to interact with other children who have the same types of disabilities (Cronin, 1992).

THE PC IS MY LIFELINE ➤

Imagine yourself blindfolded with your ears plugged. No light, no sound. That's what it means to be deaf and blind. How would you be able to use a PC? Read the manuals that come with dBASE IV? Communicate with others? Hold a full-time job as a computer professional?

It's all possible.

I was born deaf and sighted and gradually lost my vision. Adaptive devices did not exist when I enrolled as a student at New York University, so I depended on my usable sight to complete the required reading; I received my bachelor's degree summa cum laude with a major in mathematics. When I was doing graduate work in statistics at NYU, I began using a VTEK magnification system, which I continued to use in my work as a computer programmer. The system enlarges printed material and displays it on a TV-like monitor.

Since then, my vision has deteriorated, and I use other devices in my work and in my life. I have worked for several high-tech companies and am currently a senior programmer/analyst at Wang Laboratories in Lowell, Massachusetts. I work as a telecommuter from home and make weekly trips to the office. Though I still rely on fingerspelling for face-to-face conversations, I use a variety of devices in my work.

Optacon gives me immediate and independent access to printed material—computer manuals, books, and magazines. It uses a handheld scanner to reproduce characters, symbols, and even simple graphic images on a bed of vibrating pins that I feel with my index finger, one character at a time.

With VersaBraille II Plus, I can operate the AT-compatible Wang PC280 that I use at home. A portable braille terminal that can stand alone or connect to a PC or mainframe, it provides a 20-character braille display, or window, of what is on the screen. Special software enables me to navigate a 25-line-by-80-character PC screen.

These devices allow me to use off-the-shelf MS-DOS software such as WordPerfect, Lotus 1-2-3, dBASE III Plus and dBASE IV, ProComm, and PC programming language compilers.

I write software and documentation on the PC in languages such as COBOL, C, and dBASE III Plus using a regular text editor (KEdit from Mansfield Software Group). I compile, test, and debug the programs on the PC. When I'm working on mainframe programs, I use a high-speed modem and a terminal emulator to turn the PC into a workstation that runs off the Wang mainframe in Lowell, several miles away. In this mode, my VersaBraille helps me navigate the mainframe menus and get access to the company's electronic mail system, Wang Office. Through electronic mail, I also discuss technical issues and exchange information with my colleagues.

But the PC is more than a professional device for me. With the PC, I can hold telephone communications with anyone else who has a PC and modem. I have met many people through nationwide computer services like Delphi and CompuServe. On Delphi, I participate in computer conferences several times a week, chat with other computer enthusiasts around the country, and use electronic mail to keep in touch with them at other times. I also get news and weather reports online and occasionally play games; my favorite is a word game called Scramble. Because my disabilities are not visible to other users online, they have been surprised, on the rare occasions when I mention it, to find out that I am deaf and blind.

Adaptive device technology is at a point now where it can help disabled people like myself to live constructive and productive lives. However, these sophisticated devices must keep up with changes in PC technology. Most devices work only on MS-DOS-based systems and do not address operating systems such as Unix and OS/2. Not all special software can tell the user where highlighted words appear on the screen; the PC community must consider putting graphics into a format accessible to those who can't see the screen. And the equipment must be made affordable.

But with all that remains to be done, the technology is helping people. Without the PC and adaptive devices, my life would be much more lonely and solitary. I could not read all the books I want to read, and I probably wouldn't be working in a field that interests me. I would have far fewer opportunities to communicate and joke with others. Optacon, VersaBraille, and the PC have enhanced my life professionally, socially, and intellectually.

—Barbara Wegreich

Barbara Wegreich is a senior programmer and analyst at Wang Laboratories.

SOURCE: From H. Brody, The great equalizer: PCs empower the disabled, *PC Computing*, July 1989, 2(7) p. 87. Copyright © 1989. Reprinted with permission.

Although special classes and resource rooms are sometimes used, itinerant teaching arrangements are gaining favor today. Because of the low prevalence of blindness, itinerant teachers do not have a class of their own but travel from school to school, working and consulting with regular teachers. For mainstream-

Issues in Special Education — Is Braille Literacy Necessary for All Children Who Are Blind?

CNN

*T*he system of printed language developed in the early 19th century by Louis Braille made the world of literature available to those with visual impairments. By learning a system of 63 raised dot patterns, persons with visual impairment could actually "read" with their fingertips.

However, due largely to technological developments whereby one can use printed language without actually "seeing" it—computers, recorders, etc.—Braille use has declined markedly during the last 25 years. According to statistics from the American Printing House for the Blind, in 1965 roughly 50% of visually impaired persons read Braille, compared to 12% in 1989.

This has stirred controversy between those who feel that Braille is, perhaps, dying a natural death, and those who feel that allowing it to become extinct would represent a serious loss to those with visual impairments.

Mark Maurer, president of the 50,000-member National Federation for the Blind, maintains that technology cannot fully substitute for the printed word. He maintains that blind children who learn to read with their fingertips are more likely to compete than than those who use ersatz visual methods to access a written language system that was really only designed for use by sighted persons.

Maurer also cites the stigma attached to Braille use—and to blindness in general—noting that many parents and teachers prefer children to pretend they have sight that they don't have.

On the other hand, the American Foundation for the Blind maintains that the 85% of individuals with visual impairment who do have some degree of vision are served better by using the visual skills they have to read, rather than relying on a system which asks nothing of their eyes. From this point of view, Braille is appropriate for those who have no reading or writing alternatives whatsoever, but not necessarily for those with residual vision.

- As a sighted person, does the image of a person reading or writing in Braille carry any kind of connotation?
- Do you feel it should be mandatory that all children with visual impairment be taught Braille, or should it be decided on a case-by-case basis?

ing to be successful with this population, a strong relationship must be established between the regular class teacher and a certified teacher of children with visual impairment (Erwin, 1991).

EARLY INTERVENTION

For many years, psychologists and educators considered the sighted infant as almost totally lacking in visual abilities during the first half year or so of life. We now know that the young sighted infant is able to take in a great deal of information through the visual system. This fact makes it easy to understand why professionals are usually eager to begin intensive intervention as early as possible to help the infant with visual impairment begin to explore the environment.

An area of particular importance in early intervention for children with visual impairment is mobility (Palazesi, 1986). Some infants who are totally blind are late to crawl, and some authorities have speculated that this is because they have not learned that there is something "out there" in their environment worth pursuing (Fraiberg, 1977). They may not be as motivated as sighted infants to explore their extended environment because they are more engaged in examining things close to their bodies. Parents can sometimes contribute to their infants lack of exploration. Some parents, concerned for the safety of their infants who are blind, are

Children with visual impairment should be given many opportunities to explore and learn about their environment.

reluctant to let them investigate their surroundings. Parents sometimes have difficulty assessing the proper amount of caution. By about six months of age, the sighted child spontaneously reaches out to visually perceived objects. Without specific training, the infant who is totally blind may not reach out to things he or she hears until late in the first year.

Unfortunately, as noted earlier in the discussion of mobility training, for many years professionals did not begin training motor development and mobility until children with visual impairment were in the elementary grades. Today, most authorities agree that mobility training should be a critical component of preschool programming. In addition to introducing cane techniques to children as soon as they are able to walk relatively well, some researchers are experimenting with methods of encouraging infants at the crawling stage to explore their environment more actively. For example, one study was successful in increasing the exploratory behavior of infants who were blind, using a specially constructed room containing a variety of tactile and auditory stimuli (Nielsen, 1991).

Most authorities agree that it is extremely important to involve parents of infants with visual impairment in early intervention efforts. Parents can become actively involved in working at home with their young children, helping them with fundamental skills, such as mobility and feeding. Parents, too, sometimes need support in coping with their reactions to having a baby with visual impairment. Sometimes there is an overwhelming sense of grief. Professionals working in early intervention programs for infants who are blind often recommend that initial efforts focus on helping parents cope with their own reactions to having a child who is blind (Maloney, 1981).

TRANSITION

Two closely related areas are difficult for some adolescents and adults with visual impairment—independence and employment.

Independent Living

An extremely important thing to keep in mind when working with adolescents and adults with visual impairment is that achieving a sense of independence is often difficult for them. Many authorities have pointed out that much of the problem of dependence is because of the way society treats persons without sight. A common mistake is to assume that such an individual is helpless. Many people think of blindness as a condition to be pitied. People with visual impairments have a long history of arguing against paternalistic treatment by sighted society. Back in the 1960s, Scott (1969) warned of the demeaning attitude of those who worked in agencies established to help people with visual impairments. The National Federation of the Blind has for several years argued fiercely that they want jobs and not handouts:

> What we need most is not, as the professionals would have it, medical help or psychological counseling but admission to the main channels of daily life and citizenship, not custody and care but understanding and acceptance. Above all, what we need is not more government programs or private charitable efforts. Instead, we want jobs, opportunity, and full participation in society. (Jernigan, 1985, p. 388)

Many people who are blind point to the Federal Aviation Administration's (FAA) policy toward airline travelers who are blind as an example of a paternalistic attitude. For years, the National Federation of the Blind has battled with the FAA and the airline industry over the right to sit by the exit on airplanes. The current FAA policy stipulates that a person must be able to receive visual directions and be able to assess escape paths outside of the aircraft. Individual airlines have varied in how they have interpreted these policies. Some have allowed people who are blind to take seats in the exit row while others have insisted that the person be able to see well enough, for example, to read the safety directions printed on the card in the seat pocket. The following is the reaction of a spokesperson for the National Federation of the Blind:

> It is not enough to show that a given blind person in a given instance may block an exit or pose a safety hazard. Blind persons are just as diverse and variable in their behavior and characteristics as sighted persons are. . . . It must be shown that they are not being held to a higher standard of conduct than others. . . . and that there is something about blindness that makes the blind less capable. . . .
>
> If safety is the only consideration, no one at all will fly. But just as in using automobiles, there are tradeoffs, and we are willing to accept a certain amount of risk. . . .
>
> The next fallback position for maximum safety in air travel would probably be to place trained, healthy airline officials in the exit rows, but the airlines say this is unacceptable because of the lost revenue. . . .
>
> If we go to the next fallback position for maximum safety, it would probably be to widen the exit row aisles and have no one sit in them at all . . . Again the airlines are not willing—and again for the same reason, economics. . . .
>
> Then perhaps the airlines could at least refuse to sell liquor to people who sit in the exit rows or ask for volunteers to sit there who do not intend to drink anyway. They decline to do the first of these things because of lost revenue and the second because of concern about frightening the passengers by reminding them of possible crashes or in-flight emergencies.

Of course, none of this makes the case for permitting blind persons to sit in the exit rows, but it does demonstrate that safety is not the only (or perhaps even the prime) factor being considered. . . .

Blind persons are either a greater hazard than others seated in exit rows or they aren't. If they are, they shouldn't sit there—and any blind person with any sense wouldn't want to. If they aren't a greater safety hazard than others, then prohibiting them from sitting in the exit row is discrimination. . . .

So where does this leave us? Never in the history of commercial aviation has there been a single recorded instance of a blind person's blocking an exit, slowing an evacuation, or contributing to an accident. But there are recorded instances to the contrary. At night or when the cabin has been filled with smoke, blind persons have on more than one occasion found the exits and led others out. (Jernigan, 1991, pp. 51-53)

No matter which side one takes an the issue of airline seating, there is little doubt that the public at times has been at fault in creating an environment conducive to fostering dependency in people with blindness. The accomplished author Ved Mehta has written several books dealing with his adjustment to blindness and going to school in the United States (Mehta, 1982, 1984, 1985, 1989). In the book dealing with his adolescent years at the Arkansas School for the Blind, he talks about experiences that people who are blind typically have to face, experiences that undoubtedly can foster dependence:

I decided that I didn't like going to coffee shops. I had generally eaten at a table, either with my family or with students and staff at a school, and eating alone at a counter filled me with sadness. Moreover, there were always incidents in the coffee shops that would leave me shaken. The waitresses would shout out the menu to me as if I were half deaf, and so attract the attention of everyone in the coffee shop. Even when they got to know me and treated me normally, I would have to contend with

Athletic activities need not be considered off limits for those with visual impairment.

customers who didn't know me. I remember that once when I asked for my bill the waitress said, "A man already took care of it."

"I insist on paying for myself."

The waitress refused to accept the money. "The man done gone," she said to the coffee shop. "What does the kid want me to do—take money twice for the same ham sandwich? He should be thankful there are nice people to pay for him." I felt anything but thankful, however. I thought that I'd been an object of pity.

I remember that another time Tom took me to a new coffee shop. The waitress, instead of asking me for my order, turned to him and asked, "What does he want to eat?"

"A ham sandwich," I said, speaking up for myself. She brought me the ham sandwich, but throughout lunch she ignored me, talking to Tom as if I weren't there. (Mehta, 1985, pp. 198-199)

Rickelman and Blaylock (1983) conducted a survey of persons who were blind in which, among other things, they were asked to indicate how sighted individuals might respond to them to decrease their dependent behavior. The following are their main suggestions:

1. *Respecting and encouraging the blind person's individuality, capabilities, and independence:* Do not assume that because you can do something more conveniently or quickly you should automatically do it for the blind person.
   Blind people often do not need help. Ask, "Can I be of assistance?" instead of initiating help. Do not feel embarrassed or rejected if a blind person declines your offer of assistance.
   Avoid being oversolicitous or overly protective. Blind people have the right to make mistakes, too.
   The qualities and characteristics of the blind are as individual as the sighted. Respect this individuality.

2. *Talking with the blind:* Feel free to approach and talk to a blind person. You have the right to ask any questions you wish. The blind person has the right to respond as he wishes.
   Identify yourself before beginning a conversation or offering assistance.
   Approach a blind person without embarrassment, fear, or pity.
   If you are uncomfortable being around or associating with a blind person, admit it openly to the person. Neither the sighted nor the blind profit from avoiding each other.
   When you leave the presence of a blind person, always let him or her know that you are leaving.
   Talk in a normal tone of voice. Do not assume deafness or other disability.
   If your business is with a blind person, speak directly to the person rather than to sighted companions or relatives to get information.

3. *Becoming knowledgeable about guide techniques:* Let the blind person take your arm and walk slightly behind you. Never take his or her arm and push the blind person ahead of you. Walk at a normal pace.
   Always go through a door ahead of a blind person, telling him or her which way the door opens. (Rickelman & Blaylock, 1983 pp.10-11)

Many independent living skills learned incidentally by sighted people need to be taught explicitly to those who are visually impaired, for example, how to work household appliances, prepare and cook food, and even some parenting skills. Regarding the latter, the National Federation of the Blind promotes a booklet (*Parent tips,* available from Janiece Betker, 1886 29th Ave., N.W., New Brighton, MN 55112) prepared by a parent who is blind that provides tips on

In Their Own Words VED MEHTA

Ved Mehta was born in India in 1928, and educated in India, the United States, and England. During the first half of this century, educational opportunities for children who were blind were scarce, certainly in India. In spite of being relatively wealthy, his family hoped for little more than that Ved might avoid becoming a "blind beggar boy" holding out a tin cup on the streets of Bombay or Calcutta.

His series of autobiographical novels known as "Continents of Exile," chronicles his experiences as a small child at boarding school in Bombay, through to his years at Harvard, Pomona University, and Oxford. The following excerpt is from his novel *Sound-Shadows of the New World*, which covers his adolescent years spent at The Arkansas School for the Blind, in Little Rock.

Two birds fluttered overhead. I wondered what color they were. I wondered whether in some part of my mind I could remember the colors I had seen before I went blind, and whether, if I did, that would help me to understand Wayne's hatred of Negroes. I repeated to myself, "White, Negro, white, black." Sometimes people spoke of white as clean and black as dirty, but how could "clean" or "dirty" be applied to a whole race of people? Some people thought that the blind lived in darkness, but that was nonsense. The point was that the blind had no perception of light or darkness. Perhaps darkness was like the quiet of the night. I wondered how dark I was, how much I looked like a Negro, and what my kinship with the Negro was—where I fitted into the social puzzle. I wanted somehow or other to find out where I stood in the shading from white to black, to connect myself to the rest of the world. I ached to see, even for just a moment.

SOURCE: Ved Mehta, *Sound-Shadows of the New World*, (New York: W.W. Norton and Company, 1985), p. 74.

parenting. The booklet provides useful suggestions on such topics as carrying the baby safely, taking the baby's temperature, keeping the baby's clothing color-coordinated and socks matched, and giving liquid medicine and vitamins. Regarding the latter, for example, the booklet states:

> Droppers or syringes can be purchased which draw up only 1/2 or 1 teaspoonful of liquid. Droppers can also be saved from vitamin or liquid pain-reliever bottles, washed thoroughly and used for future medicines. When the dropper can no longer reach the medicine in the bottle, the medicine can be poured into small cups such as those that come with certain cold relief liquids. The dropper or syringe is placed into the cup and the liquid medicine drawn up. The remainder is then returned to the bottle.

In some ways, it is more important for people with visual impairment to learn to be independent than it is for those who are sighted. Adults with visual impairment often find that they need to take more initiative to achieve the same level of success as the sighted. As one job counselor put it when speaking to a group of college students with visual impairment: "As blind students, you will need to spend time on activities your sighted peers never think about—recruiting and organizing readers, having textbooks prepared in alternative media, getting an early start on term papers" (Rovig, 1992, p.239).

Employment

Many working-age adults with visual impairment are unemployed, and those who are working are often overqualified for the jobs they hold (Freeman, Goetz, Richards, & Groenveld, 1991; Kirchner & Peterson, 1989). Some authorities attribute this unfortunate situation to inadequate transition programming at the secondary school level (Hanley-Maxwell, Griffin, Szymanski, & Godley, 1990; Sacks & Pruett, 1992). Even well-educated adults with visual impairment, when surveyed, indicated that they had not received training to meet their career development needs (Wolffe, Roessler, & Schriner, 1992).

As with any area of disability, job training is more likely to succeed if it takes place in regular work settings:

> The transfer of skills from a simulated environment (classroom) to an actual work environment (assembly line, clerical, or technical), for visually impaired students, might create. . . difficulties. For example, conditions such as industrial lighting and sound, physical obstacles, and social interactions with normally sighted adult co-workers cannot be simulated in a classroom environment. . . . Such an approach gives students the opportunity to develop generic work behaviors (i.e., punctuality, grooming, following directions, social skills) which will carry over to other work or community environments. (Storey, Sacks, & Olmstead, 1985, p. 481)

Although not as frequent as we would like to see, reports of adults with visual impairment who achieve successful independent living and employment are becoming more and more common. And innovative programs are being developed to meet the transition needs of students with visual impairment. For example, one successful program involved having adolescents and young adults with visual impairment come together with professionals for a three-week summer training session devoted to issues of transition (Sacks & Pruett, 1992). Among other things, this project used "job shadowing" in which students are paired with an adult with a similar visual disability and a job that matches the student's interest. The students spend a couple of days with their "partners" observing them on the job.

There is no doubt that visual impairment poses a real challenge for adjustment to everyday living, but we need to remember Don's comments in the introduction to the chapter (see p. 341). People with visual impairment share many similarities with the rest of society. Special and general educators need to achieve the delicate balance between providing special programming for students with visual impairment and treating them in the same manner as they do the rest of their students.

SUGGESTIONS FOR TEACHING ➢   E. Jane Nowacek

Students with Visual Impairment in General Education Classrooms

WHAT TO LOOK FOR IN SCHOOL

Children whose vision is severely impaired are usually diagnosed before they enter school, whereas students who have less severe visual problems often are identified during vision screenings conducted in schools. These routine examinations, however, are not foolproof. For example, they often do not measure near-point vision. Consequently, the problems of students who can read at a far distance but who cannot read materials that are near may go undetected. In addition, some students develop visual problems after the primary grades, when schools usually stop screening. Other students may experience changes in vision as they spend more time reading and as the formats of reading materials become more dense and detailed. Teachers have many opportunities to observe students reading under a variety of conditions and to provide a record of their observations by noting signs indicating possible vision problems (see p. 347).

HOW TO GATHER INFORMATION

Once you have recorded your observations, discuss them with the school nurse or the person who conducts the vision screenings in your school. They may want to conduct additional observations of the student. Share this information with the student's parents who should be encouraged to arrange a professional eye examination.

TEACHING TECHNIQUES TO TRY

Adaptation of Educational Materials

From reading the chapter, you know that the primary educational difference between students with low vision and students who are blind is their ability to read print. Students who have low vision can read print, although they may use magnifying devices and require materials written in large print. Individuals who are blind, however, must be instructed by using materials written in Braille and by aural methods, including records, cassettes, and CDs. Therefore, one required modification with students who are mainstreamed is adaptation of instructional materials. Although the itinerant or resource teacher will prepare or provide instructional materials written in Braille, you may find that tape-recording instructional lessons, assignments, and tests saves time and reduces the need for planning far in advance. In addition, several organizations, such as the Library of Congress and the American Printing House for the Blind, provide audiotapes and records of a variety of textbooks and materials for pleasure reading. Other organizations, such as Recording for the Blind, also make a large selection of books available to students and have readers who will record especially requested materials.

In addition to adapted printed materials, there are a variety of other aids that your students may find useful in your classroom:*

   A. Geography aids
     1. Braille atlases
     2. molded plastic relief maps
     3. relief globes
     4. landform models
   B. Mathematical aids
     1. abacus
     2. raised clockfaces
     3. geometric area and volume aids
     4. Braille rulers
     5. talking calculators
   C. Writing aids

     1. raised-line checkbooks
     2. signature guides
     3. long-hand writing kits
   D. Miscellaneous aids
     1. audible goal locators, used as a goal, base, or object locator or a warning device
     2. Braille or large-type answer sheets
     3. science measurement kits (including such items as thermometers, spring balances, gram weights)
     4. sports-field kit (includes raised drawings of various sports' playing fields or courts)
     5. simple machine kits (including working models of pulleys, levers, plane, wheel, and axle)

*Gearheart, Weishahn, & Gearheart (1992), p. 214.

Although students with low vision can read print, they also require adaptations of educational materials. Harley and Lawrence (1984) recommend the following modifications:

WRITTEN MATERIALS

- Use typed, rather than handwritten materials.
- Use materials that provide high contrast, such as black lettering on nongloss white or cream-colored paper.
- Use purple dittos as little as possible and then only when there is a clear, sharp copy.
- Arrange written materials on the page so they are not crowded.
- Avoid using materials in which letters are overprinted on background pictures.
- Use only one side of the paper.
- Outline dim areas of materials with a felt-tip pen.
- Keep chalkboards clean and write with white or yellow chalk to enhance the contrast.

INSTRUCTIONAL ADAPTATIONS

Besides adapting written materials, you can make other modifications that will help your mainstreamed students. For example, alternate activities that require close eye work with those that are less visually demanding and permit additional time to complete reading assignments and to take tests (Harley & Lawrence, 1984). Providing a notebook that contains the information displayed in the classroom, such as bulletin board announcements, classroom rules, word lists, and pictures, ensures that all students have access to visual information and encourages students who are visually impaired to explore their environment (MacCuspie, 1992). Best (1991) recommends these additional modifications: (a) identify potentially difficult concepts; (b) provide first-hand experiences, such as concrete materials and hands-on learning, to enrich the experiences of your students who are visually impaired; (c) repeat information you write on the chalkboard aloud; and, (d) transfer instructional material to tape-recordings.

ADAPTATIONS IN THE CLASSROOM ENVIRONMENT

When students with visual impairments first enter your class, they will require orientation to the physical arrangement of the room that includes learning the location of materials, desks, activity areas, teacher's desk, and exits. You may orient your students more rapidly if you familiarize them with these features from one focal point, such as their desk (Ashcroft & Zambone-Ashley, 1980). Once students are oriented to the classroom, they should become familiar with the school and surrounding grounds, learning the location of the gym, library, restrooms, cafeteria, water fountains, and playground. Keep students informed of changes in and additions to the classroom or school arrangements. Although you should encourage them to move about without the aid of sighted guides, you may want to assign a guide for special events and activities that occur outside of the classroom, such as fire drills and assemblies (Craig & Howard, 1981).

In addition to providing an orientation to the school and classroom, Best (1991) suggests making sure that work surfaces in the class are glare-free and large enough to accommodate a brailler; that desks are positioned near to the chalkboard and demonstrations; and that the lighting is appropriate. Natural light should come from behind or the side of the student, and a lamp should be available to illuminate the work surface, if needed. Modifications also may be necessary when using videotapes, filmstrips, and films. Torres and Corn (1990) recommend asking another student to read subtitles aloud to the class; using a rear-screen projector, which allows students who are visually impaired to sit right in front of the screen, when possible; and permitting students to view the material before or after the class to ensure they understood all the visual concepts presented.

As educators have pointed out, students with visual impairment deserve the same instruction in all content areas as their nondisabled classmates. However, they also deserve instruction in skill areas required to meet their specific needs, such as social, sensory-motor, independent, daily living skills, and orientation and mobility training (Curry & Hatlen, 1988). Although other professionals will conduct this training, you can play an important role by being aware of the times your mainstreamed students will receive instruction outside of your class and by scheduling, whenever possible, new learning and special events when all students are in your room.

HELPFUL RESOURCES

Resources

CATALOGUES OF APPLIANCES, AIDS, BOOKS

American Foundation for the Blind, 15 West Sixteenth Street, New York, NY 10011.

American Printing House for the Blind, Inc., 1839 Frankfort Avenue, Louisville, KY 40206.

Carroll Center for the Blind, 770 Centre Street, Newton, MA, (617) 969–6200.

The Communicator, (703) 766–3869.

BOOKS AND RECORDS

Braille Book Bank of the National Braille Associates, 422 Clinton Avenue South, Rochester, NY 14620.

Braille Institute of America, 741 North Vermont Avenue, Los Angeles, CA 00029.

Choice Magazine Listening, P. O. Box 10, Port Washington, NY 11050.

Complete directory of large print books and serials, Reed Reference Publishing, P. O. Box 31, New Providence, NJ 07974, (908) 464–6800.

Howe Press of the Perkins School for the Blind, 175 North Beacon Street, Watertown, MA 02171.

Library of Congress National Library Service for the Blind and Physically Handicapped, 1291 Taylor Street, NW, Washington, DC 20542.

Library Reproduction Service, The Microfilm Company of California, Inc. 1977 South Los Angeles Street, Los Angeles, CA 90011.

Oakmont Visually Handicapped Workshop, Oakmont Adult Community, 6637 Oakmont Drive, Santa Rosa, CA 94505. National Braille Press, Inc., (617) 266–6160.

Recording for the Blind, Inc., 20 Roszel Road, Princeton, NJ 08540.

Regional Libraries of the Library of Congress.

Taping for the Blind, 3935 Essex Lane, Houston, TX 77027, (713) 622–2767.

Vision Foundation, 818 Mt. Alburn Street, Watertown, MA 02172, (617) 926–4232.

TOYS AND GAMES

Touch toys and how to make them:

For information: Eleanor Timburg, 3519 Porter Street, N.W., Washington, D.C. 20016 To order: Touch Toys, P.O. Box 2224, Rockville, MD 20852.

Gallagher, P. (1978). *Educational games for visually handicapped children.* Denver: Love Publishing Company.

SERVICES

Associated Services for the Blind, 919 Walnut Street, Philadelphia, PA 19107, (215) 627 0600.

Blind Service Association, 22 West Monroe, 11th Floor, Chicago, IL: 60603, (312) 236–0808.

Center for Technology in Human Disabilities, Johns Hopkins University, (301) 338–8273.

Directory of services for blind and visually impaired persons in the United States. (23rd ed.), American Foundation for the Blind, 15 West 16th Street, New York, NY 10011.

Guide Dog Foundation for the Blind, 371 East Jericho Turnpike, Smithtown, NY 11787, (516) 265–2121.

Guiding Eyes for the Blind, 611 Granite Springs Road, Yorktown Heights, NY 10598, (914) 245–4024.

National Braille Press, Inc., (617) 266–61160.

New York Lighthouse Low Vision Service, 111 East 59th Street, New York, NY 10022.

The Carroll Center for the Blind, (617) 969–6200.

Visions, Services for the Blind and Visually Impaired, 817 Broadway, 11th Floor, New York, NY 10003, (212) 477–3800.

Instructional Methods

Aiello, B. (1981). *The visually handicapped child in the regular class.* Washington, D.C,: Teachers Network for Education of the Handicapped.

Barraga, N. C., & Erin, J. N. (1992). *Visual handicaps and learning* (3rd ed.). Austin, TX: Pro-Ed.

Best, A. B. (1991). *Teaching children with visual impairments.* Philadelphia: Open University Press.

Bishop, V. E. (1986). Identifying the components of success in mainstreaming. *Journal of Visual Impairment & Blindness, 80,* 939–946.

Chapman, E. K., & Stone, J. M. (1988). *The visually handicapped child in your classroom.* London: Cassell.

Rogow, S. M. (1988). *Helping the visually impaired child with developmental problems: Effective practice in home, school, and community.* New York: Teachers College Press.

Shallow, R. M., & Conner, A. (1982). Aural reading. In S. S. Mangold (Ed.), *A teacher's guide to the special educational needs of blind and visually impaired children.* New York: American Foundation for the Blind.

Scott, E. P. (1982). *Your visually impaired student: A guide for teachers.* Baltimore, MD: University Park Press.

Torres, I. (1990). *When you have a visually handicapped child in your classroom: Suggestions for teachers* (2nd ed.). New York: American Foundation for the Blind.

Wisconsin Department of Public Instruction (1990). *A guide to curriculum planning in education for the visually impaired.* Milwaukee, WI: Wisconsin Department of Public Instruction.

Literature about Individuals with Visual Impairment

ELEMENTARY

Aiello, B., & Shulman, J. (1988). *Business is looking up.* Frederick, MD: Twenty-first Century Books. (Juvenile) (Fiction=F, includes factual information about visual aids)

Christian, M. B. (1986). *Mystery at Camp Triumph.* Niles: IL: Whitman. (Juvenile) (F)

Clifford, E. (1987). *The man who sang in the dark.* Boston: Houghton Mifflin. (Juvenile) (F)

Cohen. M. (1989). *See you tomorrow, Charles.* New York: Dell Young Yearling Books. (Juvenile) (F)

Fine, A. (1978). *The summer-house lion.* New York: Crowell. (Ages 5–7) (F)

First, J. (1985). *The absolute, ultimate end.* New York: Watts. (Ages 9–12) (F)

Fort, P. (1988). *Redbird.* New York: Orchard Books. (F)

Frevert, P. D. (1983). *Patrick, yes you can.* Mankato, MN: Creative Education, (Ages 9–12) (Nonfiction - NF)

Giff, P. R., (1986). *Watch out, Ronald Morgan.* New York: Puffin Books. (Juvenile) (F)

Hall, L. (1988). *Murder at the spaniel show.* New York: Scribner. (Ages 9–12) (F)

Herman, H. (1986). *Jenny's magic wand.* New York: Watts. (Juvenile) (F)

Holland, I. (1989). *The unfrightened dark.* Boston: Little, Brown. (Ages 9–12) (F)

Loreto, J. M. (1986). *A song for Susan.* Surry,ME: Special Children's Friends. (Juvenile) (F)

MacLochlan, P. (1980). *Through grandpa's eyes.* New York: Harper & Row. (Ages 5–8) (F)

Marcus, R. B. (1981). *Being blind.* New York, NY: Hastings. (Ages 9–12) (NF)

Martin, B., & Archambault, J. (1987). *Knots on a counting rope.* New York: Holt. (Juvenile) (F)

Milton, H. (1980). *Blind flight.* New York: Watts. (Ages 9–12) (F)

Paterson, K. (1978). *The great Gilly Hopkins.* New York: Crowell. (Ages 9–12) (F)

Rounds, G. (1989). *The blind colt.* New York: Holiday House. (Ages 9–12) (F)

Weiss, M. E. (1980). *Blindness.* New York, NY: Franklin Watts. (Ages 9–12) (NF)

Yeatman, L. (1988). *Perkins: The cat who was more than a friend.* New York: Barron. (F)

ADOLESCENT/ADULT

Mark, J. (1979). *Divide and rule.* New York: Crowell. (Ages 16–18) (F)

Ure, J. (1985). *After Thursday.* New York: Delacourt Press. (Ages 13–15) (F)

Computer Software

Arithmetic 1,2, and 3 with Speech, Life Science Associates, 1 Fenimore Road, Bayport, NY 11705, (516) 472–2111. (Requires Echo II Speech Synthesizer)

Elementary Volume 1: Mathematics, American Printing House for the Blind, 1839 Frankfort Avenue, Lousiville, KY 40206, (502) 895–2405. (Requires Echo speech synthesizer)

Keyboarding for the Visually Limited, Educational Electronic Techniques,LTD., 1088 Wantagh Avenue, Wantagh, NY 11793, (800) 433–8872.

Keys to Success: Computer Keyboard skills for Blind Children, Life Science Associates, 1 Fenimore Road, Bayport, NY 11705 (516) 472–2111.

Pix Cells, Raised Dot Computing, Inc. 408 South Baldwin Street, Madison, WI 53703.

MECC Software adapted for blind students, American Printing House for the Blind,1839 Frankfort Avenue, Louisville, KY 40206, (502) 895–2405.

Speaking Speller, American Printing House for the Blind, P.O. Box 6085, Louisville, KY 40206 (502) 895–2405.

Talking Checkbook and Talking File Box, Access Unlimited, 3535 Briarpark Drive, Suite 102, Houston, TX 77042–5235, (800) 848–0311 (Requires Echo speech synthesizer)

Texttalker, American Printing House for the Blind, P.O. Box 6085, Louisville, KY 40206, (502) 895–2405. (A text to speech program for many Apple programs, requires a speech synthesizer)

Word Processing Programs

Dr. Peet's Talkwriter, Hartley Courseware, Inc., P.O. Box 431 Dimondale, MI 48821, (800) 247–1380.

Talking Keys, Lehigh Valley Easter Seal Society, 2200 Industrial Drive, Bethlehem, PA 18017–2198, (212)866–8092.

TEXTWRITER, AccessUnlimited, 3535 Briarpark, Drive, Suite 102, Houston, TX 77042–5235, (800) 848–0311.

Large Print Programs

1–2–3 Sequence Me, Sunburst Communications, 39 Washington Avenue, Pleasantville, NY 10570, (800) 628–8897. (Beginning readers sequence pictures or words to create a story)

Be a Writer, Sunburst Communications, 39 Washington Avenue, Pleasantville, NY 10570, (800) 628–8897. (Reading, spelling, word processing)

Beginning Mathematics Concepts, Looking Glass Learning Products, Inc. 276 Howare Avenue, Des Plaines, IL 60018–1906, (800) 545–5457.

Big Book Maker: Favorite Fairy Tales and Nursery Rhymes, Pelican Software, Inc. 768 Farmington Avenue, Farmington, CT 06032, (800) 822–DISK. (Prints strips that tape together to create Big Books)

Big Book Maker: Letters, Numbers, and Shapes, Pelican Software, Inc., 768 Farmington Avenue, Farmington, CT 06032, (800) 822–DISK.

Big Book Maker: Tall Tales and American Folk Heroes, Pelican Software, Inc., 768 Farmington Avenue, Farmington, CT 06032, (800) 822–DISK.

Big Book Maker: Feeling Good about Yourself, Pelican Software, Inc. 768 Farmington Avenue, Farmington, CT 06032, (800) 822–DISK.

Cotton Tales, Mind Play, 3130 N. Dodge Blvd., Tucson, AZ 855716, (800) 221–7911.

Railroad Snoop, Sunburst Communications, 39 Washington Avenue, Pleasantville, NY 10570, (800) 628–8897. (Story writing for fifth-seventh grades)

Ready-Set-Read, Continental Press, Inc., 520 E. Bainbridge Street, Elizabethtown, PA 17022, (800) 847–0656.

Spellist, Castle Special Computer Services,Inc., 9801 San Gabriel N. E., Albuquerque, NM 87111–3530, (505) 293–8379. (Requires a speech synthesizer)

Organizations

American Council of the Blind, 1155 Fifteenth Street, NW, Suite, 720, Washington, D.C. 20005, (202) 467–5081.

American Foundation for the Blind, 15 West 16th Street, New York, NY 10011, (212) 620–2000.

Division for the Visually Handicapped, Council for Exceptional Children, 1920 Association Drive, Reston, VA 22091, (703) 620–3660.

National Federation of the Blind, 1800 Johnson Street, Baltimore, MD 211230, (301) 659–9314.

BIBLIOGRAPHY FOR TEACHING SUGGESTIONS

Ashcroft, S. C., & Zambone-Ashley, A. M. (1980). Mainstreaming children with visual impairments. *Journal of Research and Development in Education, 13,* 22–35.

Best, A. B. (1991). *Teaching children with visual impairments.* Philadelphia: Open University Press.

Craig, R., & Howard, C. (1981). Visual impairment. In M.L. Hardman, M. W. Egan, & D. Landau (Eds.). *What will we do in the morning?* (pp. 180–209). Dubuque, IA: William C. Brown.

Curry, S. A., & Hatlen, P. H. (1988). Meeting the unique educational needs of visually impaired pupils through appropriate placement. *Journal of Visual Impairment and Blindness, 82,* 417–424.

Gearheart, B. R., Weishahn, M. W., & Gearheart, C. J. (1992). *The exceptional student in the regular classroom* (5th ed.), New York: Merrill.

Harley, R. K. & Lawrence, G. A. (1984). *Visual impairment in the schools.* (2nd ed.), Springfield, IL: Charles C. Thomas.

MacCuspie, A. (1992). Tips for teachers. *DVH Quarterly, 27,* 11.

Scott, E. P. (1982). *Your visually impaired student: A guide for teachers.* Baltimore, MD: University Park Press.

Torres, I., & Corn, A. L. (1990). *When you have a visually handicapped child in your classroom: Suggestions for teachers.* New York: American Foundation for the Blind.

Summary

There are two definitions of visual impairment—the legal and educational. The legal definition depends on the measurement of visual acuity and field of vision. A person who is legally blind has visual acuity of 20/200 or less in the better eye, even with correction, or has a very narrow (less than 20 degrees) field of vision. Individuals who are partially sighted have visual acuity between 20/70 and 20/200 in the better eye with correction. Educators, however, prefer to define blindness according to how well the person functions, especially in reading. For the educator, blindness indicates the need to read Braille or use aural methods. Those who can read print, even though they may need magnification or large-print books, have low vision.

The majority of those who are legally blind have some vision. Many students who are legally blind are not educationally blind because they can read print.

Blindness is one of the least prevalent disabling conditions in childhood but is much more prevalent in adults.

The Snellen chart, consisting of rows of letters or of *E*s arranged in different positions, measures visual acuity for far distances. Special charts measure visual acuity for near distances. There are also methods for measuring visual efficiency.

Most visual problems are the result of errors of refraction: Because of faulty structure and/or malfunction of the eye, light rays do not focus on the retina. The most common visual impairments are myopia (nearsightedness), hyperopia (farsightedness), and astigmatism (blurred vision). Eyeglasses or contact lenses can usually correct for these problems. More serious impairments include glaucoma, cataracts, diabetic retinopathy, coloboma, retinitis pigmentosa, retinopathy of prematurity (ROP), strabismus, and nystagmus. Most serious visual impairments in school-age students are due to hereditary factors. When scientists first discovered that ROP was caused by high levels of oxygen administered to premature newborns, incidents of this condition decreased. Research indicates, however, that ROP is on the rise due to medicine's efforts to keep more premature babies alive.

Most authorities believe that visual impairment may result in a few subtle language differences but not in deficient language skills. Also, blindness does not result in intellectual retardation. There are some differences in conceptual development because children with visual impairment rely more on touch to learn about the world. They also need to be more vigilant to pick up information from their environment. Research has shown that early training in the use of strategies helps children who are blind use their touch more efficiently.

A very important ability for the successful adjustment of people with visual impairment is mobility. There is no one-to-one relationship between the age at onset and the degree of visual loss and mobility skills. Mobility is greatly affected by motivation. Mobility skills depend largely on spatial ability. Those who are able to conceptualize their environment as a cognitive map have better mobility skills than do those who process their environment sequentially.

People who are blind do not, as is commonly thought, have an inherent obstacle sense. But some can develop the ability to detect obstacles by detecting changes in the pitch of echoes as they approach obstacles. Another myth is that people who are blind automatically develop better acuity in other senses. What they actually do is become adept at picking up other sensory cues in their surroundings, thus making better use of their intact senses.

Comparing the academic achievement of students with visual impairment to that of the sighted is difficult because the two are tested under different conditions. Evidence suggests, however, that students with visual impairment are behind their sighted peers in achievement.

Personality problems are not an inherent condition of visual impairment. Any social adjustment problems that students with visual impairment have are usually due to society's reaction to blindness. The stereotypic behaviors (e.g., eye poking and body rocking) exhibited by a few persons who are blind can be an impediment to social acceptance, but researchers are working on developing techniques to diminish their occurrence.

Educational experiences in regular classrooms are frequently visual. But with some modifications, teachers can usually apply the same general principles of instruction to both students with and without visual impairment. Since the mid-1960s, there has been a sharp decline in the use of Braille. Many professionals are now decrying this decrease because they believe it has led to a high rate of illiteracy. The National Federation of the Blind has lobbied for Braille bills to increase the availability of Braille and the Braille competency of vision teachers. Braille is now also being recommended for those whose low vision might worsen over the years.

In addition to Braille, large-print books and audio tapes are available. Also, scientists are developing a number of technological devices; examples are the Optacon, the Kurzweil Reading Machine, and the Kurzweil Personal Reader.

Mobility training can involve the use of the long cane, a guide dog, human guides, and electronic devices. Most mobility instructors recommend the long cane for the majority of individuals who are blind. At one time, mobility instruction did not begin until elementary or secondary school. Now, most authorities recommend that mobility instruction begin in preschool.

The four basic educational placements for students with visual impairment are the itinerant teacher/regular classroom, resource room, special class, and residential school. More and more students with visual impairment are in general education classrooms. Residential placement, at one time the most popular alternative, is now recommended infrequently. One trend is for residential institutions to offer programs coordinated with local public schools.

Without special attention, infants with visual impairment may lag behind their sighted peers, especially in mobility. Impaired vision may restrict their interaction with the environment. Early intervention often focuses on parental interaction with the child and parental reaction to the child's disability.

Education for the adolescent and adult stresses independent living and employment skills. Independence is a particularly important area because society often mistakenly treats people with visual impairment as helpless. Many adults with visual impairment are unemployed or overqualified for their jobs. Professionals are attempting to overcome the bleak employment picture with innovative approaches.

CHARLES FOGLE

Charles Fogle, a 61-year-old artist who uses a wheelchair, has been painting professionally since 1970. His work appears in numerous public and private collections. Of his work he says, "My art is a communication of an idea. . . a statement of my existence. . . something that will survive me to a time and place in the future."

*W*e thank you Lord, 'cause Freddie's walkin'
We thank you Lord, 'cause Freddie's walkin'
Freddie's wearin' a smile, and rightly so,
'cause now his feet know how to go
We thank you Lord, 'cause Freddie's walkin'

We thank you Lord, 'cause Freddie's walkin'
We thank you Lord, 'cause Freddie's walkin'
Freddie's steppin' out, holdin' his head up high,
with his pretty blue eyes lookin' toward the sky
Oh, thank the Lord, 'cause Freddie's walkin'.

> ➤ Chuck Mangione
> "Freddie's Walkin'"

Physical Disabilities

*I*n Western culture people are almost obsessed with their bodies. They
▲ ▲ ▲ don't just want to be healthy and strong; they want to be beautiful—
well-formed and attractive to others. In fact, some people seem to be more concerned about the impression their bodies make than they are about their own
well-being. They may even endanger their health in an effort to become more
physically alluring. It is not really surprising, then, that those with physical disabilities must fight two battles—the battle to overcome the limitations imposed
by their physical condition and the battle to be accepted by others.

Children with physical disabilities often face more than the problem of
acceptance, however. For many, accomplishing the seemingly simple tasks of
everyday living is a minor—or major—miracle. Learning to walk, for example,
may call for special celebration, as Chuck Mangione's song indicates on page 385.

DEFINITION AND CLASSIFICATION

In this chapter we consider children whose primary distinguishing characteristics are health or physical problems. For the purposes of this book, children with
physical disabilities are defined as those whose physical limitations or health
problems interfere with school attendance or learning to such an extent that special services, training, equipment, materials, or facilities are required. Our definition excludes children whose *primary* characteristics are visual or auditory
impairments, although some children with physical disabilities have these deficiencies as *secondary* problems. Children who have physical disabilities may also
have mental retardation, learning disabilities, emotional or behavioral disorders,
communication disorders, or special gifts or talents. Thus we consider in this
chapter those children whose physical condition is the first and foremost concern
but whose additional characteristics may be extremely varied. The child's physical condition is, of course, the proper concern of the medical profession—but
when physical problems have obvious implications for education, teaching specialists may need to enter the scene.

The fact that the primary distinguishing characteristics of children with
physical disabilities are medical conditions, health problems, or physical limitations highlights the necessity of interdisciplinary cooperation. There simply *must*
be communication between physicians and special educators to maintain the
child's health and at the same time develop whatever capabilities he or she has
(Bigge, 1991; Verhaaren & Connor, 1981a).

There is a tremendous range and variety of physical disabilities. Children
may have **congenital anomalies** (defects they are born with), or they may
acquire disabilities through accident or disease after birth. Some physical disabilities are comparatively mild and transitory; others are profound and progressive,
ending in total incapacitation and early death. So it is difficult to discuss physical
disabilities in general. Most of the remainder of the chapter will be organized
around specific conditions and diseases falling under one of several categories:
neurological impairments, musculoskeletal conditions, congenital malformations, accidents and other conditions, and child abuse and neglect.

➤ **congenital anomaly.** An
irregularity (anomaly) present
at birth; may or may not be
due to genetic factors.

PERSONS WITH PHYSICAL DISABILITIES

MYTH ➤ Cerebral palsy is a contagious disease.

FACT ➤ Cerebral palsy is not a disease. It is a nonprogressive neurological injury. It is a disorder of muscle control and coordination caused by injury to the brain before or during birth or in early childhood.

MYTH ➤ Physical disabilities of all kinds are decreasing because of medical advances.

FACT ➤ Because of advances in medical technology, the number of children with severe disabilities is increasing. The number of survivors of serious medical conditions who develop normally or have mild impairments such as hyperactivity and learning disabilities is also increasing.

MYTH ➤ The greatest educational problem involving children with physical disabilities is highly specialized instruction.

FACT ➤ The greatest educational problem is teaching people without disabilities about what it is like to have a disability and how disabilities can be accommodated.

MYTH ➤ The more severe a person's physical disability, the lower his or her intelligence.

FACT ➤ A person may be severely physically disabled by cerebral palsy or another condition but have a brilliant mind.

MYTH ➤ People with epilepsy are mentally ill.

FACT ➤ People with epilepsy (seizure disorder) are not any more or less disposed to mental illness than those who do not have epilepsy.

MYTH ➤ Arthritis is found only in adults, particularly the elderly.

FACT ➤ Arthritic conditions are found in people of any age, including young children.

MYTH ➤ People with physical disabilities have no need for sexual expression.

FACT ➤ People with physical disabilities have sexual urges and need outlets for sexual expression.

PREVALENCE AND NEED

The U.S. Department of Education, for many years, estimated that for special education purposes, approximately 0.5 percent of school-age children have physical disabilities. About half of the population with physical disabilities was assumed to have cerebral palsy or another crippling condition; the other half was assumed to have chronic health problems or diseases of one sort or another that interfered with schooling. If the 0.5 percent prevalence estimate is correct, one would expect to find about 200,000 children with physical disabilities needing special education in the United States.

Figures from the U.S. Department of Education (1989) indicate that in the late 1980s about 150,000 students were being served under three special education categories related to physical disabilities: orthopedically disabled (about 41,000), other health impaired (about 43,000), and multiply disabled (about 63,000). The needs of many students with physical disabilities appear to be unmet for many reasons, including the fact that the population of children and youths with physical disabilities is growing but health and social service programs are not (Martin, 1992).

Part of the increase in the prevalence of physical disabilities may be due to improvements in the identification of and medical services to children with certain conditions. Ironically, medical advances have not only improved the chances of preventing or curing certain diseases and disorders. They have also assured the survival of more children with severe medical problems (Blum, 1992; Brown, 1993). Many children with severe and multiple disabilities and those with severe, chronic illnesses who in the past would not have survived long today can have a normal life span. So declining mortality rates do not necessarily mean there will be fewer individuals with disabilities. And improvements in medical care may not lower the number of individuals with disabilities unless there is also a lowering of risk factors in the environment—factors such as accidents, toxic substances, poverty, malnutrition, disease, and interpersonal violence (Baumeister, Kupstas, & Klindworth, 1990).

NEUROLOGICAL IMPAIRMENTS

One of the most common causes of physical disability in children is damage to or deterioration of the central nervous system—the brain or spinal cord. Damage to the brain may be so mild as to be undetectable as far as the child's functioning is concerned, or so profound as to reduce the child's physical or cognitive functioning to a very low level. There may be focal brain damage (involving a very specific and delimited area, often with specific effects on the child's behavior) or diffuse brain damage (involving a large or poorly defined area, often with generalized behavioral effects).

A child with brain damage may show a wide variety of behavioral symptoms, including mental retardation, learning problems, perceptual problems, lack of coordination, distractibility, emotional or behavioral disorders, and communication disorders. (Of course, a child may show these behavioral manifestations and not have a damaged brain—see the discussion of brain damage and learning disabilities in Chapter 5.) Other symptoms that indicate brain damage or malfunction are impaired motor function, paralysis, and certain types of seizures.

Even though a person's brain may be intact and functioning properly, he or she may have neurological impairment because of damage to the spinal cord.

Since nerve impulses are sent to and from the extremities by way of the spinal cord, damage to the cord may mean that the child will lose sensation, be unable to control movement, or be incapable of feeling or moving certain parts of the body.

Neurological impairments have many causes, including infectious diseases, hypoxia (oxygen depletion), poisoning, congenital malformations, and physical trauma because of accidents or abuse. The diverse causes of brain damage in childhood are summarized in the box on page 390.

Poliomyelitis (polio or infantile paralysis) is an example of an infectious disease that attacks the nerves in the spinal cord or brain and often causes paralysis. Spina bifida is an example of a congenital malformation of the spine usually resulting in paralysis. In many cases of brain damage it is impossible to identify the exact cause of the impairment. The important point is that *when a child's nervous system is damaged, no matter what the cause, muscular weakness or paralysis is almost always one of the symptoms.* And because these children cannot move about like most children, their education typically requires special equipment, special procedures, or other accommodations for their disabilities. We turn now to some specific types of neurological impairments.

Cerebral Palsy

Cerebral palsy (CP) is not a disease. It is not contagious, it is not progressive (except that improper treatment may lead to complications), and there are no remissions. Although it is often thought of as a motor problem associated with brain damage at birth, it is actually more complicated. Cerebral palsy can, for practical purposes, be considered part of a syndrome that includes motor dysfunction, psychological dysfunction, seizures, or emotional or behavioral disorders due to brain damage. Some individuals show only one indication of brain damage, such as motor impairment; others may show combinations of symptoms. The usual definition of CP refers to a condition characterized by paralysis, weakness, incoordination, and/or other motor dysfunction because of damage to the child's brain before it has matured (Batshaw & Perret, 1986). Symptoms may be so mild that they are detected only with difficulty or so profound that the individual is almost completely incapacitated.

> ➤ **cerebral palsy (CP).** A condition characterized by paralysis, weakness, incoordination, and/or other motor dysfunction because of damage to the brain before it has matured.

Causes

Anything that can cause brain damage during the brain's development can cause CP. Before birth, maternal infections, chronic diseases, physical trauma, or maternal exposure to toxic substances or X-rays, for example, may damage the brain of the fetus. During the birth process the brain may be injured, especially if labor or birth is difficult or complicated. Premature birth, hypoxia, high fever, infections, poisoning, hemorrhaging, and related factors may cause harm following birth. In short, anything that results in oxygen deprivation, poisoning, cerebral bleeding, or direct trauma to the brain can be a possible cause of CP. Although CP occurs at every social level, it is more often seen in children born to mothers in poor socioeconomic circumstances. Children of the poor have a greater risk of incurring brain damage because of such factors as malnutrition of the mother, poor prenatal and postnatal care, and environmental hazards during infancy (see Baumeister, Kupstas, & Klindworth, 1990).

ACQUIRED PEDIATRIC BRAIN DAMAGE: DIVERSE CAUSES ➤   Paul Pipitone

Traumatic Causes

Every year 200,000 children sustain traumatic brain injuries; 89 percent of those injuries are caused by falls and by bicycle, motor vehicle, and sporting accidents. Other causes of traumatic damage include child abuse, gunshot wounds, and injury from other projectiles.[1]

Age is a strong predictor of the cause of brain injury in children:

- At least 80 percent of deaths from head trauma in children under 2 years of age are the result of nonaccidental trauma.[2]
- Preschoolers are the second highest risk group for brain injury.[3]
- Children between the ages of 6 and 12 are involved in twice as many pedestrian/motor vehicle accidents as younger children.[4]
- Youths, ages 15 to 25, are the highest risk group for traumatic brain injury; 220/100,000 youths under age 15 will sustain a head injury each year.[2] Teenagers, 14 to 19 years old, are most susceptible to sports and auto-occupant accidents.[4]
- Also, boys are two to four times as likely to sustain brain injury as girls.[3]

Nontraumatic Causes

Infectious diseases remain a major cause of neurologic disability in children, although early recognition and treatment substantially improve outcome. In one study, evidence of cerebral herniation was found in 25 percent of 302 children with bacterial meningitis.[5]

Environmental toxicity causes damage to many young brains. In a study conducted between 1976 and 1980, 700,000 children in the U.S. under age 6 were found to have elevated blood lead levels.[6] The effects of lead paint poisoning include learning disabilities, mental retardation, convulsions, coma, and death.[7]

Developmental abnormalities of the brain account for 30 percent to 40 percent of deaths during the first year of life. Surviving children sometimes develop intellectual impairments.[8]

Subarachnoid hemorrhage in a child with a history of seizure disorder usually suggests arteriovenous malformation(AVM). Mortality from bleeding as a result of AVM is less than that associated with ruptured aneurysms, but morbidity is higher. Periventricular-intraventricular hemorrhage occurs in 40 percent of infants born weighing less that 1500 grams.[5]

White matter abnormalities (perinatal leukoencephalopathies) are significantly higher in preterm infants. Cerebral palsy alone is 25 to 30 times greater in infants weighing less than 1.5 kg at birth. White matter destruction can also occur in children with meningitis. Cystic white matter lesions only occur in 3 percent to 7 percent of very low birthweight infants, but when these lesions occur, the association with cerebral palsy can be as high as 100 percent.[9]

Low birthweight infants have a high risk of developing bronchopulmonary dysplasia (BPD). In turn, these low-weight, BPD infants are twice as likely to develop respiratory illnesses that can lead to impaired neurologic and cognitive status.[10]

NOTES:

1. Humphreys, R. "Patterns of Pediatric Brain Injury" in Miner, M. & Wagner, K. (Eds). *Neurotrauma 3-Treatment, Rehabilitation and Related Issues,* Butterworths, 1989: 115–26.

2. Bruce, D. et al, Pediatric Annals, 1989; 18, 8: 482–94.

3. Waaland, P. "Pediatric Traumatic Brain Injury" *Special Topic Report,* The Rehabilitation Research & Training Center on Severe Traumatic Brain Injury, Medical College of Virginia, Richmond, VA, 1990.

4. Dandrinos-Smith S., *Crit. Care Nurs. Clin. North Am.,* 1991; 3, 3: 387–89.

5. LeRoux, P., et al, *Childs Nerv Syst,* 1991; 7: 34–39.

6. Rabin, R., *Am J Pub Health,* 1989; 79, 12: 1668–74.

7. Centers for Disease Control, *JAMA,* 1990; 265, 16: 2050–52.

8. Weisberg, L., et al, "Neurologic Disorders of Childhood" *Essentials of Clinical Neurology,* Aspen, 1989: 219–243.

9. Leviton, A., & Paneth, N. *Early Hum Dev,* 1990; 24: 1–22.

10. Vohr, B., et al, *Dev. Med. Child Neurol,* 1991; 33, 690–97.

SOURCE: Headlines, 1992, *3*(5), p. 5.

Cases in which genetic (chromosomal) factors cause CP are rare. In some cases of genetically determined biochemical disorders associated with mental retardation, the child may show evidence of brain damage or CP. Although there are many possible causes of CP, the actual causes are often unknown. The cause can be identified in only about 60 percent of cases (Batshaw & Perret, 1986).

Types of Cerebral Palsy

It may seem reasonable to classify CP according to the time period during which brain damage occurred (prenatal, natal, or postnatal), but ordinarily it is impossible to pinpoint the exact time of the damage. Classification according to degree of involvement (severity) or the extent and nature of the damage to the brain has not been successful either because severity involves subjective judgments. Brain damage cannot be assessed precisely except by autopsy and recently developed technologies. The two means of classification that have been most widely accepted specify the limbs involved and the type of motor disability.

Classification according to the extremities involved applies not just to CP but also to all types of motor disability or paralysis. The most common classifications and the approximate percentage of individuals with CP falling into each class may be summarized as follows:

- **Hemiplegia:** One-half (right or left side) of the body is involved (35 to 40 percent).
- **Diplegia:** Legs are involved to a greater extent than arms (10 to 20 percent).
- **Quadriplegia:** All four limbs are involved (15 to 20 percent).
- **Paraplegia:** Only the legs are involved (10 to 20 percent).

Classification according to type of brain damage and consequent type of motor disability includes *pyramidal*, *extrapyramidal*, and *mixed* types. These may be described as follows:

- **Pyramidal (spastic):** Individuals with this type have suffered damage to the motor cortex or to the pyramidal tract of the brain. This results in problems with voluntary movements and in spasticity—stiffness or tenseness of muscles and inaccurate voluntary movement. About 50 percent of cases show spasticity.
- **Extrapyramidal (choreoathetoid, rigid, and atonic):** Damage is outside the pyramidal tracts and results in abrupt, involuntary movements and difficulty maintaining posture (choreoathetoid), malleable rigidity or "lead pipe stiffness" (rigid), or floppy muscle tone (atonic). About 25 percent of cases show symptoms associated primarily with extrapyramidal damage.
- **Mixed:** Damage is to both pyramidal and extrapyramidal regions of the brain, and the child shows a mixture of effects (e.g., spasticity in the legs and rigidity in the arms). About 25 percent of cases are classified as mixed.

The regions of the brain that are damaged and the resulting paralysis for several types of CP are depicted in Figure 10–1. Emotional state and general activity level may affect a child's movements, the disorder becoming more apparent when the child is under stress and/or moving about than when he or she is at ease.

Although there is no "cure" for CP, advances in medical and rehabilitation technology offer increasing hope of overcoming disabilities imposed by neurological damage. Today, for example, intensive, long-term physical therapy in combination with a surgical procedure called selective posterior rhizotomy—in which the surgeon cuts selected nerve roots below the spinal cord that cause spasticity in the leg muscles—allow some children with spastic CP to better control certain muscles. Such treatment allows some nonambulatory children to walk and helps others to walk more normally (Dyar, 1988).

> **hemiplegia.** A condition in which one half (right or left side) of the body is paralyzed.

> **diplegia.** A condition in which the legs are paralyzed to a greater extent than the arms.

> **quadriplegia.** A condition in which all four limbs are paralyzed.

> **paraplegia.** A condition in which both legs are paralyzed.

> **pyramidal cerebral palsy.** Types of cerebral palsy caused by damage to the pyramidal cells in the cerebral cortex, resulting in difficulty in making voluntary movements; spasticity.

> **spastic cerebral palsy.** Types of cerebral palsy resulting in stiffness of the muscles and inaccurate voluntary movement.

> **extrapyramidal cerebral palsy.** Types of cerebral palsy caused by damage to areas of the brain other than the pyramidal cells of the cerebral cortex, resulting in involuntary movements, stiffness, or floppiness of the muscles.

> **choreoathetoid cerebral palsy.** A type of cerebral palsy characterized by abrupt involuntary movements and difficulty in maintaining posture.

Figure 10–1

➤ Different regions of the brain are affected in various forms of cerebral palsy. The darker the shading, the more severe the involvement.

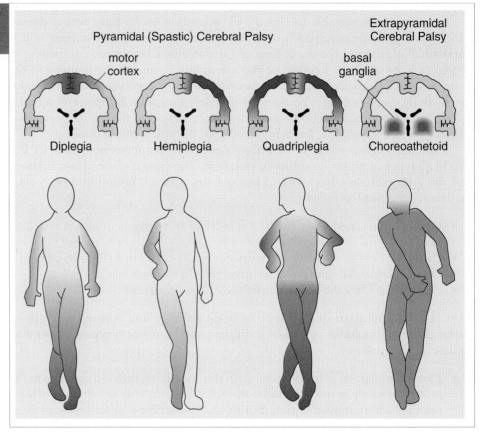

Pyramidal (Spastic) Cerebral Palsy

Extrapyramidal Cerebral Palsy

motor cortex

basal ganglia

Diplegia   Hemiplegia   Quadriplegia   Choreoathetoid

SOURCE: M. L. Batshaw and Y. M. Perret, *Children with handicaps: A medical primer*, 2nd ed. Copyright © 1986 by Paul H. Brookes. Reprinted with permission. p. 302.

➤ **atonic cerebral palsy** A type of cerebral palsy characterized by lack of muscle tone or "floppiness."

➤ **mixed cerebral palsy.** A type of cerebral palsy in which two or more types, such as *athetosis* and *spasticity*, occur together.

➤ **rigid cerebral palsy.** A rare type of cerebral palsy that is characterized by diffuse, continuous muscle tension and consequent "lead-pipe" stiffness.

Prevalence

The prevalence of CP is difficult to determine accurately. In the past a great deal of stigma was attached to the condition, and many parents hesitated to report their children's problems. Many cases occur among the poor and disadvantaged segment of the population and so may not be identified or receive medical treatment. In addition, prevalence estimates are confused by the many disabilities, such as mental retardation and emotional or behavioral disorders, that can accompany CP. There are data indicating that CP occurs at a rate of approximately 1.5 to 3.0 per 1,000 live births—between 0.15 percent and 0.3 percent of the child population (Batshaw & Perret, 1986; Bigge, 1991). A higher percentage of male than female and white than black children are affected.

Associated Disabilities and Educational Problems

Research during the past few decades has made it clear that CP is a developmental disability—a multidisabling condition far more complex than a motor disability alone (Cruickshank, 1976; Batshaw & Perret, 1986). When the brain is damaged, sensory abilities, cognitive functions, and emotional responsiveness as well as motor performance are usually affected. A high proportion of children with CP are found to have hearing impairments, visual impairments, perceptual disorders, speech defects, behavior disorders, mental retardation, or some combination of several of these disabling conditions in addition to motor disability. They may also exhibit such characteristics as drooling or facial contortions.

Some individuals with CP have normal or above-average intellectual capacity, and a few test within the gifted range. The *average* tested intelligence of children with CP, however, is clearly lower than the average for the general population (Batshaw & Perret, 1986). A comparison between the normal distribution of IQs and that for children with CP is shown in Figure 10–2. As Cruickshank and others point out, proper testing of these children requires a great deal of clinical sophistication because many intelligence tests or specific test items are inappropriate for children with multiple disabilities. Consequently, one must be cautious in interpreting test results for such children.

The educational problems of children who have CP are as multifaceted as their disabilities. Not only must special equipment and procedures be provided because the children have physical disabilities, but also the same special educational procedures and equipment required to teach children with vision, hearing, or speech and language disorders, learning disabilities, emotional or behavioral disorders, or mental retardation are often needed. Careful and continuous educational assessment of the individual child's capabilities is particularly important. Teaching the child who has CP demands competence in many aspects of special education and experience in working with a variety of disabling conditions in a multidisciplinary setting (Bigge, 1991; Verhaaren & Connor, 1981a, 1981b; Zadig, 1983).

Seizure Disorder (Epilepsy)

A person has a **seizure** when there is an abnormal discharge of electrical energy in certain brain cells. The discharge spreads to nearby cells, and the effect may be loss of consciousness, involuntary movements, or abnormal sensory phenomena. The effects of the seizure will depend on the location of the cells in which the discharge starts and how far the discharge spreads.

People with epilepsy have recurrent seizures. About 6 percent of the population will have a seizure at some time during life, but most of them will not be diagnosed as having epilepsy because they do not have repeated seizures (Batshaw & Perret, 1986).

> **seizure (convulsion).** A sudden alteration of consciousness, usually accompanied by motor activity and/or sensory phenomena; caused by an abnormal discharge of electrical energy in the brain.

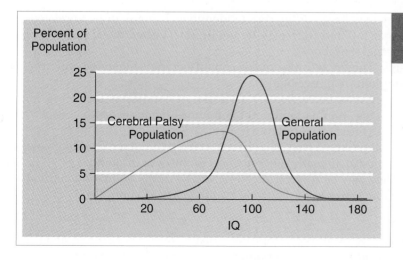

Figure 10–2

> *Hypothetical curves showing distribution of IQs for the cerebral palsy population and the general population.*

SOURCE: Data provided from T. W. Hopkins, H. V. Bice, and K. C. Kolton, *Evaluation and education of the cerebral-palsied child.* Copyright © 1954 by The Council for Exceptional Children. Reprinted with permission.

Most seizures first occur before the individual is six years old or when he or she has reached old age; seizures are primarily a phenomenon of early childhood and old age (Hauser & Kurland, 1975). Seizures beginning before the age of two years are usually associated with developmental defects (Cavazzuti, Ferrari, & Lalla, 1984); those with onset after age twenty-five are usually a sign of organic brain disease. Seizures reflect abnormal brain activity, so it is not surprising that they occur more often in children with developmental disabilities (e.g., mental retardation or cerebral palsy) than in children without disabilities (Batshaw & Perret, 1986; Jacobs, 1983; Sillanpaa, 1992).

Causes

Seizures apparently can be caused by almost any kind of damage to the brain. The most common causes include lack of sufficient oxygen (hypoxia), low blood sugar (hypoglycemia), infections, and physical trauma. Certain conditions, like those named, tend to increase the chances that neurochemical reactions will be set off in brain cells (Batshaw & Perret, 1986). In many cases, the cause is unknown (Wolraich, 1984). Some types of seizures may be progressive. That is, they may damage the brain or disrupt its functioning in such a way that having a seizure increases the probability of having another (Girvin, 1992).

Types of Seizures

The International League Against Epilepsy suggests two major types of seizures: *generalized* and *partial*. A **generalized seizure** involves the discharge of cells in a large part of the brain; a **partial seizure** begins in a localized area, and only a small part of the brain is involved. Several subtypes of both generalized and partial seizures have been classified. Other terminology used in classifying seizures includes **tonic/clonic**—the person loses consciousness, becomes rigid due to strong muscle contractions (the tonic stage), and then begins to jerk rapidly or shake (the clonic stage). **Absence** seizures are those in which the person loses consciousness for a brief period but does not show convulsive movements. The important point here is that seizures may take many forms. They may differ along at least the following dimensions:

- Duration: They may last only a few seconds or for several minutes.
- Frequency: They may occur as frequently as every few minutes or only about once a year.
- Onset: They may be set off by certain identifiable stimuli or be unrelated to the environment, and they may be totally unexpected or be preceded by certain internal sensations.
- Movements: They may cause major convulsive movements or only minor motor symptoms (e.g., eye blinks).
- Causes: They may be caused by a variety of conditions including high fever, poisoning, trauma, and other conditions mentioned previously; but in many cases the cause is unknown.
- Associated disabilities: They may be associated with other disabling conditions or be unrelated to any other medical problem or disability.
- Control: They may be controlled completely by drugs, so that the individual has no more seizures, or they may be only partially controlled.

Prevalence

Seizure disorders of all types (but not isolated seizures) occur in about 0.5 percent to 0.7 percent of the general population (Sillanpaa, 1992; Wolraich, 1984).

➤ **generalized seizure.** A seizure involving a large part of the brain.

➤ **partial seizure.** A seizure beginning in a localized area and involving only a small part of the brain.

➤ **tonic/clonic seizure.** Loss of consciousness (usually for 2 to 5 minutes) followed by repeated tonic and clonic contractions of muscles of the limbs, trunk, and head (i.e., convulsions); also called grand mal seizure.

➤ **absence seizures.** Brief, generalized seizures manifested by a brief "absence" or lapse of consciousness lasting up to 30 seconds; the individual suddenly stops any activity in which he or she is engaged and then resumes the activity following the seizure; also called petit mal seizures.

*S*ociety applauds the emergence of individuals with physical or mental impairments into mainstream society, into the workforce, into schools, restaurants, and public venues. But when participation in "normal" activities includes romantic love, sexuality, and childbearing, society has been less accepting.

When most persons considered mentally retarded were institutionalized, budding romances were squelched immediately. Usually one of the offending parties was transferred to another institution.

Particularly on the issue of sex and pregnancy, fears prevail that couples who are disabled will necessarily bear children who are disabled, and necessarily be incompetent parents. After all, children are entitled to a "normal" upbringing, which supposedly parents with disabilities are unable to provide.

However, medical knowledge has shown many such fears to be based on myths about disabilities and their causes. In the case of mental retardation, different degrees of retardation are now recognized, and their causes differentiated. While some cases are directly related to genetic influences, and others unexplained, many can be attributed to preventable causes (drugs, alcohol, malnutrition, and so forth).

As for the quality of upbringing available to children being raised by parents with disabilities, the issue is hardly seen as a black and white one any longer, perhaps least so by those within the disabled community who point out that the definition of "normal family" barely exists today anyway.

Certainly as individuals continue to merge into mainstream society, their rights to participate in one of the fundamental institutions of that society will continue to be a key issue.

- Do you feel that individuals with disabilities should in any way be prevented from coupling and/or bearing children?
- What factors should weigh in the decision of a person who is disabled to have children?

Educational Implications

About half of all children with seizure disorders have average or higher intelligence. Among those without mental retardation, however, one may expect to find a higher than usual incidence of learning disabilities (Batshaw & Perret, 1986; Westbrook, Silver, Coupey, & Shinnar, 1991). Although many children who have seizure disorders have other disabilities, some do not. Consequently, both general and special education teachers may be expected to encounter children who have seizures. Besides obtaining medical advice regarding management of the child's particular seizure disorder, teachers should know first aid for epileptic seizures (see the box on page 396).

Seizures are primarily a medical problem and require primarily medical attention. Educators are called on to deal with the problem in the following ways: (1) General and special teachers need to help dispel ignorance, superstition, and prejudice toward people who have seizures and provide calm management for the occasional seizure the child may have at school. (2) Special education teachers who work with students with severe mental retardation or teach children with other severe developmental disabilities need to be prepared to manage more frequent seizures as well as to handle learning problems. The teacher should record the length of a child's seizure and the type of activity the child was engaged in before the seizure. This information will help physicians in diagnosis and treatment. If a student is being treated for a seizure disorder, the teacher should know the type of medication and its possible side effects.

FIRST AID FOR EPILEPTIC SEIZURES ➢

A major epileptic seizure is often dramatic and frightening. It lasts only a few minutes, however, and does not require expert care. These simple procedures should be followed:

- REMAIN CALM. You cannot stop a seizure once it has started. Let the seizure run its course. Do not try to revive the child.
- If the child is upright, ease him to the floor and loosen his clothing.
- Try to prevent the child from striking his head or body against any hard, sharp, or hot objects, but do not otherwise interfere with his movement.
- Turn the child's face to the side so that saliva can flow out of his mouth.
- DO NOT INSERT ANYTHING BETWEEN THE CHILD'S TEETH.

- Do not be alarmed if the child seems to stop breathing momentarily.
- After the movements stop and the child is relaxed, allow him to sleep or rest if he wishes.
- It isn't generally necessary to call a doctor unless the attack is followed almost immediately by another seizure or the seizure lasts more than ten minutes.
- Notify the child's parents or guardians that a seizure has occurred.
- After a seizure, many people can carry on as before. If, after resting, the child seems groggy, confused, or weak, it may be a good idea to accompany him or her home.

SOURCE: Courtesy of Epilepsy Foundation of America.

Some children who do not have mental retardation but have seizures exhibit learning and behavior problems. (Huberty, Austin, Risinger, & McNelis, 1992; Westbrook et al., 1991). Learning and behavior problems may result from damage to the brain that causes other disabilities as well. The problems may also be the side effects of anticonvulsant medication or the result of mismanagement by parents and teachers. Teachers must be aware that seizures of any type may interfere with the child's attention or the continuity of education. Brief seizures may require the teacher to repeat instructions or allow the child extra time to respond. Frequent major convulsions may prevent even a bright child from achieving at the usual rate.

Children with seizure disorders have emotional and behavioral problems more often than most children (Freeman, Jacobs, Vining, & Rabin, 1984; Hoare, 1984). One must not, however, conclude that seizure disorders cause emotional and behavioral problems directly. The stress of having to deal with seizures, medications, and stigma, as well as adverse environmental conditions, is more likely to cause these problems. Moreover, Freeman and his research group have shown that the school adjustment of students with seizure disorders can be improved dramatically if they are properly assessed, placed, counseled, taught about seizures, and given appropriate work assignments.

Spina Bifida

During early fetal development, the two halves of the embryo grow together or fuse at the midline. When the closure is incomplete, a congenital "midline defect" is the result. Cleft lip and cleft palate are examples of such midline defects (see Chapter 7). **Spina bifida** is a congenital midline defect resulting from failure of the bony spinal column to close completely during fetal development. The defect may occur anywhere from the head to the lower end of the spine. Because the spinal column is not closed, the spinal cord (nerve fibers) may protrude, resulting in damage to the nerves and paralysis and/or lack of function or

➢ **spina bifida.** A congenital midline defect resulting from failure of the bony spinal column to close completely during fetal development.

sensation below the site of the defect. This is called a **myelomeningocele** (or **meningomyelocele**) (see Figure 10–3). A myelomeningocele is often accompanied by paralysis of the legs and of the anal and bladder sphincters because nerve impulses are not able to travel past the defect.

Surgery to close the spinal opening is performed in early infancy, but this does not repair the nerve damage. The mortality rate for children with spina bifida is being lowered, meaning that more severely impaired children are surviving and attending school (Korabek & Cuvo, 1986).

Cause and Prevalence

The cause of spina bifida is not known, although many factors are suspected (Batshaw & Perret, 1986). Prevalence is estimated at 0.1 percent, making it one of the most common birth defects causing physical disability.

Educational Implications

The extent of the paralysis resulting from myelomeningocele depends on the location of the spinal cord defect (how high or low on the spinal column it is). Some children will walk independently, some will need braces, and others will have to use a wheelchair. Some children will have acute medical problems, which may lead to repeated hospitalizations for surgery or treatment of infections. Among the other considerations for teachers are the following:

- Spina bifida is often accompanied by hydrocephalus, a condition in which there is excessive pressure of the cerebrospinal fluid, sometimes leading to an enlarged head or to attention disorders, learning disabilities, or mental retardation (see Chapter 4). Hydrocephalus is typically treated surgically by installing a shunt to drain the cerebrospinal fluid into a vein. Another possible complication of spina bifida is meningitis (bacterial infection of the linings of the brain or spinal cord).
- Damage to nerves along the spine may result in complications in which the child is likely to fracture bones in the lower extremities.

> **myelomeningocele (meningomyelocele).** A tumorlike sac containing part of the spinal cord itself; a type of spina bifida.

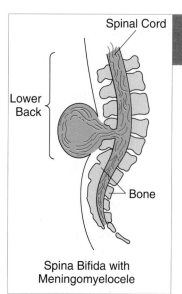

Spinal Cord

Lower Back

Bone

Spina Bifida with Meningomyelocele

Figure 10–3

> *Spina bifida*

SOURCE: *Spina bifida: Hope through research*, PHS pub. no. 1023, Health Information Series No. 103, 1970.

*N*eurological or musculoskeletal conditions that impair ability to sit or stand require physical therapy.

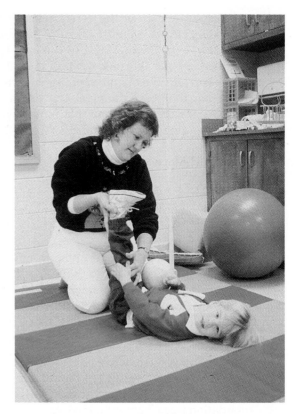

- Lack of sensation in certain areas of the skin may increase the risk of burns, abrasions, and pressure sores. The child may need to be positioned periodically during the school day and monitored carefully during some activities in which there is risk of injury. Because the student has deficiencies in sensation below the myelomeningocele, he or she may have particular problems in spatial orientation, spatial judgment, sense of direction and distance, organization of motor skills, and body image or body awareness.
- Lack of bowel and bladder control in some children will require periodic catheterization. Many children can be taught to do the procedure known as clean intermittent **catheterization** themselves, but teachers should know what to do or obtain help from the school nurse.
- Spina bifida generally has no effect on a child's stamina, and most children with myelomeningocele can participate in a full day of school activities.

Traumatic Head Injury

An increasingly frequent cause of neurological impairment in children and youths is traumatic head injury. Savage (1988) refers to such injury as a "pervasive epidemic in our children and young adults" (p. 2). Bigge (1991) notes that although the assessment and treatment of traumatic head injury have improved dramatically in recent years, "the sheer number of cases is depressing" (p. 13). It is all the more depressing because so many cases are entirely preventable or avoidable. The most frequent causes are car accidents (including many in which young children are not properly restrained or older passengers do not wear seatbelts), motorcycle or other vehicular accidents (including many in which cyclists

➤ **catheterization.** Insertion of a tube into the urethra to drain urine from the bladder.

THE STORY OF MY HEAD INJURY >

I was 8 years old when I got my head injury. I was riding my bike on the sandpit road when a high school kid came around the corner and hit me. I don't remember anything about it. My brother Ian was with me and he saw the car smack me and me fly over the car into the bushes. My bike got run over cause the kid that hit me was drinking. And he didn't even stop until he saw my brother and his friends up the road. That's all stuff that Ian told me because I was unconscious.

I don't remember the hospital much. I remember my mom holding me and rubbing my head. My leg hurt the most cause it got broke in the accident. My mom says I was unconscious for 16 days and nights. She says they had to feed me with tubes and I had another tube to help me breath. Mrs. R. had the kids in school send me cards. My mom read them to me over and over. I wanted to be back in school real bad. I missed our Halloween party.

After I got home a teacher worked with me. Then I went back to school. I only remember how happy I was to be back. I didn't remember where my desk was. I guess I cried the first day cause everything was so hard and the kids were way ahead of me. My mom says I cried all week. I had to take two medicines for my head injury. I don't know what they were.

Now I'm in the 5th grade and I am doing much better. I got 2 B's, and 3 C's on my last report card. My mom says to say that it is still hard for me to read and think for a long time. As for me, I hate spelling. But I hated it before my head injury too. It takes me a while to get things and sometimes I have to bring work to my special teacher Mr. M. He helps me every afternoon for 45 minutes. When I first went back to school I saw him all afternoon. He says cause of me he is a head injury expert—Ha, Ha.

One thing I remember in grade 3 is not being able to stay awake long. I was tired a lot. I even fell asleep in school. And I hated lunch, not the food. But I got mixed up cause everything was so loud. Mrs. R used to let me eat lunch with her. This was good except she made me practice my math as we ate lunch.

I am suppose to tell you about my friends too. Ian, my brother, is still my best friend. He helps me with my homework and he is teaching me his computer. He said to say that I also have friends like Tommy, Jason, Franky, and Mica. We are on the same baseball team. We ride our bikes almost every day. I got a new bike after a year. My dad sent it from New York. My mom wasn't too happy about it. But I told her not to worry.

Right now I feel very good. I only take one medicine for my head injury. I think I am the same but sometimes it is still hard for me to learn stuff like reading for ideas and stuff. My teacher says I have come a long ways. Next year will be better, I hope.

The End,
Bobby G.

SOURCE: From *An educator's manual: what educators need to know about students with traumatic head injury.* National Head Injury Foundation, Southborough, MA: Author, 1988, pp. 89–90.

do not wear helmets), gunshot wounds, falls, and child abuse. "Not all individuals who sustain head injuries survive, and only a fraction of those who do survive recover completely" (Bigge, 1991, pp. 12–13).

Traumatic head injury results in brain injury, which may range from mild to profound and be temporary or permanent. The brain injury may affect emotional and social behavior as well as physical and cognitive functioning (National Head Injury Foundation, 1988; see the box above). Savage summarizes the educational implications of traumatic head injury as follows:

1. Transition from hospital (or rehabilitation center) to school requires involvement of both institutions; information must be shared to ensure a smooth transition.
2. Teachers need training about traumatic brain injury and its ramifications (materials are available from NHIF, 333 Turnpike Road, Southborough, MA 01772).
3. The school must use a team approach involving regular and special educators, other special teachers, the guidance counselor, administrators, and the student's family.
4. The educational plan for the student must be concerned with cognitive, social/behavioral, and sensorimotor domains.

5. The student should be placed into an appropriate educational service category [now traumatic brain injury].
6. Most students with traumatic head injury experience problems in focusing and sustaining attention for long periods, remembering previously learned facts and skills, and learning new things. They have difficulty with organization, abstraction, and flexible thinking. They often lose basic academic skills and learning strategies and experience high levels of frustration, fatigue, and irritability. They also have difficulty reestablishing associations with peers and controlling inappropriate social behavior.
7. Programs for students must emphasize the cognitive processes through which academic skills are learned as well as content.
8. The school needs to consider the student's long-term needs in addition to the annual IEP goals, but initial IEP goals should be reviewed at least every six weeks because rapid changes sometimes take place early in recovery.

In Chapter 1, we noted that under IDEA (Individuals with Disabilities Act of 1990) traumatic brain injury became a new category of disability under which students may be eligible for special education. Consequently, some colleges and universities are now developing special training programs for teachers of students with traumatic brain injury.

We now know that the effects of brain injury may not all be seen immediately; some effects may appear months or years after the injury (Allison, 1992; Mira & Tyler, 1991). About half of the children and youths who experience a severe or serious traumatic brain injury will require special education, and those who return to regular classes will require modifications if they are to be successful (Mira & Tyler, 1991).

Other Neurological Impairments

In addition to the conditions arising from spina bifida and traumatic head injury, a variety of other rare diseases, disorders, hereditary syndromes, and accidents can result in neurological impairment. The effects of these impairments vary widely and include sensory, motor, emotional, and intellectual deficits. The educational needs of students with neurological impairments must be considered on a case-by-case basis.

MUSCULOSKELETAL CONDITIONS

Some children are physically disabled because of defects or diseases of the muscles or bones. Even though they are not neurologically impaired, their ability to move about is affected. Most of the time muscular and skeletal problems involve the legs, arms, joints, or spine, making it difficult or impossible for the child to walk, stand, sit, or use his or her hands. The problems may be congenital or acquired after birth, and the causes include genetic defects, infectious diseases, accidents, or developmental disorders. We will describe two of the most common musculoskeletal conditions: muscular dystrophy and juvenile rheumatoid arthritis.

Muscular Dystrophy

Some children are disabled by a weakening and wasting away of muscular tissue. If there is neurological damage or the muscles are weak because of nerve degeneration, the condition is called **atrophy.** When there is no evidence of a neurological disease or impairment, the condition is called **myopathy.** The term **dystrophy** is applied to cases in which the myopathy is progressive and hereditary. Although there are many varieties of muscular atrophy and myopathy, some of the most common serious conditions of this type fall under the general heading of **muscular dystrophy,** a hereditary disease characterized by progressive weakness caused by degeneration of muscle fibers. The exact biological mechanisms responsible for muscular dystrophy are not known, nor is there at present any cure (Batshaw & Perret, 1986).

The most common type of muscular dystrophy is the pseudohypertrophic (Duchenne) form, which occurs only in males. It is usually first noticed when the child is learning to walk, and it progresses throughout childhood. By early adolescence the child needs to use a wheelchair. Pseudohypertrophy (literally false growth) of the muscles of the pelvic girdle, shoulder girdle, legs, and arms gives the child the outward appearance of health and strength, but the muscles are actually being replaced by fatty tissue. The individual seldom lives beyond young adulthood.

Problems associated with muscular dystrophy are impairment of physical mobility and the prospect of early total disability or death. In advanced cases complications involving the bones and other body systems are common. One of the primary considerations is maintaining as normal a pattern of activity as possible so that the deterioration or degeneration of muscle tissue is minimized (Bigge, 1991). Although muscular dystrophy itself does not affect intellectual functioning, research indicates that children with the Duchenne form tend to have lower than average verbal IQs (Batshaw & Perret, 1986). Furthermore, when a child with muscular dystrophy has low intelligence, he or she tends to lose ambulation ability sooner, possibly because of lower motivation to continue exercise programs and use braces properly (Ziter & Allsop, 1976).

Juvenile Rheumatoid Arthritis

Pain in and around the joints can be caused by many factors, including a large number of debilitating diseases and conditions known as **arthritis.** Many people think of arthritis as a condition found exclusively in adults, especially the elderly. But arthritic conditions may be found in people of any age, including young children. **Rheumatoid arthritis,** the most common form, is a systemic disease with major symptoms involving the muscles and joints. The cause and cure are unknown. Juvenile rheumatoid arthritis is a relatively uncommon disorder with about 3 new cases per 100,000 population per year (Bigge, 1991, pp. 7–8), and there are complete remissions in 75 to 80 percent of the cases. Girls are affected more often than boys—by a ratio of about 2 to 1. Arthritis may vary greatly in severity, from relatively mild inflammation, swelling, and stiffness in the joints and connective tissues to extremely debilitating symptoms accompanied by atrophy and joint deformity. Sometimes there are complications such as fever, respiratory problems, heart problems, and eye infections. Educational considerations for children with arthritis consist of making the school experience as normal as possible (see the box on p. 402).

Among children with disabilities, **osteoarthritis** is the most common form. The cartilage around the joint is damaged, the space between the bones becomes smaller and loses its lubrication, and movement becomes painful or impossible. Osteoarthritis is especially likely to occur when the child has a condition in

➢ **atrophy.** Degeneration of tissue, such as muscles or nerves.

➢ **myopathy.** A weakening and wasting away of muscular tissue in which there is no evidence of neurological disease or impairment.

➢ **dystrophy.** Hereditary, progressive weakening and wasting away of muscle tissue in which there is no evidence of neurological disease.

➢ **muscular dystrophy.** A hereditary disease characterized by progressive weakness caused by degeneration of muscle fibers.

➢ **arthritis.** A disease involving inflammation of the joints.

➢ **rheumatoid arthritis.** A systemic disease with major symptoms involving the muscles and joints.

➢ **osteoarthritis.** A type of arthritis common among children with disabilities in which movement is painful or impossible because of damage to the cartlige around the joint.

JUVENILE RHEUMATOID ARTHRITIS ⮞

"I feel more and more like a regular person these days," Amy Levendusky says. This is not the sort of thing a 9-year-old girl should have to say. But Amy has juvenile rheumatoid arthritis, which affects 71,000 children in this country. The disease gripped Amy at the age of 4 and spread from her feet to every joint in her body. "She'd be sitting there not able to move because it hurt so much," says her father, John. "I'd have to pick her up to take her from one place to another." Now a fourth grader, Amy attends a school outside her home district in Whitefish Bay, Wis., because it has an elevator. Most days she doesn't go outside for recess—even a bump might send a shock of pain through her whole body.

Still, Amy has shown signs of improvement in the last year. She has a daily regimen of joint exercises, and an anti-inflammatory drug called methotrexate seems to be helping. "There's not as much pain or stiffness most of the time," she says. "I can walk up the stairs normally now. Before, I had to pull myself up with my hands." She began piano lessons as therapy two years ago and discovered a love for the keyboard. "She just wants to be seen as a normal little girl," says her mother, Susan. But in one unexpected way the disease may have made Amy special. "I think she has developed a keener sensitivity," Susan says. "There will be times when she'll notice how beautiful things look outside and say, 'Let's take a walk.' Most kids her age wouldn't pay attention to things like that."

SOURCE: From Melinda Beck with Mary Hager and Vern E. Smith, Living with arthritis, *Newsweek,* March 20, 1989, p. 67. Copyright © 1989, Newsweek, Inc. All rights reserved. Reprinted by permission.

which a joint has been dislocated. Children with cerebral palsy, for example, may have recurring dislocations and suffer from painful arthritis. Surgery to correct the dislocation may also involve repair of the joint to reduce the risk of arthritis (Batshaw & Perret, 1986).

Other Conditions

A wide variety of other congenital conditions, acquired defects, and diseases can affect the musculoskeletal system (see Batshaw & Perret, 1986; Bigge, 1991; 1986; Blackman, 1984). Some of these are listed in Table 10–1. In all these conditions, as well as in cases of muscular dystrophy and arthritis, intelligence is unaffected unless there are additional associated disabilities. Insofar as the musculoskeletal problem itself is concerned, special education is necessary only to overcome the child's mobility deficit, to see that proper posture and positioning are maintained, to provide for education during periods of confinement to hospital or home, and otherwise to make the educational experience as normal as possible.

CONGENITAL MALFORMATIONS

Several of the conditions we have described are always congenital (spina bifida, for example); others are sometimes congenital and sometimes acquired after birth (e.g., cerebral palsy). Babies can be born with a defect or malformation of any body part or organ system; here we will give examples of only some of the more common or obvious ones. Congenital defects occur in about 3 percent of live births (Batshaw & Perret, 1986). Some congenital anomalies are not noticed at birth but discovered during the first year. Not all these defects are debilitating.

Table 10–1 ➤ Additional Musculoskeletal Conditions

CONDITION	DESCRIPTION
Clubfoot	One or both feet turned at the wrong angle at the ankle
Scoliosis	Abnormal curvature of the spine
Legg-Calve-Perthes disease	Flattening of the head of the femur or hipbone
Osteomyelitis	Bacterial infection of the bone
Arthrogryposis	Muscles of the limbs missing or smaller and weaker than normal
Osteogenesis imperfecta	Bones formed improperly and break very easily

Common Malformations

Congenital malformations of the heart and/or blood vessels leading to or from the heart are particularly serious. More children with congenital heart defects are surviving as advances are being made in heart surgery. Today defects that once would have required an extremely sheltered or restricted life are being repaired so successfully that many children with congenital heart defects can look forward to a life of normal activity.

Congenital dislocation of the hip is a fairly common problem, occurring in about 1.5 of every 1,000 live births; eight times more females than males are affected. The defect appears to be genetically determined and tends to run in families. It can usually be corrected with the use of casts or braces until the hip socket grows properly.

Congenital malformations of the extremities may range from relatively minor abnormalities of the foot or hand (webbing of the fingers or an extra toe) to profound malformations of the legs and arms. Some babies are born with arms or legs completely or partly missing. Minor malformations of the extremities can ordinarily be corrected by plastic or reconstructive surgery; major malformations require the fitting of prosthetic (artificial) devices, perhaps in addition to corrective or reconstructive surgery, and instruction in how to make the best use of the existing extremities (Bigge, 1991).

Congenital malformations of the head and face (craniofacial abnormalities) are serious not only because they are cosmetic defects but also because the brain, eyes, ears, mouth, and nose may be involved. In addition to bizarre appearance, the child may suffer brain damage, visual impairment, auditory impairment, no sense of smell or taste, or inability to eat or talk normally. Advances in medicine, especially in plastic and reconstructive surgery, have had two obvious consequences: First, more children with major craniofacial anomalies are surviving than previously; second, children who formerly had to go through life markedly deformed can now often be made quite normal in appearance and be given the ability to see, smell, taste, or eat more normally.

Congenital Malformations and Teratogens

Some children are born with malformed bodies because of a genetic defect—that is, they are destined to be malformed from conception because of the chromosomes contributed by the mother and/or father. Others are damaged at some time during fetal development. In some cases viruses, bacteria, radiation, or chemical substances—**teratogens**—damage the chromosomes of the parent(s) or interfere with normal fetal development. An almost endless list of diseases, drugs taken by the mother, and poisonous substances to which the mother may have been exposed during the course of pregnancy can cause a deformed fetus. Although in the vast majority of cases a specific teratogenic agent cannot be identified, the list of drugs, chemicals, and bacteria known to be capable of producing deformed fetuses is constantly growing.

A particular factor may be teratogenic *only* if the mother (and, indirectly, of course, the fetus) is exposed to it at a certain critical interval. In general, the first trimester is the crucial stage of fetal development. By the end of this first three months of pregnancy all the body parts have developed, although they have not completed their growth in size. For example, if a woman contracts **German measles (rubella)** during the first trimester, her baby may be born with a deformity. After this period, maternal rubella ordinarily presents no danger to the fetus.

Perhaps the most dramatic, and infamous, teratogenic drug is thalidomide. This apparently "safe" sedative or antinausea drug, taken by many pregnant women in the late 1950s and early 1960s (especially in Europe), was responsible for the birth of thousands of babies with extremely deformed or missing limbs and other peculiar anomalies (Batshaw & Perret, 1986). "Thalidomide babies" typically showed a deformity that is called **phocomelia,** in which the limbs are extremely short or are missing completely, and the hands and feet are attached directly to the torso.

Not as dramatic and infamous, but probably the most frequently used teratogenic drug in contemporary life, is alcohol. Ethanol, the type of alcohol found in beer, wine, and liquor, is known to be capable of causing cancer, mutations, and birth defects (Wilsnack, Klassen, & Wilsnack, 1984). A pregnant woman who drinks alcohol excessively runs the risk of having a baby with **fetal alcohol syndrome** (or **alcohol embryopathy**). Fetal alcohol syndrome is now the most frequent teratogenic damage seen in humans. The syndrome can range from mild to severe and includes effects such as fetal and postnatal growth retardation, brain damage, mental retardation, hyperactivity, anomalies of the face, and heart failure.

➤ **teratogens.** Deformity-producing factors that interfere with normal fetal development.

➤ **German measles (rubella).** A serious viral disease, which, if it occurs during the first trimester of pregnancy, is likely to cause a deformity in the fetus.

➤ **phocomelia.** A deformity in which the limbs of the baby are very short or missing completely, the hands and feet attached directly to the torso, like flippers; many cases resulted from maternal use of the drug thalidomide during pregnancy.

➤ **fetal alcohol syndrome.** Abnormalities associated with the mother's drinking alcohol during pregnancy. Defects range from mild to severe, including growth retardation, brain damage, mental retardation, hyperactivity, anomalies of the face, and heart failure.

➤ **alcohol embryopathy.** Fetal alcohol syndrome.

Table 10-2 ➤ Additional Physical Conditions

CONDITION	DESCRIPTION
Asthma	Chronic respiratory condition characterized by repeated episodes of difficulty in breathing, especially exhalation
Cystic fibrosis	Inherited disease characterized by chronic respiratory and digestive problems, including thick, sticky mucus and glandular secretions
Diabetes	A hereditary or developmental problem of sugar metabolism caused by failure of the pancreas to produce enough insulin
Nephrosis and nephritis	Disorders or diseases of the kidneys due to infection, poisoning, burns, crushing injuries, or other diseases
Sickle-cell-anemia	Severe, chronic hereditary blood disease in which red blood cells are distorted in shape and do not circulate properly
Hemophilia	A rare, sex-linked disorder in which the blood does not have a sufficient clotting component and excessive bleeding occurs
Rheumatic fever	Painful swelling and inflammation of the joints (typically following strep throat or scarlet fever) that can spread to the brain or heart
Tuberculosis	Infection by the tuberculosis bacterium of an organ system, such as lungs, larynx, bones and joints, skin, gastrointestinal tract, genitourinary tract, or heart
Cancer	Abnormal growth of cells that can affect any organ system

ACCIDENTS AND OTHER PHYSICAL CONDITIONS

Falling, burning, poisoning, and mishaps involving bicycles, motorcycles, and automobiles are some of the ways children and youths acquire disabilities. Neurological impairments as well as disfigurement or amputation may result from such accidents; and the physical, psychological, and educational problems range from insignificant to profound. The problem of childhood accidents can hardly be overrated: More children die in accidents each year than are killed by all childhood diseases combined. Millions of children under the age of sixteen are injured in accidents each year. Spinal cord injury occurs at a particularly high rate in young persons fifteen to twenty-four years of age because of vehicular accidents. Sports injuries also contribute to temporary and permanent disabling conditions of children and youths (Vinger & Hoerner, 1986).

A variety of other physical conditions that may affect children's development and education are summarized in Table 10–2 on page 405. This is not an exhaustive list; children are susceptible to many more disorders and diseases than those given here. It is important to note the relationship between diseases and disabilities and the environmental, social, and economic conditions of our time. For example, increases in the prevalence of asthma and cancer may be related to increasing environmental pollutants. In the United States, tuberculosis was once a major disabling and often fatal disease—and it is becoming a major health concern in our country once again. "Between 1985 and 1991, American TB cases increased by 16 percent. Last year [1991], New York City alone was home to nearly 4,000 new cases of active tuberculosis. . . . Over the past decade, poverty has dramatically increased, and public-health programs have been cut back. Homelessness, meanwhile, increases the chances of exposure" (Chowder, 1992, pp. 192–193). With very large numbers of children being reared in poverty and the AIDS epidemic destroying its victims' immunity to infections, the tubercle bacterium is once again a major threat. Until poverty among children is lowered and better health care is made available to poor families, we are likely to see increasing numbers of children with tuberculosis.

An important thing to remember is that these conditions affect normal bodily functions—breathing, eating, digestion, growth, elimination, healing, or movement. And because these bodily functions are adversely affected, the child may lack vitality, require special medical treatment or therapy, or be unable to participate in some ordinary school activities.

Congenital Infections

At least 40,000 babies are born each year in the United States with congenital infections, including rubella (German measles), toxoplasmosis (a parasitic infection acquired from raw or poorly cooked infected meat), syphilis, and various forms of the herpes virus (Williamson & Demmler, 1992). All of these infections can cause significant developmental problems, including long-term impairments in sensory or neurological functioning. Early intervention to minimize the disabling effects of these infections is critically important. Social services to address family needs as well as medical and educational services are necessary. Moreover, "close, ongoing coordination among medical and educational service providers is necessary to ensure that programs are effective, appropriate, and safe" (Williamson & Demmler, 1992, p. 8).

Acquired Immunodeficiency Syndrome (AIDS)

Perhaps the most feared and controversial disease currently known is **Acquired Immunodeficiency Syndrome (AIDS)**. The virus that causes the disease—HTLV-III—interferes with the body's immune system, leaving the individual vulnerable to chronic and ultimately fatal infections from a variety of microbes.

First described as a disease of homosexual men, AIDS was soon detected among Haitians, intravenous drug users, persons with hemophilia (see Table 10–2), others who had received blood transfusions, heterosexual prostitutes, and young children. Today it is known that the disease can be transmitted through

➤ **Acquired Immunodeficiency Syndrome (AIDS).** A fatal virus-caused illness resulting in a breakdown of the immune system. Currently, no known cure exists.

intimate sexual contact with an AIDS patient or a carrier of the virus, through transfusions of blood from patients or carriers, and from contaminated hypodermic needles.

The seriousness of AIDS and the medical concern regarding its control can hardly be overemphasized. Church, Allen and Stiehm (1986) describe AIDS as a "devastating epidemic disorder of extraordinary morbidity and mortality" (p. 423). HIV infection is now one of the leading causes of death of children and young women, and HIV infection is growing especially fast among Hispanic and African-American women and children (Indacochea & Scott, 1992). Although "the number of children with HIV infection continues to rise" (Rudigier, Crocker, & Cohen, 1990, p. 26), the problem is not only the number of individuals with the disease but the devastating effects of HIV infection (Armstrong, Seidel, & Swales, 1993).

> Central nervous system (CNS) involvement is a prominent clinical finding in children with HIV infection, with estimates of the prevalence of CNS dysfunction ranging from 78 to 93%. . . The neurologic implications for children with HIV infection derive from encephalopathy and may include: global developmental delay, loss of previously achieved milestones, cognitive disorders, motor function abnormalities, spasticity, sensory impairment and acquired microencephaly. . . It is expected that as the number of children with HIV infection continues to grow, the virus will become the leading infectious cause of mental retardation and developmental disability in children (Rudigier et al., 1990, p. 28.).

AIDS is a particularly serious concern because many young people contract the disease through sexual behavior or intravenous drug use. Adolescents who are drug abusers and sexually active are at particularly high risk; and females are at risk not only for contracting the disease themselves but for giving birth to babies infected in utero with the HIV virus.

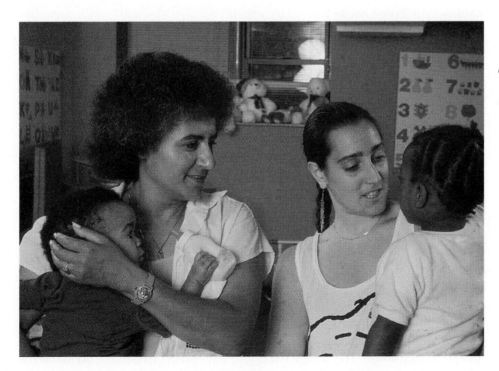

An increasingly common health problem involves children born with AIDS.

Both the U.S. Surgeon General and the National Academy of Sciences have called for massive education programs to prevent a worsening of the epidemic. However, AIDS education and the matter of education for students with AIDS are controversial for two reasons: (1) The disease is usually sexually transmitted, and therefore sex education is involved; (2) fear of the disease creates pressure to exclude infected children and adults from classrooms.

"In the 1990s AIDS will spare no school" (Merina, 1989). The issue involves teachers and other school personnel with AIDS, as well as pupils (Reed, 1988). AIDS will be a particular problem for special education because of the increasing number of infants and young children who are contracting the disease from their mothers and because the complications of AIDS, in addition to frequent infections, include a variety of cognitive, behavioral, and neurological symptoms (Crocker, 1989; Rudigier et al., 1990). As children born with AIDS survive longer, we will see an increasing number needing special medical and educational services. These services will be required not only because of the children's fragile and declining physical health but also because of other effects the disease may produce, including psychotic behavior, mental retardation, seizures, and neurological impairments similar to cerebral palsy. Because the medical and psychological conditions of children with HIV infection are extremely varied from individual to individual and for a given individual over time, it is important to create flexible and comprehensive program alternatives. The components of the program may include the home, a developmental clinic, a hospital, and both regular and special education classrooms. Teachers should be aware that "there is no serious concern regarding transmission of HIV infection in the setting of usual developmental services" (Rudigier et al., 1990, p. 28). Most states now have policies emphasizing the education of children with AIDS in regular classrooms (Katsiyannis, 1992).

Adolescent Pregnancy

Adolescent pregnancy is not a physical disability, but to the extent that it interferes with a young person's schooling, special educational provisions are necessary. Furthermore, teenage mothers are more likely than women over 20 to give birth to premature babies, to have babies with disabilities, and to be abusive to their children. The problem is not just one of maternal health; it also involves prevention of disabling conditions (Baumeister, Kupstas, & Klindworth, 1990).

Each year over a million American girls between the ages of 15 and 19 become pregnant (about 10 percent of this age group). A large percentage of these pregnancies end in miscarriage or abortion. At least 500,000 babies are born to teenage mothers annually (Stevens-Simon, 1992). Clearly, massive efforts to educate teenagers about pregnancy and child care and to provide for the continued schooling of teenagers who are pregnant or mothers or fathers are needed. Federal law now disallows federal funds to any school system that does not include pregnant girls in its education programs.

Teenage mothers are more likely than older women to give birth to premature or low-birth-weight babies. Children with very low birth weight are at risk for a wide variety of physical and psychological problems when they reach school age (McCormick, Brooks-Gunn, Workman-Daniels, Turner, & Peckham, 1992). Adolescent pregnancy also carries high risk for the health of both the mother and the baby because it is so often associated with sexual promiscuity and substance abuse. The sexual activity of adolescents frequently occurs in the context of drug use (Gilchrist, Gillmore, & Lohr, 1990). This increases the chance that the mother will contract the HIV virus or venereal disease and, of course, the chance that the baby will be born with the infection. Moreover, maternal use of drugs during pregnancy carries a high risk of direct damage to the fetus.

Children Born to Substance-Abusing Mothers

We have already mentioned fetal alcohol syndrome, which results in disabilities acquired by children of mothers who abuse alcohol during pregnancy. In recent years, babies born to mothers who use crack cocaine during pregnancy have increased dramatically in number. The effects of maternal cocaine addiction involve not only multiple physiological, emotional, and cognitive problems of newborns, but also a high probability of neglect and abuse by the mother after her baby is born. Many women who are intravenous drug users not only risk chemical damage to their babies but also give them venereal diseases such as syphilis, which can result in disabilities. As the number of substance-abusing mothers increases, the number of infants and young children with severe and multiple disabilities will increase as well.

There is no question that the percentage of babies exposed to drugs before birth has increased dramatically in the 1980s and 1990s (Sautter, 1992). The consequences of this prenatal exposure to drugs are very serious and can result in severe or mild disabilities that are seen in the children when they come to school (Van Dyke & Fox, 1992). However, initial reaction to the problems of "crack babies"—the assumption that these children are uniquely, severely, and permanently damaged—was unfounded. We now realize that "crack baby" is a misnomer. Many of the pregnant women who abuse crack cocaine are multiple drug users, and we seldom know which drug was responsible for their babies' problems. Furthermore, many of the problems of babies born exposed to drugs also occur if mothers have received inadequate prenatal care and live in conditions of poverty, further complicating the causal factors involved in the child's developmental problems. In spite of the multiple causal factors involved, the prospects of effective early intervention with children exposed prenatally to drugs are much better than previously thought. True, many such children will have developmental disabilities. Like the developmental disabilities having other causes, however, those of children exposed before birth to drugs are amenable to modification. The box on pages 410–411 provides recommendations for educators dealing with children exposed to drugs prenatally.

Children Who Are Medically Fragile and Children Dependent on Ventilators or Other Medical Technology

Children who are medically fragile are those who have special health needs that demand immediate attention to preserve life or to prevent or retard further medical deterioration. Delicate medical conditions may arise from a variety of diseases and disorders, and it is important to make distinctions among students whose condition is episodic, those whose condition is chronic, and those whose condition is progressive.

> These students include those with special health needs who are having a temporary medical crisis, those who are consistently fragile, and those whose diseases are progressive in nature and will eventually lead to a fragile state. The concept that must be remembered is that any student with a special health need can be fragile at times, but only a small portion of those who are fragile will remain fragile (Bigge, 1991, p. 71).

EN RECOMMENDATIONS FOR EDUCATORS ➤

At the federal level, the U.S. Department of Education (ED) does not take any particular position on how schools ought to educate children exposed to drugs prenatally. But Shirley Jackson, director of ED's Comprehensive School Health Education Program, has just completed her own two-year nationwide study of school programs for prenatally drug-exposed children.

Jackson makes 10 recommendations to help guide schools and teachers.

1. Cease using the labels *crack babies* and *crack children.* "We don't know whether crack children exist," insists Jackson. "We know from research on other self-fulfilling prophecies on grouping children that when you identify children with derogatory terms, you set low expectations for them that are likely in and of themselves to be fulfilled," she explains.

   "And I've seen many cases of schools that worried hysterically about 'crack kids' and how different these children are. But they did not actually know that the children were born prenatally exposed. Lots of people don't know what they are talking about.

   "As important, the literature and researchers say that most drug-abusing mothers are polysubstance abusers. So it is not clear which drug may or may not have done damage to the child. For example, alcohol and tobacco are in many cases far more detrimental in terms of effect on the child. Additionally, many children are misdiagnosed by teachers or schools that have no medical evidence for their fears. So that's why it makes little sense to label these children."

2. Do not identify, label, and segregate children because it is believed that they have been prenatally exposed to drugs. "There appears to be no educational reason to set up an early identification system," Jackson says. "If the child has been prenatally exposed to crack cocaine, how will the teacher treat that differently from a case of prenatal expo-

sure to alcohol or just coming from a dysfunctional environment? The manifesting behaviors are the same.

   "Children affected by psychosocial trauma and children who may be affected by prenatal exposure to drugs have the same kind of behaviors. The researchers cannot tell the difference between children exposed to drugs in utero and those with postnatal psychosocial traumatic conditions.

   "So there is no need for [teachers] to do anything differently. All they could do is label and segregate the children and start a cycle of self-fulfilling prophecies. These students for the most part will be in regular classrooms. About 40% have developmental lags, but they are the same kind of things you find among children traumatized by poverty — attention disorders, the restlessness that these children show, and some of the antisocial behaviors are similar.

   "If a child is living in an environment with the using parents, then that child is being exposed to a lot of neglect and trauma," Jackson explains. "Whether it is prenatal or postnatal, you have to deal with the behavior of that particular child.

   "Identification systems by schools could also lead to legal entanglements. If they get mothers to 'tell' of their prenatal drug use, many states have laws that punish those whom the schools help to self-incriminate. The schools may get involved in something that they do not really need."

3. Provide all teachers with staff development to prepare and encourage them to use practices that have been learned from research about the ways to successfully teach children who are experiencing psychosocial trauma. "All regular classroom teachers need to know how to teach children who are experiencing some kind of difficulty because of psychosocial trauma," Jackson says. "More and more of our schools, even in the richest school

Programs for students who are medically fragile must be particularly flexible and open to revision. Daily health care plans and emergency plans are essential, as are effective lines of communication among all who are involved with the student's treatment, care, and schooling. Decisions regarding placement of these students must be made by a team including health care providers and school personnel as well as the student and his or her parents.

An increasing number of children are returning home from hospitalization able to breathe only with the help of a ventilator (a mechanical device forcing oxygen into the lungs through a tube inserted into the trachea). Many of these children are also returning to public schools, sometimes with the assistance of a full-time nurse. The conditions under which it is appropriate for children depen-

districts, are finding a lot more of their children with a lot of behaviors that in the past were associated with poor children.

"There is a lot of destabilization going on in the society," she notes, "economic destabilization, lots of latchkey children. The schools—whether the richest or the poorest—are seeing a different kind of child. So teachers are going to have to learn, from some of the excellent techniques that have been developed through special education and through Head Start, ways to deal with children who have less readiness or eagerness to learn."

4. Schools should provide developmentally appropriate early childhood education programs for all children—but especially poor children. "If these kids don't receive the sound early intervention, then it is unlikely that they are going to experience success in school," Jackson asserts.

5. Plan the guidance of social and emotional development as an integral part of the curriculum. Positive social behaviors should be modeled and taught directly, not incidentally, especially for children experiencing behavioral difficulties. Such behaviors "include perseverance, industry, independence, cooperation, negotiating, solving interpersonal problems nonviolently, self-control, dealing with fears, and intrinsic motivation," explains Jackson. "Some children just don't come from environments where they have learned these things. If they come to school not knowing these things, especially in the primary grades, our job has to be the guidance of social/emotional development as an integral part of the curriculum."

6. Schools should remember that classroom limits of two adults for every 20 children are recommended for the preschool and primary years. Early childhood educators concur on this standard for developmentally appropriate programs. "In all of the programs I contacted," says Jackson, "the directors spoke emphatically to the question of class size."

7. Schools should organize multidisciplinary trans-agency teams of providers of health and social services to assist children and families in solving problems that transcend the reach of schools and teachers. "Teachers can only do so much, and we have to support them" so that they have time enough "to actually teach children as their number-one priority," Jackson argues. This requires an easy system of teacher referral to medical or counseling aid. Schools have to reach out to public health-care providers to create these networks.

"The schools see a lot of things that need attention, but the teacher should not be responsible for solving all the problems. But so many of these problems are presenting barriers to learning that we can't ignore them anymore."

8. Establish effective home/school partnerships that help care givers become actively involved in the education of their children. "The important thing to emphasize is the real care giver," says Jackson, "whether grandmother or foster parent or other family member. We must deal with the reality of the new family."

9. Schools should plan active and intensive drug-prevention programs for all children, especially those living in communities with a widespread drug culture.

10. Schools should cooperate with others in the community to provide drug-prevention treatment or seminars for women of child-bearing age, including middle and high school students.

Jackson insists that the entire area is a "rapidly emerging field that schools need to keep track of as new developments occur. We want to give these children the best chance." —RCS

SOURCE: R. C. Sautter, (1992). Crack: Healing the children. *Phi Delta Kappan, 74,* K8-K9 [Kappan Special Report]. Copyright © 1992, Phi Delta Kappan. Reprinted with permission of R. C. Sautter.

---

dent on ventilators or other medical technology to attend regular classrooms are still a matter for debate. Educators and parents together must make decisions in the individual case, weighing medical judgment regarding danger to the child as well as the interest of the child in being integrated into as many typical school activities as possible with his or her peers.

CHILD ABUSE AND NEGLECT

Since the early 1960s there has been national interest among child health specialists in the **battered child syndrome.** Klein and Stern (1971) define the syndrome

> ➣ **battered child syndrome.** Evidence of physical, psychological, and/or sexual abuse or neglect of a child that is threatening to the child's health or life.

PROTECTING ABUSED KIDS ➤

Q. Is child abuse still a problem in this country?
A. Emphatically, yes. We have succeeded in making the problem visible but not in reducing it. It remains a pervasive, debilitating societal problem that affects many, many children and adults.

Q. How common is child abuse?
A. A conservative estimate is that at least 30 percent of our population will be abused at some time during childhood. Every year two or three percent of all U.S. children are reported as having been abused or neglected.

Q. What are the various forms of abuse?
A. The usual classifications are neglect, physical abuse (causing physical injury), sexual abuse, and emotional abuse.

Q. Does abuse "run" in families?
A. Persons who have abused their children very often say they themselves were abused as children.

Q. Who abuses children? Is there a specific "abusing" personality?
A. That depends on the type of abuse. Generally, people who have already abused children are quite likely to do it again. The trick is finding out who has that kind of history.

Potential child abusers don't have any obvious physical or mental features that make them stand out in a crowd. When there's no available record of abuse, you need to know a lot of personal things about someone to recognize that potential.

Q. How can child abuse be detected? What kind of physical symptoms or injuries are present?
A. Teachers can learn to recognize signs of physical abuse. They should be concerned if a child repeatedly comes to class in the morning with swellings and bruises. Teachers also should be concerned if a child habitually wears long sleeves or layers of clothing even when the weather is warm. Some kids will tell a teacher they're being abused if the teacher just comes out and asks them.

School-based child abuse education programs emphasize the importance of telling someone about the abuse. Often a sexually abused child in such a program will tell someone about his or her situation. When you give children definitions of abuse—especially sexual abuse—they'll more clearly understand that what is happening to them is wrong, and they'll be more likely to report it.

Teachers also can pick up on abuse by keeping an eye out for behavioral problems. A child who all of a sudden starts acting out or becomes violent could just be displaying something learned at home. Teachers should wonder, "Where did this child pick up this behavior? Where did he or she learn this violence?" Most likely it came from a parent.

Q. What should a teacher do who suspects a student is being abused?
A. Every state has a law requiring teachers to report cases of child abuse. So it's imperative that teachers receive training on how to deal with the issue and how to handle the situation. Unfortunately, not enough of this kind of instruction is going on.

Q. What determines how much psychological damage an abused child suffers, and when is such damage likely to show up?
A. The amount of damage depends on how severe and intense the abuse is, how long it lasts, and when it starts. The earlier in life abuse begins, the worse effects it's likely to have later in life.

Abuse causes more psychological damage to children at certain ages than at others. But even those children who are abused at particularly vulnerable points in their development may not show any abnormality from abuse until later in life.

as "frank unexplained skeletal trauma or severe bruising or both, or such neglect as to lead to severe medical illness or immediate threat to life" (p. 15). Public Law 93–247, passed in 1974, defines child abuse and neglect as "physical or mental injury, sexual abuse, negligent treatment, or maltreatment of a child under the age of 18 by a person who is responsible for the child's welfare under circumstances which indicate that the child's health or welfare is harmed or threatened." Although the definition of child abuse is not simple and current prevalence estimates are not reliable, it is known that many thousands of children ranging in age from newborns to adolescents are battered or abused each year in the United States. They are beaten, burned, sexually molested, starved, or otherwise neglected or brutalized by their parents or other older persons.

Sexually abused children, for example, usually don't manifest problems until they're older, when they're beginning to develop and understand their own sexuality.

Q. Do some children withstand abuse better than others?

A. It appears that they do, but the exact reasons are hard to sort out. Some children survive severe abuse and emerge as successful, healthy adults; others become virtually disabled psychologically.

Genetic factors seem to play some role, but a lot of evidence indicates that the most important factor in "surviving" child abuse may be a long-term relationship with a supportive, healthy adult, perhaps a relative or a teacher, who stays interested and available.

Q. How can child abuse be prevented or at least reduced?

A. In-home services are quite effective in combatting either neglect or physical abuse—except for sexual abuse. Someone (usually a social worker from the school or a local social service agency) comes into the home on friendly terms with the family and provides any kind of support that's possible. This person teaches parents to be parents—often they don't know how—and serves as a role model.

This kind of friendly relationship with the family takes a long time to develop. In-home service people often drop in five or six times a day. They teach abusive parents to live for the next day. All too often, abusive people live only for today because they don't know whether there will be a tomorrow.

It's important to know that abuse is compulsive, repetitive behavior. It's habitual, like an addiction.

And, again like substance abusers, child abusers can find help and support in groups of people who share their problem. One group, "Parents Anonymous," has been around for over 30 years and has a chapter in almost every city. Its program is modeled after the 12-step Alcoholics Anonymous program.

Q. Has child abuse declined with the increase in education and publicity over the years?

A. In the '70s we did fairly well in managing the situation and preventing abuse, but in the '80s services for abused children and their families deteriorated dramatically. Although reporting of cases has improved and society's consciousness has been raised, little has been done in recent years to actually improve the situation for these children.

Q. Beyond reporting the problem, what role can school employees play in helping abused children?

A. School employees can play a crucial role. First, they can teach about abuse and prevention. In California, for example, school districts must provide every child with at least three child abuse education courses between kindergarten and high school.

Second, abused children lack a sense of security. We know that comfortable relationships with adults—and school employees can be very important adults in this respect—can make a big difference in abused children's health. Beyond recognizing the problems and getting help for the victims, that's a very important contribution school employees can make.

SOURCE: D. Chadwick, Protecting abused kids, *NEA Today, 8*(5) (1989), 23. Copyright © by National Education Association. Rerprinted with permission.

The consequences of child abuse may be permanent neurological damage, other internal injuries, skeletal deformity, facial disfigurement, sensory impairment, or death. Psychological problems are an inevitable outcome of abuse. Evidence indicates that the abuse of children is increasing. Abuse and neglect by adults is now a leading cause of injury—both physical and psychological—and death among children. Unfortunately, congressional action to prevent abuse and provide services to abusive families has been weak (Chadwick, 1989).

Child abuse and neglect constitute one of the most complex problems confronting our society today. There is a need for better understanding of the nature and extent of the problem among both the general public and professionals. Education for parenting and child management, including family life education in the public schools, is an obvious need in our society. In perhaps as high as 50 percent of cases of serious child mistreatment, the adults responsible for the child's welfare have substance abuse problems (Murphy et al., 1991). Thus progress in preventing child abuse and neglect may be partly limited by the extent of our progress in lowering the prevalence of substance abuse. Without concerted effort on the part of all professionals, as well as a strong coalition of political constituencies, the problem will not be satisfactorily addressed. Since abuse and injury vary so greatly from case to case, the special educational provisions appropriate for abused and neglected children range from special attention by regular classroom teachers to residential or hospital teaching.

Teachers can play an extremely important role in detecting, reporting, and preventing child abuse and neglect because, next to parents, they are the people who spend the most time with children. It is therefore vital that teachers be aware of the indicators that a child is being abused or neglected at home (see the box on pp. 412–413). Teachers must also be aware of the reporting procedures that should be followed when they suspect abuse or neglect. These vary from one area and state to another, but ordinarily the teacher is required to report suspected cases of child abuse or neglect to a school administrator or public health official. A professional who fails to report child abuse or neglect may be held legally liable.

Children who are already disabled physically, mentally, or emotionally are more at risk for abuse than are nondisabled children (Grayson, 1992; Zirpoli, 1986). Because children with disabilities are more vulnerable and dependent, abusive adults find them easy targets. The poor social judgment and limited experience of many children with disabilities make them even more vulnerable to sexual abuse. Moreover, some of the characteristics of children with disabilities are sources of additional stress for their caretakers and may be contributing factors in physical abuse—they often require more time, energy, money, and patience than children without disabilities. Parenting any child is stressful; parenting a child with a disability can demand more than some parents are prepared to give. It is not surprising that children with disabilities are disproportionately represented among abused children and that the need for training is particularly great for parents of children with disabilities.

PSYCHOLOGICAL AND BEHAVIORAL CHARACTERISTICS

Academic Achievement

It is impossible to make many valid generalizations about the academic achievement of children with physical disabilities because they vary so widely in the nature and severity of their conditions. Many students with physical disabilities have erratic school attendance because of hospitalization, visits to physicians, the requirement of bed rest at home, and so on. Some learn well with ordinary teaching methods; others require special methods because they have mental retardation or sensory impairments in addition to physical disabilities. Because of the frequent interruptions in their schooling, some fall considerably behind their age-mates in academic achievement, even though they have normal intelligence and motivation. Some children with mild or transitory physical problems have no academic deficiencies at all; others have severe difficulties. Some students who have serious and chronic health problems still manage to achieve at a high level. Usually these high-achieving children have high intellectual capacity, high motivation, and teachers and parents who make every possible special provision for their education. Children with neurological impairments are, as a group, most likely to have intellectual and perceptual deficits and therefore to be behind their age-mates in academic achievement (see Batshaw & Perret, 1986; Bigge, 1991; Verhaaren & Connor, 1981a, 1981b).

Personality Characteristics

Research does not support the notion that there is a "personality type" associated with any physical disability (DeLoach & Greer, 1981; Lewandowski & Cruickshank, 1980). Children and youths with physical disabilities are as varied in their psychological characteristics as nondisabled children, and they are apparently responsive to the same factors that influence the psychological development of other children. How they adapt to their physical limitations and how they respond to social-interpersonal situations greatly depends on how parents, siblings, teachers, peers, and the public react to them (Bigge, 1991).

Public Reactions

Public attitudes can have a profound influence on how children with physical disabilities see themselves and on their opportunities for psychological adjustment, education, and employment. If the reaction is one of fear, rejection, or discrimination, they may spend a great deal of energy trying to hide their stigmatizing differences. If the reaction is one of pity and an expectation of helplessness, people with disabilities will tend to behave in a dependent manner. To the extent that other people can see children with physical disabilities as persons who have certain limitations but are otherwise just like everyone else, children and youths with disabilities will be encouraged to become independent and productive members of society.

Several factors seem to be causing greater public acceptance of people with physical disabilities. Professional and civic groups encourage support and decrease fear of people who are disabled through information and public education. Government insistence on the elimination of architectural barriers that prevent citizens with disabilities from using public facilities serves to decrease discrimination. Programs to encourage hiring of workers with disabilities help the public to see those with physical disabilities as constructive, capable people. Laws that protect *every* child's right to public education are bringing more individuals into contact with people who have severe or profound disabilities. Public agencies are including youths with physical disabilities in their programs. For example, the National Park Service has begun a program in which young people with a variety of physical disabilities—including severe arthritis, cerebral palsy, multiple sclerosis, and spinal cord injuries—work as staff members during the summer (Satz, 1986). This program has not only benefited the participants who are disabled, but also made the public and the Park Service more sensitive to the needs of persons with disabilities. All these changes are encouraging more positive attitudes toward children and adults with disabilities (DeLoach & Greer, 1981). But there is no doubt that many children with physical disabilities are still rejected, feared, pitied, or discriminated against. The more obvious the physical flaw, the more likely it is that the person will be perceived in negative terms by the public.

Public policy regarding children's physical disabilities has not met the needs of most such children and their families (Baumeister, Kupstas, & Klindworth, 1990; Hobbs, Perrin, & Ireys, 1984; Hobbs, Perrin, Ireys, Moynahan, & Shayne, 1984). Particularly, as successful medical treatment prolongs the lives of more and more children with severe chronic illnesses and other disabilities, issues of who should pay the costs of treatment and maintenance (which are often enormous) and which children and families should receive the limited available resources are becoming critical (Lyon, 1985).

Children's Reactions

As suggested earlier, children's reactions to their own physical disabilities are largely a reflection of the way they have been treated by others. Shame and guilt are learned responses; children will have such negative feelings only if others respond to them by shaming or blaming them (and those like them) for their physical differences. Children will be independent and self-sufficient (within the limits of their physical disability) rather than dependent and demanding only to the extent that they learn how to take care of their own needs. And they will have realistic self-perceptions and set realistic goals for themselves only to the extent that others are honest and clear in their appraisal of their condition.

However, certain psychological reactions are inevitable for the child with physical disabilities, no matter how he or she is treated. The wish to be nondisabled and participate in the same activities as most children, and the fantasy that the disability will disappear, are to be expected. With proper management and help, the child can be expected eventually to accept the disability and live a happy life, even though he or she knows the true nature of the condition (DeLoach & Greer, 1981). Fear and anxiety, too, can be expected. It is natural for children to be afraid when they are separated from their parents, hospitalized, and subjected to medical examinations and procedures that may be painful. In these situations, too, proper management can minimize emotional stress. Psychological trauma is not a necessary effect of hospitalization. The hospital environment may in fact be better than the child's home in the case of abused and neglected children.

Other important considerations regarding the psychological effects of a physical disability include the age of the child and the nature of the limitation (e.g., whether it is congenital or acquired, progressive or not). But even these factors are not uniform in their effects. A child with a relatively minor and short-term physical disability may become more maladjusted, anxious, debilitated, and disruptive than another child with a terminal illness because of the way the child's behavior and feelings are managed. Certainly understanding the child's and the family's feelings about the disability are important. But it is also true that managing the consequences of the child's behavior is a crucial aspect of education and rehabilitation.

It may seem reasonable to expect more frequent psychological depression and suicide attempts among adolescents and young adults with disabilities than among their nondisabled peers because disability does impose psychological stress. However, Bryan and Herjanic (1980) concluded that "the association between handicaps and depression, suicide attempts, and suicide has not been clearly established" (p. 64). It is true that a youth who is disabled must go through a difficult period of learning to accept a disability, its permanence, and its personal and social implications. It is equally true that adolescents without physical disabilities find the task of establishing an identity difficult.

PROSTHETICS, ORTHOTICS, AND ADAPTIVE DEVICES FOR DAILY LIVING

A **prosthesis** is an artificial replacement for a missing body part (e.g., an artificial hand or leg); an **orthosis** is a device that enhances the partial function of a part of a person's body (a brace or a device that allows a person to do something; see Figures 10–4 to 10–7). **Adaptive devices** for daily living include a variety of

➤ **prosthesis.** A device designed to replace, partially or completely, a part of the body (e. g. , artificial teeth or limbs).

➤ **orthosis.** A device designed to restore, partially or completely, a lost function of the body (e. g. , a brace or crutch).

➤ **adaptive devices.** Special tools that are adaptations of common items to make accomplishing self-care, work, or recreation activities easier for someone who has a physical disability.

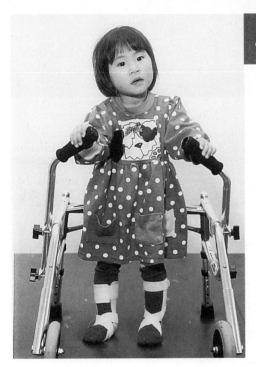

Figure 10–4

➤ *Examples of thermoform leg braces. The braces are molded to fit the contour of the wearer's leg and hold the knee, ankle, and/or foot in a more correct or acceptable position. The orthoses are lighter in weight, more functional, and cosmetically more acceptable than older-style braces and can be worn with a variety of footwear.*

Figure 10–5

➤ *Devices to assist a person with a physical disability in eating: plate attached to table to keep it from moving; rim around plate keeps food from being accidentally pushed off and helps in getting food on utensil; cuff on wrist and hand allows someone with weak grasp to hold utensil.*

Figure 10–6

➤ *A device to help someone who uses a wheelchair to pick up objects on the floor or on shelves too high to reach from a sitting position.*

Figure 10–7

➤ *A mouth stick or wand allows people who cannot use their hands to point, turn pages, type, paint, and so on. The wand may also be attached to head straps to allow the person to use neck and head motion (see Figure 10–13).*

adaptations of ordinary items found in the home, office, or school—such as a device to aid bathing or handwashing or walking—that make performing the tasks required for self-care and employment easier for the person who has a physical disability.

The most important principles to keep in mind are use of residual function, simplicity, and reliability. For example, an artificial hand is operated by the muscles of the arm, shoulder, or back. This may be too complicated or demanding for an infant or young child with a missing or deformed upper limb. Depending on the child's age, the length and function of the amputated limb, and the child's

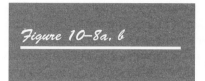

➤ *Rehabilitation engineers are redesigning wheelchairs for use in off-the-street recreational and work environments; (a) chairs suitable for use at the beach or in other soft terrain; (b) a chair specially designed for racing.*

(a)

(b)

other abilities, a passive "mit" or a variety of other prosthetic devices might be more helpful (Gover & McIvor, 1992). Choice of the most useful prosthesis will depend on careful evaluation of each individual's needs. A person without legs may be taught to use his or her arms to move about in a wheelchair, or to use torso and arms to get about on artificial legs (perhaps using crutches or a cane in addition). Again, each individual's abilities and preferences must be evaluated in designing the prosthesis.

Two points regarding prosthetics, orthotics, and residual function must be kept in mind. First, residual function is often important even when a prosthesis, orthosis, or adaptive device is not used. For example, it may be crucial for the child with cerebral palsy or muscular dystrophy to learn to use the affected limbs as well as possible without the aid of any special equipment because using residual function alone will make the child more independent and may help to prevent or retard physical deterioration. Too, it is often more efficient for a person to learn not to rely completely on a prosthesis or orthosis as long as he or she can accomplish a task without it.

Second, spectacular technological developments often have very limited meaning for the immediate needs of the majority of individuals with physical disabilities. It may be years before expensive experimental equipment is tested adequately and marketed at a cost most people can afford, and a given device may be applicable only to a small group of individuals with an extremely rare condition (Moore, 1985). For a long time to come, common "standby" prostheses, orthoses, and other equipment adapted to the needs of the individual will be the most practical devices. A few common devices that are helpful to persons with various physical disabilities are shown in Figures 10–5 through 10–8. (See Bigge, 1991; DuBose & Deni, 1980; Fraser & Hensinger, 1983; Verhaaren & Connor, 1981b, for additional illustrations of such devices.)

We do not mean to downplay the importance of technological advances for people with physical disabilities. Our point here is that the greatest significance of a technological advance often lies in how it changes seemingly "ordinary" items or problems. For example, technological advances in metallurgy and plastics have led to the design of much more functional braces and wheelchairs. The heavy metal-and-leather leg braces—which were cumbersome, difficult to apply, and not very helpful in preventing deformity or improving function—formerly used by many children with cerebral palsy or other neurological disorders have been largely supplanted by braces constructed of thermoform plastic (see Figure 10–4). Wheelchairs are being built of lightweight metals and plastics and redesigned to allow users to go places inaccessible to the typical wheelchair (see Figure 10–8). And an increasing number of computerized devices are improving the movement and communication abilities of people with disabilities.

The greatest problem today is not devising new or more sophisticated assistive technology, but rather the accurate evaluation of children and youths to determine what would be most useful and then making that technology available. Many children and youths who need prostheses or other assistive devices, such as computers, special vehicles, and self-help aids, are not carefully evaluated and provided with the most appropriate equipment (Parette & VanBiervliet, 1991).

EDUCATIONAL CONSIDERATIONS

Too often we think of people who have physical disabilities as being helpless or unable to learn. It is easy to lower our expectations for them because we know that they are indeed unable to do some things. We forget that many people with physical disabilities can learn to do most or all of the things most nondisabled persons do, although sometimes they must perform these tasks in a different way (e.g., a person who does not have the use of the hands may have to use the feet or mouth). Accepting the limitations imposed by physical disabilities without trying to see how much people can learn or how the environment can be changed to allow them to respond more effectively is an insulting and dehumanizing way of responding to physical differences.

Educating students with physical disabilities is not so much a matter of special instruction for children with disabilities as it is of educating the nondisabled population. People with physical disabilities solve many of their own problems, but their lives are often needlessly complicated because the nondisabled give no thought to what life is like for someone with specific physical limitations. Design adaptations in buildings, furniture, household appliances, and clothing can make it possible for someone with a physical disability to function as efficiently as a nondisabled person in a home, school, or community.

Individualized Planning

➤ **individualized family service plan (IFSP).** A plan for services for young children with disabilities (under 3 years of age) and their families drawn up by professionals and parents, similar to an IEP for older children, mandated by PL 99–457.

Students with complex physical disabilities typically require a wide array of related services as well as special education. The IEPs (individualized education programs) for such students tend to be particularly specific and detailed. The instructional goals and objectives often include seemingly minute steps, especially for young children with severe disabilities. Many of the children under the age of three years who need special education and related services are children with physical disabilities. These children are required by law (PL 99–457) to have an **individualized family service plan (IFSP)** rather than an IEP (see Chapters 1 and 12). These plans must specify how the family will be involved in intervention as well as what other services will be provided.

Educational Placement

Children with physical disabilities may be given an education in any one of several settings, depending on the type and severity of the condition, the services available in the community, and the medical prognosis for the condition. If such children ordinarily attend regular public school classes but must be hospitalized for more than a few days, they may be included in a class in the hospital itself. If they must be confined to their homes for a time, a visiting or homebound teacher may provide tutoring until they can return to regular classes. In these cases, which usually involve accident victims or conditions that are not permanently and severely disabling, relatively minor, commonsense adjustments are required to continue the children's education and keep them from falling behind their classmates. At the other extreme, usually involving serious or permanent disabilities, the child may be taught for a time in a hospital school or a special public school class designed specifically for children with physical disabilities. Today most are being integrated into the public schools because of advances in medical treatment: new developments in bioengineering, allowing them greater mobility and functional movement; decreases in or removal of architectural barriers and transportation problems; and the movement toward public education for *all* children (Bigge, 1991).

Educational Goals and Curricula

It is not possible to prescribe educational goals and curricula for children with physical disabilities as a group because their limitations vary so greatly from child to child. Even among children with the same condition, goals and curricula must be determined after assessing the individual child's intellectual, physical, sensory, and emotional characteristics.

A physical disability, especially a severe and chronic one that limits mobility, may have two implications for education. The child may be deprived of experiences that nondisabled children have, and the child may find it impossible to manipulate educational materials and respond to educational tasks the way most children do. For example, a child with severe cerebral palsy cannot take part in most outdoor play activities and travel experiences and may not be able to hold and turn pages in books, write, explore objects manually, or use a typewriter without special equipment.

For children with an impairment that is only physical, curriculum and educational goals should ordinarily be the same as for nondisabled children: reading, writing, arithmetic, and experiences designed to familiarize them with the world about them. In addition, special instruction may be needed in mobility skills, daily living skills, and occupational skills. That is, because of their physical impairments, these children may need special, individualized instruction in the use of mechanical devices that will help them perform tasks that are much simpler for those without disabilities. For children with other disabilities in addition to physical limitations, curricula will need to be further adapted (Bigge, 1991; Hanson & Harris, 1986).

Educational goals for students with severe or profound disabilities must be related to their functioning in everyday community environments. Only recently have educators begun to address the problems of analyzing community tasks (e.g., crossing streets, using money, riding public transportation, greeting neighbors) and planning efficient instruction for individuals with severe disabilities

A Key to Success

HELEN M. COYLE

Teacher of students who have multiple disabilities Hollymead Elementary School, Charlottesville, Virginia; B.S., Education, State College at Fitchburg, Massachusetts

DENISE PILGRIM

First-grade teacher, Hollymead Elementary School; B.S., Early Childhood, North Carolina A&T State University; M.Ed., Reading, University of Virginia

➤ **Helen** I have six children in my self-contained class, five boys and a girl. They range in age from eight to eleven and in grade level from one to four. One is nonverbal, three have speech that is difficult to understand, one is on a respirator, and one has behavior problems. All of them are nonambulatory, and they're all mainstreamed for about 60 percent of the school day. They participate in whatever regular classes they can. The greatest handicap my students have is how other people see them. Too often, nondisabled people see wheelchairs, adaptive equipment, respirators, communication devices, and so on; their vision of someone with a disability ends there. My goal is to help nondisabled children see the kids I teach as regular kids who have some physical limitations. I've been a regular classroom teacher too, and I know that all children learn with and from other children. I want my students to participate in regular class activities, not just be physically present. I think you'll understand what I mean when

we describe how we worked with Brett, an eight-year-old with spina bifida (myelomeningocele). He is nonambulatory and has poor expressive language. His speech is difficult to understand. He has good trunk control and is able to write with a pencil, cut with scissors, use a computer keyboard independently, and transfer himself from his wheelchair to other types of seating with minimal assistance. He's very shy and doesn't initiate conversations with strangers.

➤ **Denise** At the beginning of the year, Helen and I discussed the possibility of mainstreaming Brett into my class of twenty-one students. We discussed the amount of time he'd spend in my class, the best time of day, appropriate instruction levels, and because Brett's in a wheelchair, space for movement in my classroom.

➤ **Helen** Brett wasn't eager to go to Denise's class at first. Last year he devel-

oped confidence in me, though. We started planning for mainstreaming when we wrote his IEP for this year.

➤ **Denise** We started mainstreaming Brett after the fourth week of school, first just in the morning during math when Helen could spend some time in my class. This made it a lot easier for him. At first, Brett was reluctant to participate in my class, but with Helen's encouragement and mine—and especially his new classmates'—his fear soon disappeared. Then we added language arts, which follows math. Helen would come into my classroom periodically to reassure Brett that he wasn't alone and to see what we were doing so she'd know what he was working on. Eventually, we dropped that support. Brett now comes to my classroom as soon as he gets to school so that he can interact with his classmates during free activity time and be with them during our initial activities of the day. This allows him to participate when I go over the day's schedule and we do the calendar and sing our song for the month.

➤ **Helen** Denise is responsible for Brett's academic learning only. He gets the same report card as the regular students, he's graded by the same criteria as others, he takes the same standardized tests, participates in class activities, and goes on class field trips. He goes to assembly programs, music, art, and library with the regular first-graders, as well as the academic classes Denise mentioned. For field trips, I arrange for the special bus and determine whether the place the class is going is wheelchair accessible. I provide the adaptive equipment Brett requires—a floor table and a computer, for example. Brett wears a body jacket to prevent further scoliosis. Because of this, spinal exercises such as stretching and twisting are imperative. He has to have some special therapies.

➤ **Denise** Brett's special therapies cause him to miss some assignments in my room, which are made up as homework or in Helen's class. I don't alter my instruction or goals for Brett, but I do make adjustments that will enable him to complete his work and get the most out of instruction. For example, I place him in the front of the room when he's copying from the board and provide a pointer when he needs to point to words we're reading from the board or pocket chart. My aide and I had to learn how to lift Brett correctly to get him from his chair to the floor so he can work at his floor desk, which he prefers. The occupational therapist made large link letters that enable Brett to work on individual sight words. All this seems simple, but our success required shared responsibilities and understanding. It involved teamwork for follow-up, scheduling, and being aware of Brett's condition—his capabilities, strengths, and weaknesses.

➤ **Helen** Time is a very important commodity in Brett's day, so I try to incorporate as much therapeutic movement into his regular activities as I can. When he's manipulating objects in math and working at his floor table, I put the materials behind him and to his right and left. This way he needs to twist and stretch to get the materials. Brett also needs to stand during the day. When time doesn't permit this in my classroom, I take his standing table into Denise's class. I'm responsible to see that Brett's required therapies are scheduled, that he's getting alternate positioning, and that his bathroom and eating needs are met. Denise doesn't need to take care of these concerns. She and I meet frequently during the week to discuss his needs, achievement, and goals. I look to Denise to meet his academic needs, and I try to reinforce the concepts she presents. I've made some materials that are easier for him to use, and I try to give him as much access to a computer as I can. Brett can write legibly with a pencil, but he can write faster with the computer. I try to have Brett develop his physical and mental abilities as much as possible. If he can do something without adaptive equipment, I encourage him to do that and not get used to equipment that would keep him dependent.

➤ **Denise** The most difficult thing for me is not to allow Brett to just get by.

Sometimes he doesn't finish work or gets tired and doesn't want the challenge. I had to make myself keep the expectations and goals the same as for other children. Helen kept reminding me that Brett is here to learn and asking what she could do to help make it easier for me. You might think that Brett's poor speech and manual dexterity would have been issues, but they weren't. True, he might have to tell me something several times before I understand, and it takes him longer to complete an assignment. But I learned to be patient, and his difference doesn't interfere with the rest of the class.

➤ **Helen** When Brett began going into Denise's class, the other children were very curious about why he had to be in a wheelchair. Denise arranged a time when I could speak to her class about Brett's physical condition. I brought in a plastic

> *He's learning self-worth. What more important lesson can we teach our students?*

skeleton and a model of the brain and began to describe the nature of Brett's disability and why he couldn't walk or feel his legs. The children accepted what they were able to understand, asked questions, and then accepted Brett as one of their group. They put no conditions on their friendship and didn't exclude him. The most difficult part of mainstreaming Brett doesn't have anything to do with Denise. It comes from other school personnel who are not used to having a child with physical disabilities during regular activities. They're not used to having students like Brett participate in standardized testing, school performances, and so on. The more activities I can involve them in, the more the curtain of fear and disbelief is lifted and the easier it gets.

➤ **Denise** I think the greatest barriers to special and general education teachers' working together are not having enough time to talk and plan and general education teachers' belief that they'll have to alter their instruction too much. I think we general educators tend to forget why we are doing what we're doing—forget that we're not here just for the general population but also for special kids who may take a little longer to understand or complete a task. Kids in special education need to see what the "real world" is like, too, not experience just the special class with its small student-teacher ratio and teachers who are trained to meet their special needs. We general educators mustn't forget that we went into our profession to prepare all students to achieve whatever they can and that we must accept all students and what they bring to the classroom. Special education teachers have to find the right classroom teachers to make this work—those with the right personality, classroom setup, and a willingness to talk.

➤ **Helen** The most rewarding aspect of our teamwork for me is Brett's progress. He now willingly goes to Denise's class and doesn't need me to be with him. He initiates and participates in conversations with other kids and adults. He's more outgoing and sociable, and he's beginning to read. He's excited about learning new things, and he's eager to share what he's learned with his family and me. It's almost like a metamorphosis. It's brought a lot of joy to his family. They see him now as capable, and their hopes are lifted. Brett is gaining pride in himself and his accomplishments. He's learning self-worth. What more important lesson can we teach our students?

➤ **Denise** I agree with Helen. Another rewarding aspect of working with Brett is knowing that I have the support of the special education team and Brett's family. The other children cheer him on, and they're always willing to give a helping hand—sometimes too much so!

(Bigge, 1991; Snell & Browder, 1986). Efficient instruction in such skills requires that teaching occur in the community environment itself.

The range of educational objectives and curricula for children with physical disabilities is often extended beyond the objectives and curricula typically provided for other students in school. For example, very young children and those with severe neuromuscular problems may need objectives and curricula focusing on the most basic self-care skills (e.g., swallowing, chewing, self-feeding). Older students may need not only to explore possible careers in the way all students should but also to consider the special accommodations their physical limitations demand for successful performance.

Although all students may profit from discussion of death and dying, death education may be particularly important in classrooms in which a student has a terminal illness. As Bigge notes regarding the teacher's responsibilities in dealing with students who are terminally ill, "The role of educators is complex, requiring them to deal directly with the dying child as well as with the family, classmates, and peers" (1991, p. 124). Teachers should be direct and open in their discussion of death and dying. Death should not be a taboo subject, nor should teachers deny their own feelings or squelch the feelings of others. Confronted with the task of educating a child or youth with a terminal illness, teachers should seek available resources and turn to other professionals in other disciplines for help (Bigge, 1991).

Links with Other Disciplines

In the opening pages of this chapter we made two points: Children with physical disabilities have medical problems, and interdisciplinary cooperation is necessary in their education. It is important for the teacher to know what other disciplines are involved in the child's care and treatment, and to be able to communi-

A prosthetic device enables those who have lost a limb to participate in many activities.

cate with professionals in these areas about the physical, emotional, and educational development of each child.

It goes almost without saying that knowing the child's medical status is crucial. Many children with physical disabilities will need the services of a physical therapist and/or occupational therapist. Both can give valuable suggestions about helping the child use his or her physical abilities to the greatest possible extent, continuing therapeutic management in the classroom, and encouraging independence and good work habits. Teachers should be particularly concerned about how to handle and position the child so that the risk of further physical disability is minimized and independent movement and manipulation of educational materials are most efficiently learned.

Specialists in prosthetics and orthotics design and build artificial limbs, braces, and other devices that help individuals who are physically disabled function more conventionally. By conferring with such specialists, the teacher will get a better grasp of the function and operation of a child's prosthesis or orthosis and understand what the child can and cannot be expected to do.

Social workers and psychologists are the professionals with whom most teachers are quite familiar. Cooperation with them may be particularly important in the case of a child with a physical disability. Work with the child's family and community agencies is often necessary to prevent lapses in treatment. The child may also be particularly susceptible to psychological stress, so the school psychologist may need to be consulted to obtain an accurate assessment of intellectual potential.

Speech-language therapists are often called on to work with children with physical disabilities, especially those with cerebral palsy. The teacher will want advice from the speech-language therapist on how to maximize the learning of speech and language.

EARLY INTERVENTION

Two concerns of all who work with young children with physical disabilities are (1) early identification and intervention and (2) development of communication. Identifying signs of developmental delay so intervention can begin as early as possible is important in preventing further disabilities that can result from lack of teaching and proper care. Early intervention is also important for maximizing the outcome of therapy. Communication skills are difficult for some children with physical disabilities to learn, and they are one of the critical objectives of any preschool program (see Chapter 7).

Probably the first and most pervasive concerns of teachers of young children with physical disabilities should be handling and positioning. Handling refers to how the child is picked up, carried, held, and assisted; positioning refers to providing support for the child's body and arranging instructional or play materials in certain ways. Proper handling makes the child more comfortable and receptive to education. Proper positioning maximizes physical efficiency and ability to manipulate materials. It also inhibits undesirable motor responses while promoting desired growth and motor patterns (Bigge, 1992; Fraser & Hensinger, 1983).

What constitutes proper positioning for one child may not be appropriate for another. It is important that the teacher of children who are physically disabled be aware of some general principles of positioning and handling; in addition, he or she must work closely with physical therapists and physicians so that each child's particular needs are met.

SOURCE: Adapted from B. A. Fraser and R. N. Hensinger, *Managing physical handicaps: A practical guide for parents, care providers, and educators.* Copyright © by Paul H. Brookes. Used with permission. p. 167.

Figure 10–9

➤ *The asymmetrical tonic neck reflex. As shown in this illustration, the ATNR causes a student to assume a "fencing" position every time his head is turned.*

➤ **spastic.** Sudden, involuntary contraction of muscles that makes accurate, voluntary movement difficult; a type of cerebral palsy.

➤ **contractures.** Permanent shortening of muscles and connective tissues and consequent distortion of bones and/or posture because of neurological damage.

➤ **hypotonic.** Low muscle tone; sometimes occurs as a result of cerebral palsy.

➤ **asymmetrical tonic neck reflex (ATNR).** A normal reflex in babies up to about four months of age in which turning the head to one side results in extension of the arm and leg on the side toward which the head is turned and flexion of the opposite arm and leg. It is an abnormal reflex indicative of brain injury in infants older than about four months.

The physical problems that most often require special handling and positioning involve muscle tone. Some children have **spastic** muscles—chronic increased muscle tone. As a result, their limbs may be either flexed or extended all the time. If nothing is done to counteract the effects of the chronic imbalance of muscle tone, the child develops **contractures**—permanent shortening of muscles and connective tissues that results in deformity and further disability. Other children have athetosis or fluctuating muscle tone that results in almost constant uncontrolled movement. If these movements are not somehow restrained, the child cannot accomplish many motor tasks successfully. Still other children have muscles that are **hypotonic.** These children appear floppy—their muscles are flaccid and weak. The hypotonia may prevent them from learning to hold up their heads, sit, or stand. All these muscle tone problems can occur together in the same child, they can occur with varying degrees of severity, and they can affect various parts of the body differently.

Another major problem that involves handling and positioning is the presence of abnormal reflexes that most children exhibit during certain developmental periods but do not show after a given age. An example is the **asymmetrical tonic neck reflex (ATNR),** which babies normally show from birth to about four months but which is definitely abnormal or pathological if exhibited by a child who is a year old. The stimulus that elicits ATNR is turning the head to either side while lying on the back. The reflex is characterized by extension of the arm and leg on the side toward which the head is turned and flexion of the other arm and leg (see Figure 10–9). Four major problems are caused by a pathological ATNR: First, rolling over is difficult or impossible; second, the child who is on all fours will collapse if the face is turned to either side; third, the child may not be able to get both hands to the midline for manual activities; fourth, self-feeding and walking are difficult.

Handling and positioning the child who is physically disabled demands attention to support of the child's body at various points and how various postures influence muscle tone and ability to move. There are several key points—neck and spine, shoulder girdle, and pelvic area—where support should be given because pressure on these points controls muscle tone in the extremities and influences voluntary movement. Picking up, carrying, or handling children without attention to support at these key points may only make the child's voluntary movements more difficult (Hanson & Harris, 1986). Simple adaptive equipment is frequently required to keep the child positioned properly for movement and learning. Often such equipment can easily be made (Bigge, 1991; DuBose & Deni, 1980; Fraser & Hensinger, 1983; Hanson & Harris, 1986). Examples of such positioning equipment are shown in Figures 10–10, 10–11, and 10–12. Some adaptive equipment for positioning can be purchased, but it often needs to be tailored to the needs of the individual child.

The teacher of young children with physical disabilities must know how to teach gross motor responses, such as head control, rolling over, sitting, standing, and walking. If the child has severe neurological and motor impairments, the teacher may need to begin by focusing on teaching the child to eat (e.g., how to chew and swallow) and to make the oral movements required for speech (Bigge, 1991). Fine-motor skills, such as pointing, reaching, grasping, and releasing may be critically important. These motor skills are best taught in the context of daily lessons that involve self-help and communication. That is, motor skills are not taught in isolation but as part of daily living and learning activities that will increase the child's communication, independence, creativity, motivation, and future learning. Motor and communication skills necessary for daily living are not the only areas in which the teacher must provide instruction. Learning social responsiveness, appropriate social initiation, how to play with others, and problem solving, for example, are important goals for which the teacher must develop instructional strategies. Some children who are well beyond the typical preschooler's age may still be functioning at a very early developmental level. Consequently, the muscle tone, posture, and movement problems we discuss

Figure 10–10 a, b, c

➤ *Alternatives to allow change of position throughout the day: (a) Sidelyer, (b) Wedge, (c) Tricycle with built up back and pedals. Adult three-wheeled bikes are available for larger children.*

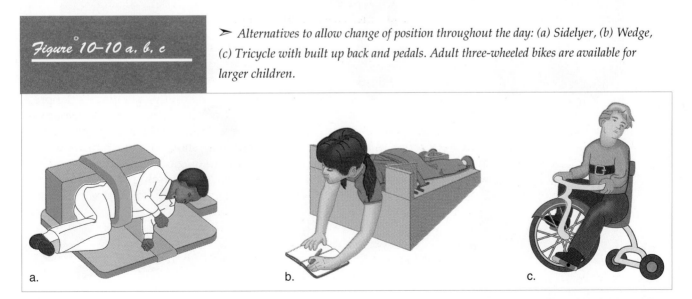

a.   b.   c.

SOURCE: Adapted from June L. Bigge, *Teaching individuals with physical and multiple disabilities* (3rd ed.). Copyright © 1991 by Macmillan Publishing Company. p. 137. Reprinted with permission.

Figure 10–11

➤ *Some children need to be supported in a tilted semistanding or kneeling position by a board so they can work at a table or counter. Special features of a prone board are its adjustability and devices to keep the child securely in place and properly positioned.*

SOURCE: Adapted from June L. Bigge, *Teaching individuals with physical and multiple disabilities* (3rd ed.). Copyright © 1991 by Macmillan Publishing Company. p. 190. Reprinted with permission.

Figure 10–12a, b, c, d, e, f

➤ *Alternative seating: (a) chair without legs and added post in front of chair to promote abduction of hips, (b) chair with arms and foot rests—runners or skis can be added to keep chair from tipping, (c) sandbags as supports, (d) and (e) corner seats (with lap straps, leg positioners and perhaps a tray), (f) partial recliner.*

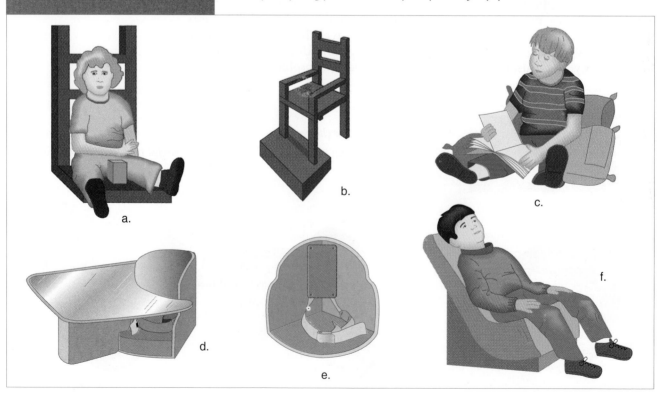

SOURCE: Adapted from June L. Bigge, *Teaching individuals with physical and multiple disabilities* (3rd ed.). Copyright © by Macmillan Publishing Company. p. 140. Reprinted with permission.

here, as well as the approach to teaching we just described, apply to some older students, too.

TRANSITION

Transition involves a turning point, a change from one situation or environment to another. When special educators speak of transition, they typically refer to change from school to work or from adolescence to adulthood. For children with physical disabilities, however, transition is perhaps a more pervasive concern than for children with other disabilities. It may involve discharge from intensive care or transition from hospital to home at any age. Neisworth and Fewell (1989) have noted that "in an era of increasingly sophisticated medical technology, transition begins for some families at or shortly after the birth of a child" (p. xi). Nevertheless, we focus our attention here on the transition concerns of adolescents and young adults.

You may recall from Chapter 1 our discussion of Matt Radcliffe (see page 9). The box on pages 430–431 is Matt's story as he wrote it, as a high school sophomore, for the school newspaper. Note the social and psychological as well as physical transitions that Matt was required to make due to his illness and its aftermath.

Two areas of concern for transition stand out clearly for adolescents and young adults with physical disabilities: careers and sociosexuality. Adolescents begin contemplating and experimenting with jobs, social relations, and sexuality in a direct and serious way. For the adolescent with a physical disability, these questions and trial behaviors are often especially perplexing, not just to themselves but to their families as well. "Can I get and hold a satisfying job?" "Can I become independent?" "Will I have close and lasting friendships?" "Will anyone find me physically attractive?" "How can I gratify my sexual needs?" Ordinary adolescents have a hard time coming to grips with these questions and the developmental tasks they imply; adolescents with physical disabilities often have an even harder time.

As we pointed out in our discussion of psychological characteristics, there is no formula for predicting the emotional or behavioral problems a person with a given physical disability will have. Much depends on the management and training the person has received. So it is particularly important to provide both career education and sociosexual education for students with physical disabilities.

Choice of Career

For the adolescent or young adult with physical disabilities, career considerations are extremely important (Fonosch, Arany, Lee, & Loving, 1982). In working out an occupational goal, it is vital to appraise realistically the individual's specific abilities and disabilities and to assess motivation carefully. Some disabilities clearly rule out certain occupational choices. With other disabilities, high motivation and full use of residual function may make it possible to achieve unusual professional status. For instance, Tom Dempsey, one of football's best field-goal kickers, had a congenitally deformed arm, hand, and foot.

One of the greatest problems in dealing with adolescents who have physical disabilities is helping them attain a realistic employment outlook. Intelligence, emotional characteristics, motivation, and work habits must be assessed at least as carefully as physical limitations. Furthermore, the availability of jobs and the

𝒞ANCER ➤

Editor's Note: The following is a true story by a student at Albemarle High School.

Cancer! Brain tumor! Malignant! To most people, when these words are pronounced, they perceive it as a death sentence and immediately lose hope. Shock, disbelief, and denial are initial reactions. People believe, "It can't happen to me. I'm too young or I'm too healthy." Cancer and diseases are a part of our everyday life. Cancer can happen to anyone, me or you. In fact, it did happen to me.

Five years ago, I was diagnosed as having a brain tumor. My reaction was, I expect, typical. "Why me? Will I live or die? It can't be happening to me, of all people."

I was almost ten years old and I wasn't ready to give in to this major setback in my life. I guess that's why I'm alive today. I fought against the disease instead of quitting before the battle had begun. I had a positive attitude and knew I had a lot to offer. My whole life was ahead of me and there were goals I wanted to accomplish like going to college, getting married, and having a family.

Before I had a brain tumor, my lifestyle was far different from what it is now. I was popular and was one of the best athletes in my class. I played soccer, basketball, baseball, and was an excellent swimmer; all the while I had good grades also. My goal was to do the very best I could in everything. I thought I had the most perfect life a kid could want at that age. But one day, I started having excruciating headaches and nausea. I had just had a yearly check-up and

the doctor said that everything was normal. Yet my headaches and sickness continued eventually becoming so severe that I was taken to UVA and Martha Jefferson hospitals, and the doctor's office for numerous tests, including bloodwork, and EEG, and neurological work-ups. The tests revealed nothing. Finally, my symptoms changed dramatically. My headaches became unbearable, I was combative, disoriented, and did not know anyone. The doctor ran a CAT scan and he found that I had an abnormal cell that was growing out of control in my brain and it was cancerous. He told my parents that I might not make it and that surgery as well as extensive follow-up therapy such as radiation would be necessary.

The illness put a lot of pressure on my parents and me. There were numerous trips to the hospital to see a number of doctors and huge medical bills. Because of a loss of my motor abilities there were things such as writing that I could no longer do which presented a problem with even the tiniest task I undertook. I lost my hair and to help relieve my double vision I had to wear an eye patch over one eye. I had to face my family, friends, and school knowing that I had cancer and that people couldn't help but think that I might die.

My parents and I were fortunate that we had a lot of friends that gave us not only moral support but they helped out with errands and chores so that my parents could spend as much time as possible with me. They were constantly fixing meals, running errands, and doing chores and especially praying for me and my family.

---

demands of certain occupations must be taken into account. The child who has moderate mental retardation and severe spastic quadriplegia is highly unlikely to have a career as a lawyer, a laboratory technician, or a clerk-typist. But what of one who has severe spastic quadriplegia and a bright mind? Such a person may well overcome both the physical limitation and the associated social stigma and be successful in a wide variety of fields in which the work is more mental than physical.

There are no simple conclusions regarding the occupational outlook for students with physical disabilities. Those with mild or transitory disabling conditions may not be affected at all in their occupational choices. Some with relatively mild physical disabilities may be unemployed, or even unemployable, because of inappropriate social and emotional behavior or poor work habits; they may need vocational rehabilitation training to function even in a vocation with limited demands. Some people with severe physical disabilities are able to use their intelligence, social skills, and residual physical abilities to the fullest and become competitive employees (or employers) in demanding occupations.

The outlook for employment of students with physical or multiple and severe disabilities has been improved dramatically by legislation and research and demonstration projects. As we mentioned in Chapter 1, the Americans with

Matt Radcliffe

It was a frightening and difficult time, but the funny thing was that I never thought that I was going to die. It may sound sort of weird, but I had faith— faith that I could overcome the odds and someday I would be as good as before I became ill.

I had to face many struggles. After I went through surgery, I realized that my head had been shaved so that the doctors could see the area more clearly. The surgery lasted five and one-half hours. I was in intensive care for less than a day, a shorter time period than the doctors had predicted. The doctor said that I had a little paralysis in my left eye causing double vision and my motor skills were impaired. I had to undergo radiation for thirty-one days, physical and occupational therapy for about two months. Physical and occupational therapy helped me to improve the motor skills that I had lost, such as writing, walking, balancing, etc. I had to have radiation so that the disease would not return and also to make sure that abnormal cells did not spread to other parts of my body. The radiation destroyed many of the good cells with the bad cells, but it did not make me sick.

The effects of the illness still aren't over. People, especially other kids, treat me differently since I've had cancer. They tease me about how I can't do things as well any more or that I look different because of my thinning hair or double vision. It's almost as if they're afraid of me.

I wish people realized that cancer is not contagious and that people who have cancer just want to be treated the same as everyone else. They still like to talk to their friends, play sports, have girlfriends and boyfriends, and goof-off. At times, having cancer made me feel like a handicapped person— lonely and that people just don't understand. I've seen that cancer causes children and young people to grow old before their time and I feel like I missed out on being a kid. Now life has a different meaning to me, because I almost lost it. I don't take things for granted and I live each day knowing that no one is promised a tomorrow.

Having cancer, I lost my popularity and good athletic abilities, and I thought I had lost everything that was ever important to me. It took a while, but then I realized that I was wrong. I had my new health, my new life, and my parents. That's a lot. I also gained a new perspective on life: caring for others. Now when I see people who are disabled or different from everyone else, I compare them to me and how my life would be in that situation.

To some people, cancer, a disease, or a handicap are reasons to give up, stop trying, but to a kid who's been there, I'm with W. Mitchell, a paralyzed millionaire who says, "All limitations are self-imposed. It's not what happens to you in life, it's what you do about it." For me, I've learned to live with life's limitations, even cancer, and I've learned that you can overcome those limitations if you put your mind to it.

SOURCE: The Patriot, 1/19/90, p. 11. Reprinted with permission.

Disabilities Act (ADA) of 1990 requires reasonable accommodations to create equal employment opportunities for people with disabilities. More accessible transportation and buildings, increased skill in using technology to allow people to accomplish tasks at work, and greater commitment to preparing people with disabilities for work are resulting in more personal independence, economic self-sufficiency, and social acceptance—good things not only for people with disabilities but for our economy and society.

We now recognize that "preparation for work begins in early childhood and continues well into adulthood" (Bigge, 1991, p. 484). Long before adolescence, children—including those with physical disabilities—need to be taught about and explore various careers. They need to be thinking about what they like to do, as well as what they are particularly good at, and the demands and rewards of various kinds of jobs. The objective should be to help students select training and enter a career that makes maximum use of their abilities in ways that they find personally gratifying.

Supported employment for people with severe disabilities is a relatively new concept that is being adopted widely. By supported employment we mean that a person with a severe disability works in regular work settings. He or she becomes a regular employee, performs a valued function in the same workplace

INVESTING IN TECHNOLOGY-ASSISTED EMPLOYABILITY ➤

Accountant Steven's workday begins when the beep on his fax machine signals the arrival of the daily transactions from ten small businesses that employ him to manage their accounts. Steven enters each transaction into his computerized accounting program and efficiently summarizes the day's business activities. Turning to his fax machine once more, Steven sends each company a print-out of their daily records and shuts off his machine with the satisfaction of a job well done. Unusual activity—no. Unusual circumstances—yes. It is three in the morning when Steven finishes his work, and he never leaves his home, in fact, Steven never leaves his bed. You see, Steven has no controlled movement below his neck and due to recent medical problems, he must remain in a special bed and constantly use respiratory support. The accounting work was accomplished through the use of a mouthstick and a home workstation arranged to allow him access to the equipment he needs to function successfully with relative independence.

When Steven was in school, little was done to prepare him for the world of work. His educational program had been based on his deficits rather than his strengths and no one assumed he would be able to compete successfully in the open marketplace. After graduation, Steven spent several years at home until he learned from a friend about a high-tech program at a local community college. This high-tech program was designed to ensure that college students with disabilities would have equal access to the available academic and training programs. Once enrolled, Steven's strengths were identified, he determined his career choice, and access to technology and to academic instruction was provided. He successfully completed a program in accounting and, with the help of the counselor in the placement office, found a job with a small accounting firm. When it became medically necessary for Steven to remain at home, with minimal expense, the accounting firm in conjunction with the Department of Rehabilitation, provided Steven with a home workstation.

Situations like this are well known to Carl Brown, Director of High Tech Center for the Disabled, California Community Colleges, who is dedicated to providing efficient, practical, and cost-effective adapted computer technology to people with disabilities in post-secondary educational settings. He and his staff have prepared extensive training guides for software and hardware adaptations, and develop intensive workshops and programs for post-secondary educators concerned with providing access to technology (Brown, Norris, & Crownover, 1987). Rather than focus on specialized mechanical devices, exotic software, or customized computer systems, Brown and staff have sought software-based solutions to the problem of access and have been very successful in finding programs that allow full and unencumbered access to the complete range of commercially available software.

Waiting until a student has reached the post-secondary level before providing academic and training access is an unacceptable educational practice. Students for whom technology offers independence and equal opportunity must be given access from the very beginning of their educational program with the integrated goals of getting an education and preparing for work.

Adequately preparing today's students for tomorrow's world of work would require a long look into a crystal ball. In lieu of access to this magic, educators must carefully examine the work skills curriculum and make instructional decisions based on concept mastery rather than specific skills mastery. This is particularly true in the area of technology because of the rapidly changing nature of the equipment and software programs used in business and industry. So, an appropriate educational objective would be to understand a technology-related process and to develop strategies for its implementation, regardless of the machine or the software program being used. For example, when a student's ability to type in information is slow and laborious, strategies for speeding up the process are critical.

SOURCE: Reprinted with the permission of Macmillan Publishing Company from *Teaching individuals with physical and multiple disabilities* (3rd ed.) by June L. Bigge. Copyright © 1991 by Macmillan Publishing Company. pp. 480–481.

as nondisabled employees, and receives fair remuneration. Training and continued support are necessary, hence the term "supported employment." Trach (1990) describes the distinguishing features of a supported employment program:

> Notably, these procedures include surveying the community for jobs, identifying and analyzing the requisite skills of potential employment sites, assessing the current skill levels of supported employees, matching jobs to prospective employees, providing systematic training in job-related skills, and providing follow-up training and maintenance of learned skills, satisfying employers, and coordinating related services. (p. 79)

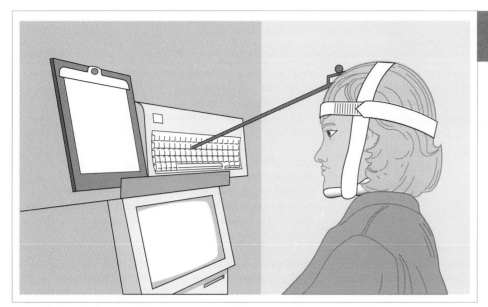

Figure 10–13

➤ *A keyboard positioned for efficient use with a headstick*

SOURCE: Adapted from June L. Bigge, *Teaching individuals with physical and multiple disabilities* (3rd ed.). Copyright © 1991 by Macmillan Publishing Co., p. 486.

New technologies, especially computing and other electronic devices, offer great promise for enabling students with physical disabilities to achieve personal independence, acquiring education and training that will make them employable, and finding employment. The box on page 432 illustrates how people with disabilities might use their abilities in successful employment as well as how schools can fail to provide appropriate education and training. In some cases, the technology is readily available and educators need only to become aware of the software (e.g., software that allows the function of keys to be altered), find ways in which keystrokes can be saved through subprogramming routines (e.g., macro or find-and-replace features in word processing), or provide substitutions for physical manipulation of materials (e.g., computer graphics programs as substitutes for paper paste-ups or model construction) (Bigge, 1991). Sometimes an individual's ability to use standard equipment is greatly enhanced by a simple modification, such as orientation or location. Figure 10–13 shows how simply placing a keyboard in a vertical position over a monitor may enhance the ability of someone who uses a headstick to use a computer. Teachers must always be looking for simple, virtually cost-free ways to facilitate the performance of students with disabilities—to prevent an environment designed for people without disabilities from handicapping those who must do things a different way. Overlooking the seemingly obvious is perhaps the way in which we most frequently handicap people with disabilities.

Sociosexuality

Until fairly recently, physical disabilities were assumed to cancel human sexuality (see Edmonson, 1988). People who were not whole physically, especially if they had limited mobility, were thought of as having no sex appeal for anyone and as

In Their Own Words   RUTH SIENKIEWICZ-MERCER

Ruth Sienkiewicz-Mercer was diagnosed with cerebral palsy during early infancy, which left her with virtually no ability to function physically except to see, hear, and digest. Born to a loving family of limited means, she was enrolled at the age of nine at the then notorious Bridgewater State Hospital in Massachusetts, where she spent the next sixteen years being treated as a mental incompetent, in spite of the fact that her intellectual functioning was unaffected by her physical condition. Such treatment consisted of utter neglect which today would qualify as outright abuse.

Her autobiographical novel, *I Raise My Eyes to Say Yes: A Memoir,* describes her years of struggle to communicate to those around her, even to her family, that with the exception of her body, she was indeed an intelligent, fully capable human being.

The following passage describes her experience when she was admitted to Bridgewater for the first time.

Just inside the building, a man and a woman dressed in white hospital clothing were waiting for us. Mother and Father spoke to them for a few minutes. Then Father came over and kissed me goodbye. Mother gave me a

long, long hug and whispered in my ear, "I love you, sweetheart, remember that." She was crying.

Then they were gone.

I was taken into an office and examined by the man who had been waiting for us, whom I will call Dr. Soong. Dr. Soong spoke English with a very thick accent. With the nurse's assistance, he placed me on the table, undressed me, removed my leg and back braces, slapped me into diapers and a hospital johnny, weighed me, measured my height, and moved my arms and legs around. He talked while this was going on, but I didn't understand a word he said.

Dr. Soong was the staff doctor at the Infirmary. Many years later I learned that the brief examination I have just described also included a "psychological evaluation." In that evaluation, Dr. Soong concluded that I was an imbecile. His method of evaluating me consisted of looking me over during the physical exam and deciding that since I didn't talk and apparently couldn't understand what he was saying, I must be an imbecile.

SOURCE: Ruth Sienkiewicz-Mercer and Steven B. Kaplan, *I Raise My Eyes to Say Yes: A Memoir,* (Boston: Houghton Mifflin, 1989), p. 38.

---

having little or no ability or right to function sexually. These ideas are reflected in the words of William L. Rush (1977), a young man with physical disabilities whose romantic feelings were rejected by the first young woman he felt he loved: "Only two roads are open for the severely physically handicapped in dealing

*P*hysical disabilities need not preclude children's participation in enjoyable and healthful activities.

with their feelings of love: the road of expecting and accepting only platonic love or the road of fantasizing. Neither is very satisfactory" (p. 6).

Fortunately, attitudes and experiences are changing. It is now recognized that people with disabilities have a right to family life education, including sex education, and to a full range of human relationships, including appropriate sexual expression (Duncan & Canty-Lemke, 1986; Edmonson, 1988). Sociosexual education for students with physical disabilities, as such education for all other children and youths, should begin early, continue through adulthood, and include information about the structure and functions of bodies, human relationships and responsibilities, and alternative modes of sexual gratification (Bigge, 1991).

Youths with physical disabilities need to experience close friendships and warm physical contact that is not sexually intimate. But it is neither realistic nor fair to expect people with physical disabilities to keep all their relationships platonic or to limit themselves to fantasy. Most physical disability, even if severe, does not in itself kill sexual desire or prevent sexual gratification; nor does it preclude marriage and children. The purpose of special education and rehabilitation is to make exceptional individuals' lives as full and complete as possible. In the case of youths with physical disabilities, this may involve teaching or providing alternative means of sexual stimulation and accepting sexual practices and relationships that are different from the norm, as discussed by Lewandowski and Cruickshank (1980). With sensitive education and rehabilitation, satisfying sociosexual expression can be achieved by all but a small minority (DeLoach & Greer, 1981; Edmonson, 1988).

SUGGESTIONS FOR TEACHING ➤   E. Jane Nowacek

Students with Physical Disabilities in General Education Classrooms

WHAT TO LOOK FOR IN SCHOOL

As you know from reading the chapter, children and adolescents attending school experience a wide range of health and physical problems. This range is increasing as medical, educational, and technological advancements make possible the integration of students with severe disabilities. Although many children with physical problems will be diagnosed before being mainstreamed, some may experience changes in their conditions or in their reactions to medication during the school year, and other students may develop illnesses or be involved in accidents after entering school. The following questions may help you to identify potential problems (Dykes & Venn, 1983; Shore, 1986). Ask yourself if your students:

- seem as energetic as usual?
- initiate contact as usual?
- have normal skin tone?
- have any sores, rashes, cuts that you haven't seen before?
- are wearing clothing that seems to fit differently than usual?
- tire easily?
- indicate verbally or nonverbally that they are experiencing discomfort or pain?

HOW TO GATHER INFORMATION

Although as a teacher you are not expected to be a medical diagnostician, you may have more opportunities than any other adult to observe your students. Therefore, you have an important responsibility to be aware of changes in your students' physical condition and to notify the school nurse and parents or guardians about your observations so they can arrange for medical examination and treatment.

For those students in your class with diagnosed physical and health impairments, you will want to gather information that enables you to answer these questions (Berdine & Blackhurst, l985, cited in Lewis & Doorlag, 1991):

Medical Concerns:

1. Does the student take medication? How frequently? In what amounts? Is the school authorized to administer the medication during school hours?
2. What are the side-effects of the medication?
3. What procedures should be followed in the event of a seizure, insulin shock, diabetic coma, or other problem?
4. Should the student's activities be restricted in any way?

Travel:

1. How will the student be transported to school?
2. Will the student arrive and leave at the usual school times?
3. Will the student need special acccommodations to travel within the school building or the classroom?

Communication:

1. Can the student write? Type? How?
2. If the student does not communicate verbally, what type of communication will be used?
3. Is an electronic communication aid used? If so, are there special instructions necessary for the student to use it or for me to understand and maintain it?
4. Can the student make his or her needs known to the teacher? How?
5. Are there other aids or devices that I should know about?

Self-Care:

1. What types of self-care help, such as feeding and toileting, does the student need? Who is responsible for providing this care?
2. What equipment does the student need?

Positioning:

1. What positioning aids or devices (braces, pillows, wedges) does the student use?
2. What particular positions are most useful for specific academic activities and for resting?
3. Are there other aids or devices that I should know about?

Reading your students' individualized educational programs (IEPs) and consulting other school personnel who work with them (see p. 424) may provide answers to these questions. For additional medical information about specific diseases and disorders and practical suggestions for teachers,

see *Physically handicapped children: A medical atlas for teachers* (Bleck & Nagel, 1982) and the chapters concerning physical disabilities and emergency medical procedures in the *Handbook of special education.* (Kauffman & Hallahan, 1981).

TEACHING TECHNIQUES TO TRY

The interventions required in school for students with physical disabilities vary greatly depending on the type and severity of their conditions. Some students may require specialized assistance or training in areas such as mobility or communications. Others may need additional support to manage the sensory, learning, and behavioral disorders that can accompany some physical disabilities (see appropriate chapters for these interventions). Still others may require no modifications or only minimal adjustments. For example, teachers simply may need to increase the length of time students have to complete assignments when they are absent or fatigued by their illnesses or the treatment of their illnesses. In fact, most students with physical and health impairments attend regular education classes for most of the school day and are expected to progress through the same curricular materials as nondisabled students (Reynolds & Birch, 1982). Many of these students, however, require some adaptation of instructional materials and activities in order to succeed in school and to maximize their independence.

Instructional Adaptations

One of the most common adaptations that teachers make for students with physical disabilities is to modify the ways in which they respond to and practice academic tasks.

WRITTEN RESPONSES

To complete written activities some students need simple modifications, such as assistance in stabilizing and selecting appropriate materials. These adaptations include (Hale, l979; Bigge, 1991):

Stabilization Techniques

- writing on a pad of paper, rather than on loose sheets
- using masking tape (two-inch width is strongest) or a clipboard to secure loose papers
- placing a rubber strip on the back of a ruler or using a magnetic ruler to prevent slipping when measuring or drawing lines
- using adhesive-backed Velcro to attach items to a desk or wheelchair laptray

Modifying/Selecting Appropriate Materials

- using pens (felt tip) and pencils (soft lead) that require less pressure
- twisting a rubber band around the shaft of the pen or pencil or slipping corrugated rubber, a form curler, or a

golf practice ball over the writing instrument to make it easier to hold.

- using an electronic typewriter, word processor, or computer
- using typing aids, such as a pointer stick attached to a head or mouthpiece to strike the keys; a keyboard guard that prevents striking two keys at once; and line spacers that hold written materials while typing
- audiotaping assignments, lectures, and other instructional activities that require extensive writing. Tape recorders can be modified so students can operate them with a single switch.

For students who have limited strength, muscular control, or mobility, selecting and designing instructional materials that require no word formation may simplify their responding to written tasks. For example, numbering problems and coding possible answers with a letter allow students to write a single letter response (Bigge, 1991). Using worksheets and tests that direct students to put a line through the correct answer requires no letter formation. It is important, however, to provide enough space between the answer alternatives so that students can indicate their choice without marking another response accidentally (Bigge, 1982).

Still other adaptations do not require students to hold a pencil or pen. Bigge (1991) indicates that students can respond to matching, sorting, classifying, and sequencing tasks by manipulating objects. For example, they can move magnetic letters and numbers on a metal cookie sheet to indicate their responses, or put a wooden block on top of their answer choice. In addition, they may indicate their comprehension of content area reading by matching a set of picture cards with a set of cards with sentences or paragraphs written on them by pushing the two correct card sets together. Students also can use this response method in practicing vocabulary, especially homonyms, synonyms, and antonyms. Similarly, they can indicate the sequence of historical events, plot episodes from literary works, and steps in scientific experiments by pushing cards in the correct order that have pictures or sentences describing each event.

In addition, special input devices for computers facilitate student responding. Computers, for example, can be equipped with a variety of switches that allow students to operate them with a single movement. Selection of the type of switch will depend on the type of movement your student can best perform. The Adaptive Firmware Card (AFC), available from Don Johnston Developmental Equipment, Inc., is a computer peripheral that permits students to use any commerical software program (Lewis & Doorlag, 1991). The AFC provides a line of letters and symbols called a scanning array on the computer screen that students select by pressing a switch. This array allows them to spell words, indicate numbers, and operate the computer. Alternate keyboards (e.g., Unicorn Expanded Keyboard) offer several features such as, providing a larger response area than standard keyboards and removing the need for simultaneous key pressing.

Consequently, they offer another means by which students with limited muscular control can use computers. Touch sensitive screens also enable students to respond to instructions and questions by touching a specific area of the screen. Still other input devices allow students to bypass keyboards completely by talking or by making consistent sounds into a microphone and by making muscular movements.

ORAL RESPONSES

Speech synthesizers voice the responses that students with severe speech impairments type on the computer and enable them to participate in class discussions and to ask questions immediately. Less expensive communication boards, charts of pictures, symbols, numbers, or words, allow students to indicate their response to specific items represented on the charts. To facilitate communication using these boards, Bigge (1982) recommends that listeners name the picture or say the letter or word quickly so the conversation moves along more rapidly. Teachers also have found less comprehensive response adaptations useful during oral activities. For example, they may give students color-coded objects, such as blocks of wood that are easy to handle and that do not slip, to indicate their response to polar questions, such as true/false; agree/disagree/don't know; same/different (Bigge, 1982).

READING TASKS

In addition to response modifications, students with physical disabilities often require equipment that facilitates reading. These devices include book holders; reading stands that adjust to reclining, sitting, and standing positions; and page turners that range from pencil erasers to electric-powered devices that can be operated with minimal mobility (Hale, 1979). Furthermore, talking books enable students who cannot hold books to tape lectures and to enjoy a variety of recorded novels, textbooks, and magazines. Specialized talking books, called compressed speech machines, play at faster than usual speeds and may be helpful to students who must learn large amounts of information (Dykes & Venn, 1983). This equipment is available at no cost from the Library of Congress. In addition to these devices, instructional materials can be adapted to facilitate student use during reading and thinking activities. For example, teachers use photo albums that have sticky backings and plastic cover sheets and plastic photo cubes to hold instructional materials, such as pictures or words cards. This latter adaptation allows students to move the cubes to respond to a variety of tasks.

HELPFUL RESOURCES

School Personnel

Because students with health impairments and physical disabilities often require the expertise of a variety of professionals, several individuals may provide services to your student. Understanding the role of each is important in coordinating instructional and medical interventions. The following list describes the functions professionals typically fulfill in the treatment of these students (Dykes & Venn, 1983, pp. 261–63):

- Physicians are licensed medical doctors who provide services that include diagnosing; prescribing medication; making referrals for physical therapy, occupational therapy, and orthopedic treatment; and recommending the extent and length of various activities and treatments. Specialized physicians include: orthopedists (specialists in diagnosing and treating joint, bones, and muscles impairments), neurologists (specialists in diagnosing and treating impairments to the nervous system such as cerebral palsy and muscular dystrophy), radiologists (specialists in using X-rays and radioactive substances to diagnose and treat conditions such as cancer).
- School nurses' responsibilities vary depending on the school system in which they are employed. Often they administer medications at school, treat medical emergencies, provide medical information to students and staff, and help in identifying community health agencies for families.
- Occupational therapists provide medically-prescribed assistance to help individuals manage their disabilities. They may teach various self-help, daily-living, prevocational, leisure-time, and perceptual-motor skills. They also provide instruction in the use of adaptive devices.
- Rehabilitation counselors perform a range of services related to vocational training and employment. For example, they may conduct vocational assessment and counseling and arrange for work training and experience. Typically they are employed by the state vocational rehabilitation agency, rather than by the school district.
- Physical therapists provide services designed to restore or improve physical functioning and engage in such activities as exercising to increase coordination, range of motion, and movement.

Instructional Methods and Materials

Bigge, J. L. (1989). *Curriculum-based instruction for special education students* (2nd ed.). Mountain View, CA: Mayfield.

Bigge, J. L. (1991). *Teaching individuals with physical and multiple disabilities* (3rd ed.). New York: Merrill/Macmillan.

Byron, E., & Katz, G. (Eds.). (1991). *HIV prevention and AIDS education: Resources for special educators*. Reston, VA: Council for Exceptional Children.

Campbell, P. H. (1989). Students with physical disabilities. In R. Gaylord-Ross (Ed.), *Integration strategies for students with handicaps*. Baltimore, MD: Brookes.

Collins, J. L., & Britton, P. O. (1990). *Training educators in HIV prevention: An inservice manual*. Santa Cruz, CA: Network Publications.

Eastman, M. K. & Safran, J. S. (1986). Activities to develop your students' motor skills. *Teaching Exceptional Children, 19*, 24–27.

Fithian, J. (Ed.). (1984). *Understanding the child with a chronic illness in the classroom*. Phoenix: Oryx Press.

Fraser, B. A. & Hensinger, R. N. (1983). *Managing physical handicaps*. Baltimore, MD: Brookes.

Fredrick, J. & Fletcher, D. (1985). Facilitating children's adjustment to orthotic and prosthetic appliances. *Teaching Exceptional Children, 17*, 228–230.

Lynch, E. W., Murphy, D. S., & Lewis, R. B., (1986). *Making things better for chronically ill children: A guide for school and families*. (Available through the Department of Special Education, c/o State Study of Chronically Ill Children, San Diego State University, San Diego, CA 92182.)

McGinnis, J. S., & Beukelman, D. R. (1989). Vocabulary requirements for writing activities for the academically mainstreamed student with disabilities. *Augmentative and Alternative Communication, 5*, 183–191.

Miller, S. E. & Schaumberg, K. (1988). Physical education activities for children with severe cerebral palsy. *Teaching Exceptional Children, 20*, 9–11.

Orelove, F. P. & Sobsey, D. (1987). *Educating children with multiple disabilities*. Baltimore, MD: Brookes.

Self, P. C. (1984). *Physical Disability: An Annotated Literature Guide*. New York: Marcel Dekker.

Smith, A. K., Thurston, S., Light, J., Parnes, P., & O'Keefe, B. (1989). The form and use of written communication produced by physically disabled individuals using microcomputers. *Augmentative and Alternative Communication, 5*, 115–124.

Umbreit, J. (Ed.). (1983). *Physical disabilities and health impairments: An introduction*. Columbus, OH: Merrill/Macmillan.

Curricular Materials

*Brown, S., Hemphill, N. J., & Voeltz (1982). *The smallest minority: Adapted regular education social studies curricula for understanding and integrating severely disabled students. Lower elementary: Understanding self and others*. Honolulu: University of Manoa, Hawaii Integration Project.

*Hemphill, N.J., Zukas, D. & Brown, S. (1982). *The smallest minority: Adapted regular education social studies curricula for understanding and integrating severely disabled students. The secondary grades: Understanding alienation*. Honolulu: University of Hawaii/Manoa, Hawaii Integration Project.

Office for the Education of Children with Handicapping Conditions (1982). *Motor impairment: Accepting individual differences*. Albany, NY: New York State Education Department.

Phi Delta Kappa (1990). *Looking into AIDS*. Bloomington, IN: Phi Delta Kappa.

*Noonan, M. J., Hemphill, N. J., & Levy, G. (1983). *Social skills curricular strategy for students with severe disabilities*. Honolulu: University of Hawaii/Manoa, Hawaii Integration Project.

Teaching AIDS (1990). Santa, Cruz, CA: ERT Associates.

*Voeltz, L., Hemphill, N. J., Brown, S., Kishi, G., Klein, R., Fruehling, R., Levy, G., Collie, J., & Kube, C. (1983). *The Special

Friends program: A trainer's manual for integrated school settings. Honolulu: University of Hawaii/Manoa, Hawaii Integration Project.

Wisconsin Department of Public Instruction (1990). *Instruction about AIDS*. Madison, WI: Wisconsin Department of Public Instruction.

*available from Media Productions and Distributions, University of Hawaii, Castle Memorial Hall, 1776 University Avenue, Honolulu, HI 96822.

Literature about Individuals with Physical Disabilities

ELEMENTARY

Aiello, B., & Shulman, J. (1989). *A portrait of me*. Frederick, MD: Twenty-first Century Books. (Ages 9–12, diabetes) (Fiction=F, includes factual information about diabetes and its treatment)

Aiello, B., & Shulman, J. (1989). *Friends for life*. Frederick, MD: Twenty-first Century Books. (Ages 9–12, AIDS) (Nonfiction =NF)

Aiello, B., & Shulman, J. (1989). *Hometown Hero*. Frederick, MD: Twenty-first Century Books. (Ages 9–12, asthma) (F, includes factual information about asthmatic episodes)

Aiello, B., & Shulman, J. (1989). *Trick or treat or trouble*. Frederick, MD: Twenty-first Century Books. (Ages 9–21, epilepsy) (F, includes factual information about responding to seizures)

Arnold, K. (1983) *Anna joins in*. New York: Abingdon. (Ages 5–8, cystic fibrosis) (F)

Bergman, T. (1989). *On our own terms: Children living with physical disabilities*. Milwaukee, WI: Gareth Stevens Children's Books (Ages 9–12, spina bifida, cerebral palsy, and spinal injuries) (NF)

Blair, M. (1989). *Kids want to know about AIDS*. Rockville, MD: National AIDS Information Clearinghouse. (Ages 9–12, AIDS) (NF)

Carlson, N. (1990). *Arnie and the new kid*. New York: Viking. (Ages 9–12) (F)

Christian, M. B. (1985). *Growin' pains*. New York: Macmillan. (Ages 9–12) (F)

Dana, M. (1988). *No time for secrets*. Mahwah, NJ: Troll Associates. (Ages 9–12) (F)

Frevert, P. D. (1983). *It's okay to look at Jamie*. Mankato, MN: Creative Education. (Ages 9–12, spina bifida) (NF)

Frevert, P. D. (1983). *Patty gets well*. Mankato, MN: Creative Education. (Ages 9–12, leukemia) (NF)

Gorman, C. (1987). *Chelsey and the green-haired kid*. Boston: Houghton Mifflin. (Ages 9–12) (F)

Gould M. (1986). *The twelfth of June*. Philadelphia: J.B. Lippincott. (Ages 9–12, cerebral palsy) (F)

Howard, E. (1987). *Edith herself*. New York: Atheneum . (Ages 9–12, Epilepsy) (F)

Kipnis, L., & Adler, S. (1979). *You can't catch diabetes from a friend*. Gainsville, FL: Triad. (Ages 9–12) (NF)

Lasker, J. (1980). *Nick joins in*. Chicago: Albert Whitman. (Ages 5–8) (F)

Muldoon, K. (1989). *Princess pooh*. Niles, IL: Albert Whitman. (Elementary, wheelchair) (F)

Rabe, B. (1981). *The balancing girl*. New York: Dutton. (Ages 5–8) (F)

Roth, D. (1980). *The hermit of Fog Hollow*. Station, NY: Beaufort. (Ages 9–12) (F)

Sanford, D. (1989). *David has AIDS*. Portland, OR: Multnomah. (Ages 9–12, AIDS) (NF)

Stern, C. (1981). *A different kind of gold*. New York: Harper & Row (Ages 9–12) (F)

Stover, M. F. (1989). *Midnight in the dollhouse*. Niles, IL: Albert Whitman. (Ages 9–12) (F)·

SECONDARY

Adler, C. S. (1981). *Down by the river*. New York: Coward, McCann, & Groghegan. (Ages 13–18) (F)

Blos, J. W. (1985). *Brothers of the heart: A story of the old northwest, 1837–1839*. New York: Chas. Scribner's. (Ages 9–15) (F)

Bruce, S. (1983). *Tomorrow is today*. Indianapolis, IN: Bobbs-Merrill. (Ages 13–18, cancer) (NF)

Carr, C. A., & McNeil, J. (Eds.). (1986). *Adolescence and death*. New York: Springer. (Ages 16–18) (NF).

Davidson, B. (1981). *Gary Coleman's medical miracle*. New York: Coward. (Ages 13–18, kidney disease) (NF).

Deford, F. (1983). *Alex, the life of a child*. New York: Viking. (Ages 13–18, cystic fibrosis) (NF)

Greenberg, J. (1983). *No dragons to slay*. New York: Farrar, Straus, and Giroux. (Ages 13–18, cancer) (F)

Levy, M. (1982). *The girl in the plastic cage*. New York: Ballantine Books/Fawcett Juniper Books. (Ages 13–15, scoliosis) (F)

McCullough, D. (1981). *Mornings on horseback*. New York: Simon and Schuster. (Ages 16–18, asthma) (NF)

Miklowitz, G. D. (1987). *Good-bye tomorrow*. New York: Delacorte Press. (Ages 13–18, AIDS) (F)

Radley, G. (1984). *CF in his corner*. Soquel: CA: Four Winds Press. (Ages 13–15, cystic fibrosis) (F)

Ress, L. (1980). *Horse of air*. New York: Methven. (Ages13–18) (F)

Richmond, S. (1985). *Wheels for walking*. New York: Atlantic Monthly Press. (Ages 13–18, quadriplegia) (F)

Seidick, K. (1984). *Or you can let him go*. New York: Delacorte. (Ages 16–18, kidney disease) (NF)

Slepian, J. (1980). *The Alfred summer*. New York: Macmillan. (Ages 13–18, cerebral palsy) (F)

Stingley, D. (1983). *Happy to be alive*. New York: Beaufort Books. (Ages 13–18, quadriplegia) (NF)

Computer Software

The following programs may be operated by an adaptive switch or touch-sensitive screens.

Academics with scanning: Language arts, ACS Software, University of Washington, Department of Speech and

Hearing Sciences JG–15, Seattle, WA 98195, (206) 543–7974. (Program includes phonics and word attack)

Academics with scanning: Math, ACS Software, University of Washington, Department of Speech and Hearing Sciences JG–15, Seattle, WA 98195, (206) 543–7974 (does not provide instruction, but allows students to use the computer as pencil/paper to complete math problems.)

Adventures of Jimmy-Jumper, Exceptional Children's Software, P.O. Box 487, Hays, KS 67601, (913) 625–9281. (Prepositions; speech synthesizer required)

Counting Critters, MECC, 3490 Lexington Avenue, North, St. Paul, MN 55126, (800) 228–3504.

Exploratory Plan, PEAL Software, 5000 North Parkway Calabasas, Ste. 105, Calabasas, CA 91302, (818) 883–7849. (Communication)

First Verbs, Laureate Learning Systems, 110 East Spring Street, Winooski, VT 05404, (800) 562–6801. (Speech synthesizer required)

First Words I and II, Laureate Learning Systems, 110 East Spring Street, Winooski, VT 05404, (800) 562–6801. (Speech synthesizer requried)

Interaction Games, Don Johnston Developmental Equipment, 1000 North Rand Road, Building 115, P.O. Box 639, Wauconda, IL 60084, (312) 526–2682. (Row and column scanning)

Keyboarding for the Physically Handicapped, Gregg/McGraw-Hill, 1221 Avenue of the Americas, New York, NY 10020, (800) 262–4729.

Keyboarding with One Hand, Educational, ComputAbility Corporation, 40000 Grand River, Ste. 109, Novi, MI 48375, (313) 477–6720.

Keytalk, PEAL Software, 5000 North Parkway Calabasas, Ste. 105, Calabasas, CA 91302, (818) 325–2001. (Electronic communcication aid)

My Words, Hartley Courseware, P. O. Box 431, Dimondale, MI 48821, (800) 247–1380. (Combines a language experience approach with a talking word processer program)

Muppet Slate, Sunburst, 39 Washington Avenue, Pleasantville, NY 10570, (800) 628–8897.

Rabbit Scanner, Exceptional Children's Software, P.O. Box 487, Hays, KS 67601, (913) 625–9281. (Scanning trainer)

Representional Play, PEAL Software, 5000 North Parkway Calabasas, Ste. 105, Calabasas, CA 91302, (818) 883–7849. (Communication)

Single Switch Game Library, Arthur Schwartz, l801 East Twelfth Street, #1119, Cleveland, OH 44114, (216) 371–3820.

Sunny Days, Don Johnston Developmental Equipment, 1000 North Rand Road, Building 115, P.O. Box 639, Wauconda, IL 60084, (312) 526–2682. (Word recognition, spelling, and reading skills)

Swtichmaster, Expert Systems Software, Ste. 316, Nashville, TV 37215, (615) 292–7667. (Operation of switches)

Touch and Match, Exceptional Children's Software, P.O. Box 487, Hays, KS 67601, (913) 625–9281.

Organizations

AIDS

National Association of People with AIDS, 2025 I Street, N.W., Suite 415, Washington, DC 20006, (202) 429–2856.

ARTHRITIS

Arthritis Foundation, 1314 Spring Street, N.W., Atlanta, GA 30309, (404) 872–7100.

ASTHMA

National Foundation for Asthma, P.O. Box 30069, Tucson, AZ 855751, (602) 323–6046.

BIRTH (CONGENITAL) DEFECTS

Association of Birth Defect Children, 5400 Diplomat Circle, Ste. 270, Orlando, FL 32812, (407) 629–1466.

March of Dimes Birth Defects Foundation, 1275 Marmaroneck Avenue, White Plains, NY 10605, (914) 428–7100.

CANCER

American Cancer Society, 1599 Clifton Road NE, Atlanta, GA 30329, (404) 320–3333.

Cancer Information Service, Boy Scout Building, Room 340, Rockville Pike, Bethesda, MD 20892, (301) 496–8664.

CEREBRAL PALSY

United Cerebral Palsy Associations, 7 Penn Plaza, Ste. 804, New York, NY 10001, (212) 268–6655.

CHILD ABUSE

American Association for Protecting Children, c/o American Humane Association, 63 Inverness Drive, E., Englewood, CO 80112, (303) 792–9900.

CHILDHELP U.S.A., Inc., 6463 Independence Avenue, Woodland Hills, CA 91370, (818) 347–7280.

DIABETES

American Diabetes Association, National Service Center, P.O. Box 25757, 1660 Duke Street, Alexandria, VA 22313, (703) 549–1500.

EPILEPSY

Epilepsy Foundation of America, 4351 Garden City Drive, Landover, MD 20785, (301) 459–3700.

MUSCULAR DYSTROPHY

Muscular Dystrophy Association, 810 Seventh Avenue, New York, NY 10019, (212) 586–0808.

MULTIPLE SCLEROSIS

National Mutliple Sclerosis Society, 205 East 42nd Street, New York, NY 10017, (212) 986–3240.

SPINA BIFIDA

Spina Bifida Association of America, 209 Shiloh Drive, Madison, WI 53705.

BIBLIOGRAPHY FOR TEACHING SUGGESTIONS

Bigge, J. L. (1982). *Teaching individuals with physcial and multiple disabilities* (2nd ed.). Columbus, OH: Merrill/Macmillan.

Bigge, J. L. (1991). *Teaching individuals with physical and multiple disabilities* (3rd ed.). New York: Merrill/Macmillan.

Bleck, E. E. & Nagel, D. A. (1982). *Physically handicapped children: A medical atlas for teachers* (2nd ed.). New York: Grune & Stratton.

Dykes, M. K., & Venn, J. (1983). Using health, physical, and medical data in the classroom. In J. Umbreit (Ed.), *Physical disabilities and health impairments: An introduction.* Columbus, OH: Merrill/Macmillan.

Hale, G. (1979). *The source book for the disabled.* Philadelphia: Saunders

Kauffman, J. M., & Hallahan, D. P. (Eds.). (1981). *Handbook of special education.* Englewood Cliffs, N J: Prentice-Hall.

Lewis, R. B. & Doorlag, D. H. (1991). *Teaching special students in the mainstream.* New York: Merrill.

Oettinger, L., & Coleman, J. (1981) Emergency medical procedures. In J. M. Kauffman & D. P. Hallahan (Eds.), *Handbook of special education.* Englewood Cliffs, NJ: Prentice-Hall.

Reynolds, M. C., & Birch. J. W. (1982). *Teaching exceptional children in all America's schools.* Reston, VA: Council for Exceptional Children.

Shore, K. (1986). *The special education handbook: A comprehensive guide for parents and educators.* New York: Teachers College Press.

Verhaaren, P., & Connor, F. P. (1981). Physical disabilities. In J. M. Kauffman & D. P. Hallahan (Eds.). *Handbook of special education.* Englewood Cliffs, NJ: Prentice-Hall.

Summary

Children with physical disabilities are those whose physical limitations or health problems interfere with school attendance or learning to such an extent that special services, training, equipment, materials, or facilities are required. These children may have other disabilities, such as mental retardation and emotional or behavioral disorders. The medical nature of the problem highlights the need for interdisciplinary cooperation in special education.

Less than 0.5 percent of the child population receives special education and related services for physical disabilities. Because of advances in medical technology, more children with severe disabilities are surviving, and many more are surviving disease or injury with mild impairments, such as hyperactivity and learning disabilities. The needs of children and youths with physical disabilities and chronic illnesses far outstrip the public programs and services for them.

Children with neurological impairments have suffered damage to or deterioration of the central nervous system. Their behavioral symptoms include mental retardation, learning problems, perceptual-motor dysfunction, paralysis, seizures, and emotional or behavioral disorders. The causes of neurological impairments include infections, diseases, hypoxia, poisoning, congenital malformations, accidents, and child abuse.

Cerebral palsy (CP), a condition characterized by paralysis, weakness, uncoordination, and/or other motor dysfunction, accounts for about half of the children with physical impairments in the United States. It is nonprogressive brain damage that occurs before or during birth or in early childhood. Classification of CP is generally made according to the limbs involved and the type of motor disability. The educational problems associated with CP are varied because of the multiplicity of symptoms; a careful clinical appraisal must be made of each individual to determine the type of special education needed.

Seizures are caused by an abnormal discharge of electrical energy in the brain. They may be generalized or partial. Recurrent seizures are referred to as epilepsy. Most people with seizure disorders are able to function normally, except when having a seizure. Intelligence is not directly affected by a seizure disorder, so educational procedures consist chiefly of attaining knowledge of the disorder and how to manage seizures, as well as a commitment to help dispel the ignorance and fear connected with seizures.

Spina bifida is a congenital midline defect resulting from failure of the bony spinal column to close completely during fetal development. The resulting damage to the nerves generally causes paralysis and lack of sensation below the site of the defect. The cause of spina bifida is not known. Educational implications of spina bifida are determined by the extent of the paralysis and medical complications, as well as the child's cognitive and behavioral characteristics. Intelligence and physical stamina are not directly affected by spina bifida, so most children with this condition attend regular classes.

An increasingly frequent cause of neurological impairment is traumatic head injury, frequently occurring as a result of vehicular accidents. The brain injury may range from mild to profound. Medical and educational personnel must work together as a team to provide transition from hospital or rehabilitation center to school. Frequent educational problems are focusing or sustaining attention, remembering, and learning new skills. Emotional, behavioral, and social problems may also be apparent. Traumatic brain injury became a separate category of disability under IDEA in 1990.

A number of physical disabilities derive from musculoskeletal conditions, in which there are defects or diseases of the muscles or bones. Children with such disabilities have a range of difficulties in walking, standing, sitting, or using their hands. Muscular dystrophy is a degenerative disease causing a progressive weakening and wasting away of muscle tissues. Progressive physical immobility and the prospect of total disability or death make this condition especially difficult to manage. But intellectual capacity is not affected, and with proper motivation and educational procedures, most of these children can benefit from regular or special education programs. Arthritis is a disease that causes acute inflammation around the joints; its symptoms vary from mild to profound, and it affects children as well as adults. These and other musculoskeletal conditions do not cause lowered intelligence, so educational considerations include overcoming the child's limited mobility so that he or she can continue learning in as normal a way as possible.

Congenital malformations can involve any organ system, including the head and face, the heart and/or blood vessels, the hip or other joints, or the extremities (e.g., webbed or extra fingers or toes or other deformities of the hands or feet). Some malformations are genetic (caused by faulty chromosomes); others are caused by teratogens. Teratogens are deformity-producing factors, such as chemicals or infections, that interfere with normal fetal development. Alcohol is now the most common teratogen.

Accidents that bring about neurological impairment, disfigurement, or amputation are an important cause of physical disabilities among children and youths. AIDS, a fatal viral infection, is now forcing schools to make controversial decisions regarding sex education and inclusion of children and adults with the disease in the classroom. The number of infants and young children with AIDS is increasing dramatically because pregnant women with AIDS transmit the disease to their babies. The complications of the disease in its advanced stages include mental retardation, psychosis, seizures, and neurological impairment similar to cerebral palsy. (Congenital infections affect a large number of children and can result in serious disabilities.)

Adolescent pregnancy often results in children with physical disabilities. Teenage mothers are more likely than older women to give birth to premature babies or babies with disabilities and more likely also to abuse or neglect their children.

Besides alcohol, women may abuse other substances during pregnancy and thereby give birth to a child with disabilities. Use of cocaine and intravenous drugs by pregnant women is resulting in the birth of more babies with severe physiological, cognitive, and emotional problems.

Children who are medically fragile or dependent on ventilators are being returned home from hospitals in increasing numbers. Many of these children are returning to public schools. Careful consideration of the mainstreaming of these children is required.

Abused and neglected children represent an alarming and large number of those with physical disabilities. Many thousands of children each year are damaged—emotionally and physically—by adults who neglect, burn, beat, sexually molest, starve, and otherwise brutalize them. Children who already have disabilities are more likely to be abused than those without disabilities. Teachers must be especially alert to signs of possible child abuse and neglect.

As a group, children with physical disabilities represent the total range of impairment, and their behavioral and psychological characteristics vary greatly.

The necessity for hospitalization, bed rest, prosthetic devices, and so on means that their academic achievement depends on individual circumstances, motivation, and the caliber of care received both at home and at school. The two major effects of a physical disability, especially if it is severe or prolonged, are that a child may be deprived of educationally relevant experiences and that he or she may not be able to learn to manipulate educational materials and respond to educational tasks the way most children do.

There does not appear to be a personality type associated with particular physical disabilities. The reactions of the public, family, peers, and educational personnel—as well as the child's own reactions to the disability—are all closely interwoven in the determination of any particular child's personality, motivation, and progress. Given ample opportunity to develop educationally, socially, and emotionally in as normal a fashion as possible, many children with physical disabilities are able to make a healthy adjustment to their impairments.

A prosthesis replaces a missing body part. An orthosis is a device that enhances the partial function of a body part. An adaptive device aids a person's daily activity. Important considerations in choosing prostheses, orthoses, and adaptive devices are simplicity, reliability, and the use of residual function.

Education for students with physical disabilities must focus on making the most of their assets. The student's individual characteristics (intellectual, sensory, physical, and emotional) must be considered when developing educational plans. Plans for young children must include service to the family. Increasingly, students with physical disabilities are being placed in regular classrooms. The problem of educating students with physical disabilities is often a problem of educating students without disabilities about the needs of people with disabilities. Along with scholastic education, the child may need special assistance in daily living, mobility, and occupational skills. Consequently, many other disciplines may be involved. The major considerations are to help each child become as independent and self-sufficient in daily activities as possible, to provide basic academic skills, and to prepare for advanced education and work.

Besides early identification and intervention to develop communication, handling and positioning are important considerations. Motor skills must be taught as part of daily lessons in self-help and communication.

Career choice and sociosexuality are two primary concerns of youths with physical disabilities. Career considerations must include careful evaluation of the young person's intellectual, emotional, and motivational characteristics as well as physical capabilities. Young people with physical disabilities have the right to the social relationships and modes of sexual expression afforded others in our society.

ALONZO CLEMONS

Alonzo Clemons, diagnosed as having Savant syndrome, has been a prolific sculptor since childhood. With no art lessons or even a visit to a zoo, his first works are remarkable likenesses of animals he has never seen. His work has been shown widely and he is recognized for his craftsmanship. A single glimpse of any animal is sufficient for him to produce astounding likenesses. Asked about the source of his genius, he replies, "My hand."

I think Jim Gillis was a much more remarkable person than his family and his intimates ever suspected. He had a bright and smart imagination and it was of the kind that turns out impromptu work and does it well, does it with easy facility and without previous preparation, just builds a story as it goes along, careless of whether it is proceeding, enjoying each fresh fancy as it flashes from the brain and caring not at all whether the story shall ever end brilliantly and satisfactorily or shan't end at all. Jim was born a humorist and a very competent one. When I remember how felicitous were his untrained efforts, I feel a conviction that he would have been a star performer if he had been discovered and had been subjected to a few years of training with a pen. A genius is not very likely to ever discover himself; neither is he very likely to be discovered by his intimates; they are so close to him that he is out of focus to them and they can't get at his proportions; they cannot perceive that there is any considerable difference between his bulk and their own. They can't get a perspective on him and it is only by a perspective that the difference between him and the rest of their limited circle can be perceived.

> *The Autobiography of Mark Twain*

Giftedness

▲ ▲ ▲

People who have special gifts, or at least have the potential for gifted per-
▲ ▲ ▲ formance, can go through life unrecognized. As Mark Twain pointed
out (see page 445), they may seem unremarkable to their closest associates.
Sometimes gifted children and youths are not discovered because their families
and intimates simply place no particular value on their special abilities.
Sometimes they are not recognized because they are not given the necessary
opportunities or training. Especially in the case of those who are poor or members
of minority groups, gifted children may be deprived of chances to demonstrate
and develop their potential. How many more outstanding artists and scientists
would we have if every talented child had the opportunity and the training necessary to develop his or her talents to the fullest possible extent? There is no way of
knowing, but it is safe to say we would have more.

Unlike mental retardation and other disabling conditions, giftedness is something to be fostered, not eliminated. Yet giftedness is not something a child can
show without risk of stigma and rejection. Many people have a low level of tolerance for those who are intellectually superior or who eclipse the ordinary individual in some area of achievement. A child who achieves far beyond the level of
his or her average peers may be subject to criticism or social isolation by other
children or their parents. Had Jim Gillis been discovered, given a few years of
training with a pen, and become a gifted writer, it is possible that some of his
intimates would have found his giftedness hard to accept.

Some of the problems presented by giftedness parallel those presented by the
disabling conditions we have discussed in the other chapters of this book. For
instance, the definition and identification of gifted children involve the same sort
of difficulties that exist in the case of children with mental retardation or an emotional or behavioral disorder. But there is an underlying philosophical question
regarding giftedness that makes us think differently about this exceptionality.
Most of us feel a moral obligation to help those who are at some disadvantage
compared to the average person, who have a deficiency that prevents them from
achieving an ordinary level of competence unless they are given special help. In
the case of gifted students, though, we may wonder about our moral obligation
to help those who are already advantaged to become even better, to distinguish
themselves further by fulfilling the highest promise of their extraordinary
resources. It is on this issue—the desirability or necessity of helping our most
capable children become even better—that special education for gifted students
is likely to founder.

DEFINITION

Children with special gifts excel in some way compared to other children of the
same age. Beyond this almost meaningless statement, you will find little agreement about how giftedness should be defined (Gallagher, 1985; Maker, 1986).
The disagreements are due primarily to differences of opinion regarding the following questions:

1. *In what ways do gifted children excel?* Do they excel in general intelligence,
   insight, creativity, special talents, and achievements in academic subjects

We are indebted to Dr. Carolyn M. Callahan of the University of Virginia for her invaluable assistance in the preparation of this chapter.

▶ ▶ PERSONS WITH GIFTEDNESS

MYTH ➤ Gifted people are physically weak, socially inept, narrow in interests, and prone to emotional instability and early decline.

FACT ➤ Although there are wide individual variations, gifted individuals as a group tend to be exceptionally healthy, well adjusted, socially attractive, and morally responsible.

MYTH ➤ Gifted individuals are in a sense "superhuman."

FACT ➤ Gifted people are not "superhuman"; rather, they are human beings with extraordinary gifts in particular areas, and like everyone else, they may have particular faults.

MYTH ➤ Gifted children are usually bored with school and antagonistic toward those who are responsible for their education.

FACT ➤ Gifted children usually like school and adjust well to their peers and teachers.

MYTH ➤ Gifted people tend to be mentally unstable.

FACT ➤ Those who are gifted are likely to be well-adjusted, emotionally healthy people.

MYTH ➤ We know that 3 to 5 percent of the population is gifted.

FACT ➤ The percentage of the population that is gifted depends on the definition of giftedness that one uses. Some definitions include only 1 or 2 percent of the population, others over 20 percent.

MYTH ➤ Giftedness is a stable trait, always consistently evident in all periods of a person's life.

FACT ➤ Some gifted people's remarkable talents and productivity develop early and continue throughout life; in other cases, a person's gifts or talents are not noticed until adulthood, and occasionally a child who shows outstanding ability becomes a nondescript adult.

MYTH ➤ Gifted people do everything well.

FACT ➤ Some people known as gifted have superior abilities of many kinds; others are clearly superior in only one area.

MYTH ➤ A person is gifted if he or she scores above a certain level on intelligence tests.

FACT ➤ IQ is only one indication of giftedness. Creativity and high motivation are as important indications as general intelligence. Gifts or talents in some areas, such as the visual and performing arts, are not assessed by IQ tests.

MYTH ➤ Gifted students will excel without special education. Students who are truly gifted need only the incentives and instruction that are appropriate for all students.

FACT ➤ Some gifted children will perform at a remarkably high level without special education of any kind. Some will make outstanding contributions even in the face of great obstacles to their achievement. But most will not come close to achieving at a level commensurate with their potential unless their talents are deliberately fostered by incentives and instruction that are appropriate for their advanced abilities.

or in a valued line of work, moral judgment, or some combination of such factors? Perhaps nearly everyone is gifted in some way or other. What kind of giftedness is most important? What kind of giftedness should we try to encourage?

2. *How is giftedness measured?* Is it measured by standardized tests of aptitude and achievement, teacher judgments, past performance in school or in everyday life, or by some other means? If it is measured in one particular way, some individuals will be overlooked. If past performance is the test, we are defining giftedness after the fact. What measurement techniques can we have confidence in? What measurements will tell us which children have the potential to become gifted?

3. *To what degree must a child excel to be considered gifted?* Must the child do better than 50 percent, 80 percent, 90 percent, or 99 percent of the comparison group? The number of gifted individuals will vary depending on the criterion (or criteria) for giftedness. What percentage of the population do we want to be gifted?

4. *Who should make up the comparison group?* Should it be every child of the same chronological age, the other children in the child's school, all children of the same ethnic or racial origin, or some other grouping? Almost everyone is the brightest or most capable in some group. What group should set the standard?

You may have concluded already that giftedness is whatever we choose to make it, just as mental retardation is whatever we choose to say it is. Someone can be considered gifted (or retarded) one day and not the next simply because we have changed an arbitrary definition. There is no inherent rightness or wrongness in the definitions professionals use. Some definitions may be more logical, more precise, or more useful than others, but we are still unable to say they are more "correct" in some absolute sense. We have to struggle with the concept of giftedness and the reasons for identifying gifted individuals before we can make any decisions about definition. Our definition of giftedness will be shaped to a large extent by what our culture believes is most useful or necessary for its survival. Giftedness is invented, not discovered (Sternberg & Davidson, 1986).

Even the terminology of giftedness can become rather confusing. Besides the word *gifted*, a variety of other terms have been used to describe individuals who are superior is some way: *talented, creative, insightful, genius,* and *precocious,* for example. **Precocity** refers to remarkable early development. Many highly gifted children show precocity in particular areas of development, such as language, music, or mathematical ability, and the rate of intellectual development of all gifted children exceeds the rate for nongifted children. **Insight** may be defined as separating relevant from irrelevant information, finding novel and useful ways of combining relevant bits of information, or relating new and old information in a novel and productive way. **Genius** has sometimes been used to indicate a particular aptitude or capacity in any area. More often, it has been used to indicate extremely rare intellectual powers (extremely high IQ or creativity). **Creativity** refers to the ability to express novel and useful ideas, to sense and elucidate novel and important relationships, and to ask previously unthought of, but crucial, questions. The word **talent** ordinarily has been used to indicate a special ability, aptitude, or accomplishment. **Giftedness,** as we use the term in this chapter, refers to cognitive (intellectual) superiority (not necessarily of genius caliber),

➤ **precocity.** Remarkable early development.

➤ **insight.** Ability to separate and/or combine various pieces of information in new, creative, or useful ways.

➤ **genius.** A word sometimes used to indicate a particular aptitude or capacity in any area; rare intellectual powers.

➤ **creativity.** Ability to express novel and useful ideas, to sense and elucidate new and important relationships, and to ask previously unthought of but crucial questions.

➤ **talent.** A special ability, aptitude, or accomplishment.

➤ **giftedness.** Refers to cognitive (intellectual) superiority, creativity, and motivation of sufficient magnitude to set the child apart from the vast majority of age-mates and make it possible for him or her to contribute something of particular value to society.

creativity, and motivation in combination and of sufficient magnitude to set the child apart from the vast majority of age-mates and make it possible for him or her to contribute something of particular value to society (Renzulli, Reis, & Smith, 1981).

Federal and State Definitions

Gifted students have special educational needs, but since giftedness is not a disability in any usual sense, it is not defined in IDEA (Individuals with Disabilities Education Act). No federal law requires special education for gifted students as it does for students with disabilities. Federal legislation does, however, encourage states to develop programs for gifted students and support research. Gifted and talented students are defined in federal law as children and youths who (1) give evidence of high performance capability in such areas as intellectual, creative, artistic, or leadership capacity or in specific academic fields and (2) require services or activities not ordinarily provided by the school in order to develop such capabilities fully.

In 1990, 26 states had mandatory programs for gifted students. Each state has its own definition of giftedness. The most common elements of state definitions in 1990 were (1) general intellectual ability, (2) specific academic aptitude, (3) creative thinking ability, (4) advanced ability in the fine arts and performing arts, and (5) leadership ability (Council of State Directors of Programs for the Gifted, 1991).

Changes in the Definition of Giftedness

The traditional definition of giftedness is based on general intelligence as measured by an individually administered intelligence test. That is, children have traditionally been considered gifted if they scored above a particular level. A definition of giftedness based solely on IQ was used in the classic studies of gifted children by Lewis Terman and his associates (published under the general title *Genetic Studies of Genius*). This definition (high IQ) has been used in many other studies and programs for the gifted. But in recent years there has been great dissatisfaction with the use of IQ as the single (or even most important) criterion for defining giftedness.

Intelligence and giftedness are more complex than the relatively narrow band of performances required to score exceptionally high on an intelligence test.* Furthermore, giftedness seems to be characterized by qualitative differences in thinking and insightfulness, which may not be clearly reflected by performance on intelligence tests (see Reis, 1989; Sternberg & Davidson, 1983). The box on the next page illustrates the type of insight that might be shown by a student who is gifted in mathematics. Because of the limitations of IQ tests, intelligence is being reconceptualized.

Reconceptualization of Intelligence

Whereas the usual tests of intelligence assess the ability to think deductively and arrive at a single answer that can be scored "right" or "wrong," tests of

---

*Recall that the limitations of IQ have become obvious also in the definition of mental retardation. An exceptionally low IQ by itself is no longer sufficient to define mental retardation but must be accompanied by deficits in adaptive behavior (see Chapter 4 and Zigler & Farber, 1985).

NSIGHT: A QUALITATIVE DIFFERENCE IN THINKING ➤

The thinking of gifted children is qualitatively different from that of ordinary people. Many times I have, in classes of gifted children, written on the blackboard:

1 + 2 + 4 + 8 + and so on + 1024 = ?

and asked the children to find the sum. Very often, I have hardly stated the problem before someone shouts out "2047!" If I ask, "How did you get it so fast?," a typical answer might be "1 + 2 is 3, and 4 more is 7, and the sum is always one less than the next number."

When I teach the same topic to average college students, I must explain the concept of a geometrical progression, how to recognize this problem as such, how to derive a formula for the sum, and then show how to apply it to this special case. The gifted children have a capacity for insights which cannot be taught at any level. If this ability exists, it can be developed and stimulated.

SOURCE: P. C. Rosenbloom, Programs for the gifted in mathematics, *Roeper Review*, 8 (1986), 243. Reprinted with permission.

creativity suggest many different potential answers. Recognition of the many facets of human intelligence led to dissatisfaction with previous conceptualizations of "general" intelligence or "primary mental abilities" (Maker, 1986). Today many researchers have concluded that "giftedness cannot possibly be captured by a single number" (Sternberg, 1991, p. 45). For example, Sternberg (1991) describes a theory of intelligence that suggests three main kinds of giftedness: analytic, synthetic, and practical. *Analytic* giftedness involves being able to take a problem apart—to understand the parts of a problem and how they are interrelated, which is a skill typically measured by conventional intelligence tests. *Synthetic* giftedness involves insight, intuition, creativity, or adeptness at coping with novel situations, skills typically associated with high achievement in the arts and sciences. *Practical* giftedness involves applying analytic and synthetic abilities to the solution of everyday problems, the kind of skills that characterize people who have successful careers.

> Of course, people do not possess just one of these different kinds of skills; rather they have some blend of the three. Moreover, this blend can change over time because intelligence can be developed in various directions.... An important part of giftedness is being able to coordinate these three aspects of abilities, and knowing when to use which. Giftedness is as much a well-managed balance of these three abilities as it is a high score on any one or more of them. I therefore sometimes refer to a gifted person as a good "mental self-manager." (Sternberg, 1991, p. 46)

Other researchers are finding evidence of multiple intelligences (Gardner & Hatch, 1989). Seven different kinds of intelligence, their end states (adult roles assumed by people high in that intelligence), and core components are shown in Table 11–1. Gardner and Hatch (1989) are convinced that these seven intelligences are highly independent and that nearly all children and adults show distinctive profiles of strength and weakness in the different kinds of intelligence. They suggest that these intelligences cannot all be measured through the usual types of testing but must be assessed in the natural contexts in which they can be exhibited. Consequently, Gardner and others are devising curriculum activities that allow children to develop and demonstrate their intelligences in common or typical contexts (Ramos, Ford, & Gardner, 1991). For example, young children's intelligences may be assessed by using the kinds of materials and activities with which they have become familiar in their preschool.

(a)

(b)

(c)

(d)

(e)

(f)

(g)

Giftedness and talent of many kinds are recognized. (a) Maya Ying Lin is a sculptor recognized for designing the Vietnam Memorial in Washington, DC; (b) Yo-Yo Ma and Bobby McFerrin for their musical talent; (c) Gabriel García Marquez for his contribution to literature; (d) Michael Jordan for his athletic ability; (e) Stephen B. Hawking for his brilliance as an astrophysicist; (f) Maya Angelou for her exquisite poetry and stories; and (g) Bill Gates, founder of Microsoft, for his computer and business acumen.

Table 11-1 ➢ The Seven Intelligences

INTELLIGENCE	END-STATES	CORE COMPONENTS
Logical-mathematical	Scientist Mathematician	Sensitivity to, and capacity to discern, logical or numerical patterns; ability to handle long chains of reasoning
Linguistic	Poet Journalist	Sensitivity to the sounds, rhythms, and meanings of words; sensitivity to the different functions of language
Musical	Composer Violinist	Abilities to produce and appreciate rhythm, pitch, and timbre; appreciation of the forms of musical expressiveness
Spatial	Navigator Sculptor	Capacities to perceive the visual-spatial world accurately and to perform transformations on one's initial perceptions
Bodily-kinesthetic	Dancer Athlete	Abilities to control one's body movements and to handle objects skillfully
Interpersonal	Therapist Salesman	Capacities to discern and respond appropriately to the moods, temperaments, motivations, and desires of other people
Intrapersonal	Person with detailed, accurate self-knowledge	Access to one's own feelings and the ability to discriminate among them and draw upon them to guide behavior; knowledge of one's own strengths, weaknesses, desires, and intelligences

SOURCE: H. Gardner & T. Hatch, Multiple intelligences go to school: Educational implications of the theory of multiple intelligences, *Educational Researcher, 18*(8) (1989), 6.

Whether intelligence should be lumped into a general characteristic or split into distinctive parts is an ongoing debate with significant implications for defining giftedness (Reis, 1989). Regardless of how the debate is ultimately resolved, it is clear that we have come a long way since the invention of the IQ in conceptualizing human intelligence.

Perhaps giftedness is not a fixed or absolute human characteristic. A person may be gifted if the conditions are right for gifted performance—if, besides possessing above-average ability and creativity, the person is given opportunities and incentives to perform at an extraordinarily high level. Perhaps we should speak of people who exhibit *gifted behavior* rather than of *gifted people* because

ifted children have superior cognitive abilities that allow them to compete with adults of average intellect.

people typically act gifted only under particular circumstances. These are relatively new ideas about giftedness that have been suggested by Keating (1980) and Renzulli and Reis (1991b).

In short, giftedness today is seen as a much more complex phenomenon than it was even a decade ago. The field is moving toward an appreciation of the neurophysiological factors involved in gifted performance and the ways in which intelligence is manifested in various domains of human endeavor.

A Suggested Definition

As mentioned earlier, an adequate definition of giftedness includes the requirement that a person show at least the *potential* for making a remarkable and valued contribution to the human condition. The problem, then, is one of predicting future performance. Given what is known about people whose achievements have been remarkable, we believe that gifted children should be defined (as suggested by Renzulli and Reis 1991b) for purposes of education as those who have demonstrated or shown potential for the following in a given domain or field:

1. High ability (including high intelligence)
2. High creativity (the ability to formulate new ideas and apply them to the solution of problems)
3. High task commitment (a high level of motivation and the ability to see a project through to its conclusion)

The reason for using the multiple-criterion definition is that all three characteristics—high ability, high creativity, and high task commitment—seem to be necessary for truly gifted performance in any field.

PREVALENCE

It has been assumed in federal reports and legislation that 3 to 5 percent of the school population could be considered gifted or talented. Obviously the prevalence of giftedness is a function of the definition chosen. If giftedness is defined as the top x percent on a given criterion, the question of prevalence has been answered. Of course, if x percent refers to a percentage of a national sample, the prevalence of gifted pupils in a given school or cultural group may vary from the comparison group. When IQ is used as the sole or primary criterion for giftedness, more gifted children will come from homes of higher socioeconomic status, have fewer siblings, and have better-educated parents. Although giftedness by nearly any definition occurs in all socioeconomic strata, gifted children are not distributed equally across all social classes when IQ is the primary means of identification. This is one of the reasons for abandoning IQ as the sole criterion for defining giftedness.

Renzulli (1982) argues convincingly that the assumption that only 3 to 5 percent of the population is gifted is needlessly restrictive and may result in many potentially gifted students' contributions being overlooked. He notes that 15 to 25 percent of all children may have sufficient ability, motivation, and creativity to exhibit gifted behavior at some time during their school career. Renzulli and Reiss (1991b) suggest identifying about 15 percent of students in most schools for a "talent pool" to serve as the major (but not the only) target group for supplementary services.

ORIGINS OF GIFTEDNESS

It is not really surprising that brilliant parents are more likely to have gifted children than are parents of average or lower intelligence. We also know that an impoverished environment is less likely to produce children who will fulfill their potential for gifted behavior than one in which models of gifted performance, opportunities for learning, and appropriate rewards are richly provided. Of course, the giftedness of some children becomes evident even though their parents are intellectually dull and even though they experience environmental disadvantages. But the statistical probability of giftedness increases when the child's parents have higher than average intelligence and provide a better than average environment for the child. Some things that are not fully understood about the origins of giftedness and will take particularly well-designed research to discover, include the *relative* contribution of **genetic** and environmental factors to giftedness and the *precise nature* of the genetic and environmental factors that contribute to giftedness.

➢ **genetics.** The biological study of heredity.

Genetic and Other Biological Factors

The proposition that intelligence and highly valued abilities are inherited is not a very popular one in our egalitarian society. It can be used as a springboard for arguments for selective reproduction of humans (with intelligence or other characteristics being the primary factors in selection of mates) and as a reason to downplay the importance of improving environmental conditions for citizens already born or conceived.

New conceptions of intelligence and giftedness might at first thought seem to allow us to sidestep the issue of genetic factors in giftedness. That is, if IQ is abandoned as the criterion for defining giftedness in favor of a variety of practical intelligences (see Table 11–1 on page 452), giftedness might be seen as something that is less affected by genetics. Research in behavioral genetics, however, suggests that every type of behavioral development is affected significantly by genes.

> The first message of behavioral genetic research is that genetic influence on individual differences in behavioral development is usually significant and often substantial. Genetic influence is so ubiquitous and pervasive in behavior that a shift in emphasis is warranted: Ask not what is heritable, ask what is not heritable. (Plomin, 1989, p. 108)

The fact that giftedness is partly inherited, regardless of how it is defined, should not be misinterpreted as an indication that environmental factors are unimportant. Although genetic influences on the development of superior abilities cannot be denied, these biological influences are clearly no more important than the environments in which children are nurtured.

Biological factors that are not genetic may also contribute to the determination of intelligence. Nutritional and neurological factors, for example, may partially determine how intellectually competent a child becomes. In previous chapters we pointed out that severe malnutrition in infancy or childhood, as well as neurological damage at any age, can result in mental retardation. But it does not follow that superior nutrition and neurological status early in life contribute to superior intelligence.

Studies of individuals with high IQ, such as Terman's classic studies, typically have shown them to be physically superior to others of lesser intelligence in characteristics such as height, weight, attractiveness, and health in adulthood as well as in childhood. However, it is not clear whether these physical characteristics are a result of generally advantaged environments or of another factor that accounts for superior intellect.

More adult males than females are considered gifted and creative. By an overwhelming margin, men achieve outstanding status and recognition more frequently than women of the same age. However, there is little evidence that these performance differences are the result of biological differences. The available research points far more clearly to social and cultural expectations as an explanation for the disproportionate number of males who are recognized as gifted (Conroy, 1989; Eccles, 1985).

In summary, genetic factors clearly are involved in the determination of giftedness. Environmental influences alone cannot account for the fact that some individuals perform so far above the average. We emphasize, however, that an individual does not inherit an IQ or talent. What is inherited is a collection of genes that, along with experiences, determine the limits of intelligence and other abilities (Zigler & Farber, 1985).

Environmental Factors

Families, schools, the peer group, and communities obviously have a profound influence on the development of giftedness (Tannenbaum, 1991). Stimulation, opportunities, expectations, demands, and rewards for performance affect children's learning. For decades, researchers have found a correlation between socioeconomic level and IQ, undoubtedly in part because the performances measured by standard intelligence tests are based on what families, schools, and communities of the upper classes expect and teach. As definitions of intelligence and giftedness are broadened to include a wider range of skills and abilities that are not so specific to socioeconomic class, we will no doubt see changes in the way we view environmental effects on giftedness.

Plomin (1989) suggests that we must recognize the important influence of genetics in behavioral development, but this is not his only message:

> The second message [of behavioral genetic research] is just as important: These same data provide the best available evidence of the importance of environment. The data . . . suggest pandemic genetic influence, but they also indicate that nongenetic factors are responsible for more than half of the variance in most complex behaviors. . . . The phrase "behavioral genetics" is in a sense a misnomer because it is as much the study of nurture as nature. (p. 108)

We must ask, therefore, how families, schools, and the larger culture can nurture children's giftedness.

Research has shown that parents differ greatly in their attitudes toward and management of their gifted children. Some parents view having a gifted child as positive, some as negative; fathers appear to see their children as gifted less often than mothers (Cornell, 1983; see also Silverman, 1991). A study of individuals who have been successful in a variety of fields has shown that the home and family, especially in the child's younger years, are extremely important (Bloom, 1982; Bloom & Sosniak, 1981). The following were found to occur in the families of highly successful persons:

- Someone in the family (usually one or both parents) had a personal interest in the child's talent and provided great support and encouragement for its development.
- Most of the parents were role models (at least at the start of their child's development of talent), especially in terms of life-style.
- There was specific parental encouragement of the child to explore, to participate in home activities related to the area of developing talent, and to join the family in related activities. Small signs of interest and capability by the child were rewarded.
- Parents took it for granted that their children would learn in the area of talent, just as they would learn language.
- Expected behaviors and values related to the talent were present in the family. Clear schedules and standards for performance appropriate for the child's stage of development were held.
- Teaching was informal and occurred in a variety of settings. Early learning was exploratory and much like play.
- The family interacted with a tutor/mentor and received information to guide the child's practice (interaction included specific tasks to be accomplished, information or specific points to be emphasized or problems to be solved, a set time by which the child could be expected to achieve specific goals and objectives, and the amount of time to be devoted to practice).
- Parents observed practice, insisted that the child put in the required amount of practice time, provided instruction where necessary, and rewarded the child whenever something was done especially well or when a standard was met.
- Parents sought special instruction and special teachers for the child.
- Parents encouraged participation in events (recitals, concerts, contests, etc.) in which the child's capabilities were displayed in public.

We may conclude that children who realize their potential for accomplishment most fully have families that are stimulating, directive, supportive, and rewarding of their abilities. Research does not indicate much else about how families encourage gifted performance. Moreover, the stresses and needs of families of gifted children are poorly understood (Silverman, 1991).

We have paid too little attention to how schools themselves may nurture children's giftedness. The ways in which schools identify giftedness, group children for instruction, design curricula, and reward performance have a profound effect on what the most able students achieve. When schools facilitate the performance of all students who are able to achieve at a superior level in specific areas, giftedness is found among children of all cultural and socioeconomic groups (Feldhusen, 1989; Frazier, 1989; Mills, Stork, & Krug, 1992; Whitmore, 1987).

*G*iftedness in children is greatly
benefited by opportunities to
learn advanced skills,
encouragement from positive adult role
models, and the right teachers.

Several studies, including Terman's early work, have found that some cultural or ethnic groups produce a higher than average number of gifted children even when differences in socioeconomic level are taken into account (Mistry & Rogoff, 1985). It may be that striving for upward social mobility and the high value attached to achievement in specific areas among certain cultural and ethnic groups contribute to giftedness. In spite of severe socioeconomic disadvantages, some cultures are able to foster high academic achievement in schools in which most other students perform very poorly (Caplan, Choy, & Whitmore, 1992).

Cultural factors work against the development and recognition of gifted females (Eccles, 1985). Females simply have not been provided with equal opportunity and motivation to enter into many academic disciplines or careers that have by tradition been dominated by males, such as chemistry, physics, medicine, and dentistry. When females do enter these fields, they have often been rewarded inappropriately (according to irrelevant criteria or with affection rather than promotion) for their performance. English literature has tended to portray females as wives, mothers, or "weaker" sisters who are either dependent on males or sacrifice themselves for the sake of males who are dominant. These barriers to giftedness in females have only recently been brought forcefully to public attention. Although the barriers to females' achieving giftedness and using their special abilities in careers have not been entirely eliminated, much progress has been made. Kerr (1991) points out that "young gifted women are choosing professional careers in almost equal proportions to gifted young men," and "business has replaced education as the most popular career choice of bright young women" (p. 402).

In summary, environmental influences have much to do with how a child's genetic endowment is expressed in performance. But neither environment nor genetics can be entirely responsible for the performance of gifted or retarded individuals. Genetic factors apparently determine the range within which a person will function, and environmental factors determine whether the individual will function in the lower or upper reaches of that range.

IDENTIFICATION OF GIFTEDNESS

Measurement of giftedness is a complicated matter. Some components cannot be assessed by traditional means. In addition, the particular definition of giftedness will determine how test scores are interpreted. But if it is indeed important to identify gifted children early so that they will achieve self-fulfillment and be aided in the development of their special potential to make a unique and valuable contribution to society, it is important that appropriate methods be used.

The most common methods of identification include IQ (based on group or individual tests), standardized achievement test scores, teacher nominations, parent nominations, peer nominations, self-nominations, and evaluations of students' work or performances. Typically, some combination of several of these methods is used. Identification practices have been extremely controversial, and best practices have frequently been ignored. Richert (1991) lists six "rampant" problems in identification practices:

1. Elitist and distorted definitions of giftedness
2. Confusion about the purpose of identification
3. Violation of education equity
4. Misuse and abuse of tests
5. Cosmetic and distorting use of multiple criteria
6. Exclusive program design (p. 81)

The concerns expressed by this list are that biased and unreliable criteria for identifying giftedness (e.g., overreliance on IQ and achievement tests) are sometimes used to provide special educational opportunities in an exclusive program that is discriminatory, even when school systems claim that they are using multiple and fair criteria (e.g., the criteria may all measure essentially the same thing). As Renzulli and Reis (1991b) put it, in some cases "the multiple criteria game ends up being a smoke screen for the same old test-based approach" (p. 118). Yet it is possible to develop identification methods that are fair, reliable, equitable, and do not result in an exclusive or discriminatory program design (Renzulli & Reis, 1991b; Shore, Cornell, Robinson, & Ward, 1991).

Renzulli and Reis (1991b) describe a six-step identification system associated with their definition of giftedness (which, as we mentioned earlier, consists of above-average ability, task commitment, and creativity). The six steps result in the nomination of students according to multiple criteria and the eventual identification of a "talent pool" of about 15 to 25 percent of the school enrollment. Step one is nomination on the basis of test scores—any single test or subtest score or other performance indicator that would put the student in the top 8 percent according to local norms. Step two is teacher nominations. Teachers are informed of which students in their classes have been nominated by test scores and are asked to name any additional students who show particularly high levels of creativity, task commitment, interest, talent, performance, or potential. Step three allows for alternative pathways to identification—nomination by parents, peers, or self, tests of creativity, product evaluations, or any other pathway that can be reviewed by a screening committee or evaluated in a case study approach. In step four, a list of all nominated students is circulated to all teachers in the school and to past teachers who may know of students' abilities that have somehow gone unrecognized in steps one through three. The idea of step four is to provide a "safety net" for recognition of students who might otherwise have been over- looked. Step five involves notification and orientation of parents. Parents and students are not told that "gifted" students have been identified; rather, the nature of the program for students in the talent pool this year is described. Step six provides another "safety valve" by seeking nominations from teachers throughout the year when they notice a student's high interest in a particular topic, area of study, issue, idea, or event taking place in or outside of school. Steps leading to the identification of a talent pool are shown in Figure 11–1 on page 460.

Although no identification system is perfect, the procedures described by Renzulli and Reis (1991b) have widespread support and are consistent with rec- ommended practices (Shore et al., 1991). The focus of identification methods should be on balancing concern for identifying only those students whose capabilities are markedly above average with concern for including all who show promise for gifted performance.

PHYSICAL, PSYCHOLOGICAL, AND BEHAVIORAL CHARACTERISTICS

Although intellectual precocity has been recognized throughout recorded history (Morelock & Feldman, 1991), the gifted individual has been persistently stereo- typed as physically weak, socially inept, narrow in interests, and prone to emo- tional instability and early decline. Terman's early studies, and many others, shattered the myth that giftedness carries with it a set of undesirable characteris- tics. In fact, it now appears that gifted children tend to be superior in every way—in intelligence, in physique, in social attractiveness, in achievement, in emotional stability, even in moral character. The danger now is a developing stereotype of the gifted child as "superhuman," as someone immune to ordinary frailties and defects.

This new stereotype probably has its roots in a misunderstanding of (or sim- ply insufficient attention to) two statistical phenomena: dispersion of scores around a mean and intercorrelation among characteristics. Although it is true that *as a group* gifted people are superior in almost every characteristic, individu- als deviate from the mean for the group. There are indeed gifted children who are weak, small, sickly, socially obtuse, underachieving, unattractive, or other- wise below par compared to age-mates of normal intelligence. Gifted children who have disabilities have been neglected, partly because it is hard for us to entertain the thought that people with disabilities can be superior in any way or that people who are gifted may have disabilities. Gifted children as a group have specific characteristics that show about as much variation around the mean as the variation shown by any other group around its mean.

Furthermore, the intercorrelation among the characteristics of gifted children can be misleading. For example, could it be that physical superiority actually is a characteristic of children of higher socioeconomic status, many of whom happen

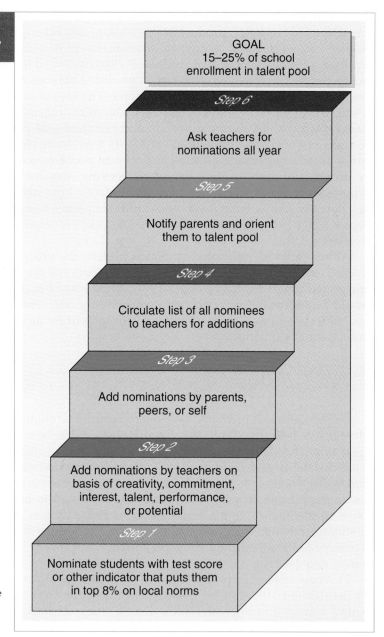

SOURCE: Based on data from J. S. Renzulli & S. M. Reis, The schoolwide enrichment model: A comprehensive plan for the development of creative productivity. In N. Colangelo & G. A. Davis (Eds.), (1991), *Handbook of gifted education*, Allyn & Bacon.

to be gifted? It is not really clear which attributes of children who are superior in ability, creativity, and motivation are just coincidental with giftedness. Here, of course, we will be making generalizations about a group, not individuals.

Physical Characteristics

As we have mentioned, study after study, beginning with Terman's work, has shown that gifted children as a group are taller, heavier, stronger, more energetic, and healthier than other children their age who have average intelligence. Terman and Oden (1959) followed gifted children identified in Terman's earlier work

(1926) into middle age and found that they maintained their superior physical characteristics. Many gifted children are outstanding in athletic ability and are superior competitors in a variety of sports.

Three cautions are in order. First, although gifted children clearly tend to outstrip their average age-mates in both mental and physical characteristics by the time they are several years old, their superiority does not appear to be detectable at birth or even during the first year in most cases. Second, since there is a sizable correlation between IQ and socioeconomic status, the apparent physical superiority of gifted children may be a result of nonintellectual factors. Third, as the definition and identification of giftedness become more equitable and inclusive of different kinds of abilities, we may find that the correlation between giftedness and physical superiority diminishes.

Educational and Occupational Characteristics

Gifted children tend to be far ahead of average children in academic achievement. Most learn to read easily; many of them are taught to read by their parents or teach themselves before they enter school. Many are more advanced in reading than in areas that require manual dexterity, such as writing and art, and more advanced in reading than in math, which depends more on sequential development of concepts and skills. Contrary to popular opinion, which pictures gifted students as constantly bored with and antagonistic toward school, most gifted children like school and love to learn (Gallagher, 1985). Many gifted students are younger than their classmates because of their superior academic performance.

Not surprisingly, gifted people tend to enter occupations demanding greater than average intellectual ability, creativity, and motivation. Most find their way into the ranks of professionals and managers, and a high proportion distinguish themselves among their peers in adulthood. Occupationally, as educationally, they tend to be winners (Gallagher, 1985; Perrone, 1991; Terman, 1926; Terman & Oden, 1959).

But again, it is important to remember that this description does not hold true for *every* gifted person. It is not unusual for a gifted child to be unrecognized by school personnel or to become unpopular with teachers because of such characteristics as inquisitiveness, unusual knowledge and wit, or boredom with unchallenging school work. It is an unfortunate fact that much talent goes to waste because school personnel are oblivious of the needs of gifted children or refuse to alter the lockstep plan of education for the sake of superior students.

Social and Emotional Characteristics

Gifted children tend to be happy and well liked by their peers. Many are social leaders at school. Most are emotionally stable and self-sufficient and are less prone to neurotic and psychotic disorders than average children. They have wide and varied interests and perceive themselves in positive terms (Coleman & Fultz, 1985; Janos & Robinson, 1985).

One area of giftedness often overlooked until recently is emotional giftedness—extraordinary sensitivity to one's own feelings and to others', for example. As a group, it appears that gifted children, youths, and adults are particularly aware of and concerned about interpersonal and intrapersonal events and issues. Piechowski (1991) summarizes as follows:

The outstanding feature of the emotional development of the gifted is their emotional sensitivity and intensity. Sometimes it is hidden; sometimes it is prominent. In an exploratory study of emotional growth of gifted adolescents, we found that only a small number followed a type of growth oriented more toward outward achievement and recognition than toward introspection and emotional awareness. The introspective type of emotional growth was rather free of the self-consciousness and egocentrism characteristic of early adolescence. Instead it displayed an awareness of one's real self, and understanding of feelings and emotions, an empathic approach to others, and much focus on inner growth through searching, questioning, carrying on an inner dialogue, and exercising self-corrective judgment. We associate these characteristics with emotional giftedness because it is in self-scrutiny and self-judgment that we find ourselves wanting; this leads us to develop a more accepting and compassionate understanding of others. Out of emotional sensitivity grows the desire to be of help to others, and the ideal of service is its fulfillment. (p. 303)

The emotional and social aspects of giftedness include concern for moral and ethical behavior. There is a tendency among most of us to hope that those who are the brightest are also the best—that moral attributes such as fairness, honesty, compassion, and justice go along with intelligence. Gifted individuals should be able to act on what is right as they see it, and they should be able to perceive what is right more quickly or more profoundly than the average person. However, the corruptibility of major figures in every profession in every society raises questions about the moral and ethical superiority of gifted persons. Here again, we must qualify the discussion by stating that there are individual differences among gifted people and that not every gifted person will be characterized by the description that fits the group. Most studies show gifted people to be superior to average individuals in concern for moral and ethical issues and in moral behavior (Gallagher, 1985; Piechowski, 1991). At an earlier age than most, gifted children tend to be concerned with abstract concepts of good and evil, right and wrong, justice and injustice (Galbraith, 1985; Hollingworth, 1942; Terman, 1926). They tend to be particularly concerned with social problems and the ways they can be resolved. The immoral, unethical gifted individual seems to be the exception rather than the rule. It may be that gifted people are the ones who have the greatest potential for helping individuals and societies resolve their moral and ethical dilemmas. It is worth remembering that almost any definition of giftedness will include people who are recognized as moral giants (Gruber, 1985; Piechowski, 1991).

When gifted students complain, what are their gripes? Galbraith (1985) studied the complaints of over 400 gifted students in six states. Approximately equal numbers of boys' and girls' responses to surveys and interviews were obtained. The students ranged in age from 7 to 18 years. The eight most frequent complaints are listed in the box on page 463. Notice that most of these gripes are not peculiar to students identified as gifted. However, Galbraith's findings do suggest that gifted students need more than intellectual challenge to feel good about themselves and use their special abilities to the fullest.

One common and persistent notion regarding gifted people, especially those who excel in the arts, is that they are prone to mental disease. It has been especially difficult to destroy the myth that creative excellence is linked to mental illness. Some great artists, musicians, and scientists have gone through periods of mental instability or psychosis, but their achievements were probably made in spite of, not because of, their emotional distress. The misconception that gifted

THE EIGHT GREAT GRIPES OF GIFTED KIDS ➤

1. No one explains what being gifted is all about—it's kept a big secret.
2. The stuff we do in school is too easy and it's boring.
3. Parents, teachers and friends expect us to be perfect, to "do our best" all the time.
4. Kids often tease us about being smart.
5. Friends who really understand us are few and far between.
6. We feel too different and wish people would accept us for what we are.
7. We feel overwhelmed by the number of things we can do in life.
8. We worry a lot about world problems and feel helpless to do anything about them.

SOURCE: From J. Galbraith, The eight great gripes of gifted kids: Responding to special needs, *Roeper Review, 7* (1985), 16. Reprinted with permission.

people tend to be social misfits and emotionally unstable was abetted by a classic study by Leta Hollingworth (1942) of children who tested at 180 or higher IQ. She reported that these children were quite isolated from their peers and not very well adjusted as adults (see Morelock & Feldman, 1991). But we should check into the representativeness of her sample of gifted children:

> In twenty-three years' seeking in New York City and the local metropolitan area, the densest center of population in this country and at the same time a great intellectual center attracting able persons, I have found only twelve children who test at or above 180 IQ (S-B). This number represents the winnowing from thousands of children tested, hundreds of them brought for the testing because of their mental gifts. (p. xiii)

To categorize gifted people as those with IQs of 180 or higher is roughly like categorizing retarded individuals as only those with IQs of 20 or less (Zigler & Farber, 1985). Certainly it is reasonable to expect that children with very high IQs might have more social problems and emotional difficulties than the more typical gifted child with an IQ in the 130 to 150 range, although follow-up research does not indicate that this is the case (White & Renzulli, 1987). All this is not to say that gifted students are immune to social and emotional problems. They may be particularly susceptible to difficulties if they are extremely precocious or if they are subject to social conditions, such as peer pressure toward mediocrity, that mitigate mental health (Janos & Robinson, 1985; Morelock & Feldman, 1991). It should come as no surprise that gifted students become upset and maladjusted when they are discriminated against and prevented from realizing their full potential. Such a reaction is not peculiar to any group of children, exceptional or average along any dimension.

ATTITUDES TOWARD GIFTED STUDENTS AND THEIR EDUCATION

It is relatively easy to find sympathy for children with disabilities, but more than a little difficult to turn that sympathy into public support for effective educational programs. It is difficult to elicit sympathy for gifted children, and next to impossible to arrange sustained public support for education that meets their needs (Reis, 1989).

As many writers have pointed out, support for education of gifted and talented students runs in cycles. When national security is a major concern, programs for the gifted flourish because excellence is seen as a means of defense; when the nation feels secure from outside threats, programs are allowed to wither in favor of emphasis on educational equity. Gallagher (1986) notes that the relative emphasis on equity and excellence is an international as well as a national phenomenon.

We can state two rational arguments for providing special education for gifted children:

1. Every child is entitled to public education that meets his or her needs. Because of their exceptional abilities, gifted children need special education if they are to realize their potential for personal fulfillment and social contribution. To deny gifted children special education suited to their needs is to deny them equal opportunity, their birthright as American citizens.
2. Society will be best served if the talents of its most capable problem solvers are cultivated. Gifted children are the most precious natural resource for solving the future problems of society, and that resource can be ignored only at great peril. As Terman remarked,

"It should go without saying that a nation's resources of intellectual talent are among the most precious it will ever have. The origin of genius, the natural laws of its development, and the environmental influences by which it may be affected for good or ill, are scientific problems of almost unequaled importance for human welfare" (1926, p. v).

These two arguments for providing special education for gifted students—do it for the sake of the children and do it for the sake of us all—are seldom enough to bring about either a wave of sentiment or a flurry of action on their behalf. In fact, the attitude we often encounter is that if gifted children are really so capable, they will find ways to help themselves.

In the mid-1980s, national interest in the education of gifted students increased, sparked by a renewed emphasis on excellence in education. Since 1990, most states have increased their support of programs for gifted and talented students. In 1989, the Jacob K. Javits Gifted and Talented Students Education Act provided federal funding for a limited number of model educational projects and for the National Research Center on the Gifted and Talented. The center brings together researchers from Yale University and the state universities of Connecticut, Georgia, and Virginia. Over 260 public and private elementary and secondary schools across the United States are involved in the center's research. Nevertheless, gifted children and youths remain the most underserved population in our nation's schools. Programs for gifted students are not yet safe from antagonistic attitudes.

Gallagher (1986) describes American society's attitude toward gifted and talented students as a love-hate relationship. Our society loves the good things that gifted people produce, but it hates to acknowledge superior intellectual performance. Opponents of special education for gifted students argue that it is inhumane and un-American to segregate gifted students for instruction, to allocate special resources for the education of those already advantaged, and that there is a danger of leaving some children out when only the ablest are selected for special programs. Yet segregation in special programs, allocation of additional resources, and stringent selectivity are practices enthusiastically endorsed by the American public when the talent being fostered is athletic. The opposition develops only when the talent is academic or artistic.

DO YOU THINK SPECIAL PROGRAMS FOR THE GIFTED ARE A GOOD IDEA? ➤

Yes!

Gifted programs give kids a chance to stay smart.
> Boy, 11, Georgia

I think gifted classes are a good idea because kids get bored in school and might start getting bad grades.
> Boy, 9, New York

I think that all schools should have gifted programs because they give gifted children a chance to *really* use their brain.
> Boy, 9, Ohio

If you're in a class that's easy, you're not learning anything.
> Boy, 11, New York

I like to be around children who are as intelligent as I am.
> Boy, 11, North Carolina

People who *can* do harder work or can go to special classes should be able to get what they deserve.
> Girl, 12, New York

Some people don't like their classmates or teachers and need to get away for part of the day. They already know most of the work in their classrooms so they need a special program.
> Boy, 12, New York

Without the gifted program I would have no reason to go to school.
> Girl, 12, New York

I believe that special programs are important because without them I wouldn't be able to learn anything extra and I wouldn't have any competition.
> Boy, 12, California

I believe you should have a special class for special kids so that they can learn faster. Because when a child is kept from learning, he or she will become frustrated.
> Girl, 12, Michigan

Schools should have gifted programs, but also they should have other special programs (such as art, physical education, music, etc.) for the rest of the kids who have other special talents.
> Girl, 12, Illinois

No!

No. Gifted programs make you miss your other classes and they make other kids jealous, too.
> Girl, 9, Illinois

I think that maybe gifted students should have a special program but it should not take up regular classroom time. Sure, the students might be getting out of class, but we miss important lessons and we have to stay in for recess to learn them.
> Girl, 11, Connecticut

Why not have anyone who is interested in something and has a special ability get time to work on it?
> Girl, 11, New York

I think that you should not have a program for children that are skilled because I think it affects the whole class and makes them feel bad. I think we could have our meetings in the classroom just as well.
> Girl, 8, Illinois

SOURCE: From *Gifted kids speak out* by James R. Delisle. Copyright © 1987. Reprinted by permission of Free Spirit Publishing Inc., Minneapolis, MN. All rights reserved. pp. 18–19.

Let us take a closer look at the arguments against special education for gifted and talented students that have been advanced by Baer (1980), Myers and Ridl (1981), and Sapon-Shevin (1984). Note that the same arguments can be used against special education for children with disabilities.

1. The children cannot be identified with great reliability (compare the difficulties in identifying students with mild disabilities).
2. More children are identified in some social classes or ethnic groups than in others.
3. Identified children receive special educational resources that others do not, although many nonidentified students could profit from those same resources.
4. Students may have special needs in one area but not in another, or at one time but not at another.
5. Identified students are set apart from their peers in a way that may stigmatize them.

In our opinion, one cannot argue against special education for gifted and talented students without arguing against special education in general, for all special education involves the recognition of individual differences and the accommodation of those differences in schooling.

The lack of research evidence supporting the effectiveness of educational programs for gifted students is also a factor underlying the fickle support of education for such children. There is simply not enough scientific research clearly indicating that gifted children become gifted adults who contribute to the social welfare or are personally fulfilled because of the influence of special education programs (Weiss & Gallagher, 1982). Although it can be argued on the basis of sound logic, common sense, and anecdotal reports that special education should be provided for gifted children, it is impossible to point to many controlled research studies showing the effects of such education. Callahan (1986) suggests that the wrong questions are often asked in evaluating programs. When the primary objective of a program is the provision of education that is appropriate for the capabilities of the students, the major evaluation questions should involve the appropriateness of the education provided, not the outcome of producing more productive citizens.

Legal arguments for education of gifted students are quite different from those for education of students with disabilities. Much of the litigation for educating children with disabilities was based on the fact that they were being excluded from school or from regular classes, leading to the argument that they were being denied equal protection of law. Gifted students are seldom denied an education or access to regular classes, so the legal basis for special provisions to meet their needs is less clear (Stronge, 1986).

Special programs for students with special gifts and talents remain highly controversial. Even among gifted students there are differences of opinion. The box on page 465 illustrates the point. These responses are only a few, obtained by Delisle (1987), from thousands of gifted students who completed questionnaires about various aspects of their education.

The Educational Reform Movement and Controversy Regarding Education of Gifted and Talented Students

The educational reform movement of the 1990s holds both promise and danger for education of gifted students (Gallagher, 1991a; Treffinger, 1991; Renzulli & Reis, 1991; VanTassel-Baska, 1991a). The promise and danger are perhaps most clearly evident when reformers emphasize both excellence and heterogeneous grouping for instruction. To the extent that the emphasis of school reform is on improving the quality of instruction and encouraging the highest performance of which students are capable, the movement holds promise for all students, including those who are gifted. To the extent that reformers reject the idea of grouping students for instruction in specific curriculum areas based on their knowledge of and facility in the subject matter, however, the movement may mean disaster—not only for the gifted, but also for those with special difficulties in learning.

Ability grouping is one of the most controversial topics related to school reform, largely because grouping by ability is seen by some as a way of perpetuating racial or ethnic inequalities in achievement and social class. Some researchers suggest that ability grouping of virtually any kind is discriminatory and ineffective and should be abolished (Oakes, 1985, 1992). Others find that ability grouping across grades and within classes has beneficial effects (Kulik &

Kulik, 1992). Grouping students for instruction based on their level of interest and achievement in specific curriculum areas should not be confused with a rigid tracking system. Flexible grouping in which students are not locked into groups or tracks but have opportunities for learning in a variety of homogeneous and heterogeneous groups is seen as highly desirable by most advocates for gifted students (Feldhusen & Moon, 1992; VanTassel-Baska, 1992).

Many school reformers have suggested that students of all ability levels learn best in heterogeneous groups in which cooperative learning and peer tutoring are used as strategies for meeting individual needs. Cooperative learning, peer tutoring, and other arrangements for addressing individual differences in heterogeneous groups may meet the needs of most students. However, students who are truly gifted in specific curriculum areas are very poorly served by these strategies. Advocates for the gifted argue that these students need instruction that is conceptually more complex and abstract than most learners of a similar chronological age can handle (Feldhusen & Moon, 1992; Renzulli & Reis, 1991).

NEGLECTED GROUPS OF GIFTED STUDENTS

There has been recent concern for neglected groups—gifted children and youths who are disadvantaged by economic needs, racial discrimination, disabilities, or sex bias—and it is not misplaced. We must face two facts: (1) Gifted children from higher socioeconomic levels already have many of the advantages, such as more appropriate education, opportunities to pursue their interests in depth, and intellectual stimulation, that special educators recommend for those who are gifted. (2) There are far too many gifted individuals who are disadvantaged by life circumstances or disabilities and who have been overlooked and discriminated against, resulting in a tremendous waste of human potential (Whitmore, 1986).

The Problem of Underachievement

Students may fail to achieve at a level consistent with their abilities for a variety of reasons. Many females achieve far less than they might because of social or cultural barriers to their selection or to progress in certain careers. Students who are members of racial or ethnic minorities are often underachievers because of bias in identification or programming for their abilities. Students with obvious disabilities are frequently overlooked or denied opportunities to achieve. Still, underachievement cannot be explained simply by discrimination; many males, nonminority, and nondisabled students also are underachievers. Underachievement of gifted and talented children can result from any of the factors that lead to underachievement in any group, such as emotional conflicts or a poor home environment. A frequent cause is an inappropriate school program—school work that is unchallenging and boring because the gifted student has already mastered most of the material. And gifted underachievers often develop negative self-images and negative attitudes toward school (Delisle, 1982; Gallagher, 1991b). When a student shows negative attitudes toward school and self, any special abilities he or she may have are likely to be overlooked.

Whitmore (1986) suggests that lack of motivation to excel is usually a result of a mismatch between the student's motivational characteristics and opportunities provided in the classroom. Students are typically highly motivated when (1) the social climate of the classroom is nurturant, (2) the curriculum content is relevant to the students' personal interests and is challenging, and (3) the instructional process is appropriate to the students' natural learning style. One way of preventing or responding to underachievement is allowing students to skip grades or subjects so school becomes more nurturing and provides a greater interest and challenge. However, acceleration is not always appropriate nor is it typically sufficient by itself to address the problems of the underachieving gifted student (Jones & Southern, 1991; Rimm & Lovance, 1992). Counseling, individual, and family therapy, and a variety of supportive or remedial strategies may be necessary alternatives or additions to acceleration (Gallagher, 1991b; VanTassel-Baska, 1990).

Underachievement must not be confused with nonproductivity (Delisle, 1981). A lapse in productivity does not necessarily indicate that the student is underachieving. Gifted students should not be expected to be constantly producing something remarkable. But this points up our difficulty in defining giftedness: How much time must elapse between episodes of creative productivity before we say that someone is no longer gifted or has become an underachiever? We noted earlier that giftedness is in the performance, not in the person. Yet we know that the unrelenting demand for gifted performance is unrealistic and can be inhumane.

Gifted Minority Students

Three characteristics may be used to define gifted students with unique needs because of their minority status: cultural diversity, socioeconomic deprivation, and geographic isolation (Baldwin, 1985). These characteristics may occur singly or in combination. They create unique needs for different reasons. Children from minority cultural groups may be viewed negatively, or the strengths and special abilities valued in their culture may conflict with those of the majority. Children reared in poverty may not have toys, reading materials, opportunities for travel and exploration, good nutrition and medical care, and many other advantages typically provided by more affluent families. Lack of basic necessities and opportunities for learning may mask intelligence and creativity. Children living in remote areas may not have access to many of the educational resources that are typically found in more populated regions.

Among the greatest challenges in the field today are the identification of culturally diverse and disadvantaged gifted students and the inclusion of these students in special programs. Some ethnic groups have been sorely neglected in programs for gifted students. For example, Patton (1992) notes that although African-American students comprise about sixteen percent of public school enrollments, they make up only about eight percent of those enrolled in programs for the gifted. Frasier (1991) observes that addressing the underrepresentation of cultural or ethnic groups is a task with many proposed solutions, none of which has yet been entirely successful.

> We know that numerous solutions have been suggested to address the underrepresentation of disadvantaged and culturally diverse students in gifted programs. These solutions have included: (a) soliciting nominations from persons other than the teacher...; (b) using checklists and rating scales specifically designed for culturally diverse and disadvantaged populations...; (c) modifying or altering traditional identification procedures...; (d) developing culture specific identification systems...; (e) using quota systems...; (f) developing programs designed to eliminate experiential and language deficits prior to evaluation for gifted programs...; (g) using a matrix to weight data from multiple sources...; and (h) modifying assessment procedures by providing students with instruction before administering test tasks...

Issues in Special Education Identifying Gifted Minority Students

*I*n the winter of 1991 two thousand delegates of the California Association for the Gifted (CAG) met in Long Beach to discuss gifted education in California and across the country. Many experts agreed that minority and culturally diverse students are seriously underrepresented in programs for gifted children.

The inadequate representation of minority and poor children, and children with disabilities is often attributed to the misuse of standardized test scores or bias on the part of teachers or administrators. Subsequent studies have shown that the standardized tests and typical checklists of gifted characteristics often fail to identify culturally diverse gifted children.

Concern about the lack of culturally diverse students in gifted programs led the schools of Palm Beach County, Florida to develop a pilot project. The Potentially Gifted Minority Student Project was begun to establish a system for identifying students with gifted potential and a course of study to meet their educational needs.

The project coordinators' research indicated that many of the students in Palm Beach County, especially those from inner-city, rural, and migrant families were struggling with limited learning experiences in the home, lack of self-confidence, low expectations for the future on the part of both parents and children, and language barriers.

To help nurture and develop these culturally diverse students, the goals of the project were divided into three components. First, an intensive thinking skills program was implemented. Second, feeling that developing self-confidence and reversing negative attitudes are as crucial as academic enrichment, the students were encouraged to use their talents and abilities. Parents provided support to their children by collaborating with teachers in playing an active role in the project. Lastly, the regular academic curriculum was presented in an accelerated manner, allowing students to move ahead in subject areas.

Coordinators of the project believe its impact has been tremendous. Annually, 25% of the project students qualify for programs for the gifted with IQ scores of 130 and above. In 1992 the Florida Department of Education revised its regulations on gifted children, allowing Florida school districts to develop plans for the identification and education of students who are underrepresented in gifted programs. The Potentially Gifted Minority Student Project has been replicated in Texas, Arkansas, and Oklahoma.

- What steps can school administrators take to identify giftedness of children who are ethnic minorities, poor, or disabled and to guide minority parents in becoming more aware of the characteristics of giftedness?
- What can parents do to provide an enriching home environment and encourage their children to learn?
- According to American Mensa, Ltd., the international society for people who score in the top 2 percent on standardized IQ tests, only 26 states require gifted children to be identified and tested. Should all states be required to identify and test gifted children?

> We know that none of these solutions has solved the problem. Few culturally diverse and disadvantaged students are being identified for participation in gifted programs. (p. 236)

Appropriate identification and programming for gifted students will result in the inclusion of approximately equal proportions of all ethnic groups. This proportionality will likely be achieved only if renewed efforts are made: to devise and adopt culturally sensitive identification criteria, to provide counseling to raise the educational and career aspirations of students in underrepresented groups, to make high-achieving models from all ethnic groups available, and to adopt a workable system to ensure the inclusion of underrepresented groups. Ultimately, the larger social-environmental issue of making families and communities safe, as well as intellectually stimulating, for children and youths of all ethnic backgrounds must be addressed. Equal opportunity for development outside the school environment would help address the underrepresentation of minority students in programs for the gifted.

Gifted Students with Disabilities

The education of gifted students with disabiities is just emerging as a field (Whitmore & Maker, 1985). The major goals of the field today are identification of gifted students with specific disabilities, research and development, preparation of professionals to work with these gifted children and youths, improvement of interdisciplinary cooperation for the benefit of such children and youths, and preparation of students for adult living.

A substantial percentage of eminent persons have had disabilities. Nevertheless, the special abilities of people with disabilities are often overlooked. Whitmore and Maker (1985) note that our stereotypic expectations for people with disabilities frequently keep us from recognizing their abilities. For example, if a child lacks the ability to speak or to be physically active or presents the image associated with intellectual dullness (e.g., drooling, slumping, dull eyes staring), we tend to assume that the child has mental retardation. The following is an example of how the gifted child with disabilities is typically overlooked:

> Kim was classified at birth as "profoundly handicapped," owing to cerebral palsy of severe degree. Early treatment began with a physical therapist and a language development specialist, but at 7 years of age, Kim still had extremely limited motor control and no expressive language. Confined to a wheelchair, she slumped considerably and had difficulty holding her head erect. Her droopy posture, continual drooling, and lack of language skills led professionals to design educational experiences for her that were identical to those provided for mentally retarded children. She was placed in a public school for the profoundly and multiply handicapped, in which development of basic self-help skills comprised the principal educational goals.
>
> Kim's parents, who were teachers, had observed through the years her increased effort to communicate with her eyes and began to believe there was more intellect within that severely limited body than they had assumed. They stimulated her with questions and problems to solve while providing her with a relatively simple means of indicating responses. When a group of students from the school for multiply handicapped were scheduled to be mainstreamed into an open-space elementary school, they insisted that Kim be included. After two months of stimulation in a normal classroom setting, the provision of an adapted communicator she could manage, and participation in a more normal instructional program, Kim evidenced remarkable development. She exhibited a capacity to learn quickly and to remember exceptionally well; superior problem-solving and reasoning skills; and a keen interest in learning. Within four months she was reading on grade level (second) despite missing two years of appropriate reading instruction in school. An adapted form of the Stanford-Binet was administered, and her performance qualified her as mentally gifted. (p. 16)

We do not want to foster the myth that giftedness is found as often among students with disabilities as among those who do not have disabilities. But, clearly, gifted students with disabilities have been a neglected population. Whitmore and Maker (1985) estimate that at least 2 percent of children with disabilities may be gifted (recall that 3 to 5 percent is the typical estimate for the general population).

VanTassel-Baska (1991b) summarizes what we know about gifted students with disabilities:

> We know that these learners exist, many times hidden inside their specific disabling condition, and we know because of their discrepant pattern, they are difficult to find and identify. Moreover, we also know that these learners require more extensive services in order to develop their potential. (pp. 261-262)

The more extensive services to which VanTassel-Baska refers can seldom be provided by a single teacher or school. A key factor in meeting these students' needs is the collaboration of a variety of disciplines and institutions to provide the appropriate technology and training (Karnes & Johnson, 1991a).

Gifted Females

Clearly, the largest group of neglected gifted students are females. As Callahan (1991) and Kerr (1991) point out, we are in a period of rapid change in *some* aspects of the way females are treated in our society. Gifted females today have many opportunities for education and choice of careers that were denied to females a generation ago.

> Yet, there is certainly convincing data that suggest that this particular group of gifted students is facing inequities, they are still not achieving at the levels we would expect, and they are not choosing career options commensurate with their abilities. (Callahan, 1991, p. 284)

Females lag behind males in many measures of achievement and aptitude (e.g., professional and career achievement, standardized test scores, grades) and tend not to pursue courses of study or careers involving science and math. In short, they are underrepresented in many fields of advanced study and in professions and careers that carry high status, power, and pay. The reasons for their underrepresentation fall into the category of what we presume to know (Callahan, 1991). Factors contributing to the situation may include lower parental expectations for females, overemphasis on and glamorization of sex differences, school and societal stereotypes of males and females, and educational practices (e.g., less attention to high achieving girls, expectations of less independence of girls) detrimental to achievement.

Recent research reviewed by Callahan (1991) and Kerr (1991) suggests that the problems of neglect and underrepresentation of gifted females are much more complex than previously believed. Like underrepresentation of ethnic minorities, the problems involving females are closely tied to cultural, social, and political issues, and they do not have simple or easy solutions. Nevertheless, the education of gifted females might be improved by encouraging females to take risks by enrolling in challenging courses, to make career choices appropriate for their abilities, and to explore avenues that break the stereotypical female role.

EDUCATIONAL CONSIDERATIONS

Today, the consensus of leaders in the field is that special education for gifted and talented students should have three characteristics: (1) a curriculum designed to accommodate the students' advanced cognitive skills, (2) instructional strategies consistent with the learning styles of gifted students in the particular content areas of the curriculum, and (3) administrative arrangements facilitating appropriate grouping of students for instruction. States and localities have devised a wide variety of plans for educating gifted students. Generally, the plans can be described as providing **enrichment** (additional experiences provided to students without placing them in a higher grade) or **acceleration** (placing the students ahead of their age-peers). Seven plans for grouping students and modifying the curriculum for gifted and talented students are described by Weiss and Gallagher (1982) as follows:

> ➤ **enrichment.** Provision of additional learning experiences for gifted students while they remain in the grade level appropriate for their chronological age.

> ➤ **acceleration.** Educating gifted students by placing them in grade levels ahead of their peers in one or more academic subjects.

1. *Enrichment in the classroom:* Provision of a differentiated program of study for gifted pupils by the classroom teacher within the regular classroom, without assistance from an outside resource or consultant teacher.
2. *Consultant teacher program:* Differentiated instruction provided within the regular classroom by the classroom teacher with the assistance of a specially trained consultant teacher.
3. *Resource room/pullout program:* Gifted students leave the classroom on a regular basis for differentiated instruction provided by a specially trained teacher.
4. *Community mentor program:* Gifted students interact on an individual basis with selected members of the community for an extended time on a topic of special interest to the child.
5. *Independent study program:* Differentiated instruction consists of independent study projects supervised by a qualified adult.
6. *Special class:* Gifted students are grouped together and receive instruction from a specially trained teacher.
7. *Special school:* Gifted students receive differentiated instruction in a specialized school established for that purpose.

Not every community offers all the options listed here. In fact, there is great variation in the types of services offered within the school systems of a given state and from state to state (Renzulli, 1986). As one might expect, large metropolitan areas typically offer more program options than small towns or rural areas. New York City, for example, has a long history of special high schools for gifted and talented students.

The future holds particularly exciting possibilities for the education of gifted and talented students. Fox and Washington (1985) note that advances in telecommunications, the presence of microcomputers in the home and classroom, and the call for excellence in American education are three developments with implications for educating our most able students. Telecommunications, including instructional television, telephone conferencing, and electronic mail, are technological means of facilitating the interaction of gifted students and their teachers over wide geographical areas. These communication systems are important for extending appropriate education to gifted students in rural and remote areas. The possible uses of microcomputers for enhancing the education of gifted students are enormous. Using software tutorials, accessing data banks, playing or inventing computer games that are intellectually demanding, writing and editing in English and foreign languages, learning computer languages, and solving advanced problems in mathematics are only a few of the possibilities.

Acceleration

Acceleration involves moving a student ahead of her or his age peers in one or more areas of the curriculum. It may mean skipping one or more grades or attending classes with students in higher grades for one or a few specific subjects. Acceleration has not been used frequently, especially in rural areas (Jones & Southern, 1992). It has been used primarily with students who are extremely intellectually precocious (i.e., those scoring 160 or higher on individually administered intelligence tests). Radical acceleration of extremely precocious students, combined with enrichment at each stage of their school careers, appears to offer these students the best social experiences as well as academic progress commensurate with their abilities (Gross, 1992).

Opponents of acceleration fear that gifted children who are grouped with older students will suffer negative social and emotional consequences or that they will become contemptuous of their age-peers. Proponents of acceleration argue that appropriate curriculums and instructional methods are available only in special schools or in regular classes for students who are older than the gifted child. Furthermore, proponents argue that by being grouped with other students who are their intellectual peers in classes in which they are not always first or correct, gifted students acquire a more realistic self-concept and learn tolerance for others whose abilities are not so great as their own. Research on the effects of acceleration does not clearly indicate that it typically has negative effects; neither does it clearly indicate benefits in all cases (Jones & Southern, 1991). Acceleration appears to be a plan that can work very well but demands careful attention to the individual case.

Models of Enrichment

Renzulli (1977) noted that many of the activities provided under the guise of "special education for the gifted and talented" cannot be justified. If gifted or average children spend their time playing games designed to foster creativity or problem-solving strategies, they are not being served well. If the traditional content-oriented curriculum (which emphasizes pouring facts into students' heads) is replaced by an equally inane process-oriented curriculum (which emphasizes pouring cognitive processes into students' heads), no real progress has been made. A defensible program for gifted pupils must state how education for them will be the same as and how it will be different from education for all students.

Renzulli and his colleagues have developed an enrichment model based on the notion that children exhibit gifted behavior in relation to particular projects or activities on which they bring to bear their above-average ability, creativity, and task commitment. Students selected into a "talent pool" through case study identification methods are engaged in enrichment activities that involve individual or small-group investigation of real-life problems; they become practicing pollsters, politicians, geologists, editors, and so on. The teacher (1) helps students translate and focus a general concern into a solvable problem, (2) provides students with the tools and methods necessary to solve the problem, and (3) assists students in communicating their findings to authentic audiences (i.e., consumers of information). Students may stay in the enrichment program as long as they have the ability, creativity, and motivation to pursue productive activities that go beyond the usual curriculum for students their age. The model has become known as the *schoolwide* enrichment model (Olenchak & Renzulli, 1989; Renzulli & Reis, 1985; 1991b). The major components of this model are shown in Table 11–2 on page 476.

The schoolwide model was designed to address the need to reduce the "separateness" of special and regular programs and to make certain that all students who can profit from enrichment activities are given opportunities to engage in more challenging activities. The goals of "curriculum compacting" are to create a challenging learning environment, guarantee proficiency in basic curriculum, and make time for enrichment and acceleration (Starko, 1986). All students' strengths are assessed, and information on their performance during general exploratory experiences (Type I enrichment) is used to plan group training activities (Type II enrichment) and individual and small-group investigations of real problems (Type III enrichment).

$\mathcal{C}$ollaboration

$\mathcal{A}$ $\mathcal{K}ey$ to $\mathcal{S}uccess$

BESSIE R. DUNCAN

Supervisor, Gifted and Talented Education, Detroit Public Schools; B.S., Medical Technology and M.A., Special Education, Wayne State University

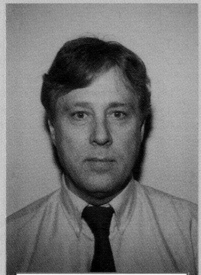

LOUIS CARNEY

English teacher, Mackenzie High School, Detroit, Michigan; B.S., Speech and English and M.A., Education Administration, Eastern Michigan University; M.S, Mathematics Education, University of Detroit

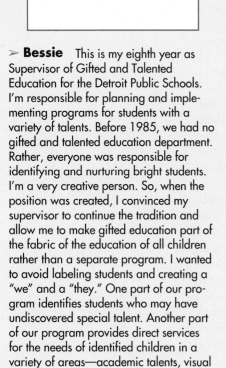

➤ **Bessie** This is my eighth year as Supervisor of Gifted and Talented Education for the Detroit Public Schools. I'm responsible for planning and implementing programs for students with a variety of talents. Before 1985, we had no gifted and talented education department. Rather, everyone was responsible for identifying and nurturing bright students. I'm a very creative person. So, when the position was created, I convinced my supervisor to continue the tradition and allow me to make gifted education part of the fabric of the education of all children rather than a separate program. I wanted to avoid labeling students and creating a "we" and a "they." One part of our program identifies students who may have undiscovered special talent. Another part of our program provides direct services for the needs of identified children in a variety of areas—academic talents, visual

and performing arts, and leadership. A part of our philosophy is that when programs are developed and implemented collaboratively with others we guard against these programs' demise because of their being person-dependent. When more people are involved, you have more champions for the program; they feel some personal ownership of the program and want to sustain it and see it grow. So the middle-school debate program first evolved in this context. Initially, I went to the supervisor of Communication Arts because, again, I don't develop programs in isolation; I always collaborate with another curriculum department. That's when I first met Lou. I had heard a lot about Lou—that he was a very fine fellow with lots of talent. So, I thought, he sounds just like the person we need—someone who cares a lot about kids, who is gentle and will help us get this program started.

➤ **Lou** Bessie and Sterling Jones, the supervisor of Communication Arts, were really enthusiastic about the success of the high school debate program. They believed that the traditional cross-examination debate format could also be effective in the middle school. The intent of the program is to promote the intellectual development of middle school students by accelerating and differentiating the curriculum through debate. Debate becomes a vehicle for stimulating middle school students' learning and encouraging them to view the world in more global terms. Reaching the goal of this program depends on a collaborative learning philosophy. Success is linked to the middle school teachers' acceptance of ownership for all decisions and by-laws. We guide them in keeping the program enthusiastic and fair for all participants. We have developed four workshops for interested middle school teachers. The first centers on basic debate terminology. Teachers receive materials describing generative thinking strategies that they can share with their students. The second workshop focuses on defining the resolution, in which the teachers write in the roles of the team members. These plans are made in collaboration with the high school science and social studies teachers. In the third workshop, teachers work in debate squads. Their task is to write a brief based upon a partial brief with supporting literature supplied by me. The opposing squad is also furnished with research to counter the brief. The goal is to redefine what they know and share this with their students. The final workshop is a practice debate among the teachers to review the format. Teachers who are seasoned debate veterans are paired with the first-year debate coaches. Rules and procedures are finalized by the coaches. The first debate is a practice meet. Students are not judged in terms of winning or losing. Instead they are critiqued and walked through the format. They are given suggestions on strengthening their stance by high school debate students, who serve as judges. All judges are given an informal inservice on format and suggestions on evaluating middle-school students.

➤ **Bessie** I want to enlarge on what Lou just brought up—our high school debaters serving as judges. These students have to be released from their classes, and many times their coaches will come to sort of cheer them on. So, it's really a collaborative project that has many layers. The collaboration is among administrators, administrators and teachers, teachers and students, and among students. I think that's what makes for the richness of the program, and I think that explains why it's so celebrated by everybody. Problems do arise, but because everybody likes the program, they work around them—arranging transportation to the meet or covering classes for coaches, for example.

➤ **Lou** I want to comment further on the high school debaters. When they debate, they often complain and are frustrated at times by judges. In competition, they sometimes don't feel that they deserve this or they should've received that. "I don't understand why the judge didn't vote for us," they say. So, now they're the judges for the middle school kids. All of a sudden they're wearing a different hat and they have to make those decisions on winning or losing and balloting for speaker points. They're required to justify their ballots and give the details in the synopsis of their decision. This changes their perspective. It gives them a comprehensive understanding of the debate process and makes their competitions more palatable. They understand that an issue might be interpreted a different way by a different listener. It seems to make them better debaters.

➤ **Bessie** I'll look at it from the perspective of another group of students—the 7th and 8th graders who participate in this project. We have heard many success stories about students who chose to participate. As I said earlier, middle school debate is a collaborative project that's

used to identify middle school students who have leadership abilities. It's certainly done that. For many of the students who have strong thinking and language skills that emerge in debate, teachers have observed that they have shown increased achievement, better attendance, and a change in their aspirations in terms of what they are going to do next. Many of the high schools who learn about these strong debate teams are courting the middle school students to come and be part of their high school debate team or the students choose a high school based on the strength of their debate team. In our first year, we started with five or six schools. In the second year we had 14, and now we're up to 18 schools with debate teams with three others watching and getting ready. That's out of a total of 60 middle schools. So, we predict that in the next three or four years we may have a pretty high ratio of our students participating. That's a reason for celebration for all of us. Living in an urban area, self-management skills are a key to students being successful in school as well as outside of school. For students involved in debate, another payoff is that even when they're upset they are able to choose, more often, appropriate responses to stress because of their thinking and language skills.

➤ **Lou** Some middle school teachers are not comfortable with the win/lose outcome of debates. They accept the fact that in basketball games there are winners and losers; in chess games, too, there are winners and losers; and in academic games there are winners and losers. But when it comes to debate, there is concern about winning and losing. The majority of people involved in the program, though, believe that what we are doing is great. They see this activity as being designed to be low-risk and low in stress, and students share their stories with their peers in the school, including faculty and administrators. It seems that the enthusiasm generated by the debate program is developing and growing

within the schools, and so as far as the little frustrations go I think the success of the program has out-weighed them.

➤ **Bessie** I certainly agree with that. We really don't have many major frustrations, and I know when I speak to people about Detroit they find it just unfathomable that we are in a district that is very friendly toward identifying and nurturing bright children. But we've done it for years even when there was no centralized leadership for gifted and talented. So, it's just part of the way we look at students, and I think that that willingness to accommodate and to do things that would help to develop talent makes everyone just very cooperative and willing to be flexible. It's had terrific benefits for students. The students have gotten involved in community service projects as a result of the topics that they've discussed and debated. For example, they gave a wonderful play on homelessness that really just mirrored all the things that they had learned.

➤ **Lou** One last point is that this debate program has also extended the collaborative effort at my high school, and I receive a lot of support from my fellow English teacher, Ellen Harcourt. In addition, several teachers in science and social studies and English are collaborating on writing across the curriculum. A collaborative class is currently being initiated at our school using teachers from various disciplines, and this is supported by funds from Bessie's office. These students will be focusing on environmental problems. They will be using their debate skills and legal terminology to write a bill and, we hope, introduce it in the state legislature. Again, this program has transcended the departmentalized atmosphere of a high school, and if it continues to nourish talent and flourish we will be way ahead of the game.

*T*able 11-2 ➤ Major Components of the Schoolwide Enrichment Model

Curriculum Compacting	Modifying or "streamlining" the regular curriculum in order to eliminate repetition of previously mastered material, upgrade the challenge level of the regular curriculum, and provide time for appropriate enrichment and/or acceleration activities while ensuring mastery of basic skills.
Assessment of Student Strengths	A systematic procedure for gathering and recording information about student's abilities, interests, and learning styles.
Type I Enrichment: General Exploratory Experiences	Experiences and activities that are designed to expose students to a wide variety of disciplines (fields of study), visual and performing arts, topics, issues, occupations, hobbies, persons, places, and events that are not ordinarily covered in the regular curriculum.
Type II Enrichment: Group Training Activities	Instructional methods and materials that are purposefully designed to promote the development of thinking and feeling processes.
Type III Enrichment: Individual and Small Group Investigations of Real Problems	Investigative activities and artistic productions in which the learner assumes the role of a first-hand inquirer; the student thinking, feeling, and acting like a practicing professional.

SOURCE: F. R. Olenchak & J. S. Renzulli, The effectiveness of the schoolwide enrichment model on selected aspects of elementary school change, *Gifted Child Quarterly, 33*(1) (1989), 37. Reprinted with permission.

Type II enrichment activities have four major objectives:

1. General skills in creative thinking and problem solving, critical thinking, and affective processes such as sensing, appreciating, and valuing
2. A variety of how-to-learn skills such as note-taking, interviewing, classifying, analyzing data, drawing conclusions
3. Skills in the appropriate use of advanced-level reference materials such as reader's guides, directories, abstracts
4. Written, oral, and visual communication skills that maximize the impact of students' products upon appropriate audiences (Renzulli & Reis, 1991b, p. 129)

All students selected for the talent pool engage in Type I and Type II activities, but Type III activities are self-selected and optional.

On the basis of an experimental study of the schoolwide enrichment model in elementary schools, Olenchak and Renzulli (1989) suggest that their approach can improve the learning environment for all students, improve attitudes of students and teachers toward education of the gifted, and make special programming for gifted students a more integral part of general education. These outcomes are critical to sustained support for special programs for the most able students. "The gains that gifted education has made in instructional technology and the commitment that this field has made to serving our most potentially able youth will only have long term endurance when they are woven into the fabric of general education rather than perceived as dangling threads that can be snipped off at any time" (p. 46).

TEACHERS OF GIFTED STUDENTS

Teaching gifted students may at first thought seem easy. Who would not like to teach students who are particularly bright, creative, and motivated? In reality, teachers of gifted students, just like other special and general education teachers, are vulnerable to burnout (Dettmer, 1982). Gifted and talented students often challenge the "system" of school, and they can be verbally caustic. Their superior abilities and unusual or advanced interests demand teachers who themselves are highly intelligent, creative, and motivated.

The teacher must be adept at assessing students' abilities, interests, and commitment to tasks and skilled at helping other teachers recognize the characteristics that indicate a student could profit from special education. Frequent communication with regular teachers, observation, interpretation of test scores, and interviews with students, parents, and other professionals are required to identify gifted students. Only a teacher with broad interests, extensive information, and abundant creative energy will be able to accomplish the identification, instruction, and guidance of gifted students.

Lindsey (1980) suggests many personal, professional, and instructional characteristics that are important for teachers of gifted students, including the following:

- Understands, accepts, respects, trusts, and likes self
- Is sensitive to, supports, respects, and trusts others
- Has high intellectual, cultural, and literary interests
- Is flexible, open to new ideas
- Desires to learn; has high achievement needs and enthusiasm
- Is intuitive, perceptive
- Is committed to excellence
- Is democratic rather than autocratic
- Is innovative and experimental rather than conforming
- Uses problem-solving; doesn't jump to unfounded conclusions
- Seeks involvement of others in discovery
- Develops flexible, individualized programs
- Provides feedback; stimulates higher mental processes
- Respects creativity and imagination

Renzulli (1980) has said that these traits are pure "American Pie" and one would hope that *all* teachers would show them. One is probably safe in assuming, however, that teachers must exceed most of their pupils in creativity, intelligence, energy, and task commitment. Consequently, a teacher of gifted students must be above the average for all teachers on many of these traits. Outstanding teachers of gifted students have been found to differ from average teachers in the following ways (Whitlock & DuCette, 1989):

- Having enthusiasm for own work with gifted students
- Having self-confidence in ability to be effective
- Being a facilitator of other people as resources and learners
- Being able to apply knowledge of theory to practice
- Having a strong achievement orientation

Teachers of gifted children may often be gifted themselves. Robin Williams's character in the film "Dead Poets Society" was a gifted teacher whose unorthodox teaching methods ran afoul of school administrators.

- Being commited to the role of educator of gifted students
- Building program support for gifted education programs

EARLY INTERVENTION

Giftedness in young children presents special problems of definition, identification, programming, and evaluation (Lewis & Louis, 1991). Karnes and Johnson (1991b) point out that, although progress has been made in building model programs and providing better services for young gifted children, negative attitudes toward such efforts persist. Barriers inhibiting the development of better education for these children include lack of parental advocacy, lack of appropriate teacher training, an emphasis on older gifted students, financial constraints, and legal roadblocks, such as laws preventing the early admission of gifted children to school.

The barriers to early identification and programming for gifted students include school policies and ideologies that Robinson and Weimer (1991) refer to as "the tyranny of the calendar."

> Very few districts pay systematic heed to kindergartners who have already mastered the goals of the curriculum, leaving it up to their already burdened teachers to make provisions. Because many districts favor only enrichment programs, special planning for advanced students does not begin until late into the elementary school years, after basic skills have been mastered. Leaving these students locked into standard grade-level curriculum, which does not match their learning pace or interest level, means that children with advanced conceptual and academic skills, so eager at first to enter school, are in clear danger of becoming casualties of the system. (p. 30)

Many questions regarding the education of young gifted children remain unanswered. We know relatively little about how advantageous it is to identify and program for gifted children before they are in third or fourth grade or how

7 THE GIFTED PRESCHOOLER: CHRIS AND JONATHAN ➤

Chris came running into the house, bubbling over with excitement, "Mommy, mommy. I did it! I put the bird back together. Its bones were scattered all around. Look. I have a skeleton of a bird! I guess I am a paleontologist for real! Let's go to the library and find out what species it is."

Chris, only 4, resembles Stephen Gould, world renowned paleontologist whose interest also began at an early age. A visit to the dinosaur exhibit at the American Museum of Natural History inspired both to the world of paleontological inquiry. Will Chris eventually become a paleontologist? Chris has both advanced knowledge and an all-consuming interest in paleontology.

From this scenario we can attest readily to his superior levels in vocabulary development and comprehension skills. Intense interest, in-depth knowledge, and accelerated development in language provide positive evidence of giftedness. But more important, these characteristics strongly imply that Chris has educational needs different from most 4-year-olds.

Will these special needs be met within the school setting? Unfortunately there are a limited number of educational programs adequately equipped to address the unique requirements of children like Chris. Chris' parents, like most parents of bright preschoolers, voice their concern since many of these youngsters are already reading, composing original stories, and computing simple addition and subtraction problems on their own.

One would only have to listen and watch children like Chris to confirm the need for such services. These children frequently demonstrate advanced vocabularies and often an early ability to read. In addition, they seem to learn easily and spontaneously. Logic appears early in some bright youngsters, often to the embarrassment of adults.

For instance, Jonathan, at 3, requested a grilled cheese sandwich at a restaurant. The waitress explained that grilled cheese was not on the menu. Jonathan, determined to have his way, queried, "Do you have cheese and bread?" The waitress nodded, "We do. . . ." "Then," Jon blurted, "do you have a pan?" Jon got his sandwich. When the sandwich arrived, the waitress took beverage orders. Jonathan ordered a milkshake, but this time the waitress was one step ahead. "Jonathan, we have milk and ice cream, but I'm sorry we don't have any syrup." To which Jon asked, "Do you have a car?"

Other youngsters may show advanced abilities in number concepts, maps, telling time, and block building. Their skills in such activities far exceed that of their age-mates. Not only do these characteristics define gifted preschoolers but they also provide a rationale and structure for intervention.

SOURCE: From S. Baum, The gifted preschooler: An awesome delight, *Gifted Child Today,* 9(4) 42–43.

best to train parents and teachers to work with gifted preschoolers. Yet we can make some statements with a high degree of confidence, as Karnes and Johnson (1991b) point out:

What We Know for Sure

1. We have not been committed to early identification and programming for the young gifted.
2. We have few advocates for young gifted children.
3. We do not have institutions of higher learning training personnel in gifted education to work with our young gifted children.
4. We are in need of financial resources to: conduct research with young gifted children and their families, develop more effective and efficient procedures and instruments for screening and assessing young gifted children, determine the most effective strategies for meeting their unique needs, including ways of differentiating instruction, and follow-up data that will give us insights into the effectiveness of our identification and programming.
5. We don't have the legislation we need to permit public schools to serve young gifted children below the age of five, nor to help public schools finance programming.
6. There is little awareness among educators and parents alike of the importance of early identification and programming for the gifted.
7. Procedures and instruments for identification of children who are handicapped and those who come from low income homes must compare children of like kind

rather than expect children to demonstrate or score on instruments at the level of their more affluent or non-handicapped peers.

8. Identification of young gifted children must be an ongoing process. This is particularly true for children from low-income and minority groups as well as children with handicapping conditions because these children need time and the opportunity to display their special gifts and talents. (pp. 279-280)

Although not a panacea for gifted students, early admission to school and acceleration through grades and subjects offer significant advantages. If gifted children are seen as essentially the same as others except that they are able to work faster and at a more advanced level than their age mates, then what young gifted children need most is the freedom to make full and appropriate use of the school system as it now exists. They need the freedom to study with older children in specific areas where their abilities are challenged. Gifted children need to be able to get around the usual eligibility rules so they can go through the ordinary curriculum at an accelerated rate. Unfortunately, relatively few gifted preschoolers receive the kind of educational programming appropriate for their abilities. This is especially the case for young gifted children who are also from minority or poor families or have disabilities.

Gifted preschoolers may be intellectually superior and have above-average adaptive behavior and leadership skills as well. Their advanced abilities in many areas, however, do not mean that their development will be above average across the board. Emotionally, they may develop at an average pace for their chronological age. Sometimes their uneven development creates special problems of social isolation, and adults may have unrealistic expectations for their social and emotional skills because their cognitive and language skills are so advanced. They may require special guidance by sensitive adults who not only provide appropriate educational environments for them but also discipline them appropriately and teach them the skills required for social competence (Baum, 1986; Roedell, 1985). They may need help, for example, in acquiring self-understanding, independence, assertiveness, sensitivity to others, friend-making skills, and social problem-solving skills.

TRANSITION

For gifted students who are achieving near their potential and are given opportunities to take on adult roles, the transitions from childhood to adolescence to adulthood and from high school to higher education or employment are typically not very problematic. In many ways, transition for gifted youths tends to be a mirror image of the problems in transition faced by adolescents and young adults with disabilities. Consider the case of Raymond Kurzweil, inventor of the Kurzweil Reading Machine for blind persons (see Chapter 9).

> A summer job, at age 12, involved statistical computer programming. Could a kid comprehend IBM's daunting Fortran manual? He very well could. Soon, in fact, IBM would be coming to young Kurzweil for programming advice.
>
> By the time he was graduated from high school, the whiz kid had earned a national reputation, particularly for a unique computer program that could compose original music in the styles of Mozart and Beethoven, among others.
>
> After carefully weighing all his options, Kurzweil decided to enroll in the Massachusetts Institute of Technology so that he could mingle with the gurus of the then-emerging science of artificial intelligence. Kurzweil was in his element. He was also rather quickly in the chips. (Neuhaus, 1988, p. 66)

ifted elementary schoolchildren demonstrate many different kinds of advanced abilities.

Today, at middle age, Kurzweil is a highly successful entrepreneur who is chairman of several high-tech corporations he founded.

Not all adolescents and young adults who are gifted take transitions in stride. Many need personal and career counseling and a networking system that links students to school and community resources (Clifford, Runions, & Smyth, 1986; Delisle, 1992). Some are well served by an eclectic approach that employs the best features of enrichment and acceleration (Feldhusen & Kolloff, 1986).

If there is a central issue in the education of gifted adolescents, it is that of acceleration versus enrichment. Proponents of enrichment feel that gifted students need continued social contact with their age-peers. They argue that gifted students should follow the curriculum of their age-mates and study topics in greater depth. Proponents of acceleration feel that the only way to provide challenging and appropriate education for those with special gifts and talents is to let them compete with older students. They argue that since the cognitive abilities of gifted students are advanced beyond their years, they should proceed through the curriculum at an accelerated pace.

Acceleration for adolescent gifted students may mean early entrance to college or enrollment in college courses while attending high school. Acceleration programs, particularly in mathematics, have been evaluated very favorably (Brody & Stanley, 1991; Kolitch & Brody, 1992). In fact, early entrance to college on a full-time or part-time basis appears to work very well for the vast majority of gifted adolescents, as long as it is done with care and sensitivity to the needs of the individual student (Brody & Stanley, 1991; Noble & Drummond, 1992). As Buescher (1991) points out, "Talented adolescents are *adolescents* first and foremost. They experience fully the regression, defensiveness, and relational fluctuations of normal adolescence" (p. 399). Thus it is important to provide counseling and support services for students who enter college early to ensure that they have appropriate, rewarding social experiences that enhance their self-esteem, as well as academic challenge and success in the courses they take.

In Their Own Words RICHARD P. FEYNMAN

Richard P. Feynman grew up during the Depression when most of his family probably did not know what to think about this unusually inquisitive boy. A Nobel Prize physicist, Feynman traveled around the world and experienced first hand many things as a painter, musician, safecracker, and gambler.

The following excerpt from his autobiography, *Surely You're Joking, Mr. Feynman,* describes the recollections of a former 11-year-old electronics whiz.

I enjoyed radios. I started with a crystal set that I bought at the store, and I used to listen to it at night in bed while I was going to sleep, through a pair of earphones. When my mother and father went out until late at night, they would come into my room and take the earphones off—and worry about what was going into my head while I was asleep.

About that time I invented a burglar alarm, which was a very simple-minded thing: it was just a big battery and a bell connected with some wire. When the door to my room opened, it pushed the wire against the battery and closed the circuit, and the bell would go off.

One night my mother and father came home from a night out and very, very quietly, so as not to disturb the child, opened the door to come into my room and take my earphones off. All of a sudden this tremendous bell went off with a helluva racket—BONG BONG BONG BONG BONG!!! I jumped out of bed yelling, "It worked! It worked!"

SOURCE: Richard P. Feynman, *Surely You're Joking, Mr. Feynman* (New York: Bantam, 1989), pp. 3–4.

Beyond acceleration and enrichment, gifted adolescents need attention to their social and personal development if they are to make a successful and gratifying transition to adulthood and a career. Like other groups with special characteristics and needs, they may benefit from opportunities to socialize and learn from other students who have similar characteristics and face similar challenges. They may be able to obtain particular benefit from reflection on the nature and meaning of life and the directions they choose for their own lives. Delisle (1992) discusses six realities that adults might use in guiding gifted adolescents in transition:

1. *Remember That the Real Basics Go Beyond Reading, Writing, and Arithmetic.* (They include play and relaxation.)

2. *You Can Be Good at Something You Don't Enjoy Doing.* (Just because you're good at something doesn't mean you have to plan your life around doing it.)

3. *You Can Be Good at Some Things That Are Unpopular with Your Friends.* (It's a good idea to connect with others who share your preferences, beliefs, and experiences and to guard against stereotyping yourself or others.)

4. *Life Is Not a Race to See Who Can Get to the End the Fastest.* (Don't become preoccupied with performance, work, or success, and don't be afraid to try something at which you might not succeed.)

5. *You Have the Ability to Ask Questions That Should Have Answers but Don't.* (Look and listen to the world around you, and become involved in making the world a better place).

6. *It's Never Too Late to Be What You Might Have Been.* (Remember that you always have career options and pursue those goals that you want most.) (pp. 137-145).

The Gifted and Talented Student in General Education Classrooms

WHAT TO LOOK FOR IN SCHOOL

As you know from reading the chapter, students who demonstrate gifted behavior are, in part, superior in some way and exhibit abilities and sensitivities that may allow them to express themselves in special ways, learn quickly, be self-sufficient, or understand their own and others' feelings, motivations, and strengths and weaknesses. Although this combination of characteristics, coupled with exceptional eagerness and curiosity, may make gifted students easy to recognize in your class, formally identifying students for gifted and talented programs may be more difficult.

HOW TO GATHER INFORMATION

Because there is no federal definition of gifted and talented, each state has established its own criteria for identifying these students and subsequently has developed programs based on these criteria. Consequently, programs differ from state to state. If you think any of your students may be gifted, ask your principal for the state guidelines to determine if the student might qualify for your district's specialized program. You may also contact the person in your building or in the central office who serves as coodinator for the gifted program and discuss the criteria your system has established. If you believe your student may meet these guidelines, collect samples of the student's work and record your observations of the student's productivity and creativity and share them with the gifted coordinator, who then may initiate a referral to the gifted and talented program.

TEACHING TECHNIQUES TO TRY

Just as school systems have different definitions and eligibility criteria, so they have different ways of meeting the educational needs of gifted students. In some schools, classroom teachers alone provide programing for their gifted students. Other schools offer resource classes taught by teachers trained in gifted education that students attend for a specified period of time each week. Still other school systems offer a variety of specialized programs, including honor classes, advanced placement courses, and special schools for students gifted in math or science or the arts. In all these arrangements, except special schools, classroom teachers assume the responsibility for providing educational experiences for their gifted students during most of the school day (Milgrim, 1989).

There are three curricular models: accelerated curricula, enrichment curricula, and independent study curricula that many teachers select to guide gifted programming. As you know, when following accelerated curricula, students progress through the grade level content rapidly and study material beyond their grade level (Feldhusen, Van Tassel-Baska, & Seleley, 1989).

Curriculum Compacting

One means by which curricula are accelerated is by curriculum compacting, a procedure in which the teacher modifies the regular curriculum to provide additional time for gifted students to pursue alternate learning activities. To make these modifications, first identify the academic strengths of your gifted students, using a variety of information sources, such as school records, previous teacher recommendations, standardized and informal test results, and observation. Then decide what curricular area(s) is most appropriate for compacting, considering the following questions:

1. What does the student already know?
2. What does the student need to learn?
3. What activities will meet the student's learning needs?

Next, outline learning experiences based on your student's strengths and interests. Finally, decide how to provide these alternative educational activities.

Mastery Learning

Teachers also use mastery learning to provide time for advanced study. In one application of mastery learning, students with high ability move sequentially through a body of knowledge at their own pace (Eby & Smutny, 1990). If these students demonstrate mastery of a new skill on a pretest, they progress immediately to the next skill in the sequence. Some schools extend the use of mastery learning from individual classrooms to a school-wide system to eliminate students' being retaught mastered skills from year to year. Mastery learning may be managed in a variety of ways. Eby and Smutny report that in some schools, one classroom teacher has the responsibility for managing the school-wide system and for teaching the non-graded material to all students. In other buildings, teachers from different grade levels team teach and the students move from classroom to classroom. In order to implement either program, however, the school day must be scheduled so that certain subjects are taught to all students in the school at the same time of day . The key is to provide alternate learning experiences appropriate for gifted students once they have progressed through grade level materials.

In the second type of curricula, enrichment, i.e., more difficult or in-depth content, supplements or enriches the learning of gifted students (Clark, 1992). Although some school districts base their gifted resource classes on one model of enrichment, this type of curricula is typically used in regular classrooms to meet the needs of gifted learners (Clark, 1992). We will examine three other types of enrichment programs schools frequently use.

Bloom's Taxonomy: Higher Levels

The first program is based on Bloom's *Taxonomy of Educational Objectives, Cognitive Domain* (Bloom, et. al., 1956) which outlines six levels of thinking: the lower levels of knowledge and comprehension and the higher levels of application, analysis, synthesis, and evaluation. Teachers enrich gifted students' learning by providing educational experiences at the four higher levels of the taxonomy in a variety of topics or subjects. For example:

> the primary social studies curriculum usually includes content on the topic of "communities." While textbooks . . . cover the basic knowledge and comprehension levels on this topic by providing students with definitions and main ideas, a gifted curriculum can be developed on the topic by writing educational objectives at the higher levels.
>   At the application level, students can be asked to draw a map of their own community.
>   At the analysis level, students can compare and contrast two or more communities.
>   At the synthesis level, students can create a play about important people in the community.
>   At the evaluation level, students can share their opinions about their own community's services. (Eby & Smutny, 1990, p,. 171).

In general developing higher level thinking skills means students' spend time exploring ideas, testing the applicability of theories, synthesizing ideas into original solution, and judging the quality of these solutions (Feldhusen et al., 1989). Consult the gifted education specialist in your building or school system for assistance in developing higher order thinking skills.

Critical Thinking

Although there are many types of thinking skills in addition to the cognitive skills represented in Bloom's Taxonomy (e.g., creative thinking skills and metacognitive skills), "teaching children to think critically has been perhaps the most popular, fastest growing part of the thinking skills movement " (French & Rhoder, 1992, p. 183). Ennis (1985) defined critical thinking as "reflective and reasonable thinking that is focused on deciding what to believe or do" (p. 45). It includes skills such as judging information and making decisions.

Raths and his colleagues (1986) provide examples of the following critical thinking skills:

Judging - examining assumptions:
1. When we hear our class is getting a new student—a girl from Vietnam—what assumptions might we make?
2. When we fill a thermos with hot soup and seal the thermos, what assumptions are we making?

Making decisions:
1. Give students a flashlight. Ask them to design investigations to show what they can find out about light.
2. When Michael sees Sarah throwing trash from her lunch on the playground, what should Michael do? What are his responsibilities?

As Eby and Smutny point out, many educators do not advocate adding new critical thinking programs, but rather suggest that teachers "remodel" existing programs so that students apply critical thinking strategies to the subject matter they study. In addition, Chaffee (1987, cited in Eby and Smutny) recommends that students apply problem-solving and critical thinking strategies to real problems in their own lives, rather than to puzzles and simulated problems. Again, the specialist in gifted education can provide assistance in the systematic development of critical thinking skills.

The final curriculum model, independent study, promotes students self-directed learning. One such model is Renzulli's Enrichment Triad Curriculum Model (Renzulli, 1977), which is designed to develop student interest in topics and higher-order thinking skills and to enable gifted students to conduct investigations in areas of interest. For more information on this model, see Renzulli and Reis' (1986) *The triad reader*.

Self-directed Learning

Treffinger developed another independent study curriculum called self-directed learning. Treffinger and Barton (1988) believe the process of self-directed learning culminates in students being able to "initiate plans for their own learning, identify resources, gather data, and develop and evaluate their own products and projects" (p. 30). Teachers use a variety of techniques, such as learning centers, independent study, and contracting, to promote self-directed learning in regular education classes.

Learning Centers

Teachers often use learning centers to provide enrichment activities for their students. To promote self-directed learning, however, these centers must offer instructional opportunities in areas that are specifically designed and sequenced to encourage student independence.

Teachers in Richland County, Ohio found they could offer activities in regular education classes that developed the productivity and creativity of their gifted students by designing interest development centers (IDC) (Burns, 1985). Unlike traditional learning centers that help students master basic curriculum skills, IDCs facilitated students' independent exploration of a wide range of topics not included in the regular curriculum. The teachers stocked their centers with manipulative and media and print materials along with several suggestions for examining and experimenting in special interest areas. In keeping with the Renzulli model (see pp. 473 and 476), they also included methodological resources that helped promote interest in long-term research. For example, one teacher developed a center about bicycling that contained materials on how to create a bike path and how to approach the city council for permission to build bike racks near businesses that students frequented. For additional information and specific independent learning center resources and ideas see Burns (1985).

Independent Study

Sometimes students will develop and/or maintain great interest in a topic they have explored. When this happens, you may decide to help students conduct an independent study on this topic. Independent study involves not only the exploration of a topic in depth but also the production of an original product that is disseminated to an appropriate audience. Because directing an independent study is time-consuming and requires an understanding of the topic, teachers often solicit the help of the gifted resource teacher or another person who is knowledgeable about the subject and willing to participate in the project (Pendarvis, Howley, & Howley, 1990). The role of the teacher and resource person(s) is not director of the study, but rather, to serve as assistants who help the students define and frame the problem, establish realistic goals and timelines, become aware of a variety of available usable resources, identify both a product that the study will produce and an audience for the product, and evaluate their study. In addition, the adults involved in the project must reinforce the students' work throughout the study and provide methodological help when necessary. To learn more about the process of guiding gifted students through independent study see Reis and Cellerino (1983) .

Contracts

You also can facilitate self-directed learning by providing individualized exploration and instruction in the form of student contracts. Like business contracts these documents are negotiated with the student and describe the area the student will study and the procedures and resources he or she will use in the investigation. When contracts are used to guide independent study, they also can specify the intended audience, the means of dissemination, deadlines for stages or steps in the study, and dates and purposes of periodic meetings with the teacher (Tuttle & Becker, 1983).

Regardless of the curricula you select, remember that the education you provide for your gifted students should be qualitatively different from what you offer nonidentified students, and it should systematically develop students' cognitive and affective processes (Renzulli, 1977).

HELPFUL RESOURCES

School Personnel

In the pursuit of ideas, information, and materials to use in self-directed learning activities, the school media specialist can be a valuable resource. He or she can orient students to the variety of materials that are available including yearbooks, geographical, political, and economic atlases; career files; subject-related dictionaries; periodical indexes; bibliographic references and databases; and information available on microfilm and microfiche. Specialists also can help students learn how to evaluate resource material by assessing such factors as the purpose of the work and its intended audience; the author's (or editor's) credentials; completeness of index and reference citations; accuracy and completeness of charts, statistics, graphs, timelines, and other illustrative materials (Flack, 1986, p. 175).

For students involved in independent studies, the media specialists may be helpful resources in the creation of research products by instructing students in the use of such processes as videotaping, laminating, and making transparencies. They also may encourage and facilitate the dissemination of the products. For example, a second grade student decided to write a children's talking book on Tchaikovsky that was intended for other elementary students and that would be housed permanently in his school's library (Reis and Cellerino, 1983).

Instructional Methods and Materials

Adams, D. M. & Hamm, M. E. (1989). *Media and literacy: Learning in an electronic age—issues, ideas, and teaching strategies.* Springfield, IL: Charles C. Thomas.

Clark, B. (1992). *Growing up gifted: Developing the potential of children at home and at school* (4th ed.). New York: Merrill/Macmillan.

Cook, C. & Carlisle, J. (1985). *Challenges for children: Creative activities for gifted and talented primary students.* West Nyack, NY: The Center for Applied Research in Education.

Cox, J., Daniel, N., & Boston, B.O. (1985). *Educating able learners: Programs and promising practices.* Austin, TX: University of Texas Press.

Cushenbery, D. C. (1987). *Reading instruction for the gifted.* Springfield, IL: Charles C. Thomas.

Davis, G.A. & Rimm, S.B. (1989). *Education of the gifted and talented.* Englewood Cliffs, NJ: Prentice Hall.

Dirkes, M.A. (1988). Self-directed thinking in the curriculum. *Roeper Review, 11*, 92–94.

Feldhuser, J., Van Tassel-Baska, J., & Seeley, K. (1989). *Excellence in educating the gifted.* Denver: Love.

French, J. N., & Rhoder, C. (1992). *Teaching thinking skills: Theory and practice.* New York: Garland.

Gallagher, J. J. (1986). *Teaching the gifted child.* (3rd. ed.). Newton, MA: Allyn & Bacon.

Greenlaw, M. J., & McIntosh, M. E. (1988). *Educating the gifted.* Chicago: American Library Association.

Kondziolka, G. & Normandeau, P. (1986). Investigation: An inter-disciplinary unit. *Gifted Child Today, 9,* 52–54.

Lewis, R. B., & Doorlag, D. H. (1991). *Teaching special students in the mainstream* (3rd ed.). New York: Merrill/Macmillan.

Lukasevich, A. (1983). Three dozen useful information sources on reading for the gifted. *Reading Teacher, 36,* 542–548.

Milgrim, R. M. (1989). *Teaching gifted and talented learners in regular classrooms.* Springfield, IL: Charles C. Thomas.

Parker, B. N. (1989). *Gifted students in regular classrooms.* Boston: Allyn & Bacon.

Parker, J. P. (1989). *Instructional strategies for teaching the gifted.* Boston: Allyn & Bacon.

Pendarvis, E. D., Howley, A. A., & Howley, C. B. (1990). *The abilities of gifted children.* Englewood Cliffs, NJ: Prentice Hall.

Romey, W. D., & Hibert, M. L. (1988). *Teaching the gifted and talented in the science classroom* (2nd ed.). Washington, D. C.: National Education Association.

Schlichter, C.L. (1988). Thinking skills instruction for all classrooms. *Gifted Child Today, 11,* 24–28.

Shore, B. M., Cornell, D. G., Robinson, A., Ward, V. S. (1991). *Recommended practices in gifted education.* New York: Teachers College Press.

Sisk, D. (1987). *Creative teaching of the gifted.* NewYork: McGraw-Hill.

Curricular Models, Adaptations, and Materials

Beyer, B. K. (1991). *Teaching thinking skills: A handbook for secondary school teachers.* Boston: Allyn & Bacon.

Betts, G. T. (1985). *Autonomous learner model for the gifted and talented.* Greeley, CO: Autonomous Learning Publications and Specialists.

Bloom, B. J., et. al., *Taxonomy of educational objectives—Handbook I: Cognitive domain.* New York: McKay.

Clausen, R. E., & Clausen, D. R. (1990). *Gifted and talented students.* Milwaukee, WI: Department of Public Instruction.

Feldhusen, J. F. (1988). *Purdue Creative Thinking Program.* West LaFayette, IN: Purdue University Media-Based Services.

Feldhusen, J. F. & Kolloff, M. B. (1988). A three-stage model for gifted education. *Gifted Child Today, 11,* 14–18.

Guilford, J. P. (1967). *The nature of human intelligence.* New York: McGraw-Hill.

Juntune, J. J. (1986). *Successful programs for the gifted and talented.* St. Paul, MN: National Association for Gifted Children.

Renzulli. J. (1977). *The enrichment triad model.* Mansfield, CT: Creative Learning Press.

Renzulli, J. S. (Ed.). (1986). *Systems and models for developing programs for the gifted and talented.* Mansfield Center, CT: Creative Learning Press.

Renzulli, J. S., & Callahan, C. M. (1986). *New directions in creativity.* Mansfield Center, CT: Creative Learning Press.

Renzulli, J. S., & Reis, S. (1985). *The schoolwide enrichment model: A comprehensive plan for educational excellence.* Mansfield Center, CT: Creative Learning Press.

Robinson, A. (1986). Elementary language arts for the gifted: Assimilation and accommodation in the curriculum. *Gifted Child Quarterly, 30,* 178–181.

Treffinger, D. J. (1975). Teaching for self-directed learning: A priority for the gifted and talented. *Gifted Child Quarterly, 12,* 46–59.

Treffinger, D. J. (1978). Guidelines for encouraging independence and self-direction among gifted students. *Journal of Creative Behavior, 12,* 14–19.

Van Tassel-Baska, J., Feldhusen, J., Seeley, K., Wheatley, G., Silverman, L., & Foster, W. (Eds.). *Comprehensive curriculum for gifted learners.* Boston: Allyn & Bacon.

Literature about Gifted and Talented Individuals
ELEMENTARY

Aliki (1984). *Feelings.* New York: Greenwillow. (Nonfiction =NF)

Berger, G. (1980). *The gifted and talented.* New York: Franklin Watts. (NF)

Calvert, P. (1980). *The snowbird.* New York: Charles Scribner's Sons. (Fiction = F)

Cooney B. (1982). *Miss Rumphius.* New York: Viking. (F)

Fitzgerald, J.D. (1967). *The great brain.* New York: Dial Press. (F)

Fitzhugh, L, (1984). *Harriet the spy.* New York: Harper & Row. (F)

Greenwald, S. (1987). *Alvin Webster's surefire plan for success (and how it failed).* Boston: Little, Brown. (F)

Hassler, J. (1981). *Jemmy.* New York: Atheneum. (F)

Heide, F. (1985). *Tales for the perfect child.* New York: Lothrop, Lee, and Shepard. (F)

Manes, S. (1982). *Be a perfect person in just three days!* Boston: Houghton Mifflin. (F)

Oneal, Z. (1980). *The language of goldfish.* New York: Viking Press. (F)

Sobol, D. J. (1963). *Encyclopedia Brown: boy detective.* New York: Thomas Nelson. (F)

MIDDLE AND HIGH SCHOOL

Evernden, M. (1985). *The dream keeper.* New York: Lothrop, Lee & Shepard Books. (F)

Pfeffer, S.B. (1989). *Dear dad, love Laurie.* New York: Scholastic. (F)

Voight, C. (1982). *Tell me if the lovers are losers.* New York: Atheneum. (F)

Voight, C. (1983). *Solitary blue.* New York: Antheneum. (F)

Zindel, P. (1989). *A begonia for Miss Applebaum.* New York: Harper and Row. (F)

Computer Software
Adventure Master, CBS Software, One Fawcett Place, Greenwich, CT 06836.

Analogies, Hartley Courseware, Box 419, Dimondale, MI 48821, (800) 247–1380.

Animate, Broderbund, 17 Paul Drive, San Rafael, CA 94913, (800) 527–6263.

Appleworks, Claris, 440 Clyde Avenue, Mountain View, CA 94043, (415) 960–1500. (Word processing)

Astronomy, The Voyager Company, 2139 Manning Avenue, Los Angeles, CA 90025.

Bank Street Music Writer, Mindscape, Inc. 344 Dundee Road, North Brook, IL 60062.

Bank Street School Filer Datatbases, Sunburst Communication, 39 Washington Avenue, Pleasantville, NY 10570, (800) 431–1934.

Creativity Unlimited, Sunburst Communications, 39 Washington Avenue, Pleasantville, NY 10570, (800) 431–1934.

Dazzle Draw, Broderbund, 17 Paul Drive, San Rafael, CA 94903.

Dinosaurs, Advanced Ideas, Inc., 680 Hawthorne Dr., Tiburon, CA 94920, (415) 425–5086.

Gears, Sunburst Communications, 39 Washington Avenue, Pleasantville, NY 10570, (800) 431–1934.

In Search of the Amazing Thing, Spinnaker, One Kendall Square, Cambridge, MA 02139, (617) 494–1200.

Mathware, Trillum Software, Box 921 Madison Square Station, New York City, NY 10159.

Music Studies, Activision, Inc., 2350 Bayshore Frontage Road, Mountain View, CA 94043.

National Gallery of Art, The Voyager Company, 2139 Manning Avenue, Los Angeles, CA 90025, (213) 475–3524.

Newsroom, Springboard, 7807 Creekridge Creek, Minneapolis, MN 55435, (800) 6554–6301.

Operation Fog, Scholastic, Inc., P.O. Box 7503, 2931 East McCarty, Jefferson City, MO 65102, (800) 654–6301.

Planetary Construction Set, Sunburst Communications, 39 Washington Avenue, Pleasantville, NY 10570, (800) 431–1934.

Science Tool Kit, Broderbund, 17 Paul Drive, San Rafael, CA 94913, (800) 527–6263.

Slide Show, Videodiscovery, P.O. Box 85878, Seattle, WA 98145, (206) 547–7981.

The Electronic Encyclopedia, Grolier Electronic Publishing, Inc., Sherman Turnpike, Danbury, CT 06816, (800) 858–8858.

The Fermi-Pico-Bagel Logo Game, Trillium Press, Box 921, Madison Square Station, New York, NY 10159, (212) 505–1440.

The Incredible Laboratory, Sunburst Communications, 39 Washington Avenue, Pleasantville, NY 10570, (800) 431–1934.

The Print Shop, Broderbund, 17 Paul Drive, San Rafael, CA 94913.

ORGANIZATIONS

Gifted Child Society, 190 Rock Road, Glen Rock, NJ 07452 (201) 444–6530.

National Association for Gifted Children, 1155 Fifteenth Street, N.W., No. 1002, Washington, D. C. 20005, (202) 785–4268.

The Association for the Gifted, the Council for Exceptional Children, 1920 Association Drive, Reston, VA 22091, (703) 620–3660.

BIBLIOGRAPHY FOR TEACHING SUGGESTIONS

Burns, D.E. (1985). Land of opportunity. *Gifted Child Today*, Issue 37, 41–45.

Clark, B. (1992). *Growing up gifted: Developing the potential of children at home and school* (4th ed.). New York: Merrill/Macmillan.

Eby, J. W., & Smutny, J. F., (1990). *A thoughtful overview of gifted education.* New York: Longman.

Ennis, R. H. (1985). A logical basis for measuring critical thinking skills. *Educational Leadership, 43,* 44–48.

Feldhusen, J., Van Tassel-Baska, J., & Seeley, K. (1989). *Excellence in educating the gifted.* Denver, CO: Love.

Flack, J.D. (1986). A new look at a valued partnership: The library media specialist and gifted students. *School Library Media Quarterly, 14,* 174–179.

French, J. N., & Rhoder, C. (1992). *Teaching thinking skills: Theory and practice.* New York: Garland.

Milgrim, R. M., (1989). *Teaching gifted and talented learners in regular classrooms.* Springfield, IL: Charles C. Thomas.

Pendarvis, E.D., Howley, A.A., & Howley, C. B. (1990). *The abilities of gifted children.* Englewood Cliffs, NJ: Prentice Hall.

Raths, L. E., Wassermann, S., Jonas, A., & Rothstein, A. (1986). *Teaching for thinking: Theory, strategies, and activities for the classroom* (2nd ed.). New York: Teachers College, Columbia University.

Reis, S. M., & Cellerino, M. (1983). Guiding gifted students through independent study. *Teaching Exceptional Children, 15,* 136–139.

Renzulli J. S. (1977). *The enrichment triad model.* Mansfield Center, CT: Creative Learning Press.

Renzulli, J. S. (1981). *The revolving door identification model.* Mansfield Center, CT: Creative Learning Press.

Renzulli, J. S., & Reis, S. M. (Eds.). (1986). *The triad reader.* Mansfield Center, CT: Creative Learning Press.

Starko, A. (1986). Meeting the needs of the gifted throughout the school day: Techniques for curriculum compacting. *Roeper Review, 9,* 27–33.

Treffinger, D. J. & Barton, B. L. (1988). Foster independent learning. *Gifted Child Today, 11,* 28–30.

Tuttle, F. B. & Becker, L. A. (1983). *Program design and development for gifted and talented students.* (2nd ed.). Washington, D.C: National Education Association.

*S*ummary

Disagreements about definitions of giftedness center on the questions of exactly how gifted children are superior; how this superiority is measured; the degree to which the individual must excel to be considered gifted; and who should make up the comparison group. Even the terms used can be confusing: *Precocity* indicates remarkable early development; *insight* involves separating relevant from irrelevant information and combining information in novel and productive ways; *genius* refers to rare intellectual powers; *creativity* has to do with the ability to express novel and useful ideas, to see novel relationships, to ask original and crucial questions; *talent* indicates a special ability within a particular area.

The use of individually administered intelligence tests as the only basis for defining giftedness has met with increasing dissatisfaction. First, traditional intelligence tests are limited in what they measure. Second, intelligence is being reconceptualized. The thinking of people with high intelligence appears to be qualitatively different from that of average people, perhaps along such dimensions as analysis, synthesis, or practical application of knowledge. Leading researchers are searching for cognitive characteristics that define either *general* intelligence or *specific* intelligences. Whether intelligence should be lumped into a general characteristic or split into distinctive parts is an ongoing controversy. Third, children exhibit gifted performance in specific domains; it would be possible, for example, for a child with physical disabilites to attain giftedness in any area not impaired by that child's specific physical disability.

Giftedness may be defined as demonstration of high ability, high creativity, and high task commitment. Therefore, a given child may be gifted at one time, in one area of performance, or in one situation and not in another.

Giftedness is not an absolute, fixed human characteristic. Furthermore, it can be defined to include many or only very few people. Consequently the prevalence of giftedness cannot be precisely established. Perhaps 15 to 25 percent of the population has the potential for exhibiting gifted behavior at some time during their schooling in at least one area of performance.

Biological factors are known to contribute significantly to behavioral development and gifted performance. Environmental factors—families, schools, and communities—are also known to influence the development of giftedness. Giftedness, then, is a result of combined biological and environmental influences—nature *and* nurture. Current research suggests that one's collection of genes sets limits of performance; the actual performance within those limits is determined by environmental factors.

Identification of giftedness is complex and involves attention to multiple criteria. Scores on intelligence and achievement tests, teacher and parent nominations, peer and self-nominations, and evaluation of students' work or performances are the most commonly used methods of identification. Identification and selection of students for special programs must be based on multiple criteria to avoid bias against neglected groups of gifted students.

The stereotype of brilliant people as physically weak, socially inept, and prone to emotional instability still exists. But considered as a group, gifted individuals tend to be superior not only in intelligence but also in physique, social attractiveness, achievement, emotional stability, and even moral character. They are not, however, "superhuman." Gifted people tend to excel in academic and occupational pursuits, although there are still many underachieving gifted children. Socially and emotionally, intellectually superior individuals tend, as a group, to be happy, well liked, stable, and less apt to have psychotic and neurotic disorders than average people. Despite outmoded psychoanalytic theories to the contrary, genius and insanity are not linked. Like most of us, brilliant people can be corrupt and unscrupulous, but the majority appear to have a great concern for moral and ethical issues and behavior.

Current attitudes toward special education for gifted students leave much to be desired. Those who argue against special education for gifted students may in reality be arguing against special education for any type of exceptional child. In recent years interest in education of gifted children has increased, but most gifted students in American public schools still receive no special services appropriate to their abilities. The educational reform movement of the 1990s holds both promise and danger for the education of gifted students. The promise derives from emphasis on excellence and attempts to move all students to a substantially higher level of performance. The danger stems from pressures to abandon all forms of ability grouping and to rely solely on strategies such as cooperative learning and peer tutoring to meet the needs of gifted students.

Neglected groups of gifted students include underachievers—those who fail to achieve at a level consistent with their abilities, whatever the reason. Underachievement is often a problem of minority students and those with disabilities, whose special abilities tend to be overlooked because of biased expectations and/or the values of the majority. Gifted females are the largest single group of neglected gifted students.

Education of gifted and talented students should have three characteristics: curriculum designed to accommodate advanced cognitive skills, instructional strategies consistent with learning styles in particular curriculum areas, and administrative facilitation of grouping for instruction. Programs and practices in the education of gifted students are extremely varied and include special schools, acceleration, special classes, tutoring, and enrichment during the school year or summer. Administrative plans for modifying the curriculum include enrichment in the classroom, use of consultant teachers, resource rooms, community mentors, independent study, special classes, and special schools. Acceleration has not been a popular plan for educating gifted students, although considerable research supports it. Models of enrichment include a schoolwide plan in which students continue to engage in enrichment activities for as long as they are able to go beyond the usual curriculum of their age-mates. This model is designed to improve the learning environment for all students.

Teachers of gifted students should exhibit characteristics that are desirable for all teachers. However, they probably must be particularly intelligent, creative, energetic, enthusiastic, and committed to excellence.

Early intervention entails early identification of special abilities, providing stimulation to preschool children to foster giftedness, and special provisions such as acceleration to make education appropriate for the young child's advanced skills. Gifted young children appear to have particular skills much like those of older nongifted children. We may need to take special care not to assume that a child's emotional and social development are advanced just because his or her language and cognitive skills are advanced.

Transitions to adolescence, adulthood, and higher education and employment are typically not the problems for high-achieving gifted children that they are for children with disabilities. Nevertheless, many do need personal and career counseling and help in making contacts with school and community resources. A major issue is acceleration versus enrichment. Programs of acceleration (especially in mathematics, in which students skip grades or complete college-level work early) have been evaluated very positively.

CHAPTER TWELVE

MARY THORNLEY

Mary Thornley, a nationally recognized artist, has recently completed a series of paintings modeled after famous artists. In the Chapter 1 opener, her painting is modeled after Rembrandt and this painting is modeled after Velasquez. She often incorporates themes surrounding hearing impairment into her artwork.

*S*un shone that day long ago in Corcloon. Yvonne was gone to school. Asleep in his blue bed Joseph looked the picture of pleasant childlike thimblework. Nora serenely simpered as she lifted him. Washed and powdered he sat on her lap. Fondly she slipped the geansai [jersey] over his blonde head. His head tilted boldly forward then suddenly it shot backwards. He faced his mother. He gazed his hurt gaze, lip protruding, eyes busy in conversation. He ordered her to look out the window at the sunshine. He looked hard at her ear ordering her to listen to the birds singing. Then jumping on her knees he again asked her to cock her ear and listen to the village children out at play in the school yard. Now he jeered himself. He showed her his arms, his legs, his useless body. Beckoning his tears he shook his head. Looking at his mother he blamed her, he damned her, he mouthed his cantankerous why, why, why me? Distracted by his youthful harshness of realization she tried to distract him. Lifting him in her arms she brought him outside into the farmyard. "Come on till I show you the calves," she coaxed. His lonely tears rushed even faster. He knew why she tried to divert his boyish questioning. . . . "All right," she said, "we'll go back inside and talk." Placing him in his chair she then sat down and faced her erstwhile boy, yes, her golden-haired accuser. Meanwhile he cried continuously, conning himself that he had beaten her to silence. Looking through his tears he saw her as she bent low in order to look into his eyes. "I never prayed for you to be born crippled," she said. "I wanted you to be full of life, able to run and jump and talk just like Yvonne. But you are you, you are Joseph not Yvonne. Listen here Joseph, you can see, you can hear, you can think, you can understand everything you hear, you like your food, you like nice clothes, you are loved by me and Dad. We love you just as you are.". . . His mother said her say and that was that. She got on with her work while he got on with his crying. The decision arrived at that day was burnt forever in his mind. He was only three years in age but he was now fanning the only spark he saw, his being alive and more immediate, his being wanted just as he was.

➤ Christopher Nolan
Under the Eye of the Clock: The Life Story of Christopher Nolan

Parents and
Families

▲ ▲ ▲

A fertile ground for conflict or harmony, the family, especially the family of the 1990s—and more especially the family of the 1990s with a family member who has a disability—is the perfect locale for the study of the interplay of human emotion and behavior. Think of your own family as you were growing up. Think of the dynamics of interaction among you and your sibling(s) and parent(s). These interactions were no doubt carried out within the full range of human emotions. Now, add to this mixture of human interaction a dose of disability. Consider how much more complex living in your family would have been if you had had a brother, like Joseph, with severe cerebral palsy (see p. 491).

In addition to underscoring the complexities of living with a family member with disabilities, the autobiographical account of Joseph and his mother also demonstrates how resilient some families can be in the face of extreme difficulties. A child with disabilities does not always threaten the well-being of a family. Reactions of family members to the individual with a disability can run the gamut from absolute rejection to absolute acceptance, from intense hate to intense love, from total neglect to total overprotection. In fact, some parents and siblings assert that having a family member with a disability has actually strengthened the family. As highlighted by the interaction between Joseph and his mother, however, coping with the stress of raising and living with a child who has a disability rarely comes easily.

In this chapter, we explore the dynamics of families with children who are disabled and discuss parental involvement in their treatment and education. Before proceeding further, however, it is instructive to consider the role of parents of children who are disabled from a historical perspective.

PROFESSIONALS' CHANGING VIEWS OF PARENTS

Today, the knowledgeable professional who works with exceptional individuals is aware of the importance of the family. We now recognize that the family of the person with a disability, especially the parents, can help us in our educational efforts. To ignore the family is shortsighted because it can lessen the effectiveness of teaching. Though today we recognize how crucial it is to consider the concerns of parents and families in treatment and educational programs for individuals who are disabled, this was not always the case.

Professionals' views of the role of parents have changed dramatically. In the not too distant past, some professionals looked to the parents primarily as a cause of some of the child's problems or as a place to lay blame when practitioners' interventions were ineffective. According to one set of authorities, negative views of parents were in some ways a holdover from the eugenics movement of the late nineteenth and early twentieth centuries (Turnbull & Turnbull, 1990). Professionals associated with the **eugenics movement** believed in the selective breeding of humans. For example, they proposed sterilization of people with mental retardation because they erroneously believed that virtually all cases of mental retardation were caused by heredity.

Although the eugenics movement had largely died out by the 1930s and few professionals any longer blamed disabilities primarily on heredity, the climate was ripe for some of them to blame a variety of disabilities, especially emotional problems, on the child-rearing practices of parents. For example, until the 1970s

➤ **eugenics movement.** A drive by some professionals to "better" the human race through selective breeding and sterilization of "unfit" parents such as people with mental retardation. This popular movement of the late nineteenth and early twentieth centuries resulted in laws restricting the marriage of individuals with mental retardation and sterilization of some of them.

MYTH ➤ Parents are to blame for many of the problems of their children with disabilities.

FACT ➤ Parents can influence their children's behavior, but so, too, can children affect how their parents behave. Research shows that some children with disabilities are born with difficult temperaments, which can affect parental behavior.

MYTH ➤ Parents must experience a series of reactions—shock and disruption, denial, sadness, anxiety and fear, anger—before adapting to the birth of a child with a disability.

FACT ➤ Parents do not go through emotional reactions in a lockstep fashion. They may experience some, or all, of these emotions, but not necessarily in any particular order.

MYTH ➤ Many parents of infants with disabilities go from physician to physician, "shopping" for an optimistic diagnosis.

FACT ➤ Just the opposite is often true. Parents frequently suspect that something is wrong with their baby but are told by professionals not to worry, the child will "outgrow" the problem. Then they seek another opinion.

MYTH ➤ Fathers are unimportant in the development of the child with a disability.

FACT ➤ Although they are frequently ignored by researchers and generally do experience less stress than mothers, fathers can play a critical role in the dynamics of the family. The father's role has become more important, but research indicates that his role is still often indirect, that is, the father can influence the mother's reactions to the child.

MYTH ➤ Siblings are usually unaffected by the addition of a child with a disability to the family.

FACT ➤ Siblings often experience the same emotional reactions as parents, and their lack of maturity can make coping with these emotions more difficult.

MYTH ➤ The primary role of the early intervention professional should be to provide expertise for the family.

FACT ➤ Many authorities now agree that professionals should help parents become more involved in making decisions for the family.

MYTH ➤ The "typical" family in the United States has two parents, is middle class, and only the father works outside the home.

FACT ➤ Demographics are changing rapidly. There are now many more families with both parents working, more single-parent families, and families living in poverty.

MYTH ➤ Parents who elect not to be actively involved (e.g., attending and offering suggestions at IEP meetings or visiting the school frequently) in their child's education and treatment are neglectful.

FACT ➤ Although it is desirable for parents to be involved, it is sometimes very difficult for them to do so because of their commitments to other family functions (e.g., work and child care).

MYTH ➤ Professionals are always in the best position to help families of persons with a disability.

FACT ➤ Informal sources of support, such as extended family and friends are often more effective than formal sources of support, such as professionals and agencies, in helping families adapt to a family member with a disability.

MYTH ➤ Teachers should respect the privacy of parents and communicate with them only when absolutely necessary, for example, when their child has exhibited serious behavior problems.

FACT ➤ Teachers should initiate some kind of contact with parents as soon as possible so that, if something like a serious behavior infraction does occur, some rapport with the parents will already have been established.

and 1980s, when research demonstrated a biochemical basis for autism, it was quite popular to pin the blame for autism on the parents, especially mothers. The leading proponent of this viewpoint, Bruno Bettelheim, asserted that mothers who were cold and unresponsive toward their children—"refrigerator moms"—produced autism in their children (Bettelheim, 1950, 1967).

In the late 1970s and early 1980s professionals became less likely to blame parents automatically for the problems of their children. There were at least two reasons for this more positive view. First, Richard Bell forwarded the notion that the direction of causation between child and adult behavior is a two-way street (Bell & Harper, 1977). Sometimes the parent changes the behavior of the child or infant; sometimes the reverse is true. With specific regard to children who are disabled, some researchers point out that children with disabilities, even as infants, sometimes possess difficult temperaments, which influence how parents respond to them (Brooks-Gunn & Lewis, 1984; Mahoney & Robenalt, 1986). Some infants who are disabled, for example, are relatively unresponsive to stimulation from their parents, making it more difficult to carry on interactions with them. With an understanding of the reciprocal nature of parent-child interaction, we are thus more likely, for example, to sympathize with a mother's frustration in trying to cuddle an infant with severe retardation or a father's anger in attempting to deal with his teenager who has an emotional or behavior disorder.

Second, professionals began to recognize the potentially positive influence of the family in the educational process. Although at first many of them tended to think that parents needed training to achieve a positive effect on their children, more and more have recognized that parents often have as much, and in some cases more, to offer than professionals regarding suggestions for the treatment of their children. The prevailing philosophy now dictates that whenever possible, professionals should seek the special insights that parents can offer by virtue of living with their child. Furthermore, authorities today are less likely to view the purpose of early intervention to be the training of parents to assume the role of quasi-therapist or quasi-teacher (Guralnick, 1991). Instead, many believe the goal should be to develop and preserve the natural parent-child relationship as much as possible, that a healthy parent-child relationship is inherently beneficial.

For at least three reasons, professionals now have a more positive attitude toward the role of parents:

1. More and more special educators are supporting the idea that early intervention that takes place in the home and/or uses the home as a basis for curricular objectives has the best chance of success (McDonnell & Hardman, 1988). Early childhood special educators have noted that education should be focused on enabling preschool children to function in the home because a large portion of their time is spent in that setting.

2. Parents themselves have become more active in advocating services in an organized and effective way for their children. In the process, they have frequently argued that they themselves should be given a voice in how schools educate their children.

3. Because of the efforts of parental and professional organizations, Congress has passed federal laws (PL 94-142 and PL 99-457) stipulating that schools make a concerted effort to involve parents and families in the education of their children with disabilities. Among other things, for example, PL 94-142 (IDEA) specifies that schools attempt to include parents of children

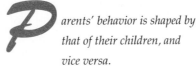

arents' behavior is shaped by that of their children, and vice versa.

with disabilities in the development of an individualized education plan (IEP) (see Chapter 1). In the case of children under three years of age, PL 99-457 dictates that schools must involve parents in the development of an **individualized family service plan (IFSP).** The focus of the IFSP is not only on the individual child who has a disability but also on his or her family. It specifies services the family needs to enhance the child's development.

THE EFFECTS OF A CHILD WITH A DISABILITY ON THE FAMILY

The birth of any child can have a significant effect on the dynamics of the family. Parents and other children in the family must undergo a variety of changes to adapt to the presence of a new member. The effects on the family of the birth of a child who has a disability can be even more profound. Infants and children with disabilities are frequently characterized by extremes of behavior, which in turn influence the interactions they have with parents and siblings. The extra care and special accommodations required by some children who are disabled often alter how parents and siblings interact with the child who has a disability as well as with nondisabled family members.

Not only is the study of families of individuals with disabilities difficult because of the complexity of the interactions that take place, but it is also complicated by the fact that studies rely so much on subjective impressions. When talking about the impact a child who is disabled has on a family, we are talking to a great extent about *feelings*—the feelings of parents toward the child and toward

> **individualized family service plan (IFSP).** A plan for services for young children with disabilities (under 3 years of age) and their families drawn up by professionals and parents; similar to an IEP for older children; mandated by PL99–457.

society's reactions to the child, the feelings of the child's siblings toward the child and society, and the feelings of the child who has a disability. When talking about feelings, of course, we are in the realm of subjectivity. Psychologists are notoriously good at describing people's emotions but poor at understanding them. The subjective and complex nature of the familial feelings aroused by children with disabilities makes our job of comprehending their nature extremely difficult.

Parental Reactions

A Stage Theory Approach

Traditionally, researchers and clinicians have suggested that parents go through a series of stages after learning they have a child with a disability. Some of these stages parallel the proposed sequence of responses that accompany a person's reactions to the death of a loved one. A representative set of stages based on interviews of parents of infants with serious physical disabilities includes shock and disruption, denial, sadness, anxiety and fear, anger, and finally adaptation (Drotar, Baskiewicz, Irvin, Kennell, & Klaus, 1975).

Several authorities have questioned the wisdom of this stage approach in understanding parental reactions (Turnbull & Turnbull, 1990). It is clear that we should not think of parents as marching through a series of stages in lockstep fashion. It would be counterproductive, for example, to think, "This mother is now in the anxiety and fear stage; we need to encourage her now to go through the anger stage so she can finally adapt."

One argument against a strict stage model comes from the fact that many parents report that they do not engage in denial. In fact, they are often the first to suspect a problem. It is largely a myth that parents of children who are disabled go from physician to physician, shopping for a more favorable diagnosis. It is all too frequently the case that they have to convince the doctor that there is something wrong with their child (Akerley, 1985).

Although they may not go through these reactions in a rigid fashion, some parents do experience some or all of these emotions at one time or another. A common reaction, they report, is guilt.

The Role of Guilt

Parents of children with disabilities frequently wrestle with the terrifying feeling that they are in some way responsible for their child's condition. Even though in the vast majority of cases there is absolutely no basis for such thoughts, guilt is one of the most commonly reported feelings of parents of exceptional children. The high prevalence of guilt is probably due to the fact that the primary cause of so many disabilities is unknown. Uncertainty about the cause of the child's disability creates an atmosphere conducive to speculation by the parents that they themselves are to blame. Mothers are particularly vulnerable. As Featherstone (1980), the mother of a boy who is blind and has hydrocephaly, mental retardation, cerebral palsy, and seizures, relates:

> Our children are wondrous achievements. Their bodies grow inside ours. If their defects originated in utero, we blame our inadequate bodies or inadequate caution. If . . . we accept credit for our children's physical beauty (and most of us do, in our hearts), then inevitably we assume responsibility for their physical defects.

he significant role of the father in the development of children is increasingly recognized.

The world makes much of the pregnant woman. People open doors for her, carry her heavy parcels, offer footstools and unsolicited advice. All this attention seems somehow posited on the idea that she is creating something miraculously fine. When the baby arrives imperfect, the mother feels she has failed not only herself and her husband, but the rest of the world as well.

Soon this diffuse sense of inadequacy sharpens. Nearly every mother fastens on some aspect of her own behavior and blames the tragedy on that. (pp. 73-74)

In addition to ambivalence concerning the cause of the child's disability, parents can also feel vulnerable to criticism from others about how they deal with their child's problems. They sometimes sense, whether deservedly or not, that they are the focus of others' attention, that their decisions regarding treatment, educational placement, and so forth, are being evaluated by others (Featherstone, 1980). It may be that the public scrutinizes parents of a child with a disability because they are curious about how the parent will deal with the relatively uncommon event of having a child with a disability. In any case, guilt is an emotion that many parents of children who are disabled must learn to deal with.

The Role of the Father

Almost all the research on parental reactions to children with disabilities has focused on the mother. There have been a couple of studies comparing the reactions of mothers and fathers (Beckman, 1991; Rousey, Best, & Blacher, 1992), but the results have been contradictory—one study indicated that mothers have more stress and the other suggested no differences in parental reactions. A good guess would be that mothers are at greater risk than fathers to experience stress because, even though today's fathers are more involved with their children than fathers were of previous generations, mothers usually assume more caretaking responsibility. Furthermore, authorities posit that fathers of children with disabilities play an even more peripheral parental role than do fathers of nondisabled children. Available evidence indicates that the father's part in influencing the development of his child who is disabled is more indirect than direct (Bristol & Gallagher, 1986; Kazak & Marvin, 1984). He can affect how the mother will interact with the child by his attitudes toward her and the family. His support, or lack of it, can have a significant effect on family harmony.

The reasons that fathers of children with disabilities play a more peripheral parenting role than fathers of nondisabled children are not known. Because society still, for the most part, expects women to engage in caretaking, it may be that men find it easy to defer to their wives when a child requires extra care. However, some have speculated that the sharp differentiation of the two roles—the mother as the caretaker and the father as the supportive spouse—may be functional for some families (Kazak & Marvin, 1984). That is, they hypothesize that specialization of parental duties may be an efficient solution to the daily pressures of raising some children who have disabilities.

Parental Adjustment

Evidence is abundant that parents of children with disabilities undergo more than the average amount of stress (Beckman, 1991; Dumas, Wolf, Fisman, & Cullingan, 1991; Hanson, Ellis, & Deppe, 1989; Singer & Irvin, 1989). The stress is usually not the result of major catastrophic events, but rather the consequence of daily burdens related to child care. It may be that a single event, such as a family member coming down with a serious illness, will precipitate a family crisis, but its effects are even more devastating if the family was already under stress because of a multitude of "daily hassles."

There is no universal parental reaction to the added stress of raising a child with a disability. Much depends on the parents' prior psychological makeup, the severity of the child's disability, and the amount of support the parents receive from friends, relatives, professionals, and each other. Although there are exceptions, it is fair to say that parents who were well adjusted and happily married before the birth of the child have a better chance of coping with the situation than those who were already having psychological or marital problems. It is also evident that parents of children with more severe disabilities usually have a more difficult time than parents of children with mild disabilities because the child-care burdens are greater. Again, however, there are exceptions. As Bronicki and Turnbull (1987) state,

> A more severe disability does not always produce greater stress. As one parent of a young adolescent commented:
>
>> Don has been labelled profoundly retarded. He is not able to do anything to take care of himself, cannot walk, and has no language. Sure, he creates strains and stresses. But I remind myself that I never have to chase him around the house, he never talks back or sasses, he doesn't have to enter the rat race of teen-age years like my other sons, and he does not try to hurt himself. (p. 23)

It is important to keep in mind that the majority of parents of children with disabilities do not have major psychological problems. The types of problems some of them may be at risk to develop, for example, would be characterized as relatively mild forms of depression (Carr, 1988; Singer & Irvin, 1989).

Some parents report that the addition of a child with a disability to the family actually has some unanticipated positive results. Some parents note, for example,

Issues in Special Education — Families With Members Who Are Disabled Hit Hard by Budget Cuts

CNN

*T*he contemporary trend to deinstitutionalize goes hand-in-hand with budgetary factors that have a direct impact on families caring for children with disabilities. When state agencies send persons with disabilities home, or out on their own, they do not necessarily send along the funds that have been used to underwrite their institutional care as well.

Children with severe or multiple disabilities often require both equipment- and personnel-intensive care that state governments can no longer financially provide. Excellent institutional care that provides physical therapy, social programs, and personal contact is often too expensive for recessionary times. Requiring families to pick up the slack by providing in-home care is often not the ideal solution. Parents often lack the finances and the expertise that such intensive care requires.

Persons with mental disabilities, particularly those who are aging, can be left in tragic situations. Among the growing population of homeless persons are many who have been turned out of institutional care and have no family or home to return to.

Now that persons with mental retardation commonly outlive their parents, parents who have provided loving in-home care all their lives worry about who will be there for their adult children when they are no longer able to do so.

- How can families be expected to shoulder the costly care needed by family members who are disabled?
- Does the government have a special financial responsibility for its exceptional members?

that they have become more concerned about social issues and are more tolerant of differences in other people than they were before. Moreover, some parents claim that the birth of their child with a disability has brought the family closer together. This is not to minimize the fact that the added stress a child with a disability often brings can have a devastating impact on the stability of some families. It is dangerous to assume, though, that the birth of a child with a disability automatically spells doom for the psychological well-being of the parents or the stability of their marriage.

Sibling Reactions

Although a relatively large body of literature pertains to parental reactions, there is much less information about siblings of persons with disabilities. What is available, however, indicates that siblings can, and frequently do, experience the same emotions—fear, anger, guilt, and so forth—that parents do. In fact, in some ways siblings may have an even more difficult time than their parents in coping with some of these feelings. First, being less mature, they may have trouble putting some of their negative sensations into proper perspective. Second, they may not have as broad a base of individuals with whom they can discuss their feelings (Featherstone, 1980). And third, they may be uncomfortable asking their parents the questions that bother them, for example, whether they will "catch" what their brother has, whether they were in some way responsible for their sister's disability, whether they will be called on to take care of their brother after their parents die.

H E'S MY BROTHER ➤

There are now many children's books that deal with the subject of exceptional children. The following excerpts from Joe Lasker's *He's My Brother* deal specifically with the feelings a brother or sister of a child with a disability often has.

Jamie's my brother.
He doesn't have many friends.
Little kids play with him.
Sometimes a big kid plays when no one else is around.
Jamie gets teased.
He doesn't know how to answer back.
When he tries, he gets in trouble, and comes home.
Becka is our sister.
She likes Jamie.
She bakes brownies for him.
When kids on the block choose up teams, they choose Jamie last.
It took Jamie a long time to learn to tie his shoelaces.
He still has trouble hanging up his clothes.
I guess I have, too.
School is easy for me.
But hard for Jamie.
Jamie gets mixed up at school.
Especially when it gets noisy.

When it's time for a test, Jamie thinks he knows the answers.
Then everything goes wrong.
Sometimes the kids make fun of Jamie.
They take his cookies or spill his milk.
Sometimes I get mad at him because he is so slow.
Then I feel sorry and play a game of checkers with him.
But there are things Jamie likes a lot.
He loves babies.
He loves animals . . .
He never hurts them.
One day Jamie said, "Wouldn't it be nice if we could be friends with all the animals in the world?"
I wish I'd thought of that! . . .
Mom helps Jamie with his schoolwork.
Dad reads to Jamie.
I make up stories for Jamie.
Stories to tell him we love him.
He laughs.
He's my brother.

SOURCE: He's My Brother by Joe Lasker. Copyright 1974 by Joe Lasker. Excerpted by permission of Albert Whitman & Company.

Although some feelings about their sibling's disability may not appear for many years, a substantial number of accounts indicate that nondisabled siblings are aware at an amazingly early age that their brother or sister is different in some way. Jewell (1985), for example, recounts how her sister would make allowances for her cerebral palsy by playing a special version of "dolls" with her, a version in which all the dolls had disabilities. Though they may have a vague sense that their sibling with a disability is different, the young nondisabled siblings may still have misconceptions about the nature of their sibling's condition, especially regarding its cause. Some parents have found children's literature useful in helping young children cope with their feelings about their disabled brother or sister. (See the box above for an example of one of these books.)

As nondisabled siblings grow older, their concerns often become more focused on how society views them and their sibling who is disabled. Adolescence can be a particularly difficult period. As Featherstone (1980) notes, it is important for teenagers not to be considered different by their peers, but at the same time to be considered special within the confines of their own family. Being the brother or sister of a child with a disability, however, often singles a person out as being different. At the same time, the nondisabled sibling can feel slighted because his or her exceptional brother or sister receives so much attention from their parents. The following account, by the sister of a brother with cerebral palsy and mental retardation, is an example of the reactions of some siblings:

I cannot pinpoint exactly the time or the circumstance when I first became aware of Robin's handicaps. Several incidents come to mind, all of which occurred around the time I was eleven years old. One involved a trip to the shoe store where Robin was to be fitted for orthopedic shoes; another, a trip to the town near our country home for dinner at the YMCA. On both of these occasions, I can remember being acutely embarrassed by the ill-concealed stares our family received as we entered pushing Robin in his wheelchair. I was certain that everyone was looking at my brother with his obvious handicap and then wondering what was wrong with the rest of us. As a result of the feelings aroused in me by these occurrences, I began to refuse to go out to dinner or shopping with my family and took precautions to avoid being seen on the street or in the yard with Robin.

These avoidance procedures on my part were not taken without an accompanying sense of guilt. I knew that it was wrong for me to be ashamed of my brother. I loved Robin dearly and realized that the opinions (real or imagined) of others should have no bearing on my relationship with him. . . .

Following my period of avoidance, I entered a phase of false pretenses. I forced myself to appear in public with him—but only if I looked my very best (freshly washed hair, make-up, snazzy outfit, etc.). My specious reasoning was that if people were going to stare, they weren't going to find anything wrong with me. Also, though I am reluctant to admit such a selfish thought, I suppose I wanted to encourage people to think along the lines of "Oh, dear, look at that sweet young girl pushing her poor crippled brother around. What a wonderful child she must be." (Turnbull & Turnbull, 1985, pp. 94-95)

Siblings' Adjustment

Children, like parents, can adapt well or poorly to a sibling with a disability. Research indicates that some siblings have trouble adjusting, some have no trouble adjusting, and some actually appear to benefit from the experience (Seligman & Darling, 1989; Senapati & Hayes, 1988). Like parents, however, siblings of children with disabilities are at a greater risk than siblings of nondisabled children to have difficulties in adjustment.

Why some individuals respond negatively, whereas others do not, is not completely understood. Authorities point to three situations that can make it particularly difficult for children to develop positive attitudes toward their sibling with a disability:

1. When the two siblings are close in age there is more chance of conflict (Simeonsson & Bailey, 1986). Apparently, the similarity in age makes the differences in ability between the two siblings more obvious.
2. Siblings of the same sex are more likely to experience conflict (Simeonsson & Bailey, 1986).
3. Nondisabled girls who are older than their siblings who have a disability are likely to have negative attitudes when they reach adolescence because they often shoulder child-care responsibilities (Stoneman, Brody, Davis, & Crapps, 1988).

FAMILY INVOLVEMENT IN TREATMENT AND EDUCATION

As noted earlier, today's professionals are more likely to recognize the positive influence parents can have on their exceptional children's development than was once the case. This more positive attitude toward parents is reflected in how parents are now involved in the treatment and education of their children. One team

➤ **professional-centered program.** Type of early intervention program; assumes that professionals have the expertise rather than families; popular at one time.

➤ **family-allied program.** Type of early intervention program; family members carry out interventions developed by professionals.

➤ **family-focused program.** Type of early intervention program; professionals view family members as more capable than professional-centered and family-allied programs but not as capable as family-centered programs; professionals and family members develop interventions together.

➤ **family-centered program.** Type of early intervention program; consumer-driven in that professionals are viewed as working *for* families; views family members as the most important decision makers.

of researchers (Dunst, Johanson, Trivette, & Hamby, 1991) has categorized early intervention programs for families with a child who has a disability as being: (1) *professional-centered*, (2) *family-allied*, (3) *family-focused*, or (4) *family-centered*. These models represent a continuum of how much credence is given to the beliefs, values, and needs of the family and how much faith is placed in the family's ability to solve its own problems. **Professional-centered** models assume that professionals have virtually all of the expertise and the family is in need of that expertise in order to function. In **family-allied** models, family members carry out interventions developed by professionals. In **family-focused** programs, the family is viewed as more capable in that professionals and family members develop interventions together; however, the family is still seen as needing professional help and formal sources. **Family-centered** models are consumer-driven in that professionals work *for* the family, looking for ways to increase the decision-making power of the family and to encourage the family to obtain access to non-professional (e.g., family and friends) as well as formal sources of support.

At one time, most family intervention programs were professional-centered or family-allied models. Most programs today, however, are either family-focused or family-centered (Dunst et al., 1991). We no longer view parents as passive recipients of professional advice. Today, we are much more likely to consider parents as equal partners in the development of treatment and educational programs for their children.

The effort to build professional-parent partnerships is consistent with the thinking of child-development theorists who stress the importance of the social context within which child development occurs. Urie Bronfenbrenner (1979), a renowned child-development and family theorist, has been most influential in stressing that we cannot understand an individual's behavior without understanding the influence of the family on the behavior of the individual. Furthermore, we cannot understand the behavior of the family without considering the influence of other social systems, such as the extended family (e.g., grandparents), friends, and professionals, on the behavior of the family. The interaction between the family and the surrounding social system is critical to how the family functions. A supportive network of professionals, and especially friends, can be beneficial to the family with a child who has a disability.

Current approaches to involving families in treatment and education of their children take into account how the family fits within the broader societal context. We now discuss two such approaches—the family systems approach of the Turnbulls (Turnbull & Turnbull, 1990) and the social support systems approach of Dunst and his colleagues (Dunst, Trivette, & Deal, 1988; Dunst, Trivette, Gordon, & Pletcher, 1989). These two approaches are very similar and overlap in many ways. They differ only with regard to emphasis. The family systems approach considers events that occur within the family as well as the broader social context. The social systems approach, although hardly ignoring the inner workings of the family unit, tends to focus more on the family's relationship with its social environment.

A Family Systems Approach

The philosophy behind a family systems approach is that all parts of the family are interrelated, so that events affecting any one family member also have an effect on the others. The more treatment and educational programs take into account the relationships and interactions among family members, the more likely they are to be successful. In other words, family systems theorists advocate that the family rather than the individual should be the focus of intervention efforts. The Turnbulls' model includes four interrelated components: **family characteristics**, **family interaction**, **family functions**, and **family life cycle** (Turnbull & Turnbull, 1990).

Family Characteristics

Family characteristics provide a description of basic information related to the family. They include characteristics of the exceptionality (e.g., the type of exceptionality and the severity of the disability), characteristics of the family (e.g., size, cultural background, socioeconomic status, and geographic location), personal characteristics of each family member (e.g., health and coping styles), and special conditions (e.g., child or spousal abuse and poverty). Family characteristics help determine how family members interact with themselves and with others outside the family. To begin to understand how a family functions, we need to have a good picture of its characteristics. It will probably make a difference, for example, whether the child with a disability is retarded or hearing impaired, the child is an only child or has five siblings, the family is upper middle-class or lives in poverty, and so forth.

Recent trends in our society make it even more important for teachers and other professionals who work with families to take into account family characteristics. Demographic changes that have occurred over the past few decades make it imperative for professionals to be prepared to encounter a wide diversity of families. The middle-class nuclear family with two parents and only the father working outside the home is no longer the norm. There has been an increase in the number of: (1) families in which both parents work outside the home (Hofferth & Phillips, 1987), (2) single-parent families (Norton & Glick, 1986), and (3) families who are living in poverty (Baumeister, Kupstas, & Klindworth, 1990).

Coupled with these demographic changes, and to a certain extent influenced by them, families today live under a great deal more stress. For one thing, today's parents have less leisure time than ever before. Compared to the late 1960s, for example, today's mothers and fathers between the ages of 18 and 39 put in 241 and 189 more annual hours of work, respectively (Leete-Guy & Schor, 1992).

The result of these demographic changes and more stressful living conditions may be a reduced amount of support that is available for children with a disability from their parents (Hallahan, 1992). Parents are so consumed with meeting their own needs that they are unable to provide as much support to their children as was once the case. A counselor, with over 20 years of experience in working with families with and without members who have a disability, has observed that:

> It has only been recently that I have observed so much anger, insecurity, and despair among all families....
>
> Families are experiencing a great deal of fatigue, and lack energy to advocate like they used to on behalf of their son or daughter, brother or sister. Both parents are working, they have no leisure time, and many are barely able to take care of their own responsibilities. (Stark, 1992, pp. 248-249)

These dramatic societal changes present formidable challenges for teachers and other professionals working with families. As the configuration of families

➤ **family characteristics.** A component of the Turnbulls' family systems model; includes type and severity of the disability as well as such things as size, cultural background, and socioeconomic background of the family.

➤ **family interaction.** A component of the Turnbulls' family systems model; refers to how cohesive and adaptable the family is.

➤ **family functions.** A component of the Turnbulls' family systems model; includes such things as economic, daily care, social, medical, and educational needs.

➤ **family life cycle.** A component of the Turnbulls' family systems model; consists of birth and early childhood (0 to 5 years), childhood (5 to 12 years), adolescence (12 to 21), and adulthood.

Collaboration

A Key to Success

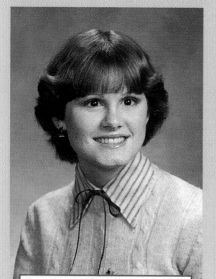

KATHY WYATT ANDREWS

Parent infant advisor for families children with hearing-impairments from birth to age three, North Harris County Cooperative for the Education of the Deaf, Houston, Texas; B.S., Education of the Deaf and Elementary Education, Ball State University; M.Ed., Educational Administration and Supervision, Sam Houston State University; pursuing master's degree in special education

SARA ANN KLIER

Married mother of two children—Katie, eight, and Daniel, four

➤ **Kathy** I have a personal interest in deafness because my sister and I have profound, unilateral, sensorineural hearing losses. Since 1985, I've been the parent infant advisor for a deaf education program. The children I serve vary greatly in ability levels and in the extent of their disabilities. Several of my students have additional disabilities involving vision impairments, mental retardation, epilepsy, emotional disturbance, cerebral palsy, and poor health. The communication modes demonstrated by the children include pointing, gestures, unintelligible vocalizations, facial expressions, physical contact, and/or meaningful one- and two-word phrases using their voices or formal signs. Where I teach in Houston

we have a mixture of black, white, and Hispanic families. I serve families with a variety of structures, including two-parent families, single mothers, and divorced parents. One of the families I work with is the Kliers, who have Daniel..

➤ **Ann** Daniel has been diagnosed as developmentally delayed, autistic, and mildly hearing impaired. His medical problems were overwhelming from birth. With his first cry, we knew he had many physical complications. He weighed 3 lbs. 14 oz., and he stopped breathing within two hours of delivery. The next month was a never-ending roller coaster ride of fear, guilt, and constant crises. When the day finally arrived for Daniel to come home, the decision to discharge him was made

by the insurance company. Although he had not achieved the minimal requirements of adequate feeding ability, weight maintenance, and body temperature maintenance, the medical staff all but washed their hands of Daniel. It was a terrifying experience, as the doctors gave us no guidance in how we should care for Daniel. The nature of his problems had not yet been diagnosed, nor could his potential be fully assessed. Our family stepped into the world of the unknown quite alone. After months of fear and frustration, medical experts finally agreed that Daniel was a gravely ill child, but they couldn't explain why. Eventually, Daniel was diagnosed as having a mild, mixed hearing loss. We were then referred to the deaf education cooperative, where we met Kathy.

➤ **Kathy** I met the Klier family when Daniel was two years and four months old. He had been recently diagnosed as having a mild, mixed hearing loss in the right ear and a moderate, primarily sensorineural hearing loss in the left ear. In addition, Daniel's hearing loss fluctuated because of chronic middle ear infections. Because of his weak condition, Daniel was sitting independently and crawling, but he was unable to support his weight in order to walk alone. His skills in the areas of socialization, self-help, motor ability, cognition, and language were all delayed by fourteen to twenty-two months. He was subsequently diagnosed as mentally retarded. Daniel preferred to perform self-stimulation behaviors, such as rocking, flicking door handles and door stops, banging his head, and staring at lights and objects. He disliked physical contact and did not seek personal attention. He displayed an increasing number of autistic characteristics and was unable to sleep through the night. He would awaken screaming and crying and begin self-abusive behavior, including scratching, biting, and hitting.

➤ **Ann** Kathy began by evaluating Daniel at home in an environment that was familiar to him. She tested him with no preconceived opinions and gave him the opportunity to demonstrate his capabilities. Afterward, she presented us with a program that would take Daniel through a series of steps toward achieving specific tasks. She scheduled weekly two-hour home visits. In introducing each new project, Kathy took the time to explain the significance of mastering the main goal and all the intermediate steps. She often adjusted the teaching procedures based on my feedback. She frequently brought articles, books, and audiovisual tapes that further explained Daniel's disibilities or offered techniques for teaching new skills. Kathy also accompanied me on doctor's visits as needed. She taught me how to prepare written questions to ask the physicians as well as how to get important information from them, including phone numbers, referrals, or another appointment as necessary. We were a team; we each played an important role in Daniel's education. When it was time for Daniel to be enrolled in a school-centered program at the age of three, Kathy explained the available preschool options and we visited each of the potential placements while the classes were in session.

➤ **Kathy** Our deaf education program uses a curriculum specifically designed to address the needs of infants with hearing impairments and their families. It's a home-based curriculum that permits the parent advisor to take advantage of the child's natural surroundings and familiar experiences. In implementing the program, I schedule weekly or biweekly home visits of an hour or two with each of the families. I act as a teacher and advisor to the families. The parents are expected to be their child's primary teachers and care givers. It's my responsibility to educate the parents in four major areas of hearing impairment: hearing aid usage, auditory training, communication skills, and oral and/or manual language skills. In addition, we monitor and address the child's progress in socialization, self-help skills, motor skills, and cognition. I have four major goals. First, I provide professional and emotional support during the early stages of identification, treatment, and placement, and throughout the delivery of the program. Second, I assess the needs of the parents and the child in conjunction with other professionals and plan the program based on the assessment. Third,

I implement my services unobtrusively within the current structure of the family's culture and philosophy. Fourth, I teach the parents new skills through modeling, while providing the rationale and several suggestions for implementing the skills.

➤ **Ann** One of our real challenges was to present a variety of activities and materials that would maintain Daniel's focus and not encourage self-stimulation. Even though Daniel needed much repetition to learn a new skill, we had to teach the task in very short intervals over a long period of time. This was really frustrating! We had to remind ourselves constantly of our objectives so we didn't lose hope.

➤ **Kathy** Another challenge was to determine Daniel's specific medical problems, according to the behaviors he displayed. Once the behaviors were diagnosed, his parents and I sought solutions

> *. . .a teacher should assist parents in acquiring the skills and confidence to raise a child with a disability . . .*

through the medical community. Medication and surgeries to remove his adenoids and place pressure-equalization tubes in his ears were really helpful. Naturally, communication is the essence of any teacher-parent relationship. Respect and honesty are the foundation for effective communication. We had to be open to each other's ideas and concerns. An honest relationship demanded that I say "I don't know" when I was uncertain of the next step or lacked the information they requested. It also required the parents to be honest about their implementation of the teaching plans and in reporting Daniel's success. The Kliers and I had to cooperate in our problem-solving. We didn't know what methods and materials would benefit Daniel. We had to develop teaching plans, imple-

ment the strategies, and finally revise those plans as needed. This effort meant that we sometimes had to accept frustration and defeat.

➤ **Ann** As we developed a common interest in Daniel and a close working relationship with Kathy, we felt comfortable in sharing personal feelings that assisted us in healing our anger, guilt, and heartache. As Kathy opened the door to our understanding Daniel's disabilities, my family became his teachers and advocates. I also learned that through active participation in Daniel's education, my family can best assist him in reaching his fullest potential. I've found that his teachers feel appreciated and respond positively to my presence. They realize that they don't have to shoulder the entire burden of Daniel's education. The results have been greater than we expected! Daniel is now able to walk independently, feed himself with minimal assistance, show affection toward others, interact appropriately with his environment, color, point to several objects, and gesture to express his wants, and he is beginning to verbalize.

➤ **Kathy** It has been exciting to see Ann and her husband develop self-confidence in their parenting skills. They are very capable of handling the new difficulties which will arise in the future. The Kliers have always had the potential to teach Daniel and to solve crises, but now they are aware of those abilities. Ultimately a teacher should assist parents in acquiring the skills and confidence to raise a child with a disability rather than make the parents dependent on educators' efforts. A child will have many teachers, but he will have the same parents all his life. Too often, teachers fail to realize all of the responsibilities and roles required of parents, which include spouse, employee, housekeeper, and parent to the child's other siblings. My greatest challenge is learning to accept the philosophies, priorities, and life-styles of individual families.

changes, professionals will need to alter their approaches. For example, the same approaches that are successful with middle-class, two-parent families may not be the ones required for single mothers. Also, professionals need to understand that today's parent is living under more and more stress and may find it more difficult to devote time and energy to working on behalf of his or her child.

Family Interaction

Family members can have a variety of functional and dysfunctional modes of interacting with one another. Turnbull and colleagues note that the amount of family cohesion and adaptability will determine how individuals within families interact. In general, families are healthier if they have moderate degrees of cohesion and adaptability.

Cohesion. Cohesion refers to the degree to which an individual family member is free to act independent of other family members. An appropriate amount of family cohesion permits the individual to be his or her "own person" while at the same time allowing him or her to draw on other family members for support as needed. Families with low cohesion may not offer the child with a disability the necessary support, whereas the overly cohesive family may overprotect the child and not allow him or her enough freedom.

It is frequently very difficult for otherwise healthy families to find the right balance of cohesion. They sometimes go overboard in wanting to help their children, and in so doing, limit their children's independence. A particularly stressful time can be adolescence, when the teenager strives to break some of the bonds that have tied him or her to the family. This need for independence is a normal behavior. What makes the situation difficult for many families of children with a disability is that the child, because of his or her disability, has often by necessity been more protected by parents. As one psychologist severely disabled by cerebral palsy has recounted,

> I remember the first time I wanted to travel alone, I had just turned sixteen. Some friends had invited me to stay with them in Baltimore. I sat down and discussed this with my parents. I said that I wanted to go by train, and that my friends would meet me in Baltimore at the train station. My parents were frightened and said so openly. They expressed their fears of my physical safety. . . . We talked and argued and cried for hours. The decision was that I was to go. . . . I'll never forget that day. My mother did not go to the train station with my father and me. She said she could give her permission for this to happen, but she couldn't watch it. My father settled me in a train seat and stood on the platform waving goodbye. I was trying not to cry and so was he. Blinking back tears, I waved goodbye to my father from the train window. He was vigorously waving goodbye with one hand—for his other was resting on the arm of my wheelchair. The train began pulling out of the station, and a panic gripped me. "My God! He still has my wheelchair. . . . Stop this train!" By this time we were a few blocks out of the station. What a ridiculous scene this must have appeared, this wriggly, little kid (I always looked young for my age) screaming at the top of my lungs to stop the train. . . . [The conductor] pulled the emergency cord and stopped the train. The words stuck in my throat as I looked up at this towering man. What a big question this little kid was about to ask, "Would you please back up the train so that I can get my wheelchair?" As the train backed up to the platform, there was my poor father still standing there waving goodbye with one hand and holding my wheelchair with the other, unaware of anything but his departing daughter. He was shocked out of his numb pose only when the conductor jumped off the train and wrenched the chair from his hand. (Diamond, 1981, pp. 41-42)

At the same time as children who are disabled ultimately need to gain as much independence from their family as possible, they also need to feel like a part of the family. They require a responsible role within the family such that other family members come to rely on them for what they contribute. Parents, for example, can consider giving household chores to the child. Certain adaptations might be necessary, such as taping a dish towel to the hands of a child with cerebral palsy so that it will not drop on the floor and allowing more time for him or her to complete the chore (Diamond, 1981), but the important thing is to provide the opportunity for the child to be a contributing member of the family.

Cohesion can also be an issue for adults with disabilities. For example, adults with mental retardation, especially those who live at home, often have special problems finding the right degree of independence from their families. Compared with those who live in the community, adults with mental retardation who live at home have a narrower range of social contacts outside the family but they do experience more support from their families (Krauss, Seltzer, & Goodman, 1992). Current thinking dictates two principles that are sometimes difficult to coordinate (Blacher & Baker, 1992). First, adults with disabilities should live in the community if at all possible. Second, family support is critical across the life span. Achieving the right degree of independence from the family, while at the same time encouraging family involvement, can be a difficult challenge.

Adaptability. Adaptability refers to the degree to which families are able to change their modes of interaction when they encounter unusual or stressful situations. Some families are so chaotic that it is difficult to predict what any one member will do in a given situation. In such an unstable environment, the needs of the family member who is disabled may be overlooked or neglected. At the other end of the continuum are families characterized by extreme rigidity. Each family member has his or her prescribed role in the family. Such rigidity makes it difficult for them to adjust to the addition of a family member with a disability. The addition of any child requires adjustment on the part of the family, but it is even more important if the child has special needs. For example, it may be that the mother's involvement in transporting the child with a disability from one therapy session to another will necessitate that the father be more involved than previously in household chores and taking care of the other children.

Family Functions

Family functions are the numerous tasks and activities in which families engage to meet their many and diverse needs. Economic, daily care, social, medical, and educational needs are just a few examples of functions to which families need to attend.

An important point for teachers to consider is that education is only one of several functions in which families are immersed. And for some students, especially those with multiple disabilities, there may be several professionals vying for the time of the parents. It is only natural, of course, that teachers should want to involve parents in the educational programming of their children as much as possible. Teachers know the positive benefits that can occur when parents are a part of the treatment program. At the same time, however, they need to respect the fact that education is just one of the many functions to which families must attend. If the child has chronic medical problems, for example, the family may be consumed by decisions regarding medical treatment (Martin, Brady, & Kotarba, 1992).

Several authorities have reported that many families of students with disabilities prefer a passive rather than an active degree of involvement in their children's education (Lynch & Stein, 1982; Vaughn, Bos, Harrell, & Lasky, 1988). Although some counselors have been troubled by the fact that many parents are not more involved, others are less perplexed. They warn that we should not automatically assume, for example, that parents who do not contribute many suggestions at their child's IEP meeting are neglectful. Given the number and diversity of functions for which families are responsible and the configuration of some families noted earlier (e.g., single-parent families), some authorities do not find it surprising when families decide to delegate most of the educational decisions to teachers (Benson & Turnbull, 1986). By so doing, they can concentrate on other needs of the child and family.

Respecting parents' desire to play a relatively passive role in their child's education does not mean that teachers should not welcome parental involvement. Teachers should encourage involvement for those families who want to be involved. Also, it may be that parents who desire not to be involved at one time will want to take a more active role at a later time.

Family Life Cycle

Several family theorists have noted that the impact of a child with a disability on the family changes over time (Beckman & Pokorni, 1988; Seligman & Darling, 1989; Turnbull & Turnbull, 1990). For this reason, some have pointed to the value of looking at families with children with a disability from a life-cycle perspective. Turnbull and Turnbull (1990), for example, have presented four major life-cycle stages that are representative of other family theorists: early childhood (zero to five years), childhood (five to twelve years), adolescence (twelve to twenty-one years), and adulthood (twenty-one years and up). Table 12–1 depicts some of the possible issues that parents and siblings of children with disabilities encounter during each of these four stages.

Transitions between stages in the life cycle are particularly stressful for families, especially families with a child who is disabled. We have already mentioned the difficulties facing families at the transition point when their child as an adult moves into more independent work and living settings. Another particularly troublesome transition can be from the relatively intimate confines of an infant or preschool program to the larger context of a kindergarten setting. For the child, the transition often requires a sudden increase in independent functioning (Fowler, Schwartz, & Atwater, 1991). For the parents, it often means giving up a sense of security for their child. As one parent relates,

> As my daughter's third birthday approached, I lived in dread, not wishing to leave the familiar, comfortable environment of her infant program. The infant program had become home away from home for me. It was supportive and intimate. I had made some lifelong friendships, as well as having established a comfortable routine in our lives. I saw making the transition to a preschool program in the school district as an extremely traumatic experience, second only to learning of Amy's diagnosis.
>
> What were my fears? First, I was concerned that my husband and I, along with professionals, would be deciding the future of our child. How could we play God? Would our decisions be the right ones? Second, I feared loss of control, as I would be surrendering my child to strangers—first to the school district's intake assessment team and then to the preschool teacher. The feeling of being at the mercy of professionals was overwhelming. In addition, I had more information to absorb and a new system with which to become familiar. Finally, I feared the "label" that would be

Table 12-1 ➤ Possible Issues Encountered at Life Cycle Stages

LIFE-CYCLE STAGE	PARENTS	SIBLINGS
Early Childhood, ages 0–5	• Obtaining an accurate diagnosis • Informing siblings and relatives • Locating services • Seeking to find meaning in the exceptionality • Clarifying a personal ideology to guide decisions • Addressing issues of stigma • Identifying positive contributions of exceptionality • Setting great expectations	• Less parental time and energy for sibling needs • Feelings of jealousy over less attention • Fears associated with misunderstandings of exceptionality
School Age, ages 5–12	• Establishing routines to carry out family functions • Adjusting emotionally to educational implications • Clarifying issues of mainstreaming v. special class placement • Participating in IEP conferences • Locating community resources • Arranging for extracurricular activities	• Division of responsibility for any physical care needs • Oldest female sibling may be at risk • Limited family resources for recreation and leisure • Informing friends and teachers • Possible concern over surpassing younger sibling • Issues of "mainstreaming" into same school • Need for basic information on exceptionality
Adolescence, ages 12–21	• Adjusting emotionally to possible chronicity of exceptionality • Identifying issues of emerging sexuality • Addressing possible peer isolation and rejection • Planning for career/vocational development • Arranging for leisure time activities • Dealing with physical and emotional change of puberty • Planning for postsecondary education	• Overidentification with sibling • Greater understanding of differences in people • Influence of exceptionality on career choice • Dealing with possible stigma and embarrassment • Participation in sibling training programs • Opportunity for sibling support groups
Adulthood, ages 21–	• Planning for possible need for guardianship • Addressing the need for appropriate adult residence • Adjusting emotionally to any adult implications of dependency • Addressing the need for socialization opportunities outside the family for individuals with exceptionality • Initiating career choice or vocational program	• Possible issues of responsibility for financial support • Addressing concerns regarding genetic implications • Introducing new in-laws to exceptionality • Need for information on career/living options • Clarify role of sibling advocacy • Possible issues of guardianship

SOURCE: *Families, professionals, and exceptionality: A special partnership.* (2nd ed.) *by* A. P.Turnbull, & H. R. Turnbull, III. Copyright © 1990 by Merrill Publishing Company. Reprinted with the permission of Merrill, an imprint of Macmillan Publishing Company.

GETTING TO KNOW YOU ➤

Parents of children with disabilities, especially those with multiple disabilities, must deal with a multitude and variety of professionals, some of whom may change from time to time. If the child is mainstreamed into general education, he or she may get a new teacher or set of teachers each year. A change from elementary to middle school or from middle to high school also brings additional changes in personnel. These many changes make it difficult for parents to keep all of the many professionals informed about their child's particular needs. The mother of a child with cerebral palsy, mental retardation, severe hearing impairment, and lack of speech has come up with a strategy for familiarizing professionals with her child. She recommends that the family develop a "My Story" booklet pertaining to the child, which can be updated periodically (Comegys, 1989). Following are excerpts from her daughter's booklet when she was in her early teens:

MY GOALS

1. I want to be as independent as I can possibly be.
2. I want to make friends with my nonhandicapped peers at the high school, and participate in all school activities which interest me, including afterschool activities.
3. I want to be included in community functions such as recreational and park activities, church, and social functions.
4. I plan on living and working in my home town after I graduate from high school.
5. I plan to work in the community (with support)—not in a sheltered workshop.

6. I want to learn to communicate with people better (eye contact, smile, and actions).
7. I want to learn to do things for people.
8. I want to learn to do more things for myself such as feed myself and participate more fully in dressing.
9. I want to develop my own sense of worth.
10. I want to be able to ride my bike by myself.
11. I am eager to operate the computer for my recreation now (Fire Organ, Sticky Bears, and Musicomp are some of the software used at home). Later, I hope to apply these skills to a real job. I enjoy working a Xerox machine now.
12. I want to make choices for: partners in activities; when to stop or start an activity, my clothes, leisure, food.
13. I want to be asked to go out by a friend spontaneously—not always preplanned.

MY INTERESTS

I enjoy lights, windows, the computer, photographs and slides of familiar activities and people, and TV (nature, sports, comedy), and watching a fire in the fireplace.
I enjoy books, magazines, newspapers and catalogues, and maps. Geometric designs, too.
I like to swim, ride horseback, ride my bike around town.
I like to go places in a car. I like the school bus.
I like warmth much better than cold—it helps my muscles— spring and summer, sunbathing, warm baths, warm feet and hands are important to me.
I like to be at the piano with people who can play it.
I like to be read to.

attached to my child and feared that this label would lower the world's expectations of her. (Hanline & Knowlton, 1988, p. 116)

Transitions between stages are difficult because of the uncertainty that each new phase presents to the family. One of the reasons for the uncertainty pertains to replacements of the professionals who work with the child who is disabled. In particular, parents of a child with multiple disabilities, who requires services from multiple professionals, can be anxious about the switches in therapists and teachers that occur many times throughout the child's life, especially at transition points. (The box above describes one strategy for alleviating some of the problems resulting from changes in professionals.)

A Social Support Systems Approach

Like a family systems approach, a social support systems approach focuses education and treatment efforts on the broader social context rather than on individuals (Dunst, Trivette, & Deal, 1988). There are two important features of this approach. First, it focuses on informal rather than formal sources of support.

I like to be hugged—if you know me well enough. I also like to be tickled.

I like birds and fish, very much! I have a parakeet: Pete!

I have long enjoyed many family slides on the Ectagraphic which I can fully operate alone with a special switch.

I am very interested in cookies and good things to drink (frappes, tonics, etc.)!

I like lots of daily physical exercise—walking two city blocks is prescribed—it helps me sleep and helps my digestion.

I MAY NOT SPEAK—BUT I DO COMMUNICATE

I use total communication (visual, audiological, physical cues). I communicate in many ways: here are three—

- **Line Drawings.** I use both single and multiple line drawings (called "Commenting Boards") which are black and white or lightly colored. They enable me to both give and receive cues. If you show me a line drawing for car, I will know we are going out for a drive and I will start to move toward the door. I tap some line drawings to let you know what I want. I use many line drawings. A few of them appear in this booklet. [not shown here]

- **Signs.** I understand some of your signs. I am learning to make some signs. Some are my own gestures and others are formal signs. Here is a list: [not shown here]

- **Body Language and Sounds.** Please *watch* me closely and you will see that I:

1. point with my knuckles, or a finger, or a sweep of my arm.
2. nod my head "yes."
3. pull you when I want you to do something.
4. push an object away (I may or may not want it).
5. pull or push the bathroom door shut for privacy.
6. tilt my head up and back which can mean I want to get up.
7. rotate my head which can mean that it's time to get moving.

Please *listen* to my tone of voice. It changes constantly, and indicates pleasure, frustration, humming, questioning, loneliness, hunger. It helps when you pair these directions with a gesture, sign, or line drawing. For example, when it is time for me to get up from the chair and go somewhere, you might sign *stand* and show me the line drawing of *car*.

Please do not talk "around or through" me as though I am not in the room. It hurts my feelings. Include me by asking my opinion, questioning me, and showing me the appropriate line drawings and signs. It will make both of us much happier.

SOURCE: A. Comegys. Integration strategies for parents of students with handicaps. In R. Gaylord-Ross (Ed.), *Integration strategies for students with handicaps.*Copyright © 1989 by Paul H. Brookes Publishing Co. Reprinted with permission. pp. 345-346.

More and more authorities are pointing to informal sources of support, such as extended family, friends, church groups, neighbors, and social clubs, as more effective than professionals and agencies in helping families cope with the stress of having a child with a disability. Unfortunately, these informal supports, once so prevalent in our society, are fast disappearing (Zigler & Black, 1989). Largely because of the demographic changes noted earlier (e.g., increases in single-parent families and poverty), families are less able today to rely on informal social networks for support.

Second, a social support systems approach focuses on helping families help themselves. Because many families do not have their own informal sources of support, a social systems approach helps to establish them. Its goal is to enhance the self-esteem of families by setting up a situation in which the help-seeker is less dependent on the help-giver than is the case in more traditional approaches.

Rather than focusing on the help-seeker as the cause of problems, the model encourages the family to accept responsibility for setting and achieving needed goals. The family, not the professional, assumes the primary decision-making role for the family's needs. The professional does not act so much on behalf of the

JAY, PAT, AND THE GREEKS: A STORY ABOUT TRANSITION ≻

BY RUD AND ANN TURNBULL

"What do you do when you graduate? What do you do when you transition?"

Ask those questions of Jay Turnbull and he'll tell you, "I hang out at SAE with Pat, Chuck, and the guys."

He might also add, "I work at KU."

In these days when one of the buzzwords is "transition" and when Developmental Disabilities Planning Councils are rightly concerned about the unacceptable rate of employment and underemployment for people with developmental disabilities, Jay's answer may come as a surprise.

It's not surprising that he works at the University of Kansas, in supported employment. That is one of the goals he and his family had for many years . . . .

What may be surprising, however, is that he has been made an honorary member of the local chapter of Sigma Alpha Epsilon Fraternity. For Jay and for the members of the SAE chapter, transition means friendship. And that means growth in many dimensions for many people.

Jay spends all of the afternoons and most of the evenings every Tuesday and Thursday at the fraternity house. That means two meals a day, twice a week, and plenty of hanging out in the members' rooms . . . .

How did all of this come about? It took only two people other than Jay to make it work. One of them is Pat, a KU junior . . . .

The other is Chuck Rhodes, the SAE resident educational advisor . . . .

Pat met Jay one afternoon at the SAE house, when Chuck, who had been training Jay in weight lifting, brought him there to meet his roommate and other SAE members. As Chuck would say, "I wanted to enlarge Jay's circle of friends, for his benefit and theirs." As it happened, Pat and some of his fraternity brothers were listening to John Denver's music . . . and Jay knows all of that music. Quite naturally, Jay began to sing the words, and soon he was accompanied by several fraternity members. From that simple beginning—from an incident that occurred very naturally and that, as luck would have it, allowed Jay to show his competence and sociability—there evolved a friendship between Pat and Jay, complementing the one that Chuck and Jay had formed. And from Pat, there grew other friendships with SAE members, all with Chuck's careful and subtle monitoring.

A few weeks later, the SAE chapter admitted Jay as an honorary member. . . .

What has it meant to everyone involved? Jay will say, by word and deed, that he has acquired new friends. When Tuesdays and Thursdays roll around, Jay has a special zip to his affect. His job coach, Sharon Donner, has observed it: "He works more to get to be with the guys than to finish his job." . . .

For "the guys," as Jay calls them, it means human development in the intellectual, spiritual, and social dimensions. J. R. Rielly, the SAE chapter president, put it well when he said,

"When we first started working with Jay, I was somewhat skeptical. I had never been around someone with mental retar-

help-seeker, "but rather creates opportunities for the help-seeker to acquire competencies that permit him or her to mobilize sources of resources and support necessary to cope, adapt, and grow in response to life's many challenges" (Dunst et al., 1988, p. 44).

When professionals do not just provide direct services but encourage families to help themselves and their children, families take more control over their own lives and avoid the dependency sometimes associated with typical professional-family relationships. Situations in which the family looks to professionals for all of its help can result in the family members becoming dependent on professionals and losing their feelings of competence and self-esteem.

Professionals can help parents establish a variety of social supports. There are often a number of untapped resources that particular communities have to offer. (One creative alternative is depicted in the box above.)

One of the most beneficial types of social support, especially for parents of recently diagnosed children, is parental support groups. These consist of parents of children with the same or similar disabilities. Such groups can be relatively unstructured, meeting infrequently with unspecified agendas, or they can be more structured. For example, some authorities have recommended that parents

dation, and I did not know what to expect or how to treat him. Now, after spending time with Jay, I realize that my ignorance was keeping me from becoming friends with a super person." . . .

The SAE guys have become such a part of Jay's life that some have begun to "hang out" at his home. They are in demand as "big brothers" to Jay's sisters, Amy (14) and Kate (11). . . .

Amy commented,

"When Jay is with the SAE guys, I can really relax about his being accepted. I don't have to interpret for Jay or always be on guard to make sure he fits in. The SAE brothers are like big brothers to all of us, because they took Jay in as one of them. Pat, for example, is doing more than most big brothers of my friends—he's the disc jockey at my birthday party next week."

Pat sums it up when he says,

"JT's my buddy, my pal. And he's really part of our house. There is no problem with him eating there or sleeping over or partying. Jay's in the community, but, with us, he can participate in the same kind of life as the rest of us. There's no difference, really. All the differences are on the surface."

Chuck notes,

"It's amazing how much Jay has grown. His self-confidence is way up. His independence is, too, because we treat him like everyone else. And he thoroughly enjoys himself here. But that's true of the members, too. They have grown and they enjoy Jay. It's a win-win situation. Nothing beats it. Nothing can." . . .

Jay Turnbull is 21 years old and has been classified as having low-moderate mental retardation. His parents are Ann and Rud Turnbull, co-directors of the Beach Center on Families and Disability, a rehabilitation research and training center funded by National Institute on Disability and Rehabilitation Research. They are the authors of "Disability and the Family: A Guide to Decisions for Adulthood," published by Paul H. Brookes Publishing Co., Baltimore, MD. That book provides advice on how families can shape the future according to their choices and those of their member with a disability. They also are the authors of "Parent, Professionals, and Exceptionality: A Special Partnership," published by Merrill (an imprint of Macmillan Publishing Co.), Columbus, Ohio. That book describes how parents and professionals can work as a team.

The Beach Center welcomes your comments about families. Write them at Beach Center, c/o Bureau of Child Research, 4138 Haworth Hall, The University of Kansas, Lawrence, Ks. 66045, and ask for their newsletter, if you are interested in families.

SOURCE: H. R. Turnbull,III & A. P. Turnbull, (1989). Jay, Pat, and the Greeks: A story about transition. *Directions: Newsletter of the Illinois Planning Council on Developmental Disabilities.*

of older children be paired with those of younger children so the latter can have the benefit of learning from the former (Turnbull & Turnbull, 1990). In any case, parental groups provide a number of benefits, "including (1) alleviating loneliness and isolation, (2) providing information, (3) providing role models, and (4) providing a basis for comparison" (Seligman & Darling, 1989, p. 44).

Communication Between Parents and Professionals

Virtually all family theorists agree that no matter what particular approach one uses to work with parents, the key to the success of the program is how well parents and professionals are able to work together. Even the most creative, well-conceived model is doomed to fail if professionals and parents are unable to communicate effectively. Unfortunately, special education does not have a long tradition of excellent working relationships between parents and teachers (Michael, Arnold, Magliocca, & Miller, 1992). This is not too surprising if you consider the ingredients of the situation. On the one hand, you have parents, who may be trying to cope with the stresses of raising a child with a disability in a complex and changing society. On the other hand, you have the professionals—teachers,

arent support groups can be helpful to many parents of children with disabilities.

speech therapists, physicians, psychologists, physical therapists, and so forth—who may be frustrated because they do not have all of the answers to the child's problems.

As the parent of a child with autism has stated:

> We don't begin in anger. We start the way all parents of all children do: with respect, reverence really, for the professional and his skills. The pediatrician, the teacher, the writer of books and articles on child development, they are the sources of wisdom from which we must draw in order to be good parents. We believe, we consult, we do as we are told, and all goes well . . . unless one of our kids has a handicap.
>
> We parents are almost always the first to notice that something is amiss, and one of our early consolations is often our pediatrician's assurance that "it's nothing—he'll outgrow it." That, of course, is exactly what we want to hear because it corresponds perfectly to the dwindling hope in our hearts, so we defer to the expert and our child loses another year. Finally, the time does come when not even the most conservative professional can deny the existence of a problem. . . . With luck, our pediatrician refers us to an appropriate specialist. . . .
>
> We transfer our trust to the new god and wait expectantly for the oracle to speak. Instead of the strong authoritative voice of wisdom, we more often hear an evasive stammer: "Can't give you a definite diagnosis . . . uh. . . . virtually untestable . . . let's see him . . . cough, cough . . . again in a year." Ironically, when the oracle is loud and clear, it is often wrong: "Seriously emotionally disturbed; it's a severe withdrawal reaction to maternal ambivalence." The parents have just been treated to their first dose of professional puffery. . . .
>
> Its one potentially redeeming feature may be realized if the parents react with sufficient anger to take charge, to assert their right to be their child's "case manager." Unfortunately, this is not likely to happen at such an early stage; it takes more than one false god to make us give up religion entirely. And when (or if) we do manage to assert ourselves, our behavior is viewed by professionals as the final stage in our own pathology; and any of us who may still be practicing religion are immediately excommunicated. (Akerley, 1985, pp. 23-24)

We can hope that this parent's frustrating experiences are not the norm. There are enough other parents who echo the same sentiments, however, to indicate that professional-parent relationships are often far from perfect and that teachers are frequently the target of parental frustrations. One of the keys to avoiding professional-parent misunderstandings is communication. It is critical that teachers attempt to communicate with the parents of their students. There are advantages to receiving information from parents as well as imparting information to parents. Given that parents have spent considerably more time with the child and have more invested in the child emotionally, they can be an invaluable source of information regarding the student's characteristics and interests. And by keeping parents informed of what is going on in the class, teachers can foster a relationship in which they can call on parents for support should the need arise. Even those parents, we mentioned earlier, who do not want to be actively involved in making decisions regarding their child's educational program should receive periodic communication from their child's teacher.

One area, in particular, that requires the cooperation of parents is homework. For mainstreamed students who are disabled, homework is often a source of misunderstanding and conflict (Mims, Harper, Armstrong, & Savage, 1991). Homework often requires that the regular educator stay in close communication with the parents of the student with a disability. Table 12-2 lists recommendations for the respective roles of regular class teachers and parents with regard to homework.

Most authorities agree that the communication between teacher and parent should take place as soon as possible and that it should not be intitiated only by negative behavior on the part of the student. Parents, especially those of students with behavior disorders, often complain that the only time they hear from school personnel is when their child has misbehaved (Kauffman, Mostert, Nuttycombe, Trent, & Hallahan, 1993). To establish a degree of rapport with parents, some teachers make a practice of sending home a brief form letter at the beginning of the school year outlining the goals for the year. Others send home periodic newsletters or make occasional phone calls to parents. Even if a teacher does not want to go to the trouble of using some of these techniques, authorities recommend that they be open to the idea of communicating with parents as soon as possible in the school year. By establishing a line of communication with parents early in the year, the teacher is in a better position to initiate more intensive and focused discussions should the need arise. Three such methods of communication are parent-teacher conferences, home-note programs, and traveling notebooks.

Parent-Teacher Conferences

Parent-teacher conferences can be an effective way for teachers to impart information to parents. Likewise, they are an opportunity for teachers to learn from parents more about the students from the parents' perspective. In addition to regularly scheduled meetings open to all parents, teachers may want to hold a

7he traditional parent-teacher conference is particularly important for parents of children with disabilities.

Table 12–2 ➤ Suggested Responsibilities of Regular Education Teachers and Parents With Regard to Homework

Suggestions for Regular Educators

- Establish a method of recordkeeping. This can be accomplished by maintaining a homework notebook or chart.
- Ensure that all homework is at the child's academic functional level.
- Inform parents and students in advance when special materials or resources are required for homework completion (e.g., study guides, a calculator, or a stopwatch).
- Make homework a review of skills that are currently being taught.
- Avoid homework that requires new knowledge or skills that have not been presented previously.
- Allow time for homework at the end of class when appropriate. If time is available for homework in class, the teacher can answer questions.
- Consider the attention span and functional level of the child when assigning homework. Lower-functioning children should not be required to complete the same amount of work as those who are higher functioning.

Suggestions for Parents

- Establish a scheduled time and place for homework to be completed.
- Decide who will supervise the homework. This does not mean that the person will always check every problem or every sentence.
- Provide an atmosphere conducive to learning. Make sure the area is well lighted and ample work space is provided.
- Monitor the noise level.
- Provide appropriate supplies.
- Provide a tutor for subject areas with which parents are unfamiliar.

SOURCE: Adapted from A. Mims, C. Harper, S. W. Armstrong, & S. Savage. Effective instruction in homework for students with disabilities. *Teaching Exceptional Children, 24*(1), 42-44. Copyright © 1991 by The Council for Exceptional Children. Reprinted with permission.

conference with the parents of a particular student. Most authorities agree that a key to conducting a successful parent-teacher conference is planning (Turnbull & Turnbull, 1990). How one initiates the meeting, for example, can be crucial. Some have recommended that the first contact be a telephone call that proposes the need for the meeting, without going into great detail, followed by a letter reminding the parent of the time and place of the meeting (Kauffman et al., 1993). Table 12–3 presents several questions authorities recommend teachers ask themselves to plan for conferences and to evaluate their performance after the conference is over (Turnbull & Turnbull, 1990).

If the focus of the meeting is the student's poor work or misbehavior, the teacher will need to be as diplomatic as possible. Most authorities recommend that the teacher find something positive to say about the student while providing an objective account of what the student is doing that is troubling. The teacher needs to achieve a delicate balance of providing an objective account of the student's transgressions or poor work while demonstrating advocacy for the student. Conveying only bad or good news can lose the parents' sense of trust:

Table 12–3 ➤ Questions for Teachers to Ask Themselves Regarding Parent-Teacher Conferences

Preconference Preparation

Notifying Families
- Did I, or the school, provide parents with written notification of the conference?
- Did I provide a means of determining that the parents knew the date and time?

Preparing for the Conference
- Did I review the student's cumulative records?
- Did I assess the student's behavior and pinpoint areas of concern?
- Did I make notes of the student's misbehavior to show to parents?
- Did I consult with other relevant professionals about the student's behavior?
- Did I mentally rehearse and review what I was going to say at the conference?

Preparing the Physical Environment
- Did the setting provide enough privacy?
- Did the setting provide enough comfort?

Conference Activities

Developing Rapport
- Did I allow time to talk informally before the start of the meeting?
- Did I express appreciation for the parents' coming to the meeting?

Obtaining Information from Parents
- Did I ask enough open-ended questions?
- Did my body language indicate interest in what parents were saying? (Did I maintain eye contact and look attentive?)
- Did I ask for clarification on points I didn't understand?

Providing Information to Parents
- Did I speak as positively as possible about the student?
- Did I use jargon-free language?
- Did I use specific examples to clarify my points?

Summarizing and Follow-up
- Did I review the main points to determine next steps?
- Did I restate who was responsible for completing the next steps and by when?
- Did I end the meeting on a positive note?
- Did I thank the parents for their interest in attending?

Postconference Follow-up

- Did I consider reviewing the meeting with the student?
- Did I share the results with the appropriate other professionals who work with the student?
- Did I make a record of the conference proceedings?

SOURCE: Reprinted with the permission of Merrill, an imprint of Macmillan Publishing Co. from *Families, Professionals, and Exceptionality: A Special Partnership* (2nd ed.) by A. P. Turnbull and H. R. Turnbull, III. Copyright © 1990 by Merrill Publishing Company.

Conveying only good news skews their perspective . . . just as much as conveying only negative information. If a serious incident arises, they have no sense of background or warning. [This] may lead them to conclude that the teacher is withholding information and provoke a sense of mistrust. When telling parents unpleasant information, it helps not only to be as objective as possible, but also state the case in a way that clearly conveys your advocacy of the student. When it is obvious to the parents that the teacher is angry or upset with their child, parents become apprehensive about the treatment the child may receive. A common response to this sense of dread is a defensiveness which polarizes parent-teacher relationships. (Kauffman, Mostert, Nuttycombe, Trent, & Hallahan, 1993, pp. 123-124)

Home-Note Programs

➤ home-note program. A system of communication between teacher and parent; the teacher evaluates the behavior of the student using a simple form, the student takes the form home, gets the parents' signatures, and returns the form the next day.

Home-note programs, sometimes referred to as home-contingency programs, are a way of communicating with parents and having them reinforce behavior that occurs at school (Kelley, 1990). By having parents dispense the reinforcement, the teacher takes advantage of the fact that parents usually have a greater number of reinforcers at their disposal than do teachers. There are a number of different types of home-notes. A typical one consists of a simple form on which the teacher records "yes," "no," or "not applicable" to certain categories of behavior (e.g., social behavior, homework completed, homework accurate, in-class academic work completed, in-class academic work accurate). The form also may contain space for the teacher and the parent to write a few brief comments. The student takes the form home, has his or her parent sign it, and returns it the next day. The parent delivers reinforcement for the student's performance. The teacher often starts out sending a note home each day and gradually decreases the frequency until he or she is using a once-a-week note.

Traveling Notebooks

➤ traveling notebook. A system of communication in which parents and professionals write "messages" to each other by way of a notebook, or log, that accompanies the child to-and-from school.

Less formal than home-notes and particularly appropriate for students who see multiple professionals are traveling notebooks. A **traveling notebook** goes back and forth between school and home. The teacher and other professionals, such as the speech and physical therapist, can write brief messages to the parents and vice versa. In addition, a traveling notebook allows the different professionals to keep up with what each of them is doing with the student. (See Figure 12–1 for excerpts from a traveling notebook of a two-year-old with cerebral palsy.)

IN CONCLUSION

Today's knowledgeable educators recognize the tremendous impact a child with a disability can have on the dynamics of a family. They appreciate the negative, as well as the positive, influence such a child can exert. Today's knowledgeable educators also realize that the family of a child with a disability can be a bountiful reservoir of support for the child as well as an invaluable source of information for the teacher. Although there have been tremendous advances, we are just beginning to tap the potential that families have for contributing to the development of their children with disabilities. We are just beginning to enable families to provide a supportive and enriching environment for their children. We are just beginning to harness the expertise of families so we can provide the best possible programs for their children.

The following short excerpts are taken at random from a notebook that accompanies two-year-old Lauren, who has cerebral palsy, back and forth to her special class for preschoolers. The notebook provides a convenient mode for an ongoing dialogue among her mother, Lyn; her teacher, Sara; her occupational therapist, Joan; and her speech therapist, Marti. As you can see from this representative sample, the communication is informal but very informative on a variety of items relating to Lauren.

Lyn,   9/7

Lauren did _very_ well—We had several criers but—She played & worked very nicely. She responds so well to instruction —that's such a plus!

She fed herself crackers & juice & did a good job. She was very vocal & enjoyed the other children too. She communicated ō me very well for the 1ˢᵗ day. Am pleased ō her first day.

Sara

Sara.   9/15

Please note that towel, toothbrush / paste + clean clothes may be removed from bag today —WED. We witnessed an apparently significant moment in her oral communication: She'll try to say "all done" after a meal. The execution is imperfect, to say the least, but she gets an "A" for effort. Could you please reinforce this after snack? Just ask her, "What do you say after you finish your snack?"

Thanks,
Lyn

9/28

Lauren had an esp. good day! She was jabbering a lot! Being very expressive ō her vocalness & jabbering. I know she said "yes" or an approximate thereof, several times when asked if she wanted something. She was so cute ō the animal sounds esp. pig & horse—she was really trying to make the sounds. It was the first time we had seen such a response. Still cruising a lot! She walked ō me around the room & in the gym. She used those consonant & vowel sounds: dadada, mamama — her jabbering was just so different & definitely progressive. I am sending her work card ō stickers home tomorrow for good working.

Several notes:

① Susie (VI) came today & evaluated Lauren. She will compile a report & be in touch with you and me. She seemed very pleased ō Lauren's performance.

② Marti (speech) will see Lauren at 11 AM for evaluation. She'll be in touch afterwards.

③ Susie informed me about the addition to the IEP meeting on Mon. Oct. 4 at 10 AM here at Woodbrook.

How are the tape & cards working at home? I know you both are pleased ō her jabbering. She seems so ready to say "something" — we are very, very pleased. See you tomorrow.

Sara

9/29

Lauren was a bit fussy during O.T. today — she stopped fussing during fine motor reaching activities (peg board, block building) but wasn't too pleased with being handled on the ball. She did a great job with the peg board & readily used her left hand.

I want to bring in some different spoons next week to see if she can become more independent in scooping with a large handle spoon or a spoon that is covered

Joan

Joan —   10/1

Although Lauren would very much approve of your idea for making her more independent during feeding, we'd rather not initiate self-feeding with an adaptive spoon at this time. Here's why:

① When I feed Lauren or get her to grip a spoon and then guide her hand, I can slip the entire bowl of the spoon into her mouth and get her to close her lips on it. When Lauren uses a spoon without help, she turns it upside-down to lick it or inserts just the tip of it into her mouth and then sucks off the food...

② Lauren has always been encouraged to do things "normally". She never had a special cup or a "Tommy Tippee", for instance. Of course it took a year of practice before she could drink well from a cup, and she still dribbles a little occasionally; but she's doing well now. We really prefer to give Lauren practice in using a regular spoon so that she doesn't get dependent on an adaptive utensil. I'd like to assure you that we appreciate your communication about sessions with Lauren and ideas for her therapy. Coordinating her school, home and CRC programs is going to be a challenge, to say the least.

                                                              Lyn

☺! Lauren walked all the way from the room to Gym & back – She also walked up & down the full length of the gym!

Several other teachers saw her and were thrilled. She fell maybe twice! But picked herself right up —

                                                              Sara

3/2

Lauren had a great speech session! We were playing with some toys and she said "I want help" as plain as day. Later she said "I want crackers" and at the end of the session, she imitated "Cindy, let's go." Super!

                                                              Marti

Summary

At one time, the prevailing attitude toward parents of persons with disabilities was negative. Professionals viewed them as causes of their children's problems, at worst, or as roadblocks to educational efforts, at best. Two factors have contributed to a much more positive attitude toward parents. First, current theory dictates that children, even young infants, can cause changes in adults' behavior. Professionals now view adult-child interaction as a two-way street—sometimes adults affect children and sometimes the reverse is true. Second, professionals began to see parents as a potential source of information about how to educate their children. This second factor came about because (1) professionals recognize that early intervention efforts that involve parents are more effective, (2) parents have become effective advocates for their children, and (3) federal legislation stipulates that parents be invited to be involved in the education of their children with disabilities. Most authorities believe that parents should not be viewed as quasi-therapists or quasi-teachers—the goal should be to preserve the natural parent-child relationship.

Many theorists believe that parents go through a series of stages after learning that they have a child with a disability. There are limitations to a stage approach, however, including the tendency to view all parents as going through all the stages in the same order. Nevertheless, many parents do have emotional reactions, for example, guilt. Most research on parents of children with disabilities is on the mother. Research on fathers indicates that they often have more of an indirect effect on the child; that is, their attitudes toward the mother and the family influence how the mother interacts with the child. Parents of children with a disability often undergo a great deal of stress, and there is reason to believe that the stress may be greater for the mother than the father. How parents cope with the stress varies. Although very few experience major psychological disturbances, they are at risk for mild forms of depression.

Siblings of children with a disability experience some of the same emotions that parents do. Because they are less mature, may not have a broad base of people with whom they can talk, and may be hesitant to talk over sensitive issues with their parents, siblings may have a difficult time coping with their emotions. As they grow older, their feelings often become centered on how society views them and their family. Like parents, most of them are able to adjust to a sibling with a disability. Adjustment may be more difficult for two siblings close in age and/or of the same sex. Also, older nondisabled girls may experience the added burden of taking care of their sibling with a disability.

Current family practitioners advocate a family-focused or family-centered approach. These models stress encouraging the family to be involved in decisions concerning the family, with the latter viewing professionals as working for families in helping them obtain access to nonprofessional (e.g., family and friends) as well as formal sources of support. Current theorists also stress the influence of the social context on child development. They note that the family as a whole affects individual family members and that society affects the family. Two educational approaches to families that consider the social context are the family systems approach and the social support systems approach.

The family systems model includes four components: family characteristics, family interaction, family functions, and family life cycle. Family characteristics comprise the type and severity of the disability as well as such things as the size, cultural background, and socio-economic background of the family. Family interaction refers to how cohesive and adaptable the family is. Family functions include such things as economic, daily care, social, medical, and educational needs. It is important for teachers to keep in mind that education is just one of many needs to which the family must attend. This is why some parents prefer more passive than active involvement in educational programming. The family life cycle is made up of birth and early childhood, childhood, adolescence, and adulthood. Transitions between stages, especially between preschool and school and between adolescence and adulthood can be very difficult for families with a disabled child. The model suggests that the impact on the family of a child with a disability as well as the impact of the family on the child are determined by the complex interactions within and between the four stages.

A social support systems approach stresses the importance of the broader societal influence on family functioning. It emphasizes the value of informal sources of social support, such as the extended family, friends, neighbors, and church groups. A particularly effective social support is that of parent support groups, made up of parents who have children with similar disabilities. A social systems philosophy is built on the assumption that it is better to enable families to help themselves than to provide only direct services to them.

Family theorists agree that the key to working and involving parents is communication. The parent-teacher conference is one of the most common avenues, and preparation is the key to a successful conference. Teachers need to consider preconference, conference, and postconference planning. A home-note program, in which teachers send home a brief checklist of student behavior that they have filled out, can keep parents informed and involve them in reinforcing the student's behavior. A traveling notebook is a log that accompanies the child to and from school in which the parent, teacher, and other professionals can write messages to one another concerning the child's progress.

GLOSSARY

▲ ▲ ▲

A

absence seizures. Brief, generalized seizures manifested by a brief "absence" or lapse of consciousness lasting up to 30 seconds; the individual suddenly stops any activity in which he or she is engaged and then resumes the activity following the seizure; also called petit mal seizures.

acceleration. Educating gifted students by placing them in grade levels ahead of their peers in one or more academic subjects.

acquired aphasia. Loss or impairment of the ability to understand or formulate language because of accident or illness.

Acquired immunodeficiency syndrome (AIDS). A fatal virus-caused illness resulting in a breakdown of the immune system. Currently, no known cure exists.

adaptive devices. Special tools that are adaptations of common items to make accomplishing self-care, work, or recreation activities easier for someone who has a physical disability.

adaptive skills. Skills needed to adapt to one's living environment, e.g., communication, self-care, home living, social skills, community use, self-direction, health and safety, functional academics, leisure, and work; usually estimated by an adaptive behavior survey; one of two major components (the other is intellectual functioning) of the AAMR definition.

adventitiously deaf. Deafness that occurs through illness or accident in an individual who was born with normal hearing.

affective disorder. A disorder of mood or emotional tone characterized by depression or elation.

aggression. Behavior that intentionally causes others harm or that elicits escape or avoidance responses from others.

alcohol embryopathy. Fetal alcohol syndrome.

Americans with Disabilities Act (ADA). Civil rights legislation for persons with disabilities ensuring nondiscrimination in a broad range of activities.

amniocentesis. A medical procedure that allows examination of the amniotic fluid around the fetus; sometimes recommended to determine the presence of abnormality.

anoxia. Loss of oxygen; can cause brain injury.

anxiety disorder. A disorder characterized by anxiety, fearfulness, and avoidance of ordinary activities because of anxiety or fear.

applied behavior analysis. The application and evaluation of principles of learning theory applied to teaching situations; used with all types of students with disabilities, but particularly appropriate for persons with severe and profound disabilities. It consists of six steps: identifying overall goals, accumulating further information through baseline measurement, specifying learning objectives, implementing the intervention, monitoring student performance, and evaluating the intervention.

apraxia. The inability to move the muscles involved in speech or other voluntary acts.

aqueous humor. A watery substance between the cornea and the lens of the eye.

arthritis. A disease involving inflammation of the joints.

articulation. Refers to the movements the vocal tract makes during production of speech sounds; enunciation of words and vocal sounds.

astigmatism. Blurred vision caused by an irregular cornea or lens.

asymmetrical tonic neck reflex (ATNR). A normal reflex in babies up to about four months of age in which turning the head to one side results in extension of the arm and leg on the side toward which the head is turned and flexion of the opposite arm and leg. It is an abnormal reflex indicative of brain injury in infants older than about four months.

atonic cerebral palsy A type of cerebral palsy characterized by lack of muscle tone or "floppiness."

atrophy. Degeneration of tissue, such as muscles or nerves.

attributions. Explanations given by people for their successes and failures. Attributions may be internal or external.

audiologist. An individual trained in audiology, a science dealing with hearing impairments, their detection, and remediation.

audiometric zero (zero decibel level). Lowest level at which normal people can hear.

auditory training. The procedure of teaching children who are deaf or hard-of-hearing to make full use of their residual hearing ability.

augmentative communication. Alternative forms of communication that do not use the oral sounds of speech.

auricle. The visible part of the ear, composed of cartilage; collects the sounds and funnels them via the external auditory canal to the eardrum.

autism. A disorder characterized by extreme withdrawal, self-stimulation, cognitive deficits, language disorders, and onset before the age of thirty months.

B

baseline. Used to assess the effects of an intervention. The therapist or teacher measures the client's or student's skill or behavior before instruction.

battered child syndrome. Evidence of physical, psychological, and/or sexual abuse or neglect of a child that is threatening to the child's health or life.

blindisms. Repetitive, stereotyped movements such as rocking or eye rubbing; also characteristic of some people who are blind, severely retarded, or psychotic; more appropriately referred to as stereotypic behaviors.

Braille bills. Legislation passed in several states making Braille more available to students with visual impairment. Specific provisions vary from state to state, but major advocates have lobbied for (a) making Braille available if parents want it, and for (b) ensuring that teachers of students with visual impairment are proficient in Braille.

Braille. A system in which raised dots are used to allow blind people to "read" with their fingertips; consists of a quadrangular cell containing from one to six dots whose arrangement denotes different letters and symbols.

C

cataracts. A condition caused by a clouding of the lens of the eye; affects color vision and distance vision.

catheterization. Insertion of a tube into the urethra to drain urine from the bladder.

cerebral palsy. (CP). A condition characterized by paralysis, weakness, incoordination, and/or other motor dysfunction because of damage to the brain before it has matured.

choreoathetoid cerebral palsy. A type of cerebral palsy characterized by abrupt involuntary movements and difficulty in maintaining posture.

chorionic villus sampling. A method of testing the unborn fetus for a variety of chromosomal abnormalities, such as Down syndrome; a small amount of tissue from the chorion (a membrane that eventually helps form the placenta) is extracted and tested; can be done earlier than amniocentesis but risk of miscarriage is slightly higher.

chromosome. A rod-shaped entity in the nucleus of the cell; contains *genes*, which convey hereditary characteristics.

chronological age. Refers to how old a person is; used in comparison with *mental age* to determine the IQ score of an individual:

$$IQ = \frac{MA}{CA} \times 100$$

cleft palate. Condition in which there is a rift or split in the upper part of the oral cavity or the upper lip (cleft lip).

cochlea. A snail-shaped organ that lies below the vestibular mechanism; its parts convert the sound coming from the middle ear into an electrical signal in the inner ear, which is transmitted to the brain.

cognition. The ability to solve problems and use strategies; an area of difficulty for many persons with learning disabilities.

cognitive-behavior modification. A training approach that emphasizes teaching individuals to control their own thought processes; often used with learning-disabled children who are in need of an educational approach that stresses self-initiative and learning strategies.

cognitive mapping. A nonsequential way of conceptualizing the spatial environment that allows a person who is visually impaired to know where several points in the environment are simultaneously; allows for better mobility than does a strictly sequential conceptualization of the environment.

cognitive training. Training procedures designed to change thoughts or thought patterns.

collaborative consultation. A special educator and a general educator collaborate to come up with teaching strategies for a student with disabilities. The relationship between the two professionals is based on the premises of shared responsibility and equal authority.

coloboma. A degenerative disease in which the central and/or peripheral areas of the retina are incompletely formed, resulting in impairment of the visual field and/or central visual acuity.

communication disorders. An impairment in the ability to use speech or language to communicate.

community residential facility (CRF). A place, usually a group home, in an urban or residential neighborhood where from about three to ten retarded adults live under supervision.

competitive employment. A workplace that provides employment at at least minimum wage and one in which most workers are nondisabled.

comprehension monitoring. The ability to keep track of one's own comprehension of reading material and to make adjustments to comprehend better while one is reading; often deficient in students with learning disabilities.

computerized tomographic scans (CT scans). A neuroimaging technique whereby X-rays of the brain are compiled by a computer to produce an overall picture of the brain.

conceptual intelligence. The traditional conceptualization of intelligence emphasizing problem solving related to academic material; what IQ tests primarily focus on assessing.

conduct disorder. A disorder characterized by overt, aggressive, disruptive behavior or covert antisocial acts such as stealing, lying, and fire setting; may include both overt and covert acts.

conductive hearing impairment. A hearing loss, usually mild, resulting from malfunctioning along the conductive pathway of the ear, i.e., the outer or middle ear.

congenital anomaly An irregularity (anomaly) present at birth; may or not be due to genetic factors.

congenitally deaf. Deafness that is present at birth; can be caused by genetic factors, by injuries during fetal development, or by injury incurred at birth.

contractures. Permanent shortening of muscles and connective tissues and consequent distortion of bones and/or posture because of neurological damage.

cooperative learning. A teaching approach in which the teacher places students with heterogeneous abilities (for example, some might have disabilities) together to work on assignments.

cooperative teaching. An approach in which regular class teachers and special educators teach together in the general classroom; it helps the special educator know the context of the regular classroom better.

cornea. A transparent cover in front of the iris and pupil in the eye; responsible for most of the refraction of the light rays in focusing on an object.

creativity. Ability to express novel and useful ideas, to sense and elucidate new and important relationships, and to ask previously unthought of but crucial questions.

criterion-referenced testing. A procedure used to determine a child's level of achievement; when this level is established, a criterion, or goal, is set to fix a level at which the child should be achieving.

cued speech. A method to aid speechreading in those with hearing impairment; the speaker uses hand shapes to represent sounds.

cultural-familial retardation. Today, a term used to refer to mild retardation due to an unstimulating environment and/or genetic factors.

curriculum-based assessment (CBA). This approach to assessment is a formative evaluation method designed to evaluate performance in the particular curriculum to which students are exposed. It usually involves giving students a small sample of items from the curriculum in use in their schools. Proponents of this assessment technique argue that it is preferable to comparing students with national norms or using tests that do not reflect the curriculum content learned by students.

D

decibels. Units of relative loudness of sounds; zero decibels (0 dB) designates the point at which people with normal hearing can just detect sound.

deinstitutionalization. A social movement of the 1960s and 1970s whereby large numbers of persons with mental retardation and/or mental illness were moved from large mental institutions into smaller community homes or into the homes of their families; recognized as a major catalyst for integrating persons with disabilities into society.

Descriptive Video Service. Provides audio narrative of key visual elements; available for several public television programs; for use of people with visual impairment.

diabetic retinopathy. A condition resulting from interference of the blood supply to the retina; the fastest-growing cause of blindness.

diplegia. A condition in which the legs are paralyzed to a greater extent than the arms.

direct instruction. A method of teaching academics, especially reading and math. It emphasizes drill and practice and immediate feedback. The lessons are precisely sequenced, fast-paced, and well-rehearsed by the teacher.

disability rights movement. Patterned after the civil rights movement of the 1960s, this is a loosely organized effort to advocate for the rights of people with disabilities through lobbying legislators and other activities. Members view people with disabilities as an oppressed minority.

discourse. Conversation; skills used in conversation, such as turn-taking and staying on the topic.

Doppler effect. Term used to describe the phenomenon of the pitch of a sound rising as the listener moves toward the source of that sound.

Down syndrome. A condition resulting from a chromosomal abnormality; characterized by mental retardation and such physical signs as slanted-appearing eyes, flattened features, shortness, tendency toward obesity. The three major types of Down syndrome are *trisomy* 21, *mosaicism*, and *translocation*.

dysarthria. A condition in which brain damage causes impaired control of the muscles used in articulation.

dystrophy. Hereditary, progressive weakening and wasting away of muscle tissue in which there is no evidence of neurological disease.

E

echolalia. The meaningless repetition (echoing) of what has been heard.

electroencephalogram (EEG). A graphic recording of the brain's electrical impulses.

encephalitis. An inflammation of the brain; can affect the child's mental development adversely.

enrichment. Provision of additional learning experiences for gifted students while they remain in the grade level appropriate for their chronological age.

eugenics movement. A drive by some professionals to "better" the human race through selective breeding and sterilization of "unfit" parents such as people with mental retardation. This popular movement of the late nineteenth and early twentieth centuries resulted in laws restricting the marriage of individuals with mental retardation and sterilization of some of them.

evoked-response audiometry. A technique involving electroencephalograph measurement of changes in brain-wave activity in response to sounds.

external otitis (swimmer's ear). An infection of the skin of the external auditory canal.

extrapyramidal cerebral palsy. Types of cerebral palsy caused by damage to areas of the brain other than the pyramidal cells of the cerebral cortex, resulting in involuntary movements, stiffness, or floppiness of the muscles.

F

facilitated communication A type of augmentative communication in which someone helps the communicator type by holding or touching the communicator's hand or arm.

family characteristics. A component of the Turnbulls' family systems model; includes type and severity of the disability as well as such things as size, cultural background, and socioeconomic background of the family.

family functions. A component of the Turnbulls' family systems model; includes such things as economic, daily care, social, medical. and educational needs.

family interaction. A component of the Turnbulls' family systems model; refers to how cohesive and adaptable the family is.

family life cycle. A component of the Turnbulls' family systems model; consists of birth and early childhood (0 to 5 years), childhood (5 to 12 years), adolescence (12 to 21), and adulthood.

family-allied program. Type of early intervention program; family members carry out interventions developed by professionals.

family-centered program. Type of early intervention program; consumer-driven in that professionals are viewed as working *for* families; views family members as the most important decision makers.

family-focused program. Type of early intervention program; professionals view family members as more capable than professional-centered and family-allied programs but not as capable as family-centered programs; professionals and family members develop interventions together.

fetal alcohol syndrome (FAS). Abnormalities associated with the mother's drinking alcohol during pregnancy. Defects range from mild to severe, including growth retardation, brain damage, mental retardation, hyperactivity, anomalies of the face, and heart failure.

fingerspelling. Spelling the English alphabet by various finger positions on one hand.

fluency. The flow with which oral language is produced.

formative evaluation methods. Measurement procedures used to monitor an individual student's progress. They are used to compare an individual to himself or herself, in contrast to standardized tests, which are primarily used to compare an individual to other students.

Fragile X syndrome. Condition in which the bottom of the X chromosome in the twenty-third pair of chromosomes is pinched off; can result in a number of physical anomalies as well as mental retardation; occurs more often in males than females; thought to be the most common hereditary cause of mental retardation.

full inclusion. The belief that all students with disabilities should be educated in regular classrooms in their neighborhood schools.

functional academics. Practical skills rather than academic learning.

G

gene. Responsible for hereditary characteristics; arranged at specific locations in the chromosomes within each cell.

generalized seizure. A seizure involving a large part of the brain.

genetics. The biological study of heredity.

genius. A word sometimes used to indicate a particular aptitude or capacity in any area; rare intellectual powers.

German measles (rubella). A serious viral disease, which, if it occurs during the first trimester of pregnancy, is likely to cause a deformity in the fetus.

giftedness. Refers to cognitive (intellectual) superiority, creativity, and motivation of sufficient magnitude to set the child apart from the vast majority of age-mates and make it possible for him or her to contribute something of particular value to society.

glaucoma. A condition of excessive pressure in the eyeball; the cause is unknown but if untreated, blindness results.

guide dog. A dog specially trained to help guide a person who is blind; not recommended for children and not used by very many adults who are blind because the user needs special training in how to use the dog properly; contrary to popular opinion, the dog does not "take" the person anywhere but serves primarily as a safeguard against walking into dangerous areas.

H

handicapism. A term used by activists who fault the unequal treatment of individuals with disabilities. This term is parallel to the term racism, coined by those who fault unequal treatment based on race.

Handicapped Children's Early Education Program (HCEEP). The first federal special education program aimed at young children with disabilities and their families. It has funded numerous demonstration and outreach projects.

hemiplegia. A condition in which one half (right or left side) of the body is paralyzed.

herpes simplex. A type of veneral disease that can cause cold sores or fever blisters; if it affects the genitals and is contracted by the mother-to-be in the later stages of fetal development, it can cause mental subnormality in the child.

Hertz (Hz) unit. A measurement of the frequency of sound; refers to highness or lowness of a sound.

home-note program. A system of communication between teacher and parent; the teacher evaluates the behavior of the student using a simple form, the student takes the form home, gets the parents' signatures, and returns the form the next day.

homophenes. Sounds identical in terms of revealing movements (visible articulatory patterns).

hydrocephalus. A condition characterized by enlargement of the head because of excessive pressure of the cerebrospinal fluid.

hyperopia. Farsightedness; usually results when the eyeball is too short.

hypotonic. Low muscle tone; sometimes occurs as a result of cerebral palsy.

I

IQ-achievement discrepancy. Academic performance markedly lower than would be expected based on a student's intellectual ability.

incus. Anvil-shaped bone in the ossicular chain of the middle ear.

individual psychology. An approach to understanding human behavior that blends psychological and behavioral principles with understanding of individual experience.

individualized education program (IEP). PL 94–142 requires an IEP to be drawn up by the educational team for each exceptional child; the IEP must include a statement of present educational performance, instructional goals, educational services to be provided, and criteria and procedures for determining that the instructional objectives are being met.

individualized family service plan (IFSP). A plan for services for young children with disabilities (under 3 years of age) and their families drawn up by professionals and parents; similar to an IEP for older children; mandated by PL 99–457.

Individuals with Disabilities Education Act (IDEA). The Individuals with Disabilities Education Act of 1990; replaced PL 94–142.

insight. Ability to separate and/or combine various pieces of information in new, creative, or useful ways.

intellectual functioning. The ability to solve problems related to academics; usually estimated by an IQ test; one of two major components (the other is adaptive skills) of the AAMR definition.

iris. The colored portion of the eye; contracts or expands depending on the amount of light striking it.

J

job coach. A person who assists adult workers with retardation or disabilities, providing vocational assessment, instruction, overall planning and interaction assistance with employers, family, and related government and service agencies.

K

Kurzweil Personal Reader. A version of the Kurzweil Reading Machine that can be used with an IBM or Apple computer.

Kurzweil Reading Machine. A computerized device that converts print into speech for persons with visual impairment. The user places the printed material over a scanner that then "reads" the material aloud by means of an electronic voice.

L

language disorders. A lag in the ability to understand and express ideas that puts linguistic skill behind an individual's development in other areas, such as motor, cognitive, or social development.

language. An arbitrary code or system of symbols to communicate meaning.

larynx. The structure in the throat containing the vocal apparatus (vocal cords); laryngitis is a temporary loss of voice caused by inflammation of the larynx.

learned helplessness. A motivational term referring to a condition wherein a person believes that no matter how hard he or she tries, failure will result.

least restrictive environment (LRE). A legal term referring to the fact that exceptional children must be educated in as "normal" an environment as possible.

legally blind. A person who has visual acuity of 20/200 or less in the better eye even with correction (e.g., eyeglasses) or has a field of vision so narrow that its widest diameter subtends an angular distance no greater than 20 degrees.

lens. A structure that refines and changes the focus of the light rays passing through the eye.

locus of control. A motivational term referring to how people attribute their successes or failures; people with an internal locus of control believe that they themselves are the reason for success or failure, whereas people with an external locus of control believe outside forces (e. g., other people) influence how they perform.

long cane. A mobility aid used by individuals with visual impairment who sweep it in a wide arc in front of them; proper use requires considerable training. It is the mobility aid of choice for most travelers who are blind.

low vision. A term used by educators to refer to individuals whose visual impairment is not so severe that they are unable to read print of some kind. They may read large or regular print, and they may need some kind of magnification.

M

macroculture. A nation or other large social entity with a shared culture.

magnetic resonance imaging (MRI). A neuroimaging technique whereby radio waves are used to produce cross-sectional images of the brain.

malleus. Hammer-shaped bone in the ossicular chain of the middle ear.

meningitis. A bacterial or viral infection of the linings of the brain or spinal cord.

mental age. Refers to the IQ test score that specifies the age level at which an individual is functioning.

metacognition. One's understanding of the strategies available for learning a task and the regulatory mechanisms to complete the task.

microcephalus. A condition causing development of a small head with a sloping forehead; proper development of the brain is prevented, resulting in mental retardation.

microculture. A smaller group existing within a larger cultural group and having unique values, style, language, dialect, ways of communicating nonverbally, awareness, frame of reference, and identification.

mild retardation. A classification used to specify an individual whose IQ test score is between 55 and 69.

minimal brain injury. A term used to describe a child who shows behavioral but not neurological signs of brain injury; the term is not as popular as it once was, primarily because of its lack of diagnostic utility—i. e., some children who learn normally show signs indicative of MBD.

mixed cerebral palsy. A type of cerebral palsy in which two or more types, such as *athetosis* and *spasticity*, occur together.

mixed hearing impairment. A hearing loss resulting from a combination of conductive and sensorineural hearing impairment.

mnemonic keyword method. A cognitive training strategy used to help children with memory problems remember curriculum content. The teacher transforms abstract information into a concrete picture, which depicts the material in a more meaningful way.

moderate retardation. A classification used to specify an individual whose IQ test score is between approximately 40 and 55.

morphology. The study within psycholinguistics of word formation; of how adding or deleting parts of words changes their meaning.

mosaicism. A type of Down syndrome in which some of the cells, owing to faulty development, have an extra chromosome and some do not.

muscular dystrophy. A hereditary disease characterized by progressive weakness caused by degeneration of muscle fibers.

myelomeningocele (meningomyelocele). A tumorlike sac containing part of the spinal cord itself; a type of spina bifida.

myopathy. A weakening and wasting away of muscular tissue in which there is no evidence of neurological disease or impairment.

myopia. Nearsightedness; usually results the eyeball is too long.

N

neologism. A coined word that is meaningless to others; meaningless words used in the speech of a person with a mental disorder.

nonsupperative otitis. Inflammation of the middle ear that occurs without an infection; often preceded by infectious otitis media.

normalization. A philosophical belief in special education that every individual, even the most disabled, should have an educational and living environment as close to normal as possible.

nystagmus. Condition in which there are rapid involuntary movements of the eyes; sometimes indicates a brain malfunction and/or inner ear problems.

O

obstacle sense. A skill possessed by some people who are blind whereby they can detect the presence of obstacles in their environment. Research has shown that it is *not* an indication of an extra sense, as popularly thought; it is the result of being able to detect subtle changes in the pitch of high frequency echoes.

Optacon. A device used to enable persons who are blind to "read"; consists of a camera that converts print into an image of letters, which are then produced by way of vibration onto the finger.

orthosis. A device designed to restore, partially or completely, a lost function of the body (e. g. , a brace or crutch).

ossicles. Three tiny bones (malleus, incus, and stapes) that together make possible an efficient transfer of sound waves from the eardrum to the oval window, which connects the middle ear to the inner ear.

osteoarthritis. A type of arthritis common among children with disabilities in which movement is painful or impossible because of damage to the cartlige around the joint.

otitis media. Inflammation of the middle ear.

oval window. Connects the middle and inner ear.

P

palate. The roof of the mouth.

paraplegia. A condition in which both legs are paralyzed.

partial participation. Students with disabilities, while in the regular classroom, engage in the same activities as nondisabled students but on a reduced basis; teacher makes adaptations in the activity to allow student to participate as much as possible.

partial seizure. A seizure beginning in a localized area and involving only a small part of the brain.

pediatric AIDS. Acquired immunodeficiency syndrome that occurs in infants or young children; can be contracted by unborn fetuses from the blood of the mother through the placenta or through blood transfusions; an incurable virus that can result in a variety of physical and mental disorders; thought to be the fastest growing infectious cause of mental retardation.

peer tutoring. A method that can be used to integrate students with disabilities in regular classrooms, based on the notion that students can effectively tutor one another. The role of learner or teacher may be assigned to either the student with a disability or the nondisabled student.

Perkins Brailler. A system making it possible to write in Braille; has six keys, one for each of the six dots of the cell, which leave an embossed print on paper.

pervasive developmental disorder. Severe disorder characterized by abnormal social relations, including bizarre mannerisms, inappropriate social behavior, and unusual or delayed speech and language.

phenylketonuria (PKU). A metabolic genetic disorder caused by the inability of the body to convert phenylalanine to tyrosine; an accumulation of phenylalanine results in abnormal brain development.

phocomelia. A deformity in which the limbs of the baby are very short or missing completely, the hands and feet attached directly to the torso, like flippers; many cases resulted from maternal use of the drug thalidomide during pregnancy.

phonological skills. The ability to understand grapheme-phoneme correspondence, the rules by which sounds go with letters to make up words; generally thought to be the reason for the reading problems of many students with learning disabilities.

phonology. The study of how individual sounds make up words.

picture cues. Illustrations or photographs that provide a visual cue for completing a task; often used with workers who are mentally retarded to help them perform more independently on the job.

PL 90–538. Congressional legislation passed in 1968 that created the Handicapped Children's Early Education Program (HCEEP).

PL 94–142. The Education for All Handicapped Children Act, which contains a mandatory provision stating that to receive funds under the act, every school system in the nation must make provision for a free, appropriate public education for every child between the ages of three and eighteen (now extended to ages three to twenty-one) regardless of how, or how seriously, he or she may be disabled.

PL 99-457. Extended the requirements of PL 94-142 to children aged three to five, with special incentive to states for instituting programs for ages birth to three years.

PL 101–476. Enacted in 1990, stipulates that schools provide transition services from secondary school to adulthood for all children with disabilities; scope includes post-secondary education, vocational training, integrated employment, continuing and adult education, independent living, and community living; stipulates that a transition plan be included in the IEP no later than 16 years of age.

postlingual deafness. Deafness occurring after the development of speech and language.

practical intelligence. The ability to solve problems related to activities of daily living; an aspect of the adaptive skills component of the AAMR definition.

pragmatics. The study within psycholinguistics of how one uses language in social situations; emphasizes functional use of language rather than its mechanics.

preacademic skills. Behaviors that are needed before formal academic instruction can begin (e. g., ability to identify letters, numbers, shapes, and colors).

precocity. Remarkable early development.

prelingual deafness. Deafness that occurs before the development of spoken language, usually at birth.

prelinguistic communication Communication through gestures and noises before the child has learned oral language.

prereferral teams (PRTs). Made up of a variety of professionals, especially regular and special educators. These teams work with regular class teachers to come up with strategies for teaching difficult-to-teach children. Designed to influence regular educators to take ownership of difficult-to-teach students and to minimize inappropriate referrals to special education.

professional-centered program. Type of early intervention program; assumes that professionals have the expertise rather than families; popular at one time.

profound retardation. A classification used to specify an individual whose IQ test score is below approximately 25.

prosthesis. A device designed to replace, partially or completely, a part of the body (e.g., artificial teeth or limbs).

psychosis. A major mental disorder exhibited in seriously disturbed behavior and lack of contact with reality; schizophrenia is a form of psychosis.

pull-out programs. Special education programs in which students with disabilities leave the regular classroom for part or all of the school day, e. g., to go to special classes or resource rooms.

pupil. The contractile opening in the middle of the iris of the eye.

pure-tone audiometry. A system whereby tones of various intensities and frequencies are presented to determine a person's hearing loss.

pyramidal cerebral palsy. Types of cerebral palsy caused by damage to the pyramidal cells in the cerebral cortex, resulting in difficulty in making voluntary movements; spasticity.

Q

quadriplegia. A condition in which all four limbs are paralyzed.

R

readiness skills. Skills deemed necessary before academics can be learned (e. g., attending skills, the ability to follow directions, knowledge of letter names).

reciprocal teaching. A teaching method in which students and teachers are involved in a dialogue to facilitate reading comprehension.

reflex audiometry. The testing of responses to sounds by observation of such reflex actions as the orienting response and the Moro reflex.

regular education initiative (REI). A philosophy that maintains that general education, rather than special education, should be primarily responsible for the education of students with disabilities.

resonance. Refers to the quality of the sound imparted by the size, shape, and texture of the organs in the vocal tract.

retina. The back portion of the eye, containing nerve fibers connected to the optic nerve.

retinitis pigmentosa. A hereditary condition resulting in degeneration of the retina; causes a narrowing of the field of vision.

retinopathy of prematurity (ROP). Formerly referred to as retrolental fibroplasia, a condition resulting from administration of an excessive concentration of oxygen at birth; causes scar tissue to form behind the lens of the eye.

reverberation. The amount of echo in a room; technically, the amount of time it takes for sound to decrease to 60 dB (decibels) after it is turned off; affects the difficulty with which people, especially those with hearing impairment, can understand speech.

reverse mainstreaming. The practice of placing nondisabled students in classes predominately composed of persons with disabilities.

rheumatoid arthritis. A systemic disease with major symptoms involving the muscles and joints.

rigid cerebral palsy. A rare type of cerebral palsy that is characterized by diffuse, continuous muscle tension and consequent "lead-pipe" stiffness.

rubella (German measles). A serious viral disease, which, if it occurs during the first trimester of pregnancy, is likely to cause a deformity in the fetus.

S

scaffolded instruction. A cognitive approach to instruction whereby the teacher provides temporary structure or support while students are learning a task; the support is gradually removed as the students are able to perform the task independently.

schizophrenic. Characterized by psychotic behavior manifested by loss of contact with reality, bizarre thought processes, and inappropriate actions.

seizure (convulsion). A sudden alteration of consciousness, usually accompanied by motor activity and/or sensory phenomena; caused by an abnormal discharge of electrical energy in the brain.

self-instruction. A type of cognitive behavior modification technique that requires individuals to talk aloud and then to themselves as they solve problems.

self-monitoring. A type of cognitive behavior modification technique that requires individuals to keep track of their own behavior.

self-regulation. Referring generally to a person's ability to regulate his or her own behavior, e.g., to employ strategies to help in a problem-solving situation; an area of difficulty for persons who are mentally retarded.

self-reinforcement. A type of behavior technique in which individuals reward themselves for job accomplishment and performance.

semantics. The study of the meanings attached to words and sentences.

sensorineural hearing impairment. A hearing loss, usually severe, resulting from malfunctioning of the inner ear.

severe retardation. A classification used to specify an individual whose IQ test score is between approximately 25 and 40.

sheltered workshop. A facility that provides a structured environment for persons with disabilities in which they can learn skills; can be either a transitional placement or a permanent arrangement.

sign language. A manual language, used by people who are deaf, to communicate a true language with its own grammar.

signal-to-noise ratio. The dB level of the speaker divided by the dB level of the rest of the room; affects the ability of a person, especially one who is hearing impaired, to understand speech.

signing English systems. Used simultaneously with oral methods in the total communication approach to teaching students who are deaf; different from American Sign Language because it maintains the same word order as spoken English.

slate and stylus. A method of writing in Braille in which the paper is held in a slate while the stylus is pressed through openings to make indentations in the paper. With this method the Braille cells are written in reverse order, and thus it is more difficult to use than the Perkins Brailler. It is more portable than the Perkins Brailler, however.

Snellen chart. Used in determining visual competence; consists of rows of letters or *E*s arranged in different positions; each row corresponds to the distance at which a normally sighted person can discriminate the letters; does not predict how accurately a child will be able to read print.

social intelligence. The ability to understand social expectations and to cope in social situations; an aspect of the adaptive skills component of the AAMR definition.

sociopathic. Behavior characteristic of a sociopath; someone whose behavior is aggressively antisocial and who shows no remorse or guilt for misdeeds.

sonography. High-frequency sound waves are converted into a visual picture; used to detect major physical malformations in the unborn fetus.

spastic cerebral palsy. Types of cerebral palsy resulting in stiffness of the muscles and inaccurate voluntary movement.

spastic. Sudden, involuntary contraction of muscles that makes accurate, voluntary movement difficult; a type of cerebral palsy.

specific language disability Language disorders not attributable to impairments of hearing, intelligence, or the physical mechanisms of speech; language disorder of unknown origin.

speech. Forming and sequencing oral language sounds during communication.

speech audiometry. A technique that tests a person's detection and understanding of speech rather than using pure tones to detect hearing loss.

speech disorders. Oral communication that involves abnormal use of the vocal apparatus, is unintelligible, or so inferior that it draws attention to itself and causes anxiety, feelings of inadequacy, or inappropriate behavior in the speaker.

speech reception threshold (SRT). The decibel level at which a person can understand speech.

speechreading. A method that involves teaching children to use visual information from a number of sources to understand what is being said to them; more than just lipreading, which uses only visual clues arising from the movement of the mouth in speaking.

spina bifida. A congenital midline defect resulting from failure of the bony spinal column to close completely during fetal development.

stapes. Stirrup-shaped bone in the ossicular chain of the middle ear.

stereotypic behaviors. Any of a variety of repetitive behaviors (e.g., eye rubbing) that are sometimes found in individuals who are blind, severely retarded, or psychotic. Sometimes referred to as stereotypies or blindisms.

stimulus reduction. A concept largely forwarded by Cruickshank; an approach to teaching distractible and hyperactive children that emphasizes reducing extraneous (nonrelevant to learning) material.

strabismus. A condition in which the eyes are directed inward (crossed eyes) or outward.

structured program. A concept largely forwarded by Cruickshank; emphasizes a teacher-directed approach in which activities and environment are structured for children who are distractible and hyperactive.

stuttering. Speech characterized by abnormal hesitations, prolongations, and repetitions; may be accompanied by grimaces, gestures, or other bodily movements indicative of a struggle to speak, anxiety, blocking of speech, or avoidance of speech.

supported competitive employment. A workplace where adults who are disabled or retarded earn at least a minimum wage and receive ongoing assistance from a specialist or job coach, and where the majority of workers are nondisabled.

supported employment. A method of integrating people with disabilities who cannot work independently into competitive employment; includes use of an employment specialist, or job coach, who helps person with disability function on the job.

syntax. The way words are joined together to structure meaningful sentences.

syphilis. A venereal disease that can cause mental subnormality in a child, especially if it is contracted by the mother-to-be during the latter stages of fetal development.

T

talent. A special ability, aptitude, or accomplishment.

Tay-Sachs disease. An inherited condition that can appear when both mother and father are carriers; results in brain damage and eventual death; it can be detected before birth through amniocentesis.

teletypewriter (TTY). A device connected to a telephone by a special adapter; allows communication between persons who are hearing impaired and the hearing over the telephone.

temperament. Inborn behavioral style, including general level of activity, regularity or predictability, approach or withdrawal, adaptability, intensity of reaction, responsiveness, mood, distractibility, and persistence. The temperament is present at birth but may be modified by parental management.

teratogens. Deformity-producing factors that interfere with normal fetal development.

tonic/clonic seizure. Loss of consciousness (usually for 2 to 5 minutes) followed by repeated tonic and clonic contractions of muscles of the limbs, trunk, and head (i.e., convulsions); also called grand mal seizure.

total communication approach. An approach for teaching the hearing impaired that blends oral and manual techniques.

Tourette's disorder. A neurological disorder beginning in childhood (about 3 times more prevalent in boys than in girls) in which stereotyped motor movements (tics) are accompanied by multiple vocal outbursts that may include grunting or barking noises or socially inappropriate words or statements.

translocation. A type of Down syndrome in which the extra chromosome (the result of faulty development) in the twenty-first set breaks off and attaches itself to another of the chromosome pairs.

traumatic brain injury. Injury to the brain, not including conditions present at birth, birth trauma, or degenerative diseases or conditions, resulting in total or partial disability or psychosocial maladjustment that affects educational performance; may affect cognition, language, memory, attention, reasoning, abstract thinking, judgment, problem solving, sensory or perceptual and motor disabilities, psychosocial behavior, physical functions, information processing, or speech.

traveling notebook. A system of communication in which parents and professionals write "messages" to each other by way of a notebook, or log, that accompanies the child to and from school.

trisomy 21. A type of Down syndrome in which the twenty-first chromosome is a triplet, making forty-seven, rather than the normal forty-six, chromosomes in all.

tympanic membrane (eardrum). The anatomical boundary between the outer and middle ear; the sound gathered in the outer ear vibrates here.

V

VersaBraille. A device used to record Braille onto tape cassettes that are played back on a reading board; the VersaBraille II Plus is a laptop computer on which a person can type Braille that can be converted into print copies.

vestibular mechanism. Located in the upper portion of the inner ear; consists of three soft, semicircular canals filled with a fluid that is sensitive to head movement, acceleration, and other movements related to balance.

visual efficiency. A term used to refer to how well one uses one's vision, including such things as control of eye movements, attention to visual detail, and discrimination of figure from background. It is believed by some to be more important than visual acuity alone in predicting a person's ability to function visually.

vitreous humor. A transparent gelatinous substance that fills the eyeball between the retina and the lens of the eye.

W

work-study program. Designed to introduce students to a variety of vocational opportunities while still in school. On-the-job training is provided, and the student's performance is evaluated.

REFERENCES

▲ ▲ ▲

Chapter 1

Bateman, B. D. (1992). *Better IEPS*. Creswell, OR: OtterInk. p. 19

Clark, D. L., & Astuto, T. A. (1988). *Education policy after Reagan—What next?* Occasional paper No. 6, Policy Studies Center of the University Council for Educational Administration, University of Virginia, Charlottesville.

Cruickshank, W. M. (1977). Guest editorial. *Journal of Learning Disabilities, 10*, 193–194.

Goodlad, J. I., & Lovitt, T. C. (Eds.) (1993). *Integrating general and special education*. Columbus, OH: Merrill/Macmillan.

Goodman, J. F., & Bond, L. (1993). The individualized education program: A retrospective critique. *Journal of Special Education, 26*, 408–422.

Hendrick, I. G., & MacMillan, D. L. (1989). Selecting children for special education in New York City: William Maxwell, Elizabeth Farrell, and the development of ungraded classes, 1900–1920. *Journal of Special Education, 22*, 395–417.

Howe, K. R., & Miramontes, O. B. (1992). *The ethics of special education*. New York: Teachers College Press.

Itard, J. M. G. (1962). *The wild boy of Averyron*. (Trans. George & Muriel Humphrey). Englewood Cliffs, NJ: Prentice-Hall.

Kanner, L. (1964). *A history of the care and study of the mentally retarded*. Springfield, IL: Charles C. Thomas.

Lloyd, J. W., Singh, N. N., & Repp, A. C. (Eds.). (1991). *The regular education initiative: Alternative perspectives on concepts, issues, and models*. Sycamore, IL: Sycamore.

MacMillan, D. L., & Hendrick, I. G. (1993). Evolution and legacies. In J. I. Goodlad & T. C. Lovitt (Eds.), *Integrating general and special education*. Columbus, OH: Merrill/Macmillan.

Morse, W. C. (1984). Personal perspective. In B. Blatt & R. Morris (Eds.), *Perspectives in special education: Personal orientations*. Glenview, IL: Scott, Foresman.

Patterson, G. R., Reid, J. B., & Dishion, T. J. (1992). *Antisocial boys*. Eugene, OR: Castalia.

Sarason, S. B. (1990), *The predictable failure of educational reform: Can we change course before it's too late?* San Francisco: Jossey-Bass.

U. S. Department of Education. (1992). *Fourteenth annual report to Congress on implementation of the Individuals with Disabilities Education Act*. Washington, DC: Author.

Verstegen, D. A., & Clark, D. L. (1988). The diminution of federal expenditures for education during the Reagan administration. *Phi Delta Kappan, 70*, 134–138.

Werner, E. E. (1986). The concept of risk from a developmental perspective. In B. K. Keogh (Ed.), *Advances in special education, Vol. 5. Developmental problems in infancy and the preschool years*. Greenwich, CT: JAI Press.

Winzer, M. A. (1986). Early developments in special education: Some aspects of Enlightenment thought. *Remedial and Special Education, 7*(5), 42–49.

Yanok, J. (1986). Free appropriate public education for handicapped children: Congressional intent and judicial interpretation. *Remedial and Special Education, 7*(2), 49–53.

Ysseldyke, J. E., Algozzine, B., & Thurlow, M. L. (1992). *Critical issues in special education* (2nd ed.). Boston: Houghton Mifflin.

Zelder, E. Y. (1953). Public opinion and public education for the exceptional child—court decisions 1873–1950. *Exceptional Children, 18*, 187–198.

Chapter 2

Bank-Mikkelsen, N. E. (1969). A metropolitan area in Denmark: Copenhagen. In R. B. Kugel & W. Wolfensberger (Eds.), *Changing patterns of residential services for the mentally retarded* (pp. 227–254). Washington DC: President's Committee on Mental Retardation.

Baumeister, A. A., Kupstas, F., & Klindworth, L. M. (1990). New morbidity: Implications for prevention of children's disabilities. *Exceptionality, 1*(1), 1–16.

Bauwens, J., & Hourcade, J. J. (1991). Making co-teaching a mainstreaming strategy. *Preventing School Failure, 35*(4), 19–24.

Bauwens, J., Hourcade, J. J., & Friend, M. (1989). Cooperative teaching: a model for general and special education integration. *Remedial and Special Education, 10*(2), 17–22.

Blatt, B., & Kaplan, F. (1966). *Christmas in Purgatory: A photographic essay on mental retardation*. Boston: Allyn & Bacon.

Bogdan, R. (1986). The sociology of special education. In R. J. Morris & B. Blatt (Eds.), *Special education: Research and trends* (pp. 344–359). New York: Pergamon Press.

Bogdan, R., & Biklen, D. (1977). Handicapism. *Social Policy, 7*(5), 14–19.

Brantlinger, E. A., & Guskin, S. L. (1987). Ethnocultural and social-psychological effects on learning characteristics of handicapped children. In M. C. Wang, M. C. Reynolds, & H. J. Walberg (Eds.), *Handbook of special education: Research and practice. Vol. 1. Learner characteristics and adaptive education* (pp. 7–34). New York: Pergamon Press.

Bricker, D. D. (1986). An analysis of early intervention programs: Attendant issues and future directions. In R. J. Morris & B. Blatt (Eds.), *Special education: Research and trends* (pp. 28–65). New York: Pergamon Press.

Bybee, J., Ennis, P., & Zigler, E. (1990). Effects of institutionalization on the self-concept and outerdirectedness of adolescents with mental retardation. *Exceptionality, 1*(4), 215–226.

Cavalier, A., & Mineo, B. A. (1986). The application of technology in the home, classroom, and work place: Unvoiced premises and ethical issues. In A. Gartner & T. Joe (Eds.), *Images of the disabled/disabling images.* New York: Praeger.

Chalfant, J. C., Pysh, M. V., & Moultrie, R. (1979). Teacher assistance teams: A model for within-building problem solving. *Learning Disability Quarterly, 2,* 85–96.

Children's Museum of Boston, with WGBH Boston. (1978). *What if you couldn't? An elementary school program about handicaps.* Weston, MA: Burt Harrison & Co.

Cohen, S. (1977). *Accepting individual differences.* Allen, TX: Developmental Learning Materials.

Crissey, M. S., & Rosen, M. (Eds.) (1986). *Institutions for the mentally retarded: A changing role in changing times.* Austin, TX: Pro-Ed.

DeStefano, L., & Wermuth, T. R. (1992). IDEA (P.L. 101–476): Defining a second generation of transition services. In F. R. Rusch, L. DeStefano, J. Chadsey-Rusch, L. A. Phelps, & E. Szymanski (Eds.), *Transition from school to adult life* (pp. 537–549). Sycamore, IL: Sycamore Publishing Co.

Edgar, E. (1987). Secondary programs in special education: Are many of them justifiable? *Exceptional Children, 53*(6), 555–561.

Fiedler, C. R., & Simpson, R. L. (1987). Modifying the attitudes of nonhandicapped high school students toward handicapped peers. *Exceptional Children, 53,* 342–349.

Fowler, S. A., Schwartz, I., & Atwater, J. (1991). Perspectives on the transition from preschool to kindergarten for children with disabilities and their families. *Exceptional Children, 58*(2), 136–145.

Fuchs, D., & Fuchs, L. S. (1991). Framing the REI debate: Abolitionists versus conservationists. In J. W. Lloyd, N. N. Singh, & A. C. Repp (Eds.), *The regular education initiative: Alternative perspectives on concepts, issues, and models* (pp. 241–255). Sycamore, IL: Sycamore Publishing Co.

Fuchs, D., & Fuchs, L. S. (in press). Limitations of a feel-good approach to consultation, *Journal of Educational and Psychological Consultation. 3* 93–97.

Gallagher, J. J. (1972). The special education contract for mildly handicapped children. *Exceptional Children, 38,* 527–535.

Gallagher, J. J. (1992). The roles of values and facts in policy development for infants and toddlers with disabilities and their families. *Journal of Early Intervention, 16*(1), 1–10.

Gartner, A., & Joe, T. (1986). Introduction. In A. Gartner and T. Joe (Eds.), *Images of the Disabled/ Disabling Images.* New York: Praeger.

Gerber, M. M., & Kauffman, J. M. (1981). Peer tutoring in academic settings. In P. S. Strain (Ed.), *The utilization of classroom peers as behavior change agents* (pp. 155–187). New York: Plenum.

Gerber, M. M., & Semmel, M. I. (1984). Teacher as imperfect test: Reconceptualizing the referral process. *Educational Psychologist, 19,* 137–148.

Gerber, M. M., & Semmel, M. I. (1985). Microeconomics of referral and reintegration: A paradigm for evaluation of special education. *Studies in Educational Evaluation, 11*(1), 13–29.

Giangreco, M. F., & Putnam, J. W. (1991). Supporting the education of students with severe disabilities in regular education environments. In L. H. Meyer, C. A. Peck, L. Brown (Eds.), *Critical issues in the lives of people with severe disabilities* (pp. 245–270). Baltimore, MD: Paul H. Brookes.

Greenspan, S., & Cerreto, M. (1989). Normalization, deinstitutionalization, and the limits of research: Comment on Landesman and Butterfield. *American Psychologist, 44,* 448–449.

Guralnick, M. J. (1991). The next decade of research on the effectiveness of early intervention. *Exceptional Children, 58*(2), 174–183.

Halpern, A. S. (1985). Transition: A look at the foundations. *Exceptional Children, 51*(6), 479–486.

Halpern, A. S. (1992). Transition: Old wine in new bottles. *Exceptional Children, 58*(3), 202–211.

Hebbeler, K. M., Smith, B. J., & Black, T. L. (1991). Federal early childhood special education policy: A model for the improvement of services for children with disabilities. *Exceptional Children, 58*(2), 104–112.

Hendrick, I. G., MacMillan, D. L., & Balow, I. H. (1989, April). *Early school leaving in America: A review of the literature.* Riverside: University of California, California Educational Research Cooperative.

Hershey, L. (1991, July/August). Pride. *The Disability Rag,* pp. 1, 4–5. Louisville, KY: Advocato Press.

The ICD Survey III. (1989, June). *A report card on special education.* New York: Louis Harris and Associates, Inc. Conducted for International Center for the Disabled in cooperation with National Council on Disability.

Jenkins, J. R., & Jenkins, L. M. (1987). Making peer tutoring work. *Educational Leadership, 44*(6), 64–68.

Johnson, D. W., & Johnson, R. (1986). Mainstreaming and cooperative learning strategies. *Exceptional Children, 52,* 553–561.

Karnes, M. B., & Stayton, V. D. (1988). Model programs for infants and toddlers with handicaps. In J. B. Jordan, J. J. Gallagher, P. L. Hutinger, & M. B. Karnes (Eds.), *Early childhood special education: Birth to three* (pp. 67–106). Reston, VA: Council for Exceptional Children and the Division for Early Childhood.

Kauffman, J. M. (1989). The regular education initiative as a Reagan-Bush education policy: A trickle-down theory of education of the hard-to-teach. *The Journal of Special Education*, 23(3), 256–278.

Kauffman, J. M., Gerber, M. M., Semmel, M. I. (1988). Arguable assumptions underlying the regular education initiative. *Journal of Learning Disabilities*, 21(1). 6–11.

Kauffman, J. M., & Hallahan, D. P. (1992). Deinstitutionalization and mainstreaming exceptional children. In M. C. Alkin (Ed.), *Encyclopedia of educational research: Vol.1* (6th ed.) (pp. 299–303). New York: Macmillan Publishing Co.

Kauffman, J. M., & Hallahan, D. P. (1993). Toward a comprehensive delivery system: The necessity of identity, focus, and authority for special education and other compensatory programs. In J. I. Goodlad & T. C. Lovitt (Eds.), *Integrating general and special education*. Columbus, OH: Charles E. Merrill. 73–102

Klobas, L. (1985, January-February). TV's concept of people with disabilities: Here's lookin' at you. *The Disability Rag*, pp. 2–6. Louisville, Ky: Advocado Press.

Landesman, S., & Butterfield, E. C. (1987). Normalization and deinstitutionalization of mentally retarded individuals: Controversy and facts. *American Psychologist*, 42, 809–816.

Laski, F. J. (1991). Achieving integration during the second revolution. In L. H. Meyer, C. A. Peck, L. Brown (Eds.), *Critical issues in the lives of people with severe disabilities* (pp. 409–421). Baltimore, MD: Paul H. Brookes.

Lieberman, L. M. (1992). Preserving special education . . . for those who need it. In W. Stainback & S. Stainback (Eds.), *Controversial issues confronting special education: Divergent perspectives* (pp. 13–25). Boston: Allyn & Bacon.

Lloyd, J. W., Crowley, E. P., Kohler, F. W., & Strain, P. S. (1988). Redefining the applied research agenda: Cooperative learning, prereferral, teacher consultation, and peer-mediated interventions. *Journal of Learning Disabilities*, 21, 43–52.

Longmore, P. K. (1985). Screening stereotypes: Images of disabled people. *Social Policy*, 16, 31–37.

Lord, W. (1991, November). Parent point of view: What is the least restrictive environment for a deaf child? *Michigan Statewide Newsletter*, p. 4.

MacMillan, D. L., Widaman, K. F., Balow, I. H., Borthwick-Duffy, S., Hendrick, I. G., & Hemsley, R. E. (1992). Special education students exiting the educational system. *The Journal of Special Education*, 26(1), 20–36.

McCann, S. K., Semmel, M. I., & Nevin, A. (1985). Reverse mainstreaming: Nonhandicapped students in special education classrooms. *Remedial and Special Education*, 6(1), 13–19.

McMurray, G. L. (1986). Easing everyday living: Technology for the physically disabled. In A. Gartner & T. Joe (Eds.), *Images of the disabled/disabling images*. New York: Praeger.

Neel, R. S., Meadows, N., Levine, P., Edgar, E. (1988). What happens after special education: A statewide follow-up study of secondary students who have behavioral disorders. *Behavioral Disorders*, 13, 209–216.

Nowacek, E. J. (1992). Professionals talk about teaching together: Interviews with five collaborating teachers. *Intervention in School and Clinic*, 27(5), 262–276.

Odom, S. L., Deklyen, M., & Jenkins, J. R. (1984). Integrating handicapped and nonhandicapped preschoolers: Developmental impact on nonhandicapped children. *Exceptional Children*, 51, 41–48.

Padden, C. & Humphries, T. (1988). *Deaf in America: Voices from a culture*. Cambridge, MA: Harvard University Press.

Position Statement of National Association for the Education of Young Children and National Association of Early Childhood Specialists in State Departments of Education. (1991). *Young Children*, 46(3), 21–38.

Raynes, M., Snell, M., & Sailor, W. (1991). A fresh look at categorical programs for children with special needs. *Phi Delta Kappan*, 73(4), 326–331.

Rusch, F. R., & Hughes, C. (1990). Historical overview of supported employment. In F. R. Rusch (Ed.), *Supported employment: Models, methods, and issues* (pp. 5–14). Sycamore, IL: Sycamore Publishing Co.

Rusch, F. R., Szymanski, E. M., & Chadsey-Rusch, J. (1992). The emerging field of transition services. In F. R. Rusch, L. DeStefano, J. Chadsey-Rusch, L. A. Phelps, & E. Szymanski (Eds.), *Transition from school to adult life* (pp. 5–15). Sycamore, IL: Sycamore Publishing Co.

Sailor, W. (1991). Special education in the restructured school. *Remedial and Special Education*, 12(6), 8–22.

Schram, L., Semmel, M. I., Gerber, M. M., Bruce, M. M., Lopez-Reyna, N., & Allen, D. (1984). Problem solving teams in California. Unpublished manuscript, University of California at Santa Barbara.

Scruggs, T. E., & Richter, L. (1986). Tutoring learning disabled students: A critical review. *Learning Disability Quarterly*, 9, 2–14.

Semmel, M. I., Abernathy, T. V., Butera, G., & Lesar, S. (1991). Teacher perceptions of the regular education initiative. *Exceptional Children*, 58(1), 9–24.

Slavin, R. E. (1988). Cooperative learning and student achievement. *Educational Leadership*, 46(2), 31–33.

Slavin, R. E. (1991). Synthesis of research on cooperative learning. *Educational Leadership*, 48(5), 71–82.

Slentz, K. L., & Bricker, D. (1992). Family-guided assessment for IFSP development: Jumping off the family assessment bandwagon. *Journal of Early Intervention*, 16(1), 11–19.

Stainback, S., & Stainback, W. (1992). Schools as inclusive communities. In W. Stainback & S. Stainback (Eds.), *Controversial issues confronting special education: Divergent perspectives* (pp. 29–43). Boston: Allyn & Bacon.

Trent, S. C. (1992). *Collaboration between special education and regular education teachers: A cross-case analysis.* Doctoral dissertation, University of Virginia, Charlottesville VA.

Turnbull, A. P., & Turnbull, H. R. (1990). *Families, professionals, and exceptionality: A special partnership* (2nd ed.). Columbus, OH: Charles E. Merrill.

U.S. Department of Education. (1990). *National goals for education.* Washington DC: U. S. Government Printing Office.

Walker, H. M., & Bullis, M. (1991). Behavior disorders and the social context of regular class integration: A conceptual dilemma? In J. W. Lloyd, N. N. Singh, & A. C. Repp (Eds.), *The regular education initiative: Alternative perspectives on concepts, issues, and models* (pp. 75–93). Sycamore IL: Sycamore Publishing Co.

Wesson, C., & Mandell, C. (1989). Simulations promote understanding of handicapping conditions. *Teaching Exceptional Children, 22*(1), 32–35.

West, J. F., & Idol, L. (1990). Collaborative consultation in the education of mildly handicapped and at-risk students. *Remedial and Special Education, 11*(1), 22–31.

Will, M. (1984). *OSERS programming for the transition of youth with disabilities: Bridges from school to working life.* Washington DC: U. S. Department of Education, Office of Special Education and Rehabilitative Services.

Will, M. C. (1986). Educating children with learning problems: A shared responsibility. *Exceptional Children, 52,* 411–415.

Wolery, M. (1991). Instruction in early childhood special education: "Seeing through a glass darkly . . . Knowing in part." *Exceptional Children, 58*(2), 127–135.

Wolf, B. (1974). *Don't feel sorry for Paul.* Philadelphia: Lippincott.

Wolfensberger, W. (1972). *The principle of normalization in human services.* Toronto: National Institute on Mental Retardation.

Wolman, C., Bruininks, R., & Thurlow, M. (1989). Dropouts and drop out programs: Implications for special education. *Remedial and Special Education, 10*(5), 6–20, 50.

Zigler, E., Hodapp, R. M., & Edison, M. R. (1990). From theory to practice in the care and education of mentally retarded individuals. *American Journal on Mental Retardation, 95*(1), 1–12.

Zigmond, N., & Miller, S. E. (1992). Improving high school programs for students with learning disabilities: A matter of substance as well as form. In F. R. Rusch, L. DeStefano, J. Chadsey-Rusch, L. A. Phelps, & E. Szymanski (Eds.), *Transition from school to adult life* (pp. 17–31). Sycamore IL: Sycamore Publishing Co.

CHAPTER 3

Ascher, C. (1992). School programs for African-American males . . . and females. *Phi Delta Kappan, 73,* 777–782.

Banks, J. A. (1988). *Multiethnic education: Theory and practice* (2nd ed.). Boston: Allyn & Bacon.

Bauer, G. B., Dubanoski, R., Yamauchi, L. A., & Honbo, K. M. (1990). Corporal punishment and the schools. *Education and Urban Society, 22,* 285–299.

Bempechat, J., & Omori, M. (1990). Meeting the educational needs of Southeast Asian children. *Digest.* New York: ERIC Clearinghouse on Urban Education, Institute for Urban and Minority Education, Teachers College, Columbia University.

Bender, W. N. (1988). The other side of placement decisions: Assessment of the mainstream learning environment. *Remedial and Special Education, 9*(5), 28–33.

Boutte, G. S. (1992). Frustrations of an African–American parent: A personal and professional account. *Phi Delta Kappan, 73,* 786–788.

Caplan, N., Choy, M. H., & Whitmore, J. K. (1992, February). Indochinese refugee families and academic achievement. *Scientific American, 266*(2), 36–42.

Chinn, P. C., & Hughes, S. (1987). Representation of minority students in special education classes. *Remedial and Special Education, 8*(4), 41–46.

Council for Children with Behavioral Disorders. (1989). White paper. Best assessment practices for students with behavioral disorders: Accommodation to cultural diversity and individual differences. *Behavioral Disorders, 14,* 263–278.

Delpit, L. D. (1988). The silenced dialogue: Power and pedagogy in educating other people's children. *Harvard Educational Review, 58,* 280–298.

Deno, S. L. (1985). Curriculum-based measurement: The emerging alternative. *Exceptional Children, 52,* 219–232.

Devore, W., & Schlesinger, E. G. (1987). *Ethnic-sensitive social work practice* (2nd ed.). Columbus, OH: Merrill/Macmillan.

Duke, D. L. (1990). *Teaching: An introduction.* New York: McGraw-Hill.

Farrington, D. P. (1986). The sociocultural context of childhood disorders. In H. C. Quay & J. S. Werry (Eds.), *Psychopathological disorders of childhood* (3rd ed.). New York: Wiley.

Franklin, M. E. (1992). Culturally sensitive instructional practices for African-American learners with disabilities. *Exceptional Children, 59,* 115–122.

Garcia, R. (1978). *Fostering a pluralistic society through multiethnic education.* Bloomington, IN: Phi Delta Kappa.

Gollnick, D., & Chinn, P. (Eds.). (1990). *Multicultural education in a pluralistic society* (3rd ed.). Columbus, OH: Merrill/Macmillan.

Hanna, J. (1988). *Disruptive school behavior: Class, race and culture.* New York: Holmes & Meier.

Harrison-Ross, P., & Wyden, B. (1973). *The black child.* Berkeley, CA: Medallion.

Hilliard, A. G. (1989). Teachers and cultural styles in a pluralistic society. *NEA Today, 7*(6), 65–69.

Hilliard, A. G. (1992). The pitfalls and promises of special education practice. *Exceptional Children, 59*, 168–172.

Hirsch, E. D. (1987). *Cultural literacy: What every American needs to know.* Boston: Houghton Mifflin.

Horton, P., & Hunt, C. (1968). *Sociology* (2nd ed.). New York: McGraw-Hill.

Howell, K. W., & Morehead, M. K. (1987). *Curriculum-based evaluation for special and remedial education.* Columbus, OH: Merrill/Macmillan.

Hunter, J. D. (1991). *Culture wars: The struggle to define America.* New York: Basic Books.

Hyman, I. A. (1988). *Eliminating corporal punishment in schools: Moving from advocacy research to policy development.* Paper presented at the 96th annual convention of the American Psychological Association, Atlanta.

Jacob, E., & Jordan, C. (Eds.). (1987). Explaining the school performance of minority students. *Anthropology and Education Quarterly, 18*(4), [special issue].

Johnson, D. W., & Johnson, R. (1986). Mainstreaming and cooperative learning strategies. *Exceptional Children, 52*, 553–561.

Kauffman, J. M., Mostert, M. P., Nuttycombe, D. G., Trent, S. C., & Hallahan, D. P. (1993). *Managing classroom behavior: A reflective case-based approach.* Boston: Allyn & Bacon.

Kidder, J. T. (1989). *Among school children.* Boston: Houghton Mifflin.

Leake, D., & Leake, B. (1992). African-American immersion schools in Milwaukee: A view from inside. *Phi Delta Kappan, 73*, 783–785.

Martin, D. S. (1987). Reducing ethnocentrism. *Teaching Exceptional Children, 20*(1), 5–8.

McDowell, E., & Friedman, R. (1979). An analysis of editorial opinion regarding corporal punishment: Some dynamics of regional differences. In I. A. Hyman & J. H. Wise (Eds.), *Corporal punishment in American education* (pp. 384–393). Philadelphia, PA: Temple University Press.

McIntyre, T. (1987). Teacher awareness of child abuse and neglect. *Child Abuse and Neglect, 11*(1), 33–35.

McIntyre, T. (1992a). The "invisible culture" in our schools: Gay and lesbian youth. *Beyond Behavior, 3*(3), 6–12.

McIntyre, T. (1992b). The culturally sensitive disciplinarian. In R. B. Rutherford & S. R. Mathur (Eds.), *Monograph in behavioral disorders: Severe behavior disorders of children and youth, 15*, 107–115.

McIntyre, T. (1992c). A primer on cultural diversity for educators. *Multicultural Forum, 1*(1), 6–7, 12.

McIntyre, T., & Silva, P. (1992). Culturally diverse childrearing practices: Abusive or just different? *Beyond Behavior, 4*(1), 8–12.

McLoughlin, J. A., & Lewis, R. B. (1990). *Assessing special students.* Columbus, OH: Merrill/Macmillan.

McNergney, R. F. (1992). *Teaching and learning in multicultural settings: The case of Hans Christian Anderson School.* Video Cassette. Boston: Allyn & Bacon.

Mehta, V. (1989). *The stolen light.* New York: W. W. Norton.

Miller, W. (1959). Implications of urban lower class culture for social work. *Social Service Review, 33*, 232–234.

Minow, M. (1985). Learning to live with the dilemma of difference: Bilingual and special education. In K. T. Bartlett & J. W. Wegner (Eds.), *Children with special needs* (pp. 375–429). New Brusnwick, NJ: Transaction Books.

Ogbu, J. U. (1990). Understanding diversity: Summary comments. *Education and Urban Society, 22*, 425–429.

Ogbu, J. U. (1992). Understanding cultural diversity and learning. *Educational Researcher, 21*(8), 5–14.

Ortiz, A., Yates, J. R., & Garcia, S. B. (1990). Competencies associated with serving exceptional language minority students. *Bilingual Special Education Newsletter*, Vol. 9. Austin, TX: University of Texas, College of Education, Office of Bilingual Education.

Padden, C., & Humphries, T. (1988). *Deaf in America: Voices from a culture.* Cambridge, MA: Harvard University Press.

Patterson, O. (1992). Black like all of us: Celebrating multiculturalism diminishes blacks' role in American culture. *The Washington Post*, Sunday, February 7, 1993, p. C2.

Patton, J. M. (1992). Assessment and identification of African-American learners with gifts and talents. *Exceptional Children, 59*, 150–159.

Persky, B. (1974). Urban health problems. In L. Golubchick & B. Persky (Eds.), *Urban, social, and educational issues.* Dubuque, IA: Kendall/Hunt.

Price, H. B. (1992). Multiculturalism: Myths and realities. *Phi Delta Kappan, 74*, 208–213.

Reschly, D. J. (1987). Learning characteristics of mildly handicapped students: Implications for classification, placement, and programming. In M. C. Wang, M. C. Reynolds, & H. J. Walberg (Eds.), *Handbook of special education: Research and practice. Vol. 1: Learner characteristics and adaptive education.* New York: Pergamon.

Rodriguez, R. (1982). *Hunger of memory: The education of Richard Rodriguez. An autobiography.* Boston: D. R. Godine.

Rodriguez, R. (1992). *Days of obligation: An argument with my Mexican father.* New York: Viking.

Rogoff, B., & Morelli, G. (1989). Culture and American children. *American Psychologist, 44*, 341–342.

Rosenfeld, G. (1971). *Shut those thick lips! A study of slum school failure.* New York: Holt, Rinehart, & Winston.

Russell, K. Y. (1992). *The color complex: The "last taboo" among African Americans.* San Diego, CA: Harcourt Brace Jovanovich.

Shor, I. (1986). *Culture wars: School and society in the conservative restoration, 1969–1984*. Boston: Routledge & K. Paul.

Silverstein, B., & Krate, R. (1975). *Children of the dark ghetto: A developmental psychology*. New York: Praeger.

Slavin, R. E. (1988). Cooperative learning and student achievement. *Educational Leadership, 46*(2), 31–33.

Spinetta, J. J., & Rigler, D. (1972). The child-abusing parent: A psychological review. *Psychological Bulletin, 77*, 296–304.

Stack, C. (1974). *All our kin: Strategies for survival in a black community*. New York: Harper & Row.

Steele, C. M. (1992, April). Race and the schooling of black Americans. *The Atlantic Monthly*, 68–78.

Swisher, K. (1990, January). Cooperative learning and the education of American Indian/Alaskan Native students: A review of the literature and suggestions for implementation. *Journal of American Indian Education*, 36–43.

Uribe, V., & Harbeck, K. M. (1992). *Coming out of the classroom closet: Gay and lesbian students, teachers, and curricula*. Binghamton, NY: Hayworth Press.

U.S. Department of Education. (1992). *Foureenth annual report to Congress on the implementation of the Individuals with Disabilities Education Act*. Washington, DC: Author.

Wallace, G., Larsen, S. C., & Elksnin, L. K. (1992). *Educational assessment of learning problems: Testing for teaching* (2nd ed.). Boston: Allyn & Bacon.

Wortham, A. (1992, September). Afrocentrism isn't the answer for black students in American society. *The Executive Educator, 14*, 23–25.

Ysseldyke, J. E., & Christenson, S. L. (1987). Evaluating students' instructional environments. *Remedial and Special Education, 8*(3), 17–24.

Ysseldyke, J. E., & Marston, D. (1988). Issues in the psychological evaluation of children. In V. B. Van Hasselt, P. S. Strain, & M. Hersen (Eds.), *Handbook of developmental and physical disabilities* (pp. 21–37). New York: Pergamon.

CHAPTER 4

AAMR Ad Hoc Committee on Terminology and Classification. (1992). *Mental retardation: definition, classification, and systems of support.* (9th ed.) Washington, DC: American Association on Mental Retardation.

Allore, R., O'Hanlon, D., Price, R., Neilson, H., Willard, H. F., Cox, D. R., Marks, A., & Dunn, R. J. Gene encoding the ß subunit of S100 protein on chromosome 21: Implications for Down syndrome. (1988, March 11). *Science*, pp. 1311–1313.

Baker, L. (1982). An evaluation of the role of metacognitive deficits in learning disabilities. *Topics in Learning and Learning Disabilities, 2(1)*, 27–35.

Bates, P., Renzaglia, A., & Wehman, P. (1981). Characteristics of an appropriate education for severely and profoundly handicapped students. *Education and Training of the Mentally Retarded, 16*, 142–149.

Batshaw, M. L., & Perret, Y. M. (1986). *Children with handicaps: A medical primer* (2nd ed.). Baltimore: Paul H. Brookes.

Baumeister, A. A., Kupstas, F., & Klindworth, L. M. (1990). New morbidity: Implications for prevention of children's disabilities. *Exceptionality, 1*(1), 1–16.

Berkell, D. (1988). Identifying programming goals for productive employment. In B. L. Ludlow, A. P. Turnbull, & R. Luckasson (Eds.), *Transitions to adult life for people with mental retardation: Principles and practices* (pp. 159–175). Baltimore: Paul H. Brookes.

Berrueta-Clement, J. R., Schweinhart, L. J., Barnett, W. S., Epstein, A. S., & Weikart, D. P. (1984). *Changed lives: The effects of the Perry Preschool Program on youths through age 19.* (Monograph of the High/Scope Educational Research Foundation No. 8.) Ypsilanti, MI: High/Scope Press.

Blacher, J., & Baker, B. L. (1992). Toward meaningful family involvement in out-of-home placement settings. *Mental Retardation, 30*(1), 35–41.

Blackman, J. A. (1984a). Down syndrome. In J. A. Blackman (Ed.), *Medical aspects of developmental disabilities in children birth to three,* (Rev. 1st ed., pp. 92–95). Rockville, Md.: Aspen Systems Corp.

Blackman, J. A. (1984b). Low birth weight. In J. A. Blackman (Ed.), *Medical aspects of developmental disabilities in children birth to three* (Rev. 1st ed., pp. 143–146). Rockville, MD: Aspen Systems Corp.

Brooks, P. H., & McCauley, C. (1984). Cognitive research in mental retardation. *American Journal of Mental Deficiency, 88*, 479–486.

Brown, L., Shiraga, B., Ford, A., Nisbet, J., Van Deventer, P., Sweet, M., York, J., & Loomis, R. (1986). Teaching severely handicapped students to perform meaningful work in nonsheltered vocational environments. In R. J. Morris & B. Blatt (Eds.), *Special education: Research and trends* (pp. 131–189). New York: Pergamon Press.

Capron, C., & Duyme, M. (1989, August 17). Assessment of effects of socio-economic status on IQ in a full cross-fostering study. *Nature*, pp. 552–553.

Chadsey-Rusch, J., Rusch, F. R., & O'Reilly, M. F. (1991). Transition from school to integrated communities. *Remedial and Special Education, 12*(6), 23–33.

Craik, F. I. M., & Lockhart, R. S. (1972). Levels of processing: A framework for memory research. *Journal of Verbal Learning and Verbal Behavior, 11*, 671–684.

Craik, F. I. M., & Tulving, E. (1975). Depth of processing and the retention of words in episodic memory. *Journal of Experimental Psychology: General, 104*, 268–294.

Cravioto, J., & DeLicardie, E. R. (1975). Environmental and nutritional deprivation in children with learning disabilities. In W. M. Cruickshank & D. P. Hallahan (Eds.), *Perceptual and learning disabilities in children.* Vol. 2:

Research and theory. Syracuse, NY: Syracuse University Press.

Cunningham, P. J., & Mueller, C. D. (1991). Individuals with mental retardation in residential facilities: Findings from the 1987 national medical expenditure survey. *American Journal on Mental Retardation, 96*(2), 109–117.

Diamond, G. W., & Cohen, H. J. (1987, December). AIDS and developmental disabilities. *Prevention Update,* National Coalition on Prevention of Mental Retardation.

Finucane, B. (1988). *Fragile X syndrome: A Handbook for families and educators.* Elwyn, PA: Elwyn.

Garber, H. L., Hodge, J. D., Rynders, J., Dever, R., Velu, R. (1991). The Milwaukee Project: Setting the record straight. *American Journal on Mental Retardation, 95*(5), 493–525.

Greenspan, S., & Granfield, J. M. (1992). Reconsidering the construct of mental retardation: Implications of a model of social competence. *American Journal on Mental Retardation, 96*(4), 442–453.

Guthrie, R. (1984). Explorations in prevention. In B. Blatt & R. Morris (Eds.), *Perspectives in special education: Personal orientations* (pp. 157–172). Glenview, IL: Scott, Foresman.

Hallahan, D. P., & Cruickshank, W. M. (1973). *Psychoeducational foundations of learning disabilities.* Englewood Cliffs, NJ: Prentice-Hall.

Hansen, H. (1978). Decline of Down's Syndrome after abortion reform in New York State. *American Journal of Mental Deficiency, 83,* 185–188.

Hasazi, S. B., & Clark, G. M. (1988). Vocational preparation for high school students labeled mentally retarded: Employment as a graduation goal. *Mental Retardation, 26*(6), 343–349.

Hasazi, S. B., Collins, M., & Cobb, R. B. (1988). Implementing transition programs for productive employment. In B. L. Ludlow, A. P. Turnbull, & R. Luckasson (Eds.), *Transitions to adult life for people with mental retardation—Principles and practices* (pp. 177–195). Baltimore: Paul H. Brookes.

Hasazi, S. B., Gordon, L. R., Roe, C. A., Hull, M., Finck, K., & Salembier, G. (1985). A statewide follow-up on post-high school employment and residential status of students labeled "mentally retarded." *Education and Training of the Mentally Retarded, 20*(6), 222–234.

Heal, L. W., Gonzalez, P., Rusch, F. R., Copher, J. I., DeStefano, L. (1990). A comparison of successful and unsuccessful placements of youths with mental handicaps into competitive employment. *Exceptionality, 1*(3), 181–195.

Heber, R. F. (1959). A manual on terminology and classification in mental retardation. *American Journal of Mental Deficiency Monograph.*

Hetherington, E. M., & Parke, R. D. (1986). *Child psychology: A contemporary viewpoint* (3rd ed.). New York: McGraw-Hill.

Kamphaus, R. W. & Reynolds, C. R. (1987). Clinical and research applications of the K-ABC. Circle Pines, MN: American Guidance.

Kopp, C. B., Baker, B. L., & Brown, K. W. (1992). Social skills and their correlates: Preschoolers with developmental delays. *American Journal on Mental Retardation, 96*(4), 357–366.

Krauss, M. W., Seltzer, M. M., Goodman, S. J. (1992). Social support networks of adults with mental retardation who live at home. *American Journal on Mental Retardation, 96*(4), 432–441.

Lagomarcino, T. R., Hughes, C., & Rusch, F. R. (1989). Utilizing self-management to teach independence on the job. *Education and Training of the Mentally Retarded, 24*(2), 139–148.

Lambert, N., & Windmiller, M. (1981). *AAMD Adaptive Behavior Scale—School Edition.* Washington, DC: American Association of Mental Deficiency.

Levy, J. M., Jessop, D. J., Rimmerman, A., & Levy, P. H. (1992). Attitudes of Fortune 500 corporate executives toward the employability of persons with severe disabilities: A national study. *Mental Retardation, 30*(2), 67–75.

Luftig, R. L. (1988). Assessment of the perceived school loneliness and isolation of mentally retarded and nonretarded students. *American Journal of Mental Retardation, 92*(5), 472–475.

MacMillan, D. L. (1982). *Mental retardation in school and society* (2nd ed.). Boston: Little, Brown.

Martin, J. E., Rusch, F. R., Tines, J. J., Brulle, A. R., and White, D. M. (1985). *Mental Retardation, 23*(3), 142–147.

McCall, R. B. (1983). Environmental effects on intelligence: The forgotten realm of discontinuous non-shared within family factors. *Child Development, 54,* 408–415.

McCall, R. B., Appelbaum, M. I., & Hogarty, P. S. (1973). Developmental changes in mental performance. *Monographs of the Society for Research in Child Development, 38,* (Ser. No. 150).

McGue, M. (1989, August 17). Nature-nurture and intelligence. *Nature,* pp. 507–508.

Mercer, J. R. (1973). *Labelling the mentally retarded.* Berkeley: University of California Press.

Mercer, J. R., & Lewis, J. F. (1977). *Adaptive behavior inventory for children, parent interview manual: System of multicultural pluralistic assessment.* New York: The Psychological Corporation.

Patterson, D. (1987). The causes of Down syndrome. *Scientific American, 257*(2), 52–57, 60.

Patton, J. R., Payne, J. S., & Beirne-Smith, M. (1990). *Mental retardation* (3rd ed.). Columbus OH: Merrill.

Plomin, R. (1989). Environment and genes: Determinants of behavior. *American Psychologist, 44*(2), 105–111.

Ramey, C. T., & Campbell, F. A. (1984). Preventive education for high-risk children: Cognitive consequences of the Carolina Abecedarian Project. *American Journal of Mental Deficiency*, 88, 515–523.

Ramey, C. T., & Campbell, F. A. (1987). The Carolina Abecedarian Project: An educational experiment concerning human malleability. In J. J. Gallagher & C. T. Ramey (Eds.), *The malleability of children* (pp. 127–139). Baltimore, MD: Paul H. Brooke.

Robinson, N. M., & Robinson, H. B. (1976). *The mentally retarded child: A psychological approach* (2nd ed.). New York: McGraw-Hill.

Rowe, D. C., & Plomin, R. (1981). The importance of non-shared (E.) environment influences in behavioral development. *Developmental Psychology*, 17, 517–531.

Rubinstein, A. (1989). Background, epidemiology, and impact of HIV infection in children. *Mental Retardation*, 27(4), 209–211.

Rusch, F. R., & Hughes, C. (1988). Supported employment: Promoting employee independence. *Mental Retardation*, 26(6), 351–355.

Rusch, F. R., Martin, J. E., & White, D. M. (1985). Competitive employment: Teaching mentally retarded employees to maintain their work behavior. *Education and Training of the Mentally Retarded*, 20(3), 182–189.

Sailor, W., Halvorsen, A., Anderson, J., Goetz, L., Gee, K., Doering, K., & Hunt, P. (1986). Community intensive instruction. In R. H. Horner, L. H. Meyer, & H. D. Fredericks (Eds.), *Education of learners with severe handicaps: Exemplary service strategies* (pp. 251–288). Baltimore: Paul H. Brookes.

Salend, S. J., & Giek, K. A. (1988). Independent living arrangements for individuals with mental retardation: The landlords' perspective. *Mental Retardation*, 26(2), 89–92.

Salzberg, C. L., Lignugaris/Kraft, B., & McCuller, G. L. (1988). Reasons for job loss: A review of employment termination studies of mentally retarded workers. *Research in Developmental Disabilities*, 9, 153–170.

Schalock, R. L., & Harper, R. S. (1978). Replacement from community-based mental retardation programs: How well do clients do? *American Journal of Mental Deficiency*, 83, 240–247.

Schalock, R. L., Harper, R. S., & Carver, G. (1981). Independent living placement: Five years later. *American Journal of Mental Deficiency*, 86, 170–177.

Schalock, R. L., McGaughey, M. J., & Kiernan, W. E. (1989). Placement into nonsheltered employment: Findings from national employment surveys. *American Journal of Mental Retardation*, 94(1), 80–87.

Schultz, E. E., Jr. (1983). Depth of processing by mentally retarded and MA-matched nonretarded individuals. *American Journal of Mental Deficiency*, 88, 307–313.

Schultz, F. R. (1984). Fetal alcohol syndrome. In J. A. Blackman (Ed.), *Mental aspects of developmental disabilities in children birth to three* (rev. 1st ed., pp. 109–110). Rockville, MD: Aspen Systems Corp.

Skeels, H. M. (1966). Adult status of children with contrasting early life experiences. *Monographs of the Society for Research in Child Development*, 31 (Ser. No. 105). University of Chicago Press.

Skeels, H. M., & Dye, H. B. (1939). A study of the effects of differential stimulation on mentally retarded children. *Convention Proceedings*, American Association on Mental Deficiency, 44, 114–136.

Snell, M. E. (1988). Curriculum and methodology for individuals with severe disabilities. *Education and Training in Mental Retardation*, 23(4), 302–314.

Sparrow, S. S., Balla, D. A., & Cicchetti, D. V. (1984). *Vineland Adaptive Behavior Scales*. Circle Pines, MN: American Guidance Service.

Stodden, R. A., & Browder, P. M. (1986). Community-based competitive employment preparation of developmentally disabled persons: A program description and evaluation. *Education and Training of the Mentally Retarded*, 21, 43–53.

Streissguth, A. P., Barr, H. M., & Martin, D. C. (1983). Maternal alcohol use and neonatal habituation assessed with the Brazelton Scale. *Child Development*, 54(5), 1109–1118.

U.S. Department of Education (1989). *Eleventh Annual Report to Congress on The Implementation of the Education of the Handicapped Act*. Washington, DC: U.S. Government Printing Office.

Walker, H. M., McConnell, S., Holmes, D., Todis, B., Walker, J., & Golden, N. (1983). *The Accepts Program*. Austin, TX: Pro-Ed.

Warren, S. F., & Abbeduto, L. (1992). The relation of communication and language development to mental retardation. *American Journal of Mental Retardation*, 97(2), 125–130.

Wasik, B. H., Ramey, C. T., Bryant, D. M., & Sparling, J. J. (1990). A longitudinal study of two early intervention strategies: Project CARE. *Child Development*, 61(6), 1682–1696.

Wehman, P., Moon, M. S., Everson, J. M., Wood, W., & Barcus, J. M. (1988). *Transition from school to work: New challenges for youth with severe disabilities*. Baltimore: Paul H. Brookes.

Wheeler, J. J., Bates, P., Marshall, K. J., & Miller, S. R. (1988). Teaching appropriate social behaviors to a young man with moderate mental retardation in a supported competitive employment setting. *Education and Training in Mental Retardation*, 23(2), 105–116.

Whitman, T. L. (1990). Self-regulation and mental retardation. *American Journal on Mental Retardation*. 94(4), 347–362.

Wolery, M., Bailey, D. B., & Sugai, G. M. (1988). *Effective teaching: Principles and procedures of applied behavior analysis with exceptional students*. Boston: Allyn & Bacon.

Zeaman, D., & House, B. J. (1963). The role of attention in retardate discrimination learning. In N. R. Ellis (Ed.), *Handbook of mental deficiency*. New York: McGraw-Hill.

Zetlin, A. G., & Murtaugh, M. (1988). Friendship patterns of mildly handicapped and nonhandicapped high school students. *American Journal of Mental Retardation, 92*(5), 447–454.

CHAPTER 5

Baker, L. (1982). An evaluation of the role of metacognitive deficits in learning disabilities. *Topics in Learning and Learning Disabilities, 2*(1), 27–35.

Baumeister, A. A., Kupstas, F., & Klindworth, L. M. (1990). New morbidity: Implications for prevention of children's disabilities. *Exceptionality, 1*(1), 1–16.

Borkowski, J. G. (1992). Metacognitive theory: A framework for teaching literacy, writing, and math skills. *Journal of Learning Disabilities, 25*(4), 253–257.

Bos, C. S., & Filip, D. (1982). Comprehension monitoring skills in learning disabled and average students. *Topics in Learning and Learning Disabilities, 2*(1), 79–85.

Brown, A. L., & Campione, J. C. (1984). Three faces of transfer: Implications for early competence, individual differences, and instruction. In M. E. Lamb, A. L. Brown, & B. Rogoff (Eds.), *Advances in developmental psychology*, (Vol. 3, pp. 143–192). Hillsdale, NJ: Lawrence Erlbaum.

Bryan, T. H., & Bryan, J. H. (1986). *Understanding learning disabilities*. Palo Alto, CA: Mayfield Publishing Company.

Bryan, T. H., Donahue, M., Pearl, R., and Sturm, C. (1981). Learning disabled children's conversational skills—The "TV Talk Show." *Learning Disability Quarterly, 4*(3), 250–260.

Case, L. P., Harris, K. R., & Graham, S. (1992). Improving the mathematical problem-solving skills of students with learning disabilities. *The Journal of Special Education, 26*(1), 1–19.

Cawley, J. F., & Parmar, R. S. (1992). Arithmetic programming for students with disabilities: An alternative. *Remedial and Special Education, 13*(3), 6–18.

Ch.A.D.D. (1992). *Ch.A.D.D. educators manual: An in-depth look at attention deficit disorders from an educational perspective*. Plantation, FL: Ch.A.D.D.

Cravioto, J., & DeLicardie, E. R. (1975). Environmental and nutritional deprivation in children with learning disabilities. In W. M. Cruickshank & D. P. Hallahan (Eds.), *Perceptual and learning disabilities in children. Vol. 2: Research and Theory*. Syracuse, NY: Syracuse University Press.

Cruickshank, W. M., Bentzen, F. A., Ratzeburg, F. H., & Tannhauser, M. T. (1961). *A teaching method for brain-injured and hyperactive children*. Syracuse, NY: Syracuse University Press.

Deci, E. L., & Chandler, C. L. (1986). The importance of motivation for the future of the LD field. *Journal of Learning Disabilities, 19*(10), 587–594.

Deno, S. L. (1985). Curriculum-based measurement: The emerging alternative. *Exceptional Children, 52*(3), 219–232.

Deshler, D. D., & Schumaker, J. B. (1986). Learning strategies: An instructional alternative for low-achieving adolescents. *Exceptional Children, 52*(6), 583–590.

DiGangi, S. A., Maag, J. W., & Rutherford, R. B. (1991). Self-graphing of on-task behavior: Enhancing the reactive effects of self-monitoring on on-task behavior and academic performance. *Learning Disability Quarterly, 14*(3), 221–230.

Ellis, E. S., Deshler, D. D., & Schumaker, J. B. (1989). Teaching adolescents with learning disabilities to generate and use task-specific strategies. *Journal of Learning Disabilities, 22*(2), 108–119, 130.

Englemann, S. E. (1977). Sequencing cognitive and academic tasks. In R. D. Kneedler & S. G. Tarver (Eds.), *Changing perspectives in special education*. Columbus, OH: Chas. E. Merrill.

Engelmann, S., Carnine, L., Johnson, G., & Meyers, L. (1988). *Corrective reading: Decoding*. Chicago: Science Research Associates.

Engelmann, S., Carnine, L., Johnson, G., & Meyers, L. (1989). *Corrective reading: Comprehension*. Chicago: Science Research Associates.

Englert, C. S. (1992). Writing instruction from a sociocultural perspective: The holistic, dialogic, and social enterprise of writing. *Journal of Learning Disabilities, 25*(3), 153–172.

Englert, C. S., Raphael, T. E., Anderson, L. M., Anthony, H. M., Fear, K. L., & Gregg, S. L. (1988). A case for writing intervention: Strategies for writing informational text. *Learning Disabilities Focus, 3*(2), 98–113.

Englert, C. S., Raphael, T. E., Anderson, L. M., Anthony, H. M., & Stevens, D. D. (1991). Making strategies and self-talk visible: Writing instruction in regular and special education classrooms. *American Educational Research Journal, 28*(2), 337–372.

Fletcher, J. M. (1992). The validity of distinguishing children with language and learning disabilities according to discrepancies with IQ: Introduction to the series. *Journal of Learning Disabilities, 25*(9), 546–548.

Federal Register (1977, December 29). Procedures for evaluating specific learning disabilities. Washington, DC: Department of Health, Education and Welfare.

Fernald, G. M. (1943). *Remedial techniques in basic school subjects*. New York: McGraw-Hill.

Finucci, J., and Childs, B. (1983). Dyslexia: Family studies. In C. Ludlow & G. Cooper (Eds.), *Genetic aspects of speech and language disorders*. New York: Academic Press.

Foorman, B. R., & Liberman, D. (1989). Visual and phonological processing of words: A comparison of good and poor readers. *Journal of Learning Disabilities, 22*(6), 349–355.

Frostig, M., & Horne, D. (1964). *The Frostig program for the development of visual perception. Teacher's guide*. Chicago: Follett.

Fuchs, L. S. (1986). Monitoring progress among mildly handicapped pupils: Review of current practice and research. *Remedial and Special Education, 7*(5), 5–12.

Fuchs, L., Deno, S. L., & Mirkin, P. K. (1984). The effects of frequent curriculum-based measurement and evaluation of pedagogy, student achievement and student awareness of learning. *American Educational Research Journal, 24*(2), 449–460.

Fuchs, L. S., & Fuchs, D. (1986). Effects of systematic formative evaluation: A meta-analysis. *Exceptional Children, 53*(3), 199–208.

Fuchs, L. S., Fuchs, D., & Strecker, P. M. (1989). Effects of curriculum-based measurement on teachers' instructional planning. *Journal of Learning Disabilities, 22*(1), 51–59.

Gajar, A. H. (1989). A computer analysis of written language variables and a comparison of compositions written by university students with and without learning disabilities. *Journal of Learning Disabilities, 22*(2), 125–130.

Gerber, P. J., Ginsberg, R., & Reiff, H. B. (1992). Identifying alterable patterns in employment success for highly successful adults with learning disabilities. *Journal of Learning Disabilities, 25*(8), 475–487.

Gerber, P. J., & Reiff, H. B. (1991). *Speaking for themselves: Ethnographic interviews with adults with learning disabilities.* Ann Arbor, MI: University of Michigan Press.

Germann, G., & Tindal, G. (1985). An application of curriculum-based assessment: The use of direct and repeated measurement. *Exceptional Children, 52*(3), 244–265.

Hall, R. V., Lund, D., & Jackson, D. (1968). Effects of teacher attention on study behavior. *Journal of Applied Behavior Analysis, 1*(1), 1–12.

Hallahan, D. P. (1975). Comparative research studies on the psychological characteristics of learning disabled children. In W. M. Cruickshank & D. P. Hallahan (Eds.), *Perceptual and learning disabilities in children. Vol. 1: Psychoeducational practices.* Syracuse, NY: Syracuse University Press.

Hallahan, D. P. (1992). Some thoughts on why the prevalence of learning disabilities has increased. *Journal of Learning Disabilities, 25*(8), 523–528.

Hallahan, D. P., & Bryan, T. H. (1981). Learning disabilities. In J. M. Kauffman & D. P. Hallahan (Eds.), *Handbook of special education.* Englewood Cliffs, NJ: Prentice Hall.

Hallahan, D. P., & Cruickshank, W. M. (1973). *Psychoeducational foundations of learning disabilities.* Englewood Cliffs, NJ: Prentice Hall.

Hallahan, D. P., Gajar, A. H., Cohen, S. B., & Tarver, S. G. (1978). Selective attention and locus of control in learning disabled and normal children. *Journal of Learning Disabilities, 4*, 47–52.

Hallahan, D. P., & Kauffman, J. M. (1977). Labels, categories, behaviors: ED, LD, and EMR reconsidered. *The Journal of Special Education, 11*, 139–149.

Hallahan, D. P., Kauffman, J. M., & Ball, D. W. (1973). Selective attention and cognitive tempo of low achieving and high achieving sixth grade males. *Perceptual and Motor Skills, 36*, 579–583.

Hallahan, D. P., Kauffman, J. M., & Lloyd, J. W. (1985). *Introduction to learning disabilities.* Englewood Cliffs, NJ: Prentice Hall.

Hallahan, D. P., Kneedler, R. D., & Lloyd, J. W. (1983). Cognitive behavior modification techniques for learning disabled children: Self-instruction and self-monitoring. In J. D. McKinney & L. Feagans (Eds.), *Current topics in learning disabilities,* Vol 1. Norwood, NJ: Ablex.

Hallahan, D. P., Lloyd, J., Kosiewicz, M. M., Kauffman, J. M., & Graves, A. W. (1979). Self-monitoring of attention as a treatment for a learning disabled boy's off-task behavior. *Learning Disability Quarterly, 2*, 24–32.

Hallahan, D. P., Lloyd, J. W., & Stoller, L. (1982). *Improving attention with self-monitoring: A manual for teachers.* Charlottesville: University of Virginia Learning Disabilities Research Institute.

Hallahan, D. P., & Reeve, R. E. (1980). Selective attention and distractibility. In B. K. Keogh (Ed.), *Advances in special education. Vol. 1: Basic constructs and theoretical orientations.* Greenwich, CO: J.A.I. Press.

Hallgren, B. (1950). Specific dylexia (congenital word blindness: A clinical and genetic study). *Acta Psychiatrica er Neurologica, 65*, 1–279.

Hammill, D. D. (1990). On defining learning disabilities: An emerging consensus. *Journal of Learning Disabilities.*

Hammill, D. D., & Larsen, S. (1974). The effectiveness of psycholinguistic training. *Exceptional Children, 41*, 5–15.

Hammill, D. D., Leigh, J. E., McNutt, G., & Larsen, S. C. (1981). A new definition of learning disabilities. *Learning Disability Quarterly, 4*, 336–342.

Henker, B., & Whalen, C. K. (1989). Hyperactivity and attention deficits. *American Psychologist, 44*(2), 216–223.

Hynd, G. W., Marshall, R., & Gonzalez, J. (1991). Learning disabilities and presumed central nervous system dysfunction. *Learning Disability Quarterly, 14*(4), 283–296.

Kauffman, J. M., & Hallahan, D. P. (1979). Learning disability and hyperactivity (with comments on minimal brain dysfunction). In B. B. Lahey & A. E. Kazdin (Eds.), *Advances in clinical child psychology,* Vol. 2. New York: Plenum.

Kavale, K. A. (1988). The long-term consequences of learning disabilities. In M. C. Wang, M. C. Reynolds, & H. J. Walberg (Eds.), *Handbook of special education: Research and practice. Vol. 2: Mildly handicapped conditions.* New York: Pergamon Press.

Kavale, K. A., & Reese, J. H. (1992). The character of learning disabilities: An Iowa profile. *Learning Disabilities Quarterly, 15*(2), 74–94.

Keilitz, I., & Dunivant, N. (1986). The relationship between learning disability and juvenile delinquency: Current state of knowledge. *Remedial and Special Education, 7*(3), 18–26.

Keogh, B. K., & Glover, A. T. (1980, November). Research needs in the study of early identification of children with learning disabilities. *Thalamus* (Newsletter of the International Academy for Research in Learning Disabilities).

Kephart, N. C. (1971, 1975). *The slow learner in the classroom* (2nd ed.) Columbus, OH: Chas. E. Merrill.

Kirk, S. A., & Kirk, W. D. (1971). *Psycholinguistic learning disabilities: Diagnosis and remediation.* Urbana: University of Illinois Press.

Kneedler, R. D., & Hallahan, D. P. (1984). Self-monitoring as an attentional strategy for academic tasks with learning disabled children. In B. Gholson & T. Rosenthal (Eds.), *Applications of cognitive development theory.* New York: Academic Press.

Kosiewicz, M. M., Hallahan, D. P., Lloyd, J. W., & Graves, A. W. (1982). Effects of self-instruction and self-correction procedures on handwriting performance. *Learning Disability Quarterly, 5,* 71–78.

Leete-Guy, L., & Schor, J. B. (1992). *The great American time squeeze: Trends in work and leisure: 1969–1989.* (Briefing paper for the Economic Policy Institute, Washington, DC).

Liscio, M. (1986). *A guide to colleges for learning-disabled students.* Orlando, FL: Academic Press.

Lloyd, J. W. (1988). Direct academic interventions in learning disabilities. In M. C. Wang, M. C. Reynolds, & H. J. Walberg (Eds.), *Handbook of special education: Research and practice. Vol. 2: Mildly handicapped conditions.* New York: Pergamon Press.

Lloyd, J., Hallahan, D. P., Kosiewicz, M. M., & Kneedler, R. D. (1980). *Self-assessment versus self-recording: Two comparisons of reactive effects on attention to task and academic productivity.* Charlottesville: University of Virginia Learning Disabilities Research Institute, Technical Report No. 29.

Lovejoy's four-year college guide for learning disabled students. (1985). New York: Simon & Schuster.

Lovitt, T. C. (1977). *In spite of my resistance . . . I've learned from children.* Columbus, OH: Chas. E. Merrill.

Mann, V. A., Cowin, E., & Schoenheimer, J. (1989). Phonological processing, language comprehension, and reading ability. *Journal of Learning Disabilities, 22*(2), 76–89.

Marston, D., & Magnusson, D. (1985). Implementing curriculum-based measurement in special and regular education settings. *Exceptional Children, 52*(3), 266–276.

Mastropieri, M. A., & Scruggs, T. E. (1988). Increasing content area learning of learning disabled students: Research implementation. *Learning Disabilities Research, 4*(1), 17–25.

Mathinos, D. A. (1988). Communicative competence of children with learning disabilities. *Journal of Learning Disabilities, 21*(7), 437–443.

McGuire, J. M., & Shaw, S. F. (1987). A decision-making process for the college-bound student: Matching learner, institution, and support program. *Learning Disability Quarterly, 10,* 106–111.

McKinney, J. D. (1987a). Research on conceptually and empirically derived subtypes of specific learning disabilities. In M. C. Wang, M. C. Reynolds, & H. J. Walberg (Eds.), *Handbook of special education: Research and practice.* New York: Pergamon Press.

McKinney, J. D. (1987b). Research on the identification of LD children: Perspectives on changes in educational policy. In S. Vaughn & C. Bos, *Future directions and issues in research for the learning disabled.* San Diego, CA: College-Hill Press.

McKinney, J. D. (1989). Longitudinal research on the behavioral characteristics of children with learning disabilities. *Journal of Learning Disabilities, 22*(3), 141–150, 165.

McKinney, J. D., & Feagans, L. (1984). Academic and behavioral characteristics: Longitudinal studies of learning disabled children and average achievers. *Learning Disability Quarterly, 7,* 251–265.

McKinney, J. D., Short, E. J., & Feagans, L. (1985). Academic consequences of perceptual-linguistic subtypes of learning disabled children. *Learning Disabilities Research, 1*(1), 6–17.

McKinney, J. D., & Speece, D. L. (1986). Academic consequences and longitudinal stability of behavioral subtypes of learning disabled children. *Journal of Educational Psychology, 78*(5), 365–272.

Meichenbaum, D. H. (1975, June). Cognitive factors as determinants of learning disabilities: A cognitive-functional approach. Paper presented at the NATO Conference on The Neuropsychology of Learning Disorders: Theoretical Approaches, Korsor, Denmark.

Meichenbaum, D. H., & Goodman, J. (1971). Training impulsive children to talk to themselves: A means of developing self-control. *Journal of Abnormal Psychology, 77,* 115–126.

Mercer, C. D., Algozzine, B., & Trifiletti, J. (1979). Early identification—An analysis of the research. *Learning Disability Quarterly, 2,* 12–24.

Mercer, C. D., & Miller, S. P. (1992). Teaching students with learning problems in math to acquire, understand, and apply basic math facts. *Remedial and Special Education, 13*(3), 19–35, 61.

Minskoff, E. H., Wiseman, D. E., & Minskoff, J. G. (1974). *The MWM Program for Developing Language Abilities.* Ridgefield, NJ: Educational Performance Associates.

Montague, M., & Bos, C. S. (1990). Cognitive and metacognitive characteristics of eighth grade students' mathematical problem solving. *Learning and Individual Differences, 2*(3), 371–388.

Montague, M., & Graves, A. (1992). In M. Pressley, K. Harris, & J. T. Guthrie (Eds.), *Promoting academic compe-*

tence and literacy in schools (pp. 261–276). New York: Academic Press.

Montague, M, Graves, A., & Leavell, A. (1991). Planning, procedural facilitation, and narratvie composition of junior high students with learning disabilities. *Learning Disabilities Research & Practice*, 6(4), 219–224.

Murphy, D. M. (1986). The prevalence of handicapping conditions among juvenile delinquents. *Remedial and Special Education*, 7(3), 7–17.

Murphy, S. T. (1992). *On being L.D.: Perspectives and strategies of young adults.* New York: Teachers College Press.

National Joint Committee on Learning Disabilities (1989, September 18). *Letter from NJCLD to member organizations.* Topic: Modifications to the NJCLD definition of learning disabilities.

Newcomer, P. L., & Barenbaum, E. M. (1991). The written composing ability of children with learning disabilities: A review of the literature from 1980 to 1990. *Journal of Learning Disabilities*, 24(10), 578–593.

Olson, R., Wise, B., Conners, F., Rack, J., & Fulker, D. (1989). Specific deficits in component reading and language skills: Genetic and environmental influences. *Journal of Learning Disabilities*, 22(6), 339–348.

Owen, F. W., Adams, P. A., Forrest, T., Stolz, L. M., & Fisher, S. (1971). Learning disorders in children: Sibling studies. *Monographs of the Society for Research in Child Development*, 36 (4, Ser. No. 144).

Palincsar, A. S. (1986). Metacognitive strategy instruction. *Exceptional Children*, 53(2), 118–124.

Pearl, R. (1992). Psychosocial characteristics of learning disabled students. In N. N. Singh & I. L. Beale (Eds.), *Current perspectives in learning disabilities: Nature, theory, and treatment* (pp. 96–125). New York: Springer-Verlag.

Pearl, R., Bryan, T., & Donahue, M. (1980). Learning disabled children's attributions for success and failure. *Learning Disability Quarterly*, 3, 3–9.

Pelham, W. E., & Murphy, H. A. (1986). Attention deficit and conduct disorders. In M. Hersen (Ed.), *Pharmacological and behavioral treatment: An integrative approach* (pp. 108–148). New York: John Wiley.

Polloway, E. A., Foley, R. M., & Epstein, M. H. (1992). A comparison of the homework problems of students with learning disabilities and nonhandicapped students. *Learning Disabilities Research & Practice*, 7(4), 203–209.

Prater, M. A., Joy, R., Chilman, B., Temple, J., & Miller, S. R. (1991). Self-monitoring of on-task behavior by adolescents with learning disabilities. *Learning Disability Quarterly*, 14(3), 164–177.

Pressley, M., Symons, S., Snyder, B. L., & Cariglia-Bull, T. (1989). Strategy instruction comes of age. *Learning Disability Quarterly*, 12(1), 16–30.

Reiff, H. B., & Gerber, P. J. (1992). Adults with learning disabilities. In N. N. Singh & D. L. Beale (Eds.), *Current perspectives in learning disabilities: Nature, theory, and treatment* (pp. 170–198). New York: Springer-Verlag.

Rivera, D., & Smith, D. D. (1988). Using a demonstration strategy to teach midschool students with learning disabilities how to compute long division. *Journal of Learning Disabilities*, 21(2), 77–81.

Robinson, F. P. (1946). *Effective study.* New York: Harper & Row.

Schumaker, J. B., Deshler, D. D., Alley, G. R., Warner, M. M., & Denton, P. H. (1982). Multipass: A learning strategy for improving reading comprehension. *Learning Disability Quarterly*, 5(3), 295–304.

Schunk, D. H. (1989). Self-efficacy and cognitive achievement: Implications for students with learning problems. *Journal of Learning Disabilities*, 22(1), 14–22.

Scruggs, T. E., & Mastropieri, M. A. (1992). Classroom applications of mnemonic instruction: Acquisition, maintenance, and generalization. *Exceptional Children*, 58(3), 219–229.

Seligman, M. E. (1992). *Helplessness: On depression, development and death.* San Francisco: W. H. Freeman.

Shaywitz, S. E., & Shaw, R. (1988). The admissions process: An approach to selecting learning disabled students at the most selective colleges. *Learning Disabilities Focus*, 3(2), 81–86.

Shaywitz, S. E., & Shaywitz, B. A. (1987). Attention deficit disorder: Current perspectives. Paper presented at National Conference on Learning Disabilities, Bethesda, MD: National Institutes of Child Health and Human Development (NIH).

Short, E. J., & Weissberg-Benchell, J. (1989). The triple alliance for learning: Cognition, metacognition, and motivation. In C. B. McCormick, G. E. Miller, & M. Pressley (Eds.), *Cognitive strategy research: From basic research to educational applications* (pp. 33–63). New York: Springer-Verlag.

Siegel, L. S. (1989). IQ is irrelevant to the definition of learning disabilities. *Journal of Learning Disabilities*, 22(8), 468–478, 486.

Siperstein, G. N. (1988). Students with learning disabilities in college: The need for a programmatic approach to critical transitions. *Journal of Learning Disabilities*, 21(7), 431–436.

Speece, D. L., McKinney, J. D., & Appelbaum, M. I. (1985). Classification and validation of behavioral subtypes of learning-disabled children. *Journal of Educational Psychology*, 77(1), 67–77.

Spekman, N. J., Goldberg, R. J., Herman, K. L. (1992). Learning disabled children grow up: A search for factors related to success in the young adult years. *Learning Disabilities Research and Practice*, 7(3), 161–170.

Sroufe, L. A. (1975). Drug treatment of children with behavior problems. In F. D. Horowitz (Ed.), *Review of child development research* (Vol. 4, pp. 347–407). Chicago: University of Chicago Press.

Stanovich, K. E. (1991a). Conceptual and empirical problems with discrepancy definitions of reading disability. *Learning Disability Quarterly. 14*(4), 269–280.

Stanovich, K. E. (1991b). Reading disability: Assessment issues. In H. L. Swanson (Ed.), *Handbook of assessment of learning disabilities: Theory, research, and practice* (pp. 147–175). Austin, TX: Pro-Ed.

Stevenson, J. (1992). Genetics. In N. N. Singh & D. L. Beale (Eds.), *Current perspectives in learning disabilities: Nature, theory, and treatment* (pp. 327–351). New York: Springer-Verlag.

Strauss, A. A., & Kephart, N. C. (1955). *Psychopathology and education of the brain-injured child. Vol. II. Progress in theory and clinic.* New York: Grune & Stratton.

Strauss, A. A., & Lehtinen, L. E. (1947). *Psychopathology and education of the brain-injured child.* New York: Grune & Stratton.

Swanson, H. L. (Ed.). (1987). *Memory and learning disabilities: Advances in learning and behavioral disabilities.* Greenwich, CT: J.A.I. Press.

Swanson, H. L. (1989). Strategy instruction: Overview of principles and procedures for effective use. *Learning Disability Quarterly, 12*(1), 3–14.

Symons, S., Snyder, B. L., Cariglia-Bull, T., & Pressley, M. (1989). Why be optimistic about cognitive strategy instruction? In C. B. McCormick, G. E. Miller, & M. Pressley (Eds.), *Cognitive strategy research: From basic research to educational applications.* New York: Springer-Verlag.

Task Force on DSM-IV. (1991). *DSM-IV options book: Work in progress.* Washington, DC: American Psychiatric Association.

Thomas, C. C., Englert, C. S., & Gregg, S. (1987). An analysis of errors and strategies in the expository writing of learning-disabled students. *Remedial and Special Education, 8*(1), 21–30, 46.

Torgesen, J. K. (1977). The role of nonspecific factors in the task performance of learning disabled children: A theoretical assessment. *Journal of Learning Disabilities, 10,* 27–34.

Torgesen, J. K. (1988). Studies of children with learning disabilities who perform poorly on memory span tasks. *Journal of Learning Disabilities, 21*(10), 605–612.

Torgesen, J. K., & Kail, R. V. (1980). Memory processes in exceptional children. In B. K. Keogh (Ed.), *Advances in special education. Vol. 1: Basic constructs and theoretical orientations.* Greenwich, CT: J.A.I. Press.

U. S. Department of Education. (1990, January 9). Reading and writing proficiency remains low. *Daily Education News,* 1–7.

Vellutino, F. R. (1987). Dyslexia. *Scientific American. 256*(3), 34–41.

Vogel, S. (1987). Issues and concerns in LD college programming. In D. Johnson & J. Blalock (Eds.), *Adults with learning disabilities* (pp. 239–275). New York: Grune & Stratton.

Werner, H., & Strauss, A. A. (1941). Pathology of figure-background relation in the child. *Journal of Abnormal and Social Psychology, 36,* 236–248.

White, O., & Haring, N. (1980). *Exceptional teaching.* Columbus, OH: Chas. E. Merrill.

Willis, W. G., Hooper, S. R., & Stone, B. H. (1992). Neurological theories of learning disabilities. In N. N. Singh & D. L. Beale (Eds.), *Current perspectives in learning disabilities: Nature, theory, and treatment* (pp. 201–245). New York: Springer-Verlag.

Zigmond, N., & Sansone, J. (1986). Designing a program for the learning disabled adolescent. *Remedial and Special Education, 7*(5), 13–17.

Chapter 6

Achenbach, T. M. (1985). *Assessment and taxonomy of child and adolescent psychopathology.* Newbury Park, CA: Sage.

Achenbach, T. M., Howell, C. T., Quay, H. C., & Conners, C. K. (1991). National survey of problems and competencies among four- to sixteen-year-olds: Parents' reports for normative and clinical samples. *Monographs of the Society for Research in Child Development, 56*(3), serial no. 225.

Bandura, A. (1973). *Aggression: A social learning analysis.* Englewood Cliffs, NJ: Prentice-Hall.

Baumeister, A. A., Kupstas, F., & Klindworth, L. M. (1990). New morbidity: Implications for prevention of children's disabilities. *Exceptionality, 1,* 1–16.

Becker, W. C. (1964). Consequences of different kinds of parental discipline. In M. L. Hoffman & L. W. Hoffman (Eds.), *Review of child development research* (Vol. 1). New York: Russell Sage Foundation.

Bettelheim, B. (1950). *Love is not enough.* New York: Macmillan.

Bettelheim, B. (1967). *The empty fortress.* New York: Free Press.

Biklen, D., & Schubert, A. (1991). New words: The communication of students with autism. *Remedial and Special Education, 12*(6), 46–57.

Bower, B. (1989). Remodeling the autistic child. *Science News, 136,* 312–313.

Bower, E. M. (1981). *Early identification of emotionally handicapped children in school* (3rd ed.). Springfield, IL: Charles C. Thomas.

Bower, E. M. (1982). Defining emotional disturbance: Public policy and research. *Psychology in the Schools, 19,* 55–60.

Brandenburg, N. A., Friedman, R. M., & Silver, S. E. (1990). The epidemiology of childhood psychiatric disorders: Prevalence findings from recent studies. *Journal of the*

American Academy of Child and Adolescent Psychiatry, 29, 76–83.

Caplan, N., Choy, M. H., & Whitmore, J. K. (1992). Indochinese refugee families and academic achievement. *Scientific American, 266*(2), 36–42.

Cline, D. H. (1990). A legal analysis of policy initiatives to exclude handicapped/disruptive students from special education. *Behavioral Disorders, 15,* 159–173.

Delpit, L. D. (1986). Skills and other dilemmas of a progressive black educator. *Harvard Educational Review, 56,* 379–385.

Drabman, R. S., & Patterson, J. N. (1981). Disruptive behavior and the social standing of exceptional children. *Exceptional Education Quarterly, 1*(4), 45–55.

Durand, V. M., & Carr, E. G. (1988). Autism. In V. B. Van Hasselt, P. S. Strain, & M. Hersen (Eds.), *Handbook of developmental and physical disabilities.* New York: Pergamon.

Edelbrock, C. S., & Achenbach, T. M. (1984). The teacher version of the Child Behavior Profile: Boys aged 6–11. *Journal of Consulting and Clinical Psychology, 52,* 207–217.

Edgar, E. B. (1987). Secondary programs in special education: Are many of them justifiable? *Exceptional Children, 53,* 555–561.

Forness, S. R. (1988). School characteristics of children and adolescents with depression. In R. B. Rutherford, C. M. Nelson, & S. R. Forness (Eds.), *Bases of severe behavioral disorders of children and youth.* Boston: Little, Brown.

Forness, S. R. (1992). Legalism versus professionalism in diagnosing SED in the public schools. *School Psychology Review, 21,* 29–34.

Forness, S. R., & Knitzer, J. (1992). A new proposed definition and terminology to replace "serious emotional disturbance" in Individuals with Disabilities Act. *School Psychology Review, 21,* 12–20.

Frank, A. R., Sitlington, P. L., & Carson, R. (1991). Transition of adolescents with behavioral disorders—Is it successful? *Behavioral Disorders, 16,* 180–191.

Fuchs, D., Fuchs, L. S., Fernstrom, P., & Hohn, M. (1991). Toward a responsible reintegration of behaviorally disordered students. *Behavioral Disorders, 16,* 133–147.

Garmezy, N. (1987). Stress, competence, and development: Continuities in the study of schizophrenic adults, children vulnerable to psychopathology, and the search for stress-resistant children. *American Journal of Orthopsychiatry, 57,* 159–174.

Goldstein, A. P. (1983). United States: Causes, controls, and alternatives to aggression. In A. P. Goldstein & M. H. Segall (Eds.), *Aggression in global perspective.* New York: Pergamon.

Gottesman, I. I. (1991). *Schizophrenia genesis: The origins of madness.* New York: W. H. Freeman.

Guetzloe, E. C. (1991). *Depression and suicide: Special education students at risk.* Reston, VA: Council for Exceptional Children.

Harris, K. R., Wong, B. Y. I., & Keogh, B. K. (Eds.). (1985). Cognitive-behavior modification with children: A critical review of the state-of-the-art. *Journal of Abnormal Child Psychology, 13,* special issue.

Hawton, K. (1986). *Suicide and attempted suicide among children and adolescents.* Newbury Park, CA: Sage.

Henggeler, S. W. (1989). *Delinquency in adolescence.* Newbury Park, CA: Sage.

Hobbs, N. (1975). *The futures of children.* San Francisco: Jossey-Bass.

Huntze, S. (1985). A position paper of the Council for Children with Behavioral Disorders. *Behavioral Disorders, 10,* 167–174.

Institute of Medicine. (1989). *Research on children and adolescents with mental, behavioral, and developmental disorders.* Washington, DC: National Academy Press.

Jordan, D., Goldberg, P., & Goldberg, M. (1991). *A guidebook for parents of children with emotional or behavioral disorders.* Minneapolis: Pacer Center, Inc.

Kazdin, A. E. (1987). *Conduct disorders in childhood and adolescence.* Newbury Park, CA: Sage.

Kazdin, A. E. (1989). Developmental psychopathology: Current research, issues, and directions. *American Psychologist, 44,* 180–187.

Kazdin, A. E. (1992). Overt and covert antisocial behavior: Child and family characteristics among psychiatric inpatient children. *Journal of Child and Family Studies, 1,* 3–20.

Kauffman, J. M. (1986). Educating children with behavior disorders. In R. J. Morris & B. Blatt (Eds.), *Special education: Research and trends* (pp. 249–271). New York: Pergamon.

Kauffman, J. M. (1993). *Characteristics of emotional and behavioral disorders of children and youth* (5th ed.). Columbus, OH: Merrill/Macmillan.

Kauffman, J. M., Mostert, M. P., Nuttycombe, D. G., Trent, S. C., & Hallahan, D. P. (1993). *Managing classroom behavior: A reflective case-based approach.* Boston: Allyn & Bacon.

Kern-Dunlap, L., Dunlap, G., Clarke, S., Childs, K. E., White, R. L., & Stewart, M. P. (1992). Effects of a videotape feedback package on the peer interactions of children with serious behavioral and emotional challenges. *Journal of Applied Behavior Analysis, 25,* 355–364.

Kerr, M. M., & Nelson, C. M. (1989). *Strategies for managing behavior problems in the classroom* (2nd ed.). Columbus, OH: Merrill/Macmillan.

Kerr, M. M., Nelson, C. M., & Lambert, D. L. (1987). *Helping adolescents with learning and behavior problems.* Columbus, OH: Merrill/Macmillan.

Klein, R. G., & Last, C. G. (1989). *Anxiety disorders in children.* Newbury Park, CA: Sage.

Knitzer, J. (1982). *Unclaimed children: The failure of public responsibility to children and adolescents in need of mental health services.* Washington, DC: Children's Defense Fund.

Knitzer, J., Steinberg, Z., & Fleisch, F. (1990). *At the schoolhouse door: An examination of programs and policies for children with behavioral and emotional problems.* New York: Bank Street College of Education.

Koegel, R. L., Rincover, A., & Egel, A. I. (1982). *Educating and understanding autistic children.* San Diego: College Hill Press.

Kovacs, M. (1989). Affective disorders in children and adolescents. *American Psychologist, 44,* 209–215.

Leone, P. E. (Ed.). (1990). *Understanding troubled and troubling youth.* Newbury Park, CA: Sage.

Leone, P. E., Rutherford, R. B., & Nelson, C. M. (1991). *Special education in juvenile corrections.* Reston, VA: Council for Exceptional Children.

Lloyd, J. W., Kauffman, J. M., & Kupersmidt, J. B. (1990). Integration of students with behavior disorders in regular education environments. In K. Gadow (Ed.), *Advances in learning and behavioral disorders,* Vol. 6. Greenwich, CT: JAI Press.

Loeber, R., Green S. M., Lahey, B. B., Christ, M. A. G., & Frick, P. J. (1992). Developmental sequences in age of onset of disruptive child behaviors. *Journal of Child and Family Studies, 1,* 21–41.

Lovaas, O. I. (1987). Behavioral treatment and normal educational and intellectual functioning in young autistic children. *Journal of Consulting and Clinical Psychology, 55,* 3–9.

Lozoff, B. (1989). Nutrition and behavior. *American Psychologist, 44,* 231–236.

Lyman, R. D. (1984). The effect of private and public goal setting on classroom on-task behavior of emotionally disturbed children. *Behavior Therapy, 15,* 395–402.

Martin, R. P. (1992). Child temperament effects on special education: Process and outcomes. *Exceptionality, 3,* 99–115.

Mattison, R. E., & Gamble, A. D. (1992). Severity of socially and emotionally disturbed boys' dysfunction at school and home: Comparison with psychiatric and general population boys. *Behavioral Disorders, 17,* 219–224.

Mattison, R. E., Morales, J., & Bauer, M. A. (1992). Distinguishing characteristics of elementary schoolboys recommended for SED placement. *Behavioral Disorders, 17,* 107–114.

McDowell, R. L., Adamson, G. W., & Wood, F. H. (Eds.). (1982). *Teaching emotionally disturbed children.* Boston: Little, Brown.

Meichenbaum, D. (1977). *Cognitive-behavior modification: An integrative approach.* New York: Plenum.

Morganthau, T., Annin, P., Wingert, P., Foote, D., Manly, H., & King, P. (1992). It's not just New York . . . *Newsweek, 119*(10), 25–29.

Morse, W. C. (1985). *The education and treatment of socio-emotionally impaired children and youth.* Syracuse, NY: Syracuse University Press.

Murphy, D. M. (1986). The prevalence of handicapping conditions among juvenile delinquents. *Remedial and Special Education, 7*(3), 7–17.

Neel, R. S., Meadows, N., Levine, P., & Edgar, E. B. (1988). What happens after special education: A statewide follow-up study of secondary students who have behavioral disorders. *Behavioral Disorders, 13,* 209–216.

Nelson, C. M. (1992). Searching for meaning in the behavior of antisocial pupils, public school education, and lawmakers. *School Psychology Review, 21,* 35–38.

Nelson, C. M., & Kauffman, J. M. (1977). Educational programming for secondary school age delinquent and maladjusted pupils. *Behavioral Disorders, 2,* 102–113.

Nelson, C. M., & Pearson, C. A. (1991). *Integrating services for children and youth with emotional and behavioral disorders.* Reston, VA: Council for Exceptional Children.

Nelson, C. M., Rutherford, R. B., Center, D. B., & Walker, H. M. (1991). Do public schools have an obligation to serve troubled children and youth? *Exceptional Children, 57,* 406–415.

Nelson, C. M., Rutherford, R. B., & Wolford, B. I. (Eds.). (1987). *Special education in the criminal justice system.* Columbus, OH: Merrill/Macmillan.

Newcomb, M. D., & Bentler, P. M. (1989). Substance use and abuse among children and teenagers. *American Psychologist, 44,* 242–248.

Osborne, S. S., Kiburz, C. S., & Miller, S. R. (1986). Treatment of self-injurious behavior using self-control techniques with a severe behaviorally disordered student. *Behavioral Disorders, 12,* 60–67.

Patterson, C. J., Kupersmidt, J. B., & Griesler, P. C. (1989). *Self-concepts of children in regular education and in special education classes.* Unpublished manuscript, Virginia Behavior Disorders Project, University of Virginia, Charlottesville, VA.

Patterson, G. R., DeBaryshe, B. D., & Ramsey, E. (1989). A developmental perspective on antisocial behavior. *American Psychologist, 44,* 329–335.

Patterson, G. R., Reid, J. B., & Dishion, T. J. (1992). *Antisocial boys.* Eugene, OR: Castalia.

Peacock Hill Working Group. (1991). Problems and promises in special education and related services for children and youth with emotional or behavioral disorders. *Behavioral Disorders, 16,* 299–313.

Petty, L. K., Ornitz, E. M., Michelman, J. D., & Zimmerman, E. G. (1984). Autistic children who become schizophrenic. *Archives of General Psychiatry, 41,* 129–135.

Plomin, R. (1989). Environment and genes: Determinants of behavior. *American Psychologist, 44,* 105–111.

Poland, S. (1989). *Suicide intervention in the schools.* New York: Guilford Press.

Prior, M., & Werry, J. S. (1986). Autism, schizophrenia, and allied disorders. In H. C. Quay & J. S. Werry (Eds.), *Psychopathological disorders of childhood* (3rd ed.). New York: Wiley.

Quay, H. C. (1986). Classification. In H. C. Quay & J. S. Werry (Eds.), *Psychopathological disorders of childhood* (3rd ed.). New York: Wiley.

Quay, H. C., & Peterson, D. R. (1987). *Manual for the Revised Behavior Problem Checklist.* Coral Gables, FL: Author.

Rogers, S. J., & DeLalla, D. (1991). A comparative study of the effects of a developmentally based instructional model on young children with autism and young children with other disorders of behavior and development. *Topics in Early Childhood Special Education*, *11*(2), 29–47.

Rogoff, B., & Morelli, G. (1989). Perspectives on children's development from cultural psychology. *American Psychologist*, *44*, 343–348.

Rutter, M. (1985). Family and school influences on behavioral development. *Journal of Child Psychology and Psychiatry*, *26*, 349–368.

Rutter, M., & Schopler, E. (1987). Autism and pervasive developmental disorders: Concepts and diagnostic issues. *Journal of Autism and Developmental Disabilities*, *17*, 159–186.

Sameroff, A. J., Seifer, R., & Zax, M. (1982). Early development of children at risk for emotional disorder. *Monographs of the Society for Research in Child Development*, *47*, serial no. 199.

Sherburne, S., Utley, B., McConnell, S., & Gannon, J. (1988). Decreasing violent and aggressive theme play among preschool children with behavior disorders. *Exceptional Children*, *55*, 166–172.

Silver, S. E., Duchnowski, A. J., Kutash, K., Friedman, R. M., Eisen, M., Prange, M. E., Brandenburg, N. A., & Greenbaum, P. E. (1992). A comparison of children with serious emotional disturbance served in residential and school settings. *Journal of Child and Family Studies*, *1*, 43–59.

Skiba, R., & Grizzle, K. (1992). Qualifications v. logic and data: Excluding conduct disorders from the SED definition. *School Psychology Review*, *21*, 23–28.

Slenkovich, J. E. (1992a). Can the language "social maladjustment" in the SED definition be ignored? *School Psychology Review*, *21*, 21–22.

Slenkovich, J. E. (1992b). Can the language "social maladjustment" in the SED definition be ignored? The final words. *School Psychology Review*, *21*, 43–44.

Strain, P. S. (1987). Comprehensive evaluation of young autistic children. *Topics in Early Childhood Special Education*, *7*(1), 97–110.

Strain, P. S., & Fox, J. E. (1981). Peers as behavior change agents for withdrawn classmates. In A. E. Kazdin & B. Lahey (Eds.), *Advances in clinical child psychology*, Vol. 4., New York: Plenum.

Strain, P. S., McConnell, S. R., Carta, J. J., Fowler, S. A., Neisworth, J. T., & Wolery, M. (1992). Behaviorism in early intervention. *Topics in Early Childhood Special Education*, *12*(1), 121–141.

Strain, P. S., Steele, P., Ellis, T., & Timm, M. (1982). Long-term effects of oppositional child treatment with mothers as therapists and therapist trainers. *Journal of Applied Behavior Analysis*, *15*, 163–169.

Tankersley, M. (1992). *Classification and identification of internalizing behavioral subtypes.* Doctoral dissertation, University of Virginia.

Thomas, A., & Chess, S. (1984). Genesis and evolution of behavioral disorders: From infancy to early adult life. *American Journal of Psychiatry*, *141*, 1–9.

U. S. Department of Education. (1992). *Fourteenth annual report to Congress on the implementation of the Individuals with Disabilities Education Act.* Washington, DC: Author.

Wagner, M., & Shaver, D. (1989). *Educational progress and achievement of secondary special education students: Findings from the national longitudinal transition study.* Menlo Park, CA: SRI International.

Walker, H. M., & Bullis, M. (1991). Behavior disorders and the social context of regular class integration: A conceptual dilemma? In J. W. Lloyd, N. N. Singh, & A. C. Repp (Eds.), *The regular education initiative: Alternative perspectives on concepts, issues, and models.* Sycamore, IL: Sycamore.

Walker, H. M., & Severson, H. H. (1990). *Systematic Screening for Behavior Disorders (SSBD): A Multiple Gating Procedure.* Longmont, CO: Sopris West.

Walker, H. M., Stieber, S., & O'Neill, R. E. (1990). Middle school behavioral profiles of antisocial and at-risk control boys: Descriptive and predictive outcomes. *Exceptionality*, *1*, 61–77.

Walther, M., & Beare, P. (1991). The effect of videotape feedback on the on-task behavior of a student with emotional/behavioral disorders. *Education and Treatment of Children*, *14*, 53–60.

Wenar, C., Ruttenberg, B. A., Kalish-Weiss, B., & Wolf, E. G. (1986). The development of normal and autistic children: A comparative study. *Journal of Autism and Developmental Disorders*, *16*, 317–333.

Wolf, M. M., Braukmann, C. J., & Ramp, K. A. (1987). Serious delinquent behavior as part of a significantly handicapping condition. *Journal of Applied Behavior Analysis*, *20*, 347–359.

C*HAPTER* 7

Alpert, C. L., & Kaiser, A. P. (1992). Training parents as milieu language teachers. *Journal of Early Intervention*, *16*(1), 31–52.

American Speech-Language-Hearing Association. (1983). Position of the American Speech-Language-Hearing Association on social dialects. *ASHA, 25,* 23–25.

Andrews, G., Craig, A., Feyer, A., Hoddinott, S., Howie, P., & Neilson, M. (1983). Stuttering: A review of research findings and theories circa 1982. *Journal of Speech and Hearing Disorders, 48,* 226–246.

Baca, L., & Amato, C. (1989). Bilingual special education: Training issues. *Exceptional Children, 56,* 168–173.

Baca, L., & Cervantes, H. (1989). *The bilingual special education interface* (2nd ed.). Columbus, OH: Merrill/Macmillan.

Bernstein, D. K., & Tiegerman, E. (1989). *Language and communication disorders in children* (2nd ed.). Columbus, OH: Merrill/Macmillan.

Bettison, S. (1991). Letter to the editor. *Journal of Autism and Developmental Disorders, 21,* 561–563.

Beukelman, D. R. (1991). Magic and cost of communicative competence. *Augmentative and Alternative Communication, 7,* 2–10.

Biklen, D. (1990). Communication unbound: Autism and praxis. *Harvard Educational Review, 60,* 291–314.

Biklen, D. (1992a). Autism orthodoxy versus free speech: A reply to Cummins and Prior. *Harvard Educational Review, 62,* 242–256.

Biklen, D. (1992b). Typing to talk: Facilitated communication. *American Journal of Speech-Language Pathology, 1*(2), 15–17.

Biklen, D., & Schubert, A. (1991). New words: The communication of students with autism. *Remedial and Special Education, 12*(6), 46–57.

Blank, M., & White, S. J. (1986). Questions: A powerful form of classroom exchange. *Topics in Language Disorders, 6*(2), 1–12.

Bloom, L. (1991). *Language development from two to three.* New York: Cambridge University Press.

Blosser, J. L., & DePompei, R. (1989). The head-injured student returns to school: Recognizing and treating deficits. *Topics in Language Disorders, 9*(2), 67–77.

Bull, G. L., Cochran, P. S., & Snell, M. E. (1988). Beyond CAI: Computers, language, and persons with mental retardation. *Topics in Language Disorders, 8*(4), 55–76.

Butler, K. G. (1986a). *Language disorders in children.* Austin, TX: Pro-Ed.

Butler, K. G. (1986b). Language research and practice: A major contribution to special education. In R. J. Morris & B. Blatt (Eds.), *Special education: Research and trends* (pp. 272–302). New York: Pergamon.

Calculator, S. N. (1992). Perhaps the emperor has clothes after all: A response to Biklen. *American Journal of Speech-Language Pathology, 1*(2), 18–20.

Calculator, S. N., & Jorgensen, C. M. (1991). Integrating AAC instruction into regular education settings: Expounding on best practices. *Augmentative and Alternative Communication, 7,* 204–212.

Campbell, S. L., Reich, A. R., Klockars, A. J., & McHenry, M. A. (1988). Factors associated with dysphonia in high school cheerleaders. *Journal of Speech and Hearing Disorders, 53,* 175–185.

Carrow-Woolfolk, E. (1988). *Theory, assessment and intervention in language disorders: An integrative approach.* Philadelphia, PA: Grune & Stratton.

Casby, M. W. (1989). National data concerning communication disorders and special education. *Language, Speech, and Hearing Services in the Schools, 20,* 22–30.

Cheng, L. L. (1989). Service delivery to Asian/Pacific LEP children: A cross-cultural framework. *Topics in Language Disorders, 9*(3), 1–14.

Crais, E. R. (1991). Moving from "parent involvement" to family-centered services. *American Journal of Speech-Language Pathology, 1*(1), 5–8.

Crawford, J. (1992). *Hold your tongue: Bilingualism and the politics of "English only."* Reading, MA: Addison-Wesley.

Crossley, R., & MacDonald, A. (1984). *Annie's coming out.* New York: Viking.

Crossley, R., & Remington-Guerney, J. (1992). Getting the words out: Facilitated communication training. *Topics in Language Disorders, 12*(4), 29–45.

Curtiss, S. (1977). *Genie: A psycholinguistic study of a modern-day "wild child."* New York: Academic Press.

Cummins, R. A., & Prior, M. P. (1992). Autism and assisted communication: A response to Biklen. *Harvard Educational Review, 62,* 228–241.

Delpit, L. (1988). The silenced dialogue: Power and pedagogy in educating other people's children. *Harvard Educational Review, 58,* 280–298.

Devany, J. M., Rincover, A., & Lovaas, O. I. (1981). Teaching speech to nonverbal children. In J. M. Kauffman & D. P. Hallahan (Eds.), *Handbook of special education* (pp. 512–529). Englewood Cliffs, NJ: Prentice-Hall.

Ensher, G. L. (1989). The first three years: Special education perspectives on assessment and intervention. *Topics in Language disorders, 10*(1), 80–90.

Falvey, M. A., McLean, D., & Rosenberg, R. L. (1988). Transition from school to adult life: Communication strategies. *Topics in Language Disorders, 9*(1), 82–86.

Felsenfeld, S., Broen, P. A., & McGue, M. (1992). A 28-year follow-up of adults with a history of moderate phonological disorder: Linguistic and personality results. *Journal of Speech and Hearing Research, 35,* 1114–1125.

Fey, M. E. (1986). *Language intervention with young children.* San Diego: College Hill Press.

Foster, H. L. (1986). *Ribin', jivin', and playin' the dozens* (2nd ed.). Cambridge, MA: Ballinger.

Fradd, S. H., Figueroa, R. A., & Correa, V. I. (1989). Meeting the multicultural needs of Hispanic students in special education. *Exceptional Children, 56*, 102–103.

Franklin, K., & Beukelman, D. R. (1991). Augmentative communication: Directions for future research. In J. F. Miller (Ed.), *Research on child language disorders: A decade of progress* (pp. 321–337). Austin, TX: Pro-Ed.

Franklin, M. E. (1992). Culturally sensitive instructional practices for African-American learners with disabilities. *Exceptional Children, 59*, 115–122.

Goldstein, H., & Strain, P. S. (1989). Peers as communication intervention agents: Some new strategies and research findings. *Topics in Language Disorders, 9*(1), 44–57.

Hallahan, D. P., Kauffman, J. M., & Lloyd, J. W. (1985). *Introduction to learning disabilities* (2nd ed.). Englewood Cliffs, NJ: Prentice-Hall.

Hoffnung, A. S. (1989). The nature of language. In P. J. Valletutti, M. McKnight-Taylor, & A. S. Hoffnung (Eds.), *Facilitating communication in young children with handicapping conditions: A guide for special educators*. Boston: Little, Brown.

Huer, M. B. (1991). University students using augmentative and alternative communication in the USA: A demographic study. *Augmentative and Alternative Communication, 7*, 231–239.

Koegel, R. L., O'Dell, M. C., & Koegel, L, C. (1987). A natural language teaching paradigm for nonverbal autistic children. *Journal of Autism and Developmental Disabilities, 17*, 187–200.

Koegel, R. L., Rincover, A., & Egel, A. L. (1982). *Educating and understanding autistic children*. San Diego: College Hill Press.

Lahey, M. (1988). *Language disorders and language development*. New York: Macmillan.

Lane, H. (1976). *The wild boy of Aveyron*. Cambridge, MA: Harvard University Press.

Langdon, H. W. (1989). Language disorders or difference? Assessing the language skills of Hispanic students. *Exceptional Children, 56*, 160–167.

LaPointe, L. L. (1986) Neurogenic disorders of speech. In G. H. Shames & E. H. Wiig (Eds.), *Human communication disorders* (2nd ed.) (pp. 495–530). Columbus, OH: Merrill/Macmillan.

Larson, V. L., & McKinley, N. L. (1985). General intervention principles with language impaired adolescents. *Topics in Language Disorders, 5*(3), 70–77.

Leonard, L. (1986). Early language development and language disorders. In G. H. Shames & E. H. Wiig (Eds.), *Human communication disorders* (2nd ed.) (pp. 291–330). Columbus, OH: Merrill/Macmillan.

Lord, C. (1988). Enhancing communication in adolescents with autism. *Topics in Language Disorders, 9*(1), 72–81.

Lovaas, O. I. (1987). Behavioral treatment and normal educational and intellectual functioning in young autistic children. *Journal of Consulting and Clinical Psychology, 55*, 3–9.

Love, R. J. (1992). *Childhood motor speech disability*. New York: Macmillan.

McCormick. L., & Schiefelbusch, R. L. (1984). *Early language intervention*. Columbus, OH: Merrill/Macmillan.

McKnight-Taylor, M. (1989). Stimulating speech and language development of infants and other young children. In P. J. Valletutti, M. McKnight-Taylor, & A. S. Hoffnung (Eds.), *Facilitating communication in young children with handicapping conditions: A guide for special educators*. Boston: Little, Brown.

McLean, J. (1992). Facilitated communication: Some thoughts on Biklen's and Calculator's interaction. *American Journal of Speech-Language Pathology, 1*(2), 25–27.

McMorrow, M. J., Foxx, R. M., Faw, G. D., & Bittle, R. G. (1986). *Looking for the words: Teaching functional language strategies*. Champaign, IL: Research Press.

McReynolds, L. V. (1986). Functional articulation disorders. In G. H. Shames & E. H. Wiig (Eds.), *Human communication disorders* (2nd ed.) (pp. 139–182). Columbus, OH: Merrill/Macmillan.

McWilliams, B. J. (1986). Cleft palate. In G. H. Shames & E. H. Wiig (Eds.), *Human communication disorders* (2nd ed.) (pp. 445–482). Columbus, OH: Merrill/Macmillan.

Meyers, S. (1986). Qualitative and quantitative differences and patterns of variability in disfluencies emitted by preschool stutterers. *Journal of Fluency Disorders, 11*, 293–306.

Moore, P. (1986). Voice disorders. In G. H. Shames & E. H. Wiig (Eds.), *Human communication disorders* (2nd ed.) (pp. 183–229). Columbus, OH: Merrill/Macmillan.

Mysak, E. D. (1986). Cerebral palsy. In G. H. Shames & E. H. Wiig (Eds.), *Human communication disorders* (2nd ed.). Columbus, OH: Merrill/Macmillan.

Naremore, R. C. (1980). Language disorders in children. In T. J. Hixon, L. D. Shriberg, & J. H. Saxman (Eds.), *Introduction to communication disorders*. Englewood Cliffs, NJ: Prentice-Hall.

Nelson, N. W. (1992). Performance is the prize: Language competence and performance among AAC users. *Augmentative and Alternative Communication, 8*, 3–18.

Nelson, N. W. (1993). *Childhood language disorders in context: Infancy through adolescence*. Columbus, OH: Merrill/Macmillan.

Ogletree, B. T., Wetherby, A. M., & Westling, D. L. (1992). Profile of the prelinguistic intentional communicative behaviors of children with profound mental retardation. *American Journal on Mental Retardation, 97*, 186–196.

Onslow, M. (1992). Choosing a treatment procedure for early stuttering: Issues and future directions. *Journal of Speech and Hearing Research, 35*, 983–993.

Ortiz, A., Yates, J. R., & Garcia, S. B. (1990). Competencies associated with serving exceptional language minority students. *Bilingual Special Education Newsletter*, Vol. 9. Austin, TX: University of Texas, College of Education, Office of Bilingual Education.

Owens, R. E. (1986). Communication, language, and speech. In G. H. Shames & E. H. Wiig (Eds.), *Human communication disorders* (2nd ed.) (pp. 27–79). Columbus, OH: Merrill/Macmillan.

Perkins, W. H., Kent, R. D., & Curlee, R. F. (1991). A theory of neuropsycholinguistic function in stuttering. *Journal of Speech and Hearing Research, 34,* 734–752.

Roberts, J. E. Babinowitch, S., Bryant, D. M., Burchinal, M. R., Koch, M. A., & Ramey, C. T. (1989). Language skills of children with different preschool experiences. *Journal of Speech and Hearing Research, 32,* 773–786.

Ruscello, D. M., St. Louis, K. O., & Mason, N. (1991). School-aged children with phonologic disorders: Coexistence with other speech/language disorders. *Journal of Speech and Hearing Research, 34,* 236–242.

Rymer, R. (1992, April). Annals of science: A silent childhood. *The New Yorker,* pp. 41–81 (April 13), 43–77 (April 20).

Schiefelbusch, R. L., & McCormick, L. P. (1981). Language and speech disorders. In J. M. Kauffman & D. P. Hallahan (Eds.), *Handbook of special education* (pp. 108–140). Englewood Cliffs, NJ: Prentice-Hall.

Schlosser, R. W., & Lloyd, L. L. (1991). Augmentative and alternative communication: An evolving field. *Augmentative and Alternative Communication, 7,* 154–160.

Seligman, J. (1992, Sept. 21). Horror story or big hoax? *Newsweek, 120,* 75.

Shames, G., & Rubin, H. (Eds.). (1986). *Stuttering: Then and now.* Columbus, OH: Merrill/Macmillan.

Shames, G. H., & Wiig, E. H. (Eds.). (1986). *Human communication disorders* (2nd ed.). Columbus, OH: Merrill/Macmillan.

Shapiro, J. P. (1992, July 27). See me, hear me, touch me. *U. S. News and World Report, 113,* 63–64.

Shprintzen, R. J. (1988). Cleft palate and craniofacial disorders: Where we have been, where we need to go. In S. E. Gerber & G. T. Mencher (Eds.), *International perspectives on communication disorders.* Washington, DC: Gallaudet University Press.

Slentz, K. L., & Bricker, D. (1992). Family-centered assessment for IFSP development: Jumping off the family assessment bandwagon. *Journal of Early Intervention, 16*(1), 11–19.

Starkweather, C. W. (1983). *Speech and language: Principles and processes of behavior change.* Englewood Cliffs, NJ: Prentice-Hall.

Stephens, M. I. (Ed.). (1985). Language impaired youth: The years between 10 and 18. *Topics in Language Disorders, 5*(3), special issue.

Stoel-Gammon, C. (1991). Issues in phonological development and disorders. In J. F. Miller (Ed.), *Research on child language disorders: A decade of progress* (pp. 255–265). Austin, TX: Pro-Ed.

Thompson, T. (1993, January). A reign of error: Facilitated Communication. *Vanderbilt University Kennedy Center News,* No. 22, 3–5.

U. S. Department of Education. (1992). *Fourteenth annual report to Congress on implementation of the Individuals with Disabilities Education Act.* Washington, DC: U. S. Government Printing Office.

Vanderheiden, G. C. (1984). High and low technology approaches in the development of communication systems for severely physically handicapped persons. *Exceptional Education Quarterly, 4*(4), 40–56.

Wallace, G., Larsen, S. C., & Elksnin, L. K. (1992). *Educational assessment of learning problems: Testing for teaching* (2nd ed.). Boston: Allyn & Bacon.

Wallach, G. P., & Miller, L. (1988). *Language intervention and academic success.* Boston: Little, Brown.

Warren, S. F., & Abbaduto, L. (1992). The relation of communication and language development to mental retardation. *American Journal on Mental Retardation, 97,* 125–130.

Wheeler, D. L., Jacobson, J. W., Paglieri, R. A., & Schwartz, A. A. (1993). An experimental assessment of facilitated communication. *Mental Retardation, 31,* 49–60.

Wilcox, M. J., Kouri, T. A., & Caswell, S. B. (1991). Early language intervention: A comparison of classroom and individual treatment. *American Journal of Speech-Language Pathology, 1*(1), 49–62.

Wong, B. Y. L., Wong, R., Darlington, D., & Jones. W. (1991). Interactive teaching: An effective way to teach revision skills to adolescents with learning disabilities. *Learning Disabilities Research and Practice, 6,* 117–127.

Yairi, E. (1983). The onset of stuttering in two- and three-year-old children: A preliminary report. *Journal of Speech and Hearing Disorders, 48,* 171–178.

Yairi, E., & Ambrose, N. (1992). A longitudinal study of stuttering in children: A preliminary report. *Journal of Speech and Hearing Research, 35,* 755–760.

Ylvisaker, M., & Szekeres, S. F. (1989). Metacognitive and executive impairments in head-injured children and adults. *Topics in Language Disorders, 9*(2), 34–49.

CHAPTER 8

Allen, T. E. (1986). Patterns of achievement among hearing-impaired students: 1974 and 1983. In A. N. Schildroth & M. A. Karchmer (Eds.), *Deaf children in America* (pp.161–206). San Diego, CA: College Hill Press.

Blennerhassett, L. (1990). Intellectual assessment. In D. F. Moores, & K. P. Meadow-Orlans (Eds.), *Educational and developmental aspects of deafness* (pp. 255–280). Washington, DC: Gallaudet University Press.

Boothroyd, A. (1987). Technology and science in the management of deafness. *American Annals of the Deaf, 132,* 326–329.

Bornstein, H., Hamilton, L., & Saulnier, K. (1983). *The comprehensive Signed English dictionary*. Washington, DC: Gallaudet University Press.

Brill, R. G., MacNeil, B., & Newman, L. R. (1986). Framework for appropriate programs for deaf children. *American Annals of the Deaf, 131*(2), 65–77.

Bull, B., & Bullis, M. (1991). A national profile of school-based transition programs for deaf adolescents. *American Annals of the Deaf, 136*(4), 339–343.

Castiglia, P. T., Aquilina, S. S., & Kemsley, M. (1983). Focus: Nonsuppurative otitis media. *Pediatric Nursing, 9*, 427–431.

Charlson, E., Strong, M., & Gold, R. (1992). How successful deaf teenagers experience and cope with isolation. *American Annals of the Deaf, 137*(3), 261–270.

Davis, H. (1978a). Abnormal hearing and deafness. In H. Davis & S. R. Silverman (Eds.), *Hearing and deafness* (4th ed.). New York: Holt, Rinehart & Winston.

Fant, L. J. (1971). *Say it with hands*. Silver Spring, Md.: National Association for the Deaf.

Fry, D. B. (1966). The development of a phonological system in the normal and the deaf child. In F. Smith & G. A. Miller (Eds.), *The genesis of language: A psycholinguistic approach*. Cambridge, MA: M.I.T. Press.

Gaustad, M. G., & Kluwin, T. N. (1992). Patterns of communication among deaf and hearing adolescents. In T. N. Kluwin, D. F. Moores, & M. G. Gaustad (Eds.), *Toward effective public school programs for deaf students: Context, process, & outcomes* (pp. 107–128). New York: Teachers College Press.

Giebink, G. S. (1990). Medical issues in hearing impairment: The otitis media spectrum. In J. Davis (Ed.), *Our forgotten children: Hard-of-hearing pupils in the schools* (pp. 49–55). Bethesda, MD: Self Help for Hard of Hearing People.

Gustason, G., Pfetzing, D., & Zawolkow, E. (1972). *Signing Exact English*. Silver Spring, MD: National Association of the Deaf.

Hawkins, D. B. (1990). Amplification in the classroom. In J. Davis (Ed.), *Our forgotten children: Hard-of-hearing pupils in the schools* (pp. 39–47). Bethesda, MD: Self Help for Hard of Hearing People.

Higgins, P. C. (1992). Working at mainstreaming. In P. M. Ferguson, D. L. Ferguson, & S. J. Taylor (Eds.), *Interpreting disability* (pp. 103–123). New York: Teachers College Press.

Janesick, V. J., & Moores, D. F. (1992). Ethnic and cultural considerations. In T. N. Kluwin, D. F. Moores, & M. G. Gaustad (Eds.), *Toward effective public school programs for deaf students: Context, process, & outcomes* (pp. 49–65). New York: Teachers College Press.

Kampfe, C. M., & Turecheck, A. G. (1987). Reading achievement of prelingually deaf students and its relationship to parental method of communication: A review of the literature. *American Annals of the Deaf, 132*(1), 11–15.

Klima, E. S., Bellugi, U. (1979). *The signs of language*. Cambridge, MA: Harvard University Press.

Kluwin, T. N. (1992). What does "local public school" mean? In T. N. Kluwin, D. F. Moores, & M. G. Gaustad (Eds.), *Toward effective public school programs for deaf students: Context, process, & outcomes* (pp. 30–48). New York: Teachers College Press.

Koester, L. S., & Meadow-Orlans, K. P. (1990). Parenting a deaf child: Stress, strength, and support. In D. F. Moores & K. P. Meadow-Orlans (Eds.), *Educational and developmental aspects of deafness* (pp. 299–320). Washington, DC: Gallaudet University Press.

Lane, H. (1984). *When the mind hears: A history of the deaf*. New York: Random House.

Lane, H. (1987, July 17). Listen to the needs of deaf children. *New York Times*.

Lane, H. (1992). *The mask of benevolence: Disabling the Deaf community*. New York: Alfred A. Knopf.

Ling, D., & Ling, A. (1978). *Aural habilitation*. Washington, DC: Alexander Graham Bell Association for the Deaf.

Loeb, R., & Sarigiani, P. (1986). The impact of hearing impairment on self-perceptions of children. *The Volta Review, 88*(2), 89–100.

Martin, F. N. (1986). *Introduction to audiology* (3rd ed.). Englewood Cliffs, NJ: Prentice Hall.

Meadow-Orlans, K. P. (1987). An analysis of the effectiveness of early intervention programs for hearing-impaired children. In M. J. Guralnick & F. C. Bennett (Eds.), *The effectiveness of early intervention for at-risk and handicapped children* (pp. 325–362). New York: Academic Press.

Meadow-Orlans, K. P. (1990). Research on developmental aspects of deafness. In D. F. Moores & K. P. Meadow-Orlans (Eds.), *Educational and developmental aspects of deafness* (pp. 283–298). Washington DC: Gallaudet University Press.

Menchel, R. S. (1988). Personal experience with speechreading. *The Volta Review, 90*(5), 3–15.

Moog, J. S., & Geers, A. E. (1991). Educational management of children with cochlear implants. *American Annals of the Deaf, 136*(2), 69–76.

Moores, D. F., Cerney, B., & Garcia, M. (1990). School placement and least restrictive environment. In D. F. Moores, & K. P. Meadow-Orlans (Eds.), *Educational and developmental aspects of deafness* (pp. 115–136). Washington, DC: Gallaudet University Press.

Moores, D. F., & Maestas y Moores, J. (1981). Special adaptations necessiated by hearing impairments. In J. M. Kauffman & D. P. Hallahan (Eds.), *Handbook of special education*. Englewood Cliffs, NJ: Prentice Hall.

Padden, C., & Humphries, T. (1988). *Deaf in America: Voices from a culture*. Cambridge, MA: Harvard University Press.

Prinz, P. M., Pemberton, E., & Nelson, K. (1985). The ALPHA Interactive Microcomputer System for teaching reading, writing, and communication skills to hearing-impaired children. *American Annals of the Deaf, 130*(4), 441–461.

Quigley, S., Jenne, W., & Phillips, S. (1968). *Deaf students in colleges and universities.* Washington, DC: Alexander Graham Bell Association for the Deaf.

Reagan, T. (1990). Cultural considerations in the education of deaf children. In D. F. Moores, & K. P. Meadow-Orlans (Eds.), *Educational and developmental aspects of deafness* (pp. 73–84). Washington, DC: Gallaudet University Press.

Sacks, O. (1989). *Seeing voices: A journey into the world of the deaf.* Berkeley: University of California Press.

Sanders, D. A. (1982). *Aural rehabilitation* (2nd ed.). Englewood Cliffs, NJ: Prentice Hall.

Saur, R., Coggiola, D., Long, G., & Simonson, J. (1986). Educational mainstreaming and the career development of hearing-impaired students: A longitudinal analysis. *The Volta Review, 88*(2), 79–88.

Schildroth, A. N., & Hotto, S. A. (1991). Annual survey of hearing impaired children and youth: 1989–1990 school year. *American Annals of the Deaf, 136*(2), 155–163.

Schildroth, A. N., & Hotto, S. (1992). Hearing impaired children under age 6: Data from the Annual Survey of Hearing Impaired Children and Youth. *American Annals of the Deaf, 137*(2), 168–175.

Schildroth, A. N., Rawlings, B. W., & Allen, T. E. (1989). Hearing-impaired children under age 6: A demographic analysis. *American Annals of the Deaf, 134*(2), 63–69.

Schow, R., & Nerbonne, M. (Eds.). (1980). *Introduction to aural rehabilitation.* Baltimore: University Park Press.

Slike, S. B., Chiavacci, J. P., & Hobbis, D. H. (1989). The efficiency and effectiveness of an interactive videodisc system to teach sign language vocabulary. *American Annals of the Deaf, 134*, 288–290.

Spencer, P. E., & Gutfreund, M. K. (1990). Directiveness in mother-infant interactions. In D. F. Moores, & K. P. Meadow-Orlans (Eds.), *Educational and developmental aspects of deafness* (pp. 350–365). Washington DC: Gallaudet University Press.

Spradley, T. S., & Spradley, J. P. (1978). *Deaf like me.* Washington, DC: Gallaudet University Press.

Stewart, D. A. (1990). Rationale and strategies for American Sign Language intervention. *American Annals of the Deaf, 135*(3), 205–210.

Stinson, M. S., & Whitmire, K. (1992). Students' views of their social relationships. In T. N. Kluwin, D. F. Moores, & M. G. Gaustad (Eds.), *Toward effective public school programs for deaf students: Context, process, & outcomes* (pp. 149–174). New York: Teachers College Press.

Stoel-Gammon, C., & Otomo, K. (1986). Babbling development of hearing-impaired and normally hearing subjects. *Journal of Speech and Hearing Disorders, 51*, 33–41.

Stokoe, W. C. (1960). *Sign language structure.* Silver Spring, MD: Linstok Press.

Stokoe, W. C., Casterline, D. C., & Croneberg, C. G. (1976). *A dictionary of American Sign Language on linguistic principles* (2nd ed.). Silver Spring, MD: Linstok Press.

Trybus, R. J., & Karchmer, M. A. (1977). School achievement scores of hearing impaired children. National data on achievement status and growth patterns. *American Annals of the Deaf, 122*, 62–69.

Viadero, D. (1992, August 5). E. D. revises policy favoring regular classes for the deaf. *Education Week*, p. 39.

Vygotsky, L. S. (1962). *Thought and language.* New York: Wiley.

Walker, L. A. (1986). *A loss for words: The story of deafness in a family.* New York: Harper & Row.

Wolk, S., & Allen, T. E. (1984). A five-year follow-up of reading comprehension achievment of hearing-impaired students in special education programs. *Journal of Special Education, 18*( ), 161–176.

Wolk, S., & Schildroth, A. N. (1986). Deaf children and speech intelligibility: A national study. In A. N. Schildroth & M. A. Karchmer (Eds.), *Deaf children in America* (pp. 139–159). San Diego: College-Hill Press.

Wolkomir, R. (1992). American Sign Language: 'It's not mouth stuff—it's brain stuff.' *Smithsonian, 23*(4), 30–38, 40–41.

Wood, D. (1991). Communication and cognition: How the communication styles of hearing adults may hinder—rather than help—deaf learners. *American Annals of the Deaf, 136*(3), 247–251.

CHAPTER 9

Aitken, S., & Bower, T. G. R. (1982). The use of the Sonicguide in infancy. *Journal of Visual Impairment and Blindness, 76*, 91–100.

Andersen, E. S., Dunlea, A., & Kekelis, L. S. (1984). Blind children's language: Resolving some differences. *Journal of Child Language, 2*, 645–664.

Bambring, M., & Troster, H. (1992). On the stability of stereotyped behaviors in blind infants and preschoolers. Journal of Visual Impairment & Blindness, 86(2), 105–110.

Barraga, N. C. (1983). *Visual handicaps and learning* (rev. ed.). Austin, TX: Exceptional Resources.

Barraga, N. C., & Collins, M. E. (1979). Development of efficiency in visual functioning: Rationale for a comprehensive program. *Journal of Visual Impairment and Blindness, 73*, 121–126.

Baumeister, A. A. (1978). Origins and control of stereotyped movements. In C. E. Meyers (Ed.), *Quality of life in severely and profoundly retarded people: Research foundations for improvment* (pp. 353–384). Washington, DC: American Association on Mental Deficiency.

Berla , E. P. (1981). Tactile scanning and memory for a spatial display by blind students. *Journal of Special Education, 15*, 341–350.

Bigelow, A. (1991). Spatial mapping of familiar locations in blind children. *Journal of Visual Impairment & Blindness, 85*(3), 113–117.

Bischoff, R. W. (1979). Listening: A teachable skill for visually impaired persons. *Journal of Visual Impairment and Blindness, 73*, 59–67.

Bishop, V. E. (1991). Preschool visually impaired children: A demographic study. *Journal of Visual Impairment & Blindness, 85*(2), 69–74.

Bower, T. J. R. (1977). Blind babies see with their ears. *New Scientist, 73*, 255–257.

Brody, H. (1989, July). The great equalizer: PCs empower the disabled. *PC Computing*, pp. 82–93.

Caton, H. (Ed.) (1991). *Print and Braille literacy: Selecting appropriate learning media*. Louisville, KY: American Printing House for the Blind.

Cheadle, B. (1991, October). Canes and preschoolers: The eight-year revolution. *The Braille Monitor*, 533–538.

Collins, M. E., & Barraga, N. C. (1980). Development of efficiency in visual functioning: An evaluation process. *Journal of Visual Impairment and Blindness, 74*, 93–96.

Conant, S., & Budoff, M. (1982). The development of sighted people's understanding of blindness. *Journal of Visual Impairment and Blindness, 76*, 86–90.

Cronin, P. J. (1992). A direct service program for mainstreamed students by a residential school. *Journal of Visual Impairment & Blindness, 86*(2), 101–104.

Cronin, B. J., & King, S. R. (1990). The development of the Descriptive Video Service. *Journal of Visual Impairment & Blindness, 84*(12), 503–506.

Davidson, P. W., Dunn, G., Wiles-Kettenmann, M., & Appelle, S. (1981). Haptic conservation of amount in blind and sighted children: Exploratory movement effects. *Journal of Pediatric Psychology, 6*, 191–200.

Dekker, R. Drenth, P. J. D., & Zaal, J. N. (1991). Results of the Intelligence Test for Visually Impaired Children (ITVIC). *Journal of Visual Impairment & Blindness, 85*(6), 261–267.

Dekker, R., Drenth, P. J. D., Zaal, J. N., & Koole, F. D. (1990). An intelligence series for blind and low vision children. *Journal of Visual Impairment & Blindness, 84*(2), 71–76.

Erwin, E. J. (1991). Guidelines for integrating young children with visual impairments in general education settings. *Journal of Visual Impairment & Blindness, 85*(6), 253–260.

Farmer, L. W. (1975). Travel in adverse weather using electronic mobility guidance devices. *New Outlook for the Blind, 69*, 433–451.

Farmer, L. W. (1980). Mobility devices. In R. L. Welsh & B. B. Blasch (Eds.), *Foundations of orientation and mobility*. New York: American Foundation for the Blind.

Ferrell, K. A. (1980). Can infants use the Sonicguide? Two years' experience of Project VIEW! *Journal of Visual Impairment and Blindness, 74*, 209–220.

Ferrell, K. A., Trief, E., Dietz, S. J., Bonner, M. A., Cruz, D., Ford, E., Stratton, J. M. (1990). Visually impaired infants research consortium (VIIRC): First year results. *Journal of Visual Impairment & Blinndness, 84*(10), 404–410.

Fichten, C. S., Judd, D., Tagalakis, V., Amsel, R., & Robillard, K. (1991). Communication cues used by people with and without visual impairments in daily conversations and dating. *Journal of Visual Impairment & Blindness, 85*(9), 371–378.

Foy, C. J., Von Scheden, M., & Waiculonis, J. (1992). The Connecticut Pre-cane: Case study and curriculum. *Journal of Visual Impairment & Blindness, 86*(4), 178–181.

Fraiberg, S. (1977). *Insights from the blind*. New York: Basic Books.

Freeman, R. D., Goetz, E., Richards, D. P., & Groenveld, M. (1991). Defiers of negative prediction: A 14-year follow-up study of legally blind children. *Journal of Visual Impairment & Blindness, 85*(9), 365–370.

Gabias, P. (1992, July). Unique features of guide dogs: Backtracking and homing. *The Braille Monitor*, 392–399.

Griffin, H. C., & Gerber, P. J. (1982). Tactual development and its implications for the education of blind children. *Education of the Visually Handicapped, 13*, 116–123.

Groenveld, M., & Jan, J. E. (1992). Intelligence profiles of low vision and blind children. *Journal of Visual Impairment & Blindness, 86*(1), 68–71.

Halliday, J. (1992, January). The future of technology. *The Braille Monitor*, 42–47.

Hanley-Maxwell, C., Griffin, S., Szymanski, E. M., & Godley, S. H. (1990). Supported and time-limited transitional employment services. *Journal of Visual Impairment & Blindness, 84*(4), 160–166.

Hanninen, K. A. (1975). *Teaching the visually handicapped*. Columbus, OH: Chas. E. Merrill.

Harris, L., Humphrey, G. K., Muir, D. M., Dodwell, P. C. (1985). Use of the Canterbury Child's Aid in infancy and early childhood: A case study. *Journal of Visual Impairment and Blindness, 79*, 4–11.

Hayes, S. P. (1942). Alternative scales for the mental measurement of the visually handicapped. *Outlook for the Blind and the Teachers Forum, 36*, 225–230.

Hayes, S. P. (1950). Measuring the intelligence of the blind. In P. A. Zahl (Ed.), *Blindness*. Princeton, NJ: Princeton University Press.

Herman, J. F., Chatman, S. P., & Roth, S. F. (1983). Cognitive mapping in blind people: Acquisition of spatial relationships in a large-scale environment. *Journal of Visual Impairment and Blindness, 77*, 161–166.

Holbrook, M. C., & Koenig, A. J. (1992). Teaching Braille reading to students with low vision. *Journal of Visual Impairment & Blindness, 86*(1), 44–48.

Hull, J. M. (1990). *Touching the rock*. New York: Pantheon Books.

Ianuzzi, J. W. (1992, May). Braille or print: Why the debate? *The Braille Monitor*, 229–233.

Jernigan, K. (1985, August-September). Blindness: The pattern of freedom. *The Braille Monitor*, 386–398.

Jernigan, K. (1991, January). Airline safety: What happens when you can see fire on the wing? *The Braille Monitor*, 51–54.

Jernigan, K. (1992, June). Equality, disability, and empowerment. *The Braille Monitor*, 292–298.

Kay, L. (1973). Sonic glasses for the blind: A progress report. *Research Bulletin: American Foundation for the Blind* (25), 25–58.

Kirchner, C., & Peterson, R. (1989). Employment: Selected characteristics. In C. Kirchner (Ed.), *Blindness and visual impairment in the U. S.* New York: American Foundation for the Blind.

McGinnis, A. R. (1981). Functional linguistic strategies of blind children. *Journal of Visual Impairment and Blindness*, 75, 210–214.

McIntire, J. C. (1985). The future role of residential schools for visually impaired students. *Journal of Visual Impairment and Blindness*, 79, 161–164.

McLinden, D. J. (1988). Spatial task performance: A meta-analysis. *Journal of Visual Impairment and Blindness*, 82, 231–236.

Maloney, P. L. (1981). *Practical guidance for parents of the visually handicapped preschooler*. Springfield, IL: Chas. C Thomas.

Matsuda, M. M. (1984). Comparative analysis of blind and sighted children's communication skills. *Journal of Visual Impairment and Blindness*, 78, 1–5.

Mauer, M. (1991, May 20). All children should learn Braille: Here's why. Scripps Howard News Service.

Mehta, V. (1982). *Vedi*. New York: W. W. Norton & Company.

Mehta, V. (1984). *The ledge between the streams*. New York: W. W. Norton & Co.

Mehta, W. (1985). *Sound-shadows of the new world*. New York: W. W. Norton & Co.

Mehta, V. (1989). *The stolen light: Continents of exile*. New York: W. W. Norton & Co.

Miller-Wood, D. J., Efron, M., & Wood, T. A. (1990). Use of closed-circuit television with a severely visually impaired young child. *Journal of Visual Impairment & Blindness*, 84(12), 559–564.

National Society for the Prevention of Blindness (1964). Pub. V-7.

National Society for the Prevention of Blindness (1972). *Teaching about vision*.

Newland, T. E. (1979). The Blind Learning Aptitude Test. *Journal of Visual Impairment and Blindness*. 73, 134–139.

Nicely, B. (1991, October). Guidelines for Braille literacy: A first step. *The Braille Monitor*, 551–556.

Nielsen, L. (1991). Spatial relations in congenitally blind infants. *Journal of Visual Impairment & Blindness*, 85(1), 11–16.

Palazesi, M. A. (1986). The need for motor development programs for visually impaired preschoolers. *Journal of Visual Impairment and Blindness*, 80, 573–576.

Pierce, B. (1991, August-September). APH figures show Braille is still declining. *The Braille Monitor*, 390–391.

Raeder, W. M. (1991, July-August). Overcoming roadblocks to literacy for blind children. *The Braille Monitor*, 363–365.

Rapp D. W., & Rapp, A. J. (1992). A survey of the current status of visually impaired students in secondary mathematics. *Journal of Visual Impairment & Blindness*, 86(2), 115–117.

Rathgeber, A. J. (1981). Manitoba vision screening study. *Journal of Visual Impairment and Blindness*, 75, 239–243.

Rickelman, B. L., & Blaylock, J. N. (1983). Behaviors of sighted individuals perceived by blind persons as hindrances to self-reliance in blind persons. *Journal of Visual Impairment and Blindness*, 77, 8–11.

Rieser, J. J., Guth, D. A., & Hill, E. W. (1982). Mental processes mediating independent travel: Implications for orientation and mobility. *Journal of Visual Impairment and Blindness*, 76, 213–218.

Ross, D. B., & Koening, A. J. (1991). A cognitive approach to reducing stereotypic head rocking. *Journal of Visual Impairment & Blindness*, 85(1), 17–19.

Rovig, L. (1992, May). Ideas for increasing your chance of job success while still in college. *The Braille Monitor*, 238–244.

Sacks, S. Z., & Pruett, K. M. (1992). Summer transition training project for professionals who work with adolescents and young adults. *Journal of Visual Impairment & Blindness*, 86(5), 211–214.

Sampaio, E. (1989). Is there a critical age for using the Sonicguide with blind infants? *Journal of Visual Impairment and Blindness*, 83, 105–108.

Schroeder, F. K. (1990, January). Literacy: The key to opportunity. *The Braille Monitor*, 33–41.

Schroeder, F. K. (1992, June). Braille bills: What are they and what do they mean? *The Braille Monitor*, 308–311.

Scott, E. P. (1982). *Your visually impaired student: A guide for teachers*. Baltimore, MD: University Park Press.

Scott, R. A. (1969). *The making of blind men*. New York: Russell Sage Foundation.

Skellenger, A. C., & Hill, E. W. (1991). Current practices and considerations regarding long cane instruction with preschool children. *Journal of Visual Impairment & Blindness*, 85(3), 101–104.

Stephens, B., & Grube, C. (1982). Development of Piagetian reasoning in congenitally blind children. *Journal of Visual Impairment and Blindness*, 76, 133–143.

Stewart, I. A., Van Hasselt, V. B., Simon, J., & Thompson, W. B. (1985). The Community Adjustment Program (CAP) for visually impaired adolescents. *Journal of Visual Impairment and Blindness, 79,* 49–54.

Storey, K., Sacks, S. Z., & Olmstead, J. (1985). Community-referenced instruction in a technological work setting: A vocational education option for visually handicapped students. *Journal of Visual Impairment and Blindness, 79,* 481–486.

Strelow, E. R. (1983). Use of the Binaural Sensory Aid by young children. *Journal of Visual Impairment and Blindness, 77,* 429–438.

Strelow, E. R., & Boys, J. T. (1979). The Canterbury Child's Aid: A binaural spatial sensor for research with blind children. *Journal of Visual Impairment and Blindness, 73,* 179–184.

Suppes, P. (1974). A survey of cognition in handicapped children. *Review of Educational Research, 44,* 145–175.

Swallow, R. M., & Conner, A. (1982). Aural reading. In S. S. Mangold (Ed.), *A teachers' guide to the special educational needs of blind and visually handicapped children.* New York: American Foundation for the Blind.

Thomas, C. L. (Ed.). (1985). *Taber's cyclopedic medical dictionary* (15th ed.). Philadelphia: F. A. Davis Co.

Thurrell, R. J., & Rice, D. G. (1970). Eye rubbing in blind children: Application of a sensory deprivation model. *Exceptional Children, 36,* 325–330.

Warren, D. H. (1981). Visual impairments. In J. M. Kauffman & D. P. Hallahan (Eds.), *Handbook of special education,* Englewood Cliffs, NJ: Prentice-Hall.

Warren, D. H. (1984). *Blindness and early childhood development* (2nd ed.). New York: American Foundation for the Blind.

Warren, D. H., & Kocon, J. A. (1974). Factors in the successful mobility of the blind: A review. *Research Bulletin: American Foundation for the Blind* (28), 191–218.

Willis, D. H. (1976). *A study of the relationship between visual acuity, reading mode, and school systems for blind students— 1976.* Louisville, KY: American Printing House for the Blind.

Wolffe, K. E., Roessler, R. T., & Schriner, K. F. (1992). Employment concerns of people with blindness or visual impairments. *Journal of Visual Impairment & Blindness, 86*(4), 185–187.

CHAPTER 10

Allison, M. (1992). The effects of neurologic injury on the maturing brain. *Headlines, 3*(5), 2–10.

Armstrong, F. D., Seidel, J. R., & Swales, T. P. (1993). Pediatric HIV infection: A neuropsychological and educational challenge. *Journal of Learning Disabilities, 26,* 92–103.

Batshaw, M. L., & Parret, Y. M. (1986). *Children with handicaps: A medical primer.* Baltimore, Paul H. Brookes.

Baumeister, A. A., Kupstas, F., & Klindworth, L. M. (1990). New morbidity: Implications for prevention of children's disabilities. *Exceptionality, 1,* 1–16.

Bigge, J. L. (1991). *Teaching individuals with physical and multiple disabilities* (3rd ed.). Columbus, OH: Merrill/Macmillan.

Blackman, J. A. (Ed.). (1984). *Medical aspects of developmental disabilities in children birth to three* (rev. ed.). Rockville, MD: Aspen.

Blum, R. W. (1992). Chronic illness and disability in adolescence. *Journal of Adolescent Health, 13,* 364–368.

Brown, R. T. (1993). An introduction to the special series: Pediatric chronic illness. *Journal of Learning Disabilities, 26,* 4–6.

Bryan, D. P., & Herjanic, B. (1980). Depression and suicide among adolescents and young adults with selective handicapping conditions. *Exceptional Education Quarterly, 1*(2), 57–66.

Cavazzuti, G. B., Ferrari, P., & Lalla, M. (1984). Follow-up study of 482 cases with convulsive disorders in the first year. *Developmental Medicine and Child Neurology, 26,* 425–437.

Chadwick, D. (1989). Protecting abused kids. *NEA Today, 8*(5), 23.

Chowder, K. (1992). How TB survived its own death to confront us again. *Smithsonian, 23*(8), 180–194.

Church, J. A., Allen, J. R., & Stiehm, E. R. (1986). New scarlet letter(s), pediatric AIDS. *Pediatrics, 77,* 423–427.

Crocker, A. C. (Ed.). (1989). Developmental disabilities and HIV infection: A symposium on issues and public policy. *Mental Retardation, 27*(4), special issue.

Cruickshank, W. M. (Ed.). (1976). *Cerebral palsy: A developmental disability* (3rd rev. ed.). Syracuse, NY: Syracuse University Press.

DeLoach, C., & Greer, B. G. (1981). *Adjustment to severe physical disability: A metamorphosis.* New York: McGraw-Hill.

DuBose, R. F., & Deni, K. (1980). Easily constructed adaptive and assistive equipment. *Teaching Exceptional Children, 12,* 116–123.

Duncan, D., & Canty-Lemke, J. (1986). Learning appropriate social and sexual behavior: The role of society. *The Exceptional Parent, 16*(5), 24–26.

Dyar, S. E. (1988). A step in the right direction. *Helix: The University of Virginia Health Sciences Quarterly, 6*(3), 5–11.

Edmonson, B. (1988). Disability and sexual adjustment. In V. B. Van Hasselt, P. S. Strain, & M. Hersen (Eds.), *Handbook of developmental and physical disabilities* (pp. 91–106). New York: Pergamon.

Fonosch, G. G., Arany, J., Lee, A., & Loving, S. (1982). Providing career planning and placement services for college students with disabilities. *Exceptional Education Quarterly, 3*(3), 67–74.

Fraser, B. A., & Hensinger, R. N. (1983). *Managing physical handicaps: A practical guide for parents, care providers, and educators.* Baltimore: Paul H. Brookes.

Freeman, J. M., Jacobs, H., Vining, E., & Rabin, C. E. (1984). Epilepsy and the inner city schools: A school-based program that makes a difference. *Epilepsia, 25,* 438–442.

Gilchrist, L. D., Gillmore, M. R., & Lohr, M. J. (1990). Drug use among pregnant adolescents. _Journal of Consulting and Clinical Psychology, 58_, 402–407.

Girvin, J. P. (1992). Is epilepsy a progressive disorder? _Journal of Epilepsy. 5_, 94–104.

Gover, A. M., & McIvor, J. (1992). Upper limb deficiencies in infants and young children. _Infants and Young Children, 5_(1), 58–72.

Grayson, J. (1992, fall). Child abuse and developmental disabilities. _Virginia Child Protection Newsletter, 37_, 1, 3–7, 10, 12–13, 16.

Gregorchik, L. A. (1992). The cocaine-exposed children are here. _Phi Delta Kappan, 73_, 709–711.

Hanson, M. J., & Harris, S. R. (1986). _Teaching the young child with motor delays._ Austin, TX: Pro-Ed.

Hauser, W. A., & Kurland, L. T. (1975). The epidemiology of epilepsy in Rochester, Minnesota, 1935 through 1967. _Epilepsia, 16_, 1–66.

Hoare, P. (1984). The development of psychiatric disorder among schoolchildren with epilepsy. _Developmental Medicine and Child Neurology, 26_, 3–13.

Hobbs, N., Perrin, J. M., & Ireys, H. T. (1984). _Chronically ill children and their families._ San Francisco: Jossey-Bass.

Hobbs, N., Perrin, J. M., Ireys, H. T., Moynahan, I. C., & Shayne, M. W. (1984). Chronically ill children in America. _Rehabilitation Literature, 45_, 206–213.

Huberty, T. J., Austin, J. K., Risinger, M. W., & McNelis, A. M. (1992). Relationship of selected seizure variables in children with epilepsy to performance on school-administered achievement tests. _Journal of Epilepsy, 5_, 10–16.

Indacochea, J. J., & Scott, G. B. (1992). HIV-1 infection and the acquired immunodeficiency syndrome in children. _Current Problems in Pediatrics, 22_, 166–204.

Jacobs, I. B. (1983). Epilepsy. In G. H. Thompson, I. L. Rubin, & R. M. Bilenker (Eds.), _Comprehensive management of cerebral palsy._ New York: Grune & Stratton.

Katsiyannis, A. (1992). Policy issues in school attendance of children with AIDS: A national survey. _Journal of Special Education, 26_, 219–226.

Klein, M., & Stern, L. (1971). Low birth weight and the battered child syndrome. _American Journal of Diseases of Children, 122_, 15–18.

Korabek, C. A., & Cuvo, A. J. (1986). Children with spina bifida: Educational implications of their medical characteristics. _Education and Treatment of Children, 9_, 142–152.

Larkin, M. (1992). New hospital-school liaisons: Ensuring success for the student with neurologic impairments. _Headlines, 3_(5), 12–17.

Lewandowski, L. J., & Cruickshank, W. M. (1980). Psychological development of crippled children and youth. In W. M. Cruickshank (Ed.), _Psychology of exceptional children and youth_ (4th ed.). Englewood Cliffs, NJ: Prentice-Hall.

Lyon, J. (1985). _Playing god in the nursery._ New York: W. W. Norton.

Martin, D. A. (1992). Children in peril: A mandate for change in health care policies for low-income children. _Family and Community Health. 15_(1), 75–90.

McCormick, M. C., Brooks-Gunn, J., Workman-Daniels, K., Turner, J., & Peckham, G. J. (1992). The health and developmental status of very low-birth-weight children at school age. _Journal of the American Medical Association, 267._ 2204–2208.

Merina, A. (1989). Is your school ready for AIDS? _NEA Today, 8_(5), 10–11.

Mira, M. P., & Tyler, J. S. (1991). Students with traumatic brain injury: Making the transition from hospital to school. _Focus on Exceptional Children, 23_(5), 1–12.

Moore, J. (1985). Technology is not magic. _The Exceptional Parent, 15_(7), 41–42.

Murphy, J. M., Jellinek, M., Quinn, D., Smith, G., Poitrast, F. G., & Goshko, M. (1991). Substance abuse and serious child mistreatment: Prevalence, risk, and outcome in a court sample. _Child Abuse and Neglect, 15_, 197–211.

National Head Injury Foundation. (1988). _An educator's manual: What educators need to know about students with traumatic brain injury._ Southborough, MA: Author.

Neisworth, J. T., & Fewell, R. R. (Eds.). (1989). Transition. _Topics in Early Childhood Special Education, 9_(4).

Parette, H. P., & VanBiervliet, A. (1991). Rehabilitation assistive technology issues for infants and young children with disabilities: A preliminary examination. _Journal of Rehabilitation, 57_(3), 27–36.

Reed, S. (1988). Children with AIDS: How schools are handling the crisis. Kappan special report. _Phi Delta Kappan, 69_, K1–K12.

Rudigier, A. F., Crocker, A. C., & Cohen, H. J.(1990). The dilemmas of childhood: HIV infection. _Children Today, 19_, 26–29.

Rush, W. L. (1977). Feelings of love. _The Exceptional Parent, 7_(6), 2–6.

Satz, J. (1986). Another first: The National Park Service opens summer work programs to students with disabilities. _The Exceptional Parent, 16_(2), 19–22.

Sautter, R. C. (1992). Crack: Healing the children. _Phi Delta Kappan, 74_, K1–K12 [Kappan Special Report].

Savage, R. C. (1988). Introduction to educational issues for students who have suffered traumatic brain injury. _An educator's manual: What educators need to know about students with traumatic brain injury._ Southborough, MA: Author.

Sillanpaa, M. (1992). Epilepsy in children: Prevalence, disability, and handicap. _Epilepsia, 33_, 444–449.

Snell, M. E., & Browder, D. M. (1986). Community-referenced instruction: Research and issues. _Journal of the Association for Severely Handicapped, 11_, 1–11.

Stevens-Simon, C. (1992). Recent developments in adolescent pregnancy. _Current Problems in Pediatrics, 22_, 295–301.

Trach, J. S. (1990). Supported employment program characteristics. In F. R. Rusch (Ed.), *Supported employment: Models, methods, and issues* (pp. 65–81). Sycamore, IL: Sycamore.

U. S. Department of Education. (1989). *Eleventh annual report to Congress on the implementation of the Education of the Handicapped Act.* Washington, DC: U. S. Government Printing Office.

Van Dyke, D. C., & Fox, A. A. (1992). Fetal drug exposure and its possible implications for learning in the preschool and school-age population. *Journal of Learning Disabilities, 23,* 160–163.

Verhaaren, P., & Connor, F. (1981a). Physical disabilities. In J. M. Kauffman & D. P. Hallahan (Eds.), *Handbook of special education.* Englewood Cliffs, NJ: Prentice-Hall.

Verhaaren, P., & Connor, F. (1981b). Special adaptations necessitated by physical disabilities. In J. M. Kauffman & D. P. Hallahan (Eds.), *Handbook of special education.* Englewood Cliffs, NJ: Prentice-Hall.

Vinger, P. F., & Hoerner, E. F. (Eds.). (1986). *Sports injuries: The unthwarted epidemic* (2nd ed.). Littleton, MA: PSG Publishing Company.

Westbook, L. E., Silver, E. J., Coupey, S. M., & Shinnar, S. (1991). Social characteristics of adolescents with ideopathic epilepsy: A comparison to chronically ill and nonchronically ill peers. *Journal of Epilepsy. 4,* 87–94.

Williamson, W. D., & Demmler, G. J. (1992). Congenital infections: Clinical outcome and educational implications. *Infants and Young Children, 4*(4), 1–10.

Wilsnack, S. C., Klassen, A. D., & Wilsnack, R. W. (1984). Drinking and reproductive dysfunction among women in a 1981 national survey. *Alcoholism: Clinical and Experimental Research, 8,* 451–458.

Wolraich, M. L. (1984). Seizure disorders. In J. A. Blackman (Ed.), *Medical aspects of developmental disabilities in children birth to three* (rev. 1st. ed., pp. 215–221). Rockville, MD: Aspen.

Zadig, J. M. (1983). The education of the child with cerebral palsy. In G. H. Thompson, I. L. Rubin, & R. M. Bilenker (Eds.), *Comprehensive management of cerebral palsy.* New York: Grune & Stratton.

Zirpoli, T. J. (1986). Child abuse and children with handicaps. *Remedial and Special Education, 7*(2), 39–48.

Ziter, F. A., & Alsop, K. G. (1976). The diagnosis and management of childhood muscular dystrophy. "Clinicians must provide the best care and support possible." *Clinical Pediatrics, 15,* 540–548.

CHAPTER 11

Baer. N. A. (1980). Programs for the gifted: A present or paradox? *Phi Delta Kappan, 61,* 621–623.

Baldwin, A. Y. (1985). Programs for the gifted and talented: Issues concerning minority populations. In F. D. Horowitz & M. O'Brien (Eds.), *The gifted and talented:*

Developmental perspectives (pp. 251–295). Washington, DC: American Psychological Association.

Baum, S. (1986). The gifted preschooler: An awesome delight. *Gifted Child Today, 9*(4), 42–45.

Bloom, B. S. (1982). The role of gifts and markers in the development of talent. *Exceptional Children, 48,* 510–522.

Bloom, B. J. et al. (1956). *Taxonomy of educational objectives. Handbook I: Cognitive domain.* New York: McKay.

Bloom, B. S., & Sosniak, L. A. (1981). Talent development vs. schooling. *Educational Leadership, 39,* 86–94.

Brody, L. E., & Stanley, J. C. (1991). Young college students: Assessing factors that contribute to success. In W. T. Southern & E. D. Jones (Eds.), *The academic acceleration of gifted children* (pp. 102–132). New York: Teachers College Press.

Buescher, T. M. (1991). Gifted adolescents. In W. T. Southern & E. D. Jones (Eds.), *The academic acceleration of gifted children* (pp. 382–401). New York: Teachers College Press.

Callahan, C. M. (1986). Asking the right questions: The central issue in evaluating programs for the gifted and talented. *Gifted Child Quarterly, 30,* 38–42.

Callahan, C. M. (1991). An update on gifted females. *Journal for the Education of the Gifted, 14,* 284–311.

Caplan, N., Choy, M. H., & Whitmore, J. K. (1992, February). Indochinese refugee families and academic achievement. *Scientific American, 266*(2), 36–42.

Clifford, J. A., Runions, T., & Smyth, E. (1986). The Learning Enrichment Service (LES): A participatory model for gifted adolescents. In J. S. Renzulli (Ed.), *Systems and models for developing programs for the gifted and talented.* Mansfield, CT: Creative Learning Press.

Coleman, J. M., & Fultz, B. A. (1985). Special class placement, level of intelligence, and the self-concepts of gifted children: A social comparison perspective. *Remedial and Special Education, 6*(1), 7–12.

Conroy, M. (1989). Where have all the smart girls gone? *Psychology Today, 23*(2), 20.

Cornell, D. G. (1983). Gifted children: The impact of positive labeling on the family system. *American Journal of Orthopsychiatry, 53,* 322–335.

Council of State Directors of Programs for the Gifted. (1991). *The 1990 state of the states gifted and talented education report.* Author.

Delisle, J. (1981). The non-productive gifted child: A contradiction. *Roeper Review, 3,* 20–22.

Delisle, J. (1982). The gifted underachiever: Learning to underachieve. *Roeper Review, 4,* 16–18.

Delisle, J. R. (1987). *Gifted kids speak out.* Minneapolis, MN: Free Spirit Publishing.

Delisle, J. R. (1992). *Guiding the social and emotional development of gifted youth: A practical guide for educators and counselors.* New York: Longman.

Dettmer, P. (1982). Preventing burnout in teachers of the gifted. *Gifted/Creative/Talented*, January-February, 37–41.

Eccles, J. S. (1985). Why doesn't Jane run? Sex differences in educational and occupational patterns. In F. D. Horowitz & M. O'Brien (Eds.), *The gifted and talented: Developmental perspectives*. Washington, DC: American Psychological Association.

Feldhusen, J. F. (1989). Synthesis of research on gifted youth. *Educational Leadership, 46*(6), 6–11.

Feldhusen, J. F., & Kolloff, P. B. (1986). The Purdue secondary model for gifted and talented youth. In J. S. Renzulli (Ed.), *Systems and models for developing programs for the gifted and talented*. Mansfield, CT: Creative Learning Press.

Feldhusen, J. F., & Moon, S. M. (1992). Grouping students: Issues and concerns. *Gifted Child Quarterly, 36*, 63–67.

Fox, L. H., & Washington, J. (1985). Programs for the gifted and talented: Past, present, and future. In F. D. Horowitz & M. O'Brien (Eds.), *The gifted and talented: Developmental perspectives* (pp. 197–221). Washington, DC: American Psychological Association.

Frasier, M. M. (1989). Poor and minority students can be gifted too! *Educational Leadership, 46*(6), 16–18.

Frasier, M. M. (1991). Disadvantaged and culturally diverse gifted students. *Journal for the Education of the Gifted, 14*, 234–245.

Gailbraith, J. (1985). The eight great gripes of gifted kids: Responding to special needs. *Roeper Review, 7*, 15–18.

Gallagher, J. J. (1985). *Teaching the gifted child* (3rd ed.). Boston: Allyn & Bacon.

Gallagher, J. J. (1986). Our love-hate affair with gifted children. *Gifted Child Today, 9*(3), 47–49.

Gallagher, J. J. (1991a). Educational reform, values, and gifted students. *Gifted Child Quarterly, 35*, 12–19.

Gallagher, J. J. (1991b). Personal patterns of underachievement. *Journal of the Education of the Gifted, 14*, 221–233.

Gardner, H., & Hatch, T. (1989). Multiple intelligences go to school: Educational implications of the theory of multiple intelligences. *Educational Researcher, 18*(8), 4–9.

Gross, M. U. M. (1992). The use of radical acceleration in cases of extreme intellectual precocity. *Gifted Child Quarterly, 36*, 91–99.

Gruber, H. E. (1985). Giftedness and moral responsibility: Creative thinking and human survival. In F. D. Horowitz & M. O'Brien (Eds.), *The gifted and talented: Developmental perspectives* (pp. 301–330). Washington, DC: American Psychological Association.

Hollingworth, L. S. (1942). *Children above 180 IQ, Stanford-Binet: Origin and development*. Yonkers-on-Hudson, NY: World Book Company.

Janos, P. M., & Robinson, N. M. (1985). Psychosocial development in intellectually gifted children. In F. D. Horowitz & M. O'Brien (Eds.), *The gifted and talented: Developmental perspectives* (pp. 149–195). Washington, DC: American Psychological Association.

Jones, E. D., & Southern, W. T. (1991). Conclusions about acceleration: echoes of debate. In W. T. Southern & E. D. Jones (Eds.), *The academic acceleration of gifted children* (pp. 223–228). New York: Teachers College Press.

Jones, E. D., & Southern, W. T. (1992). Programming, grouping, and acceleration in rural schools districts: A survey of attitudes and practices. *Gifted Child Quarterly, 36*, 112–117.

Karnes, M. B., & Johnson, L. J. (1991a). Gifted handicapped. In N. Colangelo & G. A. Davis (Eds.), *Handbook of gifted education* (pp. 428–437). Boston: Allyn & Bacon.

Karnes, M. B., & Johnson, L. J. (1991b). The preschool/primary gifted child. *Journal for the Education of the Gifted, 14*, 267–283.

Keating, D. P. (1980). Four faces of creativity: The continuing plight of the intellectually underserved. *Gifted Child Quarterly, 24*(2), 56–61.

Kerr, B. (1991). Educating gifted girls. In N. Colangelo & G. A. Davis (Eds.), *Handbook of gifted education* (pp. 402–415). Boston: Allyn & Bacon.

Kolitch, E. R., & Brody, L. E. (1992). Mathematics acceleration of highly talented students: An evaluation. *Gifted Child Quarterly, 36*, 78–86.

Kulik, J. A., & Kulik, C. C. (1992). Meta-analytic findings on grouping programs. *Gifted Child Quarterly, 36*, 73–77.

Lewis, M., & Louis, B. (1991). Young gifted children. In N. Colangelo & G. A. Davis (Eds.), *Handbook of gifted education* (pp. 365–381). Boston: Allyn & Bacon.

Lindsey, M. (1980). *Training teachers of the gifted and talented*. New York: Teachers College Press.

Maker, C. J. (1986). Education of the gifted: Significant trends. In R. J. Morris & B. Blatt (Eds.), *Special education: Research and trends* (pp. 190–221). New York: Pergamon.

Milgrim, R. M. (1989). *Teaching gifted and talented learners in regular classrooms*. Springfield, IL: Charles C. Thomas.

Mills, C. J., Stork, E. J., & Krug, D. (1992). Recognition and development of academic talent in educationally disadvantaged students. *Exceptionality, 3*, 165–180.

Mistry, J., & Rogoff, B. (1985). A cultural perspective on the development of talent. In F. D. Horowitz & M. O'Brien (Eds.), *The gifted and talented: Developmental perspectives* (pp. 125–144). Washington, DC: American Psychological Association.

Morelock, M. J., & Feldman, D. H. (1991). Extreme precocity. In N. Colangelo & G. A. Davis (Eds.), *Handbook of gifted education* (pp. 347–364). Boston: Allyn & Bacon.

Myers, D. G., & Ridl, J. (1981). Aren't all children gifted? *Today's Education, 70*, 15–20.

Neuhaus, C. (1988). Genius at work. *US Air, 10*(2), 64–68.

Noble, K. D., & Drummond, J. E. (1992). But what about the prom? Students' perceptions of early college entrance. *Gifted Child Quarterly, 36*, 106–111.

Oakes, J. (1985). *Keeping track: How schools structure inequality.* New Haven, CT: Yale University Press.

Oakes, J. (1992). Can tracking research inform practice? Technical, normative, and political considerations. *Educational Researchers, 22*(4), 12–21.

Olenchak, F. R., & Renzulli, J. S. (1989). The effectiveness of the schoolwide enrichment model on selected aspects of elementary school change. *Gifted Child Quarterly, 33*(1), 36–46.

Patton, J. M. (1992). Assessment and identification of African-American learners with gifts and talents. *Exceptional Children, 59,* 150–159.

Perrone, P. A. (1991). Career development. In N. Colangelo & G. A. Davis (Eds.), *Handbook of gifted education* (pp. 321–327). Boston: Allyn & Bacon.

Piechowski, M. M. (1991). Emotional development and emotional giftedness. In N. Colangelo & G. A. Davis (Eds.), *Handbook of gifted education* (pp. 285–306). Boston: Allyn & Bacon.

Plomin, R. (1989). Environment and genes: Determinants of behavior. *American Psychologist, 44,* 105–111.

Ramos-Ford, V., & Gardner, H. (1991). Giftedness from a multiple intelligences perspective. In N. Colangelo & G. A. Davis (Eds.), *Handbook of gifted education* (pp. 55–64). Boston: Allyn & Bacon.

Reis, S. M. (1989). Reflections on policy affecting the education of gifted and talented students: Past and future perspectives. *American Psychologist, 44,* 399–408.

Renzulli, J. S. (1980). Will the gifted child movement be alive and well in 1990? *Gifted Child Quarterly, 24*(3), 3–9.

Renzulli, J. S. (1982). Dear Mr. and Mrs. Copernicus: We regret to inform you . . . *Gifted Child Quarterly, 26*(1), 11–14.

Renzulli, J. S. (1986). *Systems and models for developing programs for the gifted and talented.* Mansfield Center, CT: Creative Learning Press.

Renzulli, J. S., & Reis, S. M. (1985). *The schoolwide enrichment model: A comprehensive plan for educational excellence.* Mansfield Center, CT: Creative Learning Press.

Renzulli, J. S., & Reis, S. M. (1991a). The reform movement and the quiet crisis in gifted education. *Gifted Child Quarterly, 35,* 26–35.

Renzulli, J. S., & Reis, S. M. (1991b). The schoolwide enrichment model: A comprehensive plan for the development of creative productivity. In N. Colangelo & G. A. Davis (Eds.), *Handbook of gifted education* (pp. 111–141). Boston: Allyn & Bacon.

Renzulli, J. S., Reis, S. M., & Smith, L. H. (1981). *The revolving door identification model.* Mansfield Center, CT: Creative Learning Press.

Richert, E. S. (1991). Rampant problems and promising practices in identification. In N. Colangelo & G. A.

Davis (Eds.), *Handbook of gifted education* (pp. 81–96). Boston: Allyn & Bacon.

Rimm, S. B., & Lovance, K. J. (1992). The use of subject and grade skipping for the prevention and reversal of underachievement. *Gifted Child Quarterly, 36,* 100–105.

Robinson, N. M., & Weimer, L. J. (1991). Selection of candidates for early admission to kindergarten and first grade. In W. T. Southern & E. D. Jones (Eds.), *The academic acceleration of gifted children* (pp. 29–50). New York: Teachers College Press.

Roedell, W. C. (1985). Developing social competence in gifted preschool children. *Remedial and Special Education, 6*(4), 6–11.

Sapon-Shevin, M. (1984). The tug-of-war nobody wins: Allocation of educational resources for handicapped, gifted, and "typical" students. *Curriculum Inquiry, 14,* 57–81.

Shore, B. M., Cornell, D. G., Robinson, A., & Ward, V. S. (1991). *Recommended practices in gifted education: A critical analysis.* New York: Teachers College Press.

Silverman, L. K. (1991). Family counseling. In N. Colangelo & G. A. Davis (Eds.), *Handbook of gifted education* (pp. 307–320). Boston: Allyn & Bacon.

Starko, A. J. (1986). *It's about time: Inservice strategies for curriculum compacting.* Mansfield Center, CT: Creative Learning Press.

Sternberg, R. J. (1991). Giftedness according to the triarchic theory of human intelligence. In N. Colangelo & G. A. Davis (Eds.), *Handbook of gifted education* (pp. 45–54). Boston: Allyn & Bacon.

Sternberg, R. J., & Davidson, J. E. (1983). Insight in the gifted. *Educational Psychologist, 18,* 51–57.

Sternberg, R. J., & Davidson, J. E. (Eds.) (1986). *Conceptions of giftedness.* New York: Cambridge University Press.

Stronge, J. H. (1986). Gifted education: Right or privilege? *Gifted Child Today, 9*(3), 52–54.

Tannenbaum, A. J. (1991). The social psychology of giftedness. In N. Colangelo & G. A. Davis (Eds.), *Handbook of gifted education* (pp. 27–44). Boston: Allyn & Bacon.

Terman, L. M. (1926). *Genetic studies of genius, Vol. I: Mental and physical traits of a thousand gifted children* (2nd ed.). Palo Alto, CA: Stanford University Press.

Terman, L. M., & Oden, M. H. (1959). *Genetic studies of genius, Vol. V: The gifted group at midlife.* Palo Alto, CA: Stanford University Press.

Treffinger, D. J. (1991). School reform and gifted education—opportunities and issues. *Gifted Child Quarterly, 35,* 6–11.

VanTassel-Baska, J. (1990). (Ed.). *A practical guide to counseling the gifted in a school setting* (2nd ed.). Reston, VA: Council for Exceptional Children.

VanTassel-Baska, J. (1991a). Gifted education in the balance: Building relationships with general education. *Gifted Child Quarterly, 35,* 20–25.

VanTassel-Baska, J. (1991b). Serving the disabled gifted through educational collaboration. *Journal for the Education of the Gifted, 14*, 246–266.

VanTassel-Baska, J. (1992). Educational decision making on acceleration and grouping. *Gifted Child Quarterly, 36*, 68–72.

Weiss, P., & Gallagher, J. J. (1982). *Report on education of gifted (Vol. II)*. Chapel Hill, NC: University of North Carolina Frank Porter Graham Child Development Center.

White, W. L., & Renzulli, J. S. (1987). A forty year follow-up of students who attended Leta Hollingworth's school for gifted students. *Roeper Review, 10*, 89–94.

Whitlock, M. S., & DuCette, J. P. (1989). Outstanding and average teachers of the gifted: A comparative study. *Gifted Child Quarterly, 33*, 15–21.

Whitmore, J. (1987). Conceptualizing the issue of underserved populations of gifted students. *Journal for the Education of the Gifted, 10*, 141–153.

Whitmore, J. R. (1986). Understanding a lack of motivation to excel. *Gifted Child Quarterly, 30*, 66–69.

Whitmore, J. R., & Maker, C. J. (1985). *Intellectual giftedness in disabled persons*. Rockville, MD: Aspen.

Zigler, E., & Farber, E. A. (1985). Commonalities between the intellectual extremes: Giftedness and mental retardation. In F. D. Horowitz & M. O'Brien (Eds.), *The gifted and talented: Developmental perspectives* (pp. 378–408). Washington, DC: American Psychological Association.

CHAPTER 12

Akerley, M. S. (1985). False gods and angry prophets. In H. R. Turnbull & A. P. Turnbull (Eds.), *Parents speak out: Then and now* (2nd ed., pp. 23–31). Columbus, OH: Chas. E. Merrill.

Baumeister, A., Kupstas, F., & Klindworth, L. M. (1990). New morbidity: Implications for prevention of children's disabilities. *Exceptionality, 1*(1), 1–16.

Beckman, P. J. (1991). Comparison of mothers' and fathers' perceptions of the effect of young children with and without disabilities. *American Journal on Mental Retardation, 95*(5), 585–595.

Beckman, P. J., & Pokorni, J. L. (1988). A longitudinal study of families of preterm infants: Changes in stress and support over the first two years. *Journal of Special Education, 22*(1), 55–65.

Bell, R. Q., & Harper, L. V. (1977). *Child effects on adults*. Hillsdale, NJ: Lawrence Erlbaum.

Benson, H. A., & Turnbull, A. P. (1986). Approaching families from an individualized perspective. In R. H. Horner, L. H. Meyer, & H. D. B. Fredericks (Eds.), *Education of learners with severe handicaps: Exemplary service strategies* (pp. 127–157), Baltimore: Paul H. Brookes.

Bettelheim, B. (1950). *Love is not enough*. New York: Macmillan.

Bettelheim, B. (1967). *The empty fortress*. New York: Free Press.

Blacher, J., & Baker, B. L. (1992). Toward meaningful family involvement in out-of-home placement settings. *Mental Retardation, 30*(1), 35–43.

Bristol, M. M., & Gallagher, J. J. (1986). In J. J. Gallagher & P. M. Vietze (Eds.), *Families of handicapped persons: Research, programs, and policy issues* (pp. 81–100). Baltimore: Paul H. Brookes.

Bronfenbrenner, U. (1979). *The ecology of human development: Experiments by nature and design*. Cambridge, MA: Harvard University Press.

Bronicki, G. J., & Turnbull, A. P. (1987). Family-professional interactions. In M. E. Snell (Ed.), *Systematic instruction of persons with severe handicaps* (pp. 9–35). Columbus, OH: Chas. E. Merrill.

Brooks-Gunn, J., & Lewis, M. (1984). Maternal responsivity in interactions with handicapped infants. *Child Development, 55*(3), 858–868.

Carr, J. (1988). Six weeks to twenty-one years old: A longitudinal study of children with Down's syndrome and their families. *Journal of Child Psychology and Psychiatry, 29*(4), 407–431.

Comegys, A. (1989). Integration strategies for parents of students with handicaps. In R. Gaylord-Ross (Ed.), *Integration strategies for students with handicaps* (pp. 339–350). Baltimore: Paul H. Brookes.

Diamond, S. (1981). Growing up with parents of a handicapped child: A handicapped person's perspective. In J. L. Paul (Ed.), *Understanding and working with parents of children with special needs*. New York: Holt, Rinehart & Winston.

Drotar, D., Baskiewicz, A., Irvin, N., Kennell, J., & Klaus, M. (1975). The adaptation of parents to the birth of an infant with a congenital malformation: A hypothetical model. *Pediatrics, 56*, 710–717.

Dumas, J. E., Wolf, L. C., Fisman, S. N., & Culligan, A. (1991). Parenting stress, child behavior problems, and dysphoria in parents of children with autism, Down syndrome, behavior disorders, and normal development. *Exceptionality, 2*(2), 97–110.

Dunst, C. J., Trivette, C. M., & Deal, A. (1988). *Enabling and empowering families*. Cambridge, MA: Brookline Books.

Dunst, C. J., Trivette, C. M., Gordon, N. J., & Pletcher, L. L. (1989). Building and mobilizing informal family support networks. In G. H. S. Singer & L. K. Irvin (Eds.), *Support for caregiving families: Enabling positive adaptation to disability* (pp. 121–141). Baltimore: Paul H. Brookes.

Dunst, C. J., Johanson, C., Trivette, C. M., Hamby, D. (1991). Family-oriented early intervention policies and practices: Family-centered or not? *Exceptional Children, 58*(2), 115–126.

Featherstone, H. (1980). *A difference in the family: Life with a disabled child*. New York: Basic Books.

Fowler, S. A., Schwartz, I., & Atwater, J. (1991). Perspectives on the transition from preschool to kindergarten for children with disabilities and their families. *Exceptional Children, 58*(2), 136–145.

Guralnick, M. J. (1991). The next decade of research on the effectiveness of early intervention. *Exceptional Children, 58*(2), 174–183.

Hallahan, D. P. (1992). Some thoughts on why the prevalence of learning disabilities has increased. *Journal of Learning Disabilities, 25*(8), 523–528.

Hanline, M. F., & Knowlton, A. (1988). A collaborative model for providing support to parents during their child's transition from infant intervention to preschool special education public school programs. *Journal of the Division for Early Childhood, 12*(2), 116–125.

Hanson, M. J., Ellis, L., & Deppe, J. (1989). Support for families during infancy. In G. H. S. Singer & L. K. Irvin (Eds.), *Support for caregiving families: Enabling positive adaptation to disability* (pp. 207–219). Baltimore: Paul H. Brookes.

The Helsel Family. (1985). The Helsels' story of Robin. In H. R. Turnbull & A. P. Turnbull (Eds.), *Parents speak out: Then and now* (2nd ed., pp. 81–89). Columbus, OH: Chas. E. Merrill.

Hofferth, S. L., & Phillips, D. A. (1987). Child care in the United States, 1970 to 1995. *Journal of Marriage and the Family, 49*, 559–571.

Jewell, G. (1985). *Geri.* New York: Ballantine Books.

Kauffman, J., Mostert, M., Nuttycimbe, D., Trent, S., & Hallahan, D. (1993). *Managing Classroom Behavior: A reflective case-based approach.* Boston, MA: Allyn & Bacon.

Kazak, A. E., & Marvin, R. S. (1984). Differences, difficulties, and adaptation: Stress and social networks in families with a handicapped child. *Family Relations, 33*, 67–77.

Kelley, M. L. (1990). *School-home notes: Promoting children's classroom success.* New York: Guilford Press.

Krauss, M. W., Seltzer, M. M., & Goodman, S. J. (1992). Social support networks of adults with mental retardation who live at home. *American Journal on Mental Retardation, 96*(4), 432–441.

Leete-Guy, L., & Schor, J. B. (1992). *The great American time squeeze: Trends in work and leisure, 1969–1989.* (Briefing paper for the Economic Policy Institute, Washington, DC).

Lynch, E. W., & Stein, R. (1982). Perspectives on parent participation in special education. *Exceptional Education Quarterly, 3*(2), 56–63.

McDonnell, A., & Hardman, M. (1988). A synthesis of "best practice" guidelines for early childhood services. *Journal of the Division for Early Childhood, 12*(2), 328–341.

Mahoney, G., & Robenalt, K. (1986). A comparison of conversational patterns between mothers and their Down syndrome and normal infants. *Journal of the Division for Early Childhood, 10*, 172–180.

Martin, S. S., Brady, M. P., & Kortarba, J. A. (1992). Families with chronically ill children: The unsinkable family.

Remedial and Special Education, 13*(2), 6–15.

Michael, M. G., Arnold, K. D., Magliocca, L. A., & Miller, S. (1992). Influences on teachers' attitudes of the parents' role as collaborator. *Remedial and Special Education, 13*(2), 24–30, 39.

Mims, A., Harper, C., Armstrong, S. W., & Savage, S. (1991). Effective instruction in homework for students with disabilities. *Teaching Exceptional Children, 24*(1), 42–47.

Nolan, C. (1987). *Under the eye of the clock: The life story of Christopher Nolan.* New York: St. Martin's Press, pp. 37–38.

Norton, A. J., & Glick, P. C. (1986). One parent families: A social and economic profile. *Family Relations, 35*(1), 9–17.

Rousey, A., Best, S., & Blacher, J. (1992). Mothers' and fathers' perceptions of stress and coping with children who have severe disabilities. *American Journal on Mental Retardation, 97*(1), 99–109.

Seligman, M., & Darling, R. B. (1989). *Ordinary families, special children: A systems approach to childhood disability.* New York: Guilford Press.

Senapati, R., & Hayes, A. (1988). Sibling relationships of handicapped children: A review of conceptual and methodological issues. *International Journal of Behavioral Development, 11*(1), 89–115.

Simeonsson, R. J., & Bailey, D. B. (1986). Siblings of handicapped children. In J. J. Gallagher & P. M. Vietze (Eds.), *Families of handicapped persons: Research, programs, and policy issues* (pp. 67–77). Baltimore: Paul H. Brookes.

Singer, G. H. S., & Irvin, L. K. (1989). Family caregiving, stress, and support. In G. H. S. Singer & L. K. Irvin (Eds.), *Support for caregiving families: Enabling positive adaptation to disability* (pp. 3–25). Baltimore: Paul H. Brookes.

Stark, J. (1992). Presidential Address 1992: A professional and personal perspective on families. *Mental Retardation, 30*(5), 247–254.

Stoneman, Z., Brody, G. H., Davis, C. H., & Crapps, J. M. (1988). Childcare responsibilities, peer relations, and sibling conflict: Older siblings of mentally retarded children. *American Journal of Mental Retardation, 93*(2), 174–183.

Turnbull, A. P., & Turnbull, H. R. (1990). *Families, professionals, and exceptionality: A special partnership* (2nd ed.). Columbus, OH: Chas. E. Merrill.

Turnbull, H. R., & Turnbull, A. P. (1985). *Parents Speak Out: Then and Now* (2nd ed.). (The Helsel Family). Colunbus, OH: Chas, E. Merrill/Macmillan.

Vaughn, S., Bos, C., Harrell, J., & Lasky, B. (1988). Parent participation in the initial placement/IEP conference 10 years after mandated involvement. *Journal of Learning Disabilities, 21*(2), 82–89.

Zigler, E., & Black, K. B. (1989). America's family support movement: Strengths and limitations. *American Journal of Orthopsychiatry, 59*(1), 6–19.

NAME INDEX

▲ ▲ ▲

SUBJECT INDEX

▲ ▲ ▲